DAN GOLDMAN

Microeconomic Theory
and Applications

Microeconomic Theory and Applications

Edgar K. Browning
University of Virginia

Jacquelene M. Browning
Sweet Briar College

Little, Brown and Company
BOSTON   TORONTO

Library of Congress Cataloging in Publication Data

Browning, Edgar K.
  Microeconomic theory and applications.

  Includes index.
  1. Microeconomics.   I. Browning, Jacquelene M.
II. Title.
HB172.B864   1983   338.5   82–80899
ISBN 0-316-11223-2

Library of Congress Catalog Card No. 82-80899

ISBN 0-316-11223-2

9 8 7 6 5 4 3 2

HAL

Published simultaneously in Canada
by Little, Brown & Company (Canada) Limited

Printed in the United States of America

Credits

Table 1–1. From J. Kearl, C. Pope, G. Whiting, and L. Wimmer, "A Confusion of
Economists," *American Economic Review,* 69 (May 1979), pp. 28–37, Table 1. Reprinted by permission of the publisher and the authors.

Table 15–2. *First National City Bank Monthly Economic Letter,* April 1957, 1958,
1967, 1968, 1978. Reprinted by permission of Citibank Economics Department.

To our families

Preface

Microeconomic theory is basically the study of how markets operate, and understanding how markets operate is essential to understanding how our economic system functions. Beyond developing a coherent view of economic reality, microeconomics provides techniques that are playing increasing roles in both public policy formulation and private decision-making. Although macroeconomic issues frequently receive more visible media attention, the ways that innumerable microeconomic issues are resolved have a far greater and more enduring impact in shaping our economic environment.

We believe microeconomics is the most important course in the undergraduate economics curriculum, and our intent in writing *Microeconomic Theory and Applications* was to develop a text that will teach students this theory and how to use it correctly. To this end, we have presented basic microeconomic principles in a clear, thorough way, using numerous applications to illustrate the use of theory and to reinforce students' understanding of it. This approach gives students the fundamental tools of analysis and teaches them how to think about problems using the analytical framework that economists have found to be so successful.

Organization and Content

Microeconomic Theory and Applications reflects the belief that it is better for students to be exposed to a thorough coverage of fundamental microeconomic concepts and techniques than to a superficial treatment of a great number of topics, many of which will never be encountered again. In determining which topics to include and which to exclude, we were guided by the results of an extensive market survey and our reviewers' suggestions. In addition, we applied two further criteria: (1) Is the concept or technique commonly used in upper level applied microeconomics courses? and (2) Will the concept or technique help students understand the economic events and issues in their daily lives — even if they never take another course in economics? These criteria suggest that an emphasis on the core principles of microeconomics and how to use them is appropriate. Apart from this emphasis, the text is conventional in structure and organization except for one feature: we have four chapters devoted exclusively to applications. These are Chapter 4, Using Consumer Choice

Theory; Chapter 10, Using the Competitive Model; Chapter 12, Using Monopoly Theory; and Chapter 16, Using Input Market Analysis.

Another feature of the text that deserves mention is the attention given to input market analysis. Traditionally, this has been a weak area in most microeconomics texts, with seldom more than two, and frequently only one, chapter on the subject. Yet in a fundamental quantitative sense, input markets and product markets are of equal importance since the sum of incomes generated in input markets (national income) equals total outlays on goods and services (national product). Moreover, public policy issues relating to input markets have become increasingly important, as suggested by recent attention given to income distribution, welfare programs, discrimination, interest rates and investment, the effects of taxation on labor supply and saving, and regulation of wages and working conditions. Consequently, we devote three chapters to the subject of input market analysis (Chapters 14–16).

Because all microeconomics courses are not taught the same way, the text is designed to give instructors great flexibility in adapting the book to their requirements. For example, in a short course emphasizing the theoretical underpinnings of partial equilibrium analysis, the instructor might cover only Chapters 1–3, 6–9, 11, 14, and 15. A longer, more theoretically oriented course could include all chapters except the applications chapters. Generally, however, we expect most instructors to steer a middle course and select three or four applications from each of these chapters (the way we normally use the material). In addition, instructors can either assign the applications as they appear in the text — following the development of the theory — or integrate them into their presentation of the theory chapters.

Applications

As the space devoted to them suggests, we believe a liberal dose of applications is an essential ingredient in a microeconomics course. Although economists know that microeconomics is important and often exciting, students have to be shown that this is so. Applications serve this purpose. In addition, they enliven the subject for students and help them appreciate the theory. Time permitting, the more applications covered, the better prepared students will be to use the theory on their own.

Each of the four applications chapters (Chapters 4, 10, 12, and 16) contains seven or eight applications that use and reinforce the graphical and logical techniques developed in the theory chapters. In Chapter 10, Using the Competitive Model, for example, competitive market theory is used to examine, among other topics, the supply of exhaustible resources, worker safety regulations, airline regulation and deregulation, and rent controls. In Chapter 16, Using Input Market Analysis, the theory is applied to discrimination, the negative income tax, the Laffer curve, and the incidence of the Social Security payroll tax.

Applications are not relegated exclusively to the four applications chapters; each of the remaining chapters also contains one or two. We feel, however, that it is appropriate to use more applications in some areas than in others. For example, it seems a misallocation of scarce textbook space to include as many applications for production or general equilibrium theory as for the competitive model. Not only are the competitive applications likely to be more interesting to students, they are also likely to provide more useful training for students' later work. As we mentioned earlier, the four applications chapters can be used in a variety of ways.

Pedagogical Aids

In addition to our use of applications, we would like to mention a few other in-text pedagogical aids.

Graphs. We have paid careful attention to the graphs used in the text. Unusually thorough explanations of graphs are given. Furthermore, the explanatory captions and the liberal use of color will help students follow the text discussion and understand graphical analysis.

End-of-Chapter Aids. At the end of each chapter is a *Summary* that highlights the important points of the chapter. More than 270 *Review Questions and Problems* help students review chapter material and require them to solve analytical exercises. Answers to about a third of these questions and problems are provided in the *Appendix* at the end of the book. The *Supplementary Readings* offer suggestions for the interested reader or for outside assignments.

Ancillaries

A *Study Guide* prepared by John Lunn (Miami University, Ohio) is available to give students further review and practice in the use of microeconomic theory. We have written an *Instructor's Manual* to accompany the text. Each chapter in the manual features a chapter outline, general comments on the chapter, specific section-by-section comments and suggestions that may help in developing lectures, and class discussion topics. The manual also contains additional review questions and problems and multiple-choice questions.

Acknowledgments

We have been fortunate to have the assistance of many helpful and able people in the preparation of this book. The following economists reviewed large segments or all of the manuscript at various stages in its development.

Larry Blume, University of Michigan
Wayne Boyet, University of Mississippi
Charles Breeden, Marquette University

Richard Caves, Harvard University
Alvin Cohen, Lehigh University
Darius Conger, Central Michigan University
Robert Ekelund, Auburn University
David Gay, University of Arkansas
John Goddeeris, Michigan State University
Warren Gramm, Washington State University
Timothy Gronberg, Texas A&M University
Barry Hirsch, University of North Carolina at Greensboro
Art Kartman, San Diego State University
Edward Kittrell, Northern Illinois University
Al Link, Auburn University
William McEachern, University of Connecticut
William Novshek, Stanford University
Stanley Stephenson, Pennsylvania State University
Roy Van Til, Bentley College

These reviewers were generous with their time and provided numerous suggestions that helped to improve the book. To them we extend our gratitude and hope the final product meets with their approval.

We would also like to thank several people at Little, Brown who were all authors could hope for in a publishing organization: Al Hockwalt, our economics editor, who oversaw the entire project with skill and good humor, and Kate Campbell, his editorial assistant, who kept us and our reviewers on schedule; Elizabeth Schaaf, our book editor, who most capably and patiently managed the production of the book; and especially Jane Tufts, our developmental editor, who truly deserves the title of "Super Reviewer."

Finally, we would like to thank colleagues at the University of Virginia — Leland Yeager, William Breit, and William Johnson — for their help. In addition, we are also grateful to June Morris for her prompt and competent typing assistance.

E.K.B.
J.M.B.
Charlottesville, Virginia

Brief Contents

Contents

Chapter 7   *The Costs of Production   183*

Chapter 8   *Profit Maximization and the Competitive Firm   215*

Chapter 9   *The Competitive Industry   237*

Chapter 10 *Using the Competitive Model*   *269*

Chapter 11 *Monopoly*   *303*

Chapter 12 *Using Monopoly Theory*   *332*

Microeconomic Theory
and Applications

Microeconomics and Market Analysis

1

If you were to poll the members of the economics profession, a sizable majority would probably agree that microeconomics is the most important subject in the economics curriculum. Microeconomics is important because it supplies the foundation for most of our understanding of how the U.S. economy, or indeed any economy, operates. Although microeconomics provides no pat answers to social problems, it does provide a set of tools to aid us in thinking about economic issues. This text will acquaint you with these analytical techniques and show how their use can help us understand economic events and issues.

In this chapter we introduce the subject of microeconomic theory by first discussing its nature and the role of theory in general. The remainder of the chapter contains a brief description of the market model of supply and demand. The supply-demand model is a good introduction to microeconomics and provides an overview of the subject matter, since it involves the analysis of human behavior as it manifests itself in interactions between buyers and sellers.

THE SCOPE OF MICROECONOMIC THEORY
1.1

The prefix *micro-* in microeconomics comes from the Greek word *mikros*, meaning small. Microeconomics is the branch of economics based on the economic behavior of "small" economic units: consumers, workers, savers, business managers, firms, individual industries and markets, and so on. Microeconomics, however, is not limited to "small" issues. Instead, it reflects the view that many "big" issues can best be understood by recognizing that they are composed of numerous smaller parts. Just as much of our knowledge of chemistry and physics is built on the study of molecules, atoms, and subatomic particles, much of our knowledge of economics is based on the study of individual behavior.

All economic decisions are ultimately made by individuals, and the totality of these decisions defines the economic environment. Consumers decide how much of various goods to purchase, workers decide what jobs to take, and business people decide how many workers to hire and how much output to produce. Microeconomics encompasses the factors that influence these choices and the way these innumerable small decisions merge to determine the workings of the entire economy. Because of the important effects that prices have on these individual decisions, microeconomics is frequently called *price theory*.

Although the basic building block of microeconomic theory is the individual, the resulting theory is capable of dealing with some of the most important social issues of the day. To name a few: environmental pollution, poverty and welfare programs, labor unions and real wages, safety regulation, monopolies and consumer well-being, rising medical costs, discrimination in employment, rent controls and housing shortages, the military draft, energy problems, punishment as a deterrent to crime, the OPEC oil cartel, taxation and work incentives. Economists have used microeconomic techniques to examine these and other important issues in recent years. Have the results demonstrated the value of microeconomic theory? We believe they have, but you can judge for yourself, since most of these topics are discussed in later chapters.

The other major branch of economics is macroeconomics; the prefix *macro-* derives from the Greek word *makros*, meaning large. Macroeconomics deals primarily with the analysis of aggregates like national output and the absolute level of prices, while microeconomics focuses on the composition of output and the relative prices of different goods and services. Thus, each branch deals with different (although sometimes overlapping) issues.

THE NATURE AND ROLE OF THEORY
1.2

In most disciplines, from physics to political science, it is essential to use a theory to make sense of a complex reality. Facts do not always "speak for themselves." In economics, facts may describe a historical episode, but facts can never explain why the episode occurred or how things would have been different had, for example, the government pursued a different policy. Moreover, facts can never demonstrate how, for instance, a change in agricultural price supports will affect agricultural production next year. For purposes of explanation or prediction we must employ a theory that shows how facts are related to one another.

Practical people frequently disparage the use of theories, claiming that experience and facts are better guides. Yet they rely on theories just as much as the student of pure science does. As Yeager and Tuerck note:

> Choosing and interpreting [facts and figures] depends on theories about which ones are relevant and how. Anyone presenting a fact or figure has *some* idea, presumably, of how it fits in, or what difference it makes; and that is his theory. The real contrast is not between people who theorize and people who use only facts but between people who theorize with the advantage of knowing what they are doing and people who theorize without real-

izing it. Facts chosen and presented on the basis of half-formed, unrecognized theories are likely to be worse than useless.[1]

Consciously or unconsciously, we are all theorists both in our personal lives and in our discussions of social or economic issues. The relevant question is whether we use good or bad theories. How can we tell? To see what is involved, consider a theory unquestioningly accepted by millions of people; let's dub it the "calorie theory." The calorie theory holds that a person's weight depends on the number of calories consumed per day: the more calories ingested, the heavier the person will be.

This theory predicts that to lose weight, a person should cut his or her calorie intake. Is this a good theory? Consider these two criticisms. First, the calorie theory is based on very unrealistic assumptions. No one has ever seen a calorie, much less observed the human body convert it into weight. Second, the calorie theory ignores a great many other factors that influence a person's weight: age, sleep, metabolism, exercise, climate, heredity, bone structure, occupation, efficiency of the digestive system. In short, the calorie theory neglects many factors that influence weight, and its assumption that something called calories is converted into body weight appears very unrealistic.

Does this mean that millions of people who count calories are wrong? Not at all; in fact, the calorie theory appears to be a good theory. In practice the posited relationship between calories and weight seems to hold. Many people have observed through personal experience that when they eat more, they gain weight, and when they eat less, they lose weight. *The test of a theory is whether it explains or predicts what it is designed to explain or predict.* The calorie theory passes this test, so we should not discard it just because its assumptions are unrealistic or because it fails to incorporate every conceivable factor related to gaining or losing weight.

We can draw two lessons from this example that are relevant for an evaluation of economic, or other, theories. First, to explain any complex phenomenon, a theory must simplify and abstract from reality. A theory can consider only a few of the many factors that influence real events. The trick is to incorporate the most important factors into the theory and ignore the rest. Microeconomic theory attempts to do this by focusing on costs, revenues, prices, incomes, and the like and neglecting other possible influences.

Second, the assumptions of a theory need not fully or precisely describe reality. The test of any scientific theory is whether it explains the phenomena it is designed to explain, not whether its assumptions exactly mirror reality. The assumptions of the calorie theory are certainly not realistic, but the theory works well. Likewise, in economics we generally assume that business firms make output and price decisions that maximize profits. Such an assumption is probably not completely accurate, but

[1] Leland B. Yeager and David G. Tuerck, *Foreign Trade and U.S. Policy* (New York: Praeger, 1976), p. 115.

the theory based on this assumption passes the same test as the calorie theory; that is, it predicts correctly. A theory does not have to be realistic to be useful.

The body of economic theory developed in the succeeding chapters passes, we believe, the basic test of theory. It explains a wide range of economic phenomena and permits valid predictions of the consequences of changes in certain conditions. This body of theory, however, does not explain all economic phenomena. In some cases the basic theory must be extended to incorporate special features of particular markets, as we will do in several examples. In addition, the degree of accuracy of the theory is likely to differ from one case to another. Better, more accurate theories may be developed over time, but at the present there is a broad consensus in the economics profession that the body of theory developed in the following chapters is the best now available.

POSITIVE ANALYSIS AND VALUE JUDGMENTS
1.3

Many people expect economics to determine which economic institutions, processes, or policies are desirable and which are not. Unfortunately, economics is unable to fulfill that expectation. Economics can sometimes help us evaluate the economic consequences of policies, but it can never by itself demonstrate whether the results are good or bad.

Consider a minimum wage law, in which the government declares it is illegal to pay workers less than some specified amount. Evaluating the desirability of this policy requires three steps:

1. Determination of the effects of the policy. How will it affect employment of workers and the prices of products? What groups will be harmed and what groups will benefit?

2. Determination of the magnitudes of the effects. How much unemployment will be created? How many workers will lose their jobs and how many will retain their jobs at higher wage rates?

3. A judgment that these effects are desirable or undesirable. Does the benefit to workers who remain employed outweigh the costs borne by others?

To decide whether a policy is good or bad depends on these steps. The first step involves identifying the nature of the consequences of the policy. This step is in the realm of *positive analysis,* involving the expected, objective outcomes. The distinguishing feature of positive analysis is that it deals with propositions that can be tested with respect to both their underlying logic and the empirical evidence. Positive analysis is scientific since it draws on accepted standards of logic and evidence that are potentially capable of being used to ascertain the truth or falsity of statements. Microeconomic theory is a form of positive analysis; it can be used, for example, to predict that a minimum wage law will reduce employment.

Identifying the nature of the effects, however, is not sufficient to resolve the question of desirability. We also need some idea of the size of the effects. It may matter a great deal whether the minimum wage causes 1 percent or 25 percent of unskilled workers to lose their jobs. Note that this step still involves positive analysis, but now in quantitative terms rather than qualitative terms. The tools of statistics and econometrics may help determine the magnitudes involved.

Knowing the consequences of an action, both qualitatively and quantitatively, however, is still not sufficient to determine whether or not a policy is desirable. A final step is necessary: we must decide whether the consequences themselves are, on balance, desirable or undesirable. To make this evaluation, each person must make a subjective judgment, a *value judgment*. By nature such a judgment is nonscientific. It cannot be proven to be right or wrong by facts, evidence, or logic. For example, a belief that it is desirable to help unskilled workers at the expense of others falls into this category. People may agree that a particular policy has this effect, but some may hold that the outcome is desirable and others that it is not. Their value judgments differ.

Microeconomic theory cannot demonstrate that a particular set of economic institutions or policies is desirable — and neither, for that matter, can any other scientific branch of knowledge. A belief that something is desirable requires a nonscientific judgment of what constitutes "desirability," and that judgment cannot be supplied by a technique of analysis. Nonetheless, microeconomic theory can assist each of us in reaching such judgments by helping us determine the likely outcomes. In other words, microeconomics helps us take the first of the three steps necessary to make an evaluation of some economic phenomenon.

A familiar joke runs along these lines: put six economists in a room and seven opinions will emerge. Economists disagree about many issues, but they disagree a good deal less about the scientific, or positive, aspects of economic questions than most people think. This statement is particularly true in the field of microeconomic theory.[2] Economists, and other people, may agree about the effects of some policy (steps 1 and 2) but disagree about whether it is desirable because they have different values. This is true in every scientific discipline: physicists, for example, may agree on how a nuclear missile can be made and what the consequences of using it will be, but they may still disagree on whether it should be made or used.

Table 1–1 illustrates this distinction. A random sample of over two hundred economists were polled and asked to express their views on a

[2] The authors of the study cited in Table 1–1 conclude: "Consensus tends to center on microeconomic issues involving the price mechanism while the major areas of disagreement involve macroeconomic and normative issues" (p. 36).

TABLE 1-1

Responses of Economists to Various Propositions

Propositions	Percentage of Respondents Who	
	Agree	Disagree
1. A minimum wage increases unemployment among young and unskilled workers.	90	10
2. A ceiling on rents reduces the quantity and quality of housing available.	98	2
3. The fundamental cause of the rise in oil prices of the past three years is the monopoly power of the large oil companies.	25	75
4. The government should be an employer of last resort and initiate a guaranteed job program.	53	47
5. The distribution of income in the United States should be more equal.	71	29
6. The level of government spending should be reduced (ignoring expenditures for stabilization).	57	43

Note: The responses "Generally Agree" and "Agree with Provisions" have been combined to form the "Agree" column here.

Source: J. Kearl, C. Pope, G. Whiting, and L. Wimmer, "A Confusion of Economists," *American Economic Review*, 69 (May 1979), Table 1.

variety of economic issues. The first three propositions are drawn from the domain of microeconomic theory and are positive statements about the objective consequences of certain economic arrangements. Note the strong consensus on these questions. The consensus, however, concerns the consequences of minimum wages, rent ceilings, and large oil companies and does not imply a value judgment about their respective desirability. (These three issues, incidentally, will be analyzed in later chapters.) Propositions 4, 5, and 6 are *normative* propositions that deal with what ought to be rather than positive propositions that deal with what is or what will be. A normative statement, frequently indicated by the use of words like should or ought, must be based in part on value judgments. Understandably, there is greater disagreement over such issues, but that does not imply that economics is unscientific or that economists disagree greatly over the positive aspects of economic theory.

MARKET ANALYSIS
1.4

Most of microeconomics involves the study of how individual markets function. *Markets*, as the term will be used here, refer to the interplay of all potential buyers and sellers involved in the production, sale, or purchase of a particular commodity or service. A little reflection will convince you that most economic issues involve the way particular markets function. The fact that economists' wages are higher than gas station attendants' wages but lower than doctors' wages reflects the workings of those three labor markets. The impacts of minimum wages and labor unions depend on how the affected labor markets respond. Rapidly rising medical care prices have emerged from transactions in markets for medical care. Economic forces in some markets have produced environmental pollution. Higher gasoline prices have induced consumers to switch to more gas-efficient automobiles, so the gasoline market has affected the automobile market. The list could be extended almost indefinitely, but the point is clear: most economic issues and events can only be understood by studying how markets work.

To analyze markets, we must concentrate on what factors influence the decisions of buyers and sellers. Innumerable factors could have an impact, but some are clearly more important than others. Prices receive special attention. Prices are the results of market transactions, but they also strongly influence the behavior of buyers and sellers in every market — or so microeconomics would suggest.

The term *price* as used in microeconomics always refers to the *relative* price of the item. The absolute, or money, price by itself does not tell us how costly an item really is. Is a 10-cent cup of coffee expensive? In 1920 it would have been outrageously expensive; today it would be a bargain. The problem with absolute prices is that the dollar is an elastic yardstick. For our purposes we need a more meaningful measure, one that does not fluctuate with every change in the price level, so we rely on relative prices.

The relative price of any good reflects its price compared with, or relative to, the prices of other things. Table 1–2 clarifies the distinction between relative and absolute prices. Between 1967 and 1980 the price level, or average price of goods and services, rose by 151.7 percent according to the Consumer Price Index (CPI). (The CPI for all items in 1980 was 251.7; it was 100 in 1967.) The CPI measures the rise in absolute, or dollar, prices. Table 1–2 indicates that the dollar prices of some goods, such as fuel oil, rose by much more than 151.7 percent, and the prices of others, like television sets, rose less. Even though the dollar price of all goods rose, the relative prices of some goods fell. Consider the last column in Table 1–2, which reflects the change in each item's price compared with the change in the average of all prices. Although the price of fuel oil in dollars rose by 485.4 percent, the overall price level more than doubled over the same period, so the relative price of fuel oil rose by "only" 132 percent [(585.4 − 251.7)/251.7]. And the relative price of television sets fell sharply, since that price rose by less than the average price of goods and services. A microeconomist examining this information would say that the prices of the first five items rose while the prices of the last five fell, because in microeconomics the term *price* always refers to a relative price.

Microeconomics emphasizes relative prices because the behavior of buyers and sellers depends on relative, not absolute, prices. Therefore, the

TABLE 1-2
Absolute and Relative Price Changes, 1967-1980

	Index of Absolute Prices in 1980 (1967 = 100)	Percent Change in Relative Prices, 1967-1980
All items	251.7	—
Fuel oil	585.4	+132%
Hospital room	428.4	+70%
Roasted coffee	426.1	+69%
Potatoes	313.2	+24%
Sirloin steak	280.9	+12%
Residential rent	195.1	−22%
New cars	181.7	−28%
Eggs	179.9	−29%
Whiskey	137.6	−45%
Televisions	105.0	−58%

Source: Consumer Price Index Detailed Report, September 1980.

prices that we repeatedly refer to and indicate in various diagrams will mean relative prices unless otherwise noted. Prices, however, will generally be measured in dollar units. This practice is legitimate as long as it is understood that we are using dollars of constant purchasing power — which is the same as measuring each price in comparison with the general price level.

With these preliminaries out of the way, in the remainder of the chapter we describe briefly the most well known, and most important, market model in microeconomics: the supply-demand model. For many readers this discussion will be a review of material learned earlier. Nonetheless, it provides a useful introduction and overview to the subject matter of microeconomics.

DEMAND AND SUPPLY CURVES
1.5

Markets are composed of buyers and sellers. Our analysis of the behavior of buyers relies on demand curves; supply curves depict the behavior of sellers. Let's begin with the buying, or demand, side of the market.

The Demand Curve

The amount of a good that any consumer, or group of consumers, wishes to purchase depends on many factors: income, age, occupation, education and experience, expectations, and so on. It also depends on the price of the good. According to the *law of demand*, the lower the price of a good, the larger the quantity consumers wish to purchase. We must add an important condition. The relationship will necessarily hold only if the other factors that affect consumption, such as income and age, do not change at the same time the price of the good changes.

Figure 1–1 shows a hypothetical market demand curve for jogging shoes. At each possible price the curve identifies the total quantity desired by consumers. At a price of $30 a pair, for example, consumers will wish to purchase 400,000 pairs. If the price is lower, at $20 a pair, consumers will want a larger quantity, 550,000 pairs. Put more briefly, at a price of $30 the *quantity demanded* will be 400,000, while at a price of $20 the *quantity demanded* is 550,000. Note that we do not say that *demand* is higher at the lower price, only that the *quantity demanded* is. When economists use the term *demand* by itself (as in demand and supply), they are referring to the entire relationship, the demand curve. *Quantity demanded*, however, refers to one particular quantity on the demand curve.

The negative slope of the demand curve — higher prices associated with lower quantities — is the graphical representation of the law of demand. Economists believe that the demand curves for all, or virtually all, goods, services, and inputs slope downward. As a consequence, the proposition

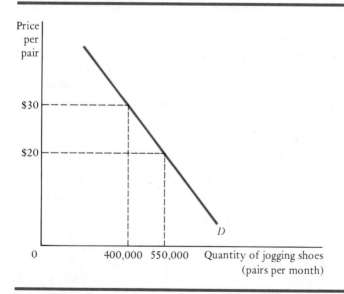

FIGURE 1–1

A Demand Curve

The demand curve *D* shows the quantity of jogging shoes that consumers will purchase at alternative prices. Its negative slope reflects the law of demand: at a lower price more shoes will be purchased.

that demand curves have negative slopes has been elevated in the economist's jargon to the position of a "law." It is probably the most universally valid and strongly supported (by evidence) proposition in economics.

A demand curve for a product must pertain to a particular period of time. For example, the demand curve in Figure 1–1 may refer to consumer buying behavior for July 1982. Another demand curve may be relevant for a different period of time. In addition, the information conveyed by the demand curve refers to alternative possibilities for the same period of time. If the price is $30 in July 1982, consumers will purchase 400,000 pairs of jogging shoes; if instead it is $20 in July 1982, consumers will purchase 550,000 pairs.

Although economists usually interpret the curve as showing *the quantities purchased at various prices*, they sometimes use an equivalent interpretation. The demand curve also identifies *the price that consumers will pay for various quantities*. If 400,000 pairs of jogging shoes are placed on the market, consumers will be willing to pay $30 per pair. If the larger quantity, 550,000, is offered on the market, consumers will purchase the quantity only at the lower price of $20. A larger quantity can only be sold at a lower price; this is another, and equivalent, way of stating the law of demand.

A final point about demand curves. Their negative slope is not due only to the presence of more consumers at lower prices. In fact, for some goods like water, the number of consumers will be the same regardless of price. The greater consumption of water at a lower price is due to more consumption per person, not to more people consuming water. At the other extreme are goods for which more consumption at lower prices results mainly from new consumers entering the market. Novels might be an example of such a good. Most goods fall between these extremes; more consumers enter the market, and more consumption per consumer occurs at lower prices.

Shifts in the Demand Curve

As mentioned earlier, many factors influence consumer purchases. A demand curve just focuses on the effect of changes in price, with other factors held constant. For example, consumers' incomes are assumed to be the same at all points on a particular demand curve. Now let's consider the other factors, besides the good's price, that might affect consumption of a good. First are the *incomes* of consumers. The level of income is certain to affect the amount of goods consumers will purchase; usually they wish to purchase more when income rises. Second are the *prices of closely related goods*. For example, at a much higher entrance fee for marathons, fewer jogging shoes would be purchased. Third are the *tastes*, or *preferences*, of consumers. Tastes mean the underlying, subjective feelings of consumers about the desirability of different goods and services. Should joggers decide that swimming is better exercise – a change in tastes — the purchases of jogging shoes would drop off. These three factors do not exhaust the possibilities, but they are almost certain to be significant for virtually all goods and services, so we will concentrate on them.

In drawing a demand curve, incomes, the prices of related goods, and consumer preferences are assumed to be the same at all points on the curve. The purpose of holding them constant is not to deny that they ever change but to identify the independent influence of the good's own price on consumer purchases. If incomes, prices of related goods, or preferences do change, the entire demand curve shifts. Figure 1–2 illustrates such a shift. (Note that here we begin to use familiar shorthand terms on the axes, price and quantity. It should be understood that we mean price per unit and quantity per time period.) Demand curve *D*, for example, reflects conditions when consumers' incomes average $10,000 and the other factors mentioned are held constant. If consumers' incomes rose to $15,000, consumers would wish to purchase more jogging shoes at every price than they did before. The change in income produces a *shift in the demand curve* from *D* to *D'*. In this case an increase in income *increases demand* for the good, meaning that the entire demand curve shifts outward. A *decrease in demand* refers to an inward, or leftward, shift in the

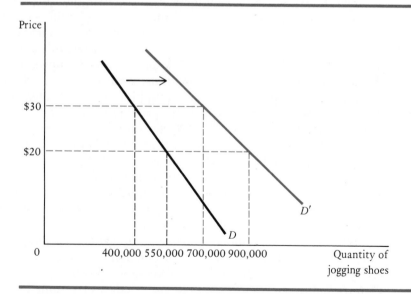

FIGURE 1–2

An Increase in Demand

In drawing a demand curve, consumers' incomes, consumers' preferences, and prices of other goods are held constant. Changes in these underlying factors normally cause the demand curve to shift. Here an increase in consumers' incomes causes the demand curve to shift from *D* to *D'*.

demand curve toward the origin. If joggers decide swimming is better exercise, the demand for jogging shoes would decrease.

To use demand curves correctly, it is important to distinguish clearly between situations that involve a *shift in demand* and ones that involve a *movement along a given demand curve*. A movement along a demand curve occurs when the quantity demanded (not demand) changes in response to a change in price while the other factors that affect consumption are held constant. A shift in demand occurs when there is a change in incomes, prices of related goods, or preferences that affects the quantities demanded at each possible price.

The Supply Curve

On the selling side of a market we are interested in the amount of a good that business firms will produce and sell. The amount firms offer for sale depends on many factors, among them the technological know-how concerning production of the good, the cost and productivity of inputs required for production, expectations, employee-management relations, and so on. The price of the good is also important since it is the reward producers receive for their efforts. The supply curve summarizes the effect of price on the quantity that firms produce and offer for sale.

Figure 1–3 shows a hypothetical market supply curve for jogging shoes. For each possible price the supply curve identifies the combined quantities the separate firms will offer for sale. Since all the firms that produce a particular product constitute the industry, this curve is generally called the industry, or market, supply curve. It shows, for example, that at a price of $20 per pair, total industry output will be 300,000 pairs of jogging shoes. The upward-sloping supply curve indicates that the industry will produce more when the price is higher. If the price is $30 instead of $20, output will be 600,000 rather than 300,000. Stated differently, at a price of $20 the *quantity supplied* will be 300,000, while at a price of $30 the *quantity supplied* will be 600,000. Note that we do not say that *supply* is greater at the higher price, only that the *quantity supplied* is. The term *supply* by itself refers to the entire supply curve while *quantity supplied* refers to one particular quantity on the curve. This terminology parallels that used for the demand curve.

Supply curves for most goods slope upward. Basically, this upward slope reflects the fact that per-unit production costs rise when more units are produced, so a higher price is necessary to elicit a greater output. In Chapter 9, though, we will see that supply curves for some products may be horizontal. Upward-sloping supply curves, however, are thought to be the most common shape, and we will draw them this way here.

Several points made in connection with demand curves are also relevant to supply curves. The supply curve must pertain to a particular period of time. For example, the curve in Figure 1–3 may refer to what

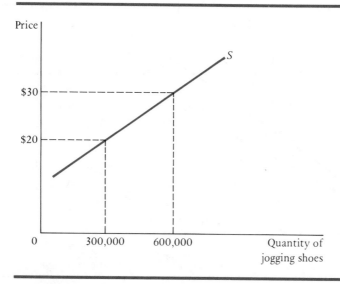

FIGURE 1-3

A Supply Curve

The supply curve *S* shows the quantity of jogging shoes producers will be willing to sell at alternative prices. It generally slopes upward, indicating that output will increase at a higher price.

firms in the industry will do in July 1982. In addition, points on the supply curve refer to alternative possibilities for the same period of time. Finally, the number of firms producing the good may vary along the supply curve. At low prices some firms may halt production and leave the industry; at high prices new firms may enter the industry.

Shifts in the Supply Curve

The supply curve shows the influence of price on quantity supplied when other factors that also influence output are held constant. When any of the other factors change, the entire supply curve shifts.

There are two important factors, other than the good's own price, that affect quantity supplied. First is the *state of technological knowledge* concerning the various ways a product can be manufactured. Second are the *conditions of supply of inputs*, like labor and energy, that are used to produce the good. Supply conditions for inputs relate to the prices that must be paid for their use. Other factors may be important in particular cases — for example, weather in the case of agricultural crops — but technology and input supply conditions influence all output markets.

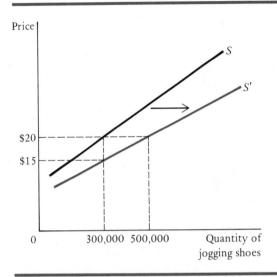

FIGURE 1-4

An Increase in Supply

In drawing a supply curve, technology and input supply conditions are held constant. Changes in these underlying factors normally cause the supply curve to shift. Here an increase in the supply of workers causes the supply curve to shift from *S* to *S'*.

In drawing a supply curve, we assume that technological knowledge and input supply conditions do not vary along the curve. The supply curve shows how variation in price alone affects output. If technology or input supply conditions do change, the supply curve shifts. For instance, if a new invention allows manufacturers to produce jogging shoes at a lower cost, the supply curve shifts to the right, as illustrated in Figure 1–4. After the technological advance, the quantity supplied is greater at each possible price, as shown by the shift in the supply curve from *S* to *S'*. The rightward and downward movement in the supply curve reflects an *increase in supply*. If there is an increase in supply, each quantity will be available at a lower price than before. For example, before the technological advance 300,000 pairs of jogging shoes would have been produced only if the price was at least $20; afterward, 300,000 would be produced at a price of $15.

Just as with demand curves, *shifts in supply* must be carefully distinguished from *movements along a given supply curve.* A movement along a supply curve occurs when the quantity supplied varies in response to a change in the product's selling price while the other factors that affect output are held constant. A shift in the supply curve occurs when the other factors that affect output change.

DETERMINATION OF PRICE AND QUANTITY
1.6

The demand curve shows what consumers wish to purchase at various prices, and the supply curve shows what producers wish to sell. When the two are put together, we see that there is only one price at which the quantity consumers wish to purchase exactly equals the quantity firms wish to sell. In Figure 1–5 that price is $25, where consumers wish to purchase 475,000 pairs of jogging shoes and firms wish to sell the same quantity. It is identified by the point of intersection between the supply and demand curves.

The intersection identifies the *equilibrium* price and quantity in the market. The concept of equilibrium involves a balancing of opposing forces. In the case of a market, equilibrium means there is no tendency for the price or quantity to change as long as the supply or the demand curve does not shift. A basic conclusion of microeconomic theory is that the independent actions of buyers and sellers will tend to establish the equilibrium price and quantity.

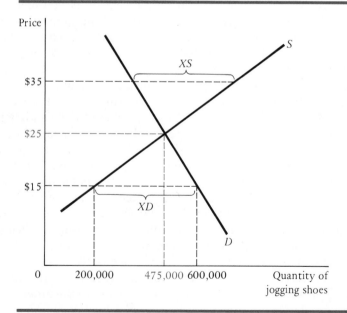

FIGURE 1–5
Determination of the Equilibrium Price and Quantity

The point of intersection of the supply and the demand curves identifies the equilibrium price and quantity. Here, at a price of $25, the quantity demanded by consumers exactly equals the quantity supplied by firms. Market forces tend to produce this outcome.

That a market composed of thousands or millions of persons, each acting independently, could by itself attain an equilibrium is really quite remarkable. Market equilibrium signifies a great degree of coordination among the activities of many separate persons and firms. Each individual consumer decides how much to purchase without regard to what other consumers are doing, and yet all consumers are able to acquire the quantities they wish. Each individual firm decides how much to produce and sell without regard to what other firms are doing, and yet all firms are able to sell what they have produced. The mutual compatibility in the plans of independent economic agents is characteristic of a market equilibrium and explains why an equilibrium will persist unless something happens to change the position of the supply or the demand curve.

We have just asserted that a market left to itself will establish the equilibrium price and quantity shown graphically by the intersection of supply and demand curves. This conclusion can best be understood by imagining that the price is not at its equilibrium level and recognizing that market participants — firms and consumers — have incentives to behave in ways that involve a movement toward the equilibrium. Suppose, for example, that the price is $15 in Figure 1–5. At $15 the demand curve indicates that consumers want 600,000 pairs of jogging shoes, but the supply curve shows that firms will only produce 200,000 pairs. This is a *disequilibrium;* the quantity demanded exceeds the quantity supplied, so the plans of buyers and sellers are inconsistent. The excess of the amount consumers want (600,000) over what firms will sell (200,000), or 400,000 pairs, is called the *excess demand (XD)*, or *shortage*, at the price of $15.

Think about how the people involved — consumers and business managers — will react in this situation. Consumers are frustrated at not getting as much as they wish, and they are willing to pay a higher price to obtain more shoes. Business managers will see that consumers want more jogging shoes and are willing to pay a higher price for them. There will therefore be a strong tendency for the actual price to rise. Whenever there is a shortage at some price, market forces — the behavior of buyers and sellers in the marketplace — tend to produce a higher price. As the price rises, quantity demanded falls below 600,000 (a movement along the demand curve), and quantity supplied increases beyond 200,000 (a movement along the supply curve). The process continues until quantity demanded equals quantity supplied at a price of $25.

Alternatively, if for some reason the price is above $25, the quantity firms wish to sell will be greater than the quantity consumers are willing to purchase. An *excess supply (XS)*, or *surplus*, will exist at a higher-than-equilibrium price. Unsold goods pile up. In this case market forces exert a downward pressure on price, because firms cut prices rather than accumulate unwanted inventories. Once again there is a tendency toward the equilibrium price and quantity.

Therefore, at any price other than the equilibrium price, market forces will tend to cause price and quantity to change in the direction of their equilibrium values. That observation is the basis for asserting that the supply-demand intersection will tend to be established. We say "tend to be" since there is no presumption that a market is always in equilibrium. The equilibrium position itself will change when demand or supply curves shift, so actual markets may, in effect, be pursuing a moving objective as they continually adjust toward equilibrium.

Adjustment to Changes in Demand or Supply

The most common application of the supply and demand model is to explain or predict how a change in market conditions affects price and output. Figure 1–6a illustrates a situation where there is an increase in demand but no change in supply. Demand might increase, for instance, following a report from the Surgeon General's Office that jogging not only reduces the risk of heart attack but also doubles life expectancy. If believed, this report would probably shift the demand curve for jogging shoes to the right but leave the supply curve unaffected.

Before demand increases, the equilibrium price and quantity are $25 and 475,000 pairs of jogging shoes. When the demand curve shifts to D', a shortage will temporarily exist at the original price of $25 — quantity demanded (650,000) will exceed quantity supplied (475,000). As a conse-

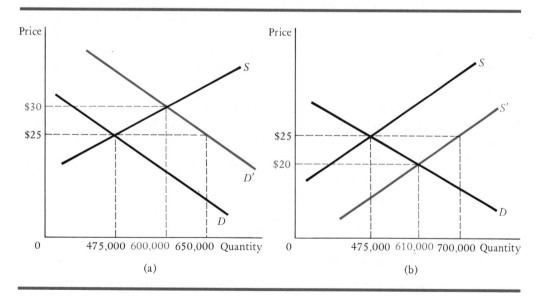

FIGURE 1–6

Market Adjustments to Changes in Demand and Supply

Part a shows that an increase in demand from *D* to *D'*, with supply unchanged, leads to a higher price and output. Part b shows that an increase in supply from *S* to *S'*, with demand unchanged, leads to a lower price and higher output.

quence, there will be upward pressure on price. Thus, price will rise, quantity supplied will increase, and quantity demanded will decline until a new equilibrium price and quantity of $30 and 600,000 pairs of shoes are determined, as indicated by the intersection of D' and S. Note that the higher output is not described as an increase in supply. Supply has not increased; the quantity supplied has (involving a movement along the unchanged supply curve).

Figure 1–6b shows the effects of an increase in supply when there is no change in demand. Suppose the Surgeon General reports that employment in the shoe industry has the aforementioned benefits. If believed, the report will cause the supply curve to shift outward as workers flood into the jogging shoe industry, depressing wages. At the initial price of $25, firms would now wish to sell more shoes than consumers would be willing to buy at that price, and a temporary surplus would result. Price would fall, and a new equilibrium with a price of $20 and an output of 610,000 would be established. Note that the greater purchases of consumers at the new equilibrium are not described as an increase in demand. Demand has not increased; quantity demanded has increased because of a lower price.

According to this theoretical analysis, changes in supply or demand conditions — or both — will affect, among other things, the price and the output of products. Do real world markets respond to the forces of supply and demand in the way suggested by the theory? Over time, economists have accumulated and evaluated a great deal of evidence with sophisticated statistical techniques and found that many real world markets function in this way. Careful attention to the news media also supplies more evidence, though of a less sophisticated sort. Here are a few examples.[3]

> The use of wood as a substitute for other, more expensive, fuels to heat homes during the winter has become more widespread.... Rising demand for firewood has sent prices soaring....[4]

(See Figure 1–6a; higher electricity and fuel oil prices increase the demand for firewood.)

> Usually U.S. farmers produce more than enough to supply all the peanuts and peanut butter Americans can consume[!], but last year the crop declined by 42 percent [due to a drought in the summer of 1980].... 12 ounce jars of Peter Pan and Skippy now cost $1.49. A year ago Peter Pan cost $1.15 and Skippy cost $1.05.[5]

(See Figure 1–6b; a decrease in supply means a shift from S' to S.)

[3] Note that the price increases reported in the examples are increases in *absolute* prices. Since the annual inflation rate at the time was about 10 percent, the *relative* prices did not rise as much as the dollar prices, but they still rose significantly.
[4] "Firewood Rustlers — A New Scourge," *Daily Progress*, November 19, 1980, p. B12.
[5] "Peanut Butter Supplies Increase, Price Decreases," *Daily Progress*, May 27, 1981, p. A12.

> ... Last year, in the first decline in more than 20 years, travel on the major [airline] carriers fell 7%. ... Higher air fares, propelled by rising fuel costs, are mainly to blame. ... In 1980 ... fares soared nearly 30%.[6]

(See Figure 1–6b; a shift from *S'* to *S.*)

> A cord of firewood in suburban New York cost $130 or more this year. ... In the St. Louis area, where wood is more plentiful, the price is $85 a cord. ...[7]

(Why?)

Hundreds of similar examples are reported in the news media each year and are one reason why economists are confident of the predictive and explanatory power of the supply-demand model.

Thomas Carlyle, the nineteenth-century essayist and historian who first christened economics the "Dismal Science," also observed that "it is easy to train an economist; teach a parrot to say Demand and Supply." It may take a bit more effort to use the supply-demand model correctly, however. The following statement, from a leading high school government text, is intended to describe how markets function.

> The *price* is determined by the market place and the operation of the *law of supply and demand*. Under the law of supply and demand, as the demand for a product goes up, as people want more of a certain product, the price tends to go up. But as the price increases, the demand tends to go down. This decrease in demand tends to lower prices, and lowered prices again tend to increase demand. Supply and demand vary with increases and decreases of prices. Eventually, supply and demand balance, creating a market price.[8]

It would be difficult to cram many more errors into this short statement. Using supply-demand analysis correctly offers powerful insights into the operation of real world markets, but working with it requires some care. On the other hand, perhaps a parrot could have said it better.

The Cost-Price Illusion

Casual observation leads many people to believe that production costs *alone* determine price. Costs do play a role — as shown by the supply curve — but they do not unilaterally determine prices. The impression that they do, however, is sometimes created by the way markets function, and it is important to understand the source of the confusion.

Let's consider the market for beef; we'll restrict our attention to a very short-run situation so there is no time to vary the number of cattle

---

[6] William M. Carley, "Ever Climbing Air Fares Cut into Travel, Raising Prospect of Long Slump for Carriers," *Wall Street Journal*, February 6, 1981, p. 23.

[7] *Wall Street Journal*, November 13, 1980, p. 1.

[8] Stanley E. Diamond and Elmer F. Pflieger, *Our American Government* (Philadelphia: Lippincott, 1973), p. 608.

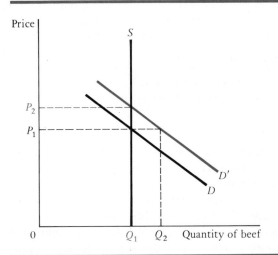

FIGURE 1–7
An Increase in Demand with Fixed Supply

With a vertical supply curve, which indicates that quantity supplied will not vary in response to changes in price, an increase in demand from *D* to *D'* leads to a higher price but an unchanged quantity sold.

brought to market.[9] In this case the supply curve is approximately vertical, like the curve in Figure 1–7. The costs of raising cattle have already been incurred in the past, so they cannot be the reason prices change in the current short-run setting. Suppose demand is shown by *D;* then the equilibrium price and quantity in this time period are P_1 and Q_1. Now assume consumer demand rises to *D'*. Price will rise to P_2, but quantity remains unchanged because we are looking at only the immediate, or very short-run, response. In this example the change in demand is responsible for the increase in price.

Now let's look at the market adjustment in more detail to see why it may appear, incorrectly, that cost increases cause the price to rise. When demand increases, butchers and beef retailers initially meet the increased demand by running down their inventories. The individual retailers are unaware that market demand has increased; they may think their increased sales just represent a temporary fluctuation. Thus, retailers do not immediately increase price. They do, however, increase their orders to replenish depleted inventories. Since the total market demand has actually increased, all retailers will try to increase their purchases of beef simultaneously.

[9] This instructive example is based on A. Alchian and W. Allen, *Exchange and Production: Competition, Coordination, and Control* (Belmont, Calif.: Wadsworth, 1977) pp. 85–87.

Retailers purchase beef from meat packers, who also keep inventories to smooth out temporary fluctuations in sales. Packers initially meet the increased demand of retailers from inventories, but then they instruct their cattle buyers to purchase more cattle. Since the quantity of cattle is fixed, as cattle buyers try to buy more than before, they bid up the price of cattle. This may be the first point at which a price actually changes.

Cattle buyers return to their employers, the meat packers, with the same total amount of cattle but purchased at a higher price. Packers view this higher price as an increase in their costs. Packers in turn charge the local butcher, or retailer, a higher price for beef, and retailers raise the price they charge consumers, also complaining of higher costs. If consumers ask why prices have risen, retailers will no doubt say, "I'm just passing along an increase in my costs." Yet in this example, we know that the true source of the higher price is increased demand by consumers.

A casual look at markets can easily give the impression that costs determine prices, even in this situation, where they play no role. Thus, a false impression can result from looking at only the final link in the process of getting goods to consumers, the retail market. The appearance that costs determine prices, and that demand does not matter, is called the *cost-price illusion*. Do you see how a person who thinks "facts speak for themselves" might conclude that higher costs caused the price of beef to increase?

This example invites two comments. First, demand is one of the determinants of prices, just as cost is. Both supply and demand matter. Second, our theoretical analysis of this situation, as illustrated in Figure 1–7, does not *describe* the entire process through which the higher price results. We just say that with an increase in demand and a vertical supply curve, the price goes up. Theory does not have to be descriptive, or realistic, for it to analyze the consequences correctly. Theory should simplify and focus on the major forces at work. If it is a good theory, it will help us reach the right conclusions without superfluous detail.

PRICE SETTING BY GOVERNMENT
1.7

Markets can be thought of as self-adjusting mechanisms; they automatically adjust to any change that affects the behavior of buyers and sellers in the market. For markets to adjust in the way we have explained, however, the price must be free to move in response to the interplay of supply and demand. In some instances, though, the government steps in and regulates price, so it is not set by the interaction of buyers and sellers. The supply-demand model can also be used to analyze this form of government intervention.

Suppose the market-determined price of gasoline is $2.00 per gallon, and the government makes it illegal to charge more than $1.50 per gallon. That is, the government imposes a legislated maximum price, or price

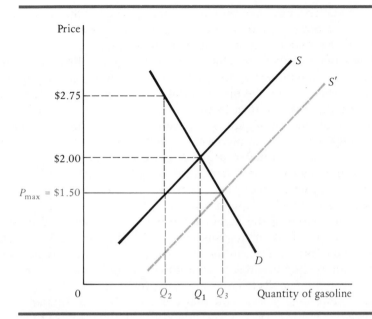

FIGURE 1–8

A Price Ceiling

With demand curve D and supply curve S. a price ceiling of $1.50 ($P_{max}$) reduces the output of gasoline from Q_1 to Q_2 but increases the quantity consumers wish to purchase from Q_1 to Q_3. The difference between Q_3 and Q_2 indicates the size of the shortage produced by the price ceiling.

ceiling. Figure 1–8 illustrates a price ceiling. The initial equilibrium quantity is Q_1, indicated by the intersection of the supply and demand curves. (Ignore the dashed supply curve for the moment.) Note that when the government sets a maximum price of $1.50, none of the underlying factors that determine the positions of the supply and demand curves are altered, so the supply and demand curves stay put. At $1.50 per gallon, producers reduce output along the supply curve to Q_2. Consumers, on the other hand, want a larger quantity at $1.50, so quantity demanded rises from Q_1 to Q_3. At the maximum legal price of $1.50, consumers wish to buy more than they did before, while producers make less available. The result is a shortage equal to $Q_3 - Q_2$. Consumers cannot get as much gasoline as they wish: quantity demanded exceeds quantity supplied.

In unregulated markets, shortages are only temporary, since they set forces in motion that quickly tend to bring quantity demanded and quantity supplied into equality. However, the normal response to a temporary shortage, a rise in price, cannot occur when a price ceiling exists. The shortage will persist unless underlying conditions of supply and demand fortuitously change to eliminate it or the government removes the price ceiling.

Although the price will not rise in response to the shortage, the market forces that put upward pressure on price still exist and will make their presence known. For example, how will the quantity that is available, Q_2, be divided, or rationed, among consumers who would like to purchase a larger quantity, Q_3? If government does not become involved in rationing the reduced quantity, some form of *nonprice rationing* is likely to arise. For example, sellers may provide gasoline on a "first come, first served" basis. Then consumers must compete with each other by trying to get to the gas station first, and the result is long lines at the gas pumps. Time spent waiting in line is a cost to consumers and makes the true cost of buying gasoline greater than $1.50 per gallon.

Another common response to a price ceiling is *quality deterioration*. Sellers don't have to offer so high a quality product to attract buyers, since there are already more buyers than can be served. In the sale of gasoline, for instance, service stations would probably remain open fewer hours per day or days per week; owners would use more self-service gas pumps; and gas station attendants would eliminate special services, such as cleaning windshields.

A third response to a price ceiling is the emergence of *black markets*, where purchases of gasoline take place illegally at prices above $1.50. Black markets occur because consumers are willing to pay more than the legal price to get more gasoline. In Figure 1–8, when the quantity Q_2 is legally available, consumers will be willing to pay as much as $2.75, as shown by the height to the demand curve at that quantity, for more gasoline. Producers will benefit if they sell gasoline at a price above $1.50, so there is scope for transactions that benefit both consumers and producers — which is why black market exchanges are likely to occur. The extent of black market activities will depend on the penalties government applies to this behavior and how stiffly they are enforced.

This example illustrates that market forces are still relevant even when the market is not allowed to determine prices. Moreover, the supply-demand model is also helpful in thinking about the ways these forces are likely to manifest themselves. We should not overlook one conclusion of this analysis: a price ceiling may harm some, or all, consumers. While producers are obviously harmed, consumers may be too. Despite the intention of supporters of price ceilings to benefit consumers, their goal may be thwarted. Although a lower price per unit for each unit purchased is a gain for consumers, there are harmful effects that diminish the benefits: a lower quantity is available, extra costs in the form of waiting time are incurred, product quality deteriorates, and black market prices may be higher than prices in an uncontrolled market. On balance, it is not clear that consumers benefit.

We have analyzed a price ceiling on gasoline as a hypothetical example, but those familiar with recent United States history will recall an episode that closely parallels this analysis. In the winter of 1973–1974 the federal government was using a general system of temporary wage and price controls, which included a price ceiling on gasoline. In late 1973 the ceiling price on gasoline was close to the market equilibrium level and therefore had little effect. In Figure 1–8, the dashed supply curve S' was the relevant one at the time. Then unexpectedly the infamous Arab oil embargo occurred, which reduced the supply of oil in United States markets, causing the supply curve to shift from S'to S. With the price control in effect, price could not rise and a shortage resulted. All the effects we deduced from our theoretical model were, in fact, observed. (Note that the price control at that time just kept the price from rising to its new equilibrium level, but the same analysis is appropriate.) When price controls were removed in the spring of 1974, waiting lines, black markets, and the like soon vanished, along with the shortage — but the price of gasoline went up sharply.

In a later chapter a more detailed analysis will be presented of a price ceiling applied to rental housing, commonly called rent control. We will also consider two cases where the government has pegged the price at a level above the market equilibrium level (a price floor): the Civil Aeronautics Board's regulation of airline fares and the government's use of agricultural price supports.

Summary

Microeconomic theory is the branch of economics that begins with the study of the behavior of individual economic units, primarily consumers and business firms, and considers how their decisions are coordinated through interactions in markets. Like all study of complex phenomena, microeconomics makes use of abstract theories or models that emphasize certain relationships and neglect others. Although these models may not be realistic, they can be very useful. The important test of any theory is whether it helps us explain or predict the phenomena it is designed to investigate.

Most economic issues and events involve the workings of individual markets. As an example of market analysis, we reviewed the most important market model, the supply-demand model. In this model the behavior of buyers is analyzed using the demand curve. The demand curve shows how much people will purchase at different relative prices when other factors that affect purchases are held constant. The demand curve slopes downward, reflecting the law of demand. Analysis of the sellers' side of the market relies on the supply curve, which shows the amount that firms will offer for sale at different relative prices, other factors being constant. The supply curve typically slopes upward.

The intersection of the demand and supply curves identifies the equilibrium price and quantity. We saw how the behavior of buyers and sellers, as they interact in the marketplace, tends to establish the equilibrium price and quantity. A shift in the supply or the demand curve produces a change in the equilibrium quantity and price. We also applied the supply-demand model to a situation where the market is not permitted to establish the equilibrium, or market-clearing, price because the government sets a maximum legal price. Even in that case, however, the market forces underlying the supply and demand curves are still relevant in analyzing the actual consequences of the price ceiling.

Review Questions and Problems

Questions or problems marked with an asterisk have answers given in the appendix.

1. Select a proposed or actual government policy that you feel is very desirable. Explain your support of this policy in terms of the

three steps set out in Section 1.3. For each step in the argument, explain how a reasonable person might disagree with your conclusion. Do you think disagreement is more likely to be due to differences in positive analysis (steps 1 and 2) or differences in value judgments?

2. Economists are frequently asked questions like these: "Is policy X really good for the country?" "What should the United States do to improve its faltering economy?" Why is it unsurprising that economists give different answers to questions like these? Do these disagreements imply that economics is not a science?

3. Explain the distinction between absolute price and relative price. Why does the law of demand relate the purchases of a commodity to its relative price but not to its absolute price?

*4. A newspaper article points out that the price of economics textbooks is up 10 percent this year over last year, and yet sales are higher this year. The author claims that these figures show that the law of demand does not apply to textbooks. What two mistakes has the author made in interpreting the law of demand?

5. A demand curve is drawn holding "other things constant." What does the "other things constant" proviso mean, and why is it important to a correct interpretation of the law of demand?

*6. "Education is expensive, but nothing is more valuable." "America needs more energy." "Social Security should cover our basic needs in retirement." Some economists get furious when they hear statements like these. Can you explain why?

7. Distinguish between increase in *demand* and increase in *quantity demanded.* Distinguish between increase in *supply* and increase in *quantity supplied.*

8. Explain why the point of intersection between a supply and demand curve identifies the equilibrium price and quantity.

9. Use demand and supply curve analysis to point out the errors in the quotation in the middle of page 19.

*10. You see an article entitled "Demand for Coal Expected to Exceed Supply by 1990." What does this statement mean in terms of supply and demand curves? Would you expect to see a shortage of coal in 1990?

11. The equilibrium price is sometimes referred to as the *market-clearing price.* What does this phrase mean?

*12. The supply and demand schedules for apples are shown below.

Demand		Supply	
Price per pound	Quantity demanded per year	Price per pound	Quantity supplied per year
$0.90	100,000	$0.60	100,000
0.80	110,000	0.70	120,000
0.70	120,000	0.80	140,000
0.60	135,000	0.90	150,000

Use graphs to answer the following questions.

a. What is the market equilibrium price and quantity?
b. The government agrees to purchase as many pounds of apples as growers will sell at a price of $0.80. How much will the government purchase, how much will consumers purchase, and how much will be produced?
c. Suppose the government policy in part b remains in effect, but consumer demand increases by 10 percent (consumers will purchase 10 percent more at each price than they did before). What will be the effects on total apple output, purchases by consumers, purchases by government, and the price of apples?

13. In economics what do we mean by the term *shortage?* In unregulated competitive markets are there ever shortages? Does monopoly ever produce a shortage? Have you ever heard noneconomists use the term *shortage* with a different meaning?

14. "A decrease in supply will lead to an increase in the price, which decreases demand, thus lowering price. Hence, a decrease in supply has no effect on the price of a good." Evaluate this statement.

15. Consider the market for taxi service in a city. Explain, by using supply and demand curves, how each of the following actions will affect the market. (Consider each case separately.)

a. Bus drivers go on strike.
b. Bus fares increase after a strike by bus drivers.
c. Taxi drivers must pass a competency test, and a third fail.
d. Gasoline prices increase.
e. Half the downtown parking lots are converted to office buildings.
f. The population of the city increases.

Supplementary Readings

Alchian, Armen, and Allen, William. *Exchange and Production: Competition, Coordination, and Control.* 2nd ed. Belmont, Calif.: Wadsworth, 1977. Chaps. 2, 3, 4.

Dorfman, Robert. *Prices and Markets.* 2nd ed. Englewood Cliffs, N.J.: Prentice-Hall, 1972.

Friedman, Milton. "The Methodology of Positive Economics." In *Readings in Microeconomics,* edited by William Breit and Harold Hochman. New York: Holt, Rinehart and Winston, 1971.

Robbins, Lionel. *The Nature and Significance of Economic Science.* 2nd ed. London: Macmillan, 1935.

The Theory of Consumer Choice

2

Consumers spend more than $2 trillion annually in the United States, purchasing a bewildering variety of goods and services. These outlays reflect hundreds of millions of decisions by consumers to buy or not to buy various goods. Why do consumers purchase some things and not others? How do incomes, prices, and tastes affect consumption decisions? In this chapter we develop the fundamentals of the theory economists use to explain how these factors interact to determine consumption choices.

One important use of the theory of consumer choice is to explain why demand curves slope downward. If the theory of consumer behavior developed here provided nothing more than a justification for drawing demand curves with negative slopes, it would hardly be worth the trouble to discuss it. The basic principles of the theory, however, have far broader applications. Economists have extended this theory to such things as consumer decisions concerning labor supply, saving and investment, charitable contributions, voting choices, and even marriage. Indeed, some believe it provides the basis for a general theory of all human choices, not just consumer choices among goods and services in the marketplace. Several applications will be examined later in Chapter 4, but first it is important to develop the theory fully as it pertains to the simple choices, among goods and services, made by a consumer.

The basic model is developed for a single consumer. Of course, we do not expect the model to explain the behavior of any *specific* person. Rather it will serve as a building block to aid in understanding the behavior of groups of consumers. As such, it focuses on what are thought to be fairly common factors that influence consumer behavior. Two factors are emphasized. First is the objective ability of the consumer to acquire goods, which is determined by income and by the prices of the goods. Second are the subjective attitudes, or tastes, of the consumer concerning the relative desirability of various combinations of goods and services.

THE BUDGET LINE

2.1

To understand how a consumer's income and the prices that must be paid for various goods limit choices, let's begin with a simple example. Consider a consumer who has a weekly income of $100 that is used to purchase only two goods, food and clothing. The price of a unit of food (P_F) is $10, and the price of a unit of clothing (P_C) is $5. Our first task is to show what combinations of food and clothing may be purchased given the income available and the prices of the two goods. Table 2–1 is one way of identifying the various *market baskets* (combinations of food and clothing) that the consumer can purchase under these conditions.

Market basket M in Table 2–1 shows what can be bought if all the consumer's income goes to purchase clothing. An income of $100 permits the consumer to buy 20 units of clothing at a price of $5, with nothing left over for food purchases. Basket N shows the other extreme, when the consumer's entire income goes for food. Since food costs $10 per unit, only 10 units can be purchased, with nothing left over for clothing. All the intermediate baskets, A through I, indicate the other mixes of food and clothing that cost a total of $100. In short, Table 2–1 lists all the alternative combinations of the two goods that a consumer can purchase with an income of $100.

Figure 2–1 shows a more convenient way of presenting this information. In this diagram the quantity of clothing consumed per week is measured on the vertical axis, and the quantity of food is measured on the horizontal axis. Both axes therefore measure *quantities* (in contrast to a supply-demand diagram that has price on one axis). The line MN plots the various market baskets a consumer may purchase, from the data in Table 2–1. This line is called the *budget line*, and it shows all the combinations of food and clothing a consumer can buy given the income and prices assumed.

TABLE 2–1
Alternative Market Baskets a Consumer May Purchase

Market Basket	Market Baskets Composed of	
	Units of Clothing per Week	Units of Food per Week
M	20	0
A	18	1
B	16	2
C	14	3
D	12	4
E	10	5
F	8	6
G	6	7
H	4	8
I	2	9
N	0	10

Note: Income = $100; P_C = $5; P_F = $10.

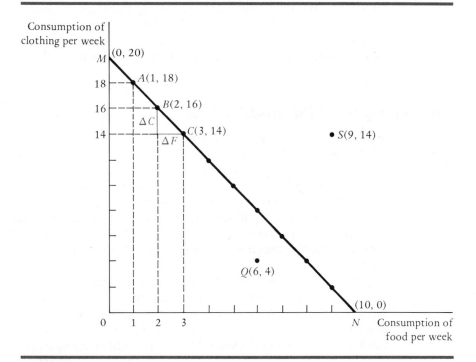

FIGURE 2-1
The Budget Line

A consumer's budget line shows the various combinations of goods that can be purchased with a given money income and prices of goods held constant. Line MN shows the budget line when income is $100, $P_C = \$5$, and $P_F = \$10$. The slope of the budget line is $-P_F/P_C$.

The budget line is drawn as a continuous line, not a collection of discrete points such as A, B, and C. This reflects an assumption of continuous divisibility: that is, fractional units may be purchased. Although the assumption of continuous divisibility may be questioned — we can purchase zero or one haircut in a week, for example, but can we purchase half a haircut? — a little reflection shows that we can purchase half a haircut per week by purchasing one every other week. Viewing consumption as the average consumption per week, rather than the precise level of consumption in any specific week, makes the assumption of a continuous budget line acceptable in most cases.

The consumer's budget line identifies the options from which the consumer can choose. In our specific example the consumer can purchase any basket on or inside the budget line MN. Any basket inside the budget line, such as Q, involves a total outlay that is smaller than the consumer's income. Any point outside the budget line, such as S, requires an outlay larger than the consumer's income and is therefore beyond reach. Consequently, the budget line reinforces the concept of scarcity to the consumer: it is impossible to have unlimited amounts of everything, so choices among possible options, which are shown by the budget line, must be made.

The Geometry of the Budget Line

A thorough understanding of the geometry of a budget line will prove helpful later on. Note that the intercepts with the axes show the maximum amount of one good that can be purchased if none of the other is bought. Point *M* indicates that 20 units of clothing can be bought if total income goes to clothing purchases alone. The vertical intercept is equal to the consumer's income (I) divided by the price of clothing (I/P_C, or \$100/\$5), since \$100 permits the purchase of 20 units of clothing costing \$5 per unit. Similarly, point *N* is equal to income divided by the price of food (I/P_F, or \$100/\$10).

The slope of the budget line indicates how many units of clothing the consumer must give up to purchase one more unit of food. For example, the slope at point *B* in Figure 2–1 is $\Delta C/\Delta F$, or $-2/1$, indicating that a movement from *B* to *C* involves sacrificing 2 units of clothing to gain an additional unit of food.[1] (Since *MN* is a straight line, the slope is constant at $-2/1$ at all points along it.) Note that the slope indicates the relative cost of each good. In this case, if the consumer wants to change the consumption mix to get 1 more unit of food, 2 units of clothing must be given up. A budget line's slope is determined by the prices of two goods. In fact, the slope is equal to (minus) the ratio of prices:

$$\Delta C/\Delta F = -P_F/P_C.$$

In this example we have

$$\Delta C/\Delta F = -2/1,$$

since

$$-P_F/P_C = -\$10/\$5 = -2/1.$$

(Note that ΔC and P_F are in the numerators, not ΔC and P_C.) To understand this important relationship, recall that $P_F = \$10$ and $P_C = \$5$ and consider the movement from *B* to *C* in the diagram. If the consumer plans to purchase 1 more unit of food (ΔF), it will cost \$10. Since clothing costs \$5, the consumer will have to purchase 2 units less of it (ΔC) to have the \$10 required to buy 1 more unit of food. Thus the slope of the budget line,

---

[1] In case the reader is unfamiliar with the Δ (Greek capital letter delta) operator, as in $\Delta C/\Delta F$, it simply means "change in." ΔC, in moving from *B* to *C* in the diagram, is the difference between 14 units of *C* at point *C* and 16 units of *C* at point *B*: $14 - 16 = -2$ units of clothing, the change in clothing consumption.

which equals 2 units of clothing per unit of food, reflects the fact that food is twice as expensive as clothing. Therefore, the slope is equal to the ratio of prices: $10 per unit of food divided by $5 per unit of clothing equals 2 units of clothing per unit of food. Put somewhat differently, the slope of the budget line is a measure of relative price — the price of one good in terms of units of the other.[2]

Shifts in Budget Lines

We have seen how income together with the prices of goods determine a consumer's budget line. Any change in income or prices will cause a shift in the budget line. In this section we will illustrate how the budget line shifts in response to a change in these two underlying factors.

INCOME CHANGES. Let's begin with the budget line described in the previous section, where the consumer's income is $100, the price of food is $10, and the price of clothing is $5. We again draw the budget line as *MN* in Figure 2–2. (Note that here, as well as later, the shorthand term *food* is used instead of *consumption of food per week*. Still, we are really measuring the rate of consumption per time period.) Now suppose the consumer's income rises to $150, but the prices of food and clothing remain unchanged. The new budget line is *M'N'*. Point *M'* shows the new maximum level of clothing consumption possible if all income is allocated to its purchase. Since income is now $150 and P_C is still $5 per unit, the consumer can purchase 30 units of clothing. (Recall that point *M'* equals I/P_C, but I has risen to $150.) Similarly, the consumer can purchase a maximum of 15 units of food if all income is spent on food.

Note that a change in income with constant prices produces a parallel shift in the budget line. The slope of the budget line has not changed, because prices have remained fixed. Even with a higher income, the consumer must still give up 2 units of clothing, at $5 per unit, to consume 1 more unit of food at $10 per unit (illustrated in the move from *G* to *H* on the new budget line). The slope of any budget line — regardless of the level of income — is equal to the price ratio, and since prices are unchanged, so is the slope. With a higher income the consumer can purchase more of both goods than before, but the cost of one good in terms of the other remains the same.

PRICE CHANGES. Now consider a change in the price of one good, with income and the price of the other good held constant. Starting again with

[2] We summarize this idea with a bit of algebra. The budget line shows market baskets where the sum of expenditures on food and expenditures on clothing equals income. Thus, $I = P_F F + P_C C$, where $P_F F$ is the price times the quantity of food (expenditures on food), and $P_C C$ is defined similarly for clothing. Since I, P_F, and P_C are constants, this equation defines a straight line. If we solve for C, we have $C = I/P_C - P_F/P_C(F)$. The slope of this line is the coefficient of F, or $-P_F/P_C$.

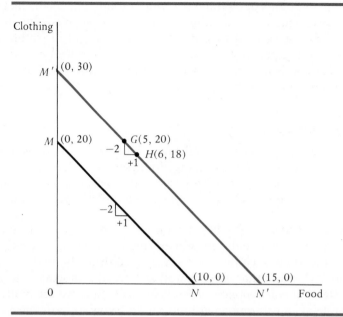

FIGURE 2–2

Effect of an Increase in Income on the Budget Line

A change in money income when product prices remain unchanged results in a parallel shift in the budget line. When income increases from $100 to $150, the budget line shifts outward from *MN* to *M'N'*, but its slope does not change.

the same initial budget line *MN*, reflecting a budget of $100, Figure 2–3 shows the effect of a reduction in the price of food from $10 to $5. *The price reduction causes the budget line to rotate about point M and become flatter, producing the new budget line MN'.* The maximum level of clothing consumption possible is unaffected, since income is still $100 and P_C is still $5. However, the maximum level of food consumption increases when its price falls. At the new price of $5 the consumer can purchase a maximum of 20 units of food (point *N'*) if the entire $100 is spent on food. A price change causes the budget line to rotate, so the slope of the line changes. When the price of food falls, the new budget line becomes flatter, since its slope, $-P_F/P_C$, is now equal to -1. With the price of both clothing and food at $5, the consumption of an additional unit of food now involves a sacrifice of only 1 unit of clothing: this is illustrated in the movement from *G* to *H* on the new budget line. *A flatter budget line means that the relative price of the good on the horizontal axis is lower.*

It is appropriate here to emphasize why we say the slope measures the relative price. A slope of $-2/1$, like the slope for line *MN*, means the price of food is double the price of clothing. Note, however, that the slope does not tell us what the absolute (money) prices are. If both prices

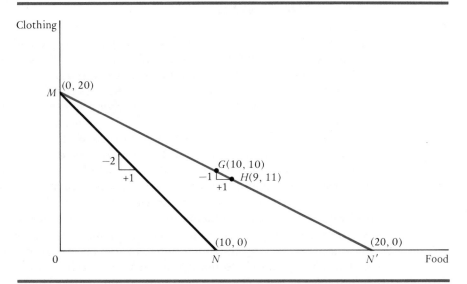

FIGURE 2-3

Effect of a Reduction in the Price of Food on the Budget Line

A change in the price of one good, with the other good's price and money income remaining unchanged, causes the budget line to rotate about one of the intercepts. When the price of food declines from $10 to $5, the budget line shifts from *MN* to *MN'*.

change by the same proportion — both doubled or halved, for instance — the ratio of the prices does not change, and so the cost of one good in terms of another is unaffected. As an example, see how a pure inflation (in which all prices, including wage rates, rise proportionately) affects the budget line. Suppose all money prices and income double: the consumer's income rises to $200 (or $2I$), and prices increase so that $P'_C = \$10$ (or $2P_C$) and $P'_F = \$20$ (or $2P_F$). Despite the absolute increases in income and prices, the budget line does not change. The budget line intercepts are now $2I/2P_C$ and $2I/2P_F$, and the slope is $-2P_F/2P_C$, which all reduce to the original values. The position and slope of budget lines always reflect relative, not absolute (money), prices.

We have confined our attention to simple budget lines in which the consumer can purchase as much of each good as desired without affecting the price per unit. Since individual consumers usually purchase only a tiny portion of the total quantity of any good, their purchases generally have no perceptible effect on price. Thus, it is appropriate for the consumer to treat price as constant, and with prices constant, the budget line is a simple straight line. As we will see later, there are cases where budget lines are not straight lines, but they are easily dealt with after the standard case has been thoroughly examined.

PREFERENCES OF THE CONSUMER
2.2

Since budget lines identify the alternatives available to the consumer, the position and shape of budget lines will affect consumption decisions. The specific market baskets that consumers actually purchase, though, will also depend on their subjective views about the desirability of alternative market baskets. In other words, their underlying preferences, or tastes, also play an important role in consumption decisions. Everyday observation tells us that consumers differ widely in their preferences: some like liver, others despise it; some guzzle beer, others drink only freshly squeezed fruit juice; some want a different pair of shoes for every occasion, others wear jogging shoes everywhere. Given such enormous diversity in preferences about goods and services, how should we incorporate the obviously important influence they have on consumer choices? To deal with this problem, economists base their analysis on some general propositions concerning consumer behavior that are believed to be widely true. These propositions do not explain *why* people have the exact tastes they do; they only identify some common characteristics shared by the preferences of virtually everyone.

Let's consider an individual consumer's subjective feelings about various combinations of goods that might be consumed. We will make two basic assumptions and an additional observation about this consumer's (and any other's) preferences. First, we assume that the consumer can rank (in order of preference) all market baskets. In other words, between two market baskets, A and B, for instance, the consumer will either prefer A to B, prefer B to A, or be *indifferent* between the two. We say a consumer is indifferent between two market baskets when both are equally satisfactory. This preference ranking reflects the relative desirability of the baskets themselves and ignores their cost. For example, it is not inconsistent for a consumer to prefer a Mercedes to a Toyota but to purchase the Toyota. A purchase decision reflects both the preference ranking and the budget line: the consumer purchases the Toyota because its lower purchase price makes it more attractive when both cost and the intrinsic merits of the vehicles are considered. Preferences and budget lines both influence consumer choice, but for the moment we will be concerned only with preferences.

Our second assumption is that the preference ranking is transitive, or logically consistent. *Transitivity* means that if the consumer prefers basket A to basket B, and B to C, then the consumer prefers A to C. For example, if a consumer likes Coke better than Pepsi, and Pepsi better than 7-Up, then logically the consumer likes Coke better than 7-Up. In a sense this condition simply requires that people be rational.

Finally, there is one other common, but not universal, characteristic of consumer preferences. Generally, a consumer will prefer to have more of a good if such a choice does not mean having less of any other good. For example, given a choice between (1) two hamburgers plus two shirts and (2) two hamburgers plus three shirts, a consumer will prefer the second basket, because it contains more shirts and the same number of hamburgers. This characteristic, sometimes called "more is preferred to less," is not a universal characteristic of preference rankings, however. There are things such as pollution, garbage, liver (for some people), and war where less is preferred to more. We call such commodities economic "bads" to distinguish them from the more frequently encountered economic "goods." An economic "good" is one where more is better than less; in effect, it is a desirable commodity in the consumer's view. Since consumers will only purchase goods that they deem desirable, the characteristic of more being preferred to less will be assumed below. Later the treatment will be extended to incorporate economic "bads" like pollution.

The ability of consumers to rank combinations of goods, the transitivity of preferences, and the notion of more being preferred to less seem unobjectionable. Probably not everyone's preferences show these common characteristics, though. Schizophrenics and small children, for example, may not display transitive preference rankings. Nonetheless, these assumptions seem reasonable enough in general to form the basis of a theory of consumer behavior. In fact, it is surprising how versatile a theory can be developed without having to resort to more and stronger assumptions.

Consumer Preferences Graphed as Indifference Curves

We can illustrate a consumer's preference ranking in a diagram. Let's return to our example in which there are two consumer goods, food and clothing. The diagram measures consumption of each good per time period along the axes, as does the budget line diagram. Every point in the diagram represents a different combination, or market basket, of food and clothing. The basic device used to show how the consumer ranks these market baskets is an indifference curve. An *indifference curve* plots all the market baskets that are viewed as equally satisfactory to a consumer. In other words, it identifies the various combinations of goods among which the consumer is indifferent. Figure 2–4 shows an indifference curve, U_1, for a specific consumer. The consumer would be equally satisfied with $10C$ plus $4F$ (basket A) or $5C$ plus $12F$ (basket B) — or any other combination of food and clothing along U_1. For those familiar with the concept of utility, the utility derived from consumption is the same at all points on an indifference curve.

From our basic assumptions we can deduce several characteristics that indifference curves must have. First, an indifference curve must slope downward if the consumer views the goods consumed as desirable goods. To see this, start with point A on U_1 in Figure 2–4. If we change the composition of the market basket so it contains more food but the same

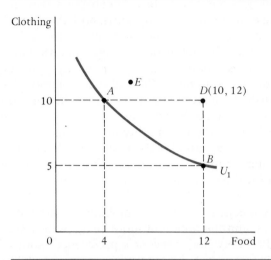

FIGURE 2-4

An Indifference Curve Relating Food and Clothing

A consumer's indifference curve, U_1, shows all the combinations of food and clothing that the consumer considers equally satisfactory. The consumer prefers any market basket lying above U_1 (like E) to all market baskets on U_1, and all market baskets on U_1 are preferred to any market basket lying below U_1.

amount of clothing (so the new basket is at a point such as D), the consumer will be better off — more food is preferred to less. Note, though, that the consumer will no longer be on U_1, the original indifference curve. If we are required to keep the consumer indifferent between alternative combinations of food and clothing, we must find a market basket that contains *more* food but *less* clothing. Market baskets that are equally satisfactory must contain more of one good and less of the other; this is simply another way of saying that the curve must have a negative slope.

A second characteristic of indifference curves is that a consumer prefers a market basket lying above (to the northeast of) a given indifference curve to every basket on the indifference curve. (Similarly, the consumer regards a basket below the indifference curve as less desirable than any on the indifference curve.) In Figure 2–4 pick any point above U_1 — for instance, E. There must be a point on U_1 that has less of both goods than E — point A, for example. Basket E will clearly be preferred to A since it contains more of both goods, and more is preferred to less. Since A is equally preferred to all points on U_1, point E must also be preferred to all points on U_1, from the transitivity assumption. Similar reasoning implies that every basket on U_1 is preferred to any basket lying below the curve.

So far we have examined only one indifference curve. To show the entire preference ranking of a consumer, we need a set of indifference curves, or an *indifference map*. Figure 2–5 shows three of the consumer's indifference curves. Since more is preferred to less, the consumer prefers higher indifference curves. Every market basket on U_2, for example, is preferred to every market basket on U_1. Although the diagram only shows three indifference curves, it should be clear that an indifference curve can be drawn through any point in the diagram. For example, an indifference curve (shown by the dashed line) that lies between U_2 and U_3 passes through point A. All baskets on this indifference curve are preferred to U_2 but are less preferred than U_3 in the view of the consumer. Thus, we could fill the diagram completely with indifference curves, and these curves would show the consumer's ranking of all conceivable market baskets of food and clothing. When using indifference curves, however, we generally draw only those indifference curves that are necessary to the analysis. To depict all the curves is unnecessary and, needless to say, cumbersome.

A set of indifference curves represents an ordinal ranking. An *ordinal ranking* arrays market baskets in a certain order, such as most preferred, second most preferred, third most preferred. It shows order of preference but does not indicate by how much one market basket is preferred to

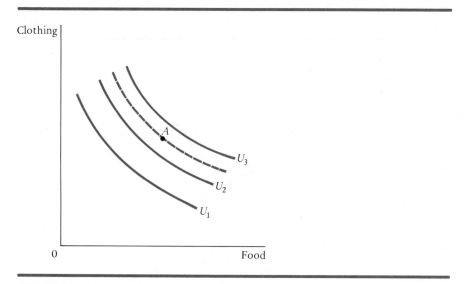

FIGURE 2–5
An Indifference Map

A set of indifference curves, or an indifference map, indicates how a consumer ranks all possible market baskets. Market baskets lying on indifference curves farther from the origin are preferred to those on curves closer to the origin.

another. There is simply no way to measure how much better off the consumer is on U_2 compared with U_1. Fortunately, we do not need this information to explain consumer choices when using indifference curves:
knowing how consumers rank market baskets is sufficient. The numbers
used to label the indifference curves measure nothing; they are simply a
means of distinguishing more preferred from less preferred market baskets.

Having described the way preferences can be represented by a set of
indifference curves, a third characteristic of indifference curves can be
stated: two indifference curves cannot intersect. We can see this feature
by incorrectly assuming that two curves intersect and then noting that this
proposition involves a violation of our basic assumptions. In Figure 2–6
two indifference curves have been drawn intersecting. Consider three
points: the point of intersection at C and two other points such that one
(B) contains more of both goods than the other (A). Now since B and C
both lie on U_2, they are equally preferred. Also, since C and A both lie on
U_1, they are equally preferred. Thus B is equal to C, and C is equal to A, so
by the transitivity assumption B should be equal to A. However, since B
has more of both goods than A, B must be preferred to A (more is preferred to less). We arrive at a contradiction: B cannot be equal to A and
preferred to A simultaneously. Consequently, intersecting indifference
curves fail to satisfy our basic assumption of transitivity and the notion of
more being preferred to less. In short, they don't make sense.

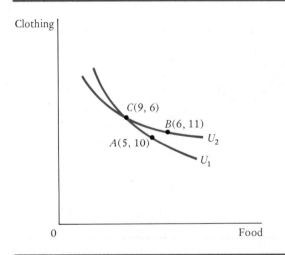

FIGURE 2–6

Intersecting Indifference Curves: A Logical Inconsistency

Indifference curves should never be drawn this way! Intersecting indifference
curves are inconsistent with rational choice; they violate the assumption that
preferences are transitive.

Curvature of Indifference Curves

We have discussed three characteristics of a set of indifference curves: each curve slopes downward, higher curves are preferred to lower ones, and indifference curves cannot intersect. These characteristics are logical implications of the assumptions about consumer preferences made earlier. Convexity is a fourth characteristic of indifference curves, but since we cannot logically deduce it from the basic assumptions about preferences, some further explanation is in order.

So far we have seen indifference curves that are convex to the origin; that is, they bow inward toward the origin so the slope of the curve becomes flatter as you move down the curve. To explain why indifference curves have this shape, we introduce the concept of *marginal rate of substitution*, or MRS. A consumer's marginal rate of substitution between, for example, food and clothing (MRS_{FC}) is the maximum amount of clothing the consumer is willing to give up to obtain an additional unit of food. Since it is a meaure of the *willingness* to trade one good for another, the MRS depends on the initial quantities held: an individual's willingness to exchange clothing for food will probably be different if he or she has 10 units of food rather than 5. Thus, a consumer's MRS is not a fixed number but will vary depending on how much of each good the consumer has.

The marginal rate of substitution is related to the slope of the consumer's indifference curves. In fact, (minus one times) the slope of the indifference curve is equal to the MRS. For example, say a market basket contains 15 units of clothing and 5 units of food. Let's assume the consumer is willing to trade a maximum of 4 units of clothing in exchange for 1 more unit of food. In other words, the MRS at this point is $4C$ per $1F$. What happens to the consumer's well-being if $4C$ is lost and $1F$ is gained so the market basket becomes $11C$ and $6F$? The individual will be no better off and no worse off than before, because we have taken away the absolute maximum amount of clothing (4 units) the consumer was willing to give up for another unit of food. In other words, if the consumer's MRS is 4 units of clothing per unit of food, and we take away 4 units of clothing and add 1 unit of food, the new market basket will be equally preferred to the original one. Both market baskets will lie on the same indifference curve.

This relationship is illustrated in Figure 2–7. Market baskets A ($15C$ and $5F$) and B ($11C$ and $6F$) are both on indifference curve U_1. Note that the slope of the indifference curve between A and B is $-4C/1F$. The slope — or, more precisely, minus one times this slope — measures the consumer's MRS. Purely for ease of communication, we define the MRS as a positive number so that the slope of the indifference curve, which is negative, must be multiplied by minus one. Don't let this definitional complication confuse you: the MRS and the slope of an indifference curve are identical concepts, both measuring the willingness of a consumer to substitute one good for another. The slope of an indifference

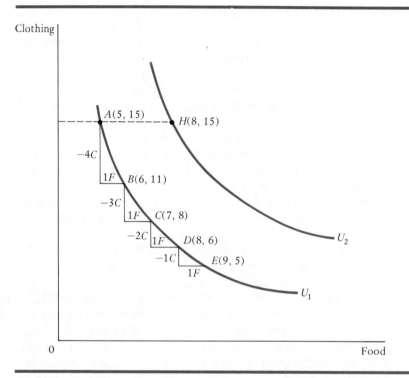

FIGURE 2-7
Diminishing MRS Along an Indifference Curve

Indifference curves are convex toward the origin, implying that the slope of each curve becomes lower as we move down the curve. The slope of U_1 at A is $4C/1F$; at D it is $1C/1F$. The slope of an indifference curve measures the consumer's marginal rate of substitution between goods. The convexity of indifference curves thus embodies the assumption of diminishing MRS along an indifference curve.

curve shows how much clothing can be exchanged for a unit of food without changing the well-being of the consumer — which is precisely what the MRS measures.[3]

Since the slope of an indifference curve and the MRS measure the same thing, drawing an indifference curve as convex (flatter slope as we move down along the curve) means that the MRS declines as we move down the curve. In Figure 2–7 the MRS declines from $4C$ for each unit of food at basket A to $3C$ per F at B, and so on. To justify drawing indif-

[3] The slope of the indifference curve at point A is not exactly $-4C/1F$. A curved line has a different slope at each point on it; its slope is measured by the slope of a straight line drawn tangent to the curve. As shown in the figure here, the slope at point A is $\Delta C/\Delta F$. Identifying the slope as we did in Figure 2–7 is an approximation to the correct measure, but for small movements along the curve the two measures are approximately equal.

ference curves as convex, we need to explain why a consumer's MRS can be expected to decline as we move down the curve.

Economists view the property of declining marginal rate of substitution along an indifference curve as a nearly universal characteristic of people's preferences, implying that indifference curves are convex. Basically, a declining MRS means that as more and more of one good is consumed along an indifference curve, the consumer is willing to give up less and less of some other good to obtain still more of the first good. Look at point _E_ on Figure 2–7. Here the consumer has a large quantity of food and very little clothing; in comparison to points such as _A_ farther up the curve, food is relatively plentiful, and clothing is relatively scarce. Under these circumstances it is probable that the consumer would be unwilling to exchange much clothing (already scarce) for more food (already plentiful). Consequently, it seems reasonable to suppose that the MRS would be lower at _E_ than at _A_. At _A_ clothing is more plentiful and food scarcer, so we might anticipate that the consumer would place a higher subjective value on food, that is, be willing to sacrifice a larger amount of clothing to obtain an additional unit of food. In other words, the assumption of a declining MRS simply embodies the belief that the relative amounts of goods are systematically related to the consumer's views about their relative importance.

This discussion is only an appeal to the intuitive plausibility of convex indifference curves; it is not a proof. Thinking along these lines, however, has convinced many people that in general it is reasonable to believe indifference curves reflect a declining MRS. (Another reason, based on observing the consumption choices people actually make, will be discussed later.) We will therefore assume that indifference curves are convex to the origin, which implies that the consumer's MRS declines as we move down each curve.

Two final points related to the convexity of indifference curves should also be mentioned. First, we have implicitly assumed that both goods in the market basket were economic "goods" (more preferred to less), the general case. In other situations, such as economic "bads," indifference curves need not be convex to the origin. Second, a declining MRS only pertains to a movement along a given indifference curve, not from one curve to another. For example, it is tempting to argue that if a consumer has more food and the same amount of clothing, the MRS_{FC} will be lower. For Figure 2–7 this argument implies that the curve U_2 is flatter at point _H_ than U_1 is at point _A_. This is not what we are assuming; we are assuming that the slope of each curve becomes flatter as we move down the curve.

Individuals Have Different Preferences

People differ widely in their underlying preferences for goods and services, and those differences are indicated by the shapes of their indifference curves. Consider the preferences of two consumers, Samantha (Sam) and Oscar, for T-shirts and beer. Figure 2–8a shows Sam's prefer-

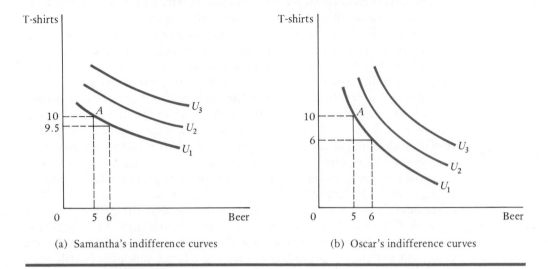

(a) Samantha's indifference curves   (b) Oscar's indifference curves

FIGURE 2–8
Indifference Maps of Two Consumers
People have different preferences, and these differences show up in the shapes of their indifference maps. Samantha's preferences are graphed in part a and Oscar's in part b. The indifference maps show that Oscar has a stronger preference for beer than does Samantha.

ences with several of her indifference curves relating T-shirts and beer consumption. Figure 2–8b shows Oscar's indifference curves. Because Oscar's curves are steeper than Sam's, we can see that Oscar has a stronger preference for beer than Sam does. To understand this idea, suppose they were both consuming the same market basket shown by point A in each graph. Since Oscar's indifference curve through this point is steeper than Sam's, Oscar's MRS_{BT} is greater than Sam's. Oscar would be willing to trade 4 T-shirts for one more beer, but Sam would only give up half a T-shirt for another beer.

Indifference curves indicate the *relative* desirability of different combinations of goods. So to say that Oscar values beer in terms of T-shirts more than Sam does is the same as saying that Sam values T-shirts in terms of beer more than Oscar does. Oscar is the "beer lover," and Sam is the "T-shirt lover" by comparison.

Can Preferences Change?

Figure 2–8 can also illustrate another point. We can show a given set of preferences or tastes as a set of indifference curves, but if a person's preferences should change, we would have to replace the original indifference curves with an entirely new set. Suppose, for example, Sam wakes up one morning and finds that she suddenly craves beer much more than before. This would be reflected as a change in her indifference map — from one such as Figure 2–8a to one such as 2–8b.

In most applications of indifference curve analysis of consumer behavior, economists assume that preferences do not change. This assumption does not rule out the possibility that preferences sometimes change; we know they do. Instead, it reflects the limitations of economic theory. Unfortunately, economists have no acceptable theory to explain the determination of the diversity of preferences observed or to explain what might cause preferences to change. Rather than try to account for the underlying factors that determine preferences, we take them as given and show how they influence the allocation of resources under different conditions.

In this context, it is worth noting that people's preferences do not seem to change erratically or frequently. If they did, we would not observe the stability in consumption patterns over time that we generally see. Moreover, we would not expect most of the phenomena economists study to affect preferences themselves. For example, the OPEC oil cartel certainly reduced the consumption of gasoline, but the reduction most likely occurred because OPEC's actions affected gas prices (affecting the budget line) rather than because people found gas intrinsically less desirable than before.

For these reasons we generally assume that underlying preferences are given, unless there is good reason to believe they have changed. If we know preferences have changed, we can, of course, apply our analysis to show what the consequences of such a change will be. (If, for example, consumers' tastes shift in favor of health food, this change would show up as an increase in demand for health food, with the usual effects.)

Graphing Different Preferences

Although our discussion of indifference curves has been restricted to choices among desirable goods, where more is preferred to less, we may depict *any* type of preferences as a set of indifference curves. While the desirable-good case is the one most generally encountered, it is a good test of your understanding of indifference curves to analyze some other situations.

For example, how would you show a person's preferences relating income per week and pollution per week with indifference curves? For a typical person, income is a desirable good, but pollution is an economic "bad." Figure 2–9a shows income and pollution on the axes. To determine the shapes of the indifference curves, we start by picking an arbitrary market basket, point *A*, for example, composed of 10 units of pollution and $50 in income. If we hold income constant at $50 but increase units of pollution — a move from *A* to *B* — the person will be worse off (on a lower

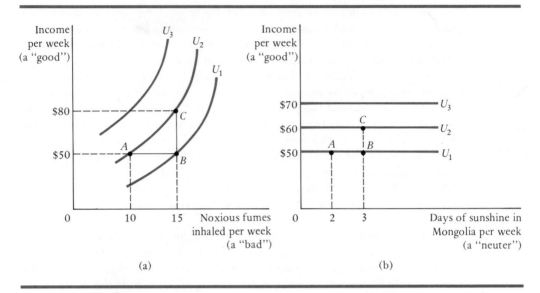

FIGURE 2–9

Indifference Maps for a "Bad" and a "Neuter"

When an economic "good" is on the vertical axis and an economic "bad" on the horizontal axis, indifference curves have the shapes shown in part a. With a "good" on the vertical axis and a "neuter" on the horizontal axis, they have the shapes shown in part b.

indifference curve) because pollution is a "bad." If a person inhales more noxious fumes and is to remain on the same indifference curve, more of the "good," income, is necessary to compensate for the additional pollution, as at point C. Thus, the indifference curve must slope upward. In addition, greater levels of well-being are shown by indifference curves above and to the northwest: U_2 is preferred to U_1. This can be seen by focusing on horizontal movements (more pollution with the same income makes the consumer worse off) and vertical movements (more income with the same pollution makes the consumer better off). We leave it as an exercise for the student to determine whether the curvature of the indifference curves in Figure 2–9a seems reasonable.

Most things are either "goods" or "bads," but an intermediate case is possible where the consumer doesn't care one way or another about something. For example, we suspect most people don't care how many days a week the sun shines in Mongolia (unless they live in Mongolia). Yet we can still draw indifference curves for Mongolian days of sunshine (an economic "neuter"?) and a second good such as income. Figure 2–9b shows these indifference curves as horizontal straight lines. Starting at A, we see that a horizontal movement to B — more sunshine but the same income — leaves the consumer on the same indifference curve. Thus the indifference curves are horizontal, implying that the MRS is zero: the consumer is unwilling to give up any income for more days of Mongolian sunshine. Any vertical movement — more income and the same amount of sunshine — will put the consumer on a higher indifference curve.

By thinking of horizontal and vertical movements, you may deduce the shape of indifference curves that relate various goods under different conditions. The most important thing, however, is to understand the general case where desirable goods are on both axes, since this is the case most frequently encountered.

THE CONSUMER'S CHOICE
2.3

Indifference curves represent the consumer's subjective attitudes toward various market baskets; the budget line shows what market baskets the consumer can afford. Putting the two separate pieces of apparatus together, we can determine what market basket the consumer will actually choose.

Figure 2–10 shows the consumer's budget line MN along with several indifference curves. We assume that the consumer will purchase the market basket, from among those that can be afforded, that will place the individual on the highest possible (most preferred) indifference curve. In other words, the consumer will select the market basket that best satisfies preferences, given a limited income and the prevailing prices. Visual inspection of this diagram shows that the consumer will choose market basket E (4 units of food and 12 units of clothing) on indifference curve U_2. Indifference curve U_2 is the highest level of satisfaction the consumer can attain, given the limitations implied by the budget line. Although the individual would be better off with any market basket on U_3, none of those baskets is affordable since U_3 lies entirely above the budget line. Any basket other than E on the budget line is affordable but yields less satisfaction since it will lie on an indifference curve below U_2. For example, basket A can be purchased, but then the consumer is on U_1; so basket A is clearly inferior to the basket at E.[4]

Note that the highest indifference curve attainable is the one that just touches, or is tangent to, the budget line: U_2 is tangent to MN at E. Point E represents the consumer's equilibrium position. Since U_2 and MN are tangent at this point, the slopes of the curves are equal. Because the slopes

---

[4] Figure 2–10 shows the consumer spending income entirely on food and clothing. It is possible that the consumer would spend less than his or her income, saving some of it for future consumption. We will neglect this possibility here and assume that all income is spent on food and clothing. Later we will see how we can incorporate the saving decision into the analysis.

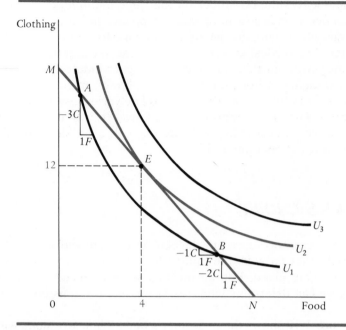

FIGURE 2-10
The Equilibrium of the Consumer

Bringing the consumer's budget line and indifference curves together, the market basket the consumer will choose is shown by point *E*, where the budget line is tangent to (has the same slope as) indifference curve U_2. Among market baskets that can be afforded — shown by *MN* — basket *E* yields the greatest satisfaction because it is on the highest indifference curve possible. The equilibrium is characterized by the equality $MRS_{FC} = P_F/P_C$.

equal the consumer's MRS and price ratio, respectively, the consumer's equilibrium is characterized by the following equality:

$$MRS_{FC} = P_F/P_C.$$

This equality indicates a balancing of the subjective valuation of the goods (MRS_{FC}) with their objective cost in the market place (P_F/P_C).

To illustrate why this equality characterizes the consumer's equilibrium, suppose that the consumer purchases some market basket other than point *E* on the budget line, for example, the basket at point *A*. The indifference curve through any point above *E* on the budget line will intersect the budget line from above, as U_1 does at point *A*.[5] Thus at *A* the

---

[5] If we tried to draw an indifference curve through *A* intersecting from below, we would find that it would intersect U_2, and intersecting indifference curves are impossible.

consumer's MRS_{FC} (3 units of clothing per unit of food) is greater than the price ratio (2 units of clothing per unit of food). At point A the consumer's subjective valuation of food and clothing indicates a willingness to exchange as much as 3 units of clothing for another unit of food, but at the given market prices the consumer only needs to give up 2 units of clothing for one more unit of food (a bargain).

In effect, the MRS is a measure of the consumer's subjective marginal benefit. *Marginal benefit* refers to the additional benefit from consuming one more unit of a good. At point A, for example, the marginal benefit of another unit of food is 3 units of clothing, the amount of clothing the consumer would give up for another unit of food. On the other hand, the price ratio is effectively a measure of marginal cost: the *marginal cost* of getting another unit of food is 2 units of clothing. At point A, therefore, the marginal benefit of one more unit of food in terms of clothing is greater than the marginal cost of one more unit of food, and the consumer will be better off consuming more food (and less clothing). Thus, by moving along the budget line in the direction of point E, the consumer will reach a higher indifference curve. In these terms the equilibrium position indicates that the consumer has chosen a market basket so that the marginal benefit of food in terms of clothing (MRS_{FC}) is exactly equal to the marginal cost of food in terms of clothing (P_F/P_C).

At points below E on the budget line, similar reasoning shows that the consumer would be better off consuming less food and more clothing, so none of these points represent an equilibrium position. At point B the consumer's MRS is less than the price ratio. The last unit of food consumed was worth only 1 unit of clothing to the consumer, yet its objective cost was 2 units of clothing, so the consumer is better off by moving back up toward point E.

Corner Equilibrium

When a consumer's preferences are such that some of both goods will be consumed, the equilibrium is characterized by an equality between the MRS and the price ratio, as we described above. In reality, however, consumers don't consume any of some goods and services. You may wish you had a Maserati, tickets to the Super Bowl, or a posh condominium in Palm Beach, but in all likelihood your consumption of these, and many more, goods is zero. The reason is that the first unit of consumption of these goods, however desirable, fails to justify the cost involved.

In our simplified two-good world, Figure 2–11 shows a situation where a consumer purchases only one of the two goods available. Equilibrium occurs at point M, where all the consumer's income goes to purchase clothing. The fact that the slope of the indifference curve at point M is less than the slope of the budget line means that the first unit of chicken livers wouldn't be worth its cost to the consumer. In this situation the

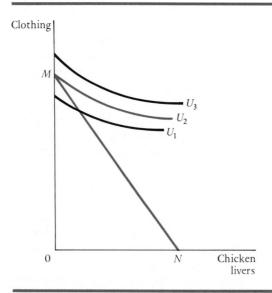

FIGURE 2-11

A Corner Equilibrium

It is possible that the consumer will not purchase any of one of the goods. In this case the equilibrium lies at one of the intercepts of the budget line, with the entire income spent on only one good. Here the equilibrium is at point M, with only clothing purchased.

consumer equilibrium is not characterized by an equality between the MRS and the price ratio, since the slopes of the indifference curve and budget line differ at point M. The equality condition only holds between pairs of goods consumed in positive amounts.

Concave Indifference Curves?

Earlier we gave an intuitive explanation of why we expect indifference curves to be convex. Since intuition is not infallible, let's contemplate the implications of indifference curves with the opposite curvature.

Figure 2-12 shows indifference curves that are concave to the origin, with the MRS increasing as you move down each curve. This shape means that the more of the good the consumer has, the more valuable still another unit becomes. Consequently, the existence of concave indifference curves does not seem too plausible. What would it mean if a consumer did have concave indifference curves as in Figure 2-12? The best position for the consumer is not where the indifference curve is tangent to the budget line at point E since the consumer can, in fact, achieve greater well-being by choosing any other point on the budget line. The basket that allows the

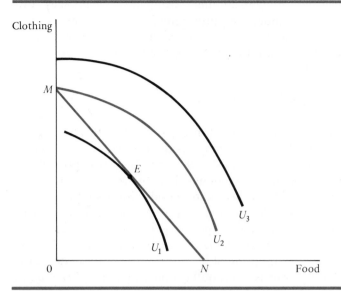

FIGURE 2-12

Concave Indifference Curves

If indifference curves are concave toward the origin, the tangency at point *E* is not the equilibrium because it implies the lowest level of well-being from among the points on the budget line. With concave indifference curves the consumer will always choose to consume only one good — in this case, clothing. Since we observe consumers purchasing many goods, indifference curves relating these goods cannot be concave.

individual to attain the highest possible indifference curve is at point *M*, a corner equilibrium. If indifference curves are concave, the equilibrium position will always be at one corner or the other, indicating that only one good will be consumed.

The implication of such a corner equilibrium provides still a second reason, in addition to intuition, for believing indifference curves to be generally convex instead of concave. If indifference curves were predominantly concave, people would consume only one good. Casual observation reveals, however, that people consume a multitude of different goods and services, which means that the indifference curves relating these goods must be convex. Convex indifference curves can explain the consumption of many goods (as in Figure 2–10) and simultaneously explain why not all goods are consumed (as in Figure 2–11), so the assumption is more consistent with observed behavior. Consequently, it seems safe to assume that people generally have convex indifference curves.

Incidentally, although we have referred to consumers having indifference curves, consumers don't actually walk around with these curves in their heads or consult them when making choices. Consumers do, however, have underlying preferences that economists or other outside observers can depict as indifference curves and thereby gain insight into the way preferences influence consumer behavior.

THE COMPOSITE-GOOD CONVENTION
2.4

We developed our analysis for a two-good world, but the general principles apply to a world of many goods. Unfortunately, many goods cannot be shown on a two-dimensional graph. Still, it is possible to deal with a multitude of goods in two dimensions by treating a number of goods as a group. Suppose there are many goods: food, clothing, housing, trips to Atlantic City, textbooks, and so on. We can continue to measure food consumption, or whatever specific good we wish to analyze, on one axis, but then treat all other goods as if they were one good; that is, as a *composite good*. Consumption of the composite good is gauged by total outlays on it; in other words, total outlays on all goods *other than food*.

Figure 2–13 illustrates a consumer equilibrium by using this approach. The consumer has $100 in weekly income and the price of food is $10 per unit. The vertical intercept of the budget line occurs at $100, since total outlays on other goods will be $100 if food consumption is zero. The consumer's income is equal to $0M$. As noted earlier, the slope of the budget line is equal to the ratio of prices, but since a $1 outlay on other goods has a price of one, the ratio reduces to the price of food ($P_F/1 = P_F$). Thus at any point on the budget line, such as B, consuming one more unit of food (which costs $10) means that outlays on other goods must be reduced by $10.

Convex indifference curves can also be drawn to relate outlays on other goods and food, since both are desirable goods to the consumer. We must now state an important assumption associated with this approach: we assume that the prices of all the other goods and services are constant. This assumption allows us to treat them as a single good. We want outlays on other goods to serve as an index of the quantities of other goods consumed, and if prices were allowed to vary, it would become a rubbery index. (That is, a larger outlay would not necessarily mean more goods were consumed unless prices were fixed.) When other prices are held constant, the consumer's preferences can be shown as indifference curves that identify a unique level of well-being for each combination of food and outlays on other goods.

The slope of an indifference curve, the MRS, now shows how much the consumer is willing to reduce outlays on other goods to obtain one more unit of food. With market basket A, for example, the consumer is willing to give up $15 worth of other goods in exchange for an additional unit of food. Note that this MRS is still a measure of the consumer's willingness to substitute among real goods, but now dollar outlays measure

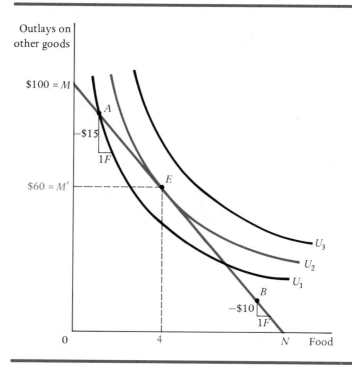

FIGURE 2-13

The Equilibrium of the Consumer

To deal graphically with the consumption of many goods, we group together all goods but one and measure total outlays on this composite good on the vertical axis. The slope of the budget line is then the dollar price of the good on the horizontal axis. The consumer equilibrium is once more a tangency between an indifference curve and the budget line at point *E*.

the quantity of other goods the consumer is willing to sacrifice in return for food.

Figure 2–13 shows the equilibrium for the consumer at point *E*, where the budget line is tangent to an indifference curve. At *E* the consumer is just willing to give up $10 of other goods for another unit of food, indicating that the individual's MRS is $10 per unit of food. This figure equals the market price that must be paid for another unit of food (the slope of the budget line, $P_F/1$, equals $10 per unit of food). It is important to understand the significance of this equilibrium. Given the individual's income and the price of food, no other market basket makes the consumer as well off. For example, at point *A* the consumer is willing to give up $15 of other goods to consume one more unit of food, but since the actual cost is only $10, the consumer will be better off purchasing an additional unit of food and moving down the budget line toward *E*. Only at point *E* is there a balance between the subjective marginal benefit of food (in dollars) and the objective marginal cost of food (in dollars), its price.

The equilibrium market basket at E consists of 4 units of food and $60 ($0M'$) devoted to the purchase of other goods. The total outlay devoted to food can also be shown as the distance MM'. Since the consumer has an income of $0M$ ($100) and, after purchasing food, has $0M'$ ($60) left to purchase other things, the difference ($0M - 0M' = MM'$), or $40, is the total cost of the 4 units of food. The difference between the consumer's total income and the amount spent on everything else (including saving as one of the other goods), except food, reflects the amount of the consumer's income spent on food.

Using this composite-good convention does not change the substance of the analysis. The consumer's equilibrium still involves a balancing of the relative subjective desirability of goods with their relative costs.

ARE PEOPLE SELFISH?
2.5

Having set out the basic components of the economic theory of consumer choice, we may now reconsider the general nature of the analysis. In particular, we wish to evaluate a commonly made objection to the way economists characterize individual behavior in economic theory. You may already have heard someone observe: "Economics assumes people are greedy and care only about material possessions"; or "Economics disregards the fact that individuals are benevolent and are concerned with the welfare of other people."

A review of our basic assumptions about preferences reveals that these criticisms are not valid. Economic analysis does not prejudge what commodities, services, or activities people consider to be economic "goods" or "bads." In fact, since many things are "goods" for some people and "bads" for others (liver, liquor, midget wrestling, ballet, chewing tobacco, roller disco, designer jeans, reading economic theory), any attempt to specify in advance what all people consider desirable would frequently lead to mistakes.

If we are unable to specify which goods people find desirable, though, how can we apply the theory to concrete situations? The answer is simple: people reveal that some commodities are desirable by the way they allocate their outlays. When we observe some consumers giving up money in return for fish, the evidence is fairly conclusive that fish is a desirable good for them. We would then draw convex indifference curves between fish and other goods for such consumers and investigate how their incomes, the price of fish, and so on, affect consumption decisions.

People give up time and resources to pursue charitable endeavors, sacrifice material wealth for a quiet life, or campaign for politicians. To understand how economic theory can be applied to examine the factors that influence such decisions, here's a hypothetical situation.

Samantha (Sam) and Oscar are friends. Sam earns $20,000 a year; Oscar earns only $3,000 a year. Let's assume that Sam cares about the material well-being of Oscar — or, more precisely, that for Sam, Oscar's income (which determines the material comforts he can enjoy) is an economic good. Does this concern imply that Sam will give some of her income to Oscar?

Figure 2–14 illustrates how we can apply indifference curve analysis to this situation. Figure 2–14a shows Sam's budget line *MN* relating her income and Oscar's. Sam's budget line does not intersect the vertical axis since we suppose she can't take income from Oscar. Point *M* shows their initial incomes. Obviously, Sam can increase Oscar's income by giving Oscar some of hers, but every dollar she gives to Oscar reduces her own income by a dollar, so the slope of the budget line is -1. Figure 2–14a shows two of Sam's indifference curves, and since both her income and Oscar's are economic goods, they have the usual shapes. Given the preferences indicated by Sam's indifference curves, at point *M* she would be willing to pay more than $1 to raise Oscar's income by $1. Thus, it is in her interest to give some of her income to Óscar, and the best-sized gift from her point of view is $2,000.

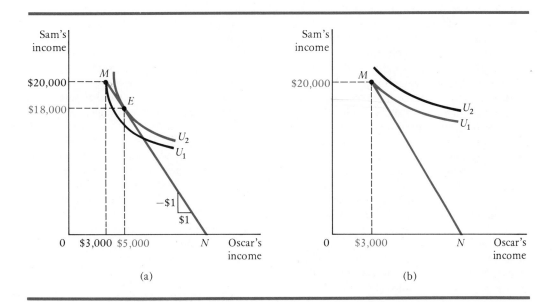

FIGURE 2–14

Transferring Income to Another Person

Altruistic preferences can also be accommodated in the analysis. In part a, Sam chooses to give $2,000 of her income to Oscar. When Sam's preferences are different as in part b, still altruistic but less so than in part a, she would not give any of her income to Oscar.

The fact that Sam cares about Oscar's income is not sufficient to imply that she will always donate money to Oscar's cause. Figure 2–14b shows an alternative set of indifference curves that Sam might have. Since these curves slope downward, they imply that Sam still views Oscar's income as an economic good. At point M, however, the slope of U_1 is less than the slope of the budget line. This means that Sam might be willing to give up, for example, 25 cents in return for Oscar having $1 more in income; unfortunately, however, it would cost her $1 to increase Oscar's income by $1 (the slope of the budget line), so she decides not to contribute anything to the Oscar fund. A corner equilibrium results.

Both parts of Figure 2–14 show preferences implying that Sam views Oscar's income as an economic good, but the intensity of preference differs. The differing intensity is shown by the different slopes of the indifference curves (the MRSs) at point M in the two diagrams. Thus, the fact that Sam cares about Oscar's income does not allow us to conclude that she will necessarily transfer any of her income to Oscar: the intensity of her preferences and the cost of giving play a critical role.

Summary

The theory of consumer choice is designed to explain why consumers purchase the combination of goods and services they do. The theory emphasizes two factors: the consumer's budget line, which shows the market baskets that can be bought; and the consumer's preferences, which indicate the subjective ranking of different market baskets.

A budget line shows the combinations of goods a consumer can purchase with a given income and with given prices for the goods. The consumer's income and the market prices of the goods determine the position and shape of the budget line. The slope of the budget line is equal to the ratio of the prices of the goods and measures the relative price of one good compared with another.

Indifference curves show graphically the consumer's tastes, or preferences. An indifference curve depicts all the combinations of goods considered equally desirable by the consumer. A set of indifference curves is a complete representation of the consumer's preferences. For economic "goods," the curves slope downward, are convex, and are nonintersecting. The slope of an indifference curve measures the marginal rate of substi-

tution (MRS). The MRS shows the willingness of the consumer to trade one good for another.

From among the market baskets that the consumer can purchase (shown by the budget line), we assume the consumer will select the one that results in the greatest possible level of satisfaction or well-being. Graphically this consumer equilibrium is shown by the tangency between the budget line and an indifference curve. At the point of tangency the consumer's MRS equals the price ratio. The analysis can also deal with more than two goods by measuring one good (food, for example) on the horizontal axis and all other goods (nonfood items), treated as a composite good, on the vertical axis. The nature of the consumer's equilibrium is the same and is still the point of tangency between the budget line and an indifference curve.

Review Questions and Problems

1. Define *budget line*. What does each axis measure? What do its vertical intercept, horizontal intercept, and its slope measure?

2. A consumer spends her entire income on pizza and record albums. Draw the budget line for each of the following situations, identifying the intercepts and slope in each case. (Measure pizza consumption horizontally.)

a. Monthly income is $1000, the price of pizza is $8, and the price of record albums is $10.
b. Same conditions as in part a, except that income is $500.
c. Same conditions as in part a, except that income is $2000 and the price of pizza is $16 (the price of record albums is unchanged).
d. Same conditions as in part a, except that record albums cost $5.
e. Compare the budget lines in parts c and d.

*3. In most cases a consumer can purchase any number of units of a good at an unchanged price per unit. Suppose, however, that a consumer must pay $10 per unit of X for the first 5 units but only $5 per unit for each unit in excess of 5 units. What does the budget line relating good X and other goods look like?

*4. Roger's budget line relating good A and good B has intercepts of 50 units of good A and 20 units of good B. If the price of good A is $12, what is Roger's income? What is the price of good B? What is the slope of the budget line?

5. Define *indifference curve*. What are the four characteristics of a set of indifference curves? Explain the justification for each characteristic.

6. Consider a commodity that is an economic "good" up to a certain level of consumption but beyond that level becomes an economic "bad." Draw several indifference curves between such a commodity and other goods. Name a commodity for which your preferences are like this.

7. With two goods, hamburger and cheese, we know that a consumer is indifferent between basket A (10H and 2C) and basket B (2H and 10C). Can we deduce whether basket C (6H and 6C) lies on a higher, lower, or the same indifference curve as baskets A and B? (Hint: Plot the three points to scale in a diagram, and draw an indifference curve through A and B.)

8. Explain why a consumer will choose a market basket so that MRS equals the price ratio.

*9. Monica spends her entire monthly income of $600 on gadgets and widgets. The price of gadgets is $30 and the price of widgets is $10. If she consumes 12 gadgets and 24 widgets, her MRS is $1W/1G$. Is she in equilibrium at this point on her budget line? Show the result in a diagram.

10. Suppose a consumer faces a zero price for gadgets. What does the budget line relating other goods and gadgets look like? By drawing indifference curves, show the equilibrium of the consumer. At the point of equilibrium, is the MRS equal to the price ratio? If so, explain the equality in words.

11. Observing that a student doesn't purchase any tutoring in economics is consistent both with convex indifference curves relating tutoring and other goods and with concave indifference curves. How, then, can we be certain that the student's indifference curves are convex?

*12. Seat belts were available as options before they were required by law in automobiles. Most motorists, however, did not purchase them. Assuming that motorists were aware that seat belts reduced injuries from accidents, were motorists irrational in not purchasing them?

13. In Figure 2–8, if Sam and Oscar have the same income and confront the same prices for beer and T-shirts, which consumer will purchase more beer? Which will purchase more T-shirts? Show by drawing in the budget lines.

14. Measure the income of Samantha on the vertical axis and the income of Oscar on the horizontal axis, as we did in Figure 2–14. Draw several of Sam's indifference curves under the following circumstances:

a. Sam doesn't care about Oscar's income; but the higher her own income is, the better off she is.

b. Sam considers both her own income and Oscar's income to be economic "goods," but only as long as her income exceeds Oscar's. When Oscar's income exceeds hers, Sam considers Oscar's income to be an economic "bad."

15. When we use the composite-good convention, what do we mean by a *composite good* and how do we measure it? What is the slope of the budget line? What is the slope of an indifference curve? Does the consumer equilibrium involve an equality between MRS and a price ratio?

Supplementary Readings

Becker, Gary. "A Theory of the Allocation of Time." *Economic Journal*, 75 (1965): 493–517.

Blaug, Mark. *Economic Theory in Retrospect.* 3rd ed. Cambridge: Cambridge University Press, 1978. Chaps. 8, 9.

Hicks, John R. *Value and Capital.* 2nd ed. Oxford: Clarendon Press, 1946. Chaps. 1, 2.

Lancaster, Kelvin. *Consumer Demand: A New Approach.* New York: Columbia University Press, 1971.

Stigler, George. "The Development of Utility Theory." *Journal of Political Economy*, 58, parts 1–2 (August–October 1950): 307–327, 373–396.

APPENDIX
THE UTILITY APPROACH TO CONSUMER CHOICE

Many students first learn about the theory of consumer choice through the concepts of total utility and marginal utility. In this appendix we explain this approach to the theory and relate it to the indifference curve approach emphasized in the text.

Total Utility and Marginal Utility

People consume goods and services because their wants, or preferences, are served by doing so: they derive satisfaction from consumption. Let's assume it is possible to measure the amount of satisfaction a consumer gets from any market basket by its utility. *Utility* is simply a subjective measure of the usefulness, or want satisfaction, that results from consumption. Units in which it is measured are arbitrary, but they are commonly referred to as utils: a util is one unit of utility.

In the minds of consumers, consumption of goods provides them with utility. But we must sharply distinguish the concepts of total utility and marginal utility. Table 2–2 illustrates the difference. Suppose the consumer purchases only clothing; so for the moment consider only the first three columns. Total utility from consumption of clothing (TU_c) is the total number of utils the consumer gets from consuming a given quantity of clothing. If clothing consumption is 2 units, total utility is 38 utils. Total utility is obviously greater at higher levels of consumption, because cloth-

TABLE 2-2
Total and Marginal Utility

Clothing	TU_C	MU_C	Food	TU_F	MU_F
1	20	20	1	50	50
2	38	18	2	85	35
3	53	15	3	110	25
4	65	12	4	130	20
5	75	10	5	145	15
6	83	8	6	155	10
7	90	7	7	161	6
8	95	5	8	163	2

ing is an economic good. The marginal utility of clothing (MU_C) refers to the amount total utility rises when consumption increases by one unit. When consumption of clothing increases from 5 to 6 units, total utility rises from 75 to 83 utils, or by 8 utils. The marginal utility of the sixth unit is thus 8 utils, the additional utility obtained by consuming an extra unit.[6]

Table 2–2 also illustrates the *law of diminishing marginal utility*. This law, or proposition, holds that as more of a given good is consumed, the marginal utility associated with the consumption of additional units tends to decline, other things equal. (In particular, the other-things-equal condition means that consumption of other goods is held fixed as consumption of the good in question is varied.) In Table 2–2 the marginal utility of the first unit of clothing is 20 utils, but it is 18 utils for the second unit (the increase in TU_C from 20 to 38 utils) and so on. Note that the MU_C of each successive unit is smaller.

Like convexity of indifference curves, diminishing marginal utility cannot be proven to be universally true. It does, however, agree with intuition. If a good has a variety of uses but only one unit is available, the consumer will assign it the most important use, the one yielding the greatest utility. If two units are available, the consumer will devote the second unit to a less important use, one yielding a smaller addition to total utility than the first unit, a smaller marginal utility. We can use water, for example, for drinking, cooking, washing, and watering lawns. When only a small amount of water is available, we will use it to sustain life by drinking it; but as the quantity increases, we will put it to less important uses that yield successively smaller increments to total utility.

---

[6] In Table 2–2 the marginal utility when consumption is 6 units is in the same row as 6 units of food. Since marginal utility refers to the change in going from 5 to 6 units, however, some writers prefer to place marginal utility halfway between the fifth and sixth row. Either procedure is acceptable as long as the correct meaning is communicated.

The law of diminishing marginal utility is assumed to hold for all goods. Table 2–2 also shows the total and marginal utility associated with different levels of consumption of a second good, food. The total utility of a market basket containing food and clothing is then the sum of TU_C and TU_F. (This statement assumes that the utility derived from food consumption is independent of clothing consumption, and vice versa. While this assumption will not always be true, its use simplifies the explanation of the theory without materially affecting the results.) With consumption of 5 units of clothing and 3 units of food, total utility is 185 utils. Obviously the consumer will choose the market basket that yields the greatest total utility, subject to the limitation implied by the individual's income and the prices of the two goods.

Consumer Equilibrium

If the consumer's income and the prices of food and clothing are specified, we could consult Table 2–2 and by trial and error eventually find the market basket of food and clothing that produces the greatest utility. With an income of $65 and the prices of food and clothing at $10 and $5, respectively, we would eventually find that the market basket composed of 5 units of food and 4 units of clothing produces more utility (205 utils) than any other market basket costing $65.

There is a simpler way to proceed. As it turns out, the utility-maximizing market basket is one for which the consumer allocates income so that the marginal utility divided by the good's price is equal for every good purchased:

$$MU_C/P_C = MU_F/P_F.$$

A market basket of $5C$ and $4F$ satisfies this equality: MU_C/P_C is equal to 10 utils per unit/$5 per unit, or 2, and MU_F/P_F is equal to 20 utils per unit/$10 per unit, or 2. These ratios measure, for a small change, how much additional utility is generated by spending a dollar on the good. With MU_C/P_C equal to 2 utils per dollar, a dollar more spent on clothing (purchasing 1/5 unit) will generate 2 utils in additional utility (one-fifth of the MU of one unit of clothing). Put slightly differently, MU/P is the marginal utility per dollar's worth of a good, and the rule for maximizing utility can equivalently be stated as allocating income among goods so the marginal utility of the last dollar spent on each good is the same.

If this equality is not satisfied, total utility can be increased by a rearrangement in the consumer's purchases. Suppose the consumer buys $3C$ and $5F$. This market basket also costs $65, but total utility is now 198 utils. With this market basket we have

$$MU_C/P_C > MU_F/P_F, \quad \text{or} \quad 15 \text{ utils}/\$5 > 15 \text{ utils}/\$10.$$

This inequality shows that the marginal dollar devoted to clothing yields 3 utils, while the marginal dollar devoted to food yields only 1.5 utils. Shifting a dollar from food consumption to clothing consumption will increase total utility: spending a dollar less on food reduces utility by 1.5 utils, but spending a dollar more on clothing increases it by 3 utils, a net gain of 1.5 utils. As long as an inequality persists, the consumer should reallocate purchases from the goods with a lower marginal utility per dollar of expenditure to goods with a higher marginal utility per dollar of expenditure. Shifting dollar outlays between food and clothing will eventually reestablish the equality condition. As clothing consumption increases, its MU falls (reducing MU_C/P_C) because of the law of diminishing marginal utility; as food consumption falls, its MU rises (increasing MU_F/P_F). When the equality condition is reestablished, at $5C$ and $4F$ in this example, the consumer is maximizing utility with the given income and prices.

Relationship to Indifference Curve Theory

Despite their surface differences, utility theory and indifference curve theory both emphasize the way preferences, incomes, and prices interact to determine the market basket a consumer will choose. Each theory, in effect, says that a consumer will choose the most preferred market basket from among those that can be afforded. We can now show formally that there is no real difference in substance between the two approaches.

To translate utility theory into indifference curve theory, we may begin by noting that an indifference curve is simply a curve showing alternative market baskets that yield the same total utility to the consumer. Figure 2–15 shows two indifference curves. The slope of U_2 at point R is $\Delta C/\Delta F$ and is equal to the consumer's MRS_{FC}. This slope, however, can also be explained in terms of the marginal utilities of the two goods.

The slope of an indifference curve equals the ratio of the marginal utilities of the two goods. Suppose $\Delta C/\Delta F = 2C/1F$. This means that 1 unit of food will replace 2 units of clothing without affecting total utility. If $1F$ will replace $2C$, then it follows that the marginal utility of 1 unit of food must be twice as great as the marginal utility of 1 unit of clothing. Thus, the slope $\Delta C/\Delta F$ equals MU_F/MU_C. The slope of the indifference curve measures the relative importance of the two goods to the consumer, which is in turn equal to their relative marginal utilities.

We can demonstrate this conclusion somewhat more formally. In Figure 2–15 the movement from R to S, ΔC, reduces total utility by an amount equal to $\Delta C \times MU_C$. (If ΔC is 2 units and MU per unit of C is 5 utils, then total utility falls by 10 utils.) Similarly, the movement from S to T, ΔF, increases total utility by an amount equal to $\Delta F \times MU_F$. Since R and T lie on the same indifference curve, the loss in utility associated with a move from R to S must be exactly offset by the gain in utility in going from S to T. Therefore, we have

$$\Delta C \times MU_C = \Delta F \times MU_F.$$

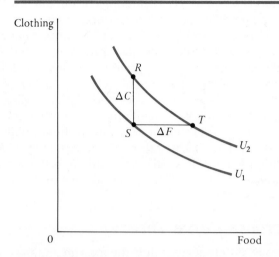

FIGURE 2-15
MRS and Marginal Utilities
The slope of an indifference curve is related to the marginal utilities of the two goods. At point R the slope is $\Delta C/\Delta F$, and this ratio equals MU_F/MU_C.

Rearranging these terms, we find

$$\Delta C/\Delta F = MU_F/MU_C.$$

Since $\Delta C/\Delta F$ equals MRS_{FC}, we can substitute terms and obtain

$$MRS_{FC} = MU_F/MU_C.$$

This equality allows us to see that the conditions for a consumer equilibrium in the two theories are essentially identical. With indifference curve analysis the consumer is in equilibrium when

$$MRS_{FC} = P_F/P_C.$$

Since MRS_{FC} equals MU_F/MU_C, we can substitute terms and rewrite the consumer equilibrium as

$$MU_F/MU_C = P_F/P_C.$$

Then by rearranging terms, we obtain

$$MU_F/P_F = MU_C/P_C,$$

which is the condition for consumer equilibrium when using the utility theory approach.

An equality between the marginal utility per dollar's worth of both goods is the same as an equality between the MRS and the price ratio. The two theories are simply different ways of viewing the same thing.

Advantages of Indifference Curve Approach

To say that we can use the two approaches to reach the same basic conclusion is not equivalent to saying that they are equally useful techniques of analysis. In actuality the indifference curve approach has at least three advantages:

1.   Compared with the utility approach, the indifference curve approach requires less restrictive assumptions. The consumer only has to be able to rank alternative market baskets by order of preference. In the utility approach the consumer must be able not only to rank baskets but also to tell how much more preferred (in utils) one basket is over another.

2.   The indifference curve approach — with its tangency between an indifference curve and the budget line — presents a more complete picture of the consumer's options and choice than the utility approach does. The indifference curve approach not only shows the equilibrium point — the tangency — but also clearly indicates all other baskets the consumer could choose (and why they are not chosen).

3.   The indifference curve approach is more flexible. In contrast, although we can derive a consumer's demand curve fairly easily with the utility approach, it does not lend itself well to the study of many other applications. We will see the importance of this implication in Chapter 4, which illustrates the wide range of applications of the indifference curve approach.

The points noted above are not intended as an indictment of the utility approach, which was historically the forerunner to the indifference curve approach. For some purposes, such as quickly arriving at an intuitive understanding of why demand curves slope downward (which is very important in introductory courses), utility theory is probably the superior approach. For the type of problems appropriate to an intermediate-level course, however, indifference curve theory is more easily handled and more versatile.

Individual and Market Demand

3

In the last chapter we developed a model that uses indifference curves and budget lines to explain consumer behavior. We found that a consumer chooses the market basket that is most preferred from among those that can be afforded — methodologically interesting but hardly a surprising or earthshaking result. The theory of consumer choice, however, has far wider uses, and its value becomes more apparent when we use it to examine the way changes in prices, income, or other circumstances affect consumption choices. This subject occupies most of this chapter and the next. For the moment our major concern is with the way changes in income and changes in the price of a good affect consumption choices. We will see how an individual's demand curve for a good can be derived, how individual demand curves are aggregated to obtain the market demand curve, and how the concept of price elasticity of demand is used in analyzing consumer choices. Chapter 4 will illustrate the wide range of applications of consumer choice theory to more unusual problems such as fringe benefits, saving and borrowing, subsidies, and taxes.

INCOME CHANGE AND CONSUMPTION CHOICES
3.1

A change in income affects consumption choices by altering the set of market baskets a consumer can afford, that is, by shifting the budget line. To examine the impact of a change in income, we will assume that the consumer's underlying preferences do not change and the prices of commodities remain fixed; only income varies.

In Figure 3-1a, the original equilibrium of the consumer is at point E,

---

FIGURE 3-1 *(facing page)*
Effect of Changes in Income on Consumer Equilibrium

An increase in income shifts the budget line outward and leads the consumer to select a different market basket. Connecting the points of equilibrium *(E, E', E'')* associated with different incomes yields the income-consumption curve in part a. Part b shows how the consumer's demand curve shifts when income changes.

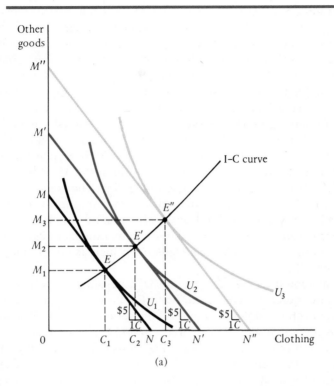

(a)

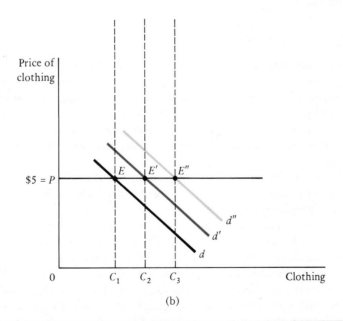

(b)

where indifference curve U_1 is tangent to budget line *MN*. Consumption of clothing is $0C_1$, consumption of other goods, as measured by total outlays on them, is $0M_1$, and income — equal to outlays on other goods if consumption of clothing were zero — is $0M$. Now suppose income increases from $0M$ to $0M'$. The budget line shifts outward to $M'N'$, but its slope (the price ratio) is unchanged since only income is assumed to vary.

This outward shift in the budget line means that the consumer is able to choose among market baskets that were previously unaffordable, but which market basket will be chosen? The answer depends on the nature of the consumer's preferences. For the set of indifference curves in Figure 3–1a, the most preferred market basket along the $M'N'$ budget line is at point E', where U_2 is tangent to the budget line. The consumer is better off (that is, the individual has attained a higher indifference curve) and is consuming $0C_2$ units of food and $0M_2$ of other goods. For the specific indifference curves shown, an increase in income from $0M$ to $0M'$ with no change in the price of clothing leads to an increase in clothing consumption, from $0C_1$ to $0C_2$.

If income increases further to $0M''$, the budget line becomes $M''N''$, and a new equilibrium occurs at point E''. Proceeding in the same way, we find that each possible income level has associated with it a unique equilibrium market basket. Only three equilibrium points are shown in the diagram, but others can be derived by considering still different levels of income for the consumer. The line that joins all the equilibrium points generated by varying income is the *income-consumption curve*, shown as the I–C curve in the diagram. It passes through the points E, E', and E'' in the diagram.

Normal Goods

The relationships in Figure 3–1a are fairly typical of what happens to the consumption of a good (clothing, in this case) when income increases. When more of a good is purchased by an individual as income rises (prices and preferences unchanged) and less is purchased as income falls, the good is a *normal good.* Calling such a good normal reflects the judgment that most goods are like this, but, as will be seen shortly, not all goods are.

Figure 3–1a indicates that consumption of clothing increases with income even though the price of clothing is unchanged. We can illustrate the same thing by using a different graph that shows the consumer's demand curve for clothing. We have not derived an entire demand curve yet, but we can identify one point on the demand curve corresponding to each income level. When income is $0M$, for example, and the price of clothing is $5 per unit, the consumer will consume $0C_1$ units. Therefore, one point on the demand curve d in Figure 3–1b can be identified: point E indicates that consumption of clothing is $0C_1$ when its price is $5. (The other points on the curve will be taken for granted at the present.)

When an increase in income combined with no change in price leads to greater consumption, it is represented by a shift in the demand curve. Thus, when income rises from $0M$ to $0M'$, the entire demand curve shifts to d', which shows an increased consumption of food, $0C_2$, at an unchanged price. Recall that a demand curve shows how price affects consumption *when other factors are held constant.* One of the more important factors held fixed is the consumer's income, so a change in income can be expected to shift the entire demand curve. Put another way, curve d is a demand curve that holds income constant at $0M$ (in Figure 3–1a) at all points along it, while d' holds income constant at a different level, $0M'$.

While our major emphasis here is on the way budget lines and indifference curves can be used to examine consumer choices, we should not lose sight of the fact that there are alternative ways to approach the same problem. Both parts of Figure 3–1 show the same thing but from a different perspective. Which approach is better really depends on the problem being examined.

Inferior Goods

Does an increase in income always lead to increased consumption? A little reflection reveals several cases when higher incomes would be expected to lead to lower consumption of some goods. For an impecunious student a higher income may lead to lower hamburger consumption since steak can now be afforded. Consumption of Hondas may fall (and consumption of Mercedes rise) for an individual whose income increases sharply. Bus transportation may fall because at higher income levels, a consumer may use airplane travel instead.

If the consumption of a good falls as individual income rises (prices unchanged), the good is called an *inferior good.* (And, conversely, if consumption rises as income falls, the good is an inferior good.) For the consumer whose preferences are shown in Figure 3–2a on page 67, hamburger is an inferior good. When income is $0M$ and the price of hamburger is \$2 per pound, the consumer is in equilibrium at point E on budget line MN. Consumption of hamburger is $0H_1$. When income rises to $0M'$, the equilibrium point E', on the new budget line, shows that hamburger consumption drops to $0H_2$. When a good is an inferior good, the income-consumption curve connecting the equilibrium points, E, E', and so on, will be backward-bending, implying lower consumption at higher income levels.

In Figure 3–2b note that the demand curve shifts inward for an inferior good when income increases: lower consumption at an unchanged price implies a reduction in demand. Another way of distinguishing between normal and inferior goods, then, is by the way a change in income affects the demand curve for the good. *An increase in income increases demand (shifts the demand curve outward) for a normal good but reduces the demand for an inferior good.*

Several other subtle points concerning the distinction between normal and inferior goods should also be kept in mind. First, a specific good may be inferior for some people and normal for others. Your consumption of hamburgers may go up if your income rises, but ours may go down if our income rises. The goods themselves are not intrinsically normal or inferior: the definitions refer to the responses of individuals to a change in income, and the responses depend ultimately on the shapes of their indifference curves. Second, a good may be a normal good for a specific individual at some income levels but an inferior good at other income levels. In Figure 3–2a, at a low level of income the good is normal (as shown by the upward-sloping income-consumption curve when income is low), but the good becomes inferior at higher levels of income. For example, you might consume more hamburger if your income increased by $50 a month, but you might consume less if your income increased by an additional $100 a month. Third, an inferior good should not be confused with an economic "bad." An inferior good is not a "bad" (where less is preferable to more), as shown by the normally shaped indifference curves in Figure 3–2a.

Further Thoughts on Normal and Inferior Goods

The formal distinction between a normal and an inferior good for a consumer depends on the shapes of the consumer's indifference curves relating one good to another, not on the objective characteristics of the good itself. However, most inferior goods have certain common objective characteristics, and understanding these characteristics is helpful in evaluating their significance.

Most inferior goods are narrowly defined goods in a general category that includes several other higher-quality (and higher-priced) goods. Take hamburger. Hamburger is a narrowly defined good belonging to the general category, meat. In the meat category there are other higher-quality and higher-priced options, such as round steak, sirloin steak, prime rib, and lamb. Understandably, some people would consume less hamburger when their incomes went up, because they could afford the better-quality alternatives that serve the same basic purpose, but serve them better. Similarly, Hondas are part of a general category, transportation. It is not

FIGURE 3–2 (facing page)
Effect of Changes in Income on Purchases of an Inferior Good
An inferior good is one that the consumer will purchase less of at a higher income and unchanged price, and is characterized by a negatively sloped income-consumption curve (part a). At a higher income the demand for an inferior good shifts inward (part b).

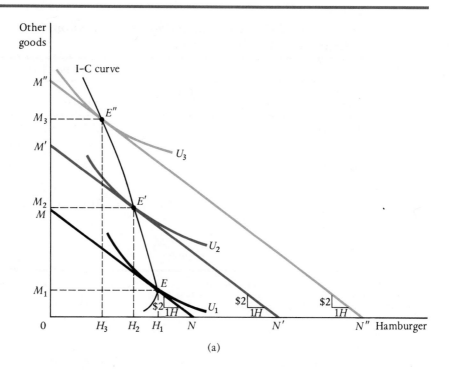

(a)

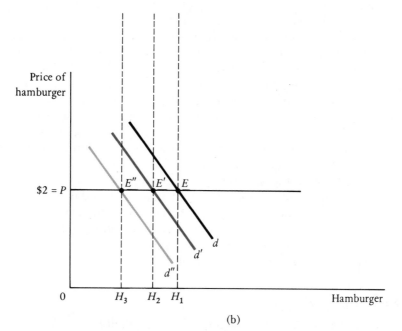

(b)

TABLE 3-1

Percentage of Consumption Outlays Expended on Selected Goods by Selected Income Classes, 1973

Consumer Good	All Classes	Income Class			
		Less than $3,000	$7-$7,999	$12-$14,999	$25,000 or more
Alcohol	1.0	0.7	1.1	0.9	1.1
Tobacco	1.6	2.1	1.9	1.8	0.9
Gasoline	4.6	3.6	4.8	5.3	3.7
Food	19.5	21.9	20.8	20.0	16.4
Housing	30.5	38.9	31.7	29.5	28.9
Health Care	6.1	6.7	6.8	5.8	5.5
Clothing	8.2	6.5	8.0	7.9	9.7
Recreation	8.2	5.2	6.0	7.8	11.3

Source: U.S. Department of Labor, Bureau of Labor Statistics, *Average Annual Expenditures for Commodity and Service Groups Classified by Nine Family Characteristics, 1972 and 1973,* Consumer Expenditure Survey Series: Interview Survey, 1972 and 1973, Report 455–3 (Washington, D.C.: Government Printing Office, 1976), Table 1b.

necessarily true that all inferior goods fit this general description, but certainly most that have been identified by economists do.

In contrast, intuition and evidence both suggest that broadly defined goods are usually normal. Meat is more likely to be a normal good than hamburger is, and food is more likely than meat. Many applications of economic theory necessarily involve broadly defined goods, which means that the normal-good case is likely to be the most relevant one. For example, the food stamp program subsidizes consumption of all kinds of food, not just hamburger, and food, considered as a composite commodity composed of many specific items, is surely a normal good.

Table 3–1 presents some data on the allocation of consumption outlays to various goods by families at different income levels. All the "goods," with the exception of gasoline, are broadly defined. Consequently, it is not surprising to find that total outlays on every good are higher for families with higher incomes. (In some cases, such as tobacco, the percentage of total consumption expenditures falls, but the absolute amount rises with income in every case.) These results suggest that most broadly defined goods are normal goods.

The Food Stamp Program

Under the federal food stamp program, eligible low-income families receive free food stamps, which can be viewed as government checks the

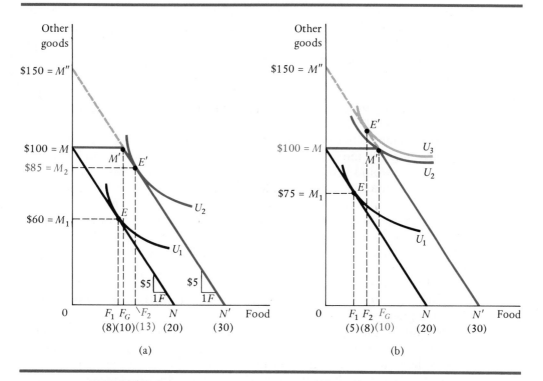

FIGURE 3–3

Effects of the Food Stamp Program on Consumption

The food stamp program shifts the budget line to $MM'N'$ by giving the consumer MM' in food stamps. The result is identical to giving the consumer cash if preferences are like those in part a, but the consumer would be better off if given cash if preferences are like those in part b.

family can use only to purchase food.[1] To illustrate how our theory can be used to examine this program, let's look at a specific example in which a consumer, Tom, receives $50 worth of food stamps each week. We will assume Tom has a weekly income of $100, and the price of food is $5 per unit.

Consider Figure 3–3a. The presubsidy budget line is MN, and the consumer purchases 8 units of food prior to receiving food stamps. The food stamp subsidy shifts the budget line to $MM'N'$. Over the MM' range

---

[1] Before 1979 the program operated differently, with low-income families having to pay something in return for the food stamps. For example, a family might have to pay $50 to receive $150 worth of food stamps. For a fuller discussion of this program see Edgar K. Browning and Jacquelene M. Browning, *Public Finance and the Price System*, 2nd ed. (New York: Macmillan, 1983), Chap. 5.

the budget line is horizontal since the $50 in free food stamps permits the recipient to purchase up to 10 units of food while leaving him his entire income of $100 to be spent on other goods. If, however, food consumption exceeds 10 units, he must purchase any additional units at the full market price of $5. Thus, the $M'N'$ portion of the budget line has a slope of $5 per unit of food, indicating the price of food over this range.

In this case the budget line is not a straight line throughout but is kinked at point M', since the subsidy terminates at the point where the $50 in food stamps is used up. Another way of visualizing this budget line is by contrasting it to the budget line that results from an increase in income of $50, which would result if the government gave Tom $50 to spend as he wished. With a $50 cash grant the budget line would be $M''N'$, coinciding with the food stamp budget line over the $M'N'$ region. The only way the food stamp subsidy differs from an outright cash grant is that options indicated on the upper part of the line, $M''M'$, are not available to the recipient, because food stamps cannot legally be used to purchase non-food items.

The food stamp subsidy will affect the recipient in one of two ways. Figure 3–3a shows one possibility. In this case Tom, if given the subsidy as a cash grant, would purchase $50 or more in food items on his own. In other words, the equilibrium occurs on the $M'N'$ part of the budget line, such as at point E'. The consequences of the food stamp subsidy are exactly the same as when the consumer is given $50 as an unrestricted cash transfer. When the budget line is $MM'N'$ under the food stamp program, the consumer chooses the market basket at point E'. If Tom receives a cash grant of $50, the budget line is $M''N'$, and Tom would still choose the same market basket E'. In this case food consumption increases, but only because food is a normal good, and more of a normal good is consumed at a higher income. Note, however, that food consumption rises by less than the amount of the subsidy. For the preferences shown in Figure 3–3a, food consumption increases by 5 units, or $25 worth. Tom uses the remainder of the subsidy to increase consumption of other goods, from $60 to $85 worth. (Since other goods, taken as a group, are certainly normal goods too, the purchase of these goods will also increase.)

Figure 3–3b shows another possible outcome of the food stamp subsidy. In this case a second consumer, Maud, if given the $50 subsidy as a cash grant, would choose to purchase less than $50 worth of food. In the diagram a $50 cash transfer produces the budget line $M''N'$, and Maud would prefer to consume at point E', where U_3 is tangent to the budget line in the $M''M'$ range, involving less than $50 spent on food. The food stamp subsidy prohibits such an outcome, however: Maud must choose among the options shown by the $MM'N'$ budget line. Faced with these alternatives, the best she can do is choose point M', since the highest indifference curve attainable is U_2, which passes through the market basket at point M'.

When the situation shown in Figure 3–3b occurs, the subsidy increases the consumer's purchases of both food and nonfood items. Indeed, it is notable that regardless of whether Figure 3–3a or Figure 3–3b is the appropriate analysis, the food stamp subsidy cannot in reality avoid being used in part to finance increased consumption of nonfood items. This result is particularly interesting since many proponents of subsidies of this sort emphasize that the subsidy should not be used to finance consumption of "unnecessary" goods (such as liquor or junk food). In practice, it is difficult to design a subsidy that will only increase consumption of the subsidized good and not affect consumption of other goods at the same time.

Note also that the consumer in Figure 3–3b will be better off if given $50 to spend as she wishes instead of $50 in food stamps. The budget line will then be $M''N'$, and the consumer will choose the market basket at point E', on indifference curve U_3. This illustrates the general proposition that recipients of a subsidy will be better off if the subsidy is given as cash. The situation in Figure 3–3a illustrates why there is a qualification to this proposition: in some cases the consumer is equally well off under either subsidy. There is no case, however, where the consumer is better off with a subsidy to a particular product than with an equivalent cash subsidy.

Since the precise outcome of the subsidy depends on the value of the food stamps relative to the preferences and incomes of the recipients, we cannot specify on theoretical grounds whether Figure 3–3a or Figure 3–3b illustrates the more common outcome. It does seem to be the case, however, that most recipients of food stamps are in the situation shown in Figure 3–3a: for them the food stamp program is equivalent to a cash subsidy.

PRICE CHANGES AND CONSUMPTION CHOICES
3.2

Now let's turn to an examination of the way a change in the price of a good affects the market basket the consumer will choose. Since we wish to isolate the effect of a price change on consumption, we will hold constant other factors that influence consumption. In particular, money income, preferences, and prices of other goods will not be allowed to vary: only the price of one good will change.

Figure 3–4a on page 73 shows the way changes in the price of clothing affect the quantity of clothing consumed. Once again the initial equilibrium occurs at point E on budget line MN. Consumption of clothing is initially $0C_1$, and outlays on other goods are $0M_1$. The price of clothing, $5.00 per unit, is indicated by the slope of the budget line.

If the price of clothing falls from $5.00 to $3.50 per unit, the budget line rotates about point M, becoming flatter. With a price of $3.50 the budget line becomes MN', where $0N'$ equals the consumer's constant money income divided by the now lower price of clothing. Confronted with this new budget line, the consumer selects the most preferred market basket from among those available on MN'. For the particular preferences shown, equilibrium occurs at point E' where the slope of U_2 (the marginal rate of substitution) equals the slope of the now flatter budget line. Consumption of clothing has increased to $0C_2$ in response to the reduction in its price. If the price of clothing falls still further to $2.00 per unit, the budget line becomes MN'', and the consumer will choose point E'', indicating consumption of $0C_3$ units of clothing.

Proceeding in this way, we can vary the price of clothing and observe the market basket that will be chosen at any price, given the indifference curves of the consumer. For every possible price a different budget line results, and the consumer selects the market basket that permits attainment of the highest possible indifference curve. Points E, E', and E'' represent three market baskets associated with prices of $5.00, $3.50, and $2.00, respectively. If we connect these equilibrium points, and those associated with other prices (not drawn in explicitly), we obtain the price-consumption curve, shown as the P–C curve in the diagram. The *price-consumption curve* identifies the equilibrium market basket associated with each possible price of clothing (always remembering that money income, other prices, and preferences are assumed to remain unchanged).

The Consumer's Demand Curve

Using the procedure described above, we can determine the consumer's demand curve for clothing. The demand curve relates clothing consumption to its price while holding money income, other prices, and preferences fixed. The price-consumption curve does the same thing. While the price-consumption curve is not itself the demand curve, it conveys the same information as the demand curve. To convert the price-consumption curve to a demand curve, all we need to do is plot the price-quantity relationships identified by the price-consumption curve in the appropriate graph.

Figure 3–4b shows the consumer's demand curve d; it indicates the quantity of clothing the consumer will purchase at alternative prices,

---

FIGURE 3–4 *(facing page)*
Derivation of the Consumer's Demand Curve

A reduction in the price of clothing, with income and the prices of other goods fixed, leads the consumer to purchase more clothing. The equilibrium market baskets associated with alternative prices for clothing are connected to form the price-consumption curve in part a. The same information is plotted as the consumer's demand curve for clothing in part b.

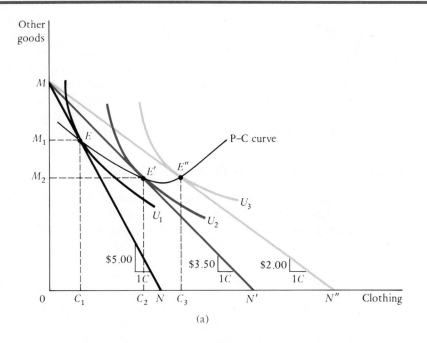

(a)

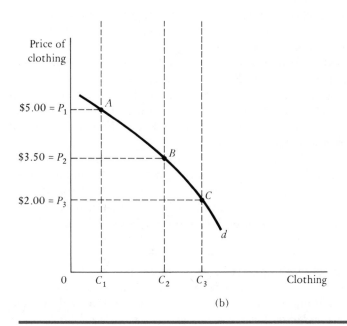

(b)

other factors held constant. The demand curve is obtained by plotting the price-quantity combinations identified by the price-consumption curve in Figure 3–4a. For example, when the price of clothing is $5.00 (the slope of *MN*), consumption of clothing is $0C_1$ units at point *E* in Figure 3–4a. Figure 3–4b shows the price per unit explicitly on the vertical axis. When the price is $5.00, consumption is $0C_1$ units, so point *A* locates one point on the demand curve. When the price is $3.50 (the slope of *MN'*), consumption is $0C_2$, and this identifies a second point, *B*, on the demand curve. Other points are obtained in the same manner to plot the entire demand curve *d*.

Some Remarks about the Demand Curve

We have just derived a consumer's demand curve from the individual's underlying preferences (with a given income and prices of other goods). This approach clarifies several points about the demand curve that should be emphasized.

1. The consumer's level of well-being varies along the demand curve. This is clear from Figure 3–4a, where the consumer reaches a higher indifference curve when the price of the product falls. Although this point is fairly obvious, the diagram shows explicitly why the consumer benefits from a lower price: the consumer can now purchase market baskets that were previously unattainable.

2. The prices of other goods are held constant along a demand curve, but the quantities purchased of these other goods are allowed to vary. Since all other goods are lumped together and treated as a composite good, the way in which consumption of any other specific good may change is not shown explicitly.

3. At each point on the demand curve the consumer's equilibrium condition $\text{MRS}_{co} = P_C/P_O$ is satisfied. (The subscript *O* refers to *other goods*, the composite good measured on the vertical axis.) As the price of clothing falls, the value of P_C/P_O becomes smaller, and the consumer chooses a market basket for which MRS_{co}, the slope of the indifference curve, is also smaller.

4. The demand curve identifies the marginal benefits associated with various levels of consumption. The height to the demand curve from the horizontal axis, at each level of consumption, indicates the marginal benefit of the good. For example, when consumption is $0C_2$ at point *B* on the demand curve (Figure 3–4b), the distance BC_2, or $3.50 per unit, is a measure of how much the marginal unit consumed is worth to the consumer. Why? Refer to Figure 3–4a; when the equilibrium is at point *E'* ($0C_2$ units of clothing), MRS_{co} is $3.50 per unit of clothing. Since the MRS is a measure of what the consumer is willing to give up for an additional unit of clothing, it is a measure of the marginal benefit. *Note that at every point on the demand curve the height to the demand curve equals the MRS,*

thereby indicating the marginal benefit of the good to the consumer. This is why economists refer to the price at which people purchase a given good as revealing the relative importance of the good to them.

Do Demand Curves Always Slope Downward?

For the specific indifference curves shown in Figure 3–4, we derived a downward-sloping demand curve. But does the demand curve always slope downward? Is it possible for a consumer to have indifference curves so that the law of demand does not hold for some good?

Figure 3–5 suggests such a possibility. When the budget line is *MN*, consumption of good *X* is $0X_1$ units. If the price of *X* falls so that the budget line becomes *MN'*, consumption of *X falls* to $0X_2$, an apparent violation of the law of demand. Note that the indifference curves that produce this result are downward-sloping, nonintersecting, and convex; that is, they do not contradict any of our basic assumptions about preferences.

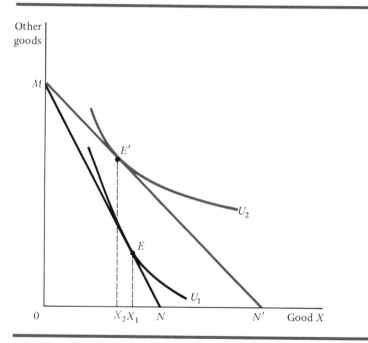

FIGURE 3–5

A Lower Price Leading to Less Consumption

This graph shows that a consumer purchases less of good *X* when its price falls, an apparent violation of the law of demand. In this case the demand curve will be upward sloping.

Just because we can draw a diagram that shows reduced consumption at a lower price does not mean such an outcome will ever be observed in reality. It does suggest, however, the importance of carefully considering exactly why consumption of a good varies in response to a change in its price, and we will do so in the following sections.

INCOME AND SUBSTITUTION EFFECTS OF A PRICE CHANGE

3.3

When the price of a good changes, the change affects consumption in two different ways. Normally, we cannot observe these two effects separately. Instead, when the consumer alters consumption in response to a price change, all we see is the combined effect of both factors. The first way a price change affects consumption is the *income effect*. When the price of a good falls, a consumer's real purchasing power increases, which affects consumption of the good. A price reduction increases *real* income — that is, makes it possible for the consumer to attain a higher indifference curve. The second way a price reduction affects consumption is the *substitution effect*. When the price of one good falls, the consumer has incentive to increase consumption of that good at the expense of other, now *relatively* more expensive goods. The individual's consumption pattern will change in favor of the now less costly good and away from other goods. In short, the consumer will substitute the less expensive good for other goods — hence the name substitution effect.

To see intuitively that there are two conceptually different factors at work when a price changes, refer to Figures 3–4 and 3–1. In Figure 3–4 a price reduction results in the consumer's reaching a higher indifference curve. In Figure 3–1 an increase in income, with no change in prices, also results in an equilibrium on a higher indifference curve. There is apparently a common factor at work here: both a reduction in price and an increase in income raise the consumer's real income, in the sense of permitting attainment of greater well-being. In both cases the budget line moves outward, allowing consumption of market baskets that were not previously attainable. This points to one of the two ways a price reduction affects consumption; namely, it augments real income (by increasing the purchasing power of a given money income), which obviously affects consumption. This is the income effect.

Although a price reduction and an income increase both have an income effect on consumption, there is also a significant difference. With a price reduction the consumer moves to a point on a higher indifference curve where the slope is lower than it was at the original equilibrium (Figure 3–4). In effect, the consumer has moved down the indifference curve to consume more of the lower-priced good: this illustrates the substitution in favor of the less costly good. When income increases, however, the consumer moves to a point on a higher indifference curve where the slope (the MRS) is the same as it was at the original equilibrium. In Figure 3–1 the slopes of the indifference curves are the same at points E and E'.

The precise distinction between these two effects, and the way they help us understand why the demand curve has the shape it does, will be clarified below using a graphical treatment.

Income and Substitution Effects Illustrated: The Normal-Good Case

In Figure 3–6 the consumer's original budget line MN relates clothing and outlays on all other goods. At a price of \$5 per unit of clothing, equilib-

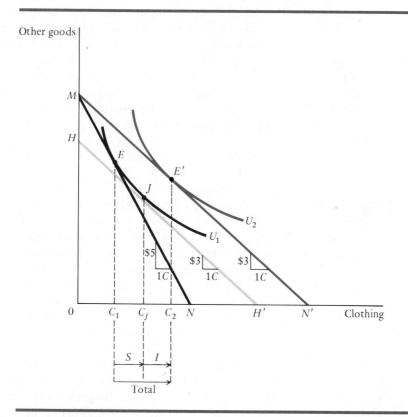

FIGURE 3–6

Income and Substitution Effects of a Price Reduction

The total effect $(C_1 - C_2)$ of a reduction in the price of clothing can be separated into two components, the income effect and the substitution effect. A hypothetical budget line HH' is drawn parallel to the new (after price change) budget line but tangent to the initial indifference curve U_1 at point J. The substitution effect is then C_1 to C_J, and the income effect is C_J to C_2, which together give the total effect on consumption of clothing.

rium occurs at point E, with $0C_1$ units of clothing purchased. If the price of clothing falls to \$3 per unit, the budget line becomes MN', and the consumer buys $0C_2$ units of clothing. The increase in clothing bought, from $0C_1$ to $0C_2$, in response to the lower price is the *total effect* of the price reduction on clothing purchases. The demand curve shows the total effect. Now we wish to show how this total effect can be conceptually decomposed into its two component parts, the income effect and the substitution effect.

The substitution effect illustrates how the change in relative prices *alone* affects consumption, independently of any change in real income or well-being. To isolate the substitution effect, we must keep the consumer on the original indifference curve, U_1, while at the same time confronting the individual with a lower price of clothing. We do so by drawing a new budget line with a flatter slope, which reflects the lower price, and then imagining that the consumer's income is reduced just enough (while holding the price of clothing at \$3) so it is possible to attain indifference curve U_1. In other words, we move the MN' budget line toward the origin parallel to itself until it is tangent to U_1. The result is the *hypothetical* budget line HH', which is parallel to MN' (both reflect the \$3 price) and tangent to U_1 at point J. This new budget line shows that if, after the price reduction, the consumer's income is reduced by MH, the preferred market basket will be at point J on U_1, the indifference curve the individual attained before the price reduction.

This manipulation permits us to separate the income and substitution effects so that each can be studied independently. *The substitution effect is shown by the difference between the market baskets at points E and J.* The lower price of clothing, looked at by itself, induces the consumer to increase consumption of clothing from C_1 to C_J and reduce consumption of other goods. In effect, the substitution effect involves sliding down the original indifference curve from point E, where its slope is \$5 per unit of clothing, to point J, where its slope is \$3 per unit of clothing. Consequently, the substitution effect of the lower price of clothing increases consumption from $0C_1$ to $0C_J$ units.

The income effect is shown by the change in consumption when the consumer moves from point J on U_1 to point E' on U_2. This change involves a parallel movement in HH' back to the MN' budget line. Recall that a parallel shift in the budget line indicates a change in income but no change in the price of clothing. Thus, the income effect of the lower price, involving the change in consumption produced by the increase in the consumer's real income, causes the consumption of clothing to rise from $0C_J$ to $0C_2$.

The sum of the substitution effect on clothing purchases ($0C_1$ to $0C_J$) and the income effect ($0C_J$ to $0C_2$) measures the total effect ($0C_1$ to $0C_2$) of the lower price. Any change in price can be separated into income and substitution effects in this manner.

Although this analysis seems highly abstract when first encountered, it is of great importance. Ultimately, we are seeking a firm basis for believing that people will consume more at lower prices; that is, that the law of demand is valid. Separating the income and substitution effects allows us to look at the issue more deeply.

Note that the substitution effect of any price change will always mean more consumption of a good at a lower price, or less consumption at a higher price. This follows directly from the convexity of indifference curves: with convex indifference curves a lower price always implies a substitution effect that involves sliding down the initial indifference curve to a point where consumption of the good is greater. Thus the substitution effect conforms to the law of demand. The income effect of a price change implies greater consumption at a lower price only if the good is a normal good. In Figure 3–6, when the budget line shifts from *HH'* to *MN'*, a parallel shift, consumption of clothing will rise if clothing is a normal good.

The demand curve for a normal good must therefore be downward sloping. Both the substitution effect and the income effect of a price change involve greater consumption of the good when its price is lower.[2] Since the total effect is the sum of the income and substitution effects, people will consume more of a normal good when its price is lower. This conclusion is a powerful one, because we know that most goods are normal goods. Some goods are inferior goods, however, and we must now determine whether the law of demand applies universally to them.

INCOME AND SUBSTITUTION EFFECTS: INFERIOR GOODS
3.4

Mechanically, the separation of income and substitution effects for a change in the price of an inferior good is accomplished in the same way as for a normal good. The results, however, differ in a significant respect. With a price reduction the substitution effect still encourages greater consumption, but the income effect works in the opposite direction. At a lower price the consumer's real income increases, and this fact, by itself, implies less consumption of an inferior good. Thus, a price reduction for an inferior good involves a substitution effect that encourages *more* consumption but an opposing income effect that encourages *less* consumption. It would appear that the total effect — the sum of the income and substitution effects — could go either way.

---

[2] Figure 3–6 shows the substitution and income effects for a price reduction. An increase is handled in a slightly different way. If we were considering an increase in the price of clothing from $3 to $5 in the diagram, we would accomplish the separation into substitution and income effects by drawing a hypothetical budget line with a slope of $5 (the new price) tangent to the indifference curve the consumer is on before the price increase, U_2.

Figure 3–7a shows one possibility. Initially, the budget line is MN, with the price of hamburger at $2 per pound and $0H_1$ units purchased. When the price falls to $1 per pound, the budget line shifts to MN', and consumption of hamburger rises to $0H_2$ units. Once again the hypothetical budget line HH' that keeps the consumer on U_1, the original indifference curve, is drawn in. The substitution effect is the movement from point E to point J on U_1, implying an increase in consumption from $0H_1$ to $0H_J$. Now see what happens to hamburger consumption when we move back from budget line HH' to MN', a movement that reflects the income effect of the lower price of hamburger. Because hamburger is an inferior good for this consumer, the income effect in this case leads to less consumption of hamburger from $0H_J$ to $0H_2$. Overall, however, the total effect of the price reduction is increased consumption because the substitution effect (greater consumption) is larger than the income effect (less consumption). In this situation the consumer's demand curve for hamburger would slope downward.

For an inferior good there is another possibility, illustrated in Figure 3–7b. Good X is also an inferior good for some consumer, and a reduction in its price shifts the budget line from MN to MN'. Here, however, the total effect of the price decrease is a reduction in the consumption of X, from $0X_1$ to $0X_2$. When the income and substitution effects are shown separately, we see how this outcome occurs. The substitution effect (point E to point J, or increased consumption of X) still shows greater consumption at a lower price. However, the income effect for this inferior good not only works in the opposing direction (less consumption, from $0X_J$ to $0X_2$) but it also overwhelms the substitution effect. Since the income effect more than offsets the substitution effect, consumption falls. This consumer's demand curve for good X, at least for the prices incorporated in the diagram, would slope upward.

Thus, for inferior goods there are two possibilities. If the substitution effect is larger than the income effect when the price of the good changes, the demand curve will have its usual negative slope. If the income effect is larger than the substitution effect for an inferior good, the demand curve will have a positive slope. This second case represents a theoretically possible exception to the law of demand. It can only happen with an inferior good, and, moreover, only for a subset of inferior goods in which income

---

FIGURE 3–7 *(facing page)*
Income and Substitution Effects for an Inferior Good
Hamburger is an inferior good with a normally shaped, downward-sloping demand curve, because the substitution effect is larger than the income effect in part a. Good X in part b is an inferior good with an upward-sloping demand curve because the income effect is larger than the substitution effect. Good X is called a Giffen good.

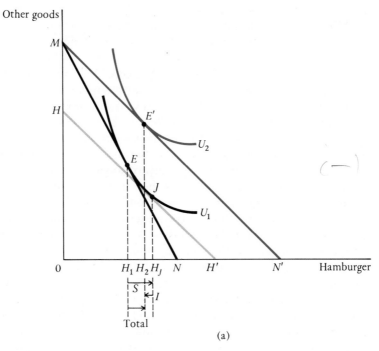

(a)

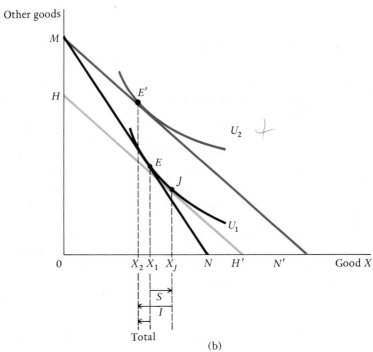

(b)

effects are larger than substitution effects. We frequently refer to a good that belongs to this class as a *Giffen good*, after the nineteenth-century English economist Robert Giffen, who believed potatoes in Ireland had an upward-sloping demand curve. (There is no evidence, however, to support his contention.)

It is difficult to find an intuitively plausible example in which the demand curve slopes upward, but consider the following hypothetical situation.[3] The Merrivale family lives in New Hampshire and typically spends the month of January in Fort Lauderdale. There is a sharp increase in the price of home heating oil. The Merrivales cut back on their use of heating oil during the other winter months, but even so their total heating costs rise so sharply they can no longer afford to vacation in Florida. Staying at home in January greatly increases their use of heating oil for that month, compared to the amount of heating oil they would have used had they been lying on the beach in Fort Lauderdale. On balance, annual heating oil purchases will rise if the increased use in January is greater than the reduction achieved during the remaining winter months. Consequently, an increase in the price of heating oil has led to greater use of heating oil by the Merrivales.

This contrived scenario illustrates the type of situation shown in Figure 3–7b. Heating oil is an inferior good for the Merrivales; a reduction in income would lead them to spend more time at home, and that fact by itself involves an increase in the use of heating oil. A price increase has an income effect that could also induce them to forgo their January vacation. If the expanded consumption in January exceeds the reduced consumption of heating oil during the other winter months, a net increase in consumption of heating oil at a higher price results.

The Giffen-Good Case: How Likely?

We might conceive of situations where the income effect for an inferior good would be larger than the substitution effect, producing an upward-sloping demand curve. However, there is no documented instance of a Giffen good, and economists generally believe that all real world inferior goods have downward-sloping demand curves, as illustrated in Figure 3–7a. This belief stems from both theoretical considerations and empirical evidence.

At a theoretical level the question is whether the income effect or the substitution effect of a price change for an inferior good will be larger. If the substitution effect is larger, the demand curve will slope downward, even for an inferior good, and there are good reasons for believing this to be the case.

---

[3] This example is adapted from E. G. Dolan, *Basic Economics*, 2nd ed. (Hinsdale, Ill.: Dryden Press, 1980), pp. 348–349.

Consider first the income effect. Its size relates closely to the fraction of the consumer's budget devoted to the good. If the price of some good falls by 10 percent, the price reduction will benefit a consumer much more (have a larger income effect) if 50 percent of the consumer's income is spent on the good than if only 2 percent is spent on it. For example, a 50 percent reduction in the price of housing will probably influence housing consumption greatly by its income effect, but a 50 percent reduction in the price of Bic pens will have a much smaller, almost imperceptible effect. Income effects from a change in price are quite small for most goods because they seldom account for as much as 10 percent of a consumer's budget. This is especially true of inferior goods, which are likely to be narrowly defined goods.

On the other hand, there is reason to believe that substitution effects for inferior goods will be relatively large. This stems from the fact that inferior goods usually belong to a general category that contains similar goods of differing qualities. Take hamburger. We would expect a reduction in its price to result in a rearrangement of the consumer's purchases away from chicken, pork, chuck roast, and so on, in favor of hamburger, thus resulting in a large substitution effect.

Consequently, we expect price changes for inferior goods to involve relatively large substitution effects but small income effects. Insofar as this is true, the demand curve would slope downward, and the case shown in Figure 3–7a would be typical. The Giffen good remains an intriguing, but remote, theoretical possibility.

Do Rats Have Downward-Sloping Demand Curves?

Logical reasoning and empirical evidence supports the proposition that humans have downward-sloping demand curves. The inquisitive reader may wonder whether the law of demand also applies to the behavior of animals. Experimental evidence suggests that it does. Consider the results of a study by several researchers at Texas A&M University.[4] The subjects of the experiment were two white male albino rats, one of Wistar stock and the other of Sprague-Dawley stock. These rats were found to have downward-sloping demand curves for root beer and Tom Collins mix.

Researchers confronted each rat with a budget line relating root beer and collins mix. They charged a "price" by requiring the rat to press a lever to receive 0.05 milliliter of each beverage. The "incomes" of the rats were determined by allocating each rat a certain number of lever presses per day. With an income of 300 lever presses and equal prices for root beer and collins mix, both rats expressed a decided preference for root

[4] John Kagel et al., "Experimental Studies of Consumer Demand Behavior Using Laboratory Animals," *Economic Inquiry*, 13 (March 1975): 22–38. See also S. E. G. Lea, "The Psychology and Economics of Demand," *Psychology Bulletin*, 85 (1978), for a survey of similar studies.

beer and spent most of their incomes on it. Then the price of collins mix
was cut in half (half as many lever presses required per unit of collins
mix) and the price of root beer doubled, with income set so that each rat
could still consume its previously chosen market basket if it wished. Economic theory would predict that consumption of collins mix would rise
and root beer fall given the new "prices." The theory proved correct: both
rats chose to consume more than four times as much collins mix as before
and less root beer.

Whether such results indirectly provide additional support for the
law of demand in human behavior is debatable. Experiments such as this
one, however, serve to emphasize once more that theory need not be realistic to yield valid predictions. No one believes that rats understand
what indifference curves and budget lines are, but apparently we can analyze their behavior accurately by using these theoretical techniques.

FROM INDIVIDUAL TO MARKET DEMAND
3.5

We have seen how to derive an individual consumer's demand curve and
why the concepts of income and substitution effects imply that it will typically slope downward. But most practical applications of economic theory require the use of the market demand curve. The reason we begin
with a discussion of individual demand is that the individual demand
curves of all the consumers in the market comprise the market demand
curve. If the typical consumer's demand curve has a negative slope, then
the market demand curve must also have a negative slope.

Figure 3–8 illustrates how individual demand curves are aggregated
to obtain the market demand curve. Assume that there are only three
consumers who purchase bananas although the process will obviously
apply to the more important case where there are a great many consumers. The individual demand curves are d_A, d_B, d_C. To derive the market demand curve, the quantities each consumer will purchase at
alternative prices are summed. For example, at P_2 consumer B will purchase 10 bananas, consumer C will purchase 15, and consumer A will
purchase none. (Note that when the price is P_2, consumer A will be at a
corner equilibrium.) The combined purchases of all consumers total 25
bananas when the price is P_2, and this identifies one point on the market
demand curve D.

Other points in the market demand curve are derived in the same
way. If the price is P_1, A will purchase 3 bananas, B will purchase 13, and
C will purchase 19, so total quantity demanded at a price of P_1 is 35 units.
The process of adding up the individual demand curves to obtain the
market demand curve is called a *horizontal summation*, because the
quantities (measured on the horizontal axis) that would be purchased at
each price are added. Note that when the individual demand curves slope
downward, the market demand also slopes downward. If all consumers

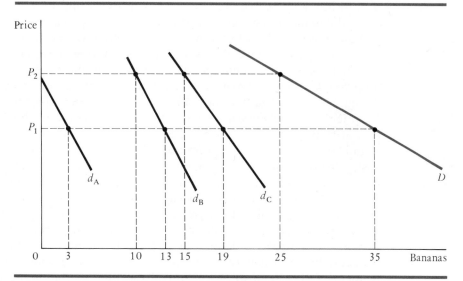

FIGURE 3-8
Summing Individual Demands to Obtain Market Demand
The market demand curve *D* is derived from the individual consumers' demand
curves by a process of horizontal summation. At each price we sum the
quantities each consumer will purchase to obtain the total quantity demanded.

purchase more at a lower price, then total purchases will rise when the
price falls.

On the other hand, a market demand curve can slope downward even
if some consumers have upward-sloping individual demand curves. In a
market with thousands of consumers, if a few dozen happened to have
upward-sloping demand curves, their contribution to the market demand
curve would be more than offset by the normal behavior of the other
consumers. So we have yet another reason not to be particularly concerned about the Giffen-good case. It is possible to imagine that the Merrivale family in New Hampshire will consume more heating oil at a higher
price, but it is difficult to believe that their behavior is typical.

COMPLEMENTS AND SUBSTITUTES
3.6

A demand curve is intended to isolate the relationship between the price
of the good and the quantity purchased, so other factors are held constant
along the curve. Among the factors held constant, we have already mentioned money income and preferences (indifference curves). (A change in
money income or in underlying preferences will generally show up as a

shift in the demand curve.) Now let's turn to the third factor that influences the demand for a good: the prices of other goods, especially goods that are closely related to the one the demand curve pertains to.

Prices of other goods must be kept constant because they can affect consumption of a particular good. If the price of margarine rises sharply, for example, we would expect an increase in the purchase of butter, even though the price of butter does not change. In other words, an increase in the price of margarine causes the entire demand curve for butter to shift outward. By contrast, a sharp increase in the price of photographic film would tend to decrease the purchase of flashbulbs: the demand curve for flashbulbs shifts inward with an increase in film prices. So a change in the price of one good can cause a shift in the demand curve for another good. In drawing a specific demand curve, we therefore must hold the prices of other goods, especially closely related goods, fixed.

Closely related goods fall into two distinct groups: *complements* and *substitutes*. The precise definitions of these terms may be difficult to understand, but their general meanings are fairly clear. Two goods are complements if they tend to be consumed together, so that consumption of both tends to rise or fall simultaneously. Examples might include automobiles and gasoline, catsup and hamburger, beer and football games, liquor and Alka Seltzer. If two goods are complements, an increase in the price of one leads to a decrease in the demand for the other. If hamburger prices rise sharply, catsup consumption will decline, because hamburger consumption will fall and the two goods are used together.

Substitutes, on the other hand, are goods that can easily replace one another in consumption. Their consumption is frequently an either-or choice since they serve similar purposes, and one or the other may be chosen. Examples might include butter and margarine, Coke and Pepsi, chicken and hamburger, and aspirin and Bufferin. If two goods are *substitutes*, an increase in the price of one leads to an increased demand for the other. If Pepsi prices rise sharply, Coke consumption will rise (the demand curve for Coke shifts out): Coke is substituted for Pepsi when Pepsi becomes more expensive.

The existence of complementary and substitute goods emphasizes that consumption decisions are interrelated. In some specific situations, this is important to keep in mind.

PRICE ELASTICITY OF DEMAND
3.7

Even though we assume that all market demand curves have negative slopes (implying that at a lower price a greater quantity will be purchased), the degree of responsiveness in quantity purchased to a price change varies widely from one commodity to another. A reduction in the price of salt may only lead to an infinitesimal increase in purchases (all the law of demand says is that there will be *some* increase, not how much), while a reduction in airplane fares may produce a veritable explosion in air travel.

For several reasons it is helpful to have an index that indicates just how responsive quantity demanded is to a change in price. This index is called the *price elasticity of demand,* or simply the elasticity of demand.

The price elasticity of demand is a measure of how sensitive quantity demanded is to a change in the price of a product. It can be defined as the percentage change in quantity demanded divided by the percentage change in price. The ratio will always be negative for any downward-sloping demand curve. For example, if a 10 percent price increase brings about a 20 percent reduction in quantity demanded, the price elasticity of demand is -20 percent/$+10$ percent, or -2.0. Frequently, economists drop the minus sign on the understanding that price and quantity always move in different directions and simply refer to the elasticity as being, in this case, 2.0. From now on we will follow this convention.

Price elasticity of demand provides a quantitative measure of the price responsiveness of quantity demanded along a demand curve. The higher the numerical value of the elasticity, the larger the effect of a price change on quantity is. If the elasticity is only 0.2, then a 10 percent price increase will reduce quantity demanded by just 2 percent (2 percent/10 percent $= 0.2$). Alternatively, if the elasticity is 4.0, a 10 percent price rise will reduce quantity by 40 percent (40 percent/10 percent $= 4.0$).

When referring to demand elasticities, economists adopt the following terminology. If the price elasticity of demand exceeds 1.0, the demand curve is said to be *elastic*. Elasticity is greater than 1.0 whenever the percentage change in quantity is greater than the percentage change in price, implying that the quantity demanded is highly responsive to a price change. If the price elasticity of demand is less than 1.0, the demand curve is said to be *inelastic*. Elasticity is less than 1.0 whenever the percentage change in quantity is less than the percentage change in price, implying that quantity demanded is relatively unresponsive to a price change. When the price elasticity of demand is equal to 1.0, the demand curve is said to be *unit elastic*, or of unitary elasticity. Unitary elasticity occurs whenever the percentage changes in price and quantity are equal.

Whether a demand curve is elastic, unit elastic, or inelastic determines how a price change will affect total expenditures on the product. Total expenditures equal price times quantity, or $p \times q$, and a change in price affects these terms in two potentially offsetting ways. A higher price increases the p term but reduces the q term (quantity demanded is lower at a higher price). The net effect on total expenditures therefore depends on how responsive quantity is to the price change: it depends on the price elasticity of demand. If a 10 percent increase in price reduces quantity by 10 percent (the unit elastic case), then total expenditures, $p \times q$, remain unchanged. But if a 10 percent increase reduces quantity by more than 10 percent (the elastic demand case), then total expenditures will fall because of the sharper reduction in quantity purchased. Finally, if a 10 percent increase reduces quantity by less than 10 percent (the inelastic demand case), then total expenditures will rise.

Let's describe these relationships more concisely. When demand is elastic, a higher price reduces total expenditures (and a lower price increases total expenditures). When demand is inelastic, a higher price increases total expenditures (and a lower price reduces total expenditures). When demand is unit elastic, a price change leaves total expenditures unchanged.

Remembering these relationships between demand elasticity and the effect of a price change on total expenditures is important, but it's unnecessary to memorize them. Instead, just by recalling what very elastic and very inelastic demand curves look like on a graph makes it possible to reproduce these relationships easily. Figure 3–9a, for example, shows a very flat demand curve for good X, which implies that a "small" price change will have a "large" effect on quantity purchased. This is an elastic demand, where the percentage change in quantity will exceed the percentage change in price. If, for example, price falls from $1.00 to $0.90, quantity increases sharply, from 100 to 200. The price reduction increases total expenditures on the good from $100 ($1.00 multiplied by 100 units) to $180 ($0.90 multiplied by 200 units). Conversely, if price rises from $0.90 to $1.00, total expenditures fall from $180 to $100. Thus, we see visually how a price change affects total expenditures when the demand curve is elastic.

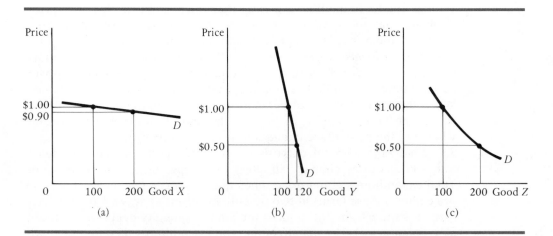

FIGURE 3-9
Price Elasticity of Demand and Total Expenditures
(a) For an elastic demand curve, at a lower price total expenditures rise. (b) For an inelastic demand curve, at a lower price total expenditures fall. (c) For a unit elastic demand curve, at a lower price total expenditures remain unchanged.

Figure 3–9b shows a demand curve for good Y that is very inelastic: a change in price has little effect on quantity. When price falls from $1.00 to $0.50, total expenditures fall from $100 to $60. When price rises from $0.50 to $1.00, total expenditures rise. Figure 3–9c shows the intermediate case of a unit elastic demand curve.[5] In this case total expenditures remain unchanged when price varies. Consumers purchase 100 units at a price of $1.00 (total expenditures of $100), and 200 units at a price of $0.50 (total expenditures still $100).

In short, when demand is elastic (elasticity greater than 1.0), price and total expenditures move in opposite directions. When demand is inelastic (elasticity less than 1.0), price and total expenditures move in the same direction. And when demand is unit elastic, total expenditures remain constant when the price varies.

Calculating the Price Elasticity

It is frequently necessary to calculate price elasticity from a pair of price-quantity points on a demand curve. Suppose we are given the following price-quantity values:

$$P_1 = \$10.00 \qquad P_2 = \$9.90$$
$$Q_1 = 1000 \qquad Q_2 = 1005$$

Our definition of *price elasticity* is the percentage change in quantity divided by the percentage change in price. Expressing this as a formula and letting η (the Greek letter eta) stand for price elasticity, we have

$$\eta = (\Delta Q/Q)\big/(\Delta P/P).$$

Here $\Delta Q/Q$ is the percentage change in quantity, and $\Delta P/P$ is the percentage change in price. In applying this formula — called the *point elasticity formula* — we encounter an ambiguity. While ΔQ and ΔP are unambiguously determined (a 5 unit change in quantity and a $0.10 change in price), what values should be used for Q and P? If we enter the values for P_1 and Q_1 into the formula, we obtain

$$(\Delta Q/Q_1)\big/(\Delta P/P_1) = (5/1000)\big/(\$0.10/\$10) = 0.50.$$

Alternatively, if we use P_2 and Q_2, we get

$$(\Delta Q/Q_2)\big/(\Delta P/P_2) = (5/1005)\big/(\$0.10/\$9.90) = 0.49.$$

Because we are dealing with small changes in this case, it makes little quantitative difference which values we choose. There is, however, a slight difference, and it reflects the fact that the percentage change between two prices, for instance, depends on the direction of the change. If price falls

---

[5] Since the product of price and quantity is unchanged at all points along a demand curve with unit elasticity, such a curve must satisfy the equation $p \times q = K$ (a constant). This equation describes a rectangular hyperbola.

from \$10 to \$5, this is referred to as a 50 percent decrease (a \$5 change in price divided by the *initial* price, \$10). Alternatively, if the price rises again from \$5 to \$10, this is a 100 percent increase (a \$5 change in price divided by the *initial* price \$5). Don't be sidetracked by this arithmetical obscurity: the important point is that some base Q and P must be selected to use in the formula, but for small changes in Q and P, it makes no significant difference to the results which base is chosen.

There is a substantial difference, however, when a large change in price and quantity is involved. Suppose instead we have the following values:

$$P_1 = \$10 \qquad P_2 = \$5$$
$$Q_1 = 1000 \qquad Q_2 = 2000$$

By inspection, we see that total expenditures are \$10,000 at both prices, so we know that demand is unit elastic. Surprisingly, though, it now makes a great difference what base values of P and Q we use if we try to apply the point elasticity formula:

$$(\Delta Q/Q_1)\big/(\Delta P/P_1) = (1000/1000)\big/(\$5/\$10) = 2.0.$$
$$(\Delta Q/Q_2)\big/(\Delta P/P_2) = (1000/2000)\big/(\$5/\$5) = 0.5.$$

According to one calculation, price elasticity of demand is 2.0; according to the other, it is 0.5. Both are wrong, and the true value, unity, lies between these estimates. The basic problem in this case is that the elasticity of demand tends to vary from one point (one P, Q combination) to another on the demand curve, and for a large change in price and quantity we need an average value over the entire range. Consequently, when we deal with large changes in price and quantity, we should use the following *arc elasticity formula:*

$$\eta = \frac{\Delta Q/(\tfrac{1}{2})(Q_1 + Q_2)}{\Delta P/(\tfrac{1}{2})(P_1 + P_2)}.$$

Note that this formula differs from the point elasticity formula only in using the average of the two quantities, $(\tfrac{1}{2})(Q_1 + Q_2)$, and the average of the two prices, $(\tfrac{1}{2})(P_1 + P_2)$. Applying this formula to the preceding figures yields the true value of the elasticity over the entire range of prices considered:

$$\frac{\Delta Q/(\tfrac{1}{2})(Q_1 + Q_2)}{\Delta P/(\tfrac{1}{2})(P_1 + P_2)} = \frac{1000/(\tfrac{1}{2})(1000 + 2000)}{\$5/(\tfrac{1}{2})(\$5 + \$10)} = 1.0.$$

Thus we have two formulas. The first works well when small changes in P and Q are involved since it then makes little difference which P or Q is used. The second formula avoids having to pick one specific point by using the average values of price and quantity and should be used with large changes in price and quantity.

Graphical Treatment of Price Elasticity

The price elasticity of demand will frequently vary from one point on the demand curve to another. In the case of a demand curve that is a straight line, the elasticity is different at every point on the curve. Figure 3–10 shows a linear demand curve AC. To see that the elasticity varies along the curve, let's consider two extreme points. At the upper end of the curve, if price falls from $25 to $24, quantity increases from 1 to 2 units. Since total expenditures increase from $25 to $48, we know the demand curve is elastic over that range. At the lower end of the curve, if price falls from $2 to $1, quantity increases from 24 to 25. Since total expenditures fall from $48 to $25, the demand curve is inelastic over that range. Note, however, that a $1 price reduction brought about a 1-unit quantity increase in both cases.

We can easily understand this result by recalling that elasticity is the ratio of the percentage changes in quantity and in price. At the upper end of the demand curve a $1 price change is a relatively small percentage change in price, but a 1-unit change in quantity (from 1 to 2) is a large percentage change in quantity. The situation is reversed at the lower end

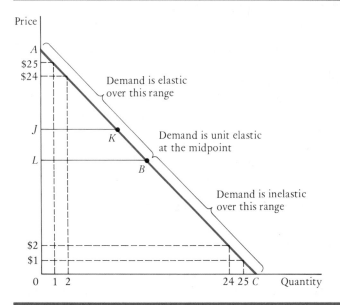

FIGURE 3–10
Elasticity of Demand Varies Along a Linear Demand Curve
The elasticity of demand is different at each point along a linear demand curve. At high prices demand is elastic; at low prices it is inelastic; at the midpoint it is unit elastic.

of the curve. The same $1 price change is now relatively large in percentage terms when the change is from $2 to $1, but the percentage change in quantity, from 24 to 25, is relatively small.

A straight-line demand curve has the same slope at all points, so *the slope and the elasticity are not the same.* Recall that the formula for point elasticity is $(\Delta Q/Q)\big/(\Delta P/P)$, which can be rewritten as $(\Delta Q/\Delta P) \times (P/Q)$. The term $\Delta Q/\Delta P$ is the inverse of the slope (1 divided by the slope), so the slope of the curve is only one of two factors that determine elasticity. The second factor is the position of the point (indicated by P/Q) at which elasticity is evaluated.

It is sometimes helpful to know how elasticity can be identified geometrically. Suppose we wish to determine price elasticity at point B in Figure 3–10. Starting with the formula for point elasticity that is relevant for a small change in price,

$$\eta = (\Delta Q/Q)\big/(\Delta P/P) = (\Delta Q/\Delta P) \times (P/Q).$$

We can interpret the various terms as distances in the diagram. Since the ratio $\Delta Q/\Delta P$ is the same for small or large changes (the slope is constant), it can be evaluated between B and A on the demand curve: $\Delta Q = LB$ and $\Delta P = LA$. Further, at point B, P equals $0L$, and Q equals LB. Substituting these values into the formula, we have

$$\eta = (\Delta Q/\Delta P) \times (P/Q) = (LB/LA) \times (0L/LB) = 0L/LA.$$

If point P is the midpoint of the demand curve, $0L$ will equal LA, and the price elasticity, $0L/LA$, will equal 1. The elasticity of demand at the midpoint of a linear demand curve is always unity. At any price above this point the demand curve will be elastic. At point K the elasticity is $0J/JA$, which is greater than 1. Similarly, at any point below B the elasticity is less than 1. In general, the elasticity rises as you move up the curve from C to A. This geometric measure is not intuitively obvious, but experimenting with numerical examples makes it clear that it is valid.[6]

PRICE ELASTICITIES VARY AMONG GOODS
3.8

Consumption of some goods is more sensitive to a change in price than consumption of other goods. For example, a 50 percent increase in the price of cigarettes would probably reduce their consumption somewhat, but not a great deal. By contrast, a 50 percent increase in the price of

---

[6] The same geometric procedure can be used with a nonlinear demand curve. In this case it is only necessary to draw a straight line tangent to the curved demand curve at the point we wish to measure the elasticity and evaluate the elasticity of that straight line at that point, exactly as we did for a linear demand curve. Since the slopes of the line and of the demand curve are the same where they are tangent ($\Delta Q/\Delta P$ is the same), and since P/Q is also the same at that point, the elasticity of the straight line is equal to the elasticity of the curve at the point of tangency.

restaurant meals would probably reduce those purchases rather sharply. What we are asserting, of course, is that the elasticities of demand differ from one good to another. Why should this be so? Unfortunately, there is no fully satisfactory answer to this question. Price elasticities ultimately reflect the willingness and ability of thousands or millions of people to change their consumption patterns. Why people respond exactly as they do we will never know. Nonetheless, there are two general factors that seem to have a pronounced effect on the price elasticity for any particular product.

The first, and most important factor, is the availability and closeness of substitutes. *The more substitutes there are for some product, and the better the substitutes, the more elastic the demand for the product will be.* When there are good substitutes, a change in the price of the product will involve a large substitution effect. The demand for margarine, for example, would probably be quite elastic, because when its price rises, many people would switch to butter. Remember that when we evaluate the price elasticity of the demand for margarine, we assume the price of butter to be unchanged. Thus a higher price of margarine (with an unchanged price of butter) leads people to shift from margarine to butter, because they are close substitutes.

This proposition has wide applicability. For example, it allows us to understand the results of one statistical study that found the elasticity of demand for Chevrolets to be 4.0, while the elasticity of demand for all automobiles was estimated at 1.5. If the price of Chevrolets falls, and other auto prices remain unchanged, many people will purchase Chevys who would otherwise have purchased another make. A large quantity response, and thus a high elasticity, is predictable, because Chevys and other cars are substitutes. When we consider the elasticity of demand for all automobiles, however, we assume that all auto prices go up and down together, and the percentage change in the quantity would be smaller.

The degree to which a good has close substitutes depends in part on how specifically it is defined. A narrowly defined good will frequently have close substitutes, and elasticity will tend to be higher. For example, the elasticity of demand for Zest soap (a very narrowly defined good with many substitutes) will be greater than the elasticity of demand for soap. For this reason the demand for any particular brand of some product (e.g., Budweiser beer) will be more elastic than the demand for all brands taken together (beer).

A second factor that is sometimes quite important is the time period over which consumers adjust to a price change. *The longer the time period involved, the fuller the adjustment consumers can make.* In part, this reflects the fact that it takes time for consumers to learn about a price change, but there are other reasons too. Consider an increase in the price of electricity. In the month following the price increase, people could cut back their usage somewhat by switching lights off more conscientiously, turning thermostats down (if electric heating is used), or turning air conditioners off. The number of ways people could economize on electricity, however, is greater when we consider what they could do over a longer period, a year, for example. They could substitute lower-wattage light bulbs for existing light bulbs, convert electric furnaces to operate on heating oil or natural gas, insulate their houses, use portable kerosene heaters, buy appliances that require less electricity, and so on. In short, demand would be more elastic the longer the time period over which consumers can adjust.

We can make this point graphically by distinguishing between a short-run demand curve, which pertains to a short period immediately following a price change, and a long-run demand curve, which pertains to time periods after consumers have fully adjusted. Figure 3–11 illustrates this difference. Suppose a $1.50-per-gallon price for gasoline has been in effect for a long period of time, and consumers are purchasing 1000 gallons per month. If the price rises to $2.25, the short-run demand curve, D_{SR}, reflects the way consumers respond in the month immediately following the price increase. Consumption falls to 900 gallons as consumers initially react by driving a little less, getting their engines tuned up, and making other easy adjustments. These responses, however, will not be the

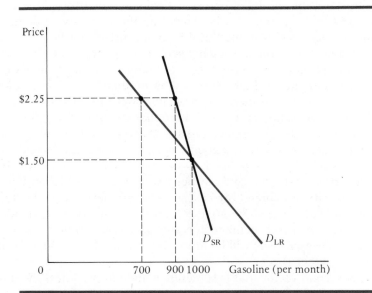

FIGURE 3–11
Elasticity of Demand Is Greater in the Long Run
In the short run an increase in the price of gasoline only leads to a modest reduction in consumption, as shown by D_{SR}. In the long run there are more ways for consumers to economize, and consumption falls more sharply, as shown by D_{LR}. Long-run demand elasticity is higher than short-run demand elasticity.

full adjustment to the higher price. Over time people will switch to more gas-efficient automobiles, use public transportation or car pools, or even choose residences closer to their place of employment. The long-run demand curve D_{LR} allows sufficient time for all these adjustments to be made and shows purchases falling to 700 gallons per month. The long-run demand curve is more elastic since it shows a larger quantity response to a given price change.[7]

For many goods consumers will not require much time to make a full adjustment to a change in price. In these cases the long-run and short-run responses will not differ substantially. We have used two goods, electricity and gasoline, as examples for which the distinction is important. Changes in the prices of electricity and gasoline will necessitate major alterations in the consumption of very durable goods (houses and cars) before consumers have fully adjusted, and those alterations take time. But for most goods (for instance, beer, shoes, wristwatches, meat, TV's, books, and so on) we would not expect the short- and long-run elasticities of demand to be much different.

The Estimation of Elasticities

In many applications of economic theory, it makes very little difference what the exact value of the price elasticity of demand for some product is; all we need to know is that the demand curve slopes downward. There are cases, however, where a knowledge of price elasticities is helpful, and, consequently, many economists have attempted to develop estimates for a variety of products. In practice, estimating elasticities of demand poses some difficult problems, because price elasticity refers to a *given demand curve*, but the demand curve itself is likely to shift over time.

Economists and statisticians have developed some sophisticated techniques to deal with this problem to permit estimation of demand elasticities. These techniques are far from perfect, so any reported estimate should be viewed with some skepticism. With that warning in mind, refer to Table 3–2, which lists some selected estimates of price elasticities for a variety of products. Before reading further, you may find it amusing to cover the numbers in the table and enter your own guesses for plausible values for the different products. You may be surprised to find that real consumer behavior sometimes differs rather sharply from what intuition suggests.

As Table 3–2 indicates, the estimates of demand elasticities differ widely among goods. Not surprisingly, salt and cigarettes are in inelastic

---

[7] Although the slope of a demand curve by itself doesn't generally allow us to deduce the elasticity, when we consider the relative elasticities of two demand curves at the point where they intersect, the curve with the lower slope (the flatter curve) is more elastic at that point. This can be seen by rewriting the formula for elasticity, $(\Delta Q/Q)/(\Delta P/P)$, as $(\Delta Q/\Delta P) \times (P/Q)$. The term P/Q is the same for both curves where they intersect, so a difference in slopes (1 divided by $\Delta Q/\Delta P$) does then imply a difference in elasticities.

TABLE 3-2
Selected Demand Elasticities

	Short Run	Long Run
Salt	—	0.1
Cigarettes	—	0.35
Water	—	0.4
Beer	—	0.7–0.9
Housing	—	1.0
Physicians' services	0.6	—
Medical and hospitalization insurance	0.3	0.9
Gasoline	0.2*	0.5*
Gasoline	—	0.8†
Gasoline	—	1.5‡
Automobiles	—	1.5
Chevrolets	—	4.0
Electricity (household utility)	0.1	1.9
Gas (household utility)	0.1	10.7
Intercity bus	2.0	2.2
Air travel	0.1	2.4
Motion pictures	0.9	3.7

Sources: Hendrik S. Houthakker and Lester D. Taylor, *Consumer Demand in the United States, 1929–1970* (Cambridge, Mass.: Harvard University Press, 1966 and 1970 editions); U.S. Department of Agriculture; Kenneth G. Elzinga, "The Beer Industry," in *The Structure of American Industry*, ed. Walter Adams (New York: Macmillan, 1977); Llad Phillips and Harold L. Votey, Jr., *Economic Analysis of Pressing Social Problems* (Chicago: Rand McNally, 1974).

*Houthakker and Taylor.

†J. L. Sweeney, "The Demand for Gasoline: A Vintage Capital Model" (Department of Engineering Economics, Stanford University).

‡J. M. Griffin, *Energy Conservation in the OECD, 1980 to 2000* (Cambridge, Mass.: Ballinger, 1979).

demand (elasticities of 0.1 and 0.35). Although people commonly think of medical care consumption as almost totally unresponsive to price, the elasticity of demand for physicians' services is 0.6. While this is inelastic, it does imply that a 50 percent increase in price would reduce consumption by fully 30 percent. Some products, such as air travel and automobiles, are apparently in highly elastic demand.

Three entries, from three different studies, are given for the long-run elasticity of demand for gasoline. They range from 0.5 to 1.5, a wide variation that serves as a reminder both of the difficulty of extracting reliable information from historical data and of the healthy skepticism that should be maintained regarding the precision of such estimates.

One implication of these estimates (and many others that could be cited) should not be missed: they all support the law of demand. Consumers do purchase more at a lower price, other things being equal. Not only that, but as a general rule the quantitative effect of price on consumer purchases is quite large (elasticities are not close to zero). This finding contrasts sharply with the view of the average noneconomist, who is generally willing to accept the proposition that price affects consumption but believes the quantitative effect to be small.

Washington, D.C., Learns About Price Elasticity

In August 1980 city officials of Washington, D.C., hard-pressed for tax revenues, levied a 6 percent excise tax on the sale of gasoline. As a first approximation (and a reasonable one, it turns out), this tax could be expected to increase the price of gasoline by 6 percent. The price elasticity of demand has an important bearing on the consequences of this action, since the more sharply the sales of gasoline fall, the less tax revenue the city will raise. Presumably, city officials hoped that gasoline sales would be largely unaffected by the higher price.

A few months later, however, the amount of gasoline sold had fallen by 33 percent.[8] A 6 percent price increase producing a 33 percent quantity reduction means the price elasticity was about 5.5. And this was only the immediate, or short-run, response. The sharp drop in sales meant that very little additional tax revenue was raised, and further indications were that when consumers had fully adjusted to the tax, tax revenues might actually fall lower. (There had been a 10-cent per-gallon tax before the 6 percent tax was added, so although the 6 percent levy was raising revenue, the gain was largely offset by the loss in revenue from the initial 10-cent tax following the reduction in sales.)

In interpreting this episode, we must recognize that price elasticities of the type reported in Table 3–2 for gasoline are irrelevant in this case. This was not a general increase in gasoline prices, but a rise only within the city limits of Washington. Gasoline sold in Washington is a narrowly defined product that has good substitutes: gasoline sold in nearby Virginia and Maryland suburbs. Higher gas prices in Washington led many consumers to fill their tanks outside the city, which accounted for the large reduction in sales within Washington. The demand for gasoline in Washington, when the prices charged in Virginia and Maryland are unchanged, will obviously be highly elastic. No economist would be surprised at the results of this tax, but apparently the city officials were. Observed one city councilman:

> We tend to think of ourselves here in the District as an island to ourselves. But we've got to realize that we're not. We've got to realize that Maryland and Virginia are right out there, and there's nothing to stop people from crossing over the line.[9]

[8] "Barry Asks Gasoline Tax Repeal," *Washington Post,* November 25, 1980, p. A1.
[9] Ibid.

The 6 percent gasoline tax was repealed in December 1980. At that time Mayor Marion Barry cited "overwhelming evidence" that the tax had not worked and that it had "caused undue hardships both on the consumers of gas . . . and those who operate retail gas businesses."[10]

PRICE ELASTICITY
AND THE PRICE-CONSUMPTION CURVE
3.9

Price elasticity can be computed for any demand curve, whether it is the total market demand curve or an individual consumer's. Admittedly, the price elasticity of market demand is generally of greatest interest, but that elasticity depends on the underlying elasticities of the demand curves of various consumers. To link our discussion of price elasticity to the individual consumer's price-consumption curve, we can now show that the slope of the price-consumption curve provides important information about the price elasticity of demand.

Figure 3–12 shows three hypothetical price-consumption curves. In Figure 3–12a the curve slopes downward. This means that the price elasticity exceeds unity: the consumer's demand curve would be elastic if plotted in a price-quantity diagram. A downward-sloping price-consumption curve shows that the consumer's total expenditures on the good rise when its price falls, which, by definition, is an elastic demand. Recall that the distance MM_1 shows total expenditures on good X when its price is given by the slope of the budget line MN. When price falls, the budget line rotates to MN', and at the new equilibrium, total expenditures on X are now MM_2, an increase from the original level.

Figure 3–12b and c show the cases of unit elastic and inelastic demand. In part b the price-consumption curve is a horizontal line, showing that total expenditures on the good remain unchanged at MM_1 when its price is varied. This situation is, by definition, one of unit elastic demand. Figure 3–12c has an upward-sloping price-consumption curve. In this case a reduction in price reduces total expenditures on the good, by definition an inelastic demand. Expenditures are initially MM_1 but fall to MM_2 when the price is reduced. Therefore, if the price-consumption curve slopes

[10] Ibid.

FIGURE 3–12 *(facing page)*
Price-consumption Curves and the Elasticity of Demand
The slope of a consumer's price-consumption curve tells us whether demand is elastic, inelastic, or unit elastic. When the price-consumption curve is negatively sloped (part a), demand is elastic. When it is zero sloped (part b), demand is unit elastic. When it is positively sloped (part c), demand is inelastic.

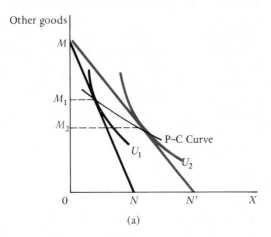

(a)

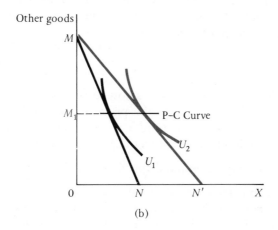

(b)

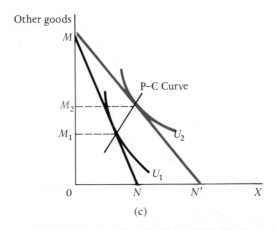

(c)

downward, the consumer's demand curve is elastic. If it is horizontal, the demand curve is unit elastic. If it slopes upward, it is inelastic. Of course, it is possible for the slope of the consumer's price-consumption curve to vary along the curve. Indeed, our original derivation of the curve (Figure 3–4) showed a U-shaped price-consumption curve. In Figure 3–4 the curve slopes downward at high prices and upward at low prices, which means that the elasticity varies along the demand curve of the consumer, with the consumer's demand curve elastic at high prices and inelastic at low prices. This is probably the typical case.

TWO OTHER ELASTICITIES
3.10

Price elasticity of demand is the most important elasticity concept in economics, but it is possible to define an elasticity to measure the responsiveness of any variable to a change in some other. Two other common elasticity measures that relate to consumer behavior are the income elasticity of demand and the cross-price elasticity of demand.

Income Elasticity

The income elasticity of demand measures how responsive consumption of some item is to a change in income: the price of the good itself is not changed. We define income elasticity as the percentage change in consumption of a good divided by the percentage change in income, or

$$\text{income elasticity of demand for } X = (\Delta X/X) \big/ (\Delta I/I).$$

For example, if income rises by 10 percent, and a consumer increases purchases of X by 5 percent, then the income elasticity is 0.5. Note that the algebraic sign of this elasticity distinguishes between normal and inferior goods. Whenever income elasticity is positive, consumption of the good rises with income, so the good must be normal. Whenever income elasticity is negative, consumption of the good falls when income rises, and the good must be inferior. A unitary income elasticity means the consumer continues to spend the same percentage of income on the good when income rises.

Cross-Price Elasticity of Demand

The cross-price elasticity of demand measures how responsive consumption of one good is to a change in the price of a different good. We define cross-price elasticity as the percentage change in consumption of a good divided by the percentage change in the price of a different good, or

cross-price elasticity of demand for X
$$\text{with respect to the price of } Y = (\Delta X/X) \big/ (\Delta P_Y/P_Y).$$

For example, if the price of margarine rises by 10 percent, and the quantity of butter purchased increases by 5 percent, then the cross-price elasticity of demand for butter is 0.5. Note that cross-price elasticity will be positive when the goods are substitutes (as are butter and margarine) and negative when the goods are complements. Indeed, the major use of this elasticity is to measure the strength of the complementary or substitute relationship between goods.

Summary

A change in a consumer's budget line will lead to a change in the market basket selected. In this chapter we began by considering a change in income when the prices of goods are held constant — a parallel shift in the budget line. We identified two possibilities: consumption of a good may go up when income rises, or it may go down. When consumption of a good rises with an increase in income, the good is a normal good. An inferior good is one for which consumption falls as income increases.

Next we discussed how a change in the price of a good affects its consumption. By rotating the budget line confronting a consumer, we can determine the market basket the consumer would select at different prices, while income, preferences, and the prices of other goods are held constant. The various price-quantity combinations identified in this way can be plotted as the consumer's demand curve.

To determine whether a demand curve must have a negative slope, we showed that the effect of a change in price on quantity demanded could be separated into two components, an income effect and a substitution effect. For a normal good both effects imply greater consumption at a lower price, so the demand curve for a normal good must slope downward. For an inferior good the income and substitution effects of a price change operate in opposing directions. If the income effect is larger, the demand curve will slope upward. However, both theoretical reasoning and empirical evidence suggest that this case is quite rare, perhaps even nonexistent.

Price elasticity of demand is a measure of how responsive quantity demanded is to a change in price. Elasticity is measured by the percentage change in quantity divided by the percentage change in price. When this ratio exceeds one, demand is elastic, and a lower price expands purchases so sharply that total outlays rise. When the ratio is less than one, demand is inelastic, and a lower price leads to a reduction in total outlays. When the ratio equals one, demand is unit elastic, and total outlays are unchanged.

Review Questions and Problems

1. An Engel curve is a relationship between the consumer's income and the quantity of some good consumed (the price of the good fixed). Income is measured on the vertical axis, and the quantity of the good consumed is measured on the horizontal axis. Draw the Engel curves for clothing and hamburger from Figures 3–1 and 3–2. How does the slope of an Engel curve identify whether the good is normal or inferior?

2. What is a normal good? What is an inferior good? Distinguish between an inferior good and an economic "bad." If Sally spends 30 percent of her income on housing when her income is $10,000, but only 25 percent when her income is $15,000, is housing an inferior good for her?

*3. Is it possible for all goods a consumer purchases to be normal goods? Is it possible for all goods a consumer purchases to be inferior goods?

*4. Consider two market baskets, A ($100 worth of other goods and 10 units of X) and B ($150 worth of other goods and 10 units of X). If good X is a normal good, will the consumer's MRS_{XO} be greater when basket *A* or basket *B* is consumed? What if good *X* is an inferior good? Show in a diagram.

5. Explain why the food stamp program can have the same effect on the consumption pattern and well-being of recipients as an outright cash transfer of the same cost. Why do you think it isn't converted into an explicit cash transfer program, thereby saving the cost of printing and redeeming food stamps?

6. Prior to 1979 the food stamp program required families to pay a certain amount for food stamps. Suppose a family can receive $150 in food stamps for a payment of $50; no other options are offered. How would this policy affect the budget line? Compared with an outright gift of $100 in food stamps, which is the way the program now works, would this policy lead to more, less, or the same food consumption?

7. Explain how the indifference curve and budget line apparatus is used to derive a consumer's demand curve. In drawing a demand curve, certain things are held constant. What are they, and how does this approach hold them constant?

8. Separate the effect of an increase in the price of beer — a normal good — into its component income and substitution effects. (Hint: See footnote 2.)

9. What is an inferior good? Must the demand curve for an inferior good slope downward? If not, what reasons do economists have for believing that the demand curves for all goods are downward sloping?

10. "A Giffen good must be an inferior good, but an inferior good need not be a Giffen good." Explain this statement fully, using the concepts of income and substitution effects.

*11. Assume that a consumer would like to purchase 50 gallons of gasoline per month at the price of $1.50 per gallon. However, the $1.50 price is the result of a government price ceiling, so there is a shortage, and the consumer can only get 25 gallons. Show what this looks like using indifference curves and the budget line. Then show that the consumer will be willing to pay a price higher than $1.50 to get additional units of gasoline. (This is the demand side reason for the emergence of a black market.)

12. "A product's price is a measure of its marginal value, or marginal benefit, to consumers." Is this statement true for all consumers who purchase the good? If a government price ceiling set below the equilibrium price is in effect, does this price equal the marginal benefit of the good?

13. What is the price elasticity of demand supposed to measure? State the point elasticity and arc elasticity formulas for measuring elasticity of demand. When should each be used?

14. "When the demand curve is inelastic, consumers will not reduce their purchases when the price rises." Evaluate this statement.

15. Suppose a consumer spends her entire income on two goods, sugar and salt. Her demand curve for salt is inelastic. If the price of salt rises, will she consume more or less sugar?

*16. Assume that the demand for heroin is inelastic, and assume further that users get the funds to pay for heroin by stealing. Suppose the government increases penalties on heroin suppliers and thereby reduces supply. What will happen to the price of heroin? What will happen to the amount of crime committed by heroin users?

17. If the price of gasoline is $2.00 and the elasticity of demand is 0.4, how much would a 10 percent reduction in quantity placed on the market increase the price? Would total spending on gasoline rise? If so, by what percentage?

18. What is the elasticity of demand for a horizontal demand curve? For a vertical demand curve?

19. Consumers purchased 600 million oranges this year at a price of 22 cents per orange. Last year purchases were 612 million at a price of 20 cents per orange. What is the elasticity of demand for oranges?

20. Is the demand for Coca-Cola more or less elastic than the demand for all cola beverages? If we know that the price elasticity of demand for Coca-Cola is 9.0, how much would purchases fall if the price is increased by 10 percent? Suppose other cola beverages were also increased in price by 10 percent. Would purchases of Coke fall by more or less in this case?

Supplementary Readings

Baumol, William. *Economic Theory and Operations Analysis*. 4th ed. Englewood Cliffs, N.J.: Prentice-Hall, 1977. Chaps. 9, 10.

Ferguson, C. E. "Substitution Effect in Value Theory: A Pedagogical Note." *Southern Economic Journal*, 24 (1960): 310–314.

Hicks, John R. *A Revision of Demand Theory*. Oxford: Oxford University Press, 1956.

Kagel, John H; Battalio, Raymond C.; Rachlin, Howard; Green, Leonard; Basmann, Robert L.; and Cleman, W. R. "Experimental Studies of Consumer Demand Behavior Using Laboratory Animals." *Economic Inquiry*, 13 (March 1975): 22–38.

Leibenstein, Harvey. "Bandwagon, Snob, and Veblen Effects in the Theory of Consumers' Demand." In *Microeconomics: Selected Readings*, 3rd ed., edited by Edwin Mansfield. New York: Norton, 1979.

Using Consumer Choice Theory

4

In the development of economic theory the most important use of consumer choice analysis is to justify the negative slope of demand curves. Once consumer choice theory provides us with a firm basis for believing the law of demand, many problems can be analyzed by using the demand curve, without having to go behind the relationship and look more deeply at consumer behavior. On the other hand, some issues are better analyzed by using the budget lines and indifference curves developed in consumer choice theory.

In this chapter we will see how we can apply consumer choice theory to several interesting and important questions. For example, we will see how subsidizing consumption of some good may lead people to consume less of it, and why higher interest rates can lead people to save less. While some of the applications in this chapter are important in themselves, they are included primarily to illustrate how the theory of consumer choice can be applied to analyze a wide variety of problems.

EXCISE SUBSIDY
4.1

An excise subsidy is a form of subsidy in which the government pays part of the per-unit price of a good and allows the consumer to purchase as many units of the good at the subsidized price as desired. For example, the government might pay half a consumer's housing costs, which effectively lowers the per-unit price of housing services to the subsidy recipient by 50 percent. The most common examples of excise subsidies are found in the income tax code. A tax credit for insulation or child care expenses, for instance, involves the government's reducing the taxpayer's tax liability when these items are purchased, and this lowers the price to the taxpayer in the same way as an outright excise subsidy.

Let's look at an excise subsidy applied to the food purchases of a particular consumer. Suppose the consumer has a weekly income of $100, the market price of food is $5, and the individual would choose to purchase 9 units of food in the absence of any subsidy. The presubsidy equilibrium is shown in Figure 4–1 by the tangency between indifference curve U_1 and the budget line *MN*. The consumer is in equilibrium at point *E*, consuming 9 units of food and $55 worth of other goods and services. Note that total outlays on other goods, which is normally measured by the distance $0M_1$, is also equal to vertical distance F_1E; this will be helpful to keep in mind later.

To subsidize the individual's food consumption, suppose the government pays $2 of the $5-per-unit cost of food. The subsidy effectively lowers the price of food to the recipient from $5 to $3 and, like any price reduction, causes the budget line to rotate. The new budget line is *MN'*. Since food is now less costly to the consumer, more will be consumed. Given the preferences shown in the diagram, the new equilibrium occurs at *E'*, where U_2 is tangent to *MN'*, and food consumption is 15 units.

What is the total cost to the government of supplying this subsidy? Since the subsidy is $2 per unit, and the consumer purchases 15 units per

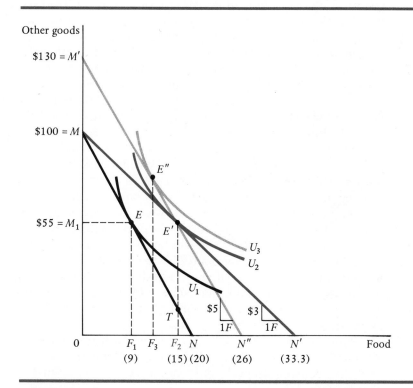

FIGURE 4-1

Excise Subsidy Versus Lump-sum Subsidy

A $2-per-unit excise subsidy to food shifts the budget line to *MN'*; the equilibrium is at *E'*, with a total cost of *E'T*. An equal-cost lump-sum subsidy produces the budget line *M'N''*, and the consumer is better off at point *E''* at no additional cost to the government.

week, the total cost is $30 per week. Figure 4–1 shows total government outlays on the subsidy as the vertical distance $E'T$, the distance between the subsidized and unsubsidized budget lines at the level of consumption chosen by the recipient. To see this, note that if the consumer had to pay the unsubsidized market price for food (still shown by budget line MN) and purchased 15 units, there would only be F_2T dollars remaining to spend on other goods. With the subsidy, however, when consumption is 15 units, there are F_2E' dollars left to spend on other goods, or $E'T$ dollars more than if the consumer had to pay the entire cost of 15 units of food. Thus, the total cost to the subsidy recipient of consuming 15 units has fallen by $E'T$, or $30, because the government is absorbing that amount.

So far in our analysis of an excise subsidy, we haven't done anything that couldn't be accomplished just as easily by using the consumer's demand curve instead of indifference curves. We have shown that when a subsidy lowers the price of a good to the consumer, consumption of the good will increase. Now, however, consider some related issues that are better analyzed by using consumer choice theory. Suppose that instead of using an excise subsidy, the government gives the consumer the same amount of assistance, $30 per week, in the form of a cash grant to be spent any way the recipient wants. How will this change in the nature of the subsidy affect the consumer's consumption pattern, and will he or she be better or worse off with a cash grant? These are important policy questions, and we can answer them by using consumer choice theory.

Substituting an unrestricted cash grant of $30 for the excise subsidy will shift the consumer's budget line in a different way. Since a cash grant is the same as an increase in the recipient's income, it produces a parallel outward shift in the budget line, from MN to $M'N''$. Note that $M'N''$ passes through point E', the equilibrium market basket under the excise subsidy. The reason is that both subsidies involve the same total cost to the government. As we saw, the total cost of the excise subsidy is $E'T$, or $30; with a cash grant of $30 the $M'N''$ budget line lies exactly $30 (vertically) above MN at all points, including point T. For example, $M'M$ equals $E'T$; both measure the size of the cash grant. Put differently, when the government uses a cash grant instead of an excise subsidy, the consumer still has the option to purchase the same market basket that was chosen under the excise subsidy of the same total cost.

Replacing the excise subsidy with the cash transfer causes the budget line to shift from MN' to $M'N''$. Confronted with the new budget line $M'N''$, the consumer's preferred market basket is at point E''. The effects of substituting the cash transfer for the excise subsidy can easily be determined. *The consumer purchases less food and more of other goods under the cash transfer and is better off* (reaches a higher indifference curve). These results must be true: since U_2 is tangent to MN' at E', it must intersect the $M'N''$ budget line at point E', indicating that preferred positions lie to the northwest of E' on the $M'N''$ line.

These conclusions can be explained in a different way. While both subsidies have an income effect that tends to expand food consumption, only the excise subsidy has a substitution effect (because of the artificially lower relative price of food) that further stimulates food consumption. Confronted with a price of only $3 per unit with the excise subsidy, the recipient purchases food up to the point where its marginal benefit (the MRS between food and other goods) is only $3, at point E'. Thus, the fifteenth unit of food purchased is only worth $3 to the recipient, but its true market cost is $5; it was only purchased because the government absorbed $2 of its cost. The recipient would rather have $5 worth of other goods instead of the fifteenth unit of food, and with a cash transfer this option is available.

This analysis generally implies that a consumer will be better off if given a cash grant instead of an excise subsidy linked to the consumption of a particular good. (We saw another example of this general proposition in the food stamp program discussed in Section 3.1.) In large part, this result explains why many economists favor converting welfare programs such as food stamps and housing subsidies into outright cash grants. If given cash, the recipients could still afford to buy the same quantities of food and housing, and if they choose to purchase something else, the presumption is that they prefer the alternative to the subsidized good they were consuming.

Our analysis does not demonstrate that cash transfers are better; it only shows that the recipients will be better off, *according to their own preferences*, if they are given cash. It is possible for a person to take a paternalistic view, such as "subsidy recipients don't know what's good for them," and favor overriding their preferences when providing them with a subsidy. For example, some people believe the poor wouldn't spend enough of the cash welfare payments on "necessities." Before accepting that position, refer to Table 3–1 and note that low-income families actually devote a larger proportion of their incomes to food, housing, and medical care than do upper-income families.

HOW A SUBSIDY CAN REDUCE CONSUMPTION OF THE SUBSIDIZED GOOD

4.2

Paying part of the price of some good, and thereby reducing the price the consumer must pay (as in the previous section), is not the only way to subsidize consumption. In fact, a more common form of subsidy is one in which the government makes a certain quantity of the good available to a consumer at no cost, or perhaps at a cost below the market price. The essential characteristic of this type of subsidy is that the quantity of the good being subsidized is beyond the control of the recipient. Food stamps, discussed in Section 3.1, are an example: the consumer receives $50 in food stamps each month, for instance, no more and no less; and if more than $50 in food is demanded, the market price must be paid for it.

In some cases, this type of subsidy may actually reduce consumption of the subsidized good. This paradoxical outcome can occur when it is impossible, or very difficult, for the consumer to supplement the quantity of the good provided or financed by the government. An example will make this point clearer. Suppose the government decides to subsidize housing consumption and offers a consumer a two-bedroom apartment at no cost. The consumer prefers a three-bedroom apartment and is willing to pay the difference in cost between a two-bedroom and a three-bedroom apartment to obtain the larger unit. This option, however, is not open: the government will provide a two-bedroom apartment or nothing. Moreover, there is no way the consumer can accept the government-financed apartment and, by paying for the cost of an extra bedroom, convert it into a three-bedroom apartment. The individual must either accept the two-bedroom apartment or forgo the subsidy altogether and pay the entire cost of any housing consumed. In this setting the consumer may decide to accept the government-financed two-bedroom apartment, whereas in the absence of the subsidy the consumer would have chosen a three-bedroom apartment.

Note how this housing subsidy differs from the food stamp subsidy discussed in Chapter 3. With the food stamp subsidy the consumer could supplement the subsidized quantity by purchasing additional units of food at the market price. With the housing subsidy the nature of the good makes it costly, if not impossible, to supplement the quantity provided by the government. Housing is typical of a good that is not highly divisible into small units; it is "lumpy," and to increase the quantity consumed usually requires moving into a larger or better housing unit. When a subsidy is limited to a specific housing unit, it is difficult to supplement.

The way this subsidy can lead to reduced consumption of housing can be clarified with a diagram. In Figure 4–2 the presubsidy budget line is MN. (Even though housing is "lumpy," the budget line showing market options is smooth, because the consumer can choose more or less housing when selecting a particular housing unit to rent.) Initial consumption of housing services is $0H_1$, and the total outlay on other goods is $0M_1$.

Now the government offers a smaller (or lower-quality) housing unit of $0H_2$ to the recipient at no cost. The budget line becomes $MM'RN$. To consume more housing than the subsidized quantity $0H_2$, the consumer must forgo the subsidized housing unit altogether and bear the entire cost of housing along the RN portion of the original budget line. If the subsidized housing unit is taken, the recipient can consume $0H_2$ units of housing, leaving $0M$ (the individual's entire income) available to spend on other goods. On the other hand, to consume more than H_2 units of housing, for example, H_2H_1 extra units, the consumer would have to give up MM_1 in other goods — a very high marginal cost associated with increased consumption beyond $0H_2$. In other words, $0H_2$ units of housing can be

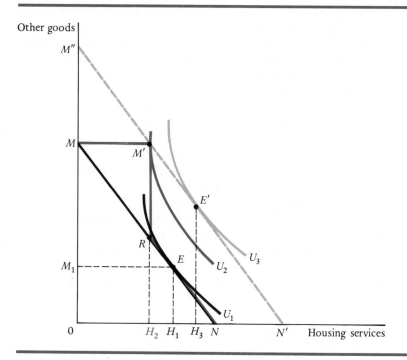

FIGURE 4-2

Fixed-quantity Subsidy: Housing

When the consumer cannot augment the quantity of the subsidized good, the result is a budget line like *MM'RN*. This situation can actually lead to lower consumption of the subsidized good than would occur with no subsidy at all. Equilibrium with the subsidy is at point *M'* with $0H_2$ units of housing, less than the $0H_1$ units that would be purchased without the subsidy.

consumed with no sacrifice in income, but to consume any larger quantity, the consumer must pay the total market cost of the housing. This explains why the budget line is *MM'RN*.

Confronted with the *MM'RN* budget line, the consumer would choose to accept the subsidized housing and consume at *M'*: this choice places the recipient on a higher indifference curve, U_2, which is better than U_1. Although the consumer gives up H_2H_1 units of housing, there is a gain of M_1M in other goods, and the indifference curves show the net effect to be an improvement.

In this case a cash transfer of equal cost to the government will lead to more housing consumed. The cost of the housing subsidy is *M'R*, equal to *M"M*, so an equal-sized cash transfer produces the *M"N'* budget line that passes through point *M'*. Faced with this budget line, the consumer would select the market basket at point *E'*, involving an increase in housing consumed, from $0H_2$ to $0H_3$, but a reduction in the consumption of other goods. Of course, the consumer is also better off with the cash transfer, because the extra H_2H_3 units of housing are worth more than their cost (as shown by the fact that E' is on a higher indifference curve than M'). This is yet another example of the general proposition that cash is usually better, from the consumer's viewpoint, than a subsidy restricted to a particular commodity.

This type of subsidy does not always lead to reduced consumption: we have only shown that it may. For a consumer with a different set of preferences, the same subsidy can produce an outcome such as the one in Figure 3–3b, in which a cash transfer leads to less consumption of the subsidized good. The exact outcome depends on the size of the subsidy in relation to the preferences and income of the subsidy recipient.

The possibility of reduced consumption from this type of subsidy is more than a theoretical curiosity. A study of public housing in New York City, for example, concluded that 49 percent of the recipients studied were consuming less housing than they would have if they had been given cash.[1] Another study found that expenditures per student would be higher for some students in the absence of state-supported colleges and universities.[2]

WHY FRINGE BENEFITS?
4.3

Employees receive compensation from their employers in two different forms: cash salaries and fringe benefits. Fringe benefits are goods or services provided directly to employees and paid for by the employer. They include such items as medical insurance, life insurance, contributions to pension funds, parking facilities, meals, and use of recreational facilities. In the last several decades fringe benefits have been growing faster than cash compensation, and today they account for as much as 25 percent of total labor compensation in some cases.

From the employer's point of view, providing fringe benefits costs the same as paying a worker cash: $100 in medical services paid for by the employer involves the same outlay as $100 in wages. From the employee's point of view, however, the two alternatives may not be equivalent. Indeed, at first glance it would seem that the employee would always prefer cash. If the worker is paid entirely in cash, the services formerly provided as fringe benefits could still be purchased if desired, but the worker would also have the option of spending some or all of the funds in other ways that might be considered more worthwhile.

[1] John Kraft and Edgar Olsen, "The Distribution of Benefits from Public Housing," in *The Distribution of Economic Well-Being*, ed. F. Thomas Juster, Studies in Income and Wealth, vol. 1 (Cambridge, Mass.: Ballinger, 1977) pp. 51–64.
[2] Sam Peltzman, "The Effect of Government Subsidies-in-Kind on Private Expenditures: The Case of Higher Education," *Journal of Political Economy*, 81, no. 1 (January/February 1973), 1–27.

Figure 4–3 illustrates the situation from the worker's viewpoint. Assume that initially the worker is paid entirely in cash at a rate of $150 per week. The budget line *MN* shows the combinations of medical services and outlays on other goods that can be purchased. Now suppose the worker is scheduled to receive a $50-per-week raise. If this raise is provided entirely as a fringe benefit, with the employer providing $50 in medical services to the worker, the budget line becomes $MM'N_1$. (Note that this is the same kind of kinked budget line that resulted from the food stamp subsidy examined earlier.) Depending on the preferences of the worker, equilibrium will occur either at point M' or somewhere along the $M'N_1$ portion of the budget line. In the diagram the worker's preferred market basket is at point M', consuming $0D_1$ in medical services and $150 in other goods and services.

Alternatively, if the worker receives $50 in extra cash income instead of medical services, the budget line will be M_1N_1, and the individual will be better off at point E', consuming less medical services and more of

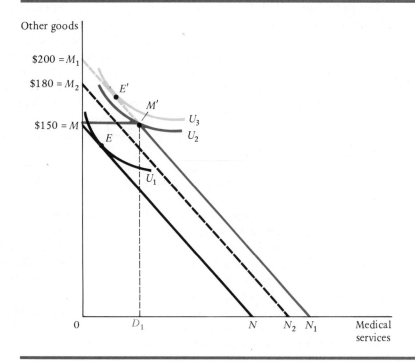

FIGURE 4–3

Fringe Benefits

Medical services provided as a fringe benefit produce the $MM'N_1$ budget line. Workers might be better off if paid in cash (budget line M_1N_1), but cash is taxable and fringe benefits are not. Thus, the aftertax cash payment budget line is M_2N_2, and the worker is better off with the fringe benefit.

other goods. For some workers — those who would be in equilibrium on the $M'N_1$ portion of the budget line — it would make no difference whether they received the raise as cash or as a fringe benefit. Consequently, it appears that some workers would prefer cash, and none would be worse off. Why, then, do employers pay workers in part with fringe benefits? Presumably, it is in the interest of employers to benefit their workers as much as possible at a given cost. Since the cost of the fringe benefit to the employer is equivalent to a $50 cash wage payment, why not pay workers entirely in cash, since this benefits them most?

We can resolve this apparent paradox by taking into account a factor so far neglected: fringe benefits are not subject to income or Social Security taxes, but cash payments are. Suppose the combined tax rate of income and Social Security taxes for the worker is 40 percent. Under these circumstances, if the worker is given $50 in medical services as a fringe benefit, that amount is not taxed; if the worker receives $50 in cash, $20 goes to the government in tax revenues. Given this option, the worker may well prefer the nontaxable fringe benefit over the taxable wage payment. Return to Figure 4–3. (The $150 initial income of the worker should now be interpreted as the aftertax income before the wage increase is granted.) If the fringe benefit is provided, the budget line becomes $MM'N_1$, as before. However, if a $50 raise is given, the aftertax income of the worker rises by only $30 to $180, so the budget line would be M_2N_2. Faced with a choice between receiving the fringe benefit and a net increase in take-home pay of $30, the worker is better off with the fringe benefit. That is, the option of a fringe benefit allows the worker to attain indifference curve U_2, which is a higher indifference curve than is possible at any point on the M_2N_2 budget line.

Our analysis of fringe benefits suggests that employers are indeed catering to the interests of workers by providing part of their compensation as nontaxable fringe benefits rather than as taxable wages. Of course, there may be factors other than taxes that also influence the compensation package preferred by workers. For example, businesses may be able to provide some services at a per-unit cost that is lower than the price the worker would have to pay for similar services. Group health insurance and life insurance plans, for instance, are frequently available at a per-person cost that is lower than the cost of individually purchased health or life insurance policies. Even in this case, however, the nontaxability of the fringe benefit will lead employees to prefer a larger part of their pay in nontaxable form than is justified by the cost advantage.

GASOLINE TAXES AND TAX REBATES
4.4

Ever since the Arab oil embargo in 1973, there have been numerous proposals designed to encourage or force American consumers to cut back on their use of gasoline. One such proposal involves the use of a large excise tax on gasoline to raise its price and thereby induce a reduction in consumption. In the 1980 presidential campaign, for example, independent candidate John Anderson's platform contained a proposal for a 50-cents per-gallon excise tax on gasoline. Realizing that such a large tax would place a heavy burden on many families, most proponents of this approach, including Anderson, recommended that the revenues raised by the tax be returned to the consumers in the form of unrestricted cash transfers, or tax rebates. Alternatively, the excise tax revenues could be used to permit a reduction in some other tax, such as the Social Security tax, with much the same results.

Although this proposal has not been enacted into law, it poses an interesting problem. One objection commonly raised to this plan involves the question of whether it would really cause gasoline consumption to fall. If the revenues from the tax are simply returned to the people, why would they curtail gas consumption? We can use consumer choice theory to show that gasoline consumption will, in fact, be reduced by a combination of an excise tax and a tax rebate.

The key to analyzing this policy package is in realizing that the tax rebate would be a cash transfer to each family that is completely unrelated to the gasoline consumption of that family. In other words, the proposal does not give a rebate of 50 cents for every gallon of gasoline purchased by each family since that would leave the effective price of gasoline unchanged and completely negate the effect of the tax. Instead, a family would receive a check for $500 per year, for example, regardless of how much gasoline it purchased. On average for all families, the rebate would equal the total tax paid, but some families would be overcompensated for the tax while others would be undercompensated.

Now let's examine the gasoline tax and rebate plan for a representative consumer. In Figure 4–4 the initial equilibrium occurs at point E with $0G_1$ gallons purchased. The excise tax by itself would increase the price to $2.00 per gallon and therefore rotate the budget line inward to MN'. This is not the end of the analysis, however, since the budget line the consumer will adjust to must reflect both the tax and the rebate. The rebate is shown as the outward parallel shift in MN' to $M'N''$, similar to an increase in income while the price of gasoline remains constant at $2.00 per gallon. With a rebate of MM' the consumer is in equilibrium at E', where U_1 is tangent to $M'N''$. Gasoline consumption has fallen from $0G_1$ to $0G_2$, while consumption of other goods has increased.

The difficult part of this analysis is to determine how far out the tax rebate will shift the MN' budget line. Since, on average, the tax rebate will equal the total gasoline tax paid, the obvious choice is to consider a consumer who receives a rebate equal to the tax paid, and this is what we have done. In Figure 4–4, with $0G_2$ in gas purchased, the total tax bill is $E'T$, the vertical distance between the budget line showing the market price, MN, and the budget line incorporating the tax, MN'. We can see that $E'T$ is the total tax bill by noting that if $0G_2$ gallons were purchased when the market price was $1.50, outlays on other goods would have been $E'G_2$. Once the tax is levied, only TG_2 in income is left (before the rebate). The

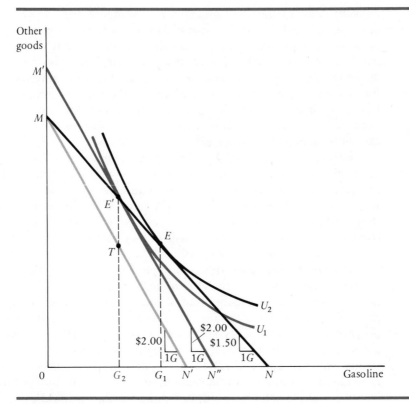

FIGURE 4–4

Tax-plus-rebate Program

An excise tax on gasoline will reduce gasoline consumption even if the revenue is returned to taxpayers as lump-sum transfers. The tax shifts the budget line to *MN'*, and the tax rebate shifts it further to *M'N''*. The combined effect reduces gasoline consumption by $G_1 G_2$.

vertical difference, $E'T$, is the total tax. Since the rebate equals the tax, the budget line must shift up by an amount equal to $E'T$, and so it passes through point E'. Thus when the consumer purchases $0G_2$ gallons, the total tax is $E'T$, and the rebate, MM', also equals this sum.

In short, the final equilibrium of the tax-plus-rebate plan must fall somewhere on the original MN budget line. This result follows intuitively, since only under that circumstance will the tax paid equal the rebate received. Moreover, since the slope of the final budget line, reflecting a higher gasoline price, is steeper than the slope of the original, the final tangency equilibrium must lie to the left of point E, involving less gasoline consumption.

While the geometry of this case is slightly complicated, the final outcome agrees with common sense. The excise tax by itself (without a rebate) has an income effect and a substitution effect, and both reduce gas consumption. The rebate in effect offsets most of the income effect of the tax (but not quite all of it, since the consumer does not return all the way to the original indifference curve). Hence the substitution effect determines the final result. Since a higher price of gasoline leads the consumer to substitute away from gasoline, the final outcome is reduced gasoline consumption.

Finally, note that this combination of tax and rebate necessarily harms the consumer. This is true, at least, for any consumer who receives a rebate exactly equal to the tax since the final outcome will be a market basket on the original budget line that is inferior to the one selected in the absence of the tax and rebate. Why does anyone propose a policy that will make the average family worse off? A good question. Perhaps some consequences are not fully reflected in this analysis. For example, decreased gasoline purchases mean decreased oil imports from the Middle East, and it is possible that decreased dependence on imported oil is beneficial in and of itself. If so, a fuller analysis of this proposal might show that it produces beneficial results, on balance.

MULTIPLE PRICE CHANGES
4.5

As we have already seen, consumer choice theory allows us to examine some issues that would be very difficult, if not impossible, to analyze by relying only on the consumer's demand curve. In this section we consider a similar example. The example is not of any great importance in itself; we selected it to illustrate how consumer choice theory can be used to analyze a different type of shift in the budget line, and it will also provide good practice for the next section.

To begin, suppose a consumer has a weekly income of $100, which is spent entirely on food and clothing. Initially, with the price of food at $2.00 and the price of clothing at $1.00, the consumer purchases 30 units of food and 40 units of clothing. Equilibrium occurs at point E, where U_1 is tangent to the budget line MN in Figure 4–5. If the price of food falls from $2.00 to $1.00, *and* the price of clothing rises from $1.00 to $1.25, how will the consumer's purchases of food and clothing be affected? Although it is tempting to predict that food purchases will rise (the price of food has fallen) and clothing purchases will fall (the price of clothing has risen), this would be an incorrect application of the law of demand. The law of demand relates purchases to a change in the price of a good *when other prices are unchanged*. Since both prices change in this example, the law of demand is not directly applicable.

Nonetheless, consumer choice theory may be used to analyze how consumption of both goods will be affected. First, we must determine how the budget line changes. When the price of food falls from $2.00 to $1.00, an unchanged $100 in income will allow the consumer to purchase 100

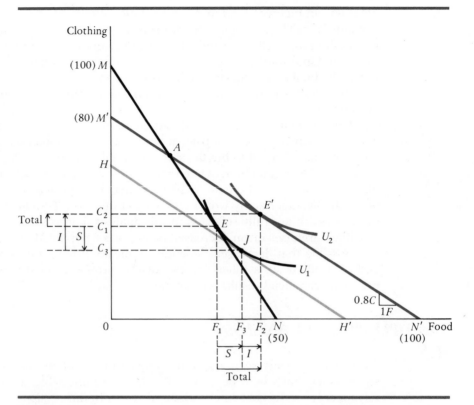

FIGURE 4–5
Income and Substitution Effects with Multiple Price Changes
When the price of food falls from $2.00 to $1.00, and the price of clothing rises from $1.00 to $1.25 (income equals $100), the budget line shifts from MN to M'N'. The diagram shows the income and substitution effects of this change in the budget line on the consumption of both food and clothing.

units of food if all income is devoted to food purchases, so the horizontal intercept of the budget line changes from N to N'. When the price of clothing rises from $1.00 to $1.25, 80 units can be purchased if all the consumer's income is devoted to clothing purchases, so the vertical intercept of the budget line shifts from M to M'. The new budget line is therefore $M'N'$, which intersects the original budget line at point A.[3] The new budget line has a slope of $0.8C/1.0F$, reflecting the new price ratio, $1.00 per F/$1.25 per C. The *relative* price of food has therefore fallen from $2C/1F$ to $0.8C/1.0F$.

[3] Point A occurs where $F = 16\text{-}2/3$ and $C = 66\text{-}2/3$. (You can see this result by solving the two equations for the budget lines, $1C + 2F = 100$ and $1.25C + 1F = 100$, for C and F.) This point is important to the analysis, because the results will obviously depend on whether the consumer is initially consuming on the AN or the MA portion of the original budget line.

With the new budget line the individual is able to reach a higher indifference curve. The consumer's new equilibrium is point E', with food purchases rising from $0F_1$ to $0F_2$ and clothing purchases increasing (despite the higher price) from $0C_1$ to $0C_2$. This simply illustrates the results for the particular preferences shown: what we want to see is whether these results can be generalized, or whether they only represent a specific set of circumstances.

To investigate, we will separate the movement from E to E' into its component income and substitution effects. In the last chapter we did this manipulation when the price of only one good changed, but it is also possible to consider the income and substitution effects produced by a more complicated change in the budget line. To isolate the substitution effect, we want to confront the consumer with the new price ratio but take away enough income to keep the individual on U_1, the original indifference curve. This is done by drawing in the hypothetical budget line, HH', that is parallel to $M'N'$ and just touches U_1 at point J. The substitution effect of this change in the budget line is thus shown by the movement from E to J, involving increased consumption of food from $0F_1$ to $0F_3$. Since the combined effect of both price changes lowers the *relative* cost of food, from $2C/1F$ to $0.8C/1F$, the substitution effect favors greater food consumption. The income effect is shown by the movement from J to E'. Since the consumer's real income has increased, the income effect also increases food consumption (from $0F_3$ to $0F_2$), assuming food is a normal good. Both the income and substitution effects act to increase food consumption, so food consumption will rise.

Our earlier discussion emphasized the way income and substitution effects relate to consumption of a good when only the price of that good changed. These same effects also influence the consumption of other goods. In the current example note that the substitution effect, the movement from point E to point J, also implies reduced consumption of clothing, from $0C_1$ to $0C_3$. The substitution effect of a reduced relative price for food involves substituting food for clothing, so it also implies lower clothing consumption. The income effect, on the other hand, acts like an increase in income and therefore tends to increase consumption of all normal goods. As a result, the income effect increases clothing consumption from $0C_3$ to $0C_2$. Therefore the net effect on clothing consumption results from opposing income and substitution effects: the substitution effect tends to lower clothing consumption, while the income effect tends to increase it. On balance, clothing consumption may increase or decrease, depending on the relative sizes of the income and substitution effects on clothing. As we have drawn the indifference curves, the income effect is larger, so clothing consumption increases.

The answer to our original question is, therefore, that such a change in the consumer's budget line will lead to greater consumption of food, and the consumption of clothing may either rise or fall, depending on the respective sizes of the income and substitution effects. As we mentioned earlier, this exercise is not important in itself, but it serves to illustrate how the concepts of income and substitution effects permit a more complete analysis of the effect of any change in the budget line on the market basket chosen by the consumer.

INTERTEMPORAL CONSUMER CHOICE
4.6

The somewhat forbidding title of this section just refers to the way consumers rearrange consumption over time (intertemporally) by saving or borrowing. Saving involves consuming less than one's current income, which makes it possible to consume more at a later date. Borrowing makes it possible to consume more than current income, but consumption in the future must fall below future income to repay the loan. A decision to save (or borrow) is therefore a decision to rearrange consumption between various time periods. By suitably adapting the theory of consumer choice, we can examine the factors that influence decisions to save or borrow.

Let's confront this topic in the simplest possible setting. Imagine a short-lived individual whose lifetime spans two time periods, year 1 (this year) and year 2 (next year). The individual's earnings in year 1 (I_1) are $10,000, but they will fall to only $2,200 in year 2 ($I_2$). The interest rate at which the individual can borrow or lend is 10 percent per year. We assume there is no inflation in the general price level so that a dollar will purchase the same quantity of goods both years. (If there is inflation, the earnings in each year can simply be expressed in dollars of constant purchasing power, and the real rate of interest can be used instead of the nominal rate. It is simpler for the moment, though, to assume no inflation.)

This information allows us to plot the budget line for the consumer. In Figure 4–6 consumption in year 1 is measured on the vertical axis and consumption in year 2 (next year's consumption) on the horizontal axis. Any point in the diagram therefore represents a certain level of consumption in each year. The budget line indicates what combinations are available to the consumer. Point *A*, for example, identifies the consumption mix where the individual's entire earnings are spent in each year: a market basket containing $10,000 in consumption in year 1 (equal to year 1 earnings of $10,000) and $2,200 in consumption in year 2 (equal to year 2 earnings of $2,200). Point *A* is sometimes called the *endowment point*, showing the consumption mix available to the individual if no saving or borrowing takes place. Alternatively, by saving or borrowing, the consumer can choose a different market basket.

To identify another point on the budget line, suppose the individual's entire income of $10,000 is saved in year 1. In this case, consumption in year 1 is zero, but in year 2 the individual could consume $13,200, equal to the sum saved the year before ($10,000), plus interest on that sum at a 10

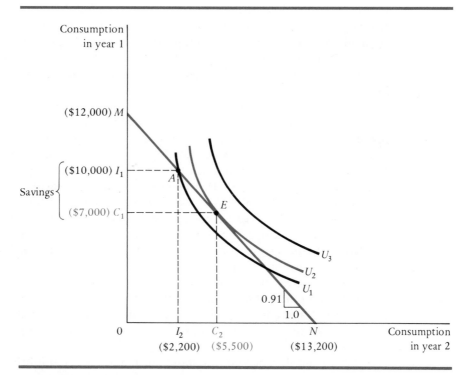

FIGURE 4-6

Intertemporal Consumer Choice

With an interest rate of 10 percent and with earnings of $10,000 in year 1 and $2,200 in year 2, the budget line relating consumption in the two years is MN with a slope of $1/(1 + i)$. Equilibrium is at point E, with saving of I_1C_1 in year 1. In year 2 consumption exceeds that year's income by I_2C_2, which is equal to the amount saved ($3,000) plus interest on this sum ($300).

percent rate ($1,000 in interest), plus earnings in year 2 ($2,200). Thus, point N shows the horizontal intercept of the budget line; if consumption in year 1 is zero, the individual can consume $13,200 in year 2. The vertical intercept shows the maximum consumption possible in year 1, which is achieved by borrowing as much as possible, limited by how much can be repaid in year 2. That is, if $2,000 is borrowed, consumption in year 1 can be $12,000 ($2,000 plus year 1 earnings); $2,000 represents the maximum the consumer can borrow, since $2,000 plus 10 percent interest, or $2,200, must be repaid the next year, and this amount equals total earnings in year 2 with nothing left over for consumption. So the vertical intercept of the budget line is at $12,000.

Points A, M, and N are possible options for the consumer and represent three points on the budget line. Connecting these points yields MN as the entire budget line. If the consumer chooses a point along the AN portion of the line, the consumer will be consuming less than earnings in year 1 (saving in year 1) and consuming more than earnings in year 2 (consuming the previous year's saving plus interest). Along the MA portion of the budget line, the consumer is borrowing in year 1 and repaying the loan in year 2.

Notice how the slope of this budget line relates to the interest rate. In fact, the slope is equal to $1/(1 + i)$, where i is the interest rate. This means that if the consumer reduces consumption by $1.00 in year 1 (saves $1.00), it is possible to increase consumption in year 2 by $1.00 plus the interest of $0.10, or by $1.10. With an interest rate of 10 percent, the slope is equal to $1/(1 + 0.10)$, or 0.91 (rounded). This tells us that the present cost of $1.00 consumed in year 2 is $0.91 in year 1, since $0.91 saved today grows to $1.00 a year later at a 10 percent interest rate — or, conversely, to have $1.00 to spend in year 2, the consumer must save $0.91 in year 1.

Now let's bring the consumer's preferences into the picture. Since consumption in both years is desirable (more is preferred to less), the indifference curves have the usual shape. The slope of an indifference curve at any point is the marginal rate of substitution between consumption in year 1 and consumption in year 2, and it shows the willingness of the individual to reduce consumption in year 1 to have greater consumption in year 2.

For the indifference curves shown in Figure 4–6, equilibrium occurs at point E. Consumption in year 1 is $7,000, and consumption in year 2 is $5,500. Note that the individual is saving some of year 1 earnings, as indicated by the choice to consume less than $10,000 in year 1. The amount of saving in year 1 is the difference between income and consumption in that year, which is shown by the distance I_1C_1, or $3,000. In year 2 the individual's consumption is $3,300 greater than year 2 earnings; this sum is equal to the amount saved, $3,000, plus interest on the saving.

Thus, the individual's equilibrium is once again characterized by a tangency between an indifference curve and the budget line. The only novel feature here is that the "commodities" consumed refer to consumption in different time periods, but that does not change the substance of the analysis.

A Change in Endowment

The budget line relevant for intertemporal choice depends on current and future income as well as the rate of interest. Any change in one or more of these variables will cause the budget line to shift and involve a change in the market basket chosen. Let's examine how a change in earnings in year 2 will affect consumption and saving. Continuing with the example just discussed, suppose the individual expects next year's earnings to be zero rather than $2,200. It may be, for example, that the part-time job expected in year 2 becomes unavailable.

A change in earnings in either year moves the endowment point in the graph. In Figure 4–7, budget line *MN* is reproduced from Figure 4–6: it shows the opportunities available when earnings are $10,000 in year 1 and $2,200 in year 2. When earnings expected in year 2 fall to zero, the endowment point moves from *A* to point I_1 on the vertical axis: if the individual's consumption equals earnings in each year, consumption will be $10,000 in year 1 and nothing in year 2. The new budget line is I_1N', and it is parallel to *MN* since the interest rate remains unchanged [both lines have a slope of $1/(1 + i)$].

A reduction in future income will not alter the relative cost of future and present consumption, but it will influence behavior through its income effect. If consumption in each year is a normal good – which is almost certain to be true since consumption is a very broadly defined good – then the shift in the budget line will lead to reduced consumption in both years. The consumer spreads the loss over both years, cutting back

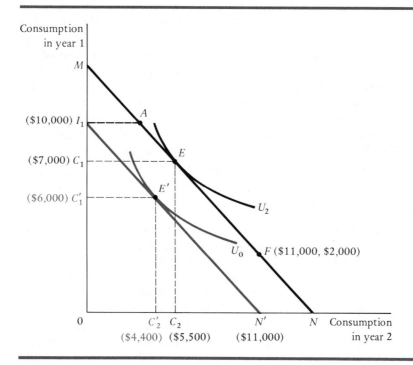

FIGURE 4–7
A Change in Income and Intertemporal Choice
If year 2 income is zero instead of $2,200, the budget line shifts from *MN* to I_1N', a parallel shift. The result is an increase in saving in year 1, from I_1C_1 to I_1C_1'. Consumption in both years falls, assuming consumption in each year is a normal good.

on consumption in year 1 and year 2. The new equilibrium point at E' illustrates this situation, with consumption reduced from $7,000 to $6,000 in year 1 and from $5,500 to $4,400 in year 2.

This analysis implies that a reduction in expected future earnings causes saving in year 1 to increase. Recall that saving is the difference between consumption and income. Before the income loss saving was I_1C_1, or $3,000, but after the loss, saving increases to I_1C_1', or $4,000. Current saving, therefore, doesn't depend exclusively on current income (which is unchanged in this example); it is also affected by expectations regarding future income.

So far we have been looking at a person who saves in year 1. Yet some people borrow in the present and repay the loan later. Under different circumstances the individual shown to be a saver in Figure 4–7 could become a borrower. For instance, suppose that instead of an income in year 1 (I_1) of $10,000 and an income in year 2 (I_2) of $2,200 (budget line MN), earnings in the first year are $2,000 and $11,000 in year 2. *The budget line doesn't change:* only the endowment point changes, from A to F on MN. The equilibrium position remains at point E, but to reach that position, the individual borrows $5,000 in year 1 and repays the loan plus interest in year 2.

This shows how the pattern of earnings over time is likely to affect saving and borrowing decisions. A relatively high present income but sharply reduced future income (such as endowment point A) is typical of middle-aged persons approaching retirement, and we expect to see them save part of current income. A low present income but a higher expected future income (such as endowment point F) is typical of students and young workers, and it is not uncommon to see such persons acquiring debt and consuming above their present incomes.

Changes in the Interest Rate

Will people save more at a higher interest rate? The answer to this question may not be the commonly anticipated "yes" response. Let's see why.

A higher interest rate changes the relative cost of present versus future consumption, which is reflected in a change in the slope of the budget line. If the interest rate rises from 10 percent to 20 percent, the slope of the budget line, $1/(1 + i)$, changes from $1/(1 + 0.1)$ to $1/(1 + 0.2)$, so the new budget line will have a slope of $1/1.2$, or 0.83. Reducing consumption by $1.00 in year 1 (saving $1.00) permits consumption of $1.20 in year 2. Put somewhat differently, the present cost of consuming $1.00 in year 2 is $0.83 in year 1, since $0.83 will grow to $1.00 in one year at a 20 percent interest rate. Or, conversely, to have $1.00 to spend in year 2, the consumer need only save $0.83 now at the higher interest rate. Thus, a higher interest rate reduces the cost of future consumption in terms of the present sacrifice required.

Figure 4–8 shows the way the budget line shifts. The initial budget line *MN* once again reflects the 10 percent interest rate, and the endowment point is *A*. *When the interest rate rises to 20 percent, the budget line pivots about point A and becomes M'N'*. Point *A* is also on the new budget line because the individual can still consume I_1 in year 1 and I_2 in year 2 if no borrowing or saving takes place. Point *A* will always be on the budget line regardless of the interest rate. A further increase in the interest rate to 30 percent yields the budget line *M"N"*, with a slope of 0.77, or $1/(1 + 0.3)$.

Incorporating the indifference curves of the individual, we can determine the preferred market basket associated with each budget line. For the indifference curves in Figure 4–8, the initial equilibrium levels of consumption are C_1 and C_2, with I_1C_1 saving in the first year. When the interest rate rises to 20 percent, the new equilibrium at E' involves a consumption

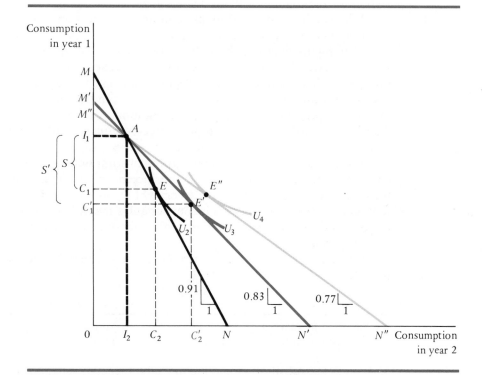

FIGURE 4–8

A Change in Interest Rates and Intertemporal Choice

A change in the interest rate pivots the budget line at endowment point *A*. When the interest rate rises from 10 to 20 percent, the budget line shifts from *MN* to *M'N'*. Consumption in year 2 will increase, but whether saving rises or falls depends on the magnitude of the income effect (encourages less saving) and the substitution effect (encourages more saving).

of C_2' in year 2 and C_1' in year 1. A lower consumption in year 1 means an increase in saving from I_1C_1 to I_1C_1'. Consequently, this individual will save more when the interest rate rises from 10 to 20 percent. We have not shown, however, that this is the general case, only that it is valid for the specific indifference curves drawn in Figure 4–8. Indeed, a further increase in the interest rate to 30 percent actually leads to less saving. With the new budget line $M''N''$, equilibrium occurs at E'', involving more consumption in both years than at E'. (Note that a higher interest rate makes it possible for a saver to increase consumption in the present and still consume more in the future.) Since consumption increases in year 1, saving falls when the interest rate rises from 20 to 30 percent.

What factors determine whether saving rises or falls when the interest rate increases? Once again, they are the familiar income and substitution effects. These are not shown explicitly in Figure 4–8, but it should be noted that the separation can be accomplished exactly as in Figure 4–5. Here only a verbal description will be given.

A higher interest rate has income and substitution effects on both consumption in year 1 and consumption in year 2. (Don't make the mistake of trying to determine how the income and substitution effects affect saving directly: think of how consumption in year 1 will be affected, and that result will determine what happens to saving.) The substitution effect associated with a higher interest rate results from the change in the relative cost of present versus future consumption. A higher interest rate reduces the cost of future consumption, which implies a substitution effect that favors future consumption at the expense of present consumption. So the substitution effect encourages future consumption instead of present consumption. On the other hand, the income effect associated with a higher interest rate enriches the saver, who is able to attain a higher indifference curve. A higher real income enables the individual to consume more in both periods, so the income effect favors increased consumption in both periods.

We can summarize the consequences of the higher interest rate in this way:

	Income Effect	Substitution Effect	Total Effect
Consumption in year 1	Plus	Minus	?
Consumption in year 2	Plus	Plus	Plus

Since both the substitution and income effects favor more consumption in year 2, it will definitely increase. However, substitution and income effects for consumption in year 1 are in opposing directions, so the outcome depends on their relative sizes. If the income effect is greater, consumption in year 1 will rise, which implies that savings will fall.

The relationship between saving and the interest rate is sometimes portrayed directly as the supply curve of saving. Figure 4–8 shows how saving varies when the interest rate changes, and the same information can be plotted as a saving supply curve. This is done in Figure 4–9. The three points identified on the curve, E, E', and E'', correspond to the same points in Figure 4–8. The supply curve indicates that more saving is supplied when the interest rate rises from 10 to 20 percent; if the interest rate rises further, though, the amount of saving falls slightly. A backward-bending supply curve of saving is, therefore, a theoretical possibility.

Intuitively it is possible to see why some people might save less at a higher interest rate. Think of a target saver, a person who is saving for a specific good, like a sailboat. A higher interest rate means the consumer can purchase the sailboat with reduced present saving. If the sailboat costs $5,000, a person would have to save $4,545 at a 10 percent interest rate but only $4,000 at a 25 percent interest rate to purchase the boat one year later. A target saver would always save less at a higher interest rate. Still, there is no reason to think that this type of behavior is common. Whether the aggregate supply curve of saving slopes upward or bends backward at current interest rates is an unresolved empirical question.

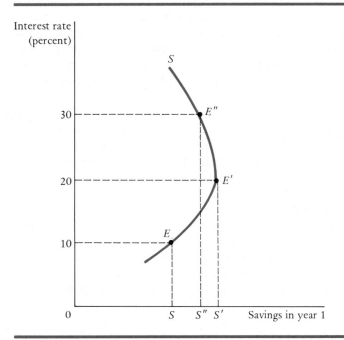

FIGURE 4–9
Supply Curve of Saving

If the income effect of a higher interest rate is larger than the substitution effect, the consumer will save less and the supply curve of saving will be backward bending. Here the substitution effect is larger up to 20 percent, yielding an upward-sloping supply curve to point E'. But beyond that point the income effect dominates, and the curve becomes backward bending.

CONSUMER SURPLUS
4.7

Consumers purchase goods and services because they are better off (on a higher indifference curve) after the purchase than they were before; otherwise the purchase would not take place. The term *consumer surplus* refers to the net benefit, or gain, secured by an individual from consuming one market basket instead of another. For example, suppose you purchase 6 pounds of steak per month at a price of $5 per pound, involving a total outlay of $30. This is one particular market basket containing 6 pounds of steak (plus other items you buy). Alternatively, you could buy no steak and spend the $30 saved on other things: this would represent a second market basket. Since you select the first market basket instead of the second, you clearly view yourself better off with the first (purchasing the steak). You secure a consumer surplus from being able to purchase 6 pounds of steak at $5 per pound. What we now wish to do is see how this surplus, or net benefit, can be measured in dollar terms.

It would be possible to obtain a measure of consumer surplus associated with steak purchases by a little introspection. Ask yourself this question: What is the maximum amount you would be willing to pay for 6 pounds of steak per month rather than do without it completely? Your answer will be the *total benefit* (or total value) of 6 pounds of steak. Your *total cost* is the $30 per month that you pay for 6 pounds of steak. The difference between these two sums is the net benefit, or consumer surplus, you receive.

The consumer's demand curve for a commodity provides another, and more direct, way to measure consumer surplus. To see how the demand curve relates to consumer surplus, consider how a consumer's demand curve for steak is actually generated. To simplify the analysis, let's initially assume steak is sold only in 1-pound packages, and start with a price so high that none is bought. We gradually lower the price until the consumer purchases 1 pound of steak when its price reaches $10. This means that the marginal benefit, or marginal value, of the first unit of steak to our carnivorous consumer is $10: this price is the maximum amount the consumer will pay for one unit. If the individual is willing to pay $10 for the first unit, the $10 reflects the subjective value placed on the first unit of steak; it is a way of measuring, in dollar terms, the benefit the consumer derives from the steak. Lowering the price further, we find the consumer will purchase a second pound of steak at a price of $9: the marginal benefit of the second unit of steak is $9. Thus, the price at which a given unit will be purchased measures the marginal benefit to the consumer.

Continuing this process, we can generate the entire demand curve, which is, in this case (where fractions of a pound cannot be purchased), the steplike graph shown in Figure 4–10. The *area* of each of the tall rectangles measures the marginal benefit of a specific unit of steak to the

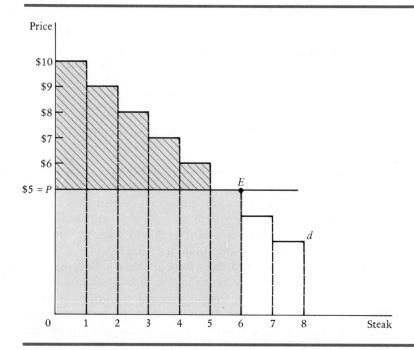

FIGURE 4-10
Consumer Surplus

The total benefit from purchasing 6 units of steak at a price of $5 per unit is the sum of the six shaded rectangles, or $45. Since the 6 units of steak involve a total cost of $30, the consumer receives a surplus of $15, which is shown by the striped area.

consumer. For instance, the tallest rectangle has an area of $10 ($10 per pound of steak multiplied by 1 pound of steak, or $10). The marginal benefit of the first pound of steak is $10; of the second, $9; of the third, $8; and so on. The *total benefit* of consuming a given quantity is the sum of the marginal benefits. If 2 units are consumed, the total benefit in dollars is $19, since the consumer would have been willing to pay as much as $10 for the first unit and $9 for the second. By determining the maximum amount the consumer will pay for each unit of steak, we can ascertain the total benefit of the steak to the consumer, which is equal to the area under the demand curve up to the quantity purchased.

Instead of having to purchase steak one package at a time at varying prices, now suppose, more realistically, that the consumer may purchase steak at a price of $5 per pound. At $5, six pounds of steak are purchased: steak is purchased up to the point where its marginal benefit is just equal to the price. Now compare the total benefit from purchasing 6 pounds of steak at $5 per pound with its total cost:

total benefit = sum of marginal benefits
= $10 + $9 + $8 + $7 + $6 + $5 = $45

total cost = sum of cost of each unit
= $5 × 6 = $30

net benefit (consumer surplus) = total benefit − total cost
= $15

The total benefit of 6 pounds of steak is $45, but the consumer has only paid $30 for the steak, so a consumer surplus, or a net gain, of $15 accrues to the consumer. Put differently, the consumer surplus ($15) is the difference between what the consumer would have been willing to pay for the steak (equal to the total benefit, or $45) and what the individual actually has to pay for it (equal to the total cost, or $30).

Geometrically, we add the areas of the six rectangles reflecting the marginal benefits; then we subtract the total cost (price times quantity) represented by the area of the large rectangle, 0PE6, or $5 times 6 units. The area that remains — the striped area in Figure 4–10 between the price line and the demand schedule — is the geometric representation of consumer surplus. An alternative way to see that this area measures consumer surplus is to imagine the consumer purchasing units of the good sequentially. The first unit is worth $10 to the consumer, but the steak only costs $5, so there is a net gain of $5 on that unit; this is the first striped rectangle above the price line. The second unit is also purchased for $5, but since the consumer would have been willing to pay as much as $9 for the second unit, there is a net gain of $4 on that unit; this is the second striped rectangle above the price line. Adding up the excess of benefit over cost on each unit purchased, we have $5 + $4 + $3 + $2 + $1 + $0 = $15, which is shown by the area between the price line and the demand curve. Note that there is no net gain on the last unit purchased. Purchases are expanded up to the point where the marginal benefit of the last unit is exactly equal to price. Previous units purchased are worth more than their price — which, of course, is why the consumer receives a net gain.

Figure 4–11 shows the same situation, but now we assume that steak is divisible into small units so a smooth demand curve can be drawn. As before, the consumer purchases 6 units at a price of $5 per unit. Consumer surplus is the triangular area PTE between the demand curve and the price line. It corresponds to the areas of the rectangles above the price line in Figure 4–10, but by letting the width of the rectangles become smaller and smaller (fractional units may be purchased), we now have a smooth line rather than discrete steps. In Figure 4–11 the total benefit from consuming 0Q units is 0TEQ, the total cost is 0PEQ, and the difference, PTE, is the consumer surplus.

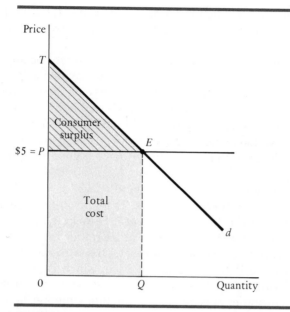

FIGURE 4-11
Consumer Surplus

With a smooth demand curve consumer surplus is the triangular area *PTE.*

Using Consumer Surplus: Two Examples

One of the most famous paradoxes in the history of economics is the water–diamond paradox. Diamonds, though attractive, clearly satisfy less important human needs than water, which is essential to life. Yet according to market prices, the essential commodity, water, is worth less than the frivolous commodity, diamonds. Why would a vital commodity such as water sell for so much less than an unnecessary commodity such as diamonds? Many a philosopher and an economist in the past have grappled with this question and concluded that something must be wrong with a system that values diamonds more than water.

We can resolve the apparent paradox by carefully distinguishing between the total benefit (or value) and the marginal benefit (or value) of each commodity. The total benefit from water consumption is indeed immense, even incalculable, but because water is so plentiful, the marginal benefit of additional amounts of water is low. How much would you pay for an extra cup of water per month? Very little, we suspect, since most municipalities price water at about 5 cents per hundred gallons. The low price reflects the low marginal benefit of water given its abundant supply (in most places). In this situation consumer surplus is large, and price is low. Diamonds, on the other hand, are scarce relative to demand, and price is high. The marginal benefit of diamonds is great, but the total benefit and consumer surplus may be small — most certainly in comparison to water.

Consumer surplus has more varied uses than might be suggested by the discussion so far. We developed the concept by considering the net benefit derived from consuming a given quantity of some good, such as water or diamonds, rather than none at all. Viewed only as a way of identifying the net benefit in an all-or-nothing situation, consumer surplus has rather limited uses. Consumer surplus, however, can also be used to identify the net benefit of a change in the price of a good or in its level of consumption.

Figure 4–12 shows a consumer's demand curve for food. At a price of $5, the consumer would purchase 9 units. The consumer surplus is given by the area *PTA*. Now let the price fall to $3. How much better off is the consumer when food can be purchased at $3 rather than $5? There are two equivalent ways to arrive at the answer. One is to note that the consumer surplus will be *P'TC* at the lower price, which is greater than the initial consumer surplus, *PTA*, by the area *PACP'*. Thus, the area *PACP'* is the increase in consumer surplus, and it identifies the net benefit to the consumer of the lower price.

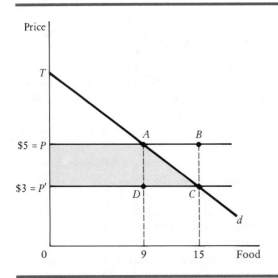

FIGURE 4–12

The Increase in Consumer Surplus with a Lower Price

At a price of $5 consumer surplus is *PTA*. At a price of $3 consumer surplus is *P'TC*. The increase in consumer surplus from the price reduction is thus the shaded area *PACP'*: this area is a measure of the dollar benefit of a reduction in price from $5 to $3.

A second way to reach the same answer is to imagine the consumer adjusting to the lower price in two steps. First, consumption is tentatively held fixed at 9 units. When the price falls, the same 9 units can be purchased for $18 less than before: this amount is equal to the area *PADP'*, and it is part of the net benefit from the lower price. Second, the lower price also makes it advantageous to expand purchases from 9 to 15 units. A net benefit is also associated with this expansion since the marginal benefit of each of these units is greater than its price. For instance, the tenth unit has a marginal benefit of just slightly below $5, but it can be purchased for $3 — a net benefit from the tenth unit of about $2. The net benefit of expanding purchases from 9 to 15 units is the area *DAC*. Combining the two areas of net benefit once again yields *PACP'* as the net benefit from the lower price.

In Figure 4–12 the consumer receives a net benefit (or increase in consumer surplus) equal to *PACP'* from the lower price. Alternatively, suppose we begin with a market price of $5 and let the government subsidize the consumer by using an excise subsidy that lowers the price to $3. We have already seen that the benefit to the consumer from the lower price (in this case the subsidy causes the price to fall to $3) is *PACP'*. What is the cost to the government? Total outlays are $30 ($2 per unit for each of the 15 units purchased), which is equal to the area *PBCP'* in Figure 4–12. Note that the total cost to the government, *PBCP'*, is greater than the benefit to the consumer, *PACP'*. Thus the consumer would prefer the subsidy in cash rather than in the form of a lower price for the commodity. The net benefit of a cash subsidy of $30 (area *PBCP'*) is exactly equal to $30, which is greater than the net benefit (*PACP'*) of the excise subsidy to the consumer. The same situation was considered in Section 4.1, where we showed that the recipient would be better off with an unrestricted cash subsidy costing the same as an excise subsidy. Using the concept of consumer surplus provides a different way of viewing the same problem.

Consumer Surplus and Indifference Curves

Consumer surplus can also be represented in our indifference curve and budget line diagrams. Let's return to our original example in which a consumer purchases 6 pounds of steak at a price of $5 per pound. Figure 4–13 shows the equilibrium at point *E*, the familiar tangency between an indifference curve and the budget line. Note that the consumer is on a higher indifference curve, U_2, when purchasing 6 pounds of steak than when buying no steak at all. If no steak is bought, equilibrium would occur at point *M* on U_1. The net benefit, or consumer surplus, from purchasing 6 units is clearly shown by the fact that the consumer reaches a higher indifference curve at point *E* than at point *M*.

Thus, the consumer receives a net benefit from purchasing 6 units instead of none. Now let's try to measure the net benefit in dollar terms.

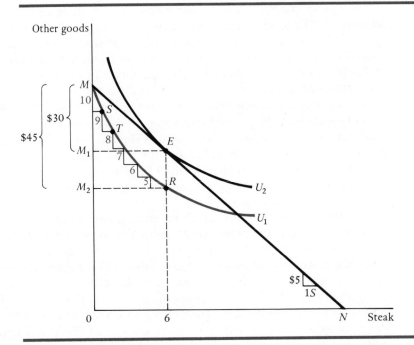

FIGURE 4-13

Consumer Surplus and Indifference Curves

The consumer surplus associated with being able to purchase steak at $5 per pound is shown by the consumer's being on U_2 rather than U_1. In dollars this net gain, or surplus, is the distance *ER*.

Starting at point *M*, where no steak is purchased, let's ask this question: What is the maximum amount of money the consumer would give up for 6 pounds of steak? Paying the *maximum* amount means the consumer will remain on U_1, the original indifference curve, and move down to point *R*, where 6 units are consumed. The distance MM_2 identifies the maximum amount the consumer would be willing to pay. Note that this amount is equal to the sum of the amounts that would be paid for each successive unit; that is, in moving from point *M* to point *S*, the consumer would pay $10 for the first unit, $9 for the second unit (*S* to *T*), and so on. The sum of these amounts equals MM_2, or $45. The distance MM_2 measures the *total benefit* from consuming 6 units, and it corresponds to the area under the demand curve in a demand curve diagram.

Total benefit is MM_2. However, the consumer actually purchases 6 units at a cost of only MM_1, or $30. The total benefit, MM_2, exceeds total cost, MM_1, by the distance M_1M_2 (also equal to the distance *ER*). The difference between total benefit and total cost, in this case $15, is the consumer surplus from purchasing 6 pounds of steak at a price of $5 per pound. The consumer surplus can be shown either by the area between the demand curve and the price line or as a vertical distance between indifference curves. Both this diagram and Figure 4–10 therefore show the same thing but from different perspectives.

Note one qualification. Under certain conditions it is possible to show that consumer surplus, as measured by the area under a demand curve, is exactly equal to the measure obtained in Figure 4–13. The certain conditions, however, require a special assumption: the income effect of price changes on consumption of the good in question must be zero. This assumption is reflected by the indifference curves being vertically parallel, having the same slope as you move up a vertical line. In Figure 4–13, for example, the slope of U_1 at point R is the same as the slope of U_2 at point E. When this assumption does not hold, the area under the demand curve is only an approximation of the true measure of consumer surplus. The approximation is still generally close enough for most applications.[4]

[4] Robert D. Willig, "Consumer Surplus Without Apology," *American Economic Review*, 65 (1976), 589–597.

Review Questions and Problems

1. With an income of $600 per month, the Jones family purchases 75 gallons of fuel oil per month when its price is $1 per gallon. The government then agrees to pay half the family's heating bill. Consumption of fuel oil rises to 100 gallons per month. Illustrate what has happened by using budget lines and indifference curves. Identify in your diagram the total cost to the government of the subsidy and the total cost the Joneses bear in purchasing fuel oil before and after the subsidy.

*2. The government has $100 per month with which to subsidize Larry's food consumption. It is considering two alternatives: giving Larry $100 worth of food stamps per month (as in Section 3.1), or paying part of the price of food, thereby lowering the price to Larry (as in Section 4.1). In the case of the excise subsidy the price is lowered to the point where the total cost of the subsidy is $100 per month. Which type of subsidy will benefit Larry more? Under which type of subsidy will he consume more food?

3. How is it possible that the government can reduce a consumer's consumption of housing by providing a housing unit at no cost? Explain in words and show in a diagram. Is the provision of public schools any different from this housing subsidy in terms of the possibility that it could reduce consumption?

4. In Figure 4–3, if the tax rate is 10 percent instead of 40 percent, would the worker prefer the raise in cash or as a fringe benefit?

5. According to recent news magazine stories, "Fringe benefits grew faster than money wages during the 1970s," and "Inflation in the 1970s pushed millions of taxpayers into higher tax rate brackets." Do you think these two events are related? In what way?

*6. When the price of gasoline is $2.00 per gallon, Harry consumes 1,000 gallons per year. The price rises to $2.50, and to offset the harm to Harry, the government gives him a cash transfer of $500 a year. Will Harry be better or worse off after the price rise plus transfer than he was before? What will happen to his gasoline consumption?

7. Sarah initially has a monthly income of $1,000, which she spends on two goods, food and clothing, with prices of $5 and $10, respectively. Suppose her income rises to $1,500 and the price of food increases to $7.50, but the price of clothing remains unchanged. Show how her budget line shifts, and explain how her consumption of food and clothing will be affected.

8. In a two-year setting Hilda has earnings of $6,000 this year (year 1) and earnings of $10,000 next year (year 2). She can borrow or lend at an interest rate of 25 percent. Draw her budget line relating consumption this year and consumption next year. What is the slope of her budget line, and what does it signify?

9. Refer to the information in question 8. Suppose Hilda decides to borrow $1,000 in year 1. Show the equilibrium in a diagram. Identify the amount borrowed in year 1, the amount repaid in year 2, consumption in year 1, and consumption in year 2.

10. "A higher interest rate lowers the present cost of future consumption." "A higher interest rate raises the future cost of present consumption." Use an example to show that both statements are correct.

11. "For a person who saves in year 1, a higher interest rate will increase consumption in year 2 but may either increase or reduce the amount saved in year 1." Explain this statement, using the concepts of income and substitution effects. Use a diagram like Figure 4–8, and separate the income and substitution effects geometrically.

12. Define *consumer surplus*, and explain how you would show it in a diagram containing a consumer's demand curve for some product.

13. State the water–diamond paradox. Using demand curves for water and diamonds, and the associated prices of the

goods, resolve the paradox. In each diagram distinguish clearly total value, marginal value, and consumer surplus.

*14. Noneconomists sometimes refer to goods like education and medical care as "invaluable," "priceless," or "worth whatever they cost." Do you think these terms may just be imprecise ways of saying that the consumer surplus associated with these goods is very large? Suppose that the consumer surplus from, say, medical care is immense. Explain why that fact is entirely irrelevant in deciding whether we should provide more medical care. What is relevant?

15. Use Harry's demand curve for gasoline and the concept of consumer surplus to answer question 6. (Hint: The analysis should be similar to that of Figure 4–12.)

*16. "If half this year's output of wheat were destroyed, the total value of the remaining amount (with inelastic demand) would be greater than the value of the initial amount. Less is worth more than more!" Discuss this statement.

Supplementary Readings

Browning, Edgar K., and Browning, Jacquelene M. *Public Finance and the Price System*, 2nd ed. New York: Macmillan, 1983. Chaps. 4, 5.

Clarkson, Kenneth. "Welfare Benefits of the Food Stamps Program." *Southern Economic Journal*, 43(1) (July 1976): 864–878.

Friedman, Milton. "The Marshallian Demand Curve." *Journal of Political Economy*, 57 (December 1949): 463–495.

Mishan, E. J. "Realism and Relevance in Consumer's Surplus." *Review of Economic Studies*, 8 (1948): 27–33.

Yeager, Leland. "*Methodenstreit* over Demand Curves." *Journal of Political Economy*, 68 (1960): 53–64.

Exchange, Efficiency, and Prices

5

In the previous three chapters we have concentrated primarily on the way a typical consumer reacts to changes in his or her budget line. Higher or lower prices or incomes, subsidies, and taxes produce generally predictable responses. The consequences of the consumer's choices for participants on the selling side of markets have so far been ignored. Of course, the budget line itself, indicating relative prices, reflects the willingness of others to trade with the consumer on specified terms, but now we wish to emphasize more explicitly that the market choices of a consumer involve exchanges between the consumer and other people.

To investigate the essential two-sidedness of market transactions, we will begin by examining the economic analysis of pure exchange. At the outset our analysis will focus on two consumers who start with specified quantities of two commodities and engage in barter exchanges. This model probably appears remote from real world behavior, and to some extent, this is true. The intention here is to focus on the nature and consequences of voluntary exchanges between people, and this model provides the simplest means possible. Most economic activity occurs through a series of voluntary exchanges: workers exchange their labor for money and then exchange money for various consumer goods, so indirectly they exchange labor for consumer goods. A model that permits us to see why voluntary exchanges occur and what their consequences are is therefore quite useful.

The analysis developed in this chapter also serves a second important purpose: it allows us to introduce the concept of *economic efficiency*. The model we discuss explains how economists use the notion of efficiency and, at the same time, illustrates the role of market-determined prices in achieving efficiency.

TWO-PERSON EXCHANGE
5.1

People engage in exchanges, or trades, because they expect to benefit. When an exchange is voluntary, with both parties agreeing to the terms of the trade, the strong presumption is that both parties benefit. Such a presumption follows from the fact that each party had the option of refusing to trade but instead chose to engage in the exchange. If I buy a can of soup, my action must mean I prefer the soup to the money I exchange for it. Also, the sale must mean the shopkeeper prefers the money to the soup. Both of us benefit from the exchange.

The fundamental point can be stated simply: *Voluntary exchange is mutually beneficial.* The truth of this basic economic proposition may appear obvious, but it is widely disbelieved. How often have you heard someone say that the prosperity of some business people must have come at the expense of their customers or workers? Economic activity, however, is not like a game or contest where, if there are winners, there must be losers. The voluntary exchanges through which economic activity is organized can be beneficial to all parties involved.

There are some qualifications to the basic proposition that voluntary exchange is mutually beneficial. First, it presupposes that fraud or trickery has not taken place. If I pay for my soup with a bad check, the seller will be worse off. Second, the benefit achieved refers to the expectations of the parties at the time of the transaction. I may purchase a book but after reading it decide I would have been better off keeping my money. Nonetheless, at the time I made the purchase, I must have believed the book was worth more than the money.

Setting aside these qualifications, let's look at the nature of voluntary exchange in more detail. Suppose there are only two consumers, Hank and Monica, and only two commodities, steak and wine. Assume Hank and Monica begin each month with certain quantities of each good. Hank's initial market basket (his endowment) is 35 bottles of wine and 5 pounds of steak; Monica's initial market basket is 5 bottles of wine and 45 pounds of steak. In the end, Hank and Monica may not choose to consume their initial market baskets. Instead, they may decide to trade with each other and end up with different combinations of steak and wine.

Under what conditions will Hank and Monica find it advantageous to trade? In this setting, whether or not trade occurs depends crucially on the relationship between the relative importance of the two goods to each consumer. Let's suppose that Hank, given his initial basket, would be willing to give up 5 bottles of wine to obtain one more pound of steak: his marginal rate of substitution is $5W/1S$. Monica, on the other hand, would be willing to give up only 1 bottle of wine for one more pound of steak: her marginal rate of substitution is $1W/1S$. In this case the relative importance of the goods differs between Hank and Monica, as indicated by their different MRSs; this means that a mutually beneficial exchange can take place. Let's see how. (The numerical data of this example are summarized in Table 5–1 for convenience.)

Given their initial holdings, Hank values steak more highly relative to wine than Monica does. He would be willing to give up as much as 5 bottles of wine to obtain another pound of steak. Monica, on the other hand, would be willing to give up 1 pound of steak if she receives at least 1 bottle of wine in return. (Note that if Monica's MRS is $1W/1S$, she would

TABLE 5-1

Gains from Exchange

Consumer	Initial Market Basket	MRS_{SW}	Trade	New Market Basket After Trade
Hank	$35W + 5S$	$5W/1S$	$-3W + 1S$	$32W + 6S$
Monica	$5W + 45S$	$1W/1S$	$+3W - 1S$	$8W + 44S$

give up $1W$ for $1S$ or, alternatively, $1S$ in return for $1W$. For a small movement along the indifference curve in either direction, $1S$ trades for $1W$ without affecting her well-being.) Put differently, Hank would pay $5W$ to get $1S$, while Monica would be willing to sell him $1S$ for $1W$. There is room for a mutually beneficial trade. Suppose Hank offers Monica 3 bottles of wine for 1 pound of steak, and she accepts. Hank will be better off after the exchange because he would have been willing to pay as much as $5W$ for the steak, but he got it for $3W$. Monica will also be better off since she would have sold the steak for as little as $1W$ but instead received $3W$. Therefore, this exchange will leave both parties better off: they prefer their new market baskets to their initial holdings. (See Table 5–1.)

The way two parties may both gain from exchange illustrates a simple idea: "You have what I want, and I have what you want, so let's trade!" While this statement conveys intuitively what is involved, a deeper understanding of the nature and consequences of voluntary exchanges is important. To go much further, however, a new graphical device, the Edgeworth box, will prove helpful.

The Edgeworth Exchange Box Diagram

The Edgeworth exchange box diagram can be used to examine the allocation of fixed total quantities of two goods between two consumers.[1] Figure 5–1 shows the box diagram appropriate for the numerical example just discussed. The horizontal and vertical dimensions of the box indicate the total quantities of the two goods. The length of the box diagram indicates the amount of steak held by the two consumers together, 50 units, and the height of the diagram indicates the total amount of wine, 40 units.

By interpreting the box diagram in a certain way, we can show all the possible ways 50 units of steak and 40 units of wine can be divided between Hank and Monica. Let's measure Hank's holdings of steak horizontally from point 0_H and his holdings of wine vertically from the same point. In effect, 0_H is the origin of the diagram for purposes of measuring the amounts of steak and wine possessed by Hank. Point A shows the

---

[1] The Edgeworth box is named for F. Y. Edgeworth, who hinted at such a construction in 1881 in his *Mathematical Psychics: An Essay on the Application of Mathematics to the Moral Sciences* (New York: August Kelly, 1953).

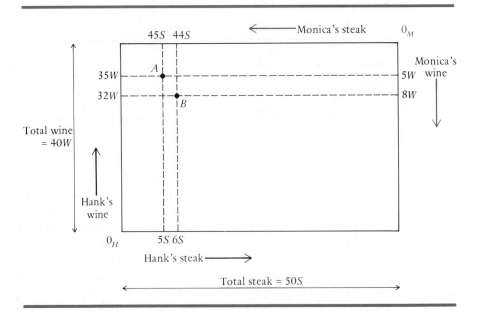

FIGURE 5–1

The Edgeworth Exchange Box

The horizontal dimension of the box measures the total amount of steak, and the vertical dimension measures the total amount of wine. When the origins of the consumers are at 0_H and 0_M, each point in the box represents a specific division of the commodities between the consumers.

market basket for Hank that contains $35W$ and $5S$; it is, in fact, his initial market basket from our numerical illustration.

One ingenious aspect of the box diagram is that point A also indicates the market basket possessed by Monica. Since the amount of steak held by both parties is fixed at 50 units, placing Hank at point A with 5 units means Monica holds the remaining 45 units. This amount is shown in the diagram by measuring Monica's holdings of steak to the left from point 0_M. Monica has 45 units of steak: point A in effect divides the horizontal dimension of the box, $50S$, between Hank ($5S$) and Monica ($45S$). Point A also indicates Monica's holdings of wine by measuring her wine holdings down from point 0_M. Since combined wine holdings are 40 units, and Hank has 35 units, the remaining 5 units belong to Monica.

Now consider point B. Point B identifies a different market basket for both Hank and Monica. Hank's market basket at B contains $32W$ and $6S$, while Monica's contains $8W$ and $44S$. (The totals still add up to $50S$ and $40W$.) In fact, the movement from point A to point B illustrates the exchange between Hank and Monica in our numerical example. In moving from A to B, Hank has given up $3W$ and gained $1S$, while Monica has gained $3W$ and given up $1S$. The movement from A to B shows graphically what happens when Hank buys 1 unit of steak from Monica and pays for it with 3 units of wine.

The Edgeworth Box Diagram with Indifference Curves

Since the points in the Edgeworth box diagram identify alternative market baskets that each party may consume, we can use indifference curves to represent each person's preferences regarding the various alternatives. This is done in Figure 5–2. Hank's indifference curves, U_3^H, U_4^H, and so on,

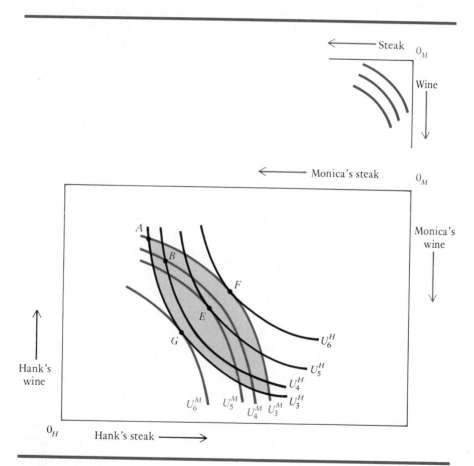

FIGURE 5–2

Gains from Trade

Point A shows the initial division of goods. Hank's and Monica's indifference curves through point A intersect, transcribing the shaded lens-shaped area. Both parties would be better off with any division of goods lying inside the lens-shaped area. It is thus in the interest of both parties to work out an exchange that will move them into this area.

require little explanation. Since Hank's market baskets are measured in the normal way, from his origin at the southwest corner, these curves have their familiar shapes.

Monica's indifference curves, U_3^M, U_4^M, and so on may appear odd at first glance. Recall that the origin for purposes of measuring Monica's consumption is the northeast corner, 0_M, and her indifference curves are relative to this origin. Compared with the usual graphic representation, all we have done is rotated Monica's indifference map 180 degrees and placed the origin in the northeast corner. The small insert in Figure 5–2 should make this manipulation clear: it shows how the normal indifference map has been inverted to place the origin at 0_M in the box diagram. Monica's indifference curves also have normal shapes; we are just looking at them upside down.

Now let's use this construction for our original example once again. Point A identifies Hank's and Monica's initial market baskets. The indifference curves corresponding to the initial market baskets (passing through point A) are U_3^H and U_3^M. Note that these curves intersect at point A, because we assume that the marginal rates of substitution differ for the two consumers. The slope of U_3^H at point A is $5W/1S$, while the slope of U_3^M is $1W/1S$. The area that lies between these two curves, the shaded area in the graph, is highly significant. *Every point inside the shaded area represents a market basket for each consumer that is preferred to basket A.* In other words, within this area both consumers would be on higher indifference curves compared with their initial curves at point A.

The shaded lens-shaped area in Figure 5–2 illustrates the potential benefit from exchange, and it is possible to arrange exchanges between Monica and Hank so that they move into this area and both benefit. For example, if Hank purchases 1 unit of steak from Monica and pays for it with 3 units of wine (as we discussed earlier), they move from A to B. Note that both Hank and Monica are better off (on higher indifference curves) at point B than they were at point A.

Starting at point A, any voluntary exchanges that occur will necessarily involve movements into the lens-shaped area of mutual gain. If they moved outside the shaded area, one or both parties would be worse off (on lower indifference curves), so such a trade would never be mutually agreed to. The basic economic proposition illustrated here is that exchanges will tend to take place as long as both parties continue to benefit. After moving from point A to point B, both parties may still benefit from further exchanges: U_4^H and U_4^M intersect at point B, carving out a smaller lens-shaped area of mutually beneficial potential exchanges. For example, Hank might trade his wine for Monica's steak again in such a way as to move to point E, where both would be better off than they were at point B.

By moving from point A to point E, both parties have benefited. However, once they reach a point such as E, where their indifference curves are tangent, no further trade is possible that will benefit both parties. Any movement from point E would harm at least one of the two parties (as an inspection will show), so the injured party would never agree to such an exchange. A tangency of indifference curves implies that the two consumers' marginal rates of substitution are equal. The process of trading from point A, where the MRSs differ, tends to bring the MRSs into equality. As Hank acquires more steak and gives up wine, his MRS becomes lower: his indifference curve is flatter at point E than it is at A. As Monica gets more wine and gives up steak, her MRS becomes greater: her indifference curve is steeper at point E than at A.

When the marginal rates of substitution differ, mutually beneficial trade between the parties is possible. Differing MRSs imply intersecting indifference curves and a corresponding lens-shaped area of potential mutual gains in the Edgeworth box diagram. Predictably, then, voluntary exchanges will occur to realize the potential gain. We should mention one final point. Our theory does not permit us to predict exactly where in the lens-shaped area the consumers will end up. While there should be a tendency for trade to continue until it is no longer mutually beneficial — until a tangency point is reached — this condition does not identify a *unique* outcome. For example, if Hank is a very astute trader, he might persuade Monica to agree to an exchange from point A to a point near F, where Monica is scarcely any better off (she would be no better off at F); then the lion's share of the potential mutual benefit goes to Hank. Conversely, if Monica is a sharp bargainer, they might end up at point G.

The reason for the indeterminacy is that we are assuming only two potential traders, one buyer and one seller, so this setting is not a competitive one (many buyers and sellers). When only two parties participate in the exchange process, elements of haggling and strategy appear, since each tries to conceal from the other how badly he or she wants the trade in order to get the best terms. Thus, we are unable to predict the exact terms of the exchange, except to note a tendency for any exchanges that occur to benefit both parties to some degree.

EFFICIENCY IN THE DISTRIBUTION OF PRODUCTS
5.2

Economic efficiency — or, as it is sometimes called, *Pareto optimality*[2] — is a characteristic of some resource allocations that is highly regarded by economists. Noneconomists do not generally hold it in such high esteem; they frequently disparage it because they believe it only relates to materialistic values or monetary costs and ignores human needs. This criticism misconstrues the meaning of economic efficiency as economists use the term. Far from being materialistically oriented, efficiency is defined in terms of the well-being of people. Roughly speaking, an efficient outcome is one that makes people as well off as possible, taking into account all the

[2] Named after the Italian economist Vilfredo Pareto (1848–1923), who first systematically formulated the concept in *Cours d' Economie Politique* (Lausanne: F. Rouge, 1897).

factors that influence their well-being. A full treatment of the concept of efficiency is important in appreciating its use in economic analysis.

In this chapter we will consider economic efficiency as it relates to the way fixed total quantities of products are distributed among consumers. Two consumers and two commodities will be analyzed, just as we did before, but the results generalize easily to larger numbers.

Suppose we have 50 units of steak and 40 units of wine to divide between our friends, Hank and Monica. There are innumerable ways to distribute $50S$ and $40W$ between two consumers. The Edgeworth box diagram not only identifies all the possibilities but also shows how alternative distributions affect the well-being of both parties. Previously, we used the Edgeworth box to show how Hank and Monica, starting with certain market baskets, could exchange products to reach a preferred position. Now, however, the box diagram will be used in a different way; we wish to consider all the points in the diagram, not just those that Hank and Monica can reach by voluntary trade starting from some initial endowment. In other words, let's imagine that a philanthropist is going to give $50S$ and $40W$ to Hank and Monica and is devising ways this might be done. Some ways are efficient, and some are inefficient, as we will see.

Figure 5–3 is an Edgeworth box diagram that shows different ways of dividing the given quantities of steak and wine between Hank and Monica. Several indifference curves for each person have been drawn so that we can see their preferences among the various possibilities. We begin by defining efficiency relative to this setting. *An efficient distribution of fixed total quantities of goods is one in which it is not possible, through any change in the distribution, to benefit one person without making some other person worse off.*

In the diagram the points where Hank's and Monica's indifference curves are tangent show efficient distributions. Point E, for example, satisfies the definition of efficiency. If we change the distribution from point E by moving to any other point, either Hank or Monica will be worse off (on a lower indifference curve). Thus, point E is an efficient distribution of steak and wine. Note, though, that it is not unique; indeed, any point of tangency between indifference curves defines an efficient distribution. At point J, for example, U_7^M is tangent to U_2^H. Any movement from point J will harm at least one of the two consumers, so point J is also an efficient distribution. So also are points G, F, K, and other points of tangency not drawn in. A line drawn through all the efficient distributions is called the *contract curve*. It is shown as CC in the diagram, and it identifies all the efficient ways of dividing the two goods between the consumers.[3]

An alternative but equivalent way of defining *efficiency* may be helpful. An efficient distribution is one that makes one party as well off as

[3] The contract curve may coincide with one of the axes over part of its length. In this case some of the efficient allocations involve one of the parties consuming only one of the two goods. For these efficient allocations the slopes of the indifference curves are not equal. The equal-slope, or tangency, characteristic of efficient points holds only for efficient points that lie completely within the box diagram.

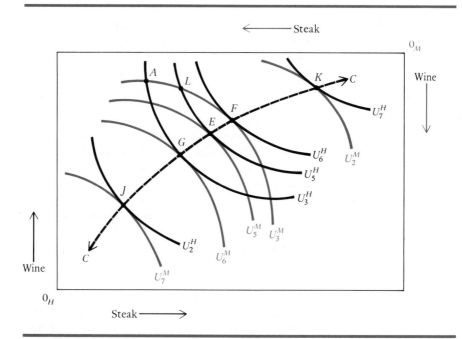

FIGURE 5–3

Efficient Distributions and the Contract Curve

A distribution of goods for which the consumers' indifference curves are tangent is efficient. We cannot change the distribution without making at least one of them worse off. There are many efficient distributions, as shown by the contract curve *CC*, which connects the points of tangency.

possible for a given level of well-being for the second party. For example, suppose we consider the given level of well-being indicated by U_3^M for Monica. She is equally well off at points *A*, *L*, *F*, or any other point on U_3^M. Among all the possible combinations of steak and wine that keep Monica on U_3^M, Hank is best off at point *F*. Point *F* places him on the highest indifference curve possible, assuming Monica stays on U_3^M. Because point *F* makes Hank as well off as possible for a given level of well-being (U_3^M) for Monica, it is thus an efficient distribution. Similarly, if we hold Monica on U_5^M instead, point *E* is best for Hank. Consequently, the same set of tangency points is defined when we look at efficiency in this way.

The contract curve defines the set of all efficient ways to divide steak and wine between Hank and Monica. In contrast, all points off the contract curve are inefficient allocations. Inefficiency may be defined as follows: *An inefficient allocation of goods is one in which it is possible, through a change in the distribution, to benefit one party without harming the other.*

In Figure 5–3 all points off the contract curve satisfy this definition of inefficiency. Consider point *A*. If we change the distribution from point *A* to point F, Hank will be better off without harming Monica — she remains on the same indifference curve, U_3^M. Alternatively, we can move from point A to point G, which benefits Monica while leaving Hank's well-being unchanged. Note, in fact, that an inefficient allocation, such as point A, permits a change that benefits both parties, such as a move from point A to point E.

If we select any point off the contract curve and draw Hank's and Monica's indifference curves through this point, the curves will intersect. The intersecting indifference curves will circumscribe a lens-shaped area within which both parties would be on higher indifference curves. Since this is true of every point off the contract curve, all these points represent inefficient distributions of the goods.

By this means all the ways the goods can be divided between Hank and Monica can be characterized as either efficient or inefficient. Inefficient distributions are shown as points where the indifference curves of the two parties intersect; that is, where $MRS_{SW}^H \neq MRS_{SW}^M$. This inequality implies, just like our initial numerical example (Table 5–1), that the consumers place different values on the two goods, so both will prefer a different distribution. Efficient distributions are shown by the contract curve, which connects the points of tangency between indifference curves. Thus, efficient distributions are characterized by an equality between marginal rates of substitution, or $MRS_{SW}^H = MRS_{SW}^M$. At those points the consumers' relative valuations of the two goods are equal, and there is no further change possible that will benefit both parties.

Efficiency and Equity

Is an efficient allocation better than an inefficient allocation? Answering this question requires making some subtle distinctions. To see what is involved, let's review again the various distributions of steak and wine shown in Figure 5–3.

First, look at any point that lies off the contract curve, such as point A. For any inefficient point there are many efficient points on the contract curve that both parties prefer. In this case points between F and G on the contract curve are better from both Hank's and Monica's viewpoints, and most people would probably agree with the judgment that the efficient points between F and G are preferred to the inefficient point A.

Now suppose two efficient points are compared, points F and G, for instance. Which of these is "better"? Since both points are efficient, the concept of efficiency provides no help in choosing between the two, yet there is a marked difference between F and G. Hank is better off at point F than at point G, while Monica is better off at point G than at point F. Moving from F to G benefits Monica at Hank's expense; moving from G to F benefits Hank at Monica's expense. To judge one efficient point superior to another would require deciding whose well-being is more important, and there is no objective basis for such a decision. In the economist's jargon, *interpersonal comparisons of utility* cannot be made scientifically, so there is no objective way to demonstrate that one efficient point is preferred to another.

If a philanthropist had to choose how to divide the steak and wine between Hank and Monica, on what basis could the choice between points *F* and *G* be made? The decision would have to be based on something other than efficiency since both points are efficient. Equity, or fairness, might provide the basis for the decision. But equity is not an objective characteristic like efficiency. Although we all have different views of what is equitable or fair, there is no generally agreed-upon definition of what constitutes equity. For that reason economists are unable to provide a formula that allows us to state that one efficient point is better than any other.

We have seen that for any inefficient point several efficient points are preferred by both parties, but a choice among efficient points requires some sort of subjective, nonscientific judgment about the relative deservingness of the parties. We should not, however, draw the conclusion that *any* efficient point is better than any inefficient one. Look at points *J* and *A* in Figure 5–3. Point *J* is efficient, and *A* is inefficient. At the inefficient point *A*, Monica is worse off than at the efficient point *J*, but Hank is better off at the inefficient point. Moving from *J* to *A* would therefore be a movement from an efficient to an inefficient point that benefits Hank but harms Monica. To compare these two points would once again necessitate having to make a judgment about whether we should help Hank at Monica's expense, or vice versa.

Efficiency is not always preferred to inefficiency. Suppose that we are initially at an efficient point, *J*, in the diagram. Assume further that Monica is wealthy and Hank is destitute. A movement from *J* to *A* would benefit poor Hank at the expense of wealthy Monica. You can see how this change might be favored on equity grounds despite the fact that it involves a move from an efficient to an inefficient resource allocation. An economist might note that if we are going to change things to benefit Hank at Monica's expense, we should at least do it by moving from *J* to a point such as *E* on the contract curve, because both parties are better off at *E* than at *A*. While we can't use the concept of efficiency to say whether point *A* or point *J* is better, point *E* is clearly preferred to point *A*.

Being able to distinguish between efficient and inefficient resource allocations, therefore, does not enable us to identify one allocation as "the best of all possible worlds." Not only are there an infinite number of efficient allocations, but some inefficient allocations might be favored over some efficient allocations on equity grounds. Efficiency is a desirable characteristic since it implies allocating resources in a way that caters effectively to people's wants. We should not forget, though, that other matters, such as equity, also play a role.

You will frequently hear claims suggesting there is one "best" way to allocate economic resources. For example, some people say we should arrange things so that we "achieve the greatest good for the greatest number" or "promote the public interest." What exactly do these slogans mean? Try to interpret them in terms of our simple two-person society in Figure 5–3. You will probably conclude that these slogans are either meaningless or too vague to be of much help. While the economic approach, with its emphasis on how various alternatives affect the well-being of people, does not identify one state of affairs as ideal, it serves to clarify the nature of the alternatives among which we must choose.

We have been looking at the concept of economic efficiency only as it pertains to the distribution of given quantities of products among consumers. The concept can also be applied in other settings, such as deciding what level of output of some good is most efficient. Clearly, overall efficiency in resource allocation involves more than just an efficient distribution of products, but an efficient distribution is an important part of the overall concept. We will discuss other aspects of economic efficiency in Chapter 18.

MANY-PERSON EXCHANGE
5.3

In the two-person model of exchange the exact outcome of bargaining cannot be predicted. We can expect the parties to haggle over the terms of exchange (the price), with the result depending on who is the superior bargainer. In real world markets, however, buyers and sellers are rarely observed haggling over price because in most cases there are many buyers and sellers in any given market. Each party is not limited to dealing with another specific party — there are alternatives. It would do you little good, for example, to try to bargain over the price of toothpaste; if you offer a price below the going rate, the storekeeper will simply wait for another customer. Similarly, if the storekeeper tries to extract a higher price from you, you will purchase your toothpaste from another seller. The existence of alternative buyers and sellers greatly limits the influence any one of them can have on the price. People simply find alternative sources if the deal offered by one person is not as good as one that can be obtained elsewhere.

With many buyers and sellers each individual will behave like a *price taker*. That is, since consumers acting individually cannot affect the price perceptibly by haggling as we just described, they take the price as given and buy or sell whatever quantities they wish at that price. What determines the given price in this many-person setting? It is, of course, the interaction of supply and demand, since we are now dealing with a competitive market.

Now let's rejoin Hank and Monica and extend our two-person model to show the outcome when there are many participants in that market. In the two-person analysis, Hank purchased steak from Monica and paid for it with wine. Assume now that there are many persons just like Hank and

Monica in the sense that they start out with the same initial holdings and have the same preferences. The Hanks have a demand curve for steak that shows how many units they would purchase at alternative prices (where the price is measured in units of wine). The Monicas have a supply curve of steak that shows how much they will sell at alternative prices. The intersection of supply and demand determines an equilibrium price for steak at which the total quantity the Hanks wish to purchase equals the total quantity the Monicas wish to sell.

We can illustrate the nature of this competitive equilibrium for a specific pair of Hanks and Monicas by using the Edgeworth box diagram. In Figure 5–4 our representative Hank and Monica begin with the initial holdings shown at point A. Suppose that the market-determined price of steak is 3 units of wine. Then each party confronts the budget line ZZ, which has a slope of $3W/1S$. At that price Hank prefers to move to point E, purchasing 4 units of steak in exchange for 12 units of wine. Confronted with ZZ, Monica also prefers point E, selling 4 units of steak for 12 units of wine. If each party takes the price ($3W/1S$) as given, the quantity of steak

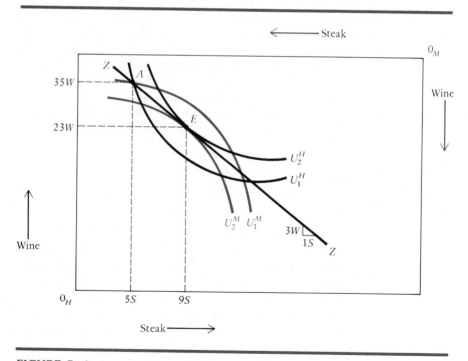

FIGURE 5–4

Many-person Competitive Exchange

With many identical Hanks and Monicas, competitive exchange will establish a uniform price of steak equal to 3 units of wine. Each party faces the budget line ZZ, and the equilibrium is at point E — an efficient outcome.

demanded by Hank, 4 units, is exactly equal to the quantity of steak Monica wants to sell at that price.

The price of 3 wine per steak is therefore an equilibrium price. Remember that there are many identical Hanks and Monicas, and we are just looking at one specific pair. If the price were lower, $2W/1S$, for example, then the Hanks would want to purchase more steaks than the Monicas would wish to sell, and the price would be pushed back to its equilibrium value. If the price were higher, there would be an excess supply of steak on the market, and the price would fall. The tangency of indifference curves at point E simply illustrates the balance between quantity demanded and supplied at the equilibrium price.

Consequently, the many-person setting is, in an important sense, simpler than the two-person case. With two parties the terms of exchange are indeterminate, but with many parties the price is determined by the combined decisions of buyers and sellers with no single individual able to affect the price.

Another implication of the market equilibrium in the many-person setting should not be missed: *The final equilibrium point is an efficient allocation.* Point E is a point of tangency between indifference curves and therefore lies on the contract curve. In a pure exchange model this illustrates Adam Smith's famous "invisible hand" theorem: each trader, concerned only with furthering his or her own interest, is led to exchange to a socially efficient result. All the potential gains from voluntary exchange are realized in a market of competitive exchange. Recall, however, that the number of efficient allocations are infinite: to show that competitive markets produce an efficient allocation is not the same as saying that competition is ideal.

CONSUMER EQUILIBRIUM
AND EFFICIENT DISTRIBUTION
5.4

As mentioned at the beginning of this chapter, the exchange model appears at first to be too abstract to have much direct applicability to the real world. Consumers, after all, don't exchange one good for another, barter style. Yet many of the implications of the Edgeworth box model remain valid in more complex settings. In this section we will show that the attainment of consumer equilibrium when consumers purchase goods from firms and not from each other implies an efficient distribution of products.

Suppose that there are only two goods, steak and wine. For any two consumers, Hank and Monica, for example, we have seen that an efficient distribution of the products requires that:

$$\text{MRS}_{SW}^{M} = \text{MRS}_{SW}^{H}. \tag{1}$$

Since Hank and Monica make their consumption decisions independently of each other in the real world (which they do not do·in our two-person exchange model), it might seem very unlikely that this condition would be satisfied. Consider, however, the equilibrium conditions that result when each person allocates his or her income in the appropriate way:

$$\text{MRS}_{SW}^{M} = P_S/P_W, \tag{2}$$

$$\text{MRS}_{SW}^{H} = P_S/P_W. \tag{3}$$

Recall from Chapter 2 that each consumer purchases a market basket such that his or her marginal rate of substitution equals the price ratio. Since the prices are the same for both consumers, each consumer's MRS is equal to the *same* price ratio, and so the MRSs are equal to one another. Thus, condition (1) is satisfied.

Let's see this matter graphically. Parts a and b in Figure 5–5 show Hank and Monica in equilibrium. In part a, Hank is consuming at point *E* on his budget line *MN*, purchasing 50 units of wine and 30 units of steak. Monica, who has a much lower income, is purchasing 15 units of wine and 10 units of steak, at point *E* in part b. *Note, however, that the slopes of their budget lines are equal.* Since they face the same market prices for steak and wine, P_S/P_W (equal to $3W/1S$ in the diagram) is the same for both of them. Thus, the slope of Hank's indifference curve at his equilibrium point, $3W/1S$, will equal the slope of Monica's indifference curve at her equilibrium point.

We can show that this distribution of wine and steak is efficient by constructing the Edgeworth box diagram for the total quantities of steak and wine, $40S$ and $65W$, consumed by Hank and Monica together. Figure 5–5c shows the result. We start with Hank's budget line, *MN*, from part a. Then Monica's budget line from part b is rotated 180 degrees, and her equilibrium point is superimposed on Hank's equilibrium point. The result is a box diagram, with dimensions of $40S$ and $65W$, that identifies the consumption of both consumers at point *E*. More importantly, Hank's and Monica's indifference curves are tangent at point *E*. This means that the distribution of products at point *E* is an efficient one: there is no other way to divide up $40S$ and $65W$ that would not make at least one of them worse off.

Over any period of time the market distributes, or rations, goods among consumers. *Although each consumer acts independently in choosing a market basket, the result is an efficient distribution of the goods.* This outcome depends on two conditions. First, the prices of goods must be the same for all consumers; this condition ensures that every consumer's budget line will have the same slope. Second, consumers must be able to purchase whatever quantity they want at those prices; this condition ensures that every consumer can select a market basket for which the marginal rate of substitution equals the ratio of the prices of the goods.

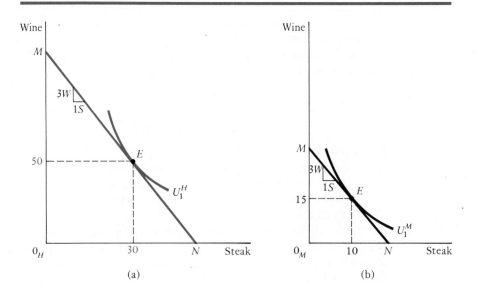

(a)   (b)

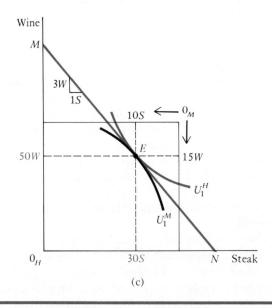

(c)

FIGURE 5-5

A Market-determined Distribution Is Efficient

(a) Hank's independently achieved equilibrium is at point E. (b) Monica's independently achieved equilibrium is at point E. (c) Even though each consumer acts independently, the result is an efficient distribution.

In our example in Figure 5–5 we have intentionally considered a case where the consumers have significantly different incomes: Hank's income is more than three times as large as Monica's. The purpose is to emphasize once more the distinction between efficiency and equity. The distribution resulting from Hank and Monica freely spending their different incomes is efficient, but it may or may not be fair. After all, other efficient distributions on the contract curve may be regarded as superior to point E on equity grounds.

Reaching an efficient distribution, albeit not the only possible efficient distribution, is no small feat. It must be emphasized that no philanthropist, or government agency, knows the preferences of millions of consumers. To attain *any* efficient outcome in this setting is a considerable achievement. When consumers must pay for the products they consume, self-interest leads them to utilize their knowledge of their own preferences, and this is reflected in the market basket they select. Since their decisions are guided by the same relative prices confronting other consumers, the result is a coordination among purchase plans that would be difficult to achieve any other way.

FOOD STAMPS AND BLACK MARKETS
5.5

We can also use the Edgeworth box diagram to investigate the incentive for black markets to emerge under the food stamp program. As explained in Section 3.1, recipients of food stamps can use those stamps only to purchase food. Yet the news media have reported vigorous illegal trading of food stamps in so-called black markets. Black market activity can take several forms. For example, the recipient of food stamps may sell some of the coupons to other people, who in turn use them to purchase food. The reasons for and consequences of this type of activity are easy to understand.

Assume that Hank receives food stamps. His budget line after the subsidy is $MM'N'$ in Figure 5–6a. Hank's equilibrium position is at point M'. From the way we have drawn his indifference curve, he would be better off if given cash (so his budget line would be M_1N') instead of food stamps. Monica receives no subsidy, and her equilibrium position is at point E in Figure 5–6b, where her indifference curve U_1^M is tangent to her budget line. At their respective equilibrium positions, the slopes of Hank's and Monica's indifference curves are different, and this difference explains why a black market exchange may occur. For Hank the marginal value of food at point M' is less than its market price. That is, the slope of U_1^H, his MRS, is less than the slope of M_1N', the price of food. Consequently, Hank would be willing to sell a food coupon redeemable for a dollar's worth of food for less than a dollar. For Monica, the marginal value of food is equal to its price so the marginal value of food to her is greater than it is to Hank. She would be willing to pay up to a dollar for a

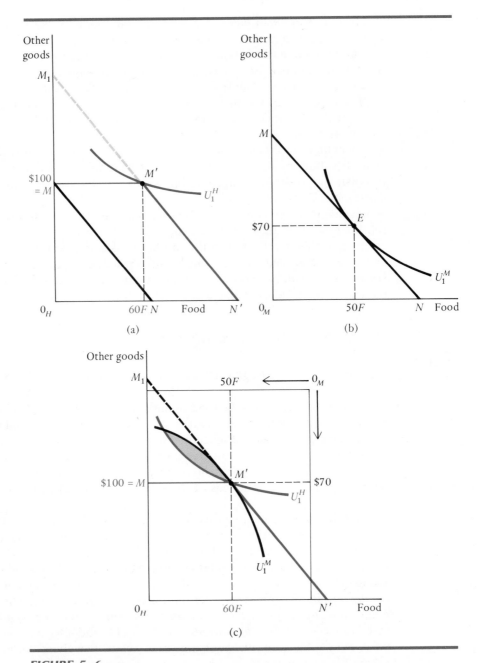

FIGURE 5-6
Food Stamps: Potential Gains from Black Market Exchange

(a) Hank's equilibrium after receiving food stamps is at point M'. (b) Monica's
unsubsidized equilibrium is at point E. (c) The distribution of goods is inefficient,
as shown by point M' in the box diagram. The lens-shaped area shows the
potential for mutually advantageous trade, but these trades are illegal, so they
can only take place in a black market.

food coupon she could use to purchase a dollar's worth of food, and Hank would be willing to sell at a price below a dollar.

To see the potential mutual benefits from black market trade explicitly, we form the Edgeworth box just as we did in the last section. In Figure 5–6c we start with Hank's budget line $MM'N'$. Then Monica's budget line from Figure 5–6b is rotated 180 degrees, and her equilibrium point is superimposed on Hank's equilibrium point M'. In this construction the box diagram has dimensions equal to Hank's and Monica's combined food consumption and total outlays on other goods. Without any black market exchange they would both be at point M' in Figure 5–6c. Since their indifference curves intersect at this point (the marginal value of food differs between them), there is a lens-shaped area identifying potential exchanges that will make both parties better off.

Figure 5–6 shows that the food stamp subsidy can lead to an inefficient distribution of products among consumers, which means that there is mutually beneficial exchange possible. Hank can sell food coupons to Monica at a price lower than $1 per dollar's worth of coupons, and both he and she will be better off, at least for trades that take place within the lens-shaped area. Black markets thus occur because the subsidy leads to an inefficient position, implying that mutually beneficial exchanges are possible.

Black market exchanges of food stamps are illegal, however, and this no doubt deters some people from engaging in these exchanges. Apparently, though, the potential benefits are sufficiently attractive for many people that they are willing to bear the risk. History, of course, provides numerous instances where the power of self-interest in consummating mutually beneficial trades led to exchanges that were illegal. Trade in liquor during Prohibition and, more recently, trade in illegal drugs are well-known examples.

Participation in black markets benefits both food stamp recipients and those who illegally purchase the food coupons — the gains from voluntary exchange again. Why, then, are black markets illegal? Consider the government's position, articulated by Carl Williamson, deputy commissioner of welfare in 1975:

> If a person gets $100 in food stamps that he wants to spend on rent or booze, he just sells them to a black marketeer, for, say $80. This middleman then sells them for $90 to a crooked grocer who gets $100 from the Government. That way, everyone makes an easy profit, and the Government gets ripped off.[4]

Commissioner Williamson recognizes the benefit to the market participants (the "easy profit"), but he claims that the government loses. In fact, government expenditures on food stamps are exactly the same whether the food stamps are used legally or illegally, so there is no financial loss for the government. However, one consequence of black markets

---

[4] Quoted in "Food Stamps, Out of Control?" *U.S. News and World Report*, September 1, 1975, p. 13.

in food stamps is that the recipients who sell food coupons consume less food (and more of other things) than they would if they did not engage in black market exchanges. (All the possibilities in the lens-shaped area in Figure 5–6c involve less food consumption for Hank.) If the government's goal is to increase food consumption, despite the recipients' own perceptions of their needs, then that goal is partially thwarted by black markets.

PRICE AND NONPRICE RATIONING AND EFFICIENCY
5.6

In open markets, prices serve a rationing function in determining how much of available quantities each consumer will get. The rationing function, and whether it is accomplished efficiently or inefficiently, is what this chapter is all about. We conclude our analysis with an example that illustrates the relationship between the demand curve treatment of rationing problems and the Edgeworth box approach emphasized in previous sections.

Figure 5–7b shows the market demand and supply curves for gasoline. Since our emphasis is on the rationing of fixed supplies, the supply curve will be drawn as vertical (perhaps reflecting a very short-run situation). With the S supply curve, price is $2.00 and quantity is 125 gallons. Now suppose there is a sharp reduction in supply to 100 gallons so that the supply curve shifts from S to S' (because of a foreign oil embargo, perhaps). The market response would be an increase in price to $3.00. Consumers are induced to restrict their use of gasoline to the available quantity by the higher price.

By looking at Figure 5–7a, we see what this price increase means for the individual consumers in the market. Once again we consider only two consumers, Hank and Monica, whose demand curves are d_H and d_M. When the price reaches $3.00, each consumer moves up his or her demand curve, cutting back on any gasoline use that is valued at less than $3.00 per gallon. The final equilibrium positions are at points A and B, with Monica purchasing 70 gallons and Hank purchasing 30 gallons. The sum of their purchases, 100 gallons, is, of course, the total quantity purchased, shown in Figure 5–7b.

Their adjustment to the higher price represents an efficient rationing of the reduced quantity available. Consider how this would appear if the final equilibrium were shown in an Edgeworth box diagram. Hank, in purchasing 30 gallons, consumes at a point where his marginal rate of substitution between outlays on other goods and gasoline is $3.00 per gallon. (Recall that the height to Hank's demand curve is equal to his MRS between money and the good in question.) Similarly, Monica, in purchasing 70 gallons, consumes at a point where her marginal rate of substitution between money and gasoline is $3.00 per gallon. Their marginal rates of substitution are equal, and if this situation were depicted in an Edgeworth

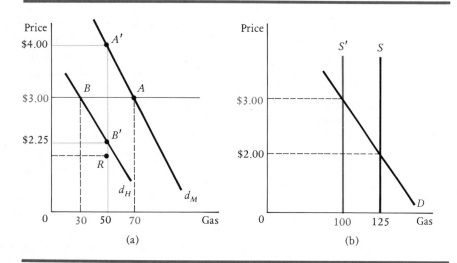

FIGURE 5-7

Gasoline Rationing

Nonprice rationing will generally lead to an inefficient distribution. Using demand curves, we can illustrate an inefficient distribution by differences in the demand prices of consumers. When each consumer gets 50 gallons of gasoline, Monica's demand price is $4.00 and Hank's is $2.25, implying that both would be better off with a different distribution.

box, it would look exactly like the one in Figure 5–5c. Hank's and Monica's indifference curves have the same slope at their equilibrium positions and so are tangent in the box diagram. Allowing the market price to ration the available quantities between the consumers consequently leads to an efficient distribution of products.

We can better appreciate the significance of the rationing problem by speculating on how it might be resolved if price was not allowed to perform this function. For example, suppose that when the supply of gasoline falls, the government doesn't allow the price to rise but instead imposes a price ceiling of $2.00 per gallon. In that event the total quantity demanded exceeds the quantity available, but somehow the combined use of Hank and Monica must be restricted to 100 gallons. Suppose the government implements a rationing scheme by using ration coupons, as it did in World War II. (In fact, during the Arab oil embargo of 1973–1974 the government again proposed the use of ration coupons and printed 3.8 billion, but the coupons were never used.) One hundred ration coupons will be printed and distributed to Hank and Monica. To purchase a gallon of gasoline, the consumer must pay $2.00 and turn in one ration coupon; since only 100 coupons are available, gasoline purchases will not exceed the available supply. (Resale of the coupons is not permitted.)

The problem, then, is how to divide the ration coupons between Hank and Monica. Suppose each receives 50 coupons: then neither could purchase more than 50 gallons. In Figure 5–7a this solution puts both Hank and Monica at point *R*, each paying $2.00 per gallon and receiving 50 gallons. Both, however, place a value greater than $2.00 on gasoline at that level of consumption. When Monica consumes 50 gallons, her marginal value of gasoline is $4.00 per gallon. This is her marginal rate of substitution between money and gasoline when only 50 gallons are available; it is measured by the height to her demand curve at point *A'*. Hank's marginal value of gasoline is $2.25 at 50 gallons, as shown by the height to his demand curve at *B'*.[5] Since Monica places a higher marginal value on gasoline than Hank does, this method of rationing gasoline is inefficient.

We could also depict this coupon-rationing equilibrium in an Edgeworth box diagram; it would be shown by a point where Hank's and Monica's indifference curves intersect. (Qualitatively it would look like Figure 5–6c.) Since Monica would be willing to pay just under $4.00 for another gallon of gas, and Hank would be willing to give up a gallon for just over $2.25, both would be better off if Monica could purchase gasoline (or coupons) from Hank. The government will not allow her to do so, however, so mutually advantageous trades cannot occur. In this situation a black market in gasoline (or coupons) would probably arise.

Thinking about how to distribute gasoline ration coupons will suggest how difficult it is to reach an efficient outcome if voluntary exchange and market-determined prices are not allowed to perform their rationing function. The essence of efficient rationing is to distribute a good so that its marginal value is the same among consumers, but without knowing the preferences of all consumers, it is a virtually impossible task. For this reason any type of nonprice rationing system is almost certain to involve some inefficiency in the way products are distributed among consumers.

As another example, many colleges deliberately sell tickets to athletic events at lower-than-market-clearing prices. This policy produces a shortage: more people want to get tickets at the prices set than are available. This practice also leads to an inefficient distribution of tickets. We know such is the case because black markets frequently arise in which illegal ticket-scalping transactions take place.

Pointing out the inefficiency that is inevitably associated with nonprice rationing programs is not the same as claiming that these forms of rationing are undesirable. The purpose of price ceilings is generally to benefit consumers at the expense of those engaged in producing and selling the commodity. It is clear that producers are harmed, but the significance of this inefficiency is that it also diminishes the benefits to consumers. In our gasoline example both consumers would be better

---

[5] This discussion assumes that income effects on demand can be neglected. If they were taken into account, however, the results would not be significantly affected.

off — without harming producers any further — if they could exchange gasoline until their marginal values are brought into equality.

Of course, the longer-run effect of the price ceiling on the quantity that will be supplied has been neglected in order to emphasize the rationing problem. Our purpose in this section was to indicate how we can show inefficiency in the distribution of a given supply by using the consumers' demand curves, since this approach provides an alternative to the use of Edgeworth box diagrams.

Summary

In this chapter we developed a model of barter exchange between two parties to demonstrate the meaning and significance of the proposition that voluntary exchange is mutually beneficial. The Edgeworth exchange box diagram was used to investigate the causes and consequences of voluntary trade. Using the box diagram, we saw that differing marginal rates of substitution imply the possibility of mutually beneficial exchange and observed that the prospect of mutual gain is what gives rise to voluntary exchange.

The Edgeworth box diagram can also be used to illustrate the concept of economic efficiency. A distribution of products between consumers is efficient if any change in the distribution will harm at least one of them. There are many distributions satisfying this definition, and they are shown by the points on the contract curve in the box diagram. Along the contract curve the consumers' MRSs are equal. Efficiency is one criterion for evaluating economic arrangements, but it is not the only criterion. Other factors such as equity must also be considered. For that reason demonstrating that a situation is efficient is not the same as saying it is desirable.

The distribution of products implied by a market equilibrium is efficient. Since each consumer is in equilibrium, with an MRS equal to the same price ratio that confronts other consumers, consumers' MRSs are equal to one another. We also saw how some economic arrangements could lead to an inefficient distribution of products. Food stamps and nonprice rationing of gasoline under price controls illustrate how policies of this sort can result in inefficient distributions of goods among consumers.

This chapter discussed efficiency only as it relates to the distribution of given quantities of products. Other aspects of efficiency relate to how inputs are combined to produce products and how much output is produced. These topics will be discussed in Chapter 18.

Review Questions and Problems

1. What do the dimensions of the Edgeworth box diagram signify? How does a point in the box identify the distribution of products between two consumers? What does a point on one of the sides of the box indicate? What does it mean if we are located at one of the corners of the box? (Examine each corner separately.)

*2. What does a vertical movement inside the box diagram signify? Would a voluntary trade ever be shown by a vertical movement? What does a horizontal movement signify? Would a voluntary trade ever be shown by a horizontal movement?

3. Roger has 40 gallons of gasoline and 20 cans of soup; for that market basket his MRS_{SG} is $3G/1S$. Jane has 40 gallons of gas and 50 cans of soup; for that market basket her MRS_{SG} is $1G/1S$. Use a numerical example to explain how a trade can benefit both of them. Illustrate the trade by using the

Edgeworth box diagram, showing that both consumers reach higher indifference curves.

4. Define *efficiency* and *inefficiency* in the context of the distribution of products between two consumers. If the distribution lies inside the box diagram, how does a knowledge of the consumers' marginal rates of substitution permit us to tell whether it is efficient or not?

*5. Roger has 40 gallons of gasoline and no cans of soup; for that market basket his MRS_{SG} is $1G/1S$. Jane has 20 gallons of gasoline and 20 cans of soup; her MRS_{SG} is $3G/1S$. Is this arrangement an efficient distribution of products? Show, using the Edgeworth box diagram.

6. Given their initial holdings of gasoline and soup, Roger's MRS_{SG} is $3G/1S$, Jane's MRS_{SG} is $1G/1S$, and Frank's MRS_{SG} is $3G/1S$. Is this arrangement an efficient distribution? If not, what type of trade would benefit all three persons?

7. What is the contract curve? Is a point on the contract curve better than every point off the curve? Is a point on the contract curve better than some points off the curve?

*8. How is an equal distribution of products shown in the Edgeworth box diagram? Is an equal distribution efficient?

9. Scrooge is the only moneylender in town — a monopolist — and he charges exorbitant interest rates. If you borrow money from Scrooge, does this practice illustrate the principle that voluntary trade is mutually beneficial?

*10. An owner of an apartment building converts the units into condominiums, throwing the current tenants out on the street. Is this situation an example of voluntary trade? Is it an example of mutually beneficial trade?

11. "Private markets ration goods among consumers in an efficient way." Explain what this statement means and why it is so. Does it imply that there is no basis for thinking that some other distribution would be better?

12. If the government pays half of Tanya's housing costs but does not subsidize Frank, will the distribution of housing and other goods between Tanya and Frank be efficient? Adapt the approaches of Figures 5–5 and 5–6 to answer this question.

Supplementary Readings

Newman, Peter. *The Theory of Exchange.* Englewood Cliffs, N.J.: Prentice-Hall, 1965.

Radford, R. A. "The Economic Organization of a P.O.W. Camp." *Economica,* (November 1945): 189–201.

Vickrey, William. *Microstatics.* New York: Harcourt, Brace & World, 1964. Chap. 3.

Production

6

In the previous four chapters we concentrated on consumer behavior, with the supply of goods and services generally taken for granted. Now we begin to develop the analysis of the factors that determine the quantities of commodities that firms will produce and offer for sale. The logical starting place is to identify the underlying physical relationships between inputs employed and output produced. The physical productivity of inputs is an important determinant of output: it specifies how much can be produced. As we will see in later chapters, the productivity of inputs underlies both the cost curves of the firm and the firm's demand curve for inputs.

Basically, this chapter explains how economists represent the technological possibilities available to the business firm. While our emphasis is on production by the firm, the same principles also apply to all organizations engaged in productive activity. In the United States business firms produce about 80 percent of the output of goods and services; government agencies, like the Department of Defense, and nonprofit organizations, like the Red Cross, produce the remainder.

RELATING OUTPUT TO INPUTS
6.1

Inputs — sometimes called *factors of production* or *resources* — are the ingredients used by a firm to produce a good or service. We may define inputs broadly or narrowly. For example, a broad definition might classify all inputs as either labor, land, or capital. When considering some questions, however, it may be more helpful to use a narrow definition and distinguish among inputs more specifically, such as engineers, mechanics, electricity, insurance, water, worker safety equipment, postal services, telephone services, and so on.

For any good or service the existing state of technology ultimately determines the maximum amount of output a firm can produce with specified quantities of inputs. By state of technology we mean, of course, the technical or engineering know-how regarding the various ways some product can be produced. The *production function* summarizes the characteristics of existing technology. The production function is a relationship between inputs and outputs: it identifies the maximum quantity of a commodity that can be produced per time period by each specific combination of inputs.

TABLE 6–1

Hypothetical Production Function for Wheat: Bushels of Wheat Produced per Year

Number of Acres Cultivated per Year	Laborers Employed per year					
	1	*2*	*3*	*4*	*5*	*6*
1	100	230	320	400	470	530
2	220	350	470	580	680	760
3	320	470	640	760	900	1000
4	400	580	760	920	1080	1180
5	470	680	860	1050	1200	1330
6	520	760	950	1120	1280	1430

We can present a production function in tabular, graphical, or mathematical form. Table 6–1 shows a hypothetical production function for a farm that uses only two inputs, labor and land, to produce wheat. If 5 workers cultivate 3 acres of land per year, for example, the table indicates that output will be 900 bushels of wheat. Moreover, it is assumed that 900 bushels are the maximum output that can be generated by using those inputs, which is another way of saying that production is *technologically efficient*. It would, of course, be possible to use 5 workers and 3 acres in ways that yield less than 900 bushels of wheat, but any such processes would be *technologically inefficient*. That is, they would not be producing the maximum level of output possible, given the available inputs.

In economic theory the production function for a commodity identifies the physical constraints the firm must deal with. We assume that the firm knows the production function for the good or service it produces and always uses this knowledge to achieve the maximum output possible from whatever combination of inputs it employs. This assumption of technological efficiency may not always be valid, but there is reason for believing it to be generally correct. Any firm that operates in a technologically inefficient way is not making as much money as possible. The firm's costs of using 3 acres and 5 workers are the same whether it uses the inputs wisely or not, but the revenues from the sale of the produce (and hence the profits) will be greatest when the firm produces the maximum amount of wheat possible given these inputs. Consequently, any profit-oriented firm has strong incentive to seek out and use the best-known techniques of production.

PRODUCTION ISOQUANTS
6.2

We can represent a firm's production function graphically by production isoquants. An *isoquant* is a curve that shows all the combinations of inputs that, when used in a technologically efficient way, will produce a certain level of output. Isoquants convey the same technological information as a table like Table 6–1, but in more convenient form. Figure 6–1 shows several isoquants for the production of wheat using labor and land; the isoquants are based on the data in Table 6–1. Isoquant Q_1, for example, shows the combinations of inputs that will produce 470 bushels of wheat per year. (Note that the axes measure the quantities of the two inputs per time period.) Five acres of land together with 1 worker will produce 470 bushels of wheat (point **B**); so will 2 acres and 3 workers (point **C**), or, indeed, any other combination on the Q_1 isoquant. Isoquants farther from the origin indicate higher levels of output.

The isoquants in Figure 6–1 portray an important economic assumption: it is possible to produce a specified level of output in a variety of different ways; that is, by using different combinations of inputs, as indicated by points **D**, **B**, and **C** on Q_1. The firm can produce 470 bushels of wheat with a small quantity of land farmed intensively with a relatively large amount of labor (point **C**) or with more acreage tended less carefully by fewer workers (point **B**). Similarly, an automobile can be custom built in a local garage with very little equipment and a great deal of labor or produced in a factory with a large quantity of specialized equipment and far less labor.

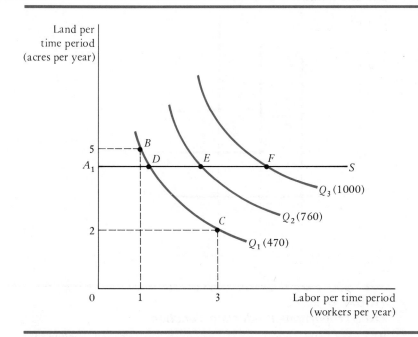

FIGURE 6–1

Production Isoquants

Production isoquants show how much output a firm can produce with various combinations of inputs. A set of isoquants graphs the production function of the firm.

When a firm can produce a commodity by using different combinations of inputs, the production function is called a *variable-proportions production function*. This term just means that a firm can combine inputs in a variety of different proportions to make the product. It should be emphasized that *every* combination of inputs shown on the isoquants in Figure 6–1 is technologically efficient: each combination shows the maximum output possible from given inputs. Since a given product can be produced in many different technologically efficient ways, knowing the technological relationships between inputs and outputs does not by itself allow us to identify the best, or least costly, input combination to use. To determine the lowest cost way to produce a given level of output, we also need to know the costs of the inputs, as we will see in the next chapter.

Economists consider variable-proportions production functions to be the general rule. However, it is possible to conceive of products that can be produced in only one way. Figure 6–2 illustrates such a situation; here a unit of product can only be produced with 2 units of land and 1 unit of labor. In this case the isoquants are drawn as right angles, with the points *A*, *B*, and *C* showing the only technologically efficient ways of producing the identified levels of output. Although it is possible to use 6 units of land

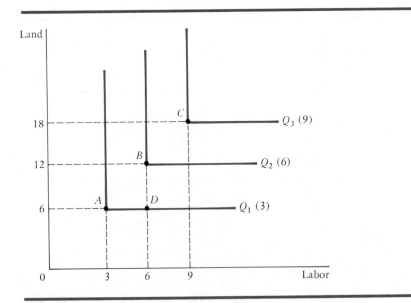

FIGURE 6-2
Fixed-Proportions Production Function

With fixed input proportions the isoquants are L-shaped, implying the impossibility of substituting one input for another without reducing output. Normally, input substitution is possible, and the isoquants will slope downward, as in Figure 6-1.

and 6 units of labor (point *D*) to produce 6 units of output, 3 units of labor are wasted since the same output can be produced with 6 units of land and 3 units of labor at point *A*. This type of production function is referred to as a *fixed-proportions production function* since technology effectively requires that inputs be used in fixed proportions, here 2 units of land per unit of labor.

SHORT-RUN AND LONG-RUN PRODUCTION RESPONSES
6.3

Production isoquants illustrate all the ways a firm can produce given levels of output. In some instances the firm may not have the option of choosing from among all the input combinations shown by an isoquant. For example, suppose the firm in Figure 6–1 is currently producing 760 bushels of wheat at point *E*. Next assume that for some reason it decides to increase the rate of production to 1,000 bushels. If it schedules this output expansion to take place within the next month, the firm may not be able to purchase additional amounts of all inputs in such a short period of time. In particular, it may not be able to acquire more land on such short notice. In that event the options on isoquant Q_3 involving more land than OA_1 are not immediately available to the firm, and it can expand output only by using more labor and operating at point *F* on Q_3.

What we are describing is a short-run output response by the firm. The *short run* is defined as a period of time in which it is impractical to change the employment levels of some inputs. Resources that a firm cannot feasibly vary over the time period involved are referred to as fixed inputs. These inputs need not be fixed in the sense that it is literally impossible for the firm to vary their use; rather they are any inputs that would be prohibitively costly to alter in a short period of time. A firm's plant and specialized equipment commonly fall in this category. Although the firm might be able to expand plant capacity in a month, doing so might require operating crews 24 hours a day at exorbitant cost. In that case, practically speaking, plant and specialized equipment are fixed inputs that the firm will not vary in the event that quick output adjustments are required.

By contrast, the *long run* is a period of time in which the firm can vary all its inputs. The farmer can acquire additional land suitable for cultivation; the business can gradually depreciate (or sell) its existing plant and replace it with a larger structure. There are no fixed inputs in the long run; all inputs are variable, and the entire range of options shown by the isoquants is open to the firm.

The distinction between the short run and the long run is necessarily somewhat arbitrary. Six months may be ample time for the clothing industry to make a long-run adjustment but insufficient time for the automobile industry to switch from production of large to small cars. Even for a given industry there is no unique time period that can be identified as *the* short run since some inputs may be variable in three months, others in six months, and still others only after a year. Despite this unavoidable imprecision, the concepts of short run and long run do emphasize that quick output changes are likely to be accomplished differently from output changes that can take place more gradually.

In discussing production functions, we have been intentionally vague about the exact relationships between inputs and outputs. These technological relationships are certain to vary over time and among different commodities. We can, however, try to identify certain common features in these relationships, and the distinction between the short run (with some inputs fixed) and the long run (with all inputs variable) is helpful here. In the next three sections we will look at short-run production relationships. In terms of Figure 6–1 we will assume that land is held fixed at some level, such as $0A_1$, and then investigate what happens to output as the labor input is varied. In other words, we will be analyzing what happens to output as we move along a horizontal line like A_1S. After examining the short-run relationship between input and output, we will turn to long-run production relationships when all inputs can be varied.

PRODUCTION WHEN ONLY ONE INPUT IS VARIABLE

6.4

Let's return to our example of a firm that combines land and labor to produce wheat. Now, we will assume that the amount of land is a fixed input (for the short-run period being considered) and that only the labor input can vary. With the amount of land held constant at 5 acres per year, we will determine how output varies as the firm employs different quantities of labor.

Table 6–2 illustrates a hypothetical relationship between output and various quantities of labor. The first column is included only to emphasize that land is fixed at 5 acres regardless of the amount of labor used. Columns 2 and 3 contain the important data, showing how much output can be produced with alternative quantities of labor. With zero workers, output is naturally zero. As the amount of labor increases, output rises. One worker applied to 5 acres of land will produce 50 bushels of wheat per year; 2 workers will produce 150 bushels; 3 will produce 300 bushels, and so on. There is, however, a limit to the quantity of wheat that the firm can produce on 5 acres by increasing the labor input, and in our example the limit is reached when 8 workers produce 610 bushels. A ninth unit of labor adds nothing to output, and using 10 workers actually causes output to fall.

Although these figures are hypothetical, the general relationship they illustrate is quite common. To examine the relationship further, we introduce the concepts of average physical product and marginal physical product of an input. The *average physical product* (or average product) of

TABLE 6–2
Diminishing Marginal Returns to Labor

Amount of Land	Amount of Labor	Total Output	Average Product of Labor	Marginal Product of Labor*
5	0	0	—	—
5	1	50	50	50
5	2	150	75	100
5	3	300	100	150
5	4	400	100	100
5	5	480	96	80
5	6	540	90	60
5	7	580	83	40
5	8	610	76	30
5	9	610	68	0
5	10	580	58	− 30

* The marginal product figures pertain to the interval between the indicated amount of labor and one unit less. Thus the marginal product at 4 units of labor is 100, because total output rises from 300 to 400 when labor increases from 3 to 4 units.

an input is defined as the total output (or total product) divided by the amount of the input used to produce that output. For example, 3 workers produce 300 bushels of wheat, so the average product of labor is 100 bushels per worker at that level of employment. The average product for each quantity of labor is, therefore, derived by dividing the total output in column 3 by the corresponding amount of labor in column 2 that produces each level of output.

The *marginal physical product* of an input can be defined as the change in total output that results from a one-unit change in the amount of the input, holding the quantities of other inputs constant. To illustrate, when labor is increased from 6 to 7 units, total output rises from 540 to 580 units, or by 40 bushels. So the marginal product of labor, when the seventh worker is employed, is 40 bushels of wheat. What the marginal product of an input measures should be thoroughly understood. In many applications it is the crucial economic variable because most production decisions relate to whether a little more or a little less of an input should be employed. The way total output responds to this variation is what the marginal product measures.

Total, Average, and Marginal Product Curves

The information from Table 6–2 can be conveniently presented graphically. Figure 6–3 shows the result. (We have assumed that labor and wheat are divisible into smaller units in drawing the graphs, so the relationships

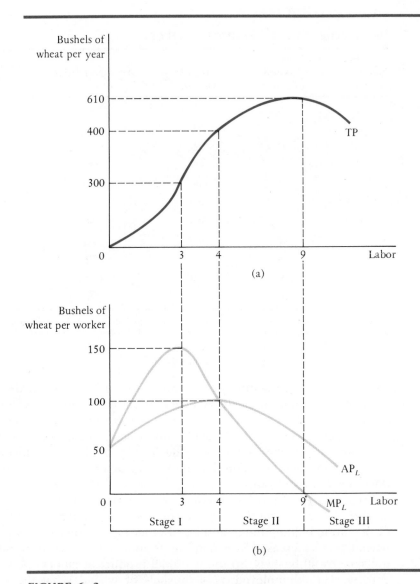

FIGURE 6-3
Total, Average, and Marginal Product Curves
(a) With the amount of land fixed, a total product curve shows the output
produced with various amounts of labor. (b) Average and marginal product
curves are derived from the total product curve.

are smooth curves rather than ten discrete points.) The total product
curve in Figure 6–3a shows how the total output of wheat varies with the
quantity of labor employed. Just as was indicated in Table 6–2, total output increases as more labor is used and reaches a maximum at 610 bushels, when 9 workers are employed; beyond 9 workers, output declines.

Figure 6–3b shows the average product and marginal product curves for labor. Note that these curves measure the output per unit of input on the vertical axis rather than total product, which is what the curve in Figure 6–3a measures. As employment of labor increases, the marginal product of labor increases at first, reaches a maximum at 3 workers, and then declines. The average product of labor also increases at low levels of employment, reaches a maximum at 4 workers, and then declines.

As is true of all marginal and average curves, definite relationships exist between the two. When marginal product is greater than average product, average product must be increasing, as is shown between 0 and 4 units of labor in Figure 6–3b. This relationship follows directly from the meaning of the terms. If the addition to total product (marginal product) is greater than the average, the average must rise. Think of the average height of people in a room. If another person enters who is taller than the average (the marginal height of the extra person is greater than the average), the average height will increase. Similarly, when marginal product is less than average product, average product must be decreasing, as is shown for labor beyond 4 units in the diagram. Since marginal product is greater than average product when the average is rising, and less than average product when the average is falling, marginal and average products will be equal when average product is at a maximum.

The relationship between the total product curve and the marginal product curve should also be mentioned briefly. As long as marginal product is positive, total product will continue to rise. That is, as long as an extra unit of labor produces some extra output (however small), the total amount produced will increase (up through 8 units of labor in Figure 6–3). When marginal product is negative, total product will fall (beyond 9 units of labor), and when marginal product is zero, total product reaches its maximum (at 9 units of labor).

THE LAW OF DIMINISHING MARGINAL RETURNS
6.5

We are now in a position to explain why the product curves have the shapes they do. Their shapes reflect the law of diminishing marginal returns, an empirical generalization about the way output responds to increases in the employment of a variable input. The *law of diminishing marginal returns* holds that as the amount of some input is increased in equal increments, while technology and other inputs are held constant, the resulting increments in output will decrease beyond some point. Put more briefly, the law holds that beyond some point, the marginal product of the variable input will decline.

Intuitively, the law of diminishing marginal returns makes sense. If we begin with 1 worker on 5 acres of land trying to grow wheat, that worker must be responsible for everything. Adding a second worker makes things easier, and they can divide the work systematically. More specialization and division of labor are possible as additional workers are employed, but eventually the marginal product of additional units of labor falls because the workers' tasks become redundant and they get in each other's way. Ultimately, the marginal product of an extra unit of labor becomes negative when there are so many workers relative to the land that they have little more to do than talk to each other and watch the wheat grow.

In Figure 6–3b diminishing marginal returns set in when the amount of labor increases beyond 3 workers. Each additional worker beyond 3 adds less to total product than the previous one: the marginal product curve slopes downward. Note that the law of diminishing marginal returns does not depend on workers' being different in their productive abilities. We are assuming all workers are alike.

It is entirely possible that diminishing marginal returns will occur from the very beginning, with the second unit of labor adding less to total output than the first unit. More commonly, marginal returns increase at very low levels of output and then decline, as in Figure 6–3.

In applying the law of diminishing marginal returns, two conditions must be kept in mind. First, some other input, or inputs, must stay fixed as the amount of the input in question is varied. The law does not apply, for example, to a situation where both labor and land are increased, if these are the only inputs. It does apply if land is held constant while labor and fertilizer, for example, are varied. The key thing is that some important input is not varied. Second, technology must remain unchanged. A change in technical know-how would cause the entire total product curve to shift. In the short run these two conditions will normally hold so that the law of diminishing returns is directly applicable.

The term *diminishing returns* is a bit of economic jargon that has crept into popular usage, and people frequently use it incorrectly, as when a student says, "I stopped studying when I reached the point of diminishing returns." Sometimes, however, even economists misapply the law. One of the most famous mistakes was made by nineteenth-century British economist Thomas Malthus. Malthus reasoned that since the amount of land is fixed, as population grows and more labor is applied to land, the productivity of labor in food production would decline. Thus, the amount of food per person would inexorably fall over time, leading to widespread famine. This prediction, in fact, is what originally led economics to be called the "dismal science."

Fortunately, both for economics and the world's population, Malthus's prediction was based on a misapplication of the law of diminishing marginal returns. Malthus confused the short run with the long run. While population was growing over time, advances in agricultural technology were also taking place. Malthus did not foresee the ways modern agricultural techniques would greatly increase labor productivity in food production. Remember that for the law of diminishing marginal returns to apply, technology must remain unchanged. Since technology will often change over long periods of time, most valid applications of the law relate to short-run production responses.

Three Stages of Production

When marginal product first rises and then falls, the product curves have the general shapes shown in Figure 6–3. Economists have found it useful to partition the product curves into three regions, shown as stages I, II, and III in Figure 6–3. Stage I occurs where the average product is rising, from 1 to 4 workers in our example. In stage I total product increases (first at an increasing rate and then at a decreasing rate); marginal product increases, reaches a maximum at 3 workers, and then falls as diminishing returns set in (but still remains positive); and average product rises and reaches a maximum at 4 workers.

Stage II ranges from 4 to 9 workers. In stage II average product falls, but total product still rises until it reaches a maximum at 9 workers; correspondingly, marginal product is positive but declines until it reaches zero at 9 workers. Thus, additional units of the variable input continue to increase total product in stage II, but not as rapidly as in stage I.

Stage III occurs for employment in excess of 9 workers. In stage III total product actually falls as more labor is used; marginal product is negative; and average product continues to decline.

It can be shown that the rational producer will never operate in stage I or stage III. It is easy to see why production would not take place in stage III. In this region output can be increased by actually using less of the variable input. This would mean that production costs would be higher in stage III than they were in stage II, but output would be lower. Even if labor were entirely free, its use would not be expanded into stage III.

To see that it is also unwise to produce in stage I, suppose the firm operates in a competitive wheat market. In stage I average product is rising, so an increase in labor increases output in greater proportion. Two workers can produce more than twice as much as one worker, so for twice the cost, wheat production more than doubles. If it is profitable to produce anywhere in stage I, profits can be increased by expanding output into stage II. In stage I using two workers rather than one, for example, only *doubles* labor costs, but since output will more than double, revenues will also *more than double:* profits rise. Thus the firm has incentive to expand production beyond the region of rising average product.

We cannot determine, from the technological information shown by the product curves, exactly where in stage II the firm will operate. Both the price of wheat and the cost of labor play a role in determining the appropriate output level. These two factors are incorporated into the analysis in the next two chapters.

The Geometry of Product Curves

As we saw in discussing Table 6–2, knowing how total output varies with the quantity of the variable input allows us to derive the average and marginal product relationships. Similarly, we can use geometrical rela-

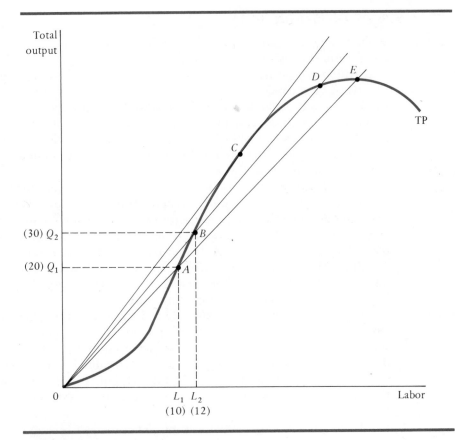

FIGURE 6-4

Deriving Average Product

The average product of labor is equal to the slope of a ray from the origin to the point on the total product curve. Thus, at point A the average product is shown by the slope of ray 0A, or 2 units of output per unit of labor.

tionships to derive the average and marginal product curves from the total product curve.

Figure 6–4 illustrates how average product is derived geometrically from the total product curve, TP. The average product of labor is total output divided by the total quantity of labor. At point A on the total product curve, average product is equal to $0Q_1/0L_1$; and since $AL_1 = 0Q_1$, then average product equals $AL_1/0L_1$, or 2 units of product per worker, in this case. Note, however, that $AL_1/0L_1$ equals the slope of the line $0A$ drawn from the origin to point A on the total product curve. *Thus, the average product at a particular point is shown geometrically by the slope of a ray from the origin to that point on the total product curve.* At point B, for example, the ray $0B$ is more steeply sloped than the ray $0A$, implying that the average product is higher at point B than at point A.

Now consider points *A*, *B*, *C*, *D*, and *E* on the total product curve. As output expands from *A* to *B* to *C*, the slopes of the rays (0*A*, 0*B*, and 0*C*) become successively greater, showing that the average product of labor rises over this region. At point *C*, in fact, average product reaches a maximum, since the ray 0*C* is the steepest ray from the origin that still touches the total product curve. (The ray 0*C* is tangent to the total product curve at point *C*.) As output expands from *C* to *D* to *E*, the rays (0*C*, 0*D*, and 0*E*) become flatter, indicating that average product falls over this region. For the points we have selected, average product is the same at points *D* and *B* and at points *E* and *A*.

Marginal product measures how much total output changes when there is a small change in the use of the input. Figure 6–5 shows how the marginal product is derived geometrically. *The marginal product of labor at a particular point on the total product curve is shown by the slope of the total product curve at that point.* The slope of the total product curve is in turn equal to the slope of a line tangent to the curve. At point *A*, for example, we have drawn a line tangent to the total product curve, with a slope of 5/1. This means that the marginal product of labor at point *A* is 5 units of output.

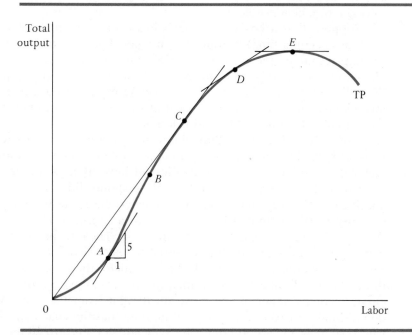

FIGURE 6–5

Deriving Marginal Product

The marginal product of labor is equal to the slope of the total product curve itself at each point. Thus, at point *A* the marginal product is equal to 5 units of output per unit of labor.

The steeper the total product curve, the faster output rises when more of the input is used, which implies a larger marginal product. In the diagram marginal product rises as we move up the curve from the origin to point *B*, but it declines (the slope becomes flatter) as we go beyond point *B*. At point *B* the total product curve is steepest, and marginal product is at a maximum. Beyond point *B*, diminishing marginal returns set in: output rises less and less when more of the input is used. Note that at point *C* marginal product and average product are equal since the slope of the total product curve at point *C* (marginal product) equals the slope of a ray from the origin (average product). This is the graphic representation of the proposition, noted earlier, that when average product is at a maximum, marginal product and average product are equal. When marginal product falls to zero at point *E*, as implied by the zero slope of the total product curve there, total output is at a maximum.

USING PRODUCT CURVES: AN EXAMPLE
6.6

Perhaps the most important relationship introduced in this chapter is the law of diminishing marginal returns. Now let's examine a hypothetical case to illustrate how the law of diminishing marginal returns can help in solving a practical problem.

Suppose that a basketball coach has a fixed quantity of resources (such as coaching time) to train two athletes. For each athlete, the more training resources received, the greater the scoring potential becomes. The input here is training resources, and the output is scoring potential. We will assume that the law of diminishing marginal returns applies to this relationship: each additional unit of training resources beyond some point applied to either athlete adds less to scoring potential than the previous unit. It makes sense that diminishing marginal returns would be relevant here since each athlete's inherent athletic ability is an important factor that is effectively fixed regardless of how intensive the training.

Our two athletes, Aaron and Ralph, respond differently to training. Specifically, let's say that when both receive the same training, Ralph's resulting scoring potential is twice as great as Aaron's. The two product curves in Figure 6–6 reflect these assumptions. The total product curve for Aaron, TP_A, shows his scoring potential for each level of resources, and TP_R is the relationship for Ralph. For simplicity these curves have been drawn to show diminishing marginal returns from the very first unit: each curve becomes flatter as we move up it right from the start. Although diminishing returns immediately set in, note that the coach will still allocate resources toward training the two athletes because there are still positive benefits; namely, the opportunity to increase the scoring capabilities of the two ballplayers.

Suppose that the available training resources are fixed in amount and are equal to two times $0T_1$. Now the problem: how should these resources be divided between the athletes if we wish their combined scoring poten-

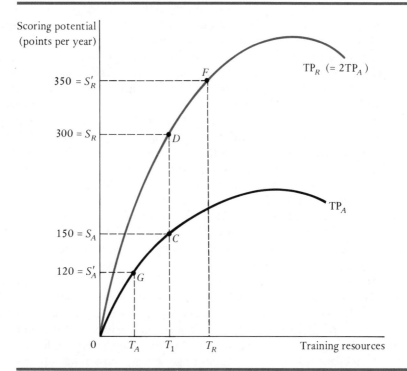

FIGURE 6–6

Using Training Resources Effectively

With a fixed amount of training resources, to mazimize combined scoring
potential, the coach should allocate resources so that the marginal products are
equal. This equality occurs at $0T_A$ and $0T_R$ in the graph.

tial to be as high as possible? We might start by supplying each athlete
with half the available amount, or $0T_1$. This allocation results in scoring
potential of S_A (150 points) for Aaron and S_R (300 points, or twice S_A) for
Ralph, a combined scoring potential of 450 points. But does any other
division of resources lead to greater combined scoring potential?

To determine how to allocate the training resources to maximize the
combined scoring potential of the players, we should think in terms of
marginal products. Given our assumption about how the athletes respond
to training, the marginal product of training for Ralph at point D is twice
as great as Aaron's marginal product at point C. With this equal division of
training resources, the marginal productivity of a unit of training resources might be 10 points (in additional scoring potential) for Ralph and
5 points for Aaron. (Look at the difference in the *slopes* of the curves at C
and D.) This means, however, that combined scoring potential will increase if we take a unit of resources away from Aaron and apply it to
Ralph; Aaron will lose 5 points, and Ralph will gain 10 points.

To maximize combined scoring potential, the coach should shift resources from Aaron to Ralph until the marginal products are equal. Since Ralph's marginal product falls as he receives more resources, and Aaron's marginal product rises as he receives fewer resources (from the law of diminishing marginal returns), shifting resources from Aaron to Ralph will eventually equalize the marginal products. This occurs when Aaron receives $0T_A$ and Ralph receives $0T_R$. (T_AT_1 units have been shifted from Aaron to Ralph: $T_AT_1 = T_1T_R$.) At points G and F the slopes (marginal products) are equal, and combined scoring potential is $S'_R + S'_A$ (470 points), which is larger than the combined scoring potential from an equal allocation of training resources between the players — the gain to Ralph (50 points) is greater than the loss of Aaron (30 points).

This example illustrates the importance of thinking in terms of marginal effects and recognizing the relevance of the law of diminishing marginal returns. For an example closer to home, consider the allocation of your time between studying for tests in economics and history. You can expect the marginal return to time spent studying each subject to diminish beyond some point: studying longer and longer hours will add less and less to your total knowledge — and presumably to your grade.

If you are interested in maximizing your grade point average, you should be dividing your study time in such a way that the marginal product is the same for both subjects. For example, suppose that by studying 6 hours for each test, you expect to get a C in economics and a B in history. By studying economics one more hour, you could raise your grade from a C to a B (the marginal product of another hour is a unit change in the letter grade); studying history one hour less would reduce your grade from a B to a B−. Since the marginal products differ, your grade point average will increase if you shift your study time from the subject where it has a lower marginal product (history) to the subject where it has a higher marginal product (economics).

As a rational student, you are in all likelihood (insofar as your goal is to maximize your combined grades) already applying this rule even if you don't think in terms of marginal products. At least, economists would predict that students in general behave this way.

LONG-RUN PRODUCTION POSSIBILITIES: ISOQUANTS FURTHER CONSIDERED
6.7

The law of diminishing marginal returns is the basic relationship governing short-run production since, in the short run, one or more inputs cannot vary. In the long run all inputs may be varied so it is necessary to consider all the possibilities identified by the firm's production function. As explained in Section 6.2, when we consider a product that is produced by using two inputs, the production options when both inputs can be varied can be shown with isoquants. In this section we will discuss further the nature of isoquants.

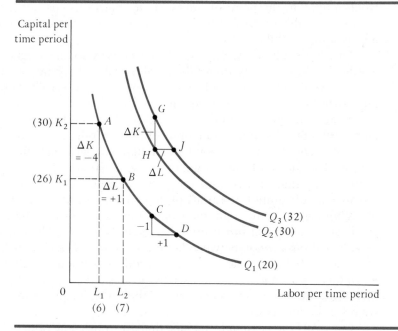

FIGURE 6–7

Marginal Rate of Technical Substitution

Isoquants have geometric properties that are similar to those of indifference curves: they are downward sloping, nonintersecting, and convex. The slope of an isoquant measures the marginal rate of technical substitution between the inputs. At point A the $MRTS_{LK}$ equals $4K/1L$, implying that 1 unit of labor can replace 4 units of capital without reducing output.

Figure 6–7 shows several isoquants relating the output of some product to two inputs, labor and capital. Isoquants are very similar to indifference curves in their characteristics.[1] By analogous reasoning we can explain several of the characteristics of isoquants briefly.

First, isoquants must slope downward as long as both inputs are productive; that is, have positive marginal products. If we increase the quantity of one input employed (which would by itself increase output) and wish to keep output unchanged, we must of necessity reduce the amount of the other input; this relationship implies a negative slope.

Second, isoquants lying farther to the northeast identify greater levels of output, again because the inputs are productive, and using more of both inputs means a higher output.

Third, two isoquants can never intersect. Intersecting isoquants

---

[1] One striking difference should be noted: while we cannot measure objectively the level of well-being implied by an indifference curve, we can frequently measure the level of output implied by an isoquant. Indeed, economists have attempted to estimate production isoquants for various products.

would imply, at the point of intersection, that the same combination of inputs is capable of producing two different *maximum* levels of output — a logical impossibility.

Finally, isoquants will generally be convex to the origin. In other words, the slope of an isoquant (in absolute value) becomes smaller as we move down the curve from left to right. To see why this is likely to be true, note that the slope of an isoquant measures the ability of one input to replace another in production. At point *A* in Figure 6–7, for example, 30 units of capital and 6 units of labor produce 20 units of output. The input combination at point *B*, though, can also produce the same output. The slope of the isoquant between *A* and *B* is −4 units of capital / +1 unit of labor, meaning that at point *A*, 1 unit of labor can replace, or substitute for, 4 units of capital without affecting output.

Without the minus sign, the slope of an isoquant measures the marginal rate of technical substitution between the inputs. The *marginal rate of technical substitution* between labor and capital ($MRTS_{LK}$) is defined as the amount by which capital can be reduced without changing output when there is a small (unit) increase in the amount of labor. At point *A* the $MRTS_{LK}$ is 4 units of capital per unit of labor, which equals the slope when we drop the minus sign.

Convexity of isoquants means that the marginal rate of technical substitution diminishes as we move down each isoquant. At point *C* on Q_1 in Figure 6–7, for example, the $MRTS_{LK}$ is only one unit of capital per unit of labor, less than it is at point *A*. The assumption of convexity of isoquants, just as with convexity of indifference curves, is an empirical generalization that cannot be proven correct or incorrect on logical grounds. It does, however, agree with intuition.[2] At point *A* capital is relatively abundant, and labor is relatively scarce, compared to point *C*. At point *A*, 1 unit of the scarce input can replace 4 units of the abundant input. Moving down the isoquant, labor becomes more abundant and capital more scarce. It makes sense that it becomes increasingly difficult for labor to replace capital in these circumstances, and this is what is implied by the convexity of the curve.

MRTS and the Marginal Products of Inputs

The degree to which inputs can be substituted for one another, as measured by the marginal rate of technical substitution, is directly linked to the marginal productivities of the inputs. Consider the MRTS, or slope, at point *A* in Figure 6–7 again. At that point, 1 unit of labor can replace 4 units of capital, so labor's marginal product must be 4 times as large as capital's marginal product when the slope of the isoquant ($MRTS_{LK}$) is 4 units of capital to 1 unit of labor. To check this reasoning, note that at

[2] It is also true that if production isoquants were not generally convex, firms would be observed employing only one input. Since most firms employ many inputs, the relevant isoquants must be convex. Again, this characteristic is closely analogous to one of the characteristics of consumer choice theory (see the discussion of Figure 2–12).

point *C* the slope of the isoquant is unity. Here the marginal products must be equal since the gain in output from an additional unit of labor (its marginal product) must exactly offset the loss in output associated with a one-unit reduction in capital (its marginal product).

Consequently, the marginal rate of technical substitution, which is equal to (minus) the slope of an isoquant, is also equal to the relative marginal productivities (MP) of the inputs. Thus,

$$\mathrm{MRTS}_{LK} = (-)\Delta K/\Delta L = \mathrm{MP}_L/\mathrm{MP}_K.$$

Note that the isoquant's slope does not tell us the absolute size of either marginal product but only their ratio.

We can also derive this relationship more formally. In Figure 6–7 consider the slope of isoquant Q_3 at point G, $\Delta K/\Delta L$. The reduction in capital, ΔK, by itself reduces output from 32 units to 30 units. This reduction in output must equal ΔK times the marginal product of capital. (For example, if $\Delta K = -\frac{1}{2}$ unit, and the marginal product of 1 unit of capital is 4 units of output, reducing capital use by $\frac{1}{2}$ unit reduces output by 2 units.) Expressing the change in output as ΔQ, we have

$$\Delta Q = \Delta K \times \mathrm{MP}_K.$$

Similarly, when labor increases from point *H* to *J*, or by ΔL, output increases by ΔL times labor's marginal product:

$$\Delta Q = \Delta L \times \mathrm{MP}_L.$$

For a movement along an isoquant, the decrease in output from reducing capital use must equal the increase in output from employing more labor, so the ΔQ terms are equal. The right-hand terms in the two expressions are equal, and by substitution, we obtain

$$\Delta K \times \mathrm{MP}_K = \Delta L \times \mathrm{MP}_L.$$

Then rearranging terms yields the desired relationship:

$$\Delta K/\Delta L = \mathrm{MP}_L/\mathrm{MP}_K.$$

Using MRTS: Speed Limits and Gasoline Consumption

Using isoquants can clarify a wide range of issues. Let's say a person drives 6000 miles per year to and from work. The speed at which the car is driven affects both the amount of gasoline used (driving faster reduces gas mileage) and the amount of time spent commuting. We can think of gasoline and time as inputs in the production of transportation. Driving slower means using less gasoline but taking more time to get to work. This relationship is shown by the isoquant in Figure 6–8. Suppose the car gets 25 miles per gallon if driven 60 miles per hour. Then commuting at 60 mph uses 240 gallons of gasoline and 100 hours; this is shown by point *A*. If the car gets 26 miles per gallon when driven 55 mph, commuting at 55 mph uses 231 gallons and 109 hours, as shown at point *B*. Driving at the slower

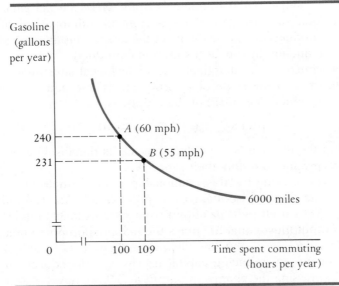

FIGURE 6-8

Isoquant Relating Gasoline and Commuting Time

When driving faster reduces gas mileage, there is a conventionally shaped isoquant relating gas consumption and time. The slope, or MRTS, shows the trade-off between gas and time implied by a change in speed.

speed saves 9 gallons but takes 9 additional hours of commuting time: the MRTS is 9 gallons/9 hours or one gallon per hour.

In debates over whether gas savings justify lower speed limits, this isoquant forces us to recognize that there is a trade-off between gasoline saved by a lower speed limit and additional time spent in transit. The trade-off is measured by the MRTS: here one gallon of gasoline per hour spent commuting (between *A* and *B*). Since reducing the speed limit from 60 to 55 mph means using less of one scarce resource (gasoline) but more of another scarce resource (driver's time), we cannot determine from the MRTS alone which speed limit is preferable. Put differently, both *A* and *B* represent technologically efficient points.

Nonetheless, the MRTS is one critical piece of information in comparing different speed limits. What else do we need to know? Basically, we need to know the relative importance of the scarce resources, gasoline and time. If gasoline costs $1.50 per gallon, the 55 mile speed limit saves our commuter $13.50. But if the commuter values time at anything more than $1.50 an hour (less than half the minimum wage), the lower speed limit costs the commuter more in lost time than is saved through reduced gasoline usage. Another trade-off is also relevant here: lower speed limits mean greater safety. Once again, the size of the trade-off between greater safety and time, the MRTS, is important. That trade-off, though, is much harder to measure.

RETURNS TO SCALE
6.8

What relationship exists between output and inputs in the long run? Since all inputs can be varied in the long run, economists approach this problem by focusing on the overall scale of operation. Specifically, we will look at how output is affected by a proportionate change in all inputs—for example, when the quantities of both labor and capital are doubled.

In this case, three possibilities arise. A proportionate increase in all inputs may increase output in the same proportion; for example, when a doubling of all inputs exactly doubles output. Here production is said to be subject to *constant returns to scale*. On the other hand, output may increase in greater proportion than input use: output more than doubles when inputs double. Production is then subject to *increasing returns to scale*. Finally, output may increase less than in proportion to input use, and then we have *decreasing returns to scale*.

These are the possibilities, but the actual relationship is not as easy to pin down. Some factors lead to increasing returns and others lead to decreasing returns; which predominate in a particular case is an empirical question.

To begin with, what factors may give rise to increasing returns? First, in a large-scale operation workers can specialize in specific tasks and carry them out more proficiently than they could if they were responsible for a multitude of jobs. This factor, the specialization and division of labor within the firm, was emphasized by the Scottish political-economist Adam Smith. Second, certain arithmetical relationships underlie increasing returns to scale. For example, a 100-foot square building (with 10,000 square feet of floor space) requires 400 feet of walls, but a 100×200-foot building, with *twice* the floor space, requires only 600 feet of walls, or 50 percent more material. Third, it may not be possible to use some techniques in a small-scale operation. Computers, blast furnaces, assembly lines, earth-moving equipment, and the like may be feasible only when output is sufficiently high.

These factors are perhaps what is meant by such phrases as the "advantages of large-scale or mass production." These factors, however, are inherently limited: after reaching a certain scale of operation, further expansion makes more economies impossible. (Even the arithmetical factors may be limited: as the building becomes larger, the ceiling and walls may have to be built with stronger materials.)

Set against these factors that tend to produce increasing returns to scale, economists emphasize one factor that tends to produce decreasing returns to scale: inefficiency of managing large operations. With large operations coordination and control become increasingly difficult. Information may be lost or distorted as it is transmitted from workers to supervisors to lower-level management to top-level management, and the reverse may be equally likely. Channels of communication become more complex and more difficult to monitor. Decisions require more time to make and implement. Problems of this sort occur in all large organizations, and they suggest that the managerial function can be a source of decreasing returns to scale.

The relative importance of the factors leading to increasing and decreasing returns to scale is likely to vary from industry to industry. As a general proposition, it seems likely that increasing returns to scale will be the case when the scale of operation is small, perhaps followed by an intermediate range when constant returns prevail, with decreasing returns to scale becoming important for large-scale operations. In other words, a production function can embody increasing, constant, and decreasing returns to scale at different levels of output. In fact, this condition is probably the general case.

Figure 6–9 shows isoquants reflecting such a production function. Since we are talking about returns to scale, we are interested in how output varies as we move along a ray from the origin, like 0R in the diagram. Along this ray the proportion in which labor and capital are used is constant: the ratio of capital to labor is 5 units of capital to 4 units of labor at

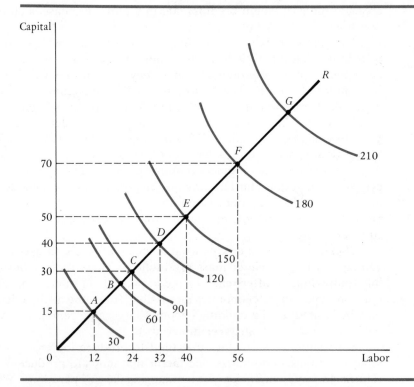

FIGURE 6–9
Returns to Scale

The spacing of isoquants indicates whether returns to scale are increasing, constant, or decreasing. From A to C there are increasing returns to scale; from C to E constant returns to scale; and from E to G decreasing returns to scale.

all points. At low rates of output, increasing returns to scale are prevalent: when labor and capital are both doubled, in moving from point *A* to point *C*, output more than doubles. Between points *C* and *E*, a range of constant returns to scale occurs: increasing both labor and capital by a third, in moving from *C* to *D*, increases output by exactly a third. Finally, beyond point *E*, decreasing returns to scale result: a 40 percent increase in inputs increases output by only 20 percent in moving from *E* to *F*. As indicated in the diagram, the spacing of isoquants along a ray indicates whether returns are increasing, constant, or decreasing.

Of course, saying that returns to scale will generally be increasing at first, then constant, and then decreasing is not saying a great deal. The exact range of output over which these relations hold is very important; as we will see in the next chapter, it helps to determine the number of firms that can survive in an industry.

Summary

This chapter deals with the relationships between the quantities of inputs used and the amount of output produced. We distinguished two relationships. In the first case the quantities of some inputs are not changed (fixed inputs) while the quantities of other inputs (variable inputs) are. This is normally a short-run output response when it is not practical to vary the quantities of some inputs. In the second case the quantities of all inputs can be varied, which is normally the case when long-run output responses are considered.

With some inputs held fixed, the total product curve shows the relationship between the quantity of the variable input and output. The important economic principle in this situation is the law of diminishing marginal returns. It holds that beyond some level, the marginal product of the variable input will decline as more of the input is used. This law implies that the total, average, and marginal product curves will have the general shapes shown in Figure 6–3.

We also discussed production isoquants, which show the relationship between inputs and output when both inputs can be varied. An isoquant shows all combinations of two inputs that will produce a given level of output. A set of isoquants is effectively a graphical representation of the firm's production function. Isoquants and indifference curves

have the same geometric characteristics. The marginal rate of technical substitution shows the technological feasibility of trading one input for another, and it is equal to the slope of an isoquant.

Finally, we discussed returns to scale, which refer to the relationship between a proportionate change in all inputs and output. If output increases in greater proportion than input use, production is said to be subject to increasing returns to scale. Constant and decreasing returns to scale are defined analogously. In general, increasing returns to scale are common at low levels of output for a firm, possibly followed by constant returns over a range; at high levels of output decreasing returns to scale will exist.

Review Questions and Problems

1. Fill in the spaces in the accompanying table.

Amount of Land	Amount of Labor	Total Output	Average Product of Labor	Marginal Product of Labor
12	0	0	—	—
12	1	75		
12	2		100	
12	3			100
12	4	380		
12	5			50
12	6		75	

2. State the law of diminishing marginal returns. How is it illustrated by the data in the table of question 1? There is a proviso to this law that certain things be held constant. What are these things? Give examples of situations where the law of diminishing marginal returns is not applicable because these "other things" are likely to vary.

*3. If the total product curve is a straight line through the origin, what do the average product and marginal product curves look like? What principle would lead you to expect that the total product curve would never have this shape?

*4. It is possible that diminishing marginal returns will set in after the very first unit of labor is employed. What do the total product, average product, and marginal product curves look like in this case?

5. Distinguish between short-run and long-run changes in output by a firm. In which case is the law of diminishing marginal returns more likely to be applicable? Why?

*6. If an employer is thinking of hiring one additional worker, will he be more concerned with the average product of labor or with the marginal product of labor? Why?

7. Define isoquant. What is measured on the axes of a diagram with isoquants? What is the relationship between the isoquant map and the production function?

8. Isoquants are downward-sloping, non-intersecting, convex curves. Explain the basis for each of these characteristics.

9. "To produce more output, we must have more of all inputs." Is this statement likely to be correct? Illustrate your answer with isoquants.

*10. When a firm uses equal amounts of labor and land, must the isoquant drawn through this point have a slope of -1? Could the isoquant have a slope of -1? If so, what would this characteristic tell us?

11. What is the marginal rate of technical substitution? How is it related to the productivities of the inputs? How is it indicated on an isoquant?

Supplementary Readings

Baumol, William. *Economic Theory and Operations Analysis*. 4th ed. Englewood Cliffs, N.J.: Prentice-Hall, 1977. Chap. 11.

Ferguson, Charles. *The Neoclassical Theory of Production and Distribution*. London: Cambridge University Press, 1969. Chaps. 1–6.

Machlup, Fritz. "On the Meaning of the Marginal Product." In *Explorations in Economics*, pp. 250–263. New York: McGraw-Hill, 1936. Reprinted in American Economic Association, *Readings in the Theory of Income Distribution*, pp. 158–174. Philadelphia: Blakiston, 1951.

Tangri, O. P. "Omissions in the Treatment of the Law of Variable Proportions." *American Economic Review*, 56 (June 1966): 484–493.

The Costs of Production
7

When a firm makes its decision about how to produce, not only must it determine what inputs are necessary to produce various levels of output, as we saw in Chapter 6, but it must also consider the costs of acquiring the inputs used to produce the product. Since production costs are important in determining a firm's output, we should understand several aspects about a firm's costs: how costs are defined (what they include), what factors affect the costs, and how costs vary with the output produced. After we have examined costs, in the next chapter we will discuss how revenue from the sale of the product is incorporated into the analysis and how costs and revenues jointly determine the profit-maximizing level of output for the competitive firm.

THE NATURE OF COSTS
7.1

Although a firm's costs of production are commonly thought of as its monetary expenses, this conception of cost is too narrow for our purposes. Since, as economists, we wish to study the way costs affect output choices, employment decisions, and the like, costs should include several factors in addition to outright monetary expenses. An example will clarify this point. Consider Mr. Dunhill, who operates a small pipe and tobacco store. He rents the premises for $10,000 a year and purchases pipes, tobacco, and related articles from wholesalers for an average of $30,000 a year. Suppose these are his only direct outlays, and his sales are $50,000 a year. What are his annual costs of operation? An accountant would only include the $10,000 rental payment and the $30,000 outlay for materials as costs. These are *explicit costs*, measured by the payments Dunhill makes to obtain these inputs, or resources. In addition to these explicit costs, however, economists would include some further costs as part of Dunhill's operating expenses.

Since Dunhill runs the store himself, he contributes his labor services to the operation, and his services involve a cost even though no contractual payment is made. This type of cost is an *implicit cost* and usually involves the use of inputs or resources owned by the owner of the operation. An obvious question follows: how should the implicit cost of Dunhill's labor be valued? The cost to Dunhill of operating his own store is the income he sacrifices by not working somewhere else. If he could earn

$25,000 working as a plumber (more precisely, if being a plumber is his best alternative job opportunity), then $25,000 measures the implicit cost associated with the use of his labor services to operate the store.

To understand why implicit costs should be regarded as a business expense, recall that our purpose is to explain how costs influence output decisions. In deciding whether to operate the store or go out of business, Dunhill will certainly be influenced by how much he could earn working somewhere else. Consequently, we must take this cost into account when attempting to understand what influences Dunhill's decision. Indeed, in this case it seems likely that he will close the store. If he stays open, the compensation for his labor is only $10,000 (revenues of $50,000 less explicit costs of $40,000), which is a good deal less than the $25,000 Dunhill could earn as a plumber. Of course, with a name like Dunhill he may choose to stay in the pipe and tobacco business (if he prefers shopkeeping to plumbing enough to offset the $15,000 financial disparity), but even so Dunhill would still take the implicit cost of his labor services into account.

In many small business operations the implicit costs associated with the owners using their own resources are an important component of total costs, and to neglect them would be a serious mistake. Consider another example: farmers not only supply their labor services to their operations but also frequently own the land and equipment they use. Implicit costs are associated with the use of the owner's land and equipment even though no explicit payment is made for the use of these resources. Land, for example, can be sold or rented: the revenue that the farmer would realize through sale or rental is sacrificed when the land is used for farming and therefore reflects an implicit cost associated with the land.

For the modern large corporation the most important implicit cost is associated with the use of the firm's productive assets, its capital. These resources are ultimately owned by the stockholders, who have provided investment funds to the corporation and expect to receive a return on their investment. Let's suppose that the stockholders could have invested their funds elsewhere and earned an annual return of 10 percent. Thus, if the corporation does not pay (in dividends or higher market valuation of the stock) at least 10 percent on the invested capital, the stockholders have incentive to withdraw their investments (by selling their stock) and invest where they will receive a 10 percent return. Although there is no contractual agreement, an implicit cost is associated with the firm's using its own (or, more precisely, its stockholders') capital: the same resources could have earned 10 percent if invested elsewhere. Viewing the rate of return that could be obtained from investing elsewhere as an implicit cost means that an average return on investment is treated as part of the firm's normal production costs. That is, a normal accounting profit is viewed as a cost of operation just like wage payments and rent.

In economic analysis a firm's costs of production are the sum of explicit and implicit costs. Explicit costs arise from transactions between the firm and other parties in which the firm purchases inputs or the services of inputs; they are what are usually counted as costs in conventional accounting statements and include labor payroll, raw materials costs, insurance, electricity, interest on debt, and so on. Implicit costs are the costs associated with the use of the firm's own resources and reflect the fact that these resources could be employed elsewhere. Although implicit costs are difficult to measure, we must take them into account in analyzing the actions taken by a firm.

The Concept of Opportunity Cost

The *opportunity cost* of using some resource in a particular way is defined as the value of that resource in its next best alternative use. This definition emphasizes that a resource can be used to produce many things: steel can be used to make cars, bicycles, refrigerators, houses, or many other goods; mechanical engineers can be used in the production of roads, airplanes, textiles, and toys, among other things. But when a resource is used to produce one good, it can't be used to produce something else. For example, when we use steel to make an automobile, we sacrifice other products that could have been produced.

What do opportunity costs have to do with the firm's production costs? We cannot fully answer this question at this point in our analysis except to observe briefly that in a competitive market, the firm's production costs, the sum of implicit and explicit costs, tend to equal the opportunity costs of the resources it uses. To see why, consider a firm's employment of workers. The firm must pay workers enough so they don't leave and work elsewhere. If the firm's wage is less than a worker's opportunity cost — what the worker could earn in the next best alternative job — the worker will quit and take the better-paying alternative. Thus, to hire a worker who could work elsewhere for $15,000, the firm must pay at least $15,000, and this wage is the opportunity cost of the worker's services.

This discussion is somewhat sketchy since it draws on conclusions of analyses we have not yet developed, such as how input prices, like wage rates, are determined. When we encounter the concept of opportunity costs in later chapters, its relationship to the firm's production costs will become clearer. Right now, the important point to remember is that the firm's production costs tend to equal the opportunity costs of the resources it uses.

Before ending this discussion, it should be emphasized that the notion of opportunity cost has even wider applicability. The very concept of opportunity costs forces us to recognize that *costs are not money payments but sacrificed alternatives.* Even if a firm somehow acquires resources without paying for them, there is still a real cost in using these resources; namely, other things that could have been produced are sacrificed. This point is relevant to the question of the military draft, for instance. Some people have argued that the United States can't afford a volunteer army in which wages are high enough to attract competent enlistees. Instead, they suggest paying lower wages and drafting the required number of recruits. The problem with this argument is that it identifies the money wage payment as the relevant cost. Clearly this position is incorrect when workers are conscripted. The cost of military personnel is the value of goods and services the draftees could produce if employed in the civilian economy. Paying military personnel less does not reduce that cost; it just shifts the cost of supporting a military force from the taxpayers to the draftees, who are forced to work for less than they could earn if they were employed in the civilian sector.

SHORT-RUN COSTS OF PRODUCTION
7.2

A firm's production costs will vary with its rate of output. Exactly how costs are likely to vary with output in the short run is discussed in this section and in Section 7.3. First, though, we will work through a numerical example that shows how short-run costs vary with output for a hypothetical firm. For the moment, it is not essential to understand why costs vary with output exactly as they do in the example; our purpose is to introduce the terminology and explain the relationships between the various measures of cost.

Measures of Short-Run Costs

Recall that the short run is a period of time over which the firm is unable to vary all its inputs. Therefore, some inputs are effectively fixed in the short run while some are variable. There are, however, costs associated with the use of both fixed and variable inputs. Let's examine Table 7–1, which shows how production costs vary at different rates of output for a hypothetical firm.

TOTAL FIXED COSTS.   *Total fixed costs* (TFC) are the costs incurred by the firm that do not depend on how much output it produces. These costs are associated with the fixed inputs the firm cannot vary in the short run, normally its plant and equipment. They include items such as the return on its own capital, interest on borrowed funds, fire insurance premiums, property taxes, and the like. (Note that some of these costs will be implicit costs, such as the costs of the firm's own capital.) The fixed costs will be the same regardless of how much output the firm produces; in particular, if the firm shuts down and produces nothing, it still incurs its total fixed costs. In Table 7–1 the firm has total fixed costs of $60 per month.

TOTAL VARIABLE COSTS.   *Total variable costs* (TVC) are the costs incurred by the firm that depend on how much output it produces. These costs are associated with the variable inputs: more output requires the use of more

TABLE 7–1
Short-Run Costs of a Hypothetical Firm

Output (units per month) (1)	Total Fixed Cost ($ per month) (2)	Total Variable Cost ($ per month) (3)	Total Cost ($ per month) (4) = (2) + (3)	Marginal Cost ($ per unit) (5)	Average Fixed Cost ($ per unit) (6) = (2) ÷ (1)	Average Variable Cost ($ per unit) (7) = (3) ÷ (1)	Average Total Cost ($ per unit) (8) = (4) ÷ (1)
1	$60	$ 30	$ 90	$30	$60.00	$30.00	$90.00
2	60	49	109	19	30.00	24.50	54.50
3	60	65	125	16	20.00	21.70	41.70
4	60	80	140	15	15.00	20.00	35.00
5	60	100	160	20	12.00	20.00	32.00
6	60	124	184	24	10.00	20.70	30.70
7	60	150	210	26	8.60	21.40	30.00
8	60	180	240	30	7.50	22.50	30.00
9	60	215	275	35	6.70	23.90	30.60
10	60	255	315	40	6.00	25.50	31.50
11	60	300	360	45	5.50	27.30	32.80
12	60	360	420	60	5.00	30.00	35.00

variable inputs, so total variable costs rise with output. To produce more in the short run, the firm must hire more workers, use more electricity, purchase more raw materials, and so on — all of which add to costs as output rises. Total variable costs are shown in column 3 of the table.

Five other measures of cost are identified in the table. Before looking at them, we should emphasize that they are all derived from the total fixed and total variable cost relationships. No new types of costs are involved: everything that we are assuming about the firm's costs is shown in columns 2 and 3. The remaining columns are just different ways of presenting the same basic cost information in a more convenient and workable form.

TOTAL COST.   *Total cost* (TC) is the sum of total fixed and total variable costs for each output level. For example, at 5 units of output, total fixed costs are $60, and total variable costs are $100, so total costs are $160. Total cost identifies the cost of all the inputs, fixed and variable, used to produce a certain output. Since total variable costs rise with output, so do total costs.

MARGINAL COST.   *Marginal cost* (MC) is the change in total cost that results from a one-unit change in output. When output increases from 7 to 8 units, for example, total cost rises from $210 to $240: the $30 increase in total cost is the marginal cost of producing the eighth unit. Marginal cost can also be defined as the change in total variable cost that results from a one-unit change in output because the only part of total cost that rises with output is variable cost. Basically, then, the marginal cost relationship shows how much additional cost a firm will incur if it increases output by one unit, or how much cost saving it will realize if it reduces output by a unit. For many purposes the concept of marginal cost is the most important cost concept.

Finally, there are three measures of average cost per unit of output.

AVERAGE FIXED COST.   *Average fixed cost* (AFC) is total fixed cost divided by the amount of output. Since fixed cost is constant, the greater the output, the lower will be the average fixed cost per unit of output. For example, the average fixed cost associated with the first unit of output is $60, but it falls to $5 for the twelfth unit.

AVERAGE VARIABLE COST.   *Average variable cost* (AVC) is total variable cost divided by the amount of output. If 8 units are produced, total variable cost is $180, so average variable cost is $180/8, or $22.50 per unit.

AVERAGE TOTAL COST.   *Average total cost* (ATC) is total cost divided by the output. We can also define it as the sum of average fixed cost and average variable cost. At 8 units of output, for instance, total cost is $240, so the average total cost is $30. Alternatively, average total cost is also the sum of average fixed cost, $7.50, and average variable cost, $22.50.

So far we have simply defined the various measures of cost and explained the arithmetical relationships among them. Having covered these matters, we can now turn to the important question of what factors determine the exact way cost varies with output for the various cost measures.

Behind Cost Relationships

A firm's costs are determined by its production function, which identifies the input combinations that can produce a given output, and the prices that must be paid for these inputs. In the short run the production function relates output to the quantity of variable inputs; fixed inputs do not vary. Recall that in a short-run setting the law of diminishing marginal returns is relevant. It specifies that increasing the variable input or inputs will, beyond some point, result in smaller and smaller increases in total output. This assumption is the only one we need to make about production relationships in the short run, and, as we will see, it largely determines how total variable costs vary with output.

The production function indicates how much of the variable input or inputs the firm needs to produce alternative levels of output. Since the total variable cost is the total amount of money the firm must spend to acquire the necessary quantity of the variable input, the price per unit of the variable input is crucial in determining the firm's short-run costs. We will assume that the firm can employ any quantity of the variable input at a given price per unit.

Figure 7–1 illustrates how these two factors — the law of diminishing marginal returns and a fixed price per unit of the variable input — combine to determine the way total variable cost varies with output. The variable input is hours of labor, and the total product curve (TP) relates the quantity of hours worked to total output. Note that the shape of the TP curve reflects diminishing marginal returns beyond point *A* (where the slope of the curve reaches a maximum).

The total product curve shows the amount of labor used to produce each level of output, and if labor is the only variable input, the cost to the firm of hiring labor is the total variable cost of production. Total variable cost can also be measured on the horizontal axis by multiplying each quantity of labor by its unit cost, here assumed to be $8 per hour. For example, from the TP curve we know that producing 200 units of output requires 40 hours of labor, and at $8 per hour, the total variable cost associated with 200 units of output is $320.

Thus, when inputs are measured in terms of their cost, the same curve relates input to output and cost to output. *The shape of the TVC curve is therefore determined by the shape of the TP curve, which in turn reflects diminishing marginal returns.* This explains why understanding the law of diminishing marginal returns is important; it ultimately determines

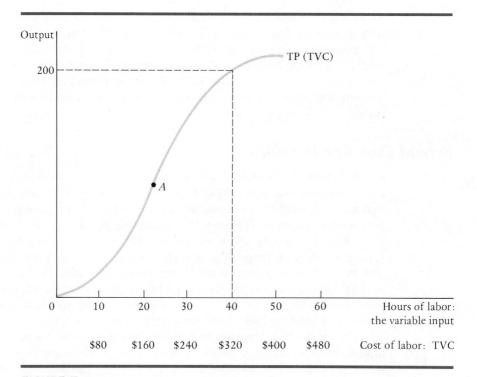

FIGURE 7-1

From Total Product to Total Variable Cost

The quantity of the variable input is related to output through the total product curve. The total product curve (TP) can be transformed into the total variable cost curve (TVC) by multiplying each quantity of the variable input by its per unit price ($8).

how total variable costs are related to output. In addition, the law also determines the behavior of marginal cost and average variable cost since they are derived from the TVC relationship. We will discuss these relationships in more detail in the next section.

By convention we draw the total variable cost curve with TVC on the vertical axis and output on the horizontal axis, the reverse of the situation in Figure 7–1, which is why the TVC curve may not look right at first glance. To see its more conventional appearance, refer to Figure 7–2a, where the axes of Figure 7–1 have been interchanged.

THE SHORT-RUN COST CURVES
7.3

Now let's take a more careful look at the relationship between cost and output by using the firm's cost curves. Figure 7–2a shows the firm's total cost curves, and Figure 7–2b shows the per-unit cost curves. The curves

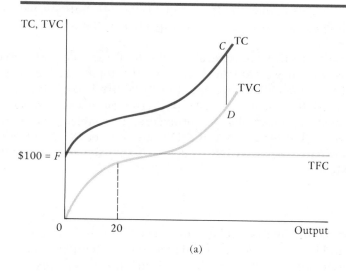

(a)

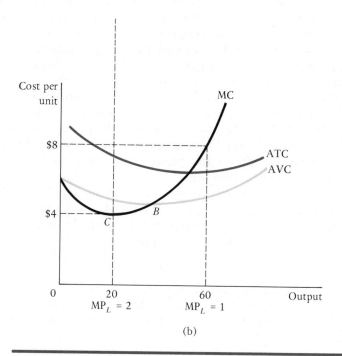

(b)

FIGURE 7-2

Short-run Total Cost Curves and Per-unit Cost Curves

(a) Adding total fixed costs (TFC) of 0F to the TVC curve yields the short-run total cost curve. (b) Three per-unit cost curves — average total cost (ATC), average variable cost (AVC), and marginal cost (MC) — are derived from the total cost curves.

have the shapes implied by the data in Table 7–1, but now we wish to see why all short-run cost curves are expected to have these same general shapes.

Little more need be said about the total variable cost curve. In the previous section we explained the way the total variable cost curve is derived from the production function. Total fixed cost, TFC, is a horizontal line at $100, indicating a $100 fixed cost regardless of output. The TC curve shows total cost, the sum of fixed and variable costs. Note that the TC curve is $100 higher than the TVC curve at each rate of output. The vertical distance between TVC and TC is total fixed cost: both *OF* and *DC* equal $100.

Marginal Cost

Most economic analysis relies more heavily on the per-unit cost curves shown in Figure 7–2b, so we will devote more attention to them. Examine the marginal cost curve first. It is U-shaped, with the cost of additional units of output first falling, reaching a minimum, and then rising. Marginal cost falls at first because the fixed plant and equipment are not designed to produce very low rates of output, and production is very expensive when output is low. Consider a striking example: the marginal cost of printing a second newspaper may be trivial compared with the marginal cost of the first (which included setting the type). Declining marginal cost comes to an end at some point (20 units of output in Figure 7–2b), and thereafter marginal cost rises with output. Eventually marginal cost must rise because the plant will ultimately be overutilized as output expands beyond the level for which it was designed. At that point and possibly before, marginal costs begin to rise, and each additional unit costs more than the previous one.

The shape of the marginal cost curve is attributable to the law of diminishing marginal returns. To see exactly why, recall that marginal cost (MC) can be defined as the change in total variable cost (ΔTVC) that is associated with a small change in output (ΔQ):

$$MC = \Delta TVC/\Delta Q.$$

A one-unit increase in output, for example, requires some additional amount of the variable input (labor), ΔL, to be employed. Using more labor increases the total variable cost by ΔL times the wage rate w. Thus, we have

$$MC = \Delta TVC/\Delta Q = w\,(\Delta L)/\Delta Q = w/MP_L$$

because the marginal product of labor (MP_L) equals $\Delta Q/\Delta L$, so the reciprocal, $\Delta L/\Delta Q$, equals $1/MP_L$.

This relationship states that short-run marginal cost equals the price of the variable input (in this case the wage rate) divided by its marginal product. Let's check to see why this makes sense. Suppose at some level of output, $w = \$8$, and $MP_L = 2$ units of output. If 1 unit of labor increases output by 2 units (MP_L), then 1 additional unit of output requires 1/2 unit of labor, at a cost of $4. So the marginal cost is $4, or $w/MP_L = \$8/2$.

Because of the law of diminishing marginal returns, the marginal product of labor varies with the amount of output and, therefore, so must marginal cost. At low levels of output MP_L is rising, so, correspondingly, marginal cost (w/MP_L) must be falling. When MP_L reaches a maximum, then MC must be at a minimum. This occurs at 20 units of output in the diagram, the rate of output at which marginal returns begin to fall. At output levels where MP_L is declining, MC must be rising. For example, at an output of 60 in the diagram, MP_L has declined to 1 unit of output. Producing another unit of output, therefore, requires 1 more unit of labor at a cost of $8, so the marginal cost is $8.

If the marginal product of the variable input rises (at low rates of output) and then falls, the marginal cost curve will first fall and then rise. Thus, the law of diminishing marginal returns lies behind the MC curve. Indeed, it is possible to restate what diminishing marginal returns mean in a way that makes this obvious. In the region of diminishing marginal returns, each additional unit of the variable input adds less to total output. That is, each additional unit of output requires more of the variable input than the previous unit required. More of the variable input per unit of output means higher costs, so marginal cost will rise in the region where marginal product is falling.

Average Cost

There are three average cost curves. To begin, let's look at average variable cost in Figure 7–2b; average variable cost is equal to total variable cost divided by output. For the very first unit of output, total variable cost, average variable cost, and marginal cost are all equal. (See Table 7–1.) Then marginal cost falls, causing the average cost to fall too. In fact, average cost will decline as long as marginal cost lies below it and pulls it down. Put differently, per-unit production costs tend to fall at low rates of output (remember the second newspaper), but beyond some point (B in the diagram), average variable cost will rise.

The physical production relationships implied by the law of diminishing marginal returns are also responsible for the shape of the average variable cost curve. Average variable cost is total variable cost divided by output:

$$AVC = TVC/Q.$$

Total variable cost is simply the total amount of the variable input (L) times its unit cost (w). Thus, we have

$$AVC = TVC/Q = w(L)/Q = w/AP_L$$

since the average product of labor (AP_L) equals Q/L (total output divided by total labor), so the reciprocal, L/Q, is equal to $1/AP_L$.

In the previous chapter we saw that the law of diminishing marginal returns leads to an average product curve shaped like an inverted U; that is, average product rises, reaches a maximum, and then falls. As a result, the AVC curve must be U-shaped. Over the region where AP_L is rising, w/AP_L (AVC) is falling. Similarly, when AP_L is falling, AVC must be rising. Point B, where AVC is at a minimum, therefore corresponds to the point at which AP_L is at a maximum.

The law of diminishing marginal returns dictates the shape of both the MC curve and the AVC curve — not a surprising conclusion since we saw that it determines TVC, and MC and AVC are derived from TVC. The shapes of the per-unit cost curves reflect the underlying physical requirements of production. As fewer units of the variable input are required per unit of output (on average for the AVC curve and for marginal changes on the MC curve), the per-unit costs fall. Conversely, they rise when physical production requirements per unit of output increase.

There are two other average cost curves, average fixed cost (AFC) and average total cost (ATC). AFC declines over the entire range of output as the fixed amount is spread over ever larger rates of output. The AFC curve is not drawn explicitly in Figure 7–2b. The ATC curve shows average total cost. It is the sum of AFC and AVC and measures the average unit cost of all inputs, both fixed and variable. The ATC curve must also be U-shaped although its minimum point is located at a higher rate of output than the minimum point of AVC. This occurs because ATC = AVC + AFC, and at the output where AVC is at a minimum, AFC is still falling, so the sum of AVC and AFC will continue to fall beyond that point. At some point, however, the rising AVC offsets the falling AFC, and thereafter ATC rises. Finally, since AVC + AFC = ATC, the average fixed cost is the vertical distance between ATC and AVC. Note that the vertical distance becomes increasingly smaller as more output is produced.

Marginal-Average Relationships

All marginal curves are related to their average curves in the same way. Since we will encounter average and marginal cost curves frequently in later chapters, the relationships bear repeating here.

When marginal cost is below average cost, average cost will decline. (Equivalently, when average cost is declining, marginal cost must be below average cost.) If average cost is currently $10, and producing one more unit costs $5, the average cost of all units will be brought down.

When marginal cost is above average cost, average cost rises. (Equivalently, when average cost is rising, marginal cost must be above average cost.) If average cost is currently $10, and producing another unit costs $15, the average cost of all units will be pulled up.

When average cost is at a minimum, marginal cost is equal to average cost. This is already implicit in the relationships above, but we can explain it in a different way. At the point where average cost is at a minimum, the curve is essentially flat over a small range of output. When the curve is neither falling nor rising, a small change in output does not change average cost. If an additional unit of output leaves the average unchanged, the marginal cost must equal average cost. For example, if average cost is $10, and it is still $10 after output increases by a unit, the marginal cost of that unit must also be $10.

The Geometry of Cost Curves

The graphical derivation of the average and marginal cost curves from a total cost curve closely parallels the derivation of average and marginal product curves from a total product curve explained in Section 6.5. As a result, the description here will be brief. Note that although we use the short-run total variable cost (TVC) curve here, the same procedure applies to the derivation of the related average cost (AC) and marginal cost (MC) curves from any total cost curve, either short-run or long-run.

Figure 7–3a shows a total variable cost curve; Figure 7–3b shows the average variable cost and marginal cost curves derived from it. To derive AVC from the TVC curve, we draw a ray from the origin to each point on the TVC curve: the slope of the ray measures AVC at that rate of output. At output Q_1, for example, the ray $0A$ has a slope equal to $AQ_1/0Q_1$, or $7 per unit ($105/15). The slope of the ray in Figure 7–3a is shown by the height to the AVC curve in Figure 7–3b. The flatter the ray from the origin, the lower is the AVC. For example, AVC is at a minimum ($5) when output is Q_2, since the ray $0C$ is the flattest ray that touches the TVC curve. Thus, AVC falls as output increases from zero to Q_2 and then rises at greater rates of output.

Marginal cost is shown by the slope of the total variable cost curve at each rate of output. At Q_3, for instance, producing another unit of output adds $8 to costs, as indicated by the slope of TVC at point D. At Q_3 in Figure 7–3b, marginal cost is $8 per unit. Starting from the origin, the TVC curve becomes flatter as we move up it to point B, implying that MC is falling, and beyond point B, it becomes steeper, indicating that MC is rising. At point C, where average variable cost is at a minimum, marginal cost equals average cost.

Cost Curves and the Court

Cost curves are more than geometry that economists use to befuddle students; sometimes they resolve important legal battles. A case in point is a suit brought by William Inglis and Sons Baking Company against ITT Continental Baking Company, a subsidiary of ITT.[1] Inglis charged that Continental (makers of Wonder Bread) had engaged in predatory pricing,

---

[1] *William Inglis & Sons v. ITT Continental Baking,* 461 F. Supplement 410 (1978), pp. 411–425.

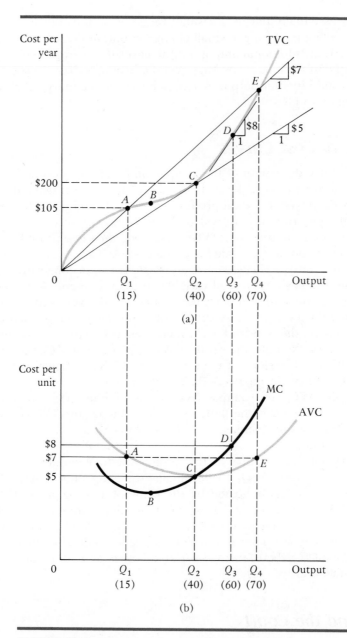

FIGURE 7-3

Graphical Derivation of Average Cost and Marginal Cost Curves

(a) Average variable cost equals the slope of a ray from the origin to a point on the total variable cost curve. For example, at point A, AVC equals the slope of the ray 0A, or $7 per unit. Marginal cost is the slope of the TVC curve at each point. For example, at point D marginal cost is $8 per unit. (b) The entire average variable cost and marginal cost curves are shown here.

driving Inglis out of business. Predatory pricing is an illegal business practice in which a firm temporarily sells at a very low price, to eliminate competitors from the field, and then raises prices. The issue was whether Continental had engaged in these tactics.

According to legal precedent, predatory pricing occurs when a firm sells at a price below short-run marginal cost. (Whether this definition is adequate proof of predatory pricing need not concern us here.) Because of the difficulty in estimating marginal cost, some courts have held that average variable cost *may* be used as evidence of marginal cost, because it is likely to approximate marginal cost. Inglis presented evidence that Continental produced bread at an AVC of 20.6 cents in 1972 but sold it at a price of 17.2 cents. On the basis of this evidence, a lower court found that Continental had engaged in predatory pricing and a jury awarded Inglis damages of $5,048,000.

On appeal, U.S. District Court Judge Spencer Williams (who had had some training in economics) overturned the lower court ruling. He argued that proof of a price below AVC is not evidence of a price below MC when there is reason to believe that the firm is operating on the downward-sloping part of its AVC curve. Because the California baking industry was characterized by surplus capacity at that time, it was evident that firms were not operating at the lowest possible average cost, and so they were on the downward-sloping portion of their AVC curves.

In his decision Judge Williams drew a diagram like Figure 7–4. Suppose output is Q_1. Inglis had argued that AVC (at P_2) was greater than price for Continental. Judge Williams used this diagram to show that price could be below AVC and still be above MC: this would be true for any price between P_1 and P_2. By a clever use of geometry, Judge Williams found that Inglis had not shown that price was below MC, which the law required for proof of predatory pricing.[2]

Postscript on Cost

It is easy to get bogged down learning seven different measures of cost (three total, three average, and one marginal), their graphical representations, and the geometrical relationships among the curves. Keep in mind, though, that only *two* crucial economic principles are involved: production relationships reflecting the law of diminishing marginal returns and the firm's ability to hire additional inputs at constant prices. All the rest involves nothing more than patiently drawing out the logical implications of these two principles and representing them in a form convenient for subsequent analysis.

[2] Judge Williams cannot be given A+ on his use of cost curves. He drew his diagram to show AVC and MC differing for the first unit of output (vertical intercepts of his MC and AVC curves occurred at different points). As Table 7–1 and our diagrams show, this is incorrect. This error does not undermine the basis of his decision, however.

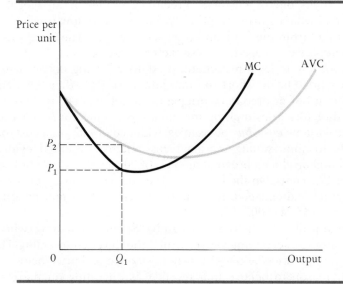

- FIGURE 7-4

When Price Is Below AVC, Must It Be Below MC?

In his decision Judge Williams drew a diagram like this one to prove his point.
When a firm is operating on the downward-sloping portion of its AVC curve, AVC
is greater than MC. Thus, even if price is less than AVC, it can still be greater
than MC.

LONG-RUN COSTS OF PRODUCTION
7.4

In the long run a firm has sufficient time to adjust its use of all inputs to
produce output in the least costly way. Because a firm can augment plant
and equipment by constructing additional facilities or by purchasing already existing facilities, all inputs are variable. Our first task is to see how
a firm will choose to combine inputs in its production process when all
factors are variable.

Isocost Lines

Consider a firm that uses just two inputs, capital (its plant and equipment)
and labor, to produce its product. We have seen how the firm's production function can be represented by isoquants, and three are shown in
Figure 7–5. The firm's costs of production can also be represented by isocost lines. An *isocost line* (equal-cost line) identifies all the combinations
of capital and labor that can be purchased at a given total cost. The diagram shows three isocost lines corresponding to three different levels of
total cost.

Since the isocost line is a new relationship, let's take a careful look at one. Look at the middle isocost line in the diagram. Suppose a firm has total funds of TC_2 to pay its inputs. The prices the firm must pay for inputs are w for labor (the wage rate) and r for capital (the rental rate for plant or equipment per time period, which may be an implicit cost if the firm owns the assets). If the firm devotes all the funds to capital, it can employ TC_2/r units of capital, leaving no money to hire workers. Thus, TC_2/r is the vertical intercept of the isocost line. Alternatively, if the firm devotes all the funds to hiring labor, it can hire TC_2/w units of labor, leaving no money for capital, so TC_2/w is the horizontal intercept. All the intermediate positions on the line show the combinations of labor and capital the firm can hire at a cost of exactly TC_2.

The slope of an isocost line is (minus) the ratio of input prices, w/r, indicating the relative prices of inputs. If, for example, the wage rate is twice the rental rate of capital ($w/r = 2$), then hiring one more unit of labor, without incurring any additional cost, means the firm must employ

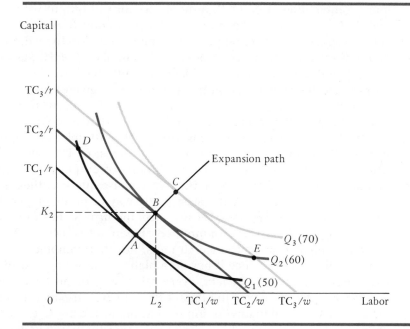

FIGURE 7–5

The Long-run Expansion Path

The point of tangency between an isoquant and an isocost line indicates the least costly combination of inputs that can produce the specified output. For example. employing $0L_2$ and $0K_2$ is the cheapest way to produce 60 units of output. The expansion path, which shows the least costly way of producing each level of output when all inputs can be varied. is formed by connecting all points of tangency.

two units less of capital. From these remarks it can be seen that there is a close analogy between the consumer's budget line and a firm's isocost line. In one respect the analogy breaks down. Consumers are usually restricted to operating within a given budget, but firms are not. Firms can expand their use of all inputs and finance the expansion by selling the increased output. The total cost of operation of a firm is not a constant but varies with output, which explains why there are three isocost lines in the diagram (among the many that could be drawn) and not just one.

Least Costly Input Combinations

Analyzing isocost lines and isoquants together allows us to determine what combinations of inputs the firm will actually use to produce various rates of output. Suppose the firm plans to spend exactly TC_2 to hire inputs. From among the input combinations it can employ (shown by the middle isocost line), the firm will clearly want to hire the combination of labor and capital that yields the greatest output. The firm could employ the input combination at point D, but only 50 units of output would be produced. By using less capital and more labor at point B, however, the firm could produce 60 units of output at the same total cost. Indeed, 60 units of output is the maximum output possible at a total cost of TC_2, as indicated by the fact that higher isoquants like Q_3 lie entirely above the isocost line. To produce the maximum output possible at a given total cost, a firm should operate at a point where an isocost line is tangent to the highest isoquant attainable: Q_2 is tangent to the isocost line at point B.

In the same manner, it is easy to see that 70 units of output is the maximum output possible at the higher total cost of TC_3, where the firm would operate at point C. Similarly, 50 units of output is the maximum output possible at a total cost of TC_1. We can also interpret these points in a different way: they show the least costly way of producing each specified level of output. Suppose, for instance, the firm wishes to produce 60 units of output: it must hire an input combination that lies on Q_2. It could operate at point E and produce 60 units, but that combination of labor and capital costs TC_3, since it lies on a higher isocost line and requires a larger outlay than TC_2. In fact, every other way of producing 60 units involves a higher total cost than point B. Point B, consequently, identifies the least costly combination of inputs that the firm can use to produce 60 units of output. *Points of tangency show the maximum output attainable at a given cost as well as the minimum cost necessary to produce that output.*

Interpreting the Tangency Points

Let's look at the tangency points more closely. At the tangencies the isoquants and isocost lines have the same slopes. Recall that the slope of an isoquant is the marginal rate of technical substitution, MRTS, and the slope of the isocost line is the ratio of the input prices. Therefore, when a firm produces an output in the least costly way, it will satisfy the condition

$$\text{MRTS}_{LK} = w/r.$$

This condition indicates that the firm will adjust its employment of inputs in such a way that the rate at which one input can be traded for another in production (MRTS_{LK}) will equal the rate at which one input can be substituted for the other in the input markets (w/r).

Let's investigate why this equality holds. Recall that the marginal rate of technical substitution equals the ratio of the marginal products of the inputs. Consequently, we can write the expression above as

$$\text{MP}_L/\text{MP}_K = w/r.$$

Rearranging terms, we obtain

$$\text{MP}_L/w = \text{MP}_K/r.$$

The last equality is equivalent to the tangency condition and indicates that to minimize costs, a firm should employ inputs in such a way that the marginal product per dollar's worth of all inputs is equal. To illustrate, suppose the firm is employing inputs at a point where $\text{MP}_L = 8$ (units of output) and $\text{MP}_K = 2$. The wage rate of labor is \$4, and the rental cost of capital is \$2. In this case $\text{MP}_L/w = 8/\$4 = 2/\$1$, implying that an additional dollar spent on labor will produce 2 more units of output. For capital, $\text{MP}_K/r = 2/\$2 = 1/\$1$, indicating that an additional dollar spent on capital will produce only one more unit of output. For this allocation of inputs, $\text{MP}_L/w > \text{MP}_K/r$; that is, a dollar's worth of labor adds more to output than does a dollar's worth of capital. The firm is not producing as much output as it could given its costs (or, equivalently, it is not producing the current output at the lowest possible cost). If the firm spends \$1 less on capital, it loses 1 unit of output ($\text{MP}_K/r = 1$), but spending this dollar on labor increases output by 2 units ($\text{MP}_L/w = 2$). So on balance output will rise by 1 unit with no change in costs.

Whenever MP_L/w is greater than MP_K/r, the firm can increase output without increasing production costs by shifting outlays from capital, where output per dollar's worth is low, to labor, where output per dollar's worth is higher. This shifting should continue until the terms are equal. (Hiring more labor tends to reduce its MP, and hiring less capital tends to increase its MP, so eventually the two ratios will be equal.) Note that the initial situation described could be shown in Figure 7–5 by a point like *D*, since at that point $\text{MRTS}_{LK} > w/r$.

The Expansion Path

The points of tangency in Figure 7–5 show the least costly way of producing each indicated output. Producing Q_2 as cheaply as possible, for instance, involves hiring L_2 units of labor and K_2 units of capital. The line formed by connecting these tangency points is the firm's *expansion path*. It identifies the least costly input combination for each rate of output and will generally slope upward, implying that the firm will expand the use of both inputs (in the long-run setting) as it increases output. Note that input prices are assumed to remain constant as the firm varies its output along the expansion path.

The expansion path is closely related to the long-run cost curves of the firm. In fact, it contains essentially the same information. The expansion path shows the lowest long-run total cost at which each output can be produced. For example, the firm can produce Q_1 for a long-run total cost of TC_1, Q_2 for TC_2, and so on. This information is usually portrayed explicitly by the firm's long-run total cost curve.

LONG-RUN COST CURVES
7.5

In many respects the firm's long-run cost curves are easier to handle than short-run cost curves. In the short run we must distinguish among three total cost curves: total fixed cost, total variable cost, and total (combined) cost. Since all inputs are variable in the long run, there is only one long-run total cost curve. There is also only one long-run average cost curve, in contrast to three in the short run.

Figure 7–6a shows a long-run total cost curve; Figure 7–6b shows the associated marginal and average cost curves. Since the graphical derivation of the AC and MC curves from the TC curve is the same for long-run curves and short-run curves (see Figure 7–3), we will not repeat it here.

Our primary concern now is to explain why the curves have the shapes they do. We have drawn the TC curve to imply a U-shaped long-run average cost curve, but why would the long-run average cost curve have this shape? With the short-run average variable cost curve, the law of diminishing marginal returns was responsible for its U shape. In the long run there are generally no fixed inputs, so the law is not directly applicable.

Nonetheless, just as the physical relationship between inputs and output underlies the short-run curves, it also underlies the long-run curves. In the long run, however, returns to scale are the factors that determine how output varies when all inputs are varied in proportion. As we explained in the previous chapter, increasing returns to scale are likely to be common at low rates of output, while decreasing returns to scale are likely to prevail at high output levels. If this is the case, the long-run average cost curve must have a U shape.

Let's see why increasing returns to scale imply a declining average cost per unit of output. Suppose 10 units of capital ($10K$) and 15 units of labor ($15L$) will produce 20 units of output: $10K + 15L = 20$. With increasing returns to scale, a proportionate increase in inputs increases output more than in proportion. So suppose doubling inputs more than doubles output; that is, $20K + 30L = 50$. Note what this implies. When output is 20, the average amount of capital per unit of output is $0.5K$, and the average amount of labor is $0.75L$. At 50 units of output average input

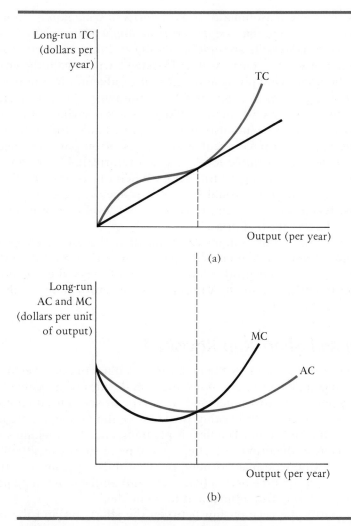

Long-run TC (dollars per year)

TC

Output (per year)

(a)

Long-run AC and MC (dollars per unit of output)

MC

AC

Output (per year)

(b)

FIGURE 7–6
Long-run Total and Per-unit Cost Curves

(a) The long-run total cost shows the minimum cost at which each rate of output may be produced, just as the expansion path does. (b) The long-run marginal cost and average cost curves are derived from the total cost curve in the same way the short-run per-unit curves are derived from the short-run total cost curves.

requirements have fallen to 0.4*K* and 0.6*L*. Increasing returns to scale mean that at higher output levels, each unit of output requires (on average) a smaller quantity of all inputs. Since inputs are available at fixed prices, however, smaller average input requirements imply smaller average unit costs. *Therefore, increasing returns to scale imply that average unit cost is falling.*

By the same reasoning, *constant returns to scale imply a constant average cost, and decreasing returns to scale imply a rising average cost.* Insofar as returns to scale are first increasing and thereafter decreasing, the long-run average cost curve will be U-shaped. Once again the cost curves reflect the underlying physical realities of production by the firm.

While a general U shape is typical for most long-run average cost curves, the average cost curve could have a somewhat different shape. Studies by several economists have suggested that for some firms, increasing returns to scale occur at low rates of output, but once output reaches a certain threshold level, constant returns hold over an extended region before decreasing returns set in. When this is true, the firm's long-run average cost curve would have this shape: ⌣_____⌣ . When average cost reaches a minimum, it stays at that level over a wide range of output before it begins to rise.

Finally, we should emphasize again that these cost curves include both explicit and implicit costs. In particular, a return on the firm's own capital is part of unit production costs even though there is no explicit contract requiring payment. A normal rate of return is one of the operating costs of the firm.

The Long Run and Short Run Revisited

It is convenient to think of the long run as a planning or investment horizon. In making long-run decisions, the firm decides what scale of plant to build or purchase, how much and what type of specialized equipment to install, whether to train existing workers for the new equipment or hire new workers, and so on. The firm is planning ahead in making such decisions. In effect, the firm is selecting what type of short-run situation it will be in later. Once the plant is built, the firm must operate with that fixed input for a certain time period (the short run) until enough time passes for a subsequent long-run adjustment to be made.

To clarify the relationship between the short run and the long run, suppose there are only five scales of plant the firm can build, and associated with each plant size is a short-run average total cost curve. Figure 7–7 shows the five short-run average cost curves as SAC_1, SAC_2, and so on. (When it is necessary to distinguish between short-run and long-run cost curves, the short-run curves will be prefixed with an S and the long-run curves with an L.) The firm can choose only one plant size: which will it be? The size of the plant depends on what output the firm expects will be appropriate — which, of course, depends on demand conditions not yet considered. Suppose, however, that the firm believes Q_1 is the appropriate output. The firm could build the smallest-sized plant (SAC_1) and produce Q_1 at a unit cost of $5.00, or it could build the next larger plant (SAC_2) and produce at a unit cost of $5.50. Of course, the firm will build the plant that permits it to produce Q_1 at the lowest average (and hence total) cost, in this instance the smallest-sized plant.

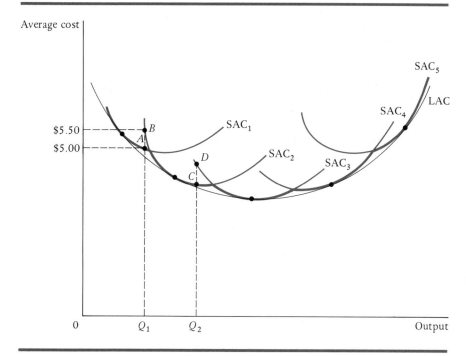

FIGURE 7–7

Relationship Between Short-run and Long-run Average Cost Curves

When the firm has only five scales of plant to choose from, the long-run average cost curve is the heavy scalloped portion of the five SAC curves. When there are intermediate scales of plant, the long-run average cost curve becomes the smooth U-shaped LAC curve.

The long-run average cost curve is defined as the lowest average cost attainable when all inputs are variable; that is, when any plant size can be constructed. In this case, with only five options, point A on SAC_1 is one point on the long-run average cost curve, since it shows the lowest unit cost for Q_1. Similarly, point C on SAC_2 is a second point on the long-run cost curve. With only five options the entire LAC curve is shown as the darker scalloped sections of the SAC curves, since each of these segments indicates the lowest unit cost possible for the corresponding level of output.

Once the firm builds the plant, its options in the immediate future will be dictated by the SAC curve selected when the long-run decision was implemented. If the firm builds the smallest-sized plant, it is temporarily stuck with that decision even if Q_1 turns out to be an inappropriate level of output after all. In that event the firm must determine whether to make another long-run decision to change its scale of operations.

In general, a firm will have many more than five scales of plant to choose from. When a large number of options exist — for example, when there are a dozen scales of plants between SAC_1 and SAC_2 — the long-run average cost curve effectively becomes a smooth curve, shown as LAC in Figure 7–7. Each point on this curve is associated with a different short-run scale of operation that the firm could choose.

IMPORTANCE OF COST CURVES
TO MARKET STRUCTURE
7.6

Although most firms have U-shaped long-run average cost curves, the level of output at which cost per unit reaches a minimum varies from firm to firm and industry to industry. The scale of operations at which average cost per unit is a minimum may be immense for automobile producers but relatively small for apparel makers. These differences occur because the increasing returns to scale that are responsible for the declining portion of the long-run average cost curve primarily reflect technological factors, and the technology governing production differs significantly from one good to another.

The level of output at which average cost is at a minimum for a typical firm in an industry has a major impact on the structure of the industry. More precisely, what matters in the level of output where average cost reaches a minimum in comparison with the total industry demand for the product. Figure 7–8 illustrates this point. When the demand curve for X is D, suppose the typical firm has a long-run average cost curve shown by LAC_1. Average cost reaches a minimum at $5 per unit of output, and at a price of $5 the total quantity demanded by consumers would be X_1. The firm can produce a total $0.05X_1$ at a unit cost of $5, or a twentieth of the total quantity demanded by consumers. Insofar as LAC_1 is typical for firms producing this product, the industry could accommodate 20 firms, each producing approximately 5 percent of the total output. With such a large number of firms the industry is likely to be highly competitive.

On the other hand, suppose that production technology dictates a cost curve like LAC_2. This curve reaches a minimum at half the total quantity demanded at a price of $5. With such cost curves the industry would tend to become dominated by a few (probably two in this case) large firms. Suppose a small firm tried to compete in this market. Operating at a small scale, the firm would have unit costs above $5; it might, for example, be operating at point A, where average cost is $8 per unit. Such a firm would tend to be driven out of business since it could easily be undersold by a larger operation producing where unit costs are $5. For this reason the industry inevitably gravitates toward a small number of large firms. Thus, technology of production, which largely determines at what output unit costs are at a minimum for a firm, is an important factor in

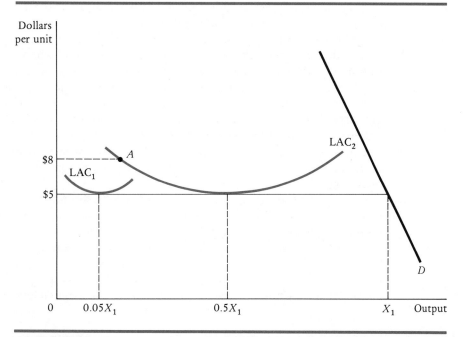

FIGURE 7-8

Cost Curves and the Structure of Industry

The level of output at which long-run average cost is at a minimum relative to market demand has important implications for the structure of the industry. If all firms have LAC curves like LAC_1, twenty firms can coexist in the industry; if the LAC_2 curve is typical, only two firms are likely to survive.

determining whether an industry is composed of a large or a small number of firms although other factors may also be involved. In later chapters we will see what difference the size of firms is likely to make for the performance of an industry.

INPUT PRICE CHANGES AND COST CURVES

7.7

It is important to remember that the prices of inputs are assumed to be unchanged when we construct a firm's cost curves. Per-unit output costs vary with output along a cost curve because the physical productivity of the inputs varies with the rate of output, not because the costs of inputs vary. Economists generally assume that one firm's output decision will not by itself influence input prices. Rarely does a single firm use a large portion of the total quantity of any input. Consequently, if a firm increases its employment of land, engineers, or gasoline, this expansion will not cause a perceptible increase in the total market demand for these inputs, and the prices will not be noticeably affected.

Although input prices do not change because of any single firm's output decision, they do occasionally change, such as when many firms simultaneously try to increase or decrease the use of some input. For example, let's take a look at the effect of a reduction in the wage rate. Figure 7–9a illustrates the firm's input choices. Initially, the firm is producing an output of Q_1 by employing labor and capital at point E on isocost line MN. The firm's original expansion path passes through point E, and from it we can derive the per-unit cost curves MC and AC, shown in Figure 7–9b. Along these curves, as along the expansion path, the prices of inputs are unchanged.

Now suppose the wage rate falls. First let's see how this affects the way inputs are combined in the least costly manner to produce the same output, Q_1. A lower wage rate means the slopes of isocost lines become flatter, because the slope is w/r. If the firm were to continue to incur the same total cost in hiring labor and capital, the relevant isocost line would be MN'. If, however, the firm operates on MN', it would produce more output, and we want to consider production of the original level of output,

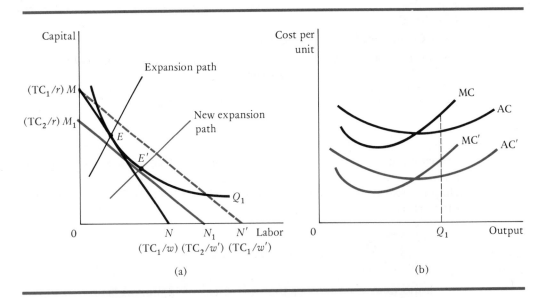

(a)   (b)

FIGURE 7–9

A Lower Input Price Shifts Cost Curves Downward

(a) With a lower wage rate, the cost of producing each level of output falls. Input combination E' becomes the least costly way to produce Q_1 after the wage reduction. (b) The change in the wage rate shifts the AC and MC curves downward to AC' and MC'. Since a firm's cost curves reflect *given* input prices, a change in input prices will cause the entire cost curves to shift.

Q_1. To produce Q_1 in the least costly way at the new wage rate, the firm should operate at point E', where Q_1 is tangent to the isocost line M_1N_1. Note that M_1N_1 is parallel to MN', reflecting the lower wage rate. Consequently, the lower wage rate makes it possible for the firm to produce the same output at a lower total cost than before: MN' shows an unchanged total cost, so M_1N_1, which is closer to the origin, represents a lower total cost. Note also that the firm will use more of the cheaper input, labor, and less of the now relatively more costly input, capital, in its production. What the movement from E to E' really shows is the *input substitution effect* that results from a change in the relative cost of inputs. Because of the lower wage rate, a new expansion path is defined.

In passing, we should warn against a common error. It is tempting to say that we could derive the firm's demand curve for labor by identifying the point at which an isoquant is tangent to MN', by analogy to the way we derive a consumer's demand curve. This is incorrect because the firm need not continue to operate at an unchanged level of total cost; it can choose any point on the new expansion path. The point that is most profitable, which will depend on demand conditions, would only by coincidence occur at the same total cost. In a later chapter we will see how the demand curve for an input is derived.

Returning to the main point, we have seen that a lower wage rate reduces the total cost of producing a given output. A lower wage rate also reduces average cost, since average cost is equal to total cost divided by output. The same reasoning, however, applies to *any* output level the firm might produce; the total cost of producing any output is now lower than it was before.

A lower price for an input shifts the AC and MC curves of the firm downward to AC' and MC', as illustrated in Figure 7–9b. The AC' and MC' curves are, of course, based on the new expansion path in Figure 7–9a, which shows the least costly method of producing each rate of output at the lower wage rate. This result is not particularly surprising, but it highlights an important distinction. Per-unit costs can vary as a result of changing output when input prices are given (a movement along given cost curves), or they can vary as a result of a change in input prices (a shift in the cost curves). Just as in the case of distinguishing between a movement along and a shift in a demand curve, it is important to keep this distinction in mind for cost curves too.

USING COST CURVES: CONTROLLING POLLUTION, PART I

7.8

Many problems can be clarified when posed in terms of marginal costs. Let's take an example of some practical importance. Two firms are located on a river, and they dispose of their wastes by dumping them in the river. (You may recall that this situation is referred to as an *externality*, a concept discussed further in Chapter 19.) Because the dumping of effluents pollutes the water and harms people living downstream, the government steps in to limit the amount of pollution by requiring each firm to curtail its pollution to 100 units (measured in some appropriate way). This restriction limits the total waste discharged into the river to 200 units.

An important question here is whether the government's program to reduce pollution to 200 units accomplishes the intended result at the lowest possible cost. To answer that question, we must think in terms of the marginal cost each firm bears in reducing pollution. Figure 7–10 illustrates the situation. In this diagram, the amount of pollution generated by each firm is measured from *right to left*. For example, before the government restricts its activities, firm A discharges $0P_1$ (300 units), and firm B discharges $0P_2$ (250 units). Measuring pollution from right to left is the same as measuring pollution abatement — the number of units by which pollution is reduced from its initial level — from left to right. For example, if firm B cuts back its pollution from 250 to 100 units, it has produced 150 units of pollution abatement, the distance P_2X.

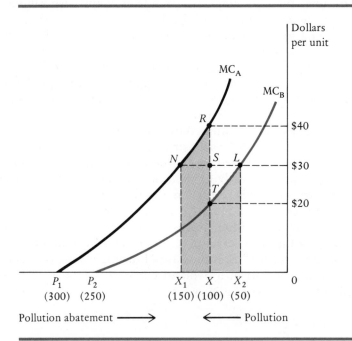

FIGURE 7–10
Costs of Pollution Abatement

To produce a given output at the lowest possible total cost, the separate firms must be producing at a point where their marginal costs are equal. This is also true for pollution abatement. To reduce pollution to 200 units in the least costly way, firm A should discharge 150 units and firm B, 50 units.

The reason for adopting these units of measurement along the horizontal axis is that each firm incurs costs from reducing pollution (abating pollution). The more pollution abatement, the greater is the total cost to the firm. In fact, we can think of each firm as having a marginal cost curve, starting from its initial position, that measures the marginal cost of pollution abatement (cutting back pollution by one unit) at each level of "output." Exactly what form these costs take is immaterial; they may involve carting away the waste by-products, burying them, or using equipment that generates less waste. Each firm would, of course, choose the least costly way of cutting back pollution. The information we require in order to find the cost of complying with the government's regulation is each firm's marginal cost curve of pollution abatement. We expect these curves to rise; as more pollution is abated, it becomes more expensive to eliminate additional units. In Figure 7–10 firm A's marginal cost curve is MC_A, and firm B's is MC_B. (Because pollution is a by-product of the production of some other good, these curves are likely to start at zero and rise throughout. Do you see why?)

When the government limits each firm to 100 units of pollution, firm A will operate at point R on MC_A, and firm B will be at point T on MC_B. (We will assume that this restriction is not so costly that either firm is put out of business.) Now only 200 units of pollution are dumped into the river, a reduction from 550. Is this the least costly way to limit pollution to 200 units? To see that it is not, we must consider the firms' marginal costs. The marginal cost of reducing pollution to firm A is $40, but firm B's cost is only $20. If firm B were to cut back pollution by one more unit, it would add only $20 to its costs. If Firm A increased pollution by one unit (produced one unit less of pollution abatement), its cost would fall by $40. Having firm B pollute one unit less and Firm A one unit more leaves the total amount of pollution unchanged, but it reduces the firms' combined costs by $20 (plus $20 for firm B and minus $40 for firm A).

As long as the marginal costs differ, the total cost of pollution abatement can be reduced by increasing pollution abatement where its marginal cost is less and reducing it where its marginal cost is greater. So shifting the production of pollution abatement from firm A to firm B should continue until B's rising marginal cost just equals A's falling marginal cost. In the diagram this equality occurs where firm B cuts back pollution to 50 units at point L on MC_B and firm A increases pollution by 50 units to point N on MC_A. At these points the marginal cost of both firms is equal to $30. Each step of this reallocation reduces A's costs by more than it increases B's costs, so the two firms still generate the same amount of total pollution (200 units) but at a lower total cost. Any further shifting of pollution abatement production from A to B would increase total costs. To limit pollution to 200 units in the least costly way, the firms should produce at a level where their marginal costs are equal.

When firm B increases its pollution abatement from P_2X to P_2X_2, its total costs rise by the shaded area TLX_2X. This area in effect sums the marginal cost of each successive unit of pollution abatement from P_2X to P_2X_2. For instance, the first unit (reduction in pollution from 100 units) beyond P_2X adds $20.00 to total cost; the next, perhaps $20.50; the third, $21.00; and so on. So the addition to total cost from the first three units in this case is $61.50. (In general, the area under a marginal cost curve between two levels of output measures how much total costs rise when moving from the lower to higher output.) Firm A's total costs fall by RNX_1X when it reduces its pollution abatement from P_1X to P_1X_1. The cost saving to firm A, RNX_1X, is clearly larger than the additional cost to firm B, TLX_2X (recall that $XX_2 = XX_1$).

If the government simply mandates that each firm restrict its pollution to the same level, this policy will normally result in a higher cost for pollution control than is necessary. The only exception to this statement is if the marginal costs of the firms are equal when they are polluting the same amount, and this situation is unlikely to happen. Our analysis, therefore, leads to an important conclusion: to minimize the costs of pollution control, firms should operate where their marginal costs are equal. The same rule also applies to automobile emissions. Emission standards for automobiles should take into account the fact that the marginal cost of limiting emissions varies from one make of automobile to another and between older and newer automobiles. Applying the same standards to all automobiles (as is done now) imposes higher total costs than are necessary.

Realistically, can the government apply this rule? In terms of Figure 7–10, to allocate pollution abatement responsibility between the firms in the least costly way, the government would need to know both firms' marginal cost curves, and such information would be virtually impossible to obtain with any degree of accuracy. Without a knowledge of the marginal cost curves, it would be impossible for the government to place a limit on each firm's pollution so that their marginal costs are equal. Does this conclusion mean that our economic analysis is of little practical value? Not at all. As we will see at the end of the next chapter, there is a way for the government to efficiently limit pollution without having to know the marginal cost curves.

Summary

In this chapter we examined the way costs vary with the output of a firm. Costs are ultimately associated with the use of inputs that have alternative uses. To economists, costs mean opportunity costs — sacrificed alternatives when inputs are used to produce one product rather than some other.

In the short run firms cannot change the quantities of some inputs (fixed inputs), so they can vary output only by varying the quantities of variable inputs. The law of diminishing marginal returns operates here, and it dictates the shapes of the short-run cost curves. The short-run marginal cost curve rises beyond the point at which diminishing marginal returns set in, and it intersects the U-shaped average variable cost and average total cost curves at their minimum points.

In the long run the firm can vary all inputs. The expansion path in an isocost-isoquant diagram shows the least costly combinations of inputs required to produce various levels of output. It identifies the lowest total cost at which the firm can produce each output when all inputs can be varied. The same information is also conveyed with the long-run cost curves of the firm.

Returns to scale are the basic determinant of the shape of long-run cost curves. With increasing returns to scale at low outputs and decreasing returns to scale at high outputs, the long-run average cost curve will be U-shaped. It shows the lowest per-unit cost at which the firm can produce each output. The level of output at which the long-run average cost curve reaches a minimum depends on technological conditions and will vary from one product to another.

It is important to remember that all cost curves for individual firms are drawn on the assumption that input prices are given. A change in one or more input prices causes the cost curves to shift.

Review Questions and Problems

*1. A firm has an attractive investment project. It can finance the project by borrowing funds at an interest rate of 10 percent. Alternatively, it can finance the project out of its current profits without borrowing. The firm's manager says it should choose the second method of finance because it is cheaper; no interest has to be paid. What do you say?

2. If a firm hires a currently unemployed worker, is the opportunity cost of using his services zero?

3. Define the following measures of short-run costs: TFC, TVC, TC, MC, AFC, AVC, and ATC. Then fill in the spaces in the accompanying table.

Output	TFC	TVC	TC	MC	AFC	AVC	ATC
1	$100	$50					
2				$30			
3						$40	
4			$270				
5							$70

*4. How is the law of diminishing marginal returns related to the shape of the short-run marginal cost curve? If the marginal product of the variable input declines from the very start, what will the short-run marginal cost and average cost curves look like? If the marginal product first rises and then falls, what will the cost curves look like?

5. Using the data from Table 6–2, construct the following relationships: (a) the average amount of labor used per unit of output at each level of output, (b) the additional amount of labor required for each additional unit of output. Show these relationships as curves, with the labor per unit of output on the vertical axis and output on the horizontal axis. How can these curves be converted into AVC and MC curves?

*6. Why do we assume that a firm will try to produce its output by using the lowest cost combination of inputs possible? Does this reason also hold for production carried out by the Post Office? The Ford Foundation?

7. What is the significance of a tangency between an isoquant and an isocost line?

8. When a firm produces an output in the least costly way, using labor and capital, $MRTS_{LK} = w/r$. Does this relationship mean that the firm sets input prices so that the ratio equals $MRTS_{LK}$?

9. At point E in Figure 7–5, is MP_K/r greater or less than MP_L/w? How do you know? Use this inequality to explain how the firm can increase output without increasing its total costs by using a different combination of inputs.

*10. A firm is employing 100 hours of labor and 50 tons of cement to produce 500 blocks. Labor costs $4 per hour and cement costs $12 per ton. For the quantities employed, $MP_L = 3$ and $MP_C = 2$. Show this situation in an isoquant-isocost diagram. Explain, and show in the diagram, how the firm can produce the same output at a lower total cost.

11. Why do we assume that the prices of inputs are constant when we draw a firm's cost curves? How does a change in the price of an input affect the AC and MC curves?

12. What is the basis for drawing the long-run average cost curve as U-shaped?

13. Figure 7–7 shows the relationship between the LAC curve and several SAC curves. What do the long-run total cost curve and the short-run total cost curves look like? Show the total cost curves in one diagram.

14. "In the United States more than 50 firms produce textiles, but only 3 produce automobiles. This statistic shows that government antimonopoly policy has been applied more harshly to the textile industry than to the automobile industry." Can you give an alternative explanation for the difference in the number of firms in the two industries?

Supplementary Readings

De Alessi, Louis. "The Short-Run Revisited." *American Economic Review,* 57(3) (June 1967): 450–461.

Maxwell, W. David. "Production Theory and Cost Curves." *Applied Economics,* 1(3) (August 1969): 211–224.

Stigler, George. "Economies of Scale." *Journal of Law and Economics,* 1 (October 1958): 54–71.

Viner, Jacob. "Cost Curves and Supply Curves." *Zeitschrift für Nationalökonomie,* 3 (September 1931): 23–46.

Profit Maximization and the Competitive Firm

8

The material presented in the previous two chapters applies to all business firms, regardless of the type of market in which they operate. The cost curves of a monopolist or an oligopolist will be influenced by the same factors that affect the cost curves of a competitive firm. As we have seen, the basic underlying determinants of costs are the prices and the productivities of inputs. But a knowledge of cost conditions alone does not permit us to explain what level of output a firm will produce. Cost curves only identify the minimum costs at which the firm may produce various outputs.

To complete the model of output determination for a competitive firm, two new elements must be incorporated into the analysis. First, the goal, or goals, of the firm must be specified. In economic analysis of business enterprises, profit maximization is usually taken as the overriding goal. Second, the demand conditions confronting the firm must be specified. The demand curve facing the firm determines the revenues the firm can realize by selling different volumes of output. After discussing these matters, we will examine the way cost and demand conditions jointly determine the most profitable output level for the competitive firm.

In this chapter, we will concentrate on the individual firm's output decisions and see how it responds to changes in price and costs. For most purposes, however, the level of industry output (supply) is more important. Consequently, in the next chapter we will show how the behavior of individual firms can be aggregated to develop the industry supply curve.

PROFIT MAXIMIZATION
8.1

Some people have no trouble accepting the assumption that a business enterprise will attempt to make as much money as possible. Yet over the years many thoughtful observers have taken issue with the assumption that profits are the single, overriding goal of the firm. Briefly, let's look at some of the major issues involved in determining how appropriate the assumption of profit maximization is.

At the outset we should recognize that any profit realized by a business belongs to the owner, or owners, of that business. In the case of a small business, where there is only one owner who actually operates the business (and there are millions of such businesses in the United States), it is plausible to suppose that each decision concerning what products to carry, who to hire or fire, what price to charge, and so on will be heavily influenced by the way the owner's profits are affected. Even in this setting, however, some objections to profit maximization can be raised. For example, the owner may be mainly concerned with achieving early retirement or sending his or her children to an expensive college. The relevant question to ask is whether such goals conflict with profit maximization. Frequently, the answer is no: money is a means to many ends, and if the owner makes more money, an early retirement or an expensive college is more easily affordable.

Another objection is that the owner-manager cannot possibly have the detailed knowledge of the costs and revenues regarding every possible action that could be taken to maximize profits, assuming profit maximization is the goal. Although there is an element of truth in this observation, economic theory does not require that firms know or think in terms of marginal costs and revenues, only that they behave as if they did. Firms may come close enough to maximizing profits by trial and error, emulation of successful firms, following rules of thumb, or blind luck for the assumption to be a fruitful one.

When we move from the small owner-managed firm to the large modern corporation, other doubts about profit maximization arise. A characteristic of most large corporations is that the owners (stockholders) themselves do not make the day-to-day decisions about prices, output, employment, advertising, and so on. Instead, salaried personnel of the corporation — the managers — make these decisions. There is a separation of ownership and control in the corporation. Managers control the firm, but the stockholders own it. It is fairly safe to assume that stockholders wish to make as much money on their investment as possible, but it is virtually impossible for them to monitor continually the managers' actions. Therefore, managers will have some degree of discretion, and some of their decisions may conflict with profit-maximizing goals.

Economists have hypothesized several alternative theories of managerial behavior that may be relevant in this setting. William Baumol, for example, has suggested that firms may seek to maximize sales rather than profits.[1] Why might a manager wish to pursue sales as a goal? Managers may feel they have more prestige and power, and possibly will receive larger salaries, when overseeing a larger operation. Managers cannot completely neglect profits, of course, since investors will withdraw their funds from a firm with below-average earnings and invest them some-

[1] William J. Baumol, *Business Behavior, Value and Growth*, rev. ed. (New York: Harcourt, Brace & World, 1976).

where else where they can earn a higher return. This threat constrains managers to some degree, and as a consequence, Baumol argues that managers will attempt to maximize sales subject to a minimum profit constraint. That is, managers will pursue sales as a goal as long as profits do not decline to such a level that investors move their capital elsewhere.

Admittedly, it is possible that managers will depart from the rule of profit maximization, but there is disagreement about the extent to which this actually occurs. Within the market, factors are at work that limit non-profit-maximizing behavior. For example, owners often relate compensation of business executives to profits, possibly even paying them in part with shares of stock or stock options, in an effort to give managers incentive to pursue profits more actively. In addition, how profitably managers run a given enterprise is likely to affect their job prospects with other firms. And finally, if managers do not make as large a profit as possible, stock prices, which tend to reflect profitability (especially expected future profitability), will be lower than need be. Undervalued stock creates an incentive for outsiders, or "raiders," to buy up a controlling interest in the firm at the depressed share prices and replace the inefficient management team with a new one. A firm that neglects profit opportunities too often leaves itself open to this type of "takeover bid," which is a fairly common occurrence in the business community.

If the firm operates in a competitive market, there is still another reason for believing that it will not stray too far from profit-maximizing goals. Suppose that several firms sell lawn mowers. Some of the firms, either through ignorance, negligence, bad luck, or intention, virtually ignore profits. Their production methods are too costly, they produce an inappropriate quantity or quality of product, they hire too many of the president's relatives, and so forth. Other firms, whether through good luck, superior management, or more conscientious attention to profits, produce the right type of lawn mower in the appropriate quantity and in the least costly way. What will happen when these firms compete for customers? Clearly, the firms that come closer to maximizing profits will make money and prosper; the others will suffer losses. Inefficient, non-profit-maximizing firms will tend to be weeded out, leaving firms that are more successful in achieving profits. In general, in competitive markets firms that do not approximate profit-maximizing behavior will fail; the survivors will be the firms that, whether intentionally or not, make the appropriate (that is, profit-maximizing) decisions. This is sometimes called the *survivor principle*, and it provides a practical defense of the assumption of profit maximization.

As these remarks may suggest, it is impossible to prove or disprove the profit maximization hypothesis on purely theoretical grounds. While it is clear that any firm, and particularly a firm in a competitive market, must pay close attention to profits, some deviation from single-minded profit maximization may occur. Most economists today, however, believe that the assumption of profit maximization provides a close enough approximation for the analysis of many problems, and it has become the standard assumption regarding the behavior of the firm. While the assumption may not be adequate to explain why Jones, the company president, hires a lazy brother-in-law, or why executives in corporation X are expected to wear dark pin-striped suits, it is not intended to serve this purpose. Instead, it is designed to explain how a firm's output will respond to a higher or lower price, a tax or a government regulation, a change in costs, and so on. Recall that the ultimate test of a theory is whether it explains and predicts well, and theories based on the assumption of profit maximization have passed that test.

THE DEMAND CURVE
FACING THE COMPETITIVE FIRM
8.2

In the remainder of this chapter we will be concerned with the implications of the profit maximization assumption for the output of a firm selling its product in a competitive market. Recall that a competitive market is characterized by a large number of firms selling the same product. Each firm supplies only a small fraction of the entire industry output. For example, one wheat producer may produce only a thousandth of the entire output of the wheat industry, or one building contractor may provide only 2 percent of the total construction services supplied in a particular city.

The nature of the demand curve confronting a single competitive firm follows directly from the relatively insignificant contribution the sales of its product make toward total supply. The price of the product is determined by the interaction of the total market supply of and the demand for the product. Since each firm produces such a small portion of the total supply, its own output decisions will have a correspondingly small effect on the market price. For simplicity the "small" effect is taken to be a "zero" effect, and the demand curve facing a competitive firm is drawn perfectly horizontal. This means that the firm can sell as much output as it wants without affecting the price of the product. Stated differently, the competitive firm is a *price taker:* since the price is largely determined by other participants in the market, each firm takes the market price as given and does not expect its decisions to affect price.

Figure 8–1 will help to clarify why the firm's demand curve is drawn as horizontal. In Figure 8–1b the total output of the good in question — the combined outputs of all the firms — is measured horizontally, and price is measured vertically. The market demand curve (the horizontal summation of all the consumers' demand curves) is shown as D. The premise is that the total quantity offered for sale by all firms together interacts with this demand curve to determine price. If the combined output of all the firms is 1050 units, the market price of the product would then be $9.50.

Firm X is one of many firms operating in this market, and it is currently selling 50 units of output at $9.50, as shown in Figure 8–1a. What we

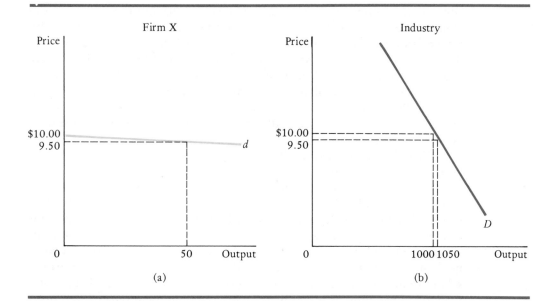

FIGURE 8–1

The Competitive Firm's Demand Curve

(b) All firms other than X produce 1000 units, and the industry demand curve is D. (a) Because an individual competitive firm supplies only a small portion of total industry output, the demand curve facing the firm will be extremely elastic, like demand curve d of firm X. For simplicity we treat the competitive firm's demand curve as perfectly elastic — that is, horizontal.

are interested in is the demand curve relevant for this one firm's output decisions. If we suppose that other firms will maintain the same output when the price varies, we can easily derive firm X's demand curve.[2] Let's imagine that firm X varies its output and observe what happens to price and output. For example, if firm X reduces output to zero, and other firms continue to sell 1000 units, total output falls from 1050 to 1000 and the price will rise to $10, as shown in Figure 8–1b. Now we have two points on firm X's demand curve: at a price of $10 or more, it can sell nothing; at a price of $9.50, it can sell 50 units. Other points on the firm's demand curve can be generated in the same way. For each level of output produced by firm X, that output is added to the 1000 units produced by other firms, and the market demand curve in Figure 8–1b shows the price.

Firm X's demand curve is thus drawn as *d* in Figure 8–1a. Just as in our earlier discussion, this figure shows that a firm producing a small part of total output has only a small effect on the market price. The demand curve for firm X is not perfectly horizontal; it slopes downward slightly.

---

[2] This assumption is not entirely correct, but it is adequate to make the major point here. This situation will be reconsidered in the next chapter.

Obviously, if other firms produced 10,000 or 100,000 units, firm X's demand curve would be, for all practical purposes, perfectly horizontal. The smaller the fraction of output produced by a firm, the more nearly its demand curve will approximate a horizontal line. While few firms may actually have perfectly horizontal demand curves, whenever the demand curve is nearly horizontal, as it is for firm X, it is a useful and fairly accurate simplification to treat it as if it were horizontal. A perfectly horizontal demand curve has an elasticity of infinity and is called an infinitely elastic demand curve.

A firm selling in a competitive market, therefore, is assumed to face a horizontal demand curve. Over the relevant range of output, the firm can sell any number of units without affecting the price. One implication is that price is equal to marginal revenue for the competitive firm. *Marginal revenue* is defined as the change in total revenue when there is a one-unit change in output. A competitive firm can sell one more unit of output without reducing the price it receives for its previous units, so total revenue will rise by an amount equal to the price. For example, if a firm is selling 10 units at a price of $5, total revenue is $50. If it sells 11 units at a price of $5 per unit, as it can with a horizontal demand curve, total revenue rises from $50 to $55, or by the $5 it receives for the eleventh unit.

Note that the assumption of a horizontal demand curve confronting a competitive firm does not mean that the price never changes. It just means that a single firm, acting by itself, cannot affect the going price. The price may vary from time to time, but not because of changes in the amount sold by one firm.

SHORT-RUN PROFIT MAXIMIZATION
8.3

In the short run a competitive firm operating with a fixed plant can vary its output by increasing or reducing its employment of variable inputs. How the firm decides on the actual level of output to produce is an important question in economics. Assuming that the firm attempts to maximize profits allows us to answer the question.

Let's begin with a numerical illustration. Table 8–1 contains the information needed to identify the profit-maximizing output for this hypothetical competitive firm; it includes the short-run costs of production and revenues from the sale of the output. We know the firm is selling in a competitive market because the price is constant at $12 per unit regardless of the level of sales. Note that total revenues are equal to price times the quantity sold, and they rise in proportion to output since the price is constant. Total costs rise with output in the familiar fashion, slowly at first and then more rapidly as the plant becomes more fully utilized and marginal costs rise. Total cost, when output is zero, is $15, reflecting the total fixed costs.

TABLE 8-1
Short-Run Cost and Revenue of a Competitive Firm

Rate of Output	Price (dollars per unit)	Total Revenue (dollars)	Total Cost (dollars)	Total Variable Cost (dollars)	Total Profit (dollars)	Marginal Cost (dollars per unit)	Marginal Revenue (dollars per unit)	
0	$12	$ 0	$ 15	$ 0	−$15	—	—	
1	12	24	25	10	−$13	$10	$12	
2	12	24	33	18	−9	8	12	
3	12	36	40	25	−4	7	12	
4	12	48	46	31	2	6	12	MR > MC
5	12	60	54	39	6	8	12	
6	12	72	63	48	9	9	12	
7	12	84	73	58	11	10	12	
8	12	96	84.9	69.9	11.1	11.9	12	MR ≈ MC
9	12	108	98	83	10	13.1	12	
10	12	120	113	98	7	15	12	
11	12	132	132	117	0	19	12	
12	12	144	155	140	−11	23	12	MC > MR
13	12	156	185	170	−29	30	12	
14	12	168	225	210	−57	40	12	

Total profits are the difference between total revenues and total costs. At low and high rates of output, profits would be negative; that is, the firm would suffer losses. In particular, note that the firm loses $15 if it produces no output at all because it still must pay fixed costs even if it temporarily shuts down. At an intermediate rate of output in this example, profits are positive. The firm, however, wishes to make as large a profit as possible, and maximum profit occurs at an output of 8 units where profits are $11.10.

Figure 8–2 shows how we identify the most profitable level of output by using the total revenue (TR) and total cost (TC) curves. The total reve-

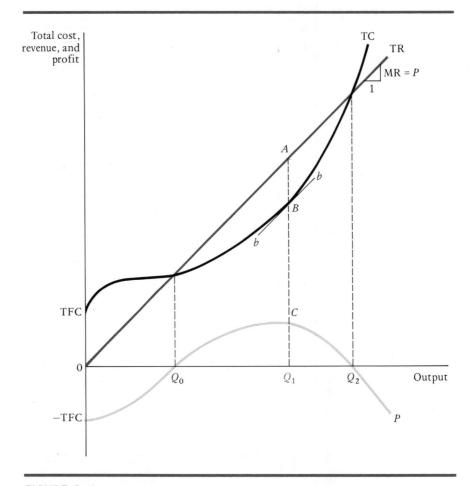

FIGURE 8–2
Short-run Profit Maximization: Total Revenue, Cost, and Profit Curves
Profits are maximized at the output where total revenues (TR) exceed total costs (TC) by the largest possible amount. This occurs at output $0Q_1$, where profits are equal to *AB*. The total profit curve (*P*), which plots the total profits explicitly at each rate of output, also shows the point of profit maximization.

nue curve is a new relationship, but it is a relatively simple one when dealing with a competitive firm. With the price per unit constant, total revenue rises in proportion to output and is, therefore, drawn as a straight line. Its slope, showing how much total revenue rises when output changes by one unit, is marginal revenue (MR). In the case of the competitive firm marginal revenue and price are always equal.

In terms of Figure 8–2, the firm wishes to select the rate of output where total revenue exceeds total cost by the largest possible amount; that is, where profits are greatest. This situation occurs at output Q_1, where total revenue, AQ_1, exceeds total cost, BQ_1, by AB. The vertical distance AB is total profit. At lower and higher rates of output, total profit is lower than AB. Note that at a lower rate of output, Q_0, for example, the TR and TC curves are diverging (becoming farther apart) as output rises, indicating that profit is greater at a higher output. This reflects the fact that marginal revenue (the slope of TR) is greater than marginal cost (the slope of TC) over this range. At Q_1 when the curves are farthest apart (with revenue above cost), the slopes of TR and TC (the slope of TC at B is equal to the slope of bb) are equal, reflecting an equality between marginal revenue and marginal cost.

In Figure 8–2 the level of total profit at each rate of output is also shown explicitly by the total profit curve *(P)*, which reaches a maximum at Q_1. The total profit curve is derived graphically by plotting the difference between TR and TC at each rate of output. For example, AB is equal to CQ_1; alternatively, when output is zero, profits are negative and equal to minus total fixed costs (TFC).

The TR and TC approach is probably the way business people are likely to think about costs, revenues, and profits. However, economists do not generally use the TR and TC curves in examining the output decisions of firms. Instead, they use the per-unit curves (marginal cost, marginal revenue, and so on), which are derived from the total cost and revenue curves since these curves clearly identify the single most profitable output. Although these two approaches amount to the same thing, it is helpful to see what the problem looks like from different vantage points.

Short-Run Profit Maximization
Using Per-unit Curves

Figure 8–3 presents the same information shown in Figure 8–2, but now we use the familiar per-unit cost and revenue relationships. With the vertical axis measuring dollars per unit of output, the firm's demand curve is shown as a horizontal line, since the firm may sell any number of units at the $12 price. The figure also shows the average (total) cost (AC), average variable cost (AVC), and marginal cost (MC) curves. The most profitable output level occurs where marginal cost and marginal revenue are equal, at Q_1 in the figure. The shaded rectangle $ABCD$ shows total profits for that output. The height of the rectangle, CD, is price minus average total cost, or the average profit per unit of output; multiplying the average profit per

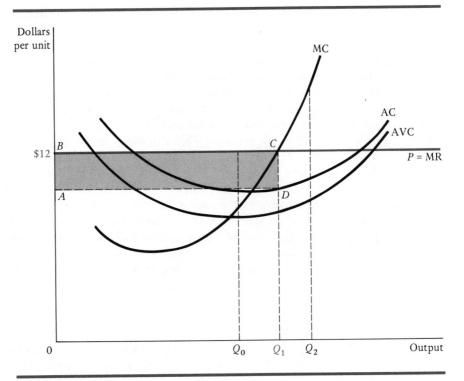

FIGURE 8–3
Short-run Profit Maximization: Per-unit Curves
In terms of the per-unit curves, the output that maximizes profits in the short run is at the point where MC = P, or $0Q_1$. At lower levels of output like $0Q_0$, P > MC, and the firm can increase profits by expanding output. At higher outputs like $0Q_2$, MC > P, and the firm can increase profits by reducing output.

unit by the number of units sold (the length of the rectangle) yields total profits.

It is very important to understand why profits are at a maximum where marginal cost and marginal revenue are equal. To see this, consider what it would mean if the firm were operating at a lower output where MR > MC, such as Q_0. At Q_0 marginal revenue is still \$12, but marginal cost is lower; let's assume it's \$8. Consequently, producing another unit adds \$12 to receipts but increases total costs by only \$8; with revenues increased more than costs, profits (the difference) will rise when another unit is produced and sold. Put differently, increasing output by one unit beyond Q_0 will add \$4 to total profits. At any rate of output where marginal revenue (price) is greater than marginal cost, the firm can earn higher profits by increasing output. As output expands, marginal cost rises, so the addition to profit from each successive unit becomes smaller (but is still positive) until Q_1 is reached, where MC = MR.

At output levels beyond Q_1 the firm would be producing too much output. At Q_2, for example, marginal cost is \$15 and is greater than marginal revenue. This implies that total profits could be increased by reducing output. If the firm produces one unit less, it loses \$12 in revenue. But costs fall by \$15, so the net effect is a \$3 increase in profits. (Refer to Table 8–1 to see what happens when output falls from 10 to 9 units if this idea is not clear.) Thus, the firm will increase profits by decreasing output if MC > MR.

Note that the firm does not necessarily maximize profits by producing where its profit margin (average profit per unit) is largest. The largest average profit per unit occurs where average cost per unit is a minimum, at the point where marginal cost equals average cost. Maximum total profits depend not only on profit per unit but also on how many units are sold. A lower profit per unit combined with a higher sales volume can lead to greater total profits, as is true in Figure 8–3.

Thus, the rule for profit maximization is to produce where MR = MC. Since marginal revenue equals price for a competitive firm, we can also express this condition as P = MC. This rule does *not* mean that the firm intentionally sets price equal to marginal cost since, for a competitive firm, price is given and beyond its control. Instead, the firm will adjust its production until the marginal cost is brought into equality with price.[3]

Operating at a Loss in the Short Run

A competitive firm may find itself in the unenviable situation of suffering a loss no matter what level of output it produces. In that event the firm has two alternatives. Either it can continue to operate at a loss or it can shut down. (Recall that we are dealing with a short-run setting; halting production may only be a temporary move until market conditions improve and is not necessarily the same as going out of business.) Yet shutting down will not avoid a loss since the firm is still liable for its fixed costs whether it operates or not (see Figure 8–2). The relevant question is whether the firm will lose *less* by continuing to operate or by shutting down.

Figure 8–4 illustrates the case where the firm's best option is to operate at a loss rather than shut down. With price at \$8 a unit and the cost curves as shown, the firm's "most profitable" output (which can also mean its "least unprofitable" output, as it does here) is where price equals marginal cost at Q_1. Since the average cost curve lies above the price line everywhere, the firm incurs losses at all levels of output. But at Q_1 the loss is the smallest, as indicated by the striped rectangle *EBCF*. The height of the rectangle, *CF*, is the difference between average cost and price, or the

---

[3] Because the MC curve is U-shaped, it is possible for MC to equal *P* at two different output levels. In this case the lower level is not the profit-maximizing output; in fact, it is the minimum profit (or maximum loss) output. If it is necessary to distinguish these two outputs, the profit-maximizing output is where *P* = MC *and* MC cuts the price line from below (that is, MC is rising).

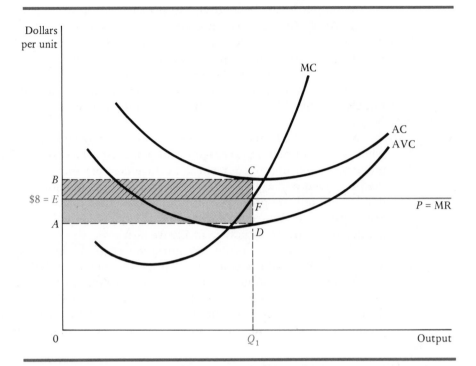

FIGURE 8–4

Operating at a Loss in the Short Run

In the short run a firm may continue to produce even though its best output yields a loss. As long as price covers AVC, it is in the firm's interest to continue operation. Output will be $0Q_1$ even though the firm's loss is *EBCF*, since the loss would be even greater — *ABCD* — if it shut down.

"negative profit margin" per unit, and the length of the rectangle, *EF*, is the number of units sold at a loss.

How do we know that the firm loses less by producing at Q_1 than by shutting down? Consider the larger rectangle *ABCD*. The height of the rectangle, *CD*, is the difference between AC and AVC at Q_1. Thus *CD* measures average fixed cost. Recall that AVC + AFC = AC; therefore, AC − AVC = AFC, and average fixed cost multiplied by the number of units produced (the length of the rectangle) equals total fixed cost (or the area of the rectangle *ABCD*). Even if the firm shuts down, it will still incur a loss; namely, total fixed cost. But since that loss (*ABCD*) is larger than the loss (*EBCF*) incurred if the firm continues to operate, the firm loses less by producing Q_1 than by shutting down. It is better to operate and lose $100 a week than to shut down and lose $200 a week.

If the price falls sufficiently low, however, the firm may lose less by shutting down, as we will see in Section 8.5. Moreover, even when it is in the firm's interest to produce at a loss, as it is in Figure 8–4, this equilibrium can only be temporary (short run). If the price remains at $8, the firm will ultimately go out of business. The point here is that a firm won't immediately liquidate its assets the moment it begins to suffer losses.

LONG-RUN PROFIT MAXIMIZATION
8.4

At any time, the short-run scale of plant the firm has built reflects a previous long-run decision. As a result, we must consider how the goal of profit maximization guides the long-run decisions of firms. The same principles we used for the short-run setting apply to long-run profit maximization, but now we employ long-run cost curves, which allow a sufficient period of time to vary all inputs.

Figure 8–5 shows the long-run cost curves LAC and LMC. The $12 price is expected to remain at that level (otherwise long-run investment decisions would not be based on that price), so the firm's most profitable output level is Q_3, where long-run marginal cost equals price. Producing Q_3 involves constructing a scale of plant that would have a related short-run average cost curve (not drawn in) tangent to LAC at point A. After building the plant, the firm realizes a total profit shown by the large shaded rectangular area. No other size plant will yield as large a profit, since the long-run cost curves reflect all possible scales of plant that the firm can construct.

Figure 8–5 also illustrates why a short-run profit-maximizing outcome may represent only a temporary equilibrium. Suppose that the price is $12 but the firm currently has a scale of plant with the short-run cost curves SAC_1 and SMC_1. With that size plant the firm's short-run profit-maximizing equilibrium is at Q_1, with the firm earning profits equal to the small striped rectangular area. If the firm expected the price of $12 to persist, however, it would immediately begin making plans to enlarge its scale of plant because it could earn significantly higher profits by building the appropriate long-run scale of plant identified by point A. By its very nature, a short-run equilibrium is only temporary unless it also coincides with a position of long-run equilibrium. Once the firm has constructed the scale of plant at point A, it will be in a position of both long- and short-run equilibrium, and it will make no further adjustments unless market conditions change.

Suppose now that the price were $7 instead of $12. The horizontal demand curve at this price is just tangent to LAC at point B. For this demand curve the most profitable output is Q_2, where price equals long-run marginal cost. Total profits, however, are zero since price just equals average cost of production.

The long-run equilibrium of the firm at Q_2, with price just covering average costs, has great significance. As we will see in the next chapter, competition among firms in an industry tends to produce this type of

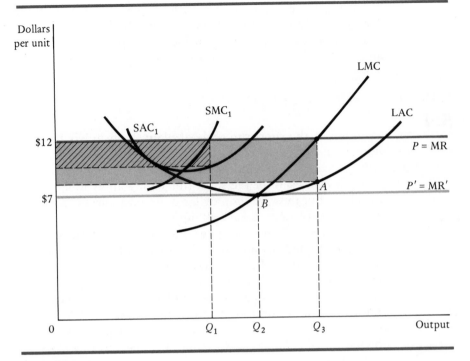

FIGURE 8–5

Long-run Profit Maximization

The firm maximizes profits in the long run by producing where $P = LMC$. With a price of $12, output will be $0Q_3$ in the long run; the large shaded area shows profits.

equilibrium for each firm. Without going into any explanation here of why this equilibrium is produced, two remarks about what it means for the firm are in order.

First, the equilibrium at Q_2 implies zero economic profit. Once again, it is essential to remember that the long-run cost curves include as costs a return to investors equal to what they can receive elsewhere; that is, a normal rate of return on investment is regarded as one of the production costs of the firm. Accountants and the financial pages of newspapers would therefore show this firm making a positive profit. (To avoid confusion because of the difference in the way economists and nearly everyone else define profits and costs, some economists prefer to describe the equilibrium at point B as one where the firm earns "normal" or "average" profits. We will continue to refer to this equilibrium as zero profit, but don't let the different terminologies confuse you.)

Second, we may question why the firm stays in business producing Q_2. Zero profit generally means that the various inputs, including capital provided by the owners, could earn just as much somewhere else. Although this is true, the relevant consideration is that they can't earn any *more* anywhere else, which is one reason the firm stays in business.

OUTPUT RESPONSE TO A CHANGE IN PRICE
8.5

Implicit in the foregoing discussion is a systematic relationship between the price of the product and the most profitable level of output. Let's analyze this relationship for the firm's short-run output choices. Figure 8–6 gives the average variable cost and marginal cost curves. Note that in this example the average total cost curve is not drawn in since it is not needed to identify the most profitable output level. The AC curve is used primarily to show total profits or losses. If the price is $9, the firm will produce at point *B*, where marginal cost equals $9, so output will be Q_1. If the price of the product were to rise from $9 to $12, the firm's profits

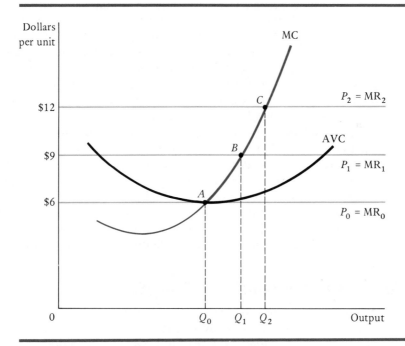

FIGURE 8–6
How the Firm Responds to Price Changes

That part of the MC curve lying above the minimum point on the AVC curve identifies the firm's most profitable output at prices above $6. At a price of $9, output will be $0Q_1$; at a price of $12, output will be $0Q_2$. Because the MC curve slopes upward, the firm will increase output at a higher price.

would change, as would the most profitable level of output. Suppose the firm maintains an output at Q_1 when the price rises to $12. Its profits will increase since revenues rise, but its costs will not change. The firm, however, can make even more profit by increasing its output. At Q_1 price ($12) is now above marginal cost ($9), signalling that an increase in output will add more to revenues than to costs. The new profit-maximizing output occurs where output has expanded until marginal cost equals the $12 price, at point C on the MC curve. Thus, a higher price gives the firm incentive to expand out from Q_1 to Q_2.

The $MC = P$ rule for profit maximization therefore implies that a competitive firm will produce more at a higher price because increased production becomes profitable at higher prices. In fact, we can think of the marginal cost curve as the firm's supply curve in the short run since it identifies the most profitable output for each possible price. For example, at a price of $9, output is Q_1 at point B on MC; at a price of $12, output is Q_2 at point C on MC; and so on.

One important qualification to this proposition should be mentioned. If price is too low, the firm will shut down. At a price of $6, the firm can just cover its variable costs by producing at point A, where average variable cost equals the price. At this point the firm would be operating at a short-run loss; in fact, the loss is exactly equal to its total fixed costs, since revenues just cover variable costs, leaving nothing to set against fixed costs. At a price below $6 the firm is unable to cover its variable costs and would shut down, at least temporarily. Consequently, point A, the minimum level of average variable costs, is effectively the *shutdown point*: if price falls below that level, the firm will close down.

As a consequence of this qualification, only the segment of the marginal cost curve that lies above the point of minimum average variable costs is relevant. Stated differently, the marginal cost curve above point A identifies the firm's output at alternative prices above $6; at any lower price output will be zero.[4] With the qualification concerning the shutdown point noted, we have established an important proposition; namely, that a competitive firm will produce more at a higher price and less at a lower price. This relationship is shown explicitly by the marginal cost curve.

Cost Curves and the Court: An Epilogue

According to the previous analysis, in the short run a firm will shut down if the price it receives is below average variable cost. However, in the case of *Inglis* v. *Continental* mentioned in Chapter 7, we noted that Inglis pre-

---

[4] In Chapter 6 we pointed out that a competitive firm will never operate in stage I of its short-run production function, where average product is rising. Figure 8–6 confirms this result by showing that the firm will not produce at any output level lower than the minimum point on AVC. The minimum point on AVC corresponds to the maximum average product of the variable inputs. In other words, stage I corresponds to the downward-sloping portion of the AVC curve.

sented evidence that Continental's price was below AVC. Was Continental making a mistake by continuing to operate?

Judge Williams had something to say on this issue too:

> The 1973 study . . . makes the average variable cost 93% of the fully allocated costs [ATC]. While all costs in the long run are variable, such a high percentage in a short-run analysis is suspect. It indicates an attribution of too many short-run fixed costs to the variable calculation.[5]

In short, Judge Williams argued that Inglis had overestimated Continental's AVC by including some costs that were really not variable in the short run. Price probably was greater than AVC but less than ATC, so Continental was correct in continuing to operate rather than shutting down.

OUTPUT RESPONSE TO A CHANGE IN INPUT PRICES
8.6

Many factors can affect the output decision of a competitive firm, but perhaps the two most common are variations in the price of the product and variations in the price of one or more inputs used in production. In reality, product prices and input prices frequently change at the same time, but at the outset it is best to examine each factor in isolation. In the previous section we looked at the way a change in the product price affected output when input prices were constant (reflected in the fact that the cost curves did not shift). Now let's study the impact of a change in input prices when the product price is constant.

Figure 8–7 illustrates a competitive firm initially producing the output Q_1 where marginal cost, shown by MC, equals the $10 price of the product. Note that only the marginal cost curve above the shutdown point, point *A*, is drawn in. Now suppose the price of one (or more) of the variable inputs falls. As we saw in Section 7.7, lower input prices cause the cost curves to shift downward, indicating a lower cost associated with each rate of output than before. In the diagram this is shown by a shift in the marginal cost curve from MC to MC'. The rule for profit maximization, MC = P, determines the new output level Q_2 that maximizes profits. To proceed to this conclusion somewhat more slowly, note that at the initial output level a lower input price decreases the marginal cost from $10 to $6. After the reduction in costs, the price ($10) is higher than marginal cost ($6), indicating that an expansion in output will now (at the lower input price) add more to revenues than to costs and thereby increase profits. Consequently, the firm will expand output along the new MC' curve until marginal cost once again equals price at Q_2.

In this and the previous section we have been concerned with predicting the reactions of a competitive firm to a change in the economic

---

[5] *William Inglis & Sons* v. *ITT Continental Baking,* 461 F. Supplement 410 (1978), p. 419.

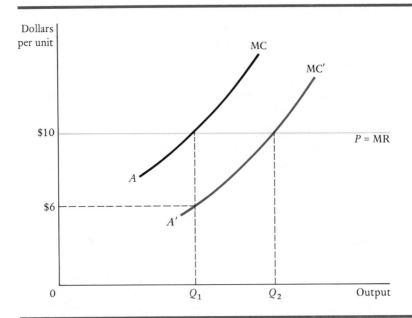

FIGURE 8-7
How the Firm Responds to Input Price Changes
A change in the price of an input, with an unchanged product price, changes the profit-maximizing output. If an input price falls, MC shifts to MC', and output increases to $0Q_2$, where MC' equals the unchanged price.

environment in which it operates, changes that are communicated to the firm in the form of variations in prices. A competitive firm by itself does not influence those prices; it is a price taker because of its small size relative to the total market. Nonetheless, the combined actions of all the competing firms materially affect the price of the product as well as input prices, as we will see when we examine the functioning of a competitive industry in the next chapter. The response of each individual firm to price changes is an integral part of the adjustment process by which the overall market attains an equilibrium.

PROFIT MAXIMIZATION
AND CONTROLLING POLLUTION, PART II
8.7

In Section 7.8 we discussed the case of two polluting firms and indicated how reducing the amount of pollution could be achieved at the lowest possible cost. The key was to divide the responsibility for abating pollution between the two firms in such a way that marginal costs were equal. Practical difficulties arose with that prescription since it seemed to require the government's knowing the firms' marginal cost curves. Now we will show how the government can achieve the efficient outcome without knowing anything about the firms' costs of pollution abatement.

Let's consider how a tax on pollution affects the firms. Specifically, suppose the government requires each firm to pay a tax equal to $30 for each unit of pollution it dumps into the river. The tax creates a strong incentive for each firm to curtail its pollution, since the firm saves $30 for each unit of pollution that it doesn't produce. If reducing pollution by one unit costs the firm less than $30, it is in the interest of the firm to incur the cost and save $30 in taxes.

Figure 8–8 shows how such a tax would affect the level of pollution. As before, pollution is measured from right to left, and the firms' marginal cost curves for pollution abatement are shown as MC_A and MC_B. Ignore firm B for the moment. A tax of $30 per unit of pollution can be shown as a horizontal line at $30 per unit. The total tax liability of the firm is $30 times the number of units of pollution. If firm A continues to pollute at its initial level, $0P_1$, it will have to pay a tax equal to $0T$ ($30) times $0P_1$, which is the area $0TT_1P_1$.

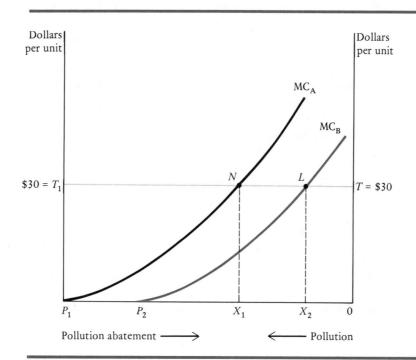

FIGURE 8–8

A Tax on Pollution

A per-unit tax on pollution effectively makes the firms competitive producers of pollution abatement. With a tax of $30 per unit of pollution, firm A produces P_1X_1 units of pollution abatement ($0X_1$ units of pollution), and firm B produces P_2X_2 units of pollution abatement ($0X_2$ units of pollution).

The tax gives the firm incentive to cut back pollution, since each unit of pollution abatement saves it $30 in taxes. Looked at from left to right, the horizontal line $T_1 T$ is much like a demand curve for pollution abatement: it shows a gain in net revenue of $30 for each unit of pollution abatement produced. Thus, the firm faces a horizontal "demand" curve for pollution abatement, and its marginal cost curve indicates the costs of abating pollution. To maximize profits, the firm has a strong incentive to cut back pollution. More precisely, if the firm can eliminate a unit of pollution for less than $30, doing so will add more to net revenues (by reducing taxes by $30) than it will to costs. In the interest of profits firm A would cut back pollution to $0X_1$ (producing $P_1 X_1$ in pollution abatement), where the marginal cost of pollution abatement is exactly equal to the per-unit tax of $30. Cutting back further would not be worthwhile since the cost of more pollution abatement exceeds the tax saving. With pollution of $0X_1$ the firm must still pay total taxes of $0TNX_1$, but this sum is significantly smaller than the sum would be if the firm continued polluting at its original level $0P_1$.[6]

Now let's turn to firm B. The same analysis is relevant when a tax of $30 per unit of pollution is levied on firm B. Firm B has incentive to cut back pollution to $0X_2$, where its marginal cost of pollution abatement equals the tax per unit. Note what this means: firm A and firm B are both operating at a level of pollution abatement where marginal cost equals $30 per unit. Their marginal costs are the same, which implies that the total reduction in pollution ($P_1 X_1$ plus $P_2 X_2$) is achieved in the least costly way. And this outcome happens without the government's knowing either firm's marginal cost curve. By applying the same tax to both firms, the government gives each firm the same incentive to curtail pollution. The result is efficient coordination of their independent production decisions.

Many economists favor taxation as a pollution control strategy, and this example helps explain why.[7] A pollution tax effectively creates market incentives for firms to reduce pollution in the least costly manner. Moreover, the size of the tax can be changed to regulate the amount of pollution: a larger tax per unit will reduce pollution further.

In the United States most environmental policies rely on regulations and quantity limitations rather than taxes. Many economists have been critical of these policies, in part because they believe the taxation approach could achieve the same results at lower cost. And the taxation approach is more than a theorist's pipe dream. Germany, for example, has successfully used pollution taxes to regulate the volume of wastes discharged into the Ruhr River for about fifty years.[8]

[6] This analysis does not show how the pollution tax affects the firm in its product market. Of course, the tax increases production costs and shifts the cost curves upward. To be accurate here, we should explicitly assume that the tax is not so large that it becomes unprofitable for the firms to stay in business.

[7] A good discussion of the use of taxes to control pollution is in Larry Ruff, "The Economic Common Sense of Pollution," *The Public Interest*, no. 19 (Spring 1970): 69–85.

[8] A. V. Kneese and B. T. Bower, *Managing Water Quality: Economics, Technology, Institutions* (Baltimore: Johns Hopkins University Press, 1968).

Summary

In this chapter we discussed the assumption economists use in analyzing the behavior of business firms: that firms attempt to maximize profits. While this assumption is probably not realistic in all cases, the profit motive appears to be sufficiently strong that a theory based on the assumption of profit maximization has wide applicability.

A competitive firm sells a product that is similar to the products sold by many other firms. Thus, the individual firm's output decision has a negligible effect on the price of the product, and the firm's demand curve can be approximated by a horizontal line at the level of the prevailing price. For any firm the most profitable output occurs where the marginal cost of producing another unit of output just equals the marginal revenue from selling it. For a competitive firm with its horizontal demand curve, price and marginal revenue are equal, so it maximizes profits by producing where marginal cost equals price. Price, however, must be at least as high as average cost or the firm will suffer losses. If price does not cover AVC in the short run, the firm will shut down; if price does not cover LAC in the long run, the firm will go out of business.

The assumption of profit maximization allows us to predict how a competitive firm will respond to changes in the product price or in input prices. An increase in the product price (with unchanged cost curves) will lead the firm to expand output as it moves up its marginal cost curve. A reduction in one or more input prices will shift the cost curves downward and so will lead the firm (with an unchanged product price) to expand output. It is important to understand how the individual firm is affected by, and will respond to, such changes since they are an integral part of the process by which a competitive industry attains an equilibrium, as we will see in the next chapter.

Review Questions and Problems

1. How can consumers have a downward sloping demand curve for peaches, and yet each peach producer face a horizontal demand curve? Explain.

*2. "The industry, or market, demand curve for avocados is the horizontal sum of the demand curves facing each avocado grower. If each avocado grower confronts a horizontal demand curve, the market demand curve must be horizontal — and that is nonsense. Thus, each avocado grower must have a downward-sloping demand curve." True or false? Explain.

3. "Price equals marginal revenue for a competitive firm." True or false? Explain.

*4. Assume that a competitive firm has the short-run costs given in Table 7–1. What is the firm's most profitable output, and how large are profits: (a) if price is $15? (b) if price is $25? (c) if price is $35?

5. Assuming that price is greater than the minimum level of AVC (why is this assumption necessary?), explain why the firm maximizes profit by producing an output at which marginal cost equals price.

6. "If price exceeds marginal cost, the firm should cut the price until the two are equal." Does this statement describe the way a competitive firm maximizes profits?

*7. The Humdrum Company produced 10,000 doldrums last year. It sold the doldrums at a price of $5 each, but each doldrum cost only $3 to make. With a profit margin of $2 per unit, should the company have produced more if it wanted to maximize profits? (Would you pay $5 for a doldrum?)

8. "The difference between price and marginal cost is the amount of profit per unit of output, which the firm wishes to be as large as possible." Why is this statement false? What does the difference, if any, between price and marginal cost measure? How would it be shown in Figure 8–2?

9. Draw long-run total cost and total revenue curves for a competitive firm, and identify the profit-maximizing output. Draw the total profit curve.

10. "If the price of the product rises, a firm will make a larger profit even if it doesn't increase its output, so there is no reason why it

should increase output." Why is the latter part of this statement false, even though the first part is correct?

11. Suppose that through ineptitude, laziness, or contrariness, a business manager always falls 10 percent short of producing the profit-maximizing output. Would a higher product price lead to greater output? Would an increase in input prices lead to a reduction in output? Does this result suggest one reason economists are not overly concerned about whether the profit-maximizing assumption is literally and exactly correct? Explain.

12. If the price of some input rises, what happens to the profit-maximizing output — assuming the product price remains unchanged? If the product price rises at the same time some input price rises, what happens to the profit-maximizing output?

*13. Suppose the firm is in the situation shown in Figure 8–5, producing Q_3 where

LMC equals the $12 price. Now the government levies an excise tax of $1 per unit of output on the firm. Assume the product price and input prices do not change. Will the firm alter its output? How? (Hint: How does the tax affect LAC? LMC?)

14. In question 13 what difference does it make whether the government taxes only one firm in a competitive industry or all firms? (Hint: Is the assumption about product price and input prices likely to be more accurate in one case than the other?)

Supplementary Readings

Baumol, William. *Economic Theory and Operations Analysis.* 4th ed. Englewood Cliffs, N.J.: Prentice-Hall, 1977. Chap. 15.

Machlup, Fritz. "Theories of the Firm: Marginalist, Behavioral, Managerial." *American Economic Review,* 57 (March 1967): 1–33.

The Competitive Industry
9

In this chapter the emphasis shifts from the individual firm to the competitive industry. Because an industry is composed of many firms producing a similar product, the analyses of the preceding three chapters concerning production, costs, and output of the individual firm are essential ingredients here. Now, however, we will build on the previous analyses to develop a model that explains the determination of the total output of a good (as distinct from the output of only one firm) and the price at which it will be sold. Basically, this involves showing the way the behavior of individual firms can be summarized by an industry supply curve, which, along with the demand curve, determines price and quantity.

The competitive model developed in this chapter is probably the most important part of microeconomic theory. Economists use this model more frequently than any other, and when circumstances require a different approach, it is usually based on an extension of the basic competitive model. Like most models, it is abstract and unrealistic, so its usefulness in analyzing real world phenomena may not be immediately apparent. In the next chapter we will discuss several applications that illustrate the ways economists have used the competitive model as the basis for studying many important problems.

THE ASSUMPTIONS OF PERFECT COMPETITION
9.1

In ordinary usage competition generally refers to intense personal rivalry among businesses. Ford and General Motors, General Electric and Westinghouse, RCA and Zenith are competitors in this sense. Each firm makes a business decision — whether to introduce a new model, advertise existing products more aggressively, or offer improved warranties — only after considering its impact on competitors and their likely response.

The economist's model of perfect competition, especially in its formal description, appears quite distant from this view of competition. Perfect competition is characterized largely by its impersonal nature. Because there are many firms, each firm recognizes that its impact on the overall market is negligible and therefore is not inclined to view other firms as personal rivals. To be more specific, in economic theory four conditions must be satisfied for an industry to be perfectly competitive.

1. Large number of buyers and sellers. A large number of independent participants on each side of the market, none of which bulks large in relation to total sales or purchases, will normally guarantee that the firms and consumers behave as price takers. Firms will view the price as market-determined and largely unaffected by their individual output decisions. Thus, each firm confronts a horizontal demand curve, which indicates that individual firms take prices as given and beyond their control. In some cases it may not require a very large number of competing firms to establish that result, but a large number (collusion aside) virtually guarantees it, so the condition is generally stated in this way.

2. Unrestricted mobility of resources. Industry adjustments to changing market conditions always involve resources entering or leaving the industry. As an industry expands, it uses more labor, energy, raw materials, capital, and so on, so resources enter the industry. Likewise, resources leave a contracting industry. A perfectly competitive market requires that there be no artificial impediments to entry or exit from an industry. Artificial impediments include such things as licenses that are legally required for firms to operate in the market; patents on productive processes that newcomers need to produce competitively; labor unions that restrict the supply of labor to certain jobs. Natural impediments, however, do not violate this condition. For example, a firm may need a large scale of plant in order to achieve low-cost production, so the financial investment required to enter the industry is quite large. Increasing returns to scale reflect the true nature of the technological factors governing production and do not imply restricted mobility in the sense intended here.

3. Homogeneous product. All the firms in the industry must be producing a standardized product. In the eyes of consumers it makes no difference which firm they purchase from. This assumption allows us to add up the outputs of the separate firms and talk meaningfully about the industry and its total output. It also contributes to the establishment of a uniform price for the product. Farmer Jones will be unable to sell his corn for a higher price than farmer Smith's if the products are viewed as interchangeable, since consumers will always purchase from the lower-priced source.

4. Possession of all relevant information. Firms and consumers must have all the information necessary to make the correct economic decisions. For firms the relevant information is knowledge of technological conditions of production (the production function), the prices that must be paid for the various inputs they need, and the price at which the product can be sold. For consumers the relevant information is a knowledge of their own preferences and the prices of the various goods and services of interest to them. Moreover, the consumers, in their role as suppliers of inputs, must know the remuneration they can receive for supplying productive services.

These four conditions are clearly very stringent, and probably no industry completely satisfies them all. Like all general theoretical models, the model of perfect competition relies on assumptions that deviate significantly from reality. Nonetheless, the theory has proven valuable in helping us understand how the economy operates. At the end of this chapter we will return to these assumptions to determine how much real world deviations from them undermine the usefulness of the competitive model. For now, let's consider the theory that follows from these assumptions.

THE SHORT-RUN SUPPLY CURVE
9.2

Moving from the determination of the most profitable output of the competitive firm, as explained in the previous chapter, to the short-run industry supply curve is a short step. In the short run a competitive firm will produce where its marginal cost equals the price, so long as the price is above the minimum point on its average variable cost curve. In other words, each firm's marginal cost curve indicates how much the firm will produce at alternative prices. *As a first approximation, the short-run industry supply curve is derived by simply adding the quantities produced by each firm, that is, by summing the marginal cost curves horizontally.*

Figure 9–1 illustrates how this is done for the three firms that compose the industry producing ball-point pens. Although three firms may not be enough to constitute a competitive industry, the derivation is the same regardless of the number of firms in the industry. The figure shows the portion of each firm's marginal cost (MC) curve that lies above the minimum average variable cost (AVC). Since the supply curve will identify the total quantity offered for sale at each price, we will add the outputs each firm would choose to produce individually.

At any price below P_0, the minimum point on firm 3's AVC curve, industry output would be zero since all three firms would be shut down. At P_0 firm 3 begins to produce. Note that its output is the only output on the market until price reaches P_1 since the other firms would not operate at such low prices. Thus, the lower portion of firm 3's marginal cost curve reflects the total industry supply curve at low prices. When price reaches P_1, however, firm 1 begins to produce, and its output must be added to firm 3's; hence, the kink in the supply curve at P_1. When price reaches P_2, firm 2 goes into production, and its output is included in the supply curve at prices above P_2. We refer to this derivation of the short-run supply curve as a horizontal summation of the firms' short-run marginal cost curves since we are summing quantities (horizontal axis) across firms. For example, at a price of P total industry supply is $0Q$, which is equal to the sum of the amounts each firm produces at that price ($0q_1 + 0q_2 + 0q_3$).

Note that the short-run supply curve, SS, slopes upward. Remember that each firm's marginal cost curve slopes upward because it reflects the

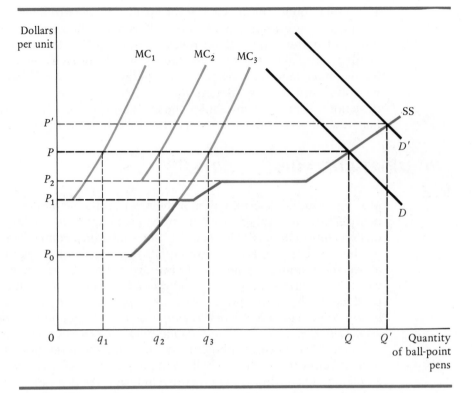

FIGURE 9–1

The Short-run Industry Supply Curve

Each firm will produce an output where MC = P to maximize profit. To derive the short-run industry supply curve, we must sum the amounts produced by the various firms in the industry, as shown by their respective MC curves. SS is thus obtained by summing the firms' MC curves.

law of diminishing marginal returns to variable inputs. Thus, the law of diminishing marginal returns is the basic determinant of the shape of the industry's short-run supply curve.

One qualification to this derivation of the short-run supply curve must be pointed out. Each firm's marginal cost curve is drawn on the assumption that the prices of its variable inputs are constant. This assumption is appropriate when we focus on one firm's individual output choices, but when we move up the industry supply curve, all firms simultaneously increase their employment of variable inputs. This could cause the prices of some of the variable inputs to rise since all the firms in the industry are attempting to use more inputs at the same time. A change in input prices would cause each firm's marginal cost curve to shift (see Section 7.7). This possibility is ignored in the derivation of the supply curve in Figure 9–1 by assuming that no shift in the MC curves occurs. If input prices do rise as the industry expands in the short run, this would reduce the intended increase in output of each firm somewhat, and the supply curve would be more inelastic than it has been drawn, but it would still slope upward. A fuller discussion of the impact of changes in input prices will be deferred until we examine the long-run adjustment process later in Section 9.4.

Price and Output Determination in the Short Run

Incorporating the consumers' market demand for the product completes the short-run competitive model. Since the consumers' demand relates total purchases (from all firms together) to the price of ball-point pens, it interacts with the supply curve to determine price and quantity. In Figure 9–1 the intersection of the demand curve D with the supply curve identifies the price where total quantity demanded equals total quantity supplied. Thus, price P is the equilibrium price in the short run, and total industry output is $0Q$. Each firm, taking price as given, produces at an output where marginal cost equals P. Firm 1 therefore produces $0q_1$; firm 2, $0q_2$; firm 3, $0q_3$; the combined output, $0q_1 + 0q_2 + 0q_3$, equals $0Q$.

Given the supply and demand relationships in Figure 9–1, if price were at a level other than P for some reason, familiar market pressures would come into play to push the price toward its equilibrium level. For example, if price were lower than P, total quantity demanded by consumers would be greater than the total quantity supplied by firms, a temporary shortage or excess demand would exist, and price would be bid up. As price rises toward P, quantity demanded by consumers becomes smaller while quantity supplied becomes larger, until the two eventually come into balance at price P. Alternatively, if price were higher than P, quantity supplied would exceed quantity demanded, a temporary surplus or excess supply would exist, and competition among firms would bring the price down.

In the short run an increase in the market demand leads to a higher price and a higher output. Suppose we begin with the equilibrium just described, and then we find demand increases to D'. A shortage would exist at the initial price of P, and price would rise. The higher price would elicit a greater output response from the firms as they move upward along their marginal cost curves. The new short-run equilibrium would be price P' with a quantity of $0Q'$.

Note that in Figure 9–1 we do not explicitly identify profits, if any, realized by the firms. If we drew in each firm's average total cost curve, we could show them, but we do not need to use the average cost curves to explain the determination of price and quantity in the short run. All the necessary information is contained in the industry supply and demand curves.

By its nature, a short-run equilibrium is generally a temporary resting place on the way toward a long-run equilibrium. Consequently, we now turn to a consideration of the long-run equilibrium in a competitive industry. In analyzing the long-run adjustments that lead to equilibrium, we will also further consider the use of the short-run model in economic analysis.

LONG-RUN COMPETITIVE EQUILIBRIUM
9.3

In a long-run competitive equilibrium the independent plans of firms and consumers mesh perfectly. Each firm has adjusted its scale of operations in light of the prevailing price and is able to sell as much as it chooses. Consumers are able to purchase as much as they want at the prevailing price. There are no incentives for any firm to alter its scale of operations or to leave the industry and no incentives for outsiders to enter the market. Unless market conditions change, the price and rate of output will remain stable.

Figure 9–2 illustrates a long-run equilibrium; Figure 9–2a shows the position from the perspective of a representative firm, and Figure 9–2b shows the interaction of total quantity bought and sold in the market. At the outset we assume that all firms in the industry have identical cost curves, so the position of any one firm will be representative of all firms. Before explaining the process by which a long-run equilibrium is reached, let's examine carefully the conditions that must hold for an industry to be in long-run equilibrium.

First, at the prevailing market price each firm must be producing the output that maximizes its profits. This condition shown graphically has each firm operating where long-run marginal cost, LMC, equals price. In Figure 9–2a the firm's profit-maximizing output is $0q$, where LMC $= P$. The reason this condition must hold is simple. If firms are not producing the appropriate amounts, they have incentive to change their production levels to increase profits. A change in output by the firms, however, affects the total quantity offered for sale by the industry, which, in turn, changes the price at which the output is sold. Therefore, the initial price could not be an equilibrium price since there would still be market pressures at work that would cause price to rise or fall as firms adjust their outputs, trying to achieve higher profits.

Second, there must be no incentive for firms to enter or leave the industry. This condition occurs when firms are making zero economic profit, or, equivalently, when they are earning a normal return on their investors' capital. If profits were higher, other firms seeking higher returns would enter the industry; if profits were lower, firms would leave the industry since they could do better elsewhere. This entry and exit would affect the level of industry output and change the price. If, however, profits in this industry are comparable to profits in other industries, there is no reason

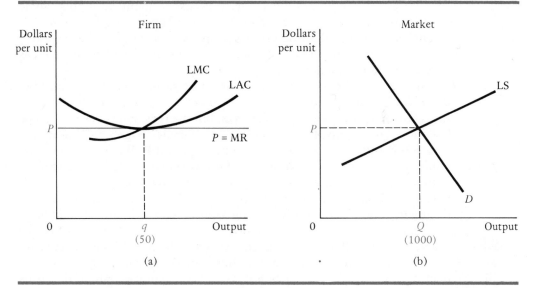

FIGURE 9–2

Long-run Competitive Equilibrium

Part b illustrates an industry in long-run equilibrium where LS and D intersect. Part a illustrates the equilibrium from the perspective of an individual firm. The firm is producing the most profitable output (P = LMC) and is making zero economic profits (P = minimum LAC).

for entry or exit to occur, and price and output will remain stable. This condition is illustrated by the zero economic profit equilibrium of each firm: price just covers long-run average cost (LAC), as shown by the tangency between the firm's demand curve and the LAC curve at output $0q$.

Third, the combined quantity of output of all the firms at the prevailing price must just equal the total quantity consumers wish to purchase at that price. This condition is illustrated in Figure 9–2b by the intersection of the long-run supply curve, LS, and the demand curve D at price P. (We have not yet derived the long-run supply curve, so we will just take its shape for granted at the moment.) If this condition is violated, there would be either an excess demand or an excess supply at the prevailing price, so the price would not be an equilibrium price.

Zero Profit When Firms' Cost Curves Differ?

When all firms in the industry have identical cost curves, every firm must be making zero economic profit in long-run equilibrium. Cost curves, however, are certain to differ among firms. While there is probably some similarity in the cost curves of firms producing the same product since they have access to the same technology of production, differences will arise because they do not always have access to identical inputs. Some farms have more fertile land than others; some businesses have more efficient management than others; some firms have more skilled workers than others. These qualitative differences in the inputs will be reflected as differences in production costs.

If firms' cost curves do differ, we must reconsider the proposition that *every* firm makes zero economic profit in a long-run equilibrium. As it turns out, this proposition is still correct, but the reason it is deserves some attention. To see why, let's examine a specific case. Figure 9–3 shows the long-run per-unit cost curves for two firms, A and B. We assume that the industry is in equilibrium at price P. Firm A (Figure 9–3a) is operating at output $0q_A$ and making zero economic profit. Firm B (Figure 9–3b), with long-run average cost curve LAC (ignore LAC' for the moment), is producing $0q_B$ and is apparently making a profit shown by the shaded area.

Can this be a long-run equilibrium with firm B making profits? To evaluate this possibility, we must first specify why firm B's cost curves are lower than firm A's. Let's suppose that firm B has some especially productive input that firm A does not have. For example, assume the firms are farms, and when they began operation, each purchased a parcel of

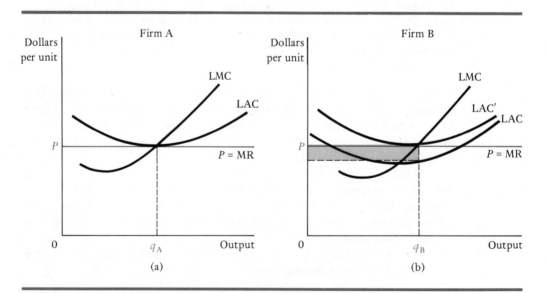

FIGURE 9–3
Zero Economic Profit in the Long Run
(a) When a competitive industry is in long-run equilibrium, every firm, like firm A, makes zero economic profit. (b) If firm B employs unusually productive inputs, will it have a cost curve like LAC and make a profit? No: these inputs will command proportionately higher prices, and the cost curve correctly drawn to show the opportunity costs of inputs is LAC'.

land. Firm **B** was lucky. Its parcel of land was far more fertile (productive) than firm **A**'s land even though they both paid the same price. The fertile land accounts for firm **B**'s lower production costs.

As a result, the shaded area of "profit" for firm **B** can really be attributed to its owning an unusually productive input. This means that the purchase price of the land understated its real economic value; that is, the cost of using the land is actually greater than its purchase price. Remember that cost reflects forgone opportunities, and once it is known that the parcel of land is highly productive, its market value — what other firms would pay for it — will rise. Since we have assumed that the firm's profits (the shaded area) are due entirely to the productivity of the land, we must increase the actual value of the land (per time period) by an amount equal to the shaded area. In the diagram we show this change as a shift in LAC to LAC′ since the original cost of the land is no longer the appropriate measure of cost. Note that the marginal cost curve is unaffected since the cost of producing additional output has not changed.

In this analysis it makes no difference whether or not firm **B** owns the land. If firm **B** rents the land, and it becomes apparent that the land is unusually productive, the rental cost will go up since other firms would be willing to pay more for highly productive land. If the firm owns the land, the same principle applies; the original purchase price is irrelevant. What counts is how much the land is worth to other potential users, that is, its opportunity cost. In this case the cost of using the land is an implicit cost, and, as explained in Chapter 7, we include implicit costs in the cost curves.

When unusually productive inputs are valued at their opportunity costs, all firms make zero economic profit in a long-run competitive equilibrium. Cost curves of firms need not be identical, but the minimum point on their LAC curves must occur at the same cost per unit. Firm **B**, for instance, may be producing a much larger output than firm **A**, but, correctly represented, both firms' LAC curves reach a minimum at the same unit cost.

The process by which unusually productive inputs receive higher compensation (implicit or explicit) is not restricted to land. Suppose you go to work for a business as a manager and are promised a salary of $20,000. When the firm hires you, it doesn't know whether or not you'll be any good at your job. Fortunately, you turn out to be truly inspiring, and even after paying your salary, the firm's net revenues rise by $10,000 because of your extraordinary managerial skills. The firm's owners will be delighted, and its books will show a $10,000 increase in profits. Once your managerial skills are recognized, however, you are in a position to command and receive a $10,000 raise, which will effectively eliminate the apparent profit of the firm. If you don't get a raise, you'll resign and accept a position with another firm that will pay you a salary closer to what you're worth—your next best alternative—and your former employer's profits will decline to their original level.

Needless to say, this process doesn't work instantaneously or with exact precision. There is a tendency, however, for inputs to receive compensation equal to their opportunity costs; that is, what they are worth to alternative users. This is the process that leads to the zero profit equilibrium. One implication of this analysis is that the accounting measure of profits may vary widely among firms in an industry even though economic profits are zero for each firm. This variation arises because a firm's own assets are frequently valued on the books at their original purchase costs instead of their opportunity costs. In our earlier example firm B's accounting profits would be higher than firm A's if they both counted only the purchase price of the land as a cost.

THE LONG-RUN SUPPLY CURVE
9.4

The long-run supply curve summarizes much of what we need to know to analyze the behavior of firms in competitive markets. It shows the total amount of a good that will be offered for sale per time period at alternative prices when firms have adequate time to adjust fully to the price. In this section we will explain the derivation of this relationship.

Economists distinguish among three different types of competitive industries: *constant cost, increasing cost,* and *decreasing cost.* The distinction depends on how a change in industry output affects the prices of inputs. As explained earlier, when only one firm changes its output, it is reasonable to assume that input prices will be unaffected. An expansion in industry output, however, is a different order of magnitude. If all firms simultaneously hire more inputs, the prices of some inputs may rise. For example, as automobile production increases, the price of steel may be bid up.

On the other hand, it is possible to conceive of industries that are able to hire more of all inputs without affecting their prices, perhaps because the industry is such a small employer relative to the overall size of the input market. An increase in safety pin production, for instance, may not perceptibly affect the price of steel or any other input used. This type of industry is called a constant-cost industry, and since it is the simplest case, we will deal with it first.

Constant-Cost Industry

To derive the long-run supply curve for a constant-cost industry, we will start from a position of equilibrium and trace the effects of a change in demand on the industry until the industry once again returns to a long-run equilibrium. Figure 9–4b shows the initial long-run equilibrium: when demand is D, output is $0Q_1$, and price is P. Assuming we start from a position of long-run equilibrium, point A will then be one point on the long-run supply curve. Figure 9–4a shows the position of a typical firm. It is producing its most profitable output $0q_1$, and making zero economic profit at price P.

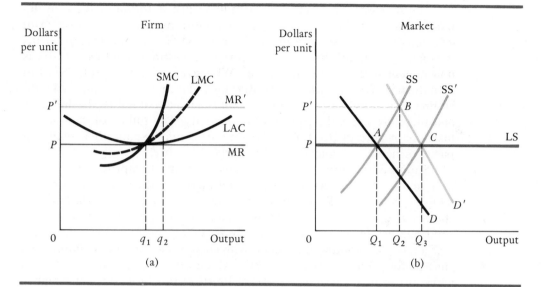

FIGURE 9–4

The Long-run Industry Supply Curve: Constant-cost Industry

The long-run industry supply curve LS of a constant-cost competitive industry is horizontal. In a constant-cost industry expansion of industry output does not bid up input prices. Thus, when industry output expands from $0Q_1$ to $0Q_3$, firms' cost curves do not shift, and the industry output expansion takes place at an unchanged cost per unit as new firms enter the market.

To identify other points on the long-run supply curve, let's imagine that there is an unexpected increase in demand to D' and work through the consequences for the industry. The immediate response to this increased demand must be a short-run one because the firms already in the industry will increase output by expanding operations in their existing plants and increasing employment of variable inputs. This response appears as a movement along the short-run supply curve of the industry, SS, from point A to point B. (Note that the initial long-run equilibrium is also a short-run equilibrium. Every firm is operating its existing plant at the appropriate level — where short-run marginal cost (SMC) equals P — so point A is also a point on the short-run supply curve drawn for the firms with their existing plant and equipment.) In the short run price rises to P', and output increases to $0Q_2$ as the industry expands along SS.

In Figure 9–4a we can see what this means for an individual firm in the industry. The higher price induces the firm to increase output along its short-run marginal cost curve SMC and produce $0q_2$ where SMC $= P'$. (Recall that the summation of all the firms' SMC curves yields the SS curve, as we explained in Section 9.2.) At this point every firm is making pure economic profits.

The industry, however, has not fully adjusted to the increase in demand; this position is only a short-run equilibrium. *The key to the long-run adjustment is profit seeking by firms.* In the short-run equilibrium, firms are making economic profits. The return on investments in this industry is now greater than in other industries. Whenever economic profits exist in an industry, investors will realize that they can make more money by investing in this industry. Economic profits attract capital to the industry and therefore expand its productive capacity. The inflow of capital can take one or both of two forms: existing firms may expand their plant capacity or new firms may enter the market.

Suppose new firms enter the industry in an attempt to share in the profitability of this market. Their output increases the total output of the industry, which, in Figure 9–4b, is shown as a rightward shift in the short-run supply curve. Recall that a short-run supply curve represents a fixed number of firms with given plants. When the number of firms increases, the total output associated with each price is greater — implying a shift in the short-run supply curve. As output expands in response to entry, price must fall along D' from its short-run level since the higher output can only be sold at a lower price. This process of firms entering, total output increasing, and price falling will continue until investment in this industry is no more profitable than investment anywhere else. In other words, a new long-run equilibrium emerges when firms are once again making only "normal profits"; that is, zero economic profit.

In the case of a constant-cost industry, the increased employment of inputs associated with expanding output occurs without an increase in the price of any inputs. With unchanged input prices the firms' cost curves do not shift. This means that price must fall back to its original level before profits return to a normal level: at any price higher than P economic profits would still persist, and entry of new firms would continue. Figure 9–4b shows the process of entry as a rightward shift in SS; it continues until SS' intersects the demand curve D' at point C, where price has returned to its original level P.

Point C is a second point on the long-run supply curve LS. With demand curve D' industry output expands until it reaches $0Q_3$ and price is P. Each firm is once again making zero economic profit. In Figure 9–4a, the firm is again confronted with price P and can do no better than cover its average costs by producing $0q_1$. The increase in total industry output from $0Q_1$ to $0Q_3$ is the result of new firms operating in the industry.

A constant-cost competitive industry is characterized by a horizontal long-run supply curve. Given time to adjust, the industry can produce a higher output with no increase in price along LS. The crucial assumption that produces this result is that input prices are not affected by expansion or contraction of the industry, so new firms can enter the market and produce at the same average cost as existing firms. The term *constant cost* refers to the fact that the cost curves of the firms do not shift; it does not mean that each firm has a horizontal LAC curve.

Increasing-Cost Industry

We can derive the long-run supply curve for an increasing-cost industry in the same way we derived it for a constant-cost industry. We assume an initial long-run equilibrium; then the demand curve shifts, and we follow the adjustment process through to its conclusion. Figure 9–5 illustrates this case. The initial long-run equilibrium price and quantity for the industry are P and $0Q_1$ in part b. The typical firm is producing $0q_1$ and is just covering its costs (shown by LAC) at the market price in part a.

Once again we assume an unexpected increase in demand to D'. The short-run equilibrium is determined by the intersection of the short-run supply curve SS and D'. Price rises to P', and output increases to $0Q_2$. Each firm expands along its short-run marginal cost curve until the typical firm is producing $0q_2$. Firms are realizing economic profits. In the long run highly profitable investment opportunities encourage new firms to enter the market or existing firms to expand their plant capacity.

Up to this point the analysis is identical to the constant-cost case. Moreover, the attainment of a new long-run equilibrium involves further expansion of industry output until profits return to a normal level (zero

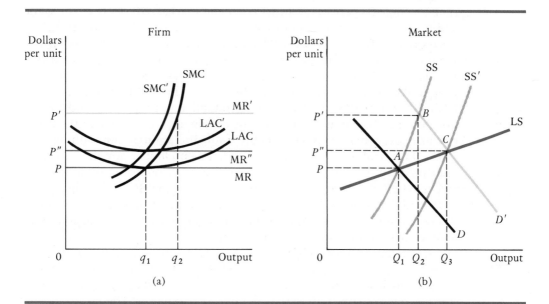

FIGURE 9–5

The Long-run Industry Supply Curve: Increasing-cost Industry

For an increasing-cost competitive industry, the long-run supply curve LS slopes upward. In an increasing-cost industry expansion of industry output bids up some input prices. Thus, when industry output expands from $0Q_1$ to $0Q_3$, firms' cost curves shift upward from LAC to LAC', and the output expansion leads to higher unit production costs.

economic profit), just as in a constant-cost industry. However, in an increasing-cost industry, the expansion of output leads to an increase in some input prices. To produce more output, firms must increase their demand for inputs, and some inputs are assumed to be available in larger quantities only at higher prices. This situation contrasts sharply with that of the constant-cost case, where we supposed that firms could hire larger quantities of all inputs without affecting their prices.

Let's see how this difference affects the long-run adjustment process. At the short-run equilibrium the temporary high level of profits leads to expansion in output — a rightward shift in the short-run supply curve. Increased output tends to reduce profits in two ways. First, just as was true before, the higher output causes price to fall, which reduces profits. Second, the increased demand for inputs that accompanies the expansion in output leads to higher input prices. Higher input prices mean higher production costs, which also reduce profits. As the industry expands in the long run, profits are caught in a two-way squeeze. Both effects result from the industrywide expansion of output. When output has expanded to a level where pure economic profits no longer exist, a new long-run equilibrium is attained.

Figure 9–5 shows this process. We start with the short-run equilibrium at point B (part b). As firms enter the market, SS shifts to the right and price falls. Each firm's horizontal demand curve shifts downward as price declines from P' toward P'', and this decline reduces profits. At the same time higher input prices shift the firms' cost curves upward, from LAC to LAC'. In Figure 9–5a profits are squeezed from above by the decline in the product price from its short-run high, and they are squeezed from below by rising unit costs of production. Rising costs and falling price ultimately eliminate profits. This occurs at price P'', when the firms can just cover their average costs by producing at the minimum point on LAC'. Once profits are squeezed out, there is no longer any incentive for industry output to increase further, and a new long-run equilibrium is reached. In Figure 9–5b, SS has shifted rightward to SS', producing a price of P'' and an output of $0Q_3$. No further shift in the short-run supply curve will occur, since economic profits have fallen to zero. Therefore, point C is another point on the long-run supply curve.

An increasing-cost competitive industry is characterized by an upward-sloping long-run supply curve. This industry can produce an increased output only if it receives a higher price because costs of production rise (the cost curves shift upward) as the industry expands. The term *increasing cost* indicates that the cost curves of all firms shift upward as the industry expands and bids up input prices.

Decreasing-Cost Industry

A decreasing-cost competitive industry is one that has a downward-sloping long-run supply curve. You might think that such a situation is impossible, and, in fact, many economists believe that it is. Others claim that a decreasing-cost industry is theoretically conceivable but admit that it is a remote possibility. Since all agree that it would be, at best, highly unusual, we will not treat it in great detail here.

Briefly, a decreasing-cost industry adjusts to an increase in demand by expanding output, just as industries in the other two cases did. In this instance, though, the expansion of output by the industry in some way lowers the cost curves of the individual firms, leading to a new long-run equilibrium with a higher output but a lower price. The tricky part is to try to explain why the cost curves shift downward. A downward shift in cost curves usually reflects a decrease in input prices, but for that to happen we have to explain how an increase in demand for some input leads to an increased quantity supplied at a lower price — not an easy task.

Although economists are in agreement about how rare decreasing-cost industries must be (if they exist), many noneconomists find the concept congenial. In large part, their view arises from the observation that prices have declined sharply as output has expanded in some industries. For example, color TVs, digital watches, and pocket calculators have all fallen in price in real terms (that is, after adjusting for inflation) by 80 to 90 percent since they were first introduced.

Before concluding that such evidence proves the existence of decreasing-cost industries, we should explore some other possibilities. One common feature in the examples mentioned is that the price was high when the product was first marketed but later fell dramatically. This suggests two possible explanations.

First, by its nature, the first firm to market a new product has a monopoly position, if only temporarily, and monopoly prices tend to be high. As other firms enter the market and begin to compete, price, of course, falls as output increases. This process suggests what we may be seeing is the emergence of competition from an initial monopoly position and not a movement along an industry's long-run supply curve.

Second, the passage of time after the product is introduced makes technological improvements in production processes possible. Particularly in the case of new and complex products, technological know-how is frequently rudimentary when firms first market the product. With experience in production over time, technological improvements may occur quickly. We emphasize that technological know-how is assumed to be unchanged along a supply curve. An improvement in technology shifts the entire supply curve to the right.

Consider Figure 9–6. The long-run supply curve for pocket calculators in 1970, LS_{70}, in conjunction with demand determines a price of $100. After five years firms found better methods of production that lower production costs, and the 1975 supply curve is LS_{75}. This shift in supply leads to a price of $50 in 1975. Further improvements in technology shift the supply curve once again, and price falls to $20 in 1980. The combination of lower prices and higher outputs over time results here from shifts in an upward-sloping supply curve, not from a slide down the negatively sloped supply curve of a decreasing-cost industry. This explanation of the phe-

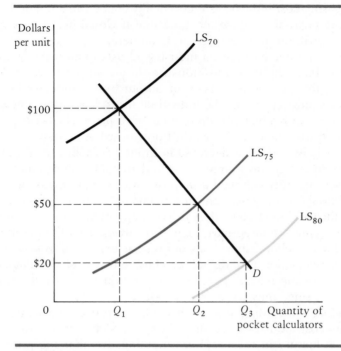

FIGURE 9-6
Technological Advances Shift the Long-run Supply Curve
Observing a reduction in price associated with greater output over a period of
time does not necessarily mean that the long-run supply curve has a negative
slope. Technological advances can occur over time, and they shift the entire
long-run supply curve downward, producing lower prices and higher outputs.

nomenon is especially appealing since new high-technology items are
known to show rapid improvements in technical knowledge in the first
years of their production.

   These remarks do not rule out the possibility of decreasing-cost industries, but if they exist, they are extremely rare, like the Giffen-good
case in demand theory. For all practical purposes the increasing-cost and
constant-cost cases are the relevant possibilities.

COMMENTS ON THE LONG-RUN SUPPLY CURVE
9.5

An industry's long-run supply curve summarizes the results of a complex
and subtle process of adjustment. Once the underlying determinants of
the supply curve are understood, it becomes a powerful tool of analysis.
In using the supply curve, it is frequently unnecessary to "go behind" this
relationship and consider the adjustment process as thoroughly as we did

in deriving the curve. Much supply-demand analysis, for example, simply posits a given supply curve and proceeds from there. To use the supply curve correctly, however, it is important to have a firm understanding of its underpinnings. To that end, we will discuss several points that are frequently misunderstood.

1.   We do not derive the long-run supply curve by summing the long-run marginal cost curves of the firms in the industry. Admittedly, every firm is producing where LMC $= P$ at each point on LS, but as the industry adjusts along LS, firms are entering or leaving the market. Therefore, it is impossible to sum the LMC curves for a given number of firms as we did in the short run. In addition, for an increasing-cost industry the LMC curves themselves shift because of changes in input prices.

2.   Just as we did with a demand curve, we assume certain things remain unchanged at all points on the long-run supply curve; that is, we use the "other things equal" or *ceteris paribus* conditions. For the supply curve there are two important assumptions. First, technology is constant. An industry expanding along its LS curve is using the same technical know-how but employing more inputs to increase output. A change in technology causes the entire supply curve to shift, as we saw in the previous section. Second, the supply curves of inputs to the industry remain unchanged. Note that we are not assuming that the prices of inputs are unchanged but rather that the conditions of supply remain constant. In a constant-cost industry input prices do not change — not because we assume them to be fixed but because the input supply curves facing the industry are horizontal. In contrast, with an increasing-cost industry input prices do change, a condition that gives rise to an upward-sloping long-run supply curve. When relevant, other factors like government regulations, tax laws, or the weather must also be assumed constant along the supply curve.

3.   In reality, an industry is never likely to fully attain a position of long-run equilibrium. Real world industries are continually buffeted by changes. For instance, input supplies, demand, technology, government regulations, and tax laws frequently change. A long-run adjustment takes time, and if underlying conditions frequently change, an industry will find itself moving toward a long-run equilibrium that is continually shifting. Recognizing the reality of frequent change, however, does not undermine the usefulness of the concept of long-run equilibrium in analysis. Although the industry may never attain a long-run equilibrium, the tendency for the industry to move in the indicated direction is what is important, and that outcome is correctly predicted by the theory.

4.   Economic profits are zero at all points along a long-run supply curve. This point is commonly misunderstood. For example, someone may say that when industry output expands following an increase in demand, the firms or producers in that industry benefit. We have seen,

however, that after an increase in demand, all firms will be making zero economic profit in the long run. (There may be temporary economic profit in the short run, of course, which benefits the owners of firms, but we are concerned with whether the benefit is permanent.)

Who does benefit as we move along the long-run supply curve? The owners of inputs whose prices are bid up by the industrywide expansion benefit. (With a constant-cost industry no input prices go up, and no input owners receive a permanent gain.) If the firms own some of the inputs and thereby gain as input prices increase, such a benefit is not considered a profit. Instead, it is akin to a worker who receives a higher wage rate. It is also possible that firms own none of the inputs whose prices rise. It may be, for example, that automobile workers who receive higher wages as industry output increases are the sole beneficiaries on the supply side of that market.

The tendency toward zero economic profit means that the rate of return on invested capital will tend to equalize among industries. If invested capital yields an annual return of 10 percent in industry X, which is comparable to earnings elsewhere, then industry X is earning zero economic profit. Accountants would, of course, generally call the 10 percent return a "profit," but economists would regard a 10 percent return as a cost necessary to attract capital to the industry.

5. In deriving the long-run supply curve, we assumed that a short-run equilibrium was first established and then long-run forces came into play. Price first went up to a short-run high and then came down to its long-run equilibrium level. The actual process of adjustment to changes in demand may not follow this pattern exactly. Identifying a short-run equilibrium and then tracing out long-run effects is merely an expedient way of explaining the determination of the final equilibrium. In fact, following an increase in demand, price may never reach its short-run level and may, in fact, never go above the ultimate long-run level. This can happen if, for example, firms anticipate the increase in demand and have time to make adjustments before demand actually rises. In this case the industry may expand output along its long-run supply curve.

These remarks also suggest that some care must be taken in using the short-run supply curve. We can use the short-run supply curve to identify the initial effects of a change in demand under only two conditions: when the demand change is unexpected, and when it is expected to be temporary. If firms expect a demand change (that is, anticipate it in advance), they can adjust their scales of plant or ready themselves to move into or out of a market before the change in demand actually occurs. An unexpected shift in demand in effect catches firms unaware, and they must operate temporarily with whatever scales of plant they have at that time. If firms expect a demand change to be temporary, they will not expand capacity or enter a market on the basis of conditions they know will not persist. Thus, in this case any change in output will result from the firms' utilizing existing plants more or less intensively, and a short-run analysis is appropriate.

Even when appropriate, a short-run analysis only identifies the temporary resting place for the industry, and subsequent long-run adjustments will continue to move the industry toward a long-run equilibrium. So in most supply-demand applications we generally use the long-run supply curve.

6.   The *price elasticity of supply* is a measure of the responsiveness of quantity supplied to a change in price. It is defined as the percentage change in quantity supplied divided by the percentage change in price. Using the Greek letter ϵ (epsilon) to represent price elasticity of supply, we can express it as

$$\epsilon = (\Delta Q/Q) \big/ (\Delta P/P).$$

We can calculate supply elasticities for either short-run or long-run supply curves. With long-run supply curves the elasticity of supply for a constant-cost industry is infinity since the supply curve is horizontal. Any upward-sloping supply curve — the increasing-cost case — has a positive elasticity since price and quantity move in the same direction.

With demand elasticities a value of unity is an intermediate value, not particularly high or unusually low. For long-run supply elasticities, however, a value of unity is extremely low. Think about what a long-run unitary supply elasticity means. If price rises by 50 percent, quantity supplied would increase by 50 percent. This result may not seem too implausible until we recall that in the long run economic profits must be zero despite a 50 percent increase in price. For this to occur, a 50 percent increase in total output would have to raise the average price of inputs by 50 percent — a result that is almost inconceivable. All industries use some inputs that would not go up in price appreciably with greater use because any single industry is just one of many that employ the same inputs. Examples might include unskilled labor, energy, land, insurance, capital. If some inputs do not rise in price, others would have to increase by more than 50 percent for the average input price to rise by 50 percent. It is difficult to believe that this situation could occur in very many industries.

Long-run elasticities of supply will typically exceed unity, and values approaching infinity (the constant-cost industry) may not be uncommon. This means that the upward-sloping supply curve of an increasing-cost industry is likely to be gently inclined and not as steep as it is sometimes drawn for emphasis.

THE LONG-RUN SUPPLY CURVE: AN ALTERNATIVE APPROACH
9.6

If we make the assumption of fixed input proportions in production (Section 6.2), we can derive the long-run supply curve in a simpler way. Recall that fixed input proportions mean that only one combination of inputs will produce a given product. Although the production function with variable input proportions is far more common, assuming fixed proportions allows us to illustrate the relationship between the product market and input markets with greater clarity than is possible in any other way.

Let's take the case of the product house painting and assume houses are painted by using only two inputs, paint and labor. The inputs are used in fixed proportions: 20 gallons of paint and 40 hours of labor will paint one house. In Figure 9–7 we derive the supply curve of houses painted. Since we assume fixed proportions, each quantity of houses painted is associated with unique quantities of the two inputs; when 10 houses are painted, for example, 200 gallons of paint and 400 hours of labor are used. This relationship means that we can use the horizontal axis to measure the quantities of the inputs as well as houses painted. Note that paint and labor are measured in blocks of 20 gallons and 40 hours, the quantities required to paint one house.

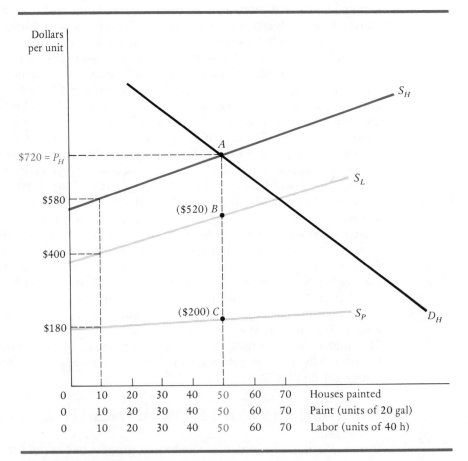

	0	10	20	30	40	50	60	70	Houses painted
0	10	20	30	40	50	60	70	Paint (units of 20 gal)
0	10	20	30	40	50	60	70	Labor (units of 40 h)

FIGURE 9–7

Product Supply Curve with Fixed Input Proportions

With fixed input proportions the output supply curve can be derived by a process of vertical addition of the input supply curves. Note that the equilibrium in the output market, shown by the intersection of D_H and S_H, implicitly determines the employment and prices of the inputs.

With the horizontal axis measuring the quantities of inputs, we can draw the supply curves of the inputs. The supply curve of paint is S_P, and it slopes upward, reflecting the assumption that an increased quantity of paint will be supplied only at a higher price. At a price of $180 per 20 gallons (or $9 per gallon), ten 20-gallon units (200 gallons, enough to paint 10 houses) will be supplied; forty 20-gallon units will be supplied at a price of $200. The supply curve of labor is S_L and also slopes upward.

The supply curve of houses painted is derived directly from the supply curves of the inputs used to produce this service. To see how this is done, recall that profits are zero on a long-run supply curve. Zero profit means that the price of the good will just cover the costs of production. For instance, an output of 10 houses painted implies that 200 gallons of paint and 400 hours of labor are required. The only costs of production are the payments for paint and labor, and when 10 houses are painted, each 20-gallon unit of paint costs $180 and each 40 hours of labor costs $400. It will therefore cost $580 to paint each house when output is 10, and competition will force the price down to the cost of production. Thus, at a price of $580 per house painted, the industry can supply 10 units and just cover the costs of production. This result identifies one zero-profit point on the supply curve of houses painted; it is derived graphically by summing the prices of the two inputs when output is 10. This is referred to as a vertical addition of input supply curves since the supply prices (shown on the vertical axis) of the inputs are added at a given quantity. Other points on the supply curve are derived in a similar manner.

This approach to the long-run supply curve makes it clear what determines the shape of the supply curve. If the supply curves of one or more inputs to the industry slope upward, then the supply curve of the product produced with those inputs will also slope upward. Input prices will vary along the output supply curve in a manner determined by the shapes of the input supply curves. Moreover, a shift in the supply curve of either input will cause the supply curve of houses painted to shift too, which is why we assume the supply curves of inputs to be given when drawing a long-run supply curve.

Supply, Demand, and Equilibrium

Now let's introduce the demand for house painting into the analysis and examine the determination of equilibrium price and quantity. When the demand curve for house painting is D_H, equilibrium occurs at the intersection of the demand curve and the industry supply curve, point A. The price of house painting is P_H, or $720 per house, and output is 50 houses painted (Figure 9–7). Note that the market equilibrium also determines the employment levels and prices of inputs, shown directly below point A at points B and C on the input supply curves. When 50 houses are painted, fifty 20-gallon units of paint are required, so the price of paint is $200, as shown at point C on the paint supply curve. Similarly, the price of labor is $520 per 40-hour unit.

This approach makes it clear that the determination of an equilibrium price and quantity in the product market simultaneously determines the prices and employment of the inputs used in the production of the product. In effect, it allows us to see what is going on behind the supply curve of a product and provides a more complete picture of the determinants of an equilibrium. Note that an increase in demand would lead to a higher price of house painting because the input supply curves slope upward, implying that input prices (and hence the firms' cost curves) will rise as more is produced. Figure 9–7 shows an increasing-cost industry since each firm's cost curves will shift upward as the industry output increases.

This analysis closely parallels our earlier derivation of the long-run supply curve for an increasing-cost industry, but now we show explicitly the crucial interrelationship with the input markets. While the fixed-input-proportion model is a special case, it serves to clarify how the shape of the supply curve depends on the supply curves of inputs. In addition, it provides a very useful technique to analyze problems where it is important to see how changes in input market conditions affect output markets, and vice versa.

WHY FIRMS EXIST
9.7

Because business firms are such familiar institutions, it is easy to take their existence for granted, which is exactly what we've done so far. In today's economy firms carry out most productive activity, but that has not always been true. Two hundred years ago business firms did not produce the bulk of goods and services in the economy. Instead, households produced many goods for themselves, and when they purchased goods from others, they frequently dealt with individuals rather than large business enterprises.

Today it is difficult to imagine our society without large business firms, yet it is possible to organize the production of goods in other ways. For example, how could automobiles be produced in the absence of business firms? If you wanted a car, you could enter into a contract directly with one individual to provide tires, with another individual to provide steel, with another to build a motor, and with still another to put all the parts together. This process would require hundreds of separate contracts, which would have to be carefully monitored and coordinated.

Obviously, automobile production could be organized in this way, but it would be tremendously expensive when the costs of entering into and enforcing the necessary transactions are taken into account. Business firms can produce automobiles more cheaply by purchasing inputs and directly overseeing the productive activities within the firm. In addition, per-unit production costs may be much lower at high levels of output because of increasing returns to scale in the production of some products. In short, *business firms exist because they are capable of producing some goods at a lower cost than can other organizational forms.*

The relative superiority of the firm as an institution to organize production varies among goods. Some goods and services, such as legal services, lawn mowing, and manuscript typing, are not typically produced by large business firms. Economists would predict that the institutions that are able to provide the product at the least cost will tend to emerge from the market process. If "Mom and Pop" operations or communes could organize production more efficiently (and therefore sell at a lower price), we would expect to see these forms of organizations drive firms out of business.

The very existence of firms sometimes obscures what is really happening in markets. Firms are artificial entities that serve as intermediaries between consumers and input suppliers. When Monica purchases an ear of corn from a grocer, what she is really doing is paying the farmer to grow the corn, the trucker to transport it, and the grocer to have it conveniently available. In short, she is compensating the owners of inputs for the services they provide. Looking beyond the firm, we can see that the result is much the same as if Monica dealt directly with all the individuals who participate in the production of corn.

The familiar slogan "Tax business, not people" typifies how misleading it can be to regard business firms as real entities rather than as intermediaries. What is a firm other than a set of working relationships among the people who own the firm, who work for it, who buy from it, and who sell to it? A tax on business must be a tax on people since it must ultimately burden either owners, suppliers, employees, or consumers.

When consumers purchase from a firm, the firm is the agency by which the consumer's demand is transmitted to the suppliers of inputs. The firm serves as an intermediary or middleman in the process, as illustrated explicitly in the fixed-proportions model discussed in the previous section. In Figure 9–7, consumers, by purchasing house painting from the firms, are clearly expressing a demand for labor and paint, a demand that the firms transmit by their purchases of inputs.

This view of firms as intermediaries in the process of exchange between households in their role as consumers and households in their role as owners of inputs is most accurate when applied to firms in a competitive market. Even there it is not entirely accurate since firms sometimes play a more active role — for instance, when they introduce new products. In addition, when markets are not competitive, firms do more than just passively serve as intermediaries, as we will see later.

WHEN DOES THE COMPETITIVE MODEL APPLY?
9.8

It is easier to explain the logic of the competitive model than to specify when it should be used. The assumptions of perfect competition are very stringent and are unlikely to be satisfied in any real world market. Yet economists use the competitive model in many instances when one or more of the assumptions are not fulfilled. In large part this practice reflects the position, discussed in Chapter 1, that the usefulness of any theory does not depend on the accuracy of its assumptions but rather on its ability to predict. And over the past two or three decades a large body of empirical evidence has accumulated that tends to support the implications of the competitive model as it applies to a large number of different industries.

We do not mean to imply that all industries can be treated as if they were competitive. In some cases economists generally agree that an industry is sufficiently noncompetitive that an alternative model must be used. In other cases economists disagree over the suitable model. For example, in the study of energy problems some economists treat the oil industry as competitive while others believe that because of collusive agreements and risk-sharing ventures, it more nearly resembles monopoly. Empirical evidence may ultimately resolve that disagreement, but this possibility provides little consolation to those who wish to analyze the oil industry now.

Economists also disagree about how to determine in practice whether some industry is "competitive enough" for the competitive model to apply. We can, however, make some observations that may help in evaluating specific cases. Consequently, we will focus on the way deviations from the assumptions of perfect competition will affect the market and explain why moderate aberrations do not significantly undermine the usefulness of the model.

Of the four assumptions of perfect competition, two are commonly regarded as relatively more significant: that resource mobility be unrestricted and that firms be sufficiently numerous that they will behave as price takers. Together these two assumptions imply that the long-run adjustment process will work approximately as we described it. The lure of profits will attract resources (inputs) to profitable industries, output will expand, price will fall, and (economic) profits will dissipate. Resources will leave unprofitable industries, output will fall, price will rise, and losses will give way to normal rates of return (zero economic profit). That, in essence, is the competitive adjustment process.

Resource Mobility

If resource mobility is restricted, the long-run adjustment process won't work as described. If for some reason resources cannot enter a profitable industry, the adjustment process is cut short at the outset. Similarly, if resources cannot leave an unprofitable industry, it may remain unprofitable. (Of course, it is much more common to have restricted entry into an industry than to have restricted exit.)

Thus, resource mobility is important to the competitive adjustment process. However, when there are restrictions on mobility, the competitive model can frequently be adapted to take them into account. This indicates another reason why the model is important: it can be extended to analyze the implications of specified departures from perfect competition. For example, suppose an industry is in long-run equilibrium and demand increases, but new firms are blocked from entering the market. It is easy to show that output will increase by less in this case, price will be higher, and economic profit will persist after the firms in the industry have made the appropriate long-run adjustment.

How Many Firms Are Enough?

If one assumption is usually associated with competitive markets more than any other, it is that there must be "many" small firms — perhaps because it is one assumption that can be readily checked directly: firms can be counted. The relationship between the number of firms and the degree of competition is not obvious, however. Indeed, the important point here is that firms face highly elastic (ideally, perfectly horizontal) demand curves, and assuming a large number of small firms guarantees this result. We will now look more carefully at how the number of firms relates to the elasticity of demand facing a given firm. Surprisingly, it is possible for the elasticity of demand facing each firm to be quite high with relatively few firms.

When we described the demand curve confronting the individual firm (Section 8.2), we assumed that other firms maintained the same output in response to a change in price. Now that we have discussed the industry supply curve, we can drop that assumption. Consider one firm. Its demand curve shows how much it can sell at different prices. At any price the amount sold must equal the total quantity purchased by consumers from all firms *minus* the amount supplied by other firms. At a lower price the amount sold will go up because the total quantity purchased increases (the market demand curve slopes downward) *and* because at a lower price the amount supplied by other firms will fall (their supply curve slopes upward).

Figure 9–8a shows how we can derive the demand curve confronting the single firm, X. Figure 9–8b illustrates the market demand curve D and the supply curve, S_O, of all the *other* firms in the market. In Figure 9–8a, if firm X produces nothing, the market price will be $10, and firm X's demand curve will begin at $10 on the vertical axis. How much can firm X sell at a price of $9? At $9 other firms reduce their output to 800 along their supply curve, but consumers are willing to purchase 1100, so firm X can sell the difference, 300 units. (This result assumes that other firms match the $9 price. If they don't, firm X could supply the entire market, 1100 units, at that price.) Now we have a second point on firm X's demand curve d. It is obviously highly elastic, with an arc elasticity (see Section 3.7) of 19, in fact.

Note how the reduction of output by other firms (200 units) and the expansion of total purchases (100 units) combine to determine how much firm X can sell at the lower price. The size of the reduction in output by

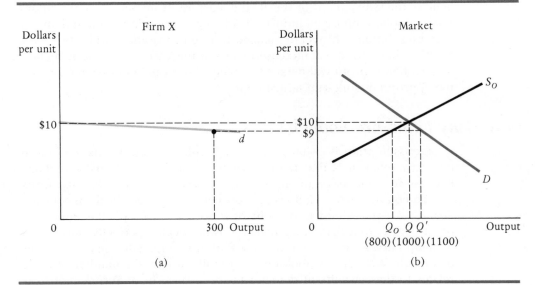

FIGURE 9–8

The Firm's Demand Curve

The demand curve facing firm X is *d*. It is derived by subtracting the quantity produced by other firms (indicated by S_o in part b) from the total quantity consumers wish to purchase (shown by *D*) at each alternative price. Taking the output response of the other firms into account, we see that the demand curve confronting any individual firm can be quite elastic, even if the firm produces a large portion of total industry output.

other firms is determined by the price elasticity of their supply curve; the size of the expansion in total purchases is determined by price elasticity of the market demand curve. Thus, the more elastic S_o and *D* are, the greater the elasticity of the demand curve confronting firm X will be.

Exactly how the elasticity of demand facing any one firm is influenced by these factors is shown by the following formula: [1]

$$\eta_i = (\eta/S_i) + [(Q_o/q_i)\epsilon_o].$$

---

[1] To derive this formula, we start with the fact that sales by firm *i* must equal total industry sales minus the sales of other firms:

$$q_i = Q_T - Q_O. \tag{1}$$

This relationship also holds for a given change in sales that results from a price change, as shown in Figure 9–8:

$$\Delta q_i = \Delta Q_T - \Delta Q_O. \tag{2}$$

Now divide by q_i, and multiply the two terms on the right by Q_T/Q_T and Q_O/Q_O:

$$\Delta q_i/q_i = (\Delta Q_T/Q_T)(Q_T/q_i) - (\Delta Q_O/Q_O)(Q_O/q_i). \tag{3}$$

Dividing the expression by $\Delta P/P$ yields the formula in the text. (The minus sign becomes a plus because we are treating the elasticity of demand as a positive number.)

In this formula η_i is the elasticity of firm i's demand curve, η is the elasticity of the market demand curve (treated as a positive number), S_i is firm i's share of total industry sales, Q_O is the output of other firms, q_i is firm i's output, and ϵ_O is the elasticity of supply of other firms. This formula just codifies our earlier conclusions. It shows that the elasticity of demand for firm i is larger the smaller its share of total industry output, the greater the elasticity of the market demand curve, and the greater the elasticity of the supply curve of the other firms.

Now let's see what this formula means in a particular instance. Suppose a firm sells a fourth of the total industry output, so $S_i = 0.25$ and $Q_O/q_i = 75\%/25\% = 3$. We don't know η and ϵ_O since these elasticities are likely to vary from case to case, so let's just use plausible intermediate values: assume η is 1 and ϵ_O is 2. (Recall that an elasticity of supply of 2 is not particularly large; indeed, it is probably smaller than the value true of most industries.) Substituting these values in the formula, we get

$$\eta_i = (1/0.25) + 3(2) = 10.$$

This firm, even though its output is equal to a fourth of the entire industry output, faces a demand curve with an elasticity of 10. This means that if the firm raises price by just 5 percent, it will lose half its sales. Now the question is, Is this demand curve *elastic enough* to treat the firm as a competitive firm? Certainly, the firm has very little ability to control the price, but is it small enough to ignore? In addition, if other firms in the industry are smaller and have even more elastic demand curves, do we get a close enough approximation to reality by analyzing the industry as a competitive industry composed of price-taking firms? Many economists would answer these questions in the affirmative, but others would probably disagree.

Wherever one chooses to draw the line, it is clear that an industry can contain a relatively small number of firms, and yet each firm can face a surprisingly elastic demand curve. To put this in perspective, let's examine some information on the degree of concentration in American manufacturing industries. Scholars in industrial organization use the *four-firm concentration ratio*, which is the share of industry sales accounted for by the four largest firms together, to measure concentration. In 1972 the average four-firm concentration ratio across all industries was 39.1 percent, and the average size of the single largest firm in each industry was 17.5 percent (implying an elasticity of 15, using the assumptions above). Seventy percent of manufacturing output was produced by industries with four-firm concentration ratios below 50 percent; 12.5 percent was produced by industries with ratios above 70 percent.[2]

---

[2] These figures come from Tables 8.3 and 8.6 in James V. Koch, *Industrial Organization and Prices,* 2nd ed. (Englewood Cliffs, N.J.: Prentice-Hall, 1980). There are well-known problems in using any concentration ratio as an indication of competitiveness, however. See F. M. Scherer, *Industrial Market Structure and Economic Performance,* 2nd ed. (Chicago: Rand McNally, 1980), pp. 59–64.

A large number of firms is not required for price-taking behavior to be a reasonably close approximation, but exactly where to draw the line can't be specified unambiguously since it depends on how close an approximation you expect the theory to provide.

Homogeneity

The assumption that firms produce a homogeneous, or standardized, product serves two purposes in the competitive model. It implies that a uniform price will prevail, and it affects the elasticity of demand facing a particular firm. In Chapter 13 we will discuss the theory of monopolistic competition, a model based on a large number of firms, each producing a slightly differentiated product. As it turns out, the implications of monopolistic competition are closer to competition than to monopoly. For the present let's turn briefly to an example of a market where the product is not homogeneous but where the competitive model seems to apply.

In the late 1960s several comparison-shopping surveys found that food prices were higher in the inner city than in the suburbs.[3] For those who expect the competitive model to be an accurate description of reality, this result violates the uniform-price implication and might suggest monopoly pricing in the inner cities. Further investigation determined that profits (in the accountant's sense) were no higher for inner-city food stores than for suburban markets, a result consistent with competition but not with monopoly.

What was going on? Basically, food sold in the inner city and food sold in the suburbs were not homogeneous products. To city residents, food sold in the inner city was worth more than food sold farther away. People were willing to pay something for the convenience of shopping nearby; and when convenience costs the retailer something, the price of the "same" product will differ. In comparison with costs in the suburbs, costs of operating a food store in the inner city are higher because rent, fire insurance, theft insurance, taxes, and the salaries of personnel all tend to be higher there. Apparently, inner-city residents were willing to pay the higher price for the added convenience.

Dropping the homogeneous product assumption means that small differentials in price can exist; but that is not often a serious problem, and the competitive model can still be used. Suppose, for example, city government passed a law that food prices in the inner city could not exceed prices in the suburbs. The competitive model applied to this setting would predict that output (food sales) would fall in the inner city, shortages would exist, some food stores would go out of business, and many inner-

---

[3] "The Inner City Poor Found to Pay More for Food than Others," *Wall Street Journal*, September 6, 1968.

city residents would be worse off because no food was conveniently available at the mandated lower price — the familiar effects of a price ceiling. These predictions would, we suspect, be borne out in practice.

Information

The assumption that firms and consumers have all the relevant information is also necessary if markets are to behave in all respects exactly as the competitive model predicts. For example, if consumers are ignorant of price, even homogeneous products can sell for different prices. Indeed, if consumers and firms were, in some sense, completely ignorant, it is not clear what would happen. Dropping the assumption of full information does not mean that we have to replace it with one of complete ignorance. One of the results of real world markets is that firms and consumers have incentives to acquire the information that is important for their economic decisions. Although they may not become fully informed, since it costs something to acquire information, we can suppose that they will become well enough informed that the assumption of complete information is not too great a distortion.

Economists have only recently begun to systematically analyze the acquisition of information and the way "information costs" influence the workings of markets. It is too early to make any sweeping generalizations in this area, but we do not want to suggest that the degree of information is irrelevant to the functioning of a market. Lack of information on the part of consumers may sometimes result in market outcomes that deviate significantly from the competitive norm. For example, many economists believe that this result is true of markets for products that are intrinsically difficult for consumers to evaluate, like medical care and auto repairs.

A Final Point

Our discussion may have suggested that any particular industry must be either competitive or noncompetitive in some specific way. That conclusion is not exactly correct. Actually, it may be appropriate to treat an industry as competitive for some purposes and as noncompetitive for others. For example, a competitive analysis of a tariff on automobile imports implies reduced imports, higher prices, lower consumer purchases, and higher domestic production. We believe that assessment would be accurate. However, when we turn to a study of the employment practices of General Motors, or of its use of franchises in marketing, it may be best to treat GM as a monopoly. Treating GM as a member of a competitive industry in one case and as a monopoly in another may produce more accurate results than assuming GM to be a monopoly or a competitive firm in both cases. The correct theoretical model depends on the problem being investigated.

As these remarks make clear, it is not an easy matter to determine when to use the competitive model, and we do not mean to suggest that all industries should be analyzed as if they were perfectly competitive. It is important to understand that the opposite position — that few, if any, industries are competitive because all the assumptions of perfect competition are not fully satisfied — is equally unsatisfactory. To repeat a point made before, theories cannot be adequately evaluated by checking the accuracy of their assumptions.

Summary

Our emphasis in this chapter was on how the selling side of a competitive market can be analyzed with a supply curve. In the short run the industry supply curve is the horizontal summation of the short-run marginal cost curves of the firms in the industry. Since the law of diminishing marginal returns implies that each firm's marginal cost curve slopes upward, the short-run industry supply curve will also slope upward.

In the long run firms have sufficient time to alter plant capacity and to enter or leave the industry. The long-run supply curve must take these adjustments into account, with the firms always guided by the search for profits. Two common shapes of the long-run supply curve are possible. First, an increasing-cost industry has an upward-sloping long-run supply curve, reflecting the increase in the prices of one or more inputs as the industry expands. Second, a constant-cost industry has a horizontal long-run supply curve, reflecting a situation where the industry can expand its use of inputs without affecting their prices.

At all points along a long-run supply curve, economic profits are zero, since only when this is true is there no incentive for firms to enter or leave the industry. Technology and input supply curves are assumed given in deriving a long-run supply curve; changes in these underlying conditions will cause the supply curve to shift. These relationships can be seen most clearly by using the supply curve based on fixed input proportions, a special but instructive case.

The model of a perfectly competitive industry developed in this chapter relies on four assumptions: a large number of buyers and sellers; unrestricted mobility of resources; firms producing a homogeneous product; and firms and consumers possessing all relevant information. Few, if any, real world industries satisfy fully these assumptions, but a theoretical model does not have to describe reality accurately to help us understand it. We explained how moderate deviations from the four conditions need not impair the usefulness of the model. There are, however, no hard-and-fast rules about when the competitive model is appropriate.

Review Questions and Problems

1. What are the four assumptions of the perfectly competitive model? Critics are fond of pointing out that few, if any, real world markets satisfy all four conditions, implying that the competitive model has little relevance for real world markets. How would you respond to these critics?

2. Starting from a long-run equilibrium, trace the effects of an unanticipated reduction in demand for (a) a constant-cost industry; and (b) an increasing-cost industry. Note: This process is just the reverse of our derivation of the supply curves in Section 9.4, but it is very good practice to think through the process. Be sure to use diagrams.

3. What is the difference between constant-cost and increasing-cost industries?

What underlying conditions determine whether a competitive industry will be one of constant or increasing costs?

*4. "In a constant-cost industry each firm has an upward-sloping marginal cost curve, yet all the firms together — the industry — have a horizontal supply curve." Explain why there is no contradiction in this statement.

5. Which of the following statements is true of a long-run competitive equilibrium? "Average cost of production equals price." "Average cost of production determines price."

*6. "In long-run equilibrium the price just covers average production cost, and every firm is making zero profit. Thus, if the price goes down, even a little bit, all the firms will have to go out of business." Discuss this statement.

*7. Following up on the suggestion on page 261, assume a constant-cost industry is in long-run equilibrium. Demand increases, but for some reason new firms are not permitted to enter the market. Analyze the determination of a new long-run equilibrium, showing the effects for a representative firm as well as the industry as a whole.

8. "Economists generally regard competitive markets favorably, despite their assumption that firms are out to make as much money as possible. Obviously, the way for a firm to make money is to sell its product at a high price while paying its workers low wages. So economists glorify a system in which businesses gouge consumers and exploit workers." Evaluate this criticism.

9. If demand increases, will the price always rise in the short run, and then fall somewhat to its final long-run equilibrium level?

10. How do we derive the long-run supply curve in the fixed-input-proportions case?

11. Assume wheat is produced by a competitive industry that uses land and labor in fixed proportions. Both input supply curves slope upward. Show an initial equilibrium, and analyze the effects of a reduction in the supply of labor on the price and quantity of wheat, the wage rate and employment of workers, and the price and amount of land employed.

12. What do we always assume to be constant in drawing a long-run supply curve? How will a change in these factors affect the supply curve? Give examples to illustrate your answer.

*13. How would each of the following phenomena affect the long-run supply curve of apples?
a. Workers in the apple industry form a union.
b. Consumers find out that apples cause cancer.
c. Hard-to-control bugs that eat apples invade from Mexico.
d. The government passes a law requiring apple trees to be planted at least 60 feet apart.
e. The government sets a maximum legal price (price ceiling) at which apples can be sold.
f. Immigration laws change to permit more itinerant apple pickers to enter the country.
g. The government passes a minimum wage law for apple pickers.

14. "Since agricultural demand is inelastic, a technological advance that lowers costs will reduce total revenues. Thus, farmers have no incentive to introduce such techniques." True or false? Explain.

15. In what way is the size of a single firm's output, compared with total industry output, relevant in deciding whether the industry is competitive? Do you think the competitive model will yield reasonably accurate predictions when the largest firm in an industry produces 10 percent of industry output? How about 20 percent? 30 percent? 40 percent? 60 percent?

16. Suppose the largest firm in an industry produces 30 percent of total output, the industry demand curve is unit elastic, and the elasticity of supply of other firms is 3.0. What

is the elasticity of demand for the largest firm? Will it be larger or smaller for the other firms?

*17. Assume the ball-point pen industry is competitive and one of the firms in the industry is located in Charlottesville. Suppose the city of Charlottesville levies an excise tax of $0.50 per pen on the output of this firm. What will be the short-run and long-run effects of this tax? (Compare with questions 13 and 14 in Chapter 8.)

18. The provision of taxicab services (in passenger miles per year) in a city is a constant-cost industry. The government requires drivers to have a license, and it gives licenses to all current drivers. It issues no more licenses. Demand for cab services rises. What happens to the price of cab services (fares) and the incomes of drivers? Do you think cab drivers would want the city to issue new licenses to anyone who wishes to drive a cab? Explain.

Supplementary Readings

Adams, Walter. *The Structure of American Industry.* 5th ed. New York: Macmillan, 1977.

Coase, Ronald. "The Nature of the Firm." In *Readings in Price Theory,* edited by K. Boulding and G. Stigler. Homewood, Ill.: Irwin, 1952.

Fama, Eugene F., and Laffer, Arthur B. "The Number of Firms and Competition," *American Economic Review,* 62 (September 1972): 670–674.

Friedman, Milton. *Price Theory.* Chicago: Aldine, 1976.

Stigler, George. "Perfect Competition, Historically Contemplated." In *Microeconomics: Selected Readings,* 3rd ed., edited by Edwin Mansfield. New York: Norton, 1979.

Using the Competitive Model

10

We can view the competitive model best perhaps as a flexible framework that can be used to analyze economic phenomena. While everyone "knows" that supply and demand determine prices, few people understand the concepts sufficiently well to analyze specific issues. An appreciation of the range of topics that can be investigated and of the ways the competitive model can be extended and adapted to take account of specific factors comes only with practice. In this chapter we will discuss several applications of the competitive model to show how economists have used it to analyze particular issues. A few examples are hypothetical, but the rest examine recent United States experience with airline regulation, rent controls, agricultural price supports and acreage restrictions, and medical care subsidies.

EXCISE SUBSIDY
10.1

Let's begin by assuming the government decides it is desirable to increase the output of a particular industry by providing an excise subsidy. We can trace the effects of this subsidy in a straightforward way by using the industry's supply and demand curves. It may prove helpful to proceed a bit more slowly at first and look at how both the industry and a representative firm in the industry are affected.

In Figure 10–1 we assume that the industry is initially in equilibrium. Figure 10–1a shows a typical firm making zero economic profit at the market-determined price of \$10. Figure 10–1b identifies the equilibrium price and output for the industry at \$10 and $0Q_1$, as determined by the intersection of the long-run supply curve LS and the demand curve D at point A. Then the government introduces the subsidy. The subsidy could be paid either to the firms or to the consumers. As we will see later, the effects are the same in both cases. For the moment, we will assume the firms receive the subsidy.

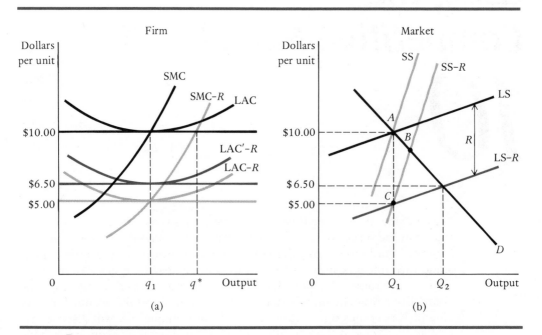

FIGURE 10-1
Effects of a Per-unit Excise Subsidy

(a) Firms continue to make zero economic profit once a new long-run equilibrium emerges. (b) A per-unit excise subsidy shifts LS downward by the amount of the subsidy to LS–R, so output increases and price falls.

Subsidizing Production

Suppose the government gives each firm $5 for every unit of output it sells. Such a subsidy is called a per-unit excise subsidy. What is the immediate impact of the subsidy on the individual firm? Before the subsidy, long-run average cost at output $0q_1$ is $10, but a subsidy reduces the *net* average cost to the firm of providing that output to $5 per unit. In fact, at any rate of output the net per-unit cost is $5 lower than before. In the diagram this is shown as a downward shift in the firm's per-unit cost curves. The long-run average cost curve LAC shifts vertically downward to LAC–R, where R is the $5 per-unit subsidy. All other cost curves shift downward too. The firm is now making economic profits at the initial output since price is greater than average cost. Note, however, that at the original level of output, price is greater than net marginal cost. The price is still $10, but the subsidy has reduced the firm's marginal cost from $10 to $5. The firm can increase profits further by expanding output along the new short-run marginal cost curve SMC–R to $0q^*$. Thus, we have identified two important consequences: the subsidy results in profits for the firm at the $10 market price, and the firm has an incentive to expand production.

All the firms in the industry have the same inducement to expand output, and a higher output can only be sold at a lower price to consumers. Figure 10–1b shows this result. The initial short-run industry supply curve SS is the sum of the SMC curves of the firms. Because the subsidy reduces the firms' marginal cost curves, it also shifts the SS curve vertically downward by $5 per unit to SS–R, since SS–R is the sum of the SMC–R curves. In other words, firms can sell a given rate of output at a price that is $5 lower to consumers because the government absorbs $5 of the per-unit cost. Consequently, as firms expand output along their SMC–R curves, the industry expands along SS–R. The short-run equilibrium is therefore at point B, with a higher output and a lower price.

Since the firms are still making profits, we have not reached a position of long-run equilibrium. Economic profits continue to provide incentive for further expansion in output, so firms will expand capacity in the long run or new firms will enter the market, a process that continues until profits are eliminated. We can identify the new long-run equilibrium by using the long-run supply curve. Since the subsidy shifts the LS curve downward by $5 per unit to LS–R, zero profits will be made at each rate of output at a consumer price that is $5 lower than the original price. Thus, SS and LS both shift down by $5, as shown by the distance AC in Figure 10–1b. In the short run the industry expands along SS–R while in the long run it expands along LS–R. The final long-run equilibrium includes a further expansion of output to $0Q_2$, and the price to consumers is $6.50.

Note that the price to consumers has only fallen by $3.50, but the subsidy is $5. The reason for this difference is that we have assumed the long-run supply curve is upward-sloping (an increasing-cost industry), implying that some input prices are bid up as the industry expands output. As a result, the cost curves of the firms shift upward as the industry expands along its long-run supply curve. Figure 10–1a shows this outcome, where the LAC'–R curve rises to LAC'–R, and the firm is making zero economic profit at the price of $6.50.

We can determine the long-run results of the subsidy more quickly by using the LS and D curves and by recognizing that the subsidy shifts LS to LS–R. This immediately identifies the outcome: greater output and lower price to consumers. However, the step-by-step analysis we have used helps reinforce the nature of the long-run adjustment process and emphasizes how the process affects an individual firm.

Of particular interest are two implications of this analysis. First, even though the subsidy is granted to firms, it ultimately benefits consumers in the form of a lower price since it creates incentive for the industry to expand output. Second, after the long-run adjustment, the firms are once again making zero economic profit even though they are receiving $11.50 per unit ($6.50 from consumers and $5 from government), which is higher than the original $10 price. Who benefits on the supply side of the market? As before, it is the owners of inputs that are bid up in price as the industry expands production.

This analysis should make one hesitant in accepting the view that all subsidies paid to business firms are in some sense "windfalls for business." For example, until 1975 (when the subsidy was eliminated for all but small producers), firms in the oil industry received what amounted to a subsidy in the form of a special tax provision called the percentage depletion allowance. Most observers viewed this provision as a benefit to the oil industry, but the analysis here suggests that the industry would pass on at least part of this subsidy to consumers in the form of lower prices for petroleum products. Prior to the emergence of OPEC as a market force in 1973, profits in the oil industry (at least insofar as they can be measured by accounting rates of return) were not above the national average, suggesting that zero economic profit was being earned despite the subsidy.[1]

Subsidizing Consumption

Now let's see what will happen if the $5 per-unit subsidy goes to the consumers rather than the firms: the government will give consumers $5 for each unit purchased. For variety, let's change the analysis in one other respect by assuming that the industry is a constant-cost industry and therefore has a horizontal long-run supply curve. In Figure 10–2 the initial demand and supply curves are D and S, output is $0Q_1$, and price is $10.

The subsidy increases the price consumers are willing to pay for the product. For example, at $0Q_1$ consumers would have paid $10 per unit for the good before receiving the subsidy. With the subsidy they will be willing to pay up to $15 per unit for the same quantity since their *net* cost will still only be $10 ($5 of the $15 is the government subsidy), and at a price of $10 their desired level of consumption is $0Q_1$ units. In effect, the subsidy is added to the price consumers will pay at each quantity, which is represented by an upward shift in the demand curve to D', where $D' = D + R$.

Once the way the subsidy affects demand is worked out, the rest of the analysis is straightforward. As far as the industry is concerned, there has been an increase in demand, and it adjusts accordingly. The final result is that output increases to $0Q_2$, and the price received by firms remains unchanged at $10. Because the industry is a constant-cost industry, firms can expand output along supply curve S without increasing their per-unit production costs. We must interpret the final equilibrium with a bit of care, however. Firms receive $10; but when consumers pay $10 for a unit, they receive a $5 reimbursement from the government. Consequently, the *net* cost to consumers is really $5 per unit, which is indicated by the height to their original demand curve, CQ_2, showing that purchases

[1] Over the period 1963–1972, the average return on net worth in petroleum production and refining was 11.7 percent while the average for all United States manufacturing was 12.2 percent. See Shyam Sunder, *Oil Industry Profits* (Washington, D.C.: American Enterprise Institute, 1977).

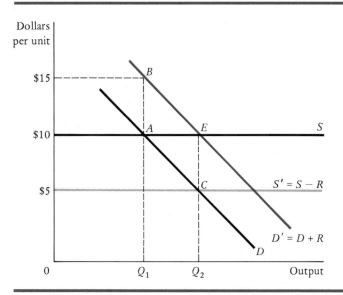

FIGURE 10-2

A Per-unit Excise Subsidy for a Constant-cost Industry

We can analyze a $5 per-unit subsidy to consumers as an upward shift in demand by $5, to D'. If instead the $5 per-unit subsidy is paid to producers, the supply curve shifts downward by $5, to S'. In both cases the final results are the same: output is $0Q_2$, and the net price to consumers is $5.

will be $0Q_2$ when the price consumers themselves must pay is $5. The distance CE between the subsidized and unsubsidized demand curves is equal to the $5 subsidy the government adds to the consumers' payments. As far as consumers are concerned, the effect of the subsidy is to lower their out-of-pocket cost from $10 to $5.

The Equivalence of the Two Subsidies

As we demonstrated earlier in more detail, if the government grants the subsidy to firms instead of consumers, the supply curve will shift down by $5, from S to S' in Figure 10–2. The final equilibrium will occur at $0Q_2$ with a price of $5 to the consumer. This analysis demonstrates a remarkable result: the outcome is the same regardless of whether the subsidy is paid to firms or to consumers. In both cases output is $0Q_2$. In both cases the net (out-of-pocket) price to consumers is $5. When consumers receive the subsidy, they pay $10 for the product but receive $5 from the government; when the firms receive the subsidy, consumers pay $5 and receive no subsidy so the net effect is the same. In both cases firms receive $10 per unit. When consumers receive the subsidy, the firms receive a price of $10 from consumers; when the firms receive the subsidy, they receive $5 from consumers plus $5 from the government for each unit they sell.

A basic proposition in economics is that it makes no difference whether firms or consumers receive the subsidy. This proposition is true whether the supply curve is upward sloping or horizontal. Analytically, we can incorporate the subsidy as an upward shift in the demand curve or a downward shift in the supply curve, regardless of who actually receives the subsidy. We can apply the same approach to taxes, as we will see when we discuss the way the Social Security payroll tax is divided between employers and employees (Chapter 16).

One other implication of the analysis is of interest. In Figure 10–2 we saw that the price to consumers fell by the full amount of the subsidy, $5 per unit. In Figure 10–1 the price only fell by $3.50 per unit. The difference is due to the shapes of the supply curves. With the upward-sloping supply curve in Figure 10–1, increased output leads to a higher unit cost, so part of the subsidy is necessary to cover the increased costs per unit, and price to consumers cannot fall by the full amount of the subsidy. With the horizontal supply curve in Figure 10–2, per-unit costs of production do not rise as output is expanded, and price to consumers falls by the full amount of the subsidy. This is sometimes summarized in this way: the more elastic the supply curve, the greater is the benefit of a given subsidy to consumers, and the less is the benefit to those engaged in producing the good. (Try rotating the supply curve at point A in Figure 10–2 and check the results.)

MEDICARE AND MEDICAID
10.2

In the previous section we examined the effects of a subsidy given to everyone who consumed some product. Yet many real world subsidies apply only to some consumers and exclude others. Examples include Medicare, Medicaid, housing subsidies, job-training programs, and food stamps. To analyze such programs, we must modify the analysis of the previous section slightly, and we will do so to examine Medicare and Medicaid.

Medicare and Medicaid were both enacted in 1965. Medicare is a subsidy of the medical care received by the elderly, and Medicaid is a subsidy of the medical care received by the poor. The subsidies, therefore, are targeted on two sometimes overlapping subsets of the population. They involve fairly heavy subsidies in the sense that the government covers virtually all the costs of medical care for Medicaid recipients and a large share of the costs for Medicare recipients. In our analysis we will assume that these programs cover all the medical costs of the subsidized groups. Although this assumption is a slight exaggeration, it does not distort the nature of the effects.

The key to analyzing programs that directly apply to only a subset of consumers is to recognize that the total market demand curve is the sum of the demand curves of the subsidized and nonsubsidized groups. In Figure 10–3 the demand curves of the two groups prior to the subsidy are D_S and D_N. The total demand curve D_T is the horizontal sum of D_S and D_N, and the intersection of D_T and the supply curve S determines price and total quantity, P and $0M_T$. At price P the (to be) subsidized group is initially consuming $0M_S$ and the nonsubsidized group, $0M_N$. Of course, $0M_S + 0M_N$ equals total consumption, $0M_T$.

Medicare and Medicaid act to increase the effective demand of the subsidized group. Assuming the government covers all medical care costs, the cost of medical care to the subsidized group is effectively zero. At a zero cost desired consumption rises to $0M'_S$. This amount, in fact, is the quantity demanded regardless of what the market price is, since Medicare and Medicaid recipients pay a zero price when the government covers all the costs. In the diagram the effect of Medicare and Medicaid is shown by a shift in D_S to D'_S, implying that desired consumption is $0M'_S$ regardless of the market price.

Medicare and Medicaid tend to increase the demand of the subsidized group for medical care, which increases the total demand for medical care services to D'_T: D'_T is equal to the sum of the unchanged demand

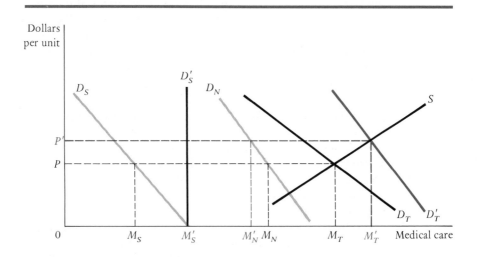

FIGURE 10-3

Medicare and Medicaid Subsidies

When government pays for all the medical care of the *S* group of consumers, D_S shifts to D'_S, which causes the total demand to shift to D'_T. Price rises to P', and the nonsubsidized group consumes less while the net-of-subsidy price to the *S* group is zero, and they consume more.

curve of the other group, D_N, and D_S'. This increase in market demand combined with an upward-sloping supply curve causes the market price to rise to P' and total output to increase to $0M_T'$. At the higher price the unsubsidized group curtails consumption to $0M_N'$ while the subsidized group increases consumption from $0M_S$ to $0M_S'$. The subsidy, although it applies only to some consumers, increases the price for everyone, but the net-of-subsidy price to the subsidized group falls (to zero). The unsubsidized group is harmed in two ways: by paying a higher price for medical care and by paying taxes to support the subsidy. Recipients of the subsidy gain, as do some owners of inputs engaged in the production of medical care.

In passing, we note that we have applied the competitive model to a market that departs significantly from the assumptions of perfect competition. Medical care is not a homogeneous product; consumers are probably not well informed about the nature of the product they receive; and some believe entry into the medical profession is partially blocked by the American Medical Association. That doesn't mean, however, that the model is inappropriate for the analysis here. It identifies an important effect of the subsidy — a major increase in the demand by some consumers — and it allows us to work out the consequences. Moreover, these consequences seem to be borne out by the available evidence.

Medicare and Medicaid were enacted in 1965. Between 1966 and 1970 medical care prices rose by 29 percent, whereas the overall consumer price index rose by only 20 percent. In other words, the relative price of medical care increased significantly shortly after the subsidies were introduced, as the analysis predicts. The analysis also suggests increased consumption by the subsidized groups. By the early 1970s the poor were consuming more medical care per person (according to some measures) than were middle- and upper-income groups, but the reverse was true before Medicare and Medicaid. For example, doctor visits per poor person rose from 4.3 per year in 1964 to 5.6 per year in 1973 while doctor visits by the nonpoor changed only slightly, from 4.6 to 4.9, over the same period.[2] These figures do not prove conclusively that Medicare and Medicaid were responsible for the changes. Possibly other factors were involved. Nevertheless, most analysts believe that these programs played a significant role in producing these results.

In analyzing these programs, we used the technique of disaggregating the total demand curve into its relevant component parts. This approach can also be used to analyze the supply side of a market. For example, the supply of automobiles available to American consumers includes both domestically produced and imported automobiles. The total supply curve of automobiles is therefore the sum of the supply curve of domestically produced automobiles and the supply curve of imported automobiles. In

---

[2] Karen Davis, *National Health Insurance: Benefits, Costs, and Consequences* (Washington, D.C.: Brookings Institution, 1975).

analyzing something that effects only one source of supply, such as a tariff or quota on imported automobiles, we must separate the supply curve into its component parts since the policy will effect them differently.

RENT CONTROLS
10.3

During World War II, many local governments in the United States applied price controls to rental housing units, a policy generally referred to as rent control. New York City was the only major city to continue rent controls after the war, and it still uses them today. Apart from New York, relatively few localities experimented with rent controls until the 1970s, when an increasing number of communities adopted the practice. By 1980 over two hundred localities were using some form of rent controls, including Los Angeles, Washington, D.C., and Boston.

We can examine the likely effects of rent controls with the aid of Figure 10–4, which shows the long-run supply and demand curves for rental housing units *in a particular community.* The fact that rent controls are generally applied by specific communities or cities has a bearing on the elasticities of these relationships. Since potential tenants have the options of living outside the community or purchasing a home rather than renting, the elasticity of demand for rental housing in one community will be higher than the elasticity of demand for housing services generally. Similarly, landlords can shift resources to nonhousing investments or to other communities if returns fall, so the supply elasticity is also likely to be high. (We are considering the long-run effects here. Later, the short-run effects will be brought into the analysis.) As we will see, high supply and demand elasticities have an impact on the quantitative effects of rent controls.

In Figure 10–4, in the absence of rent controls, the equilibrium price (rental) is *P*, or $400 per month, and 0*Q* is the quantity supplied and demanded. A rent control policy has the effect of imposing a maximum rental price on rental units that is below the equilibrium level. Suppose the price is not allowed to rise above P_M, or $350 per month. The first question to answer is whether the law can be effectively enforced. Since tenants are willing to pay a higher price, landlords have incentive to extract side payments from tenants. Although tenants cannot be forced to pay an explicit rent greater than $350, landlords may require tenants to pay a large nonrefundable key deposit, to purchase furniture as a condition for renting, or to pay for their own repairs. All these practices have been observed to result from rent controls. Unless the law explicitly blocks such practices, they will occur, and they have the effect of nullifying the policy. That is, tenants will pay $350 in explicit rent, but the extras will add $50 per month to their housing costs, leaving the effective price unchanged.

Let's assume that these methods of circumventing the law are not allowed. (The practices mentioned above are, in fact, illegal under most

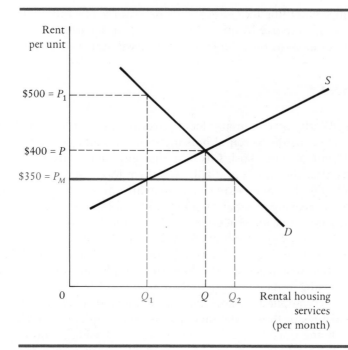

FIGURE 10–4
Rent Controls

With a legal maximum rent of $350 set below the market equilibrium level of $400, the quantity supplied falls from $0Q$ to $0Q_1$, and the quantity demanded rises to $0Q_2$. The difference, Q_1Q_2, is the excess demand, or shortage, created by the rent control policy.

rent control laws.) The price that consumers must pay is lower, and at a lower price the quantity demanded is greater; namely, $0Q_2$. At the lower price, however, the quantity supplied will fall to $0Q_1$ since investment in this market becomes less profitable. Fewer new rental units will be constructed and owners will allow existing units to deteriorate more rapidly by reducing maintenance and repairs. For example, one study of rent controls in New York City found that repair expenditures for rent-controlled apartments were only half as large as expenditures on comparable apartments not subject to rent control.[3]

The result of rent control, like that of any other price ceiling applied in a competitive market, is a shortage. The quantity that potential tenants would like to rent ($0Q_2$) is greater than the quantity available ($0Q_1$), and the excess of quantity demanded over quantity supplied, Q_1Q_2, measures the shortage. (Note that the shortage will be larger the higher the elastici-

[3] G. Sternlieb, *The Urban Housing Dilemma* (New York: New York Housing and Development Administration, 1972), p. 202.

ties of supply and demand.) Since only $0Q_1$ units are actually available, the marginal value of housing units to consumers must be at least $500 (the height to the demand curve at $0Q_1$). Price, however, cannot rise above $350, so producers have no incentive to increase quantity beyond $0Q_1$.

Rent controls are certain to have effects on other markets, too. Not all people who wish to rent are able to, so they must make other living arrangements. Apart from living in a different community, the major alternative is some form of owner-occupied housing. Therefore, the demand for such housing will increase as frustrated apartment hunters turn to home ownership. At the same time the owners of rent-controlled apartments have an incentive to convert their rental units into owner-occupied units, or condominiums, that are sold to tenants. Since the residents own condominiums, they are not subject to rent control. Conversion of rental units into condominiums is another way the quantity of rental housing will be reduced if it is permitted to occur.

In testimony before a congressional committee studying condominium conversion in 1979, Washington, D.C., Mayor Marion Barry made this observation:

> The rental housing stock in the District [of Columbia] is being reduced by conversion of apartment buildings to condominiums at a rapidly accelerating rate.... The impact is especially noticeable in our City because traditionally the District has had a housing market oriented toward rental units to accommodate its transient population.... In the District, we have attempted since 1974 to restrain the market through such legislative measures as rent control and condominium conversion regulations.[4]

Mayor Barry apparently did not connect the problem of condominium conversion with the rent control policy that had been in effect in the District of Columbia since 1974. Typically, communities with rent controls must resort to limitations on condominium conversion to prevent the supply of rental units from drying up completely.

Who Loses, Who Benefits?

Those obviously harmed by rent controls are the owners of rental units at the time the policy is implemented. They have invested in the construction or purchase of units in the expectation of being able to charge $400 (in our example), but they find that their return is reduced by law. Over time the owners, or landlords, may be able to avoid the loss recurring year after year by reducing the maintenance and repairs until the lower rent covers the cost of the lower-quality product. Recall that in the long run, when output is $0Q_1$ and price is P_M, economic profits are zero, the same as they were before rent control. The long-run harm on the supply side is to the

---

[4] U.S. Senate, *Condominium Housing Issues* (Washington, D.C.: U.S. Government Printing Office, 1978), pp. 10–12.

owners of inputs in relatively inelastic supply. (Our guess is that the most important input of this type is land.) Other groups will also be made worse off by rent controls, as we will see shortly.

Now consider who benefits from rent control. The *intended* beneficiaries are clear. In virtually all cases the proponents of rent controls expressly seek to benefit tenants. Economists, however, are skeptical over the degree to which this benefit actually occurs. Indeed, some economists believe that tenants on average are worse off under rent controls. While lower rents by themselves are good for tenants, other changes occur in the functioning of the market that are not advantageous.

First, the lower rental price is necessarily accompanied by a lower quantity (quantity falls from $0Q$ to $0Q_1$ in Figure 10–4). A lower price is good for tenants, but fewer rental units are not, and the net effect of the two is uncertain. It is conceivable that all tenants are made worse off. To see this intuitively, suppose the quantity of available rental units falls to zero under rent control. A lower price does tenants little good if they are unable to find housing.

Moreover, it is unlikely that all tenants will be affected in the same way. Instead of every tenant's getting less housing than desired, some may be able to find what they want at the lower rents, while others may be unable to locate anything suitable. In that case one group of tenants benefits while the other group loses. These "potential tenants" unable to find apartments must either purchase housing or live elsewhere.

Just as a quantity reduction acts to the detriment of tenants, so does the reduction in the quality of rental housing. Landlords will reduce maintenance and repairs when they can do it without losing tenants — which is the case when there is a shortage of rental units. Consequently, tenants get a lower-quality product for the lower price. In principle, this process of quality deterioration will eventually eliminate all the benefit of the lower rent to tenants, but the process is likely to take many years.

Second, nonprice rationing of rental units will become more prevalent, and this will work to the disadvantage of some tenants. In any market where price is not allowed to ration the available quantity among competing consumers, supply will not equal demand, and some other way of determining who gets the good and who doesn't must arise. This nonprice rationing can take many forms. Since there are many more potential tenants than dwelling units, landlords can be highly selective. For example, they are likely to favor families without children or pets (children and pets increase maintenance and repair costs) and families with histories of steady employment at good wage rates (who can be counted on to pay on time). In general, potential tenants with characteristics that make them good tenants in the eyes of landlords are likely to fare relatively better than others when price rationing is suppressed.

Another form of nonprice rationing that becomes more important is rationing on a first-come-first-served basis. Because of the lack of available units, potential tenants will incur the cost of waiting in line and searching for that rare commodity, a vacant rent-controlled apartment. This factor, of course, adds to the true cost of rental housing since not only the rent but the time spent waiting and searching must be paid by prospective tenants.

Third, the distribution of available rental units among tenants will be inefficient. We discussed efficiency in the distribution of a given quantity in Chapter 5; we saw that efficiency required the available quantity to go to consumers who placed the highest value on it. This result may not occur when nonprice rationing takes the place of price rationing. As an example, in New York it is common to find elderly couples remaining in large rent-controlled apartments long after their children have grown up and moved away. Although they no longer require as much space, they won't move because they would lose the implicit subsidy of the low rent, and they can't count on finding a smaller apartment at a low rent. At the same time a young couple with several children may be living in a small two-room rent-controlled apartment, and they are unwilling to give up their apartment for the same reasons. Both the young and the elderly couple could be better off if they switched apartments, but that outcome may not occur under rent control. As a consequence, the inefficient distribution of the available rental units means that the actual benefit to tenants is less than it could be.

For all these reasons the benefits to tenants from the lower rents under rent controls are likely to be a good deal smaller than initially anticipated. Generalizing on the outcome for tenants as a group is difficult because tenants are likely to be affected in different ways. Probably some tenants benefit, especially those occupying rental units at the time rent control takes effect; but the deterioration of the quality of the units diminishes even their benefits. Other tenants are surely made worse off because of the side effects that accompany the lower rents.

Short-Run versus Long-Run Effects

We can see why rent controls are an attractive policy to many people if we distinguish between the short-run and the long-run effects. Up to now we have emphasized the long-run effects, effects that may take several years to materialize fully. The effects immediately following implementation of controlled rents are somewhat different and largely explain why rent controls are so popular.

If a city unexpectedly applies rent controls today, the quantity and quality of rental units tomorrow will be virtually unaffected. It takes time for reduced construction and lower maintenance and repairs to have their full effects on durable goods like dwelling units. Consequently, in the short run the adverse effects on the supply side are largely absent. On the demand side, at the time when rent controls take effect, tenants are already occupying rental units suited to their needs, and most of them will not be moving in the immediate future. Thus, the various rationing problems that result from the shortage are relatively insignificant in the short run. Current tenants just stay where they are and enjoy lower rents.

What does happen in the short run is primarily a transfer of real income from landlords to tenants. Landlords have already incurred the costs of providing the housing units, and when they receive a lower rent, the result is a pure loss to them in the short run. Tenants, on the other hand, gain from the lower price, since the long-run factors that reduce benefits to tenants have not yet emerged.

Figure 10–5 illustrates the effects. The initial long-run equilibrium at P and $0Q$ is also a short-run equilibrium. The short-run supply curve is SS; we have drawn it nearly vertical to reflect the inability of the quantity of rental units to adjust significantly in the short run. When a rent control is imposed at P_M, the immediate effect is to reduce quantity only slightly below $0Q$. This outcome is a boon for the current tenants but implies losses for the landlords. The long-run adjustment begins as new construction falls and existing units are allowed to deteriorate. In the graph, this is shown as a leftward shift in the SS curve, a shift that continues until

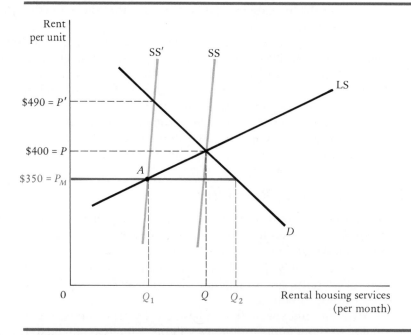

FIGURE 10–5
Short-run and Long-run Effects of Rent Controls

If rent control is unanticipated, the reduction in output in the short run will be small, as shown by SS. Over time SS shifts to SS′, and the long-run position at point A is established. If rent control is suddenly removed, output will increase only slightly, and price will rise in the short run to $490.

SS' is attained and the long-run equilibrium at point *A* is reached. In the long run tenants move among rental units and into or out of the community, so rationing problems emerge.

If we do not look beyond the short-run, or temporary, effects, rent controls appear mainly to benefit tenants at the expense of landlords. To many people, especially tenants, that result looks desirable despite the highly capricious redistribution of income involved. The beneficial effects are obvious and immediately apparent; the harmful effects take time to emerge and are difficult to understand (just as Mayor Barry didn't seem to realize why there was a rush to condominium conversion). Moreover, once the long-run effects materialize, the short-run effects of eliminating rent controls appear highly adverse. If, after quantity has fallen to $0Q_1$, rent controls are immediately removed, quantity would increase only slightly along SS', and, simultaneously, price would rise to *P'*. This result would appear to be an enormous windfall to landlords at the expense of tenants. For this reason many economists recommend gradual decontrol of rents, or an announcement that rent controls will be lifted a year or two in the future to allow new construction to occur before the ceiling on prices is lifted.

The moral of the rent control analysis is that it is important to look beyond the short-run effects. Contrary to Keynes's famous dictum, "In the long run, we are all dead," long-run adjustments generally do not take so long that they can be disregarded.

AIRLINE REGULATION AND DEREGULATION
10.4

The Civil Aeronautics Board (CAB) was formed in 1938 to regulate the airline industry. From that time until 1978 the CAB controlled, among other things, fares, routes that commercial airlines could serve, and entry of new firms into the industry. Late in 1978, after several years of national debate, Congress passed a bill deregulating the industry to a significant degree. An analysis of the consequences of the type of regulation imposed on the airline industry by the CAB will make it clear why there was widespread support for deregulation.

Our analysis will focus on the pricing policy followed by the CAB. The CAB closely regulated the fares airlines could charge, and, it turns out, the CAB kept those fares generally well above the level that would have prevailed in an open market. Even when some airlines requested fare reductions, they were regularly denied. In effect, the CAB imposed a price floor, keeping the price above the competitive level.

Even before deregulation there was persuasive evidence that regulated airline fares were artificially high. For example, the CAB was only able to regulate airlines engaged in interstate (between states) transportation. Intrastate airlines (operating entirely within a single state) were not subject to CAB regulation. The existence of unregulated airlines made some interesting comparisons possible. For instance, intrastate airlines operating in California commonly flew the Los Angeles–San Francisco route, about the same distance as a route from Washington, D.C., to Boston. The CAB-controlled fares on the Washington-Boston run were nearly twice as high as the uncontrolled fares from Los Angeles to San Francisco. A similar comparison for the uncontrolled Houston-Dallas route and the controlled Washington–New York run showed the same thing: fares twice as high when they were set by the CAB. Moreover, the federal government's General Accounting Office estimated that, on average, airline fares would have been between 22 and 52 percent lower if the CAB had not regulated them.

From this discussion we might conclude that the CAB designed the regulations to help the airlines at the expense of passengers. Airlines, after all, were receiving much higher fares as a result of the CAB's price-setting policy. Now, however, we encounter a startling fact: the airline industry was not particularly profitable during the period of regulation. In fact, over the twenty years prior to deregulation in 1978, the airline industry's accounting profits were slightly below the national average for all industries.[5]

What Happened to the Profits?

The apparent profits to airlines were dissipated in three ways. First, since the CAB also regulated routes, they required airlines to service some unprofitable routes. These routes generally provided service between sparsely populated areas where demand was insufficient for the airline to make a profit. The airlines had to set the losses on these runs against the profits on other routes. Second, unions of airline workers were in a position to demand and get higher wages when the CAB raised fares, and so some of the potential profits went to employees.

Analysts generally agree that these two reasons were far less important than the third: nonprice competition. In any market where prices are set and participants are unable to compete on the basis of price, another form of competition will emerge, as we saw with rent controls. What happened in the airline industry?

Airlines could make large potential profits at the high prices only if they could attract passengers. They could not, however, cut prices to attract passengers away from their competitors. Each airline faced the problem of making its service more attractive than its competitors' without being able to lower its fares. The solution was obvious: change the nature of the product so passengers would find it more appealing. For example, airlines began to schedule more frequent flights so that passengers would be able to get flights that were more convenient for them. In

---

[5] For interesting information regarding fares and profits, see Paul MacAvoy and John W. Snow, eds, *Regulation of Passenger Fares and Competition Among the Airlines* (Washington, D.C.: American Enterprise Institute, 1977).

addition, competition evolved among airlines to provide "frills": gourmet meals, movies, more and better attendants, complimentary Mickey Mouse ears for passengers en route to Disney World, and sometimes even live entertainment. But all these practices increased the airlines' cost of providing transportation. Costs rose, price was unchanged, and profits therefore diminished. Indeed, economic theory would predict that this process would continue until airlines were no longer making a profit at all, which explains why the airline industry was not especially profitable despite artificially high prices.

Now let's examine this process graphically. Figure 10–6b shows the supply and demand curves for airline services. For simplicity, we assume the industry to be a constant-cost industry. (Economists call this assumption a *simplifying assumption:* the results are not significantly altered by assuming a constant-cost rather than an increasing-cost industry, but the analysis is simpler.) In the absence of any regulation, price and quantity are P and $0Q$. Then the CAB sets the price P_{CAB}. Note that if the industry operated at point A on its supply curve, it would make profits shown by the shaded area. Although this will not be the final outcome, it is convenient to begin here to see why further adjustments must take place. Corresponding to point A in Figure 10–6b, the individual firm (airline) would

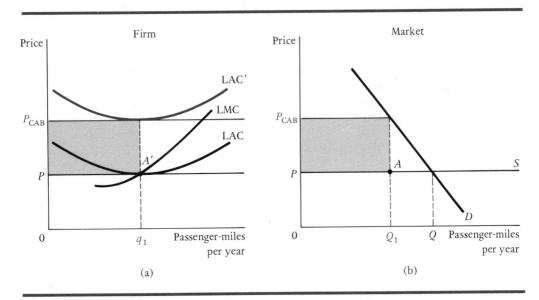

FIGURE 10–6
Airline Regulation by the CAB

A price floor of P_{CAB} implies that a representative firm (a) and the industry (b) could make profits shown by the shaded areas. However, these potential profits are dissipated through nonprice competition, which leads to cost curves shifting upward (LAC to LAC'), and firms end up with zero profit.

be at point A' in Figure 10–6a, operating at the minimum point on LAC and making a profit equal to the shaded area.

With all firms making a comfortable profit, why can't this be an equilibrium? The answer is that each airline could make still more money if it expanded its sales by attracting passengers away from other airlines. This conclusion comes from the fact that the profit-maximizing output is the point where LMC equals P_{CAB}. Since the total quantity demanded is $0Q_1$, and price cannot be lowered, the only way one airline can gain passengers is by attracting them from other airlines in some other way.

Suppose the airline attempts to attract passengers by scheduling more frequent flights. Note that every airline has incentive to initiate this practice, but more flights in total, with an *unchanged total quantity demanded*, means that fewer passengers will be carried on each flight. The result is that airlines will operate flights with empty seats, and it is in the interest of each airline to do so. Why? At a price per passenger twice as high (P_{CAB}), it is profitable to schedule a flight even if only half the seats are filled. Flying half-filled planes, however, means a higher average cost per passenger. Thus, in Figure 10–6a the LAC curve showing the cost per passenger-mile shifts upward as the number of passengers per flight declines. This shift will continue until all economic profits are eliminated. The final result is an average cost curve like LAC', with the typical airline just covering costs at the higher CAB price and with total output (passenger-miles) unchanged.[6]

Consequently, economic theory predicts that the CAB price policy will harm airline passengers and not appreciably benefit the airlines. As the significance of this analysis became more widely appreciated, the support for airline deregulation grew. Airlines were largely deregulated in 1978, and as expected, fares fell sharply on competitive routes and airline travel increased significantly. Since 1978, air fares have risen again, but the increase is the result of higher operating costs, predominantly fuel costs, which rose nearly 80 percent in 1980 alone.

FARM POLICY
10.5

Agriculture has always been a favored segment of the American economy as far as government policy is concerned. Over the years Congress has enacted a bewildering array of policies to help farmers. The mix of policies varies from one crop to another and from one year to the next. Yet certain common features are evident in these policies, so an emphasis on these elements is not likely to be misplaced. These common characteristics include price supports, acreage restrictions, and direct subsidies.

---

[6] This analysis neglects the way the change in quality affects the demand curve. Presumably, more convenient flights with "frills" are worth more to consumers, so this practice shifts the demand curve upward to some degree. Total output (in passenger-miles) would then be somewhat greater, but airlines would still be making zero profit.

Price Supports

Price support is another name for minimum price or price floor. The government sets support prices for many agricultural crops, which in effect guarantees the minimum price farmers will receive. For example, the support price for wheat might be $3 per bushel. If the market price is greater than $3 per bushel, the policy has no effect; but if the market price falls below $3, the government is obligated to take action to "support" it at $3. This generally means that the government will step in and purchase the excess if farmers can't sell all their wheat at $3.

Figure 10–7 illustrates the effects of a price support when government acts as a "purchaser of last resort." When the support price is $3, farmers are guaranteed at least that price, and they will expand output to $0Q_2$, where marginal cost is just equal to the support price. At a price of $3 the public will only purchase $0Q_1$; if any more wheat appears on the market, price would fall. To maintain the support price, then, the government must purchase the surplus, Q_1Q_2, spending an amount equal to the shaded area.

Note that once the government has purchased the wheat, it cannot be resold without driving the price below $3. Thus, a major problem confronting the government is how to dispose of the surplus. A variety of

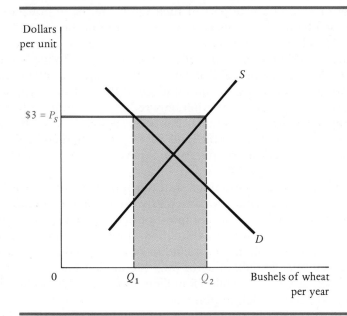

FIGURE 10–7
Farm Price Supports and Government Purchases
With a price support of $3 per bushel, consumers wish to purchase $0Q_1$, but farmers wish to sell $0Q_2$. To make the support price effective, government must purchase the difference, Q_1Q_2, at a cost shown by the shaded area.

measures were employed in the 1950s and 1960s, such as giving some of the surplus wheat to other countries as part of foreign aid programs. Some of the wheat was simply stored until it rotted in silos. At times in the early 1960s more than a billion bushels of wheat were being stored by the government.

With this policy the nonfarm public bears several costs to maintain the price of wheat. Consumers not only pay a higher price for wheat products, they also pay taxes to finance the government's wheat purchases and storage costs. The obvious waste in producing wheat that was never used to benefit the public led the government to a search for ways to avoid future surpluses.

Acreage Restriction

In the early 1960s, as the surpluses associated with price supports continued to be a problem, government implemented a new policy that attempted to induce farmers to lower production. In terms of Figure 10–7, the goal was to maintain the support price but restrict output to $0Q_1$ in some way so there would no longer be an embarrassing and wasteful surplus.

The solution was to pay farmers not to produce. More specifically, under the acreage restriction plan farmers received subsidies as an inducement not to cultivate part of their land; that is, to put part of their land in "soil banks." Land is an important input in the production of agricultural products, so acreage restriction had the effect of limiting the use of an important input and indirectly reducing output. Indeed, in the early 1970s as much as 20 percent of total United States farmland was withdrawn from production as a consequence of this policy. Surprisingly, experts agree that acreage restriction only reduced output by 2 to 5 percent. What happened was predictable. Farmers, unable to use 20 percent of their land, took their least fertile land out of production and cultivated the remaining 80 percent more intensively, thereby avoiding a large drop in output.[7]

In effect, acreage restrictions shift the supply curve leftward, but the exact way this shift occurs is particularly interesting. In Figure 10–8 the original supply curve S relates output to price before any acreage restriction. An expansion of wheat production along this supply curve would mean using more of all inputs, including land, to produce additional output. For example, 20 million acres plus 100 million hours of labor would produce $0Q_0$ at point A, while 25 million acres plus 130 million hours of labor would produce $0Q_2$ at point B.

Suppose the government acts to restrict acreage from 25 million acres to 20 million acres. This policy will not affect the supply curve below point

---

[7] D. Gale Johnson, *Farm Commodity Programs* (Washington, D.C.: American Enterprise Institute, 1973).

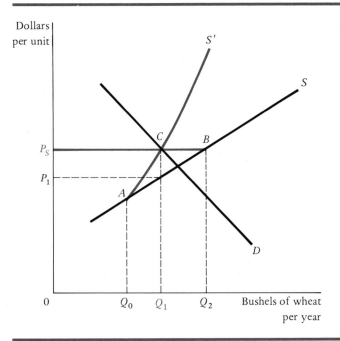

FIGURE 10-8
Acreage Restrictions

With a restriction on the acreage that farmers can devote to wheat production, the supply curve becomes AS'. Then there is no surplus produced at the support price.

A since less than 20 million acres would be used to produce relatively low levels of output. Acreage reduction does affect the supply curve above point A, however. Normally, to produce more than $0Q_0$, farmers would use more land, fertilizer, labor, machinery, and so on. With acreage restriction farmers are unable to use more land, but they can still increase production beyond $0Q_0$ by applying more of the other inputs to the fixed quantity of land. The AS' supply curve shows the cost of producing more output in this way. Note that the unit costs of production are higher under acreage restriction since farmers are not permitted to produce output in excess of $0Q_0$ in the least costly way, which involves using more land, as shown by the S curve. In fact, the supply curve under acreage restrictions, AS', is much like a short-run supply curve because an important input, land, is fixed in quantity for movements along this curve.

In short, acreage restrictions have the effect of shifting the supply curve from S to AS'. At the support price P_S farmers would then choose to produce $0Q_1$ rather than the amount ($0Q_2$) they would produce without acreage restrictions. As we have drawn the curves the acreage restriction policy completely eliminates the surplus since customers are willing to purchase the entire output $0Q_1$ at the support price. Of course, this fortuitous result cannot be guaranteed in advance. If government doesn't restrict the acreage enough, S' will lie farther to the right, output will be greater than $0Q_1$, and the government will still have to purchase the surplus. This policy of acreage restriction, however, has operated to reduce greatly the surpluses produced by the support prices in various agricultural markets.

In comparison with the competitive equilibrium, the price support combined with acreage restriction result in higher prices for consumers and a lower output. The nonfarm public also pays taxes to finance the subsidies used to induce farmers to set aside some of their land and to buy any surplus that occurs. Finally, the output $0Q_1$ is produced at a higher per-unit cost than necessary. Farmers could produce output $0Q_1$ at a per-unit cost of P_1 when they are free to vary all inputs to produce in the least costly way, as shown by the original supply curve. With acreage restrictions farmers must adopt more costly production methods — using more of other inputs but no more land — and the result is a cost per unit of P_S.

Direct Subsidies

In 1973 a new instrument of agricultural policy was adopted. This plan evolved from the concept of target prices first suggested by Charles Brannan in 1949 when he was secretary of agriculture. Under the Brannan plan a target price is set for each crop, and farmers are ensured of receiving at least that price. Farmers produce whatever output they wish, and the market determines the price. If the market price falls below the target price, the government pays farmers the difference. For example, if the target price for wheat is $3 per bushel and farmers can only sell their wheat for $2 per bushel, the government pays farmers $1 per bushel in order to bring their net price up to the target level. In this way farmers are guaranteed $3 per bushel regardless of how low the market price sinks. If the market price is greater than the target price, there is no subsidy.

Figure 10–9 clarifies this policy. The target price P_T is $3 per bushel. Farmers know they will receive $3 and plan their production accordingly. This means that the industry demand curve effectively becomes DAD' since the price farmers receive cannot fall below $3. Hence, output expands out to $0Q_2$ along the supply curve. The entire output is sold on the market for whatever it will bring. An output of $0Q_2$, with the customers' demand curve of DD_1, will only sell at a price of P_C, or $2 per bushel. The government is then obligated to pay farmers the difference between the target price and the market price, or $1 per bushel. The promise of this subsidy is why farmers can expect to receive $3 per bushel on balance. The total subsidy paid by the government is the shaded area, which equals $1 times the number of bushels $0Q_2$.

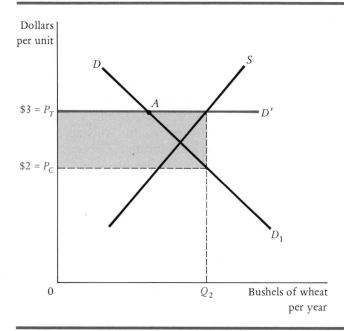

Dollars
per unit

$3 = P_T$

$2 = P_C$

D

S

A

D'

D_1

0

Q_2

Bushels of wheat
per year

FIGURE 10-9
Target Price Subsidies

A target price subsidy guarantees farmers a price of $3 per bushel, and at that price output is $0Q_2$. Consumers buy this output at a price of $2, and the government pays farmers $1 per bushel to bring the realized price to $3.

Note that this subsidy is really a variant of the excise subsidy discussed in Section 10.1. Farmers receive a certain sum per unit of output, the basic characteristic of an excise subsidy. The difference here is that the target price subsidy is a variable excise subsidy since the size of the subsidy per unit varies with the market price paid by customers. In Section 10.1 we analyzed an excise subsidy that was a fixed amount, $5 per unit, regardless of market conditions. Both subsidies operate to expand output in much the same way.

With the two previous agricultural policies discussed, consumers paid taxes to finance the subsidies and, in addition, paid higher prices for farm products. Under the target price program they continue to pay taxes to finance the subsidy but now get lower farm prices in return.

In 1981 agricultural policy consisted primarily of a mix of these three policies and several other less important programs. The relative importance of each type of policy has varied greatly in the recent past, but it seems likely that price supports, acreage restrictions, and target price subsidies will continue to be significant components of United States agricultural policy.

Who Benefits?

Most people would say that farmers benefit from these agricultural policies. Like most short answers, this one is not entirely correct and may, in fact, be quite misleading.

Farmers receive higher prices or subsidy payments under these programs. As a first and somewhat rough approximation, the total benefit of a higher farm price is greater the larger the farmer's output, so we would expect large farms to receive greater benefits. This outcome is also generally true under acreage restriction subsidies. Consequently, it is no surprise that about 60 percent of the subsidies in the late 1960s went to the 20 percent of farmers who together produced 70 percent of the output. In addition, the average income of these farmers was about one and a half times greater than the national average. Farm programs are clearly not welfare programs for the poor. Although some poor farmers may benefit, most of the benefits go to nonpoor farmers. The point we emphasize here is that theoretical reasoning alone makes it possible to predict this outcome. Several studies, furthermore, support these expectations.[8]

Looking at who receives the subsidy or higher price is only a first approximation to the question of who benefits. Observe that the effects of both the support price and the target price programs are an expansion along the industry supply curve (Figures 10–7 and 10–9). As emphasized before, the people who benefit are individuals who own inputs in scarce (upward-sloping) supply to the industry, since these inputs are bid up in price. What inputs have upward-sloping supply curves to agriculture? Viewing all agricultural products as a group, most agricultural economists agree that land has a sharply upward-sloping supply curve. The reason is that most fertile land is already used in farming, and to bring more under cultivation by bidding it away from commercial, residential, or other uses would require significantly higher prices.

In contrast, economists regard other inputs to agriculture to be in highly elastic supply. Farmers can purchase more tractors or fertilizer without bidding up their prices appreciably. More farm workers can also be hired without affecting wage rates significantly.

A relatively inelastic supply of land and a relatively elastic supply of other inputs mean that the owners of farmland will receive the bulk of the benefits. (To see this explicitly, analyze the price support and target price cases with the fixed-input-proportions model, using an upward-sloping supply curve for land and a horizontal supply curve for other inputs.) Farmers who rent farmland will receive little or no benefit; they will just pay higher rents. Similarly, farm employees are unlikely to receive any significant benefits from the various farm policies.

One final point. If you purchase farmland, do not expect to receive any *net* benefits under the various farm policies. The current owners will

---

[8] Charles L. Schultze, *The Distribution of Farm Subsidies: Who Gets the Benefits?* (Washington, D.C.: Brookings Institution, 1971).

charge a higher price for farmland to reflect the fact that they are selling you not only land but also the rights to receive future government subsidies. The present high price of farmland is due in part to the fact that ownership carries with it the right to participate in future subsidy programs. In principle, new purchasers of farmland will receive no more than a competitive return on their investment. Actually, it may not even be the present owners of the farmland who benefit from the subsidies but rather people in the past who sold them the land at prices that reflected the expected later benefits of farm subsidies. Thus, farmers and nonfarmers who owned farmland when these policies were introduced or expanded are thought to be the major beneficiaries.

SAFETY REGULATIONS
10.6

In recent years the federal government has become increasingly active in setting safety standards for workers. The Occupational Safety and Health Administration (OSHA) is the agency empowered to issue regulations governing worker safety in various industries. We will construct a hypothetical example of worker safety regulations applied to a competitive industry to see what types of effects we can expect.

Suppose that workers are initially earning $8 per hour in an industry that produces good X. Then the government requires the firms to provide protective clothing for their employees to reduce the risk of injury. The cost of the protective clothing, expressed as a cost per hour of employment (to make it comparable to the hourly wage rate), is $2. How will this cost affect the price and output of good X, and the employment and wage rates of workers?

At first glance, this question may seem very simple. After all, won't the safety regulation simply increase production costs of firms, reducing output and raising the price? The reaction to this regulation is likely to be more complicated than that. Greater worker safety is beneficial to workers, and they would be willing to work for lower money wages in safer working conditions. Greater safety is, in this respect, much like improved fringe benefits. Whether or not the firms' costs rise, therefore, depends on whether the reduction in money wages is greater or less than the cost of the protective clothing. If workers believe the greater safety is worth $3 per hour (more than it actually costs employers to provide), they would be willing to work for a wage of $5 per hour under safer conditions. In this case the hourly cost to firms would fall from $8 per hour to $7 ($5 money wage plus $2 cost of protective clothing). On the other hand, if the greater safety is worth only $1 per hour to workers, the hourly cost to firms would rise from $8 to $9 per hour ($7 wage plus $2 cost of protective clothing).

From this discussion it may appear that the net result can go either way, depending on how valuable workers perceive safer working conditions to be. However, we must remember the incentive firms had to provide safer working conditions before the regulation. If the value to the workers of protective clothing was more than its costs, firms have incentive to provide it without any regulation. If workers will work for $3 an hour less when firms supply protective clothing that costs $2, firms' net labor costs are reduced by supplying the greater safety. If firms are maximizing their profits, they will supply any safety equipment (and other fringe benefits) that is valued by workers at more than its cost.

Thus, if firms are not providing protective clothing for workers, it must be because workers don't view it as worth what it costs. Consequently, when the government requires firms to provide protective clothing, firms' net labor costs will rise. This result does not mean that the greater safety has no value to workers — just that it is worth less than $2 per hour. With higher labor costs, output falls and price to consumers rises.

We can present a more complete analysis of this issue by using the fixed-input-proportions model. This model is ideally suited to analyzing a problem where the interrelationship between input and output markets is important, as it is here. In Figure 10–10 the industry is initially using labor and capital, with supply curves S_L and S_K, to produce good X. The supply curve of good X, obtained by summing S_L and S_K vertically, is shown as

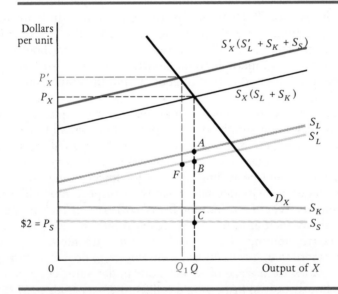

FIGURE 10-10

Regulation Requiring Worker Safety Equipment

The cost of mandatory safety equipment is S_S. With safer working conditions workers will supply labor services at a lower wage rate; S_L shifts down to S'_L. The combined effect shifts the output supply curve up to S'_X, and the price to consumers rises.

S_X. With the demand curve D_X industry output is $0Q$, and price is P_X. The wage rate for workers is AQ, which we earlier assumed to be $8 per hour.

When the government requires firms to provide protective clothing for workers, it is effectively requiring firms to use a third input in production. The supply curve of protective clothing is S_S and is assumed to be horizontal at $2. When firms provide the protective clothing, however, workers are willing to work for lower money wage rates. This result is shown by the downward shift in S_L to S'_L. Note that the supply curve of labor shifts downward by AB, which is less than the cost of protective clothing, CQ, indicating that workers do not view the benefits of the protective clothing as equal to its costs. This outcome causes a shift in the supply curve of X. Because the reduction in the wage rate at the initial level of employment is less than the added cost of protective clothing, S_X shifts upward to S'_X (since $S'_X = S'_L + S_K + S_S$). Higher total per-unit costs at output $0Q$ mean that the industry cannot cover its costs at the initial price, and output contracts along S'_X. The new equilibrium is at P'_X and $0Q_1$, so consumers pay a higher price.

Workers are also worse off on balance. If workers received a money wage of BQ plus the protective clothing, they would think themselves just as well off as they were before the regulation was implemented since the greater net safety is worth exactly the AB reduction in the money wage. However, because the industry reduces output, it also reduces employment of labor along S'_L, and the final wage rate is FQ_1, lower than BQ. As a result, the money wage rate falls by more than the safety is worth to workers, and they are, therefore, made worse off. Both workers and consumers end up bearing net costs from the policy despite the fact that workers are employed in safer working conditions.

Inadequate Information

The implication that workers and consumers are both harmed may be surprising in view of the support that exists for safety regulations. But there is one apparent assumption in the analysis that many people would question; namely, that workers can evaluate accurately how safe their working conditions are. In many industries the existence of hazardous working conditions may not be apparent to workers until too late. Years after working with asbestos, for example, workers may be subject to a higher risk of cancer. Under these circumstances workers themselves may want an impartial judge to evaluate their working environment and ensure that it is reasonably safe, and the government may fill this role. Reasoning along these lines, in fact, seems to underlie much of the support for safety regulations.

Accepting the view that workers are inadequately informed is no reason to completely reject the previous analysis. Instead, it is important to determine what that change in assumptions would mean for the analysis. What difference does it make if workers are uninformed? In responding to that question, we must distinguish two possibilities. First is the possibility that workers are unaware of how safe working conditions are before the firms are required to provide safety equipment, and they remain unaware after it is provided. In this event it appears that the workers' labor supply curve, S_L, would not shift at all when working conditions become safer. Note what this would mean: costs of production rise, output falls, and price rises. As output falls, fewer workers are employed, and the money wage rate falls. Since workers are unaware of the degree of safety, they will view themselves as worse off at the lower money wage rate. In other words, all our earlier conclusions remain valid as long as it is understood that we are referring to the well-being of workers as they themselves judge it and not as it is evaluated by someone else.

A second possibility is that workers are unaware of the potential benefits of safety equipment before it is provided, but afterward they realize they secure some benefits from it. The question then is whether they view the benefit as greater or less than the costs. If they view the greater safety as worth less than its cost, the conclusions of our earlier analysis remain valid. The other case is perhaps the most interesting. If, after the safety equipment is provided, workers realize that it is worth more than its cost, their supply curve will shift downward (in our example) by more than $2. The effects of this are (you may wish to work it out) a greater output of X at a lower price, and workers are better off. One problem with this possibility is that firms still have incentive to provide the safety equipment without the government regulation if they believe workers will come to realize it is worth the cost to them even if they aren't initially aware of the benefits.

Our purpose here is not to provide a detailed treatment of safety regulation but to indicate the usefulness of economic theory. Just because an assumption is at variance with reality is no reason to reject the model and rely on intuition. The competitive model provides a very flexible framework that can often be modified to incorporate special features of some problem, as we have done here in discussing the significance of inadequate information on the part of workers.

THE SUPPLY OF EXHAUSTIBLE RESOURCES
10.7

One of the most talked about issues in recent years has been the "energy crisis." One aspect of this issue is the widespread concern that we are depleting our stock of natural resources so quickly that we will run out in the near future. In thinking about this alarming prospect, we must understand how market forces operate to determine how fast natural resources are depleted.

Natural resources can be conveniently, if somewhat imprecisely, classified as either exhaustible or nonexhaustible. An exhaustible resource, like oil, coal, or natural gas, exists within the earth's crust in a certain quantity. Once it is used up, there is no more — at least not for several million years. A nonexhaustible resource, like people, wildlife, forests, rivers, and fish, is replaceable, and there is no inherent reason to run out of such resources. Our concern here is with exhaustible resources.

Let's develop a simple model to analyze the way competitive markets allocate an exhaustible resource over time. Suppose there are only two time periods, year 1 (this year) and year 2 (next year). At the beginning of year 1 there are 1000 million barrels of oil in the hands of enough different firms for the assumption of competition to be appropriate. (In Chapter 12 we will discuss the case in which the owners of the exhaustible resource operate as a monopoly.) All the oil will be sold either this year or next year; the more sold this year, the less will be available for sale next year. To make matters simple, we will assume that there is zero production cost: oil is just oozing around waiting to be sold. (Dropping this assumption complicates the analysis but affects the results only slightly — another simplifying assumption.)

Will competitive profit-maximizing firms sell all the oil in year 1, taking a quick profit and leaving consumers without oil in year 2? Consider a single oil producer. If the firm sells oil in year 1, it receives the current price P_1. Or the firm has the option of holding the oil until year 2 and selling it at the prevailing price then, P_2. Each barrel of oil sold in year 1 reduces the quantity that can be sold in year 2 by one barrel: this is the crucial distinguishing feature of an exhaustible resource. From this, it follows that the marginal cost of selling each barrel of oil in year 1 is the revenue of P_2 in year 2 that is sacrificed. Note that this cost is an implicit opportunity cost. Even though there is no production cost, there is a forgone opportunity when oil is sold in year 1, and the value of that forgone opportunity, P_2, is a cost to the firm.

Obviously, whether the firm will sell the oil in year 1 or hold it until year 2 depends on the current price relative to the expected future price. One other factor is important: a price of $50, for example, received next year is not worth as much as $50 received today. If the firm receives $50 today, it can invest the money at the market interest rate and the $50 will grow to a larger sum by year 2. Therefore, a dollar received next year is less valuable than a dollar received today. If P_2 is the price of oil in year 2, its *present value* in year 1 is $P_2/(1 + i)$, where i is the prevailing interest rate. If P_2 is $36, for example, and the interest rate is 20 percent, then the present value is $P_2/(1 + i) = \$36/1.2 = \$30$. A $30 price received today is equivalent to a $36 price one year later since the $30 invested at a 20 percent interest rate will grow to $36 in one year.   .

From the firm's point of view, it can make more money by holding the oil and selling it in year 2 if the price in year 2 is expected to be more than 20 percent above the current price. In other words, if $P_2/(1 + i)$ is greater than P_1, the firm can increase profits by shifting sales of oil from year 1 to year 2. Remember that $P_2/(1 + i)$ is the current value of the price P_2 to be received next year, so if this amount is greater than the price that can be received today, it is better for the firm to wait until year 2. Conversely, if P_1 is greater than $P_2/(1 + i)$, the firm can increase profits by shifting sales of oil from year 2 to year 1. Thus, the expected future price and the current rate of interest have a strong influence on the firm's decision to sell oil now or to hold it until next year.

We can illustrate the determination of prices and sales in each year with a diagram. In Figure 10–11 the horizontal axis measures the existing 1000 million barrels of oil. From left to right we will measure the quantity sold in year 1; the quantity not sold in year 1 will be sold in year 2. If 350 million barrels are sold in year 1, 650 million barrels (1000−350) will be available for sale in year 2. Any point on the horizontal axis, therefore, identifies the division of sales between year 1 and year 2. Reading from right to left, we measure the sales of oil in year 2. The demand curve in year 1 is D_1. Note that the more oil sold in year 1, the lower is its current price. The demand curve in year 2 is D_2, and it slopes downward with respect to the origin at the right-hand corner.

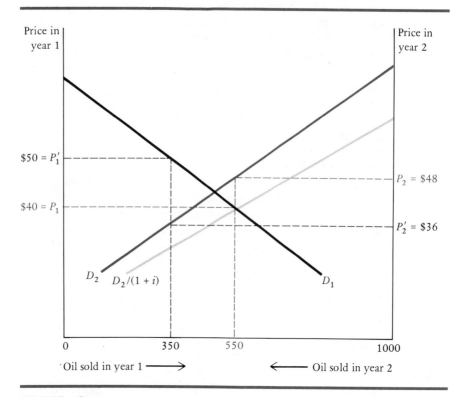

FIGURE 10-11

Supply of Exhaustible Resources Over Time

The total quantity of oil to be sold in both years is 1000 million units. The firms will sell 550 million units in year 1 at a price of $40 and 450 million units in year 2 at a price of $48, as determined by the intersection of D_1 and $D_2/(1 + i)$.

If, for example, 350 million barrels are sold in year 1, the price in year 1 will be $50, which leaves 650 million barrels to be sold in year 2, and from D_2 we see that the price in year 2 would be $36. If instead 550 million barrels are sold in year 1, price in year 1 will be $40, which leaves 450 million barrels for sale in year 2 at $48 a barrel. The more sold in year 1, the lower year 1's price will be and the higher year 2's price will be since less will be left for future sales.

To identify the competitive equilibrium, we need to express each alternative year 2 price in terms of its value in year 1. We do so by using the curve $D_2/(1 + i)$, which indicates the present value, $P_2/(1 + i)$, for each possible price on D_2. Suppose firms are currently selling 350 million barrels in year 1. Price in year 1 is $50, but price in year 2 will only be $36 when the remaining 650 million barrels are sold. The present value of $36 next year is $30 in year 1. This means that a firm can add $50 to its revenues by selling one more barrel in year 1; holding the oil and selling it next year will only bring in $30. Consequently, the firms can increase profits by selling more in year 1 and less in year 2 since P_1 is greater than $P_2/(1 + i)$. The firms can continue to increase profits as long as $P_1 > P_2/(1 + i)$ by selling more in year 1, so present sales will expand to the point where P_1 is equal to $P_2/(1 + i)$. This equality occurs where D_1 intersects $D_2/(1 + i)$.

The competitive equilibrium is thus at 550 million barrels sold in year 1 at $40 a barrel and 450 million barrels sold in year 2 at $48. At any lower rate of sales in year 1, the firms can increase profits by selling more in the present and less in the future. At any higher rate of sales in year 1, the firms can increase profits by selling less in the present and more in the future. The equilibrium condition is

$$P_1 = P_2/(1 + i)$$

since firms can then make as much (in present-value terms) selling in either period.

Further Implications

This competitive adjustment implies that the price of exhaustible resources will be rising over time at a rate equal to the rate of interest. (This analysis can be generalized to any number of years.) Price in year 2 is expected to be 20 percent higher than it was in year 1, assuming the current interest rate is 20 percent. The prospect of higher prices in the future is what gives firms the incentive to conserve part of their supply for the future.

An important implication of this analysis is that it is in the firms' interests to "conserve" exhaustible natural resources. Firms take into account future demands for the resource in determining present quantities to sell. Of course, firms do not know the future with certainty, and one might object that present owners of oil do not anticipate future market conditions accurately. While this outcome is possible, we emphasize that for this process to work as described, it isn't necessary for all present owners of oil, or even any of them, to be able to anticipate future needs. It is only necessary that some people correctly anticipate future demand. Suppose, for example, that current owners of oil decide to sell it all in year 1. People or businesses who recognize that profits can be made by buying at low current prices and selling at high future prices will then buy some oil and hold it for the future. This action tends to increase the current price and reduce the future price. These speculators perform the important function of conserving the resource for the future, and if they correctly anticipate future demand, the result will be exactly the same as if the original owners of the resources had correctly forecast the future.

Since the basic implication of this analysis is steadily rising prices of natural resources over time, it is interesting to consider how actual prices have changed in the past. One study of 29 exhaustible resources found that most of their prices actually *fell* over the 1890–1957 period.[9] This result seems to suggest that actual markets over time have conserved the resources more than our analysis implied. (Note that prices fall over time when less is sold in the present, that is, when more is conserved for the future.) Is the analysis wrong? Not really, since our analysis ignores certain factors that significantly affect resource markets. Over long periods of time two factors we neglected are likely to be important. First, new supplies of the resource may be discovered; second, technological improvements in the method of extracting the resources from the earth may be developed. Both factors serve to keep the price from rising so rapidly. For instance, in our example suppose that a new deposit of 100 million barrels was discovered in year 2. Then sales in year 2 would be 550 million barrels rather than 450, and price would be lower than $48. Improvements in technology have the same effect. Our hunch is that these two factors are largely responsible for the failure of resource prices to rise earlier in this century.

Consequently, our model, assuming no technological improvements and no new discoveries, reflects rather pessimistic assumptions. Even in the absence of these favorable developments, the resource is automatically conserved. Note also that the rising price over time serves several important functions. First, it gives owners the incentive to withhold part of the resource from the current market, to conserve it. Second, the higher price gives consumers incentive to economize on the use of a resource that is becoming scarcer and to search for substitute products. Third, higher prices of resources provide incentive for businesses to develop substitutes. For example, as the price of oil rises, firms and individuals have incentive to invest in the development of alternative energy sources, such as solar energy, and consumers have incentive to switch to more energy-efficient homes and cars.

---

[9] Chandler Morse and Harold Barnett, *Scarcity and Growth: The Economics of Natural Resource Availability* (Baltimore: Johns Hopkins University Press, 1963).

This analysis explains why economists are very skeptical of all the prophecies that predict catastrophes as society runs out of various resources. These predictions generally ignore the way markets ration exhaustible resources over time. We will not wake up one day and find that we are out of oil. Long before that happens, rising prices of oil will lead to a gradual change in consumption patterns and a switch to alternative sources of energy.

Review Questions and Problems

1. Show, using only the industry demand curve and the long-run supply curve (increasing-cost case), the effects on price and output of an excise subsidy paid to the firms. Who benefits from the subsidy? Is it correct to say that businesses benefit from the subsidy? Explain.

2. Can you think of any type of subsidy that, if given to firms in a competitive market, would in the long run benefit firms (more precisely, the owners of firms)? Why wouldn't entry of new firms into the subsidized market always occur until economic profits are zero?

*3. Suppose the government collects an excise tax from the firms in a competitive market. How will this tax affect price and output? Will the price to consumers rise more if the industry is one of increasing costs or if it is one of constant costs? (Hint: This situation is just the reverse of the excise subsidy analysis — the supply curve shifts up.) Contrast your answer here and your answer to question 17 in Chapter 9.

4. Suppose an import quota on imported automobiles places an upper limit on imports that is lower than the current level. How will this quota affect the price of automobiles, the total quantity produced, and the number of imports? (Hint: See the last paragraph of Section 10.2.)

5. "Consumers understandably like lower prices, but it is important that they understand there is a great difference between a lower price produced by a government price ceiling and a lower price that comes about through normal market channels; one benefits the consumer, the other may not." How does our analysis of rent controls relate to this pronouncement?

6. Explain why rent controls are likely to produce a housing shortage. What other effects do they have? Why is it important to distinguish between long-run and short-run effects? Do you think the personal animosity between tenants and landlords will be greater in a city with rent controls or in one without?

*7. Rent controls have several effects that are harmful to tenants. What are they? Do you think these effects fall equally on poor and nonpoor tenants? In other words, are poor tenants more or less likely to benefit from rent controls than are nonpoor tenants?

8. Why is it not inconsistent to say that airline fares, when regulated by the CAB, were above the competitive level, and yet airlines did not achieve above-normal profits from the above-normal prices?

9. The airlines generally favored CAB regulation and were opposed to fares' being determined in open markets. Since, apparently, airline profits were not unusually high when the CAB regulated the industry, what reasons could account for this support?

10. As a consumer of farm products as well as a taxpayer, how would you rank the three farm policies of Figures 10–7, 10–8, and 10–9? That is, under which would you be best off and under which worst off? If you were a farmer, how would you rank them?

*11. Under the target price agricultural subsidy, what would be the effects of an increase in demand (supply unchanged)? Of an increase in the target price (demand and supply unchanged)? In each case identify the effects on the price paid by consumers, the price received by farmers, the output, and total outlays by government.

12. When firms are required to provide a fringe benefit — greater safety — to their workers, the workers may end up worse off. Explain this situation. Can you think of a combination of circumstances under which workers would benefit from this form of regulation?

13. Government sometimes protects consumers by requiring firms to provide safer products — for example, medicine bottles that can't be opened by small children. Apply the same approach we used to analyze worker safety legislation to determine under what conditions this policy would benefit consumers.

14. "If we continue to use oil at current rates, we will run out in 1999." This statement implies that there is a certain amount of oil remaining. Does the existence of a fixed amount provide a basis for predicting when we will run out? Explain how markets would function to produce a gradual transition to a no-oil world rather than the "here today, gone tomorrow" outcome suggested by the quotation.

*15. Use the intertemporal supply model of Figure 10–11 to explain how an expected increase in future demand will lead to greater conservation in the present.

Supplementary Readings

Adams, Walter. *The Structure of American Industry.* 5th ed. New York: Macmillan, 1977.

Block, Walter, and Olsen, Edgar, eds. *Rent Control.* Vancouver: Frazer Institute, 1981.

Browning, Edgar, and Browning, Jacquelene. *Public Finance and the Price System.* 2nd ed. New York: Macmillan, 1983.

Goodman, John, and Dolan, Edwin. *Economics of Public Policy: The Micro View.* St. Paul: West, 1979.

Griffin, James, and Steele, Henry. *Energy Economics.* New York: Academic Press, 1980.

Johnson, D. Gale. *Farm Commodity Programs.* Washington, D.C.: American Enterprise Institute, 1973.

MacAvoy, Paul, and Snow, John W., eds. *Regulation of Passenger Fares and Competition Among the Airlines.* Washington, D.C.: American Enterprise Institute, 1977.

Schultze, Charles L. *The Distribution of Farm Subsidies: Who Gets the Benefits?* Washington, D.C.: Brookings Institution, 1971.

Monopoly

11

While perfect competition is characterized by many firms selling in the same market, monopoly is characterized by only one firm selling in a given market. If we classified market structures by the number of competing firms, perfect competition would stand at one end of the spectrum and monopoly at the other. Neither the model of perfect competition nor the model of monopoly is precisely descriptive of very many real world markets, but they are nonetheless the two most important market structures you should understand thoroughly. As we have emphasized, theoretical models need not be descriptively accurate in order to explain many features of real world markets. In addition, most models of other market structures build on elements developed in the monopoly and competitive models, so once you understand these basic models, it is relatively easy to extend the analysis to other market forms.

In this chapter we explain how a monopoly determines price and output, and we compare the results with those of the competitive industry. In the next chapter we will apply the basic monopoly model to several topics such as regulation of monopoly, suppression of invention by monopoly, exhaustible resources and monopoly, price discrimination, and OPEC.

THE NATURE OF MONOPOLY
11.1

A *monopoly* may be defined as the sole producer of some product that has no close substitutes. As the only producer of the product, the monopolist need not be concerned with the possibility that other firms may undercut its price. In effect, the monopoly *is* the industry since it is the only producer in the market. As a result, the demand curve confronting the monopoly is also the total market demand curve for the product, and that curve, like all market demand curves, slopes downward.

In the definition of monopoly we stated that there were no close substitutes for the monopolist's product. If close substitutes existed, the firm would be competing with some other firm or firms and would be unable to exercise much control over price. For example, Anheuser-Busch is the sole producer of Budweiser beer, but it would be a serious mistake analytically to treat Anheuser-Busch as a monopoly. Beers produced by other companies are close substitutes for Budweiser, which means that the demand curve for Budweiser is highly, though probably not perfectly, elastic. As a consequence, Anheuser-Busch, in contrast to a monopoly, has little control over the price it can charge.

The existence of close substitutes implies competition, and close substitutes are ruled out in the definition of monopoly. But an ambiguity in the definition of monopoly should be mentioned: how "close" is a close substitute? Is steel (or plastic or wood) a close enough substitute for aluminum so that even if there is only one aluminum producer, it should not be viewed as a monopoly? The role of substitutes is an important one in antitrust law in determining the degree of market, or monopoly, power exercised by a firm. In 1956, for example, the government brought antitrust action against E. I. duPont, claiming that duPont had monopolized the cellophane market in violation of the Sherman Antitrust Act. During the period relevant to the case, duPont produced nearly 75 percent of all the cellophane sold in the United States. The court found duPont not guilty on the grounds that the relevant market was not limited to cellophane but included other flexible wrapping materials such as waxed paper, Saran, and aluminum foil. When all flexible wraps were considered, duPont's share of the market fell to 20 percent. The court held that duPont had no monopoly power because of the availability of close substitutes. In the duPont cellophane case and many others, a great deal of emphasis is placed on how the market is defined, and in this process the availability of substitutes plays a key role.

The ambiguity concerning the closeness of substitutes is unavoidable. Since we are dealing with matters of degree, any precise dividing line will be arbitrary to some extent. The important point is that the degree of monopoly power possessed by any one firm depends on how many substitutes exist and how close those substitutes are. Most economists believe that local electricity companies have substantial potential monopoly power in their provision of electricity for purposes of lighting (their use of that power, however, is regulated by government). While flashlights, kerosene lamps, and candles are substitutes for electric lights, they are viewed as poor substitutes. At the same time electricity for heating purposes has close substitutes — oil, natural gas, wood stoves — and, consequently, the market for home heating is felt to be relatively competitive.

Another qualification regarding the definition of monopoly should be noted. Quite possibly a firm could become the sole producer of a product by charging a lower price than other firms can match. If the price rose, however, rival firms would find it profitable to enter the market. In this case the threat of entry can greatly restrain a firm's pricing policy even though rival firms are not currently operating in the market. The definition of monopoly is generally interpreted to rule out this possibility. When we say the firm is the sole producer, we mean that it will remain the sole producer regardless of the price charged. This interpretation is relevant in assessing the degree of monopoly in local markets. Although only one barber may be located in a small town, the threat of potential rivals (as well as the ability of consumers to shop in other towns) robs him of much monopoly power.

As these remarks may suggest, probably few instances of pure, or absolute, monopoly can be found in the American economy. Writing more than four decades ago, Clair Wilcox listed only aluminum, telephone communications, shoe machinery, Pullman railroad cars, nickel, magnesium, and molybdenum as markets approaching pure monopoly.[1] Most of these can no longer be called monopolies today, and currently the best examples are local public utilities (electricity, telephone, water) and the post office. Many firms, however, do possess some degree of monopoly power even if they are not examples of the pure theoretical construct. Moreover, industries containing several firms may not appear to be monopolies, but collectively they may behave in a monopolistic way if they collude with one another in their pricing policies.

SOURCES OF MONOPOLY POWER
11.2

For a firm to be the sole supplier of a product, there must be some reason why other firms cannot enter the market and produce the same product. If a monopoly is making an economic profit by charging a price above the cost of production, what prevents entry by other firms in an effort to realize profits themselves? Something must impede entry, or else the monopoly could not maintain its monopolistic position. For this reason economists generally find the source of monopoly to lie in *barriers to entry*. Barriers to entry are legal or technical conditions that make it impossible, or prohibitively costly, for a new firm to enter a given market. The following five types of entry barriers have historically been associated with the presence of monopoly.

Control of Inputs

A firm may own the total supply of a raw material that is essential in the production of some product. The classic example was the Aluminum Company of America (Alcoa), which was the sole producer of aluminum in the United States from the late nineteenth century until the 1940s. For a time Alcoa controlled all sources of bauxite in the United States, and bauxite is the ore from which aluminum is made. More recent examples are hard to come by. DeBeers Consolidated Mines of South Africa, through its ownership of mines and its central sales organization, controls 85 percent of the world's diamond output, but perhaps a more infamous example is OPEC. In 1975 the countries belonging to the Organization of Petroleum Exporting Countries (OPEC) possessed 70 percent of the

---

[1] James V. Koch, *Industrial Organization and Prices*, 2nd ed. (Englewood Cliffs, N.J.: Prentice-Hall, 1980), p. 25.

world's proven crude oil reserves.[2] Strictly speaking, OPEC is not a monopoly but a cartel, although a successful cartel has much the same impact as a monopoly, as we will see in the next chapter.

Economies of Scale

The technology of production for a product may be such that one large producer can supply the entire market at a lower per-unit cost than can several smaller firms sharing the same market. In other words, the long-run average cost curve for a single firm slopes downward over the entire range of market output. Consequently, it would be wasteful to have more than one firm operating in such a market since production costs are lowest if one firm supplies the entire output. In this situation the industry is a *natural monopoly*. Natural monopoly is most common in the public utilities — in the provision of power, water, and telephone services in a given locality.

Patents

A firm may have unique access to a technique that is useful or essential in the production of some good or have the sole right to produce a particular product. Frequently, the exclusive right to use some productive technique or to produce a certain product is granted by the government in the form of a patent. Patents are granted to the inventor of a technique or product, and they amount to the legal right to a temporary monopoly. Since patents expire in seventeen years, they are not a permanent source of monopoly power. Although patents are an instance of government-created and -sanctioned monopoly power, there is an economic rationale for their use; namely, that firms and individuals will underinvest in innovation and inventive activities if the fruits of these activities can immediately be copied by others who have not shared in the research and development costs. As we will see in Chapter 19, this is generally regarded as a valid argument for granting some protection to inventors, but agreement on the duration of a patent does not come as easy. Some economists believe that seventeen years is too long; others believe that given the length of time it takes to develop and market a product, seventeen years is too short.

Licenses

Governments sometimes block entry into particular markets by requiring firms to have a governmentally provided license as a condition for operating in that market. Licensing is sometimes defended as a method of ensuring minimum standards of competency, but it can be (and many feel has been) used as a barrier to entry that insulates existing holders of licenses from new competition. One cannot enter the postal service, airline, television and radio broadcasting, public utility, or trucking markets

[2] James M. Griffin and Henry B. Steele, *Energy Economics and Policy* (New York: Academic Press, 1980), p. 20.

without a governmentally provided license. Similarly, hundreds of occupations require licenses, among them barbers, funeral directors, taxi drivers, plumbers, bakers, and tailors. Often these licenses are granted by state government boards composed largely of existing license holders.

Entry Lags

The time it takes to enter a market can act temporarily to shield an existing producer from competition. Thus, the first firm to market some product will usually enjoy a temporary monopoly position. If the product turns out to be profitable, entry is likely to occur as rapidly as technological conditions permit. One well-known example of this process was the introduction of the ball-point pen by the Reynolds International Pen Company in 1945. Reynolds held a patent on the ball-point pen, which it initially sold at a price of $12.50 (more than $50.00 in current prices!), although it cost less than $1.00 to produce. Reynolds's early success prompted competitors to enter the market selling similar pens, but not similar enough to be judged patent violations. (Patents are not always the protection they seem.) A year after Reynolds marketed its first ball-point pen, over a hundred firms were selling similar items, some priced below $3.00. Within three years the price fell to less than $1.00. For a short time, though, Reynolds enjoyed a monopoly position.

A monopoly cannot exist unless it is fully protected from competition by a barrier to entry, but the existence of a barrier to entry will not automatically transform a competitive market into a pure or absolute monopoly. Barriers to entry may be no more than a minor hindrance to entry, in which case an industry could remain reasonably competitive. For example, suppose a firm receives a patent on a process that enables it to produce at a per-unit cost 1 percent below the costs of other firms. The patent holder will temporarily make higher profits, but the patent does not insulate it completely from competition by other firms. Similarly, if licenses are required to operate in a market and the government grants licenses to 99 percent of those who wish to enter the market, the outcome would be close to the competitive result even though entry is blocked to some degree. As these examples suggest, the significance of barriers to entry is likely to vary from one case to another.

THE MONOPOLIST'S DEMAND
AND MARGINAL REVENUE CURVES
11.3

A monopoly faces the market demand curve for the product it produces since it is, by definition, the only seller of the product. Thus, a monopoly's demand curve will slope downward. This situation contrasts sharply with the horizontal demand curve facing the competitive firm. While the competitive firm is a price taker, a monopoly is a price maker. A monopoly supplies the total market and can set any price it wants. Since the monopoly faces a downward-sloping market demand curve, if it raises price, the amount it can sell will fall. Much of the analysis of monopoly and the differences in output and pricing decisions between a monopoly and a competitive industry stems from this difference in the demand curves.

In determining what output to produce, any profit-oriented firm will be concerned with the way output is related to total revenues. Will an increase in output increase total revenues and, if so, by how much? Recall that marginal revenue is defined as the change in total revenue associated with a one-unit change in output. Marginal revenue thus indicates how a change in output affects total revenue. Understanding the significance of marginal revenue for the firm's output decision and the way marginal revenue is related to the firm's demand curve is central to the analysis of monopoly and other noncompetitive market structures.

For a competitive firm marginal revenue is equal to the price of the product. This follows directly from the firm's horizontal demand curve. Suppose, for example, that the firm is currently selling 3 units per week at a price of $8 per unit, yielding a total revenue of $24. With a horizontal demand curve, the firm may also sell 4 units per week at $8 per unit. Total revenue rises from $24 to $32, so marginal revenue is $8 and equal to the price of the product. With a downward-sloping demand curve, the situation is different. The only way 4 units per week can be sold is by reducing price below $8. If price must be reduced to $7 to sell 4 units, then total revenue increases to $28 ($7 times 4 units) from $24. The marginal revenue associated with increasing sales from 3 to 4 units is only $4, well below the market price of $7.

When the demand curve slopes downward, marginal revenue is always less than price. Figure 11–1 shows why. When price is $8, the firm can sell 3 units, and total revenue is equal to the rectangle $0PEQ$, or $24. To sell 4 units, the firm must reduce price to $7 since the demand curve slopes downward. Total revenue for 4 units sold is $0P'E'Q'$, or $28. Note how total revenue changes when sales increase from 3 to 4 units. The rectangular measure of total revenue decreases by area A: this area indicates how much revenue is sacrificed on the first 3 units when they are sold for $7 instead of $8 (area A equals $3). The rectangular measure of total revenue, however, increases by area B: this area indicates the additional contribution to revenue received from selling the fourth unit for $7. Area B is equal to the price of the product, $7. When the firm sells 4 units instead of 3, total revenue rises by area B (the price received for the fourth unit) minus area A (the reduced revenues from selling the first 3 units at a lower price), or by $7 minus $3, or $4. The increase in total revenue is marginal revenue, and it is less than the price (area B) because the price of the first 3 units must be reduced to sell 4 units. This reasoning applies to any downward-sloping demand curve and shows why *marginal revenue is always less than price when the demand curve slopes downward*, except for the first unit sold, as explained below.

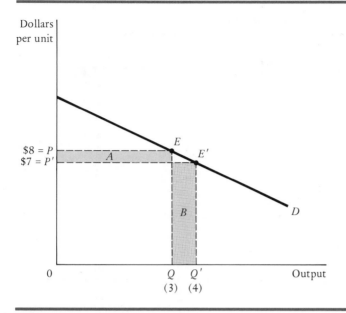

FIGURE 11-1

The Monopolist's Demand Curve

A monopolist confronts a downward-sloping market demand curve. Marginal revenue is lower than price with a downward-sloping demand curve. If price falls from $8 to $7, total revenues change by an amount equal to area *B* (the price at which the fourth unit is sold) minus area *A*.

Marginal revenue is not a fixed amount but varies with the quantity sold. Table 11-1 illustrates the relationships among the demand schedule, total revenue, and marginal revenue. The first two columns reflect the assumption of a downward-sloping demand curve, with quantity sold rising as price declines. Total revenue (price times quantity) at alternative rates of output is shown in the third column, and marginal revenue in the last column. Marginal revenue and price are equal for the first unit sold, but for all other rates of output, marginal revenue is less than price. When sales increase from 1 to 2, for example, total revenue rises from $10 to $18. So marginal revenue for the second unit of output is $8, but the price is $9.

Note that marginal revenue becomes negative over the range of prices where the demand curve is inelastic. (Recall that demand is inelastic when price and total revenue move in the same direction: when price falls so does total revenue, and vice versa.) If output increases from 7 to 8 units, the marginal revenue of the eighth unit is minus $4, meaning that the increase in sales actually generates lower total revenue. A negative marginal revenue also indicates that the firm can increase total revenue by reducing the quantity sold since the negative sign means that quantity

TABLE 11–1
Demand and Marginal Revenue

Price	Quantity Sold	Total Revenue	Marginal Revenue
$11	0	$ 0	—
10	1	10	$10
9	2	18	8
8	3	24	6
7	4	28	4
6	5	30	2
5	6	30	0
4	7	28	−2
3	8	24	−4
2	9	18	−6
1	10	10	−8

sold and total revenue are moving in opposite directions. Over the range of prices where demand is elastic, marginal revenue is positive, implying that quantity sold and total revenue change in the same direction.

Demand, Marginal Revenue, and Total Revenue Curves

Figure 11–2 illustrates graphically the relationships among demand, marginal revenue, and total revenue. Figure 11–2a shows a demand curve *D* and its associated marginal revenue curve MR. For a negatively sloped demand curve, marginal revenue is less than price at all levels of output. Another way to see the relationship between the demand curve and marginal revenue curve is to recognize that the demand curve is really an average revenue (AR) curve. When a firm sells 15 units at a price of $12, the average revenue per unit of output is also $12. Viewed in this way, the demand curve is a declining average revenue curve; and whenever the average is falling, the marginal curve associated with it must lie below the average.

In using the marginal revenue and demand curves in the analysis of monopoly, we should remember that they relate price, marginal revenue, and quantity *along a vertical line.* For example, at an output of 11, by looking directly above that output, we see that marginal revenue is $9 and price is $15. This means that if the firm sells a twelfth unit, the additional revenue generated will be $9; or if the firm reduces output from 11 to 10 units, total revenue will fall by $9. Figure 11–2b shows marginal revenue

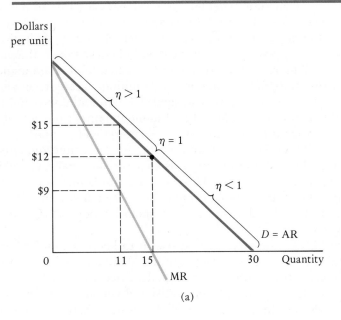

(a)

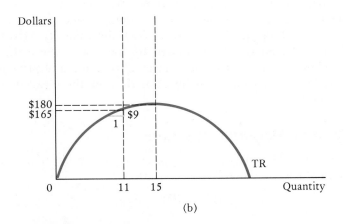

(b)

FIGURE 11-2

The Monopolist's Demand, Marginal Revenue, and Total Revenue Curves

(a) The MR curve lies below the *D* curve. At each output level the height to MR shows how much total revenues change when one unit more or less is sold. Marginal revenue is zero at the output where total revenues are at a maximum.
(b) Marginal revenue is shown by the slope of the total revenue curve.

as the slope of the total revenue curve (TR) at each rate of output. So, for example, the slope of the total revenue curve at 11 units of output is $9.

Over the range of output where the demand curve is elastic, marginal revenue must be positive. An elastic demand curve means that an increase in output will increase total revenue; and when total revenue increases as output rises, marginal revenue is, by definition, greater than zero. In Figure 11–2, since we are using a straight-line demand curve, the price elasticity of demand (η) is greater than 1 along the upper portion of the curve (between zero and 15 units of output), so marginal revenue is positive over this range. When demand is unit elastic, total revenue remains constant when an additional unit of output is sold; so marginal revenue is zero, as shown when output is 15 units. When demand is inelastic, an increase in quantity sold reduces total revenue; so marginal revenue is negative at quantities where the demand curve is inelastic, beyond 15 units of output in the graph.

One bit of geometry may be useful to keep in mind when drawing marginal revenue curves for straight-line demand curves: the slope of the MR curve is, in absolute value, exactly twice the slope of the demand curve. The MR curve falls twice as fast and becomes zero exactly halfway between the origin and the level of output where the demand curve touches the quantity axis. In the diagram marginal revenue becomes zero at 15 units of output while the demand curve reaches zero at 30 units of output. (Alternatively, recall that at the midpoint of the demand curve, the price elasticity is 1, so marginal revenue will be zero at that output.) Knowing this relationship allows us to identify one point on the MR curve; that is, where the MR curve crosses the quantity axis. A second point on the MR curve is determined by the point where the demand curve touches the price axis since marginal revenue and price are equal for the first unit of output. Drawing a line through these two points yields the marginal revenue curve.

Price, Elasticity, and Marginal Revenue

We may express the exact relationships among price, elasticity of demand, and marginal revenue as follows:[3]

$$MR = P[1 - 1/\eta].$$

---

[3] Refer to Figure 11–1 and note that the change in total revenue (ΔTR) associated with a change in quantity sold (ΔQ) is equal to area B minus area A. Area B equals $P(\Delta Q)$ and area A equals $Q(\Delta P)$. Thus,

$$\Delta TR = P(\Delta Q) - Q(\Delta P). \tag{1}$$

Since $\Delta TR/\Delta Q$ is marginal revenue, dividing (1) by ΔQ yields

$$MR = P - (\Delta P/\Delta Q)\, Q. \tag{2}$$

Since the elasticity of demand η equals (when expressed as a positive number) $- (\Delta Q/Q)/(\Delta P/P)$, $\Delta P/\Delta Q$ equals $(-1/\eta) \cdot (P/Q)$. Substituting $(-1/\eta) \cdot (P/Q)$ for $\Delta P/\Delta Q$ in (2) produces:

$$MR = P + Q[(-1/\eta) \cdot (P/Q)] = P - (P/\eta) = P[1 - (1/\eta)]. \tag{3}$$

This formula relates marginal revenue at a particular quantity of output to elasticity and price at the same quantity. We will use it later in the analysis of price discrimination, but for the moment let's interpret several relationships (that have already been discussed) among price, elasticity of demand, and marginal revenue in terms of this formula.

1. When the elasticity of demand is infinity (a horizontal demand curve), marginal revenue equals price: $MR = P[1 - (1/\infty)] = P(1 - 0) = P$.

2. When demand is unit elastic, marginal revenue equals zero: $MR = P[1 - (1/1)] = P(0) = 0$.

3. When demand is elastic ($\eta > 1$), marginal revenue is greater than zero. For example, when $\eta = 3$, marginal revenue is two-thirds the price: $MR = P[1 - (\frac{1}{3})] = P(\frac{2}{3}) = \frac{2}{3}P$.

4. When demand is inelastic ($\eta < 1$), marginal revenue is negative. For example, when $\eta = \frac{1}{2}$, marginal revenue is equal to minus the price: $MR = P[1 - (1/0.5)] = P(1 - 2) = P - 2P = -P$.

This formula implies that the more elastic the demand curve, the closer marginal revenue is to the price of the product. When demand is highly elastic, a small reduction in price will increase sales sharply; so revenue will go up by almost as much as the price received for the additional units (area *A* in Figure 11–1 is small).

In this section we have covered a good bit of material, much of it explaining the graphical and arithmetical relationships among marginal revenue, price elasticity, and total revenue. However, do not lose sight of two crucial points. First, remember the meaning of marginal revenue; it measures the contribution to total revenue produced by a change in output. Second, remember that marginal revenue is less than price at all points (except the first unit of output) along a downward-sloping demand curve.

PROFIT-MAXIMIZING OUTPUT OF A MONOPOLY
11.4

Conditions of demand and cost jointly determine the most profitable output for a monopoly, just as they do for a competitive firm. Analytically, the only difference is that a monopoly faces a downward-sloping demand curve while a competitive firm faces a horizontal demand curve. Before examining how this affects the pricing and output decisions of a monopoly, though, two preliminary matters deserve brief attention.

First, we assume that the monopoly attempts to maximize profits. As pointed out in Section 8.1, the assumption of profit maximization is probably more questionable for a monopoly than it is for a competitive firm because a monopoly may be in a position to generate positive economic profits even if it doesn't earn the maximum profit possible. So a monopoly may have some leeway to pursue other nonprofit goals (like hiring lazy relatives), if it chooses — an indulgence a competitive firm typically can't afford. Nonetheless, we will retain the assumption of profit maximization since it is generally believed to provide a sufficiently close approximation for most purposes.

Second, we will assume that the monopoly hires its inputs in competitive markets. Consequently, our firm is a monopoly in the output market but has no monopoly power in its input markets. This means that the monopoly can hire as much of any input as it wants without affecting the price of the input; that is, the monopoly is a price taker in input markets. With this assumption the cost curves of the monopoly will reflect the same underlying conditions examined in Chapter 7.

A Numerical Example

Just as with the competitive firm, there are two equivalent ways to identify the most profitable price-quantity combination for a monopoly. We may work either with the total revenue and cost relationships or with the marginal revenue and cost relationships. Table 11–2 presents cost and revenue data for a hypothetical monopoly, and these figures will be used to illustrate both approaches.

We know the firm is a monopoly by the cost and revenue data in the

TABLE 11-2
Profit Maximization by a Monopolist

Price (1)	Quantity (2)	Total Revenue (3)	Total Cost (4)	Profit (5)	Marginal Cost (6)	Marginal Revenue (7)	
—	0	0	0	0	—	—	
$10	1	$10	$ 8	$ 2	$ 8	$10.00	
9.80	2	19.60	15	4.60	7	9.60	
9.60	3	28.80	21	7.80	6	9.20	MR > MC
9.40	4	37.60	27.50	10.10	6.50	8.80	
9.20	5	46.00	34.50	4.50	7.00	8.40	
9.00	6	54.00	41.80	12.20	7.30	8.00	
8.80	7	61.60	49.35	12.25	7.55	7.60	MR ≈ MC
8.60	8	68.80	57.00	11.80	7.65	7.20	
8.40	9	75.60	65.00	10.60	8.00	6.80	
8.20	10	82.00	74.00	8.00	9.00	6.40	MC > MR
8.00	11	88.00	84.00	4.00	10.00	6.00	
7.80	12	93.60	95.00	−1.40	11.00	5.60	

tersection of the marginal revenue (MR) and marginal cost (MC) curves, at point C. Since marginal revenue equals marginal cost at output $0Q_1$, this output is the most profitable level of production. The price charged by the monopolist is shown by the point on the demand curve directly above point C. In this example the monopolist would charge a price of $10. At any other rate of output, marginal revenue is not equal to marginal cost, and profits would be lower. For example, at output $0Q_0$ marginal revenue is $8 and marginal cost is $5. Selling an additional unit of output would therefore add more to revenues ($8) than to costs ($5), and profits would increase. At any output where marginal revenue exceeds marginal cost, the firm can increase profit by expanding output. So in Figure 11–3b output should be increased up to the point where the falling MR curve meets the rising MC curve, at point C.

This explanation conceives of the monopolist's settling on a particular output rather than setting a specific price. Recall, however, that the demand curve shows the *price-quantity combinations* that are possible. We may proceed by thinking that either quantity or price is set because once one is set, the other is automatically determined. If price is set, the demand curve identifies the corresponding quantity that can be sold; if quantity is set, the demand curve shows the price that can be charged. We could recast the analysis in terms of what price the monopolist should charge and reach the same conclusion. For example, suppose the monopolist is currently producing $0Q_1$ and charging $10 a unit. Should the monopolist charge a lower price? At a lower price the firm can sell more output. Looking directly below the point on the demand curve specifying the lower price, though, we note that the marginal revenue associated with the sale of additional output is less than the cost of producing it. Thus, the lower price in combination with the greater output would reduce profit. By similar reasoning, a higher price would also cause profit to fall. Once again, we arrive at the same result; namely, that the price-quantity combination of $0Q_1$ and $10 is the profit-maximizing outcome.

As the discussion may suggest, it is simpler to think of the monopolist's determining output, with price implied by the output selected. This approach does not ignore the role played by the price since each point on the marginal revenue curve has a specific price associated with it, as shown by the corresponding point on the demand curve lying directly above it.

Figure 11–3b identifies the most profitable level of output, where marginal cost and marginal revenue are equal; it does not show exactly how much profit is realized. To identify the amount of profit explicitly, we must draw in the average cost curve. We do so in Figure 11–4. The most profitable output is, once more, $0Q_1$, with a price of $10 charged. The difference between price (average revenue per unit) and average cost at $0Q_1$ is the average profit per unit of sales, in this case $2 per unit. Multiplying this amount times the number of units sold, $0Q_1$, gives total profit, shown in the diagram by the shaded area.

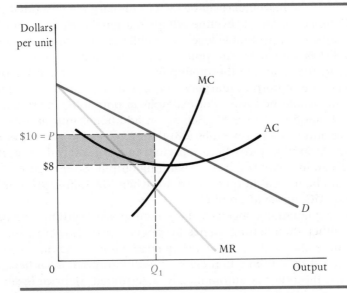

FIGURE 11-4
Profit Maximization
Profits are maximized at $0Q_1$ where MC = MR. Total profit is the shaded area.

We have been implicitly using long-run cost curves, as shown by the fact that there are no fixed costs. But the same graphical analysis applies when we use short-run cost curves. Just as was true in the competitive case, a short-run analysis is appropriate when an unexpected or temporary change occurs in market conditions.

Conditions for Profit Maximization: Monopoly and Competition Compared

We have assumed that the monopolist is motivated by a desire to maximize profits, just as the competitive firm is. In one respect, it is more difficult for a monopoly to locate the exact price-quantity combination that maximizes profits because monopolies in the real world don't know exactly what their demand curves look like. While a competitive firm can find out what price it can charge by observing its competitors, a monopoly has no competitors and lacks a similar source of information. The monopoly must therefore make price-quantity decisions on the basis of what it expects the consumer response to be. Obviously, the firm will make mistakes. Yet to the extent that the monopoly succeeds in maximizing profits — whether through trial and error or statistical estimation of demand — the end result will correspond to the outcome predicted by our analysis where we assumed that the monopolist had a knowledge of demand conditions.

Both competitive firms and monopolies are assumed to make the best of whatever market conditions they face. In both cases we can express the condition for profit maximization in the same way:

$$MC = MR \quad \text{(competitive firm and monopoly).}$$

Either firm should produce at the output where marginal revenue equals marginal cost. A competitive firm, however, faces a horizontal demand curve, so marginal revenue equals price. Thus, for a competitive firm that is maximizing profits:

$$P = MC \quad \text{since} \quad MR = P \quad \text{(competitive firm).}$$

On the other hand, a monopoly faces a downward-sloping demand curve, which implies that marginal revenue is less than price. For a monopoly that is maximizing profits:

$$P > MC \quad \text{since} \quad P > MR \quad \text{(monopoly).}$$

Price is greater than marginal cost for monopoly, but price is equal to marginal cost for a competitive firm. This important difference is apparent from the graphical representations of the equilibrium for the two cases.

FURTHER IMPLICATIONS OF MONOPOLY ANALYSIS
11.5

In this section we'll extend our discussion of monopoly to clarify several less obvious points.

1. We are so accustomed to analyzing markets in supply and demand terms that it is tempting to apply the same reasoning to a monopoly, but doing so can lead to mistakes. For example, if demand for a monopolist's product rises and the monopolist has an upward-sloping marginal cost curve, we might anticipate that both output and price would necessarily rise. Take a look at Figure 11–5. With demand curve D_1 price is $0P_1$ and output is $0Q_1$. When demand increases to D_2, the new marginal revenue curve MR_2 intersects the MC curve at the original output level. Output will remain at $0Q_1$, but a price of $0P_2$ will be charged.

To guard against thinking of supply and demand (appropriate for a competitive model but not for a monopoly), we note that *a monopoly has no supply curve*. A supply curve relates output to price when the firms have no control over price (each firm is a price taker), but it is not appropriate for a monopoly that determines price and quantity jointly. The absence of a monopoly supply curve does not mean that we are unable to analyze the output choice of a monopoly (since we have been doing just that). It simply means that the intersection of a supply curve and a demand curve does not determine output and price when the product is produced by a monopoly.

The peculiar outcome shown in Figure 11–5 is not the typical response of a monopoly to increased demand. Instead, it was contrived by

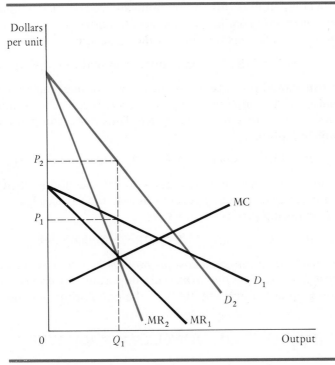

FIGURE 11-5

Increased Demand May Not Increase Output

A monopoly does not have a supply curve that uniquely relates output to price. The monopoly may produce the same output at different prices following an increase in demand. When demand increases from D_1 to D_2, output remains $0Q_1$ but price rises from P_1 to P_2.

having the higher demand curve become much less elastic (at the initial quantity). As a general proposition, we suspect that monopolies will find it profitable to expand output when demand increases. For example, if the demand curve shifts outward parallel to the original curve, or if it rotates about the price axis, output will rise, and so will price, as long as the marginal cost curve slopes upward.

2. Monopolies are usually thought of as making huge profits, but a monopoly may not always be able to make a profit. A monopoly can always charge a price above cost, but it cannot force consumers to purchase at that price. The position of the demand curve ultimately limits its ability to make money. If the average cost curve lies entirely above the demand curve, then any output the firm produces would have to be sold at a loss. In that case the monopoly would do better to produce nothing.

Thousands of monopolists each year find out that monopoly power does not guarantee profits. Among others, this group includes many who receive patents on their inventions. Many items granted patents — which gives the inventor the exclusive right to sell the product — are never marketed at all because it is believed that potential customers would not pay enough to cover production costs. For example, the following items have been given patents: a chewing gum preserver, a trap for tapeworms, a device for producing dimples, an air-cooled rocking chair, a vermin electrocutor, a safety coffin (with an escape tunnel and alarm "so that, should a person be interred ere life is extinct, he can, on recovery of consciousness, ascend . . . or ring the bell . . . and thus save himself from premature burial and death"), and goggles for chickens (resembling a pince-nez).[4] Actually, almost eighty years after the chicken goggles were patented, a firm called Animal Optics is about to market contact lenses for chickens. Before they were domesticated, chickens pecked one another to establish flock hierarchy (or pecking order!). Domesticated chickens peck, too, sometimes causing chicken ranchers to lose as much as 25 percent of their flocks. Animal Optics has discovered that for some reason rose-tinted contact lenses inhibit pecking, and it soon will be selling a lens for hens at 20 cents a pair. But will the contacts stand the market test? When surveyed, one chicken farmer puzzled, "Can you imagine putting contact lenses on one million chickens and checking them every week to see if they're still there?"[5]

All a monopoly position guarantees is that the seller can make the best of whatever demand and cost conditions exist. In many cases, however, this position does mean the monopoly will be able to make positive economic profits, as illustrated in Figure 11–4.

3. Monopolists are frequently believed to make more money if the product they sell is in inelastic demand. Yet it is easy to see that a monopolist who is maximizing profits will always be selling at a price where demand is elastic. (Recall that the elasticity of demand varies along most demand curves, with the elastic portion usually occurring at higher prices.) If, for some reason, the monopoly is producing an output where demand is inelastic, it could increase its profits by cutting back output and raising price. A lower output means higher total revenue (when demand is inelastic) and lower total costs, so profits will necessarily increase. The monopoly should reduce output until it is operating somewhere in the elastic portion of the demand curve. Another way to see this is by recalling that profits are maximized when marginal revenue equals marginal cost. Since marginal cost is always greater than zero, marginal revenue must always be positive when profits are maximized. But a positive marginal revenue implies an elastic demand curve since it means greater output (lower price) will increase total revenue.

---

[4] A. E. Brown and H. A. Jeffcott, Jr., *Absolutely Mad Inventions* (New York: Dover, 1960).
[5] Laurel Leff, "Question: Why Did the Chicken Wear Contact Lenses?" *Wall Street Journal*, December 16, 1980, p. 1.

Simple as this point is, notice how it allows us to see the inconsistency in the following statements: (a) the oil companies collude with one another, charging a monopoly price for gasoline; (b) gasoline is a virtual necessity that is in highly inelastic demand. These two statements cannot both be correct. If gasoline is in inelastic demand at the current price, that price is not a monopoly price. If the price is a monopoly price, the demand must be elastic. Yet many people believe both statements to be correct.

THE EFFECTS OF MONOPOLY
11.6

The way the form of market organization affects the functioning of a market has always been a major concern in economics. Having examined competitive and monopoly markets separately, we should now turn to a careful comparison of the two market forms. To do so, we need to determine how a change in market structure from, for example, competition to monopoly will affect price, output, employment in the industry, and so on.

To make this comparison, we will assume that the industry is initially competitive and that it is a constant-cost competitive industry. The assumption of constant costs means that input prices will be the same under competition or monopoly. This assumption allows us to isolate the impact of monopoly in the output market more easily. In Figure 11–6 the competitive demand and supply curves are D and LS, so the competitive outcome is a price of $0P$ and output $0Q$. The marginal revenue curve associated with the *industry* demand curve is MR, but it plays no role in determining output under competitive conditions since each firm adjusts to its own marginal revenue curve. In the competitive case each individual firm faces a horizontal marginal revenue curve at the market-determined price.

Now suppose the industry becomes a monopoly. The monopoly confronts the *industry's* demand and marginal revenue curves, but what about the monopoly's cost curves? If we assume that the monopoly can operate the separate plants at the same costs as those of the individual competitive firms, then the competitive supply curve in effect becomes the monopoly's average cost curve. Since this curve is horizontal, implying constant average cost regardless of output, marginal cost will equal average cost. Thus, the horizontal competitive supply curve is both the average and the marginal cost curve for the monopoly.

At the initial competitive output $0Q$, the monopoly's marginal cost (CQ) is greater than marginal revenue (EQ), so the monopolist is in a position to increase profits (from the zero profit level of the competitive equilibrium) by reducing output. By restricting output, the monopolist is able to charge a higher price. The profit-maximizing output occurs where MR = MC at output $0Q_M$. The monopoly will produce $0Q_M$, charge a price of $0P_M$, and realize economic profits of PP_MBA. *For the same demand and*

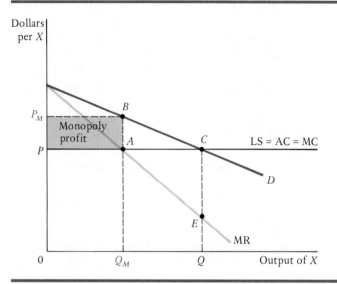

FIGURE 11-6
Monopoly and Competition Compared
The competitive long-run supply curve is LS: if the industry is competitively
organized, output is 0Q and price is P. Under monopoly conditions LS becomes
the monopolist's long-run AC and MC curves, and the monopolist's
profit-maximizing output is 0Q_M at a price of P_M. Price is higher and output lower
under monopoly. The shaded area shows monopoly profit.

*cost conditions, price will be higher and output lower under monopoly than
they will be under competition.* This conclusion is one of the most important and best-known conclusions of microeconomic theory.

Monopoly and the Distribution of Income

If a competitive industry becomes a monopoly, there will be a change in
the distribution of real income among members of society. The owners of
the monopoly — sometimes called "the" monopolist, for short — will gain.
The economic profits of the monopoly are a measure of the increase in the
income of the monopolist since they represent a return on investment in
excess of what could have been earned in the absence of the monopoly
power. On the other hand, consumers lose when a competitive industry
becomes a monopoly because of the higher price they pay. The higher
price reduces the real purchasing power, or real income, of the consumers. Thus, by charging a price above average cost, the monopolist
gains at the expense of the consumers — a redistribution of income from
consumers to the owners of the monopoly.

Can we say that monopoly is undesirable because of its effect on the distribution of income? When consumers pay a price above cost, they are harmed, but the excess of price over cost becomes profit to the monopolist. One group gains and another group loses. Economists are reluctant to label this outcome as undesirable because doing so implicitly makes the value judgment that the well-being of one group (the consumers) is more important than the well-being of another group (the owners of monopoly). We do not mean to say that each of us cannot make a judgment about the desirability of the change in income distribution accomplished by monopoly, only that economics as a scientific discipline cannot demonstrate that one distribution of income is better than another.

We can look at this issue in another way. Most people would judge the distributional effects of the exercise of monopoly power differently when the monopolists are wealthy owners of giant corporations and when they are unskilled workers. (Some unskilled workers gain from a higher-than-competitive wage rate because of the minimum wage law in much the same way that a monopolistic corporation gains from a higher-than-competitive price for what it sells.) Microeconomic theory just identifies the distributional effect; each person must supply his or her own value judgment about its desirability.

The Welfare Cost of Monopoly

Since the monopoly profit is a transfer of income from consumers to the monopolist, it is not a net loss when we count all members of society — the monopolist as well as consumers. But monopoly has another effect that does involve a net loss in welfare, or well-being, because it leads to an inefficient level of output. Economists refer to this net loss as a *welfare cost,* or *deadweight loss,* of monopoly.

To understand the nature of this loss, recall that the monopoly reduces the output of the monopolized good, good X, from $0Q$ to $0Q_M$ in Figure 11–6. This reduction in output is not fully a net loss because resources that were previously employed to produce the Q–Q_M units of X can now be used to produce something else. When the monopoly restricts output and employs less labor, land, energy, and so on, these displaced resources can find employment in other markets; they do not remain idle. Therefore, a more complete statement of the effect of monopoly on resource allocation is that *less of the monopolized good X and more of other goods are produced.*

Calling all other goods Y for short, suppose that under competitive conditions outputs are $2000X$ and $3000Y$. When X is monopolized, suppose outputs become $1000X$ and $4500Y$. If consumers prefer the competitive output mix to the monopoly output mix, they are harmed by the change in outputs produced by the monopoly. This harm is what we call the welfare cost. This effect on consumers is, in principle, distinct from, *and in addition to,* the harm they bear from paying a higher price for X

and thereby generating profit for the monopoly. Even if the government could tax away the entire monopoly profit and return it to consumers, consumers would still be worse off if they prefer $2000X$ and $3000Y$ to the monopoly outcome, $1000X$ and $4500Y$.

We can now show that consumers prefer the competitive output mix to the monopoly output mix. Look at what happens as the monopoly reduces output from $0Q$ to $0Q_M$ in Figure 11–7. The reduction in output releases resources that have a market value of $ACQQ_M$. In this example area $ACQQ_M$ represents $5000 worth of labor, capital, and so on ($5 per unit times 1000 units). If other markets are competitive, these resources will produce additional output of other goods worth $5000 to consumers. The additional output must be valued at $5000 by consumers because in other markets marginal cost equals price, so each additional dollar's worth of resources generates additional output valued at a dollar by consumers.

Consequently, consumers *gain* $5000 worth of other products because of the monopoly, but they *lose* $Q_M - Q$ units of X. Still, we can see that the loss of X is valued at more than $5000, so there will be a net loss from the

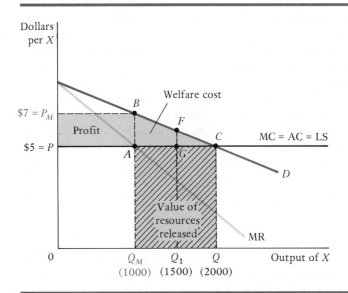

FIGURE 11–7

Welfare Cost of Monopoly

The reduction in output under monopoly from $0Q$ to $0Q_M$ releases resources that can increase output of other goods by an amount that is worth $ACQQ_M$ to consumers. However, consumers lose QQ_M of good X that is worth $BCQQ_M$ to them, so there is a net loss, or welfare cost, which is measured by the triangle ABC.

change in the output mix. The position of the demand curve relative to the marginal cost curve tells us this. Each unit of X between 2000 and 1000 units is valued by consumers at more than the $5 worth of resources released when it is not produced. For example, when the monopoly chooses not to produce the 1500th unit of X, consumers lose a product worth FQ_1 ($6) to them; not producing that unit of X permits the production of other goods to increase, but these goods are only worth GQ_1 to consumers ($5, equal to marginal cost), so a net loss of FG, or $1, on that unit results. The triangular area ABC is the sum of the net loss in benefits for all the units from 1000 to 2000. *This area is a measure of the net loss, or welfare cost, due to the monopoly restriction of output.*

We can arrive at this same conclusion from the opposite direction. At the monopoly output of $0Q_M$, price ($7) is above marginal cost ($5). This means that consumers value additional output of X at more than it costs the monopolist to produce. (Remember that price reflects the marginal value of the good.) The 1001st unit is worth $7 to consumers, but it uses resources that can produce other goods worth only $5 (marginal cost). Consequently, a gain of $2, or AB, results if the 1001st unit is produced. Each successive unit of output would yield a smaller net benefit than the previous one until output reaches 2000, where price equals marginal cost. The excess of value over cost associated with increasing output from 1000 to 2000 is area ABC. The monopoly, however, chooses not to produce these units, so consumers are unable to realize the potential net gain. It remains a net loss because the monopoly produces only 1000 units. Under competition, output expands to 2000 units, where price is equal to marginal cost.[6]

The welfare cost of monopoly is thus due to the production of an inappropriate level of output. Monopolies produce an inefficient (too low) level of output, and the triangular measure of the welfare cost is a dollar measure of the net loss involved. Consumers bear this cost in addition to the cost they bear from paying the higher monopoly price for the product.

HOW IMPORTANT IS THE WELFARE COST OF MONOPOLY?

11.7

Given sufficient information, we can estimate the magnitude of the welfare cost due to the monopoly restriction in output. Two items of information are required. First, the excess of the monopoly price over marginal cost $(P - \text{MC})$ provides us with the height of the welfare cost triangle, the

---

[6] If you have read the section on consumer surplus (Section 4.7), there is still another way to see that the area ABC is a net loss. When the price rises from $5 to $7, a loss in consumer surplus equal to P_MBCP results. This loss is not the welfare cost since the monopolist gains part of this area, P_MBAP, as profit. Note, however, that the cost to consumers, P_MBCP, is larger than the gain to the monopolist, P_MBAP, by the area ABC. Consumers lose more than the monopolist gains, and the difference is the net loss, or welfare cost, of monopoly.

distance AB in Figure 11–7. Second, the restriction on output gives us the base of the triangle, the distance AC in the diagram. (This distance can be estimated from the elasticity of the demand curve if we assume that marginal cost is constant.) Since the area of a triangle is one-half the base times the height, for the triangle in Figure 11–7 the welfare cost is $(1/2)$ (AB) (AC), or $(1/2)$ ($2) (1000), or $1000.

Knowing the size of the combined welfare cost due to monopolistic restrictions in output for the American economy would be quite important, and several economists have made ambitious attempts to develop such an estimate. The first was Arnold Harberger, whose 1954 study concluded that the welfare cost of monopoly in American manufacturing corporations equaled a scant 0.1 percent (or a thousandth) of gross national product (GNP). The trivial size of this estimate surprised many economists, but later studies, using different data and methodologies, have tended to support Harberger's conclusion that the welfare cost is not large relative to GNP. After reviewing all the studies, F. M. Scherer concluded that the welfare cost of monopoly in the United States "lies somewhere between 0.5 and 2 percent of gross national product, with estimates nearer the lower bound inspiring more confidence than those on the higher side."[7]

Needless to say, there are difficulties, relating to both data and methodology, in estimating the welfare cost of monopoly, and as yet no firm consensus has emerged on the matter. It is easy, however, to explain why we can expect the welfare cost to be small in comparison to GNP. Note that in Figure 11–7 the welfare cost of $1000 is a seventh of the $7000 sales revenues of the monopoly. In the United States only some markets are monopolized, and when we compare the welfare cost in those markets with total net sales in all markets (GNP), the ratio will be even smaller. For example, if a tenth of GNP is produced by monopolies, and the welfare cost of each monopoly is a seventh of its sales, then the total is 1/10 times 1/7, or 1/70 (1.4 percent) of GNP.

Furthermore, virtually no pure monopolies operate in the United States that are not regulated by government. Studies of the welfare cost of monopoly are really examining the monopoly power in industries where a few large firms dominate a market (such as the automobile industry), not in industries where there is only one producer. In concentrated industries it is likely that the outcome lies somewhere between the absolute monopoly and perfect competition results (between $0Q_M$ and $0Q$ in Figure 11–7). For example, in Figure 11–7, if two or three firms dominate the market, output might be at $0Q_1$. In that event, with a price of $6 and an output of 1500 units, the welfare cost (now area FGC) would only be $250, or less

[7] F. M. Scherer, *Industrial Market Structure and Economic Performance*, 2nd ed. (Chicago: Rand McNally, 1980), p. 464. Scherer provides a good review of the Harberger study and other studies and discusses the difficulties involved in constructing such estimates on pages 459–464.

than 3 percent of industry sales. And if one industry in ten exercised this degree of monopoly power on average, the total welfare cost for the economy would be 0.3 percent of GNP.

A crucial factor that influences the size of the welfare cost is the excess of price over marginal cost; that is, the height of the welfare triangle. If marginal cost is constant, this is equal to price minus average cost, or average profit per unit of sales. Consequently, data on profits per dollar of sales provide information on how much prices may exceed the competitive level. Unfortunately, the data report accounting profits, which normally will overstate economic profits. Nonetheless, they provide an interesting clue to the likely magnitude of the welfare cost.

Considering all American corporations, how much accounting profit do you think businesses on average make per dollar of sales? The typical response from college students in a Gallup opinion survey was 45 cents.[8] The correct answer is actually about 5 cents of aftertax profits per dollar of sales. In the same survey students also indicated that they thought a "fair" profit for corporations would be 25 cents per dollar of sales. Of course, the 5 percent profit margin is an average for all corporations, and firms in some industries do significantly better, but rare indeed is the industry with a 20 percent profit margin. This fact, together with our discussion above, makes it clear why the welfare cost of monopolistic output distortions is not likely to be large compared with GNP. A figure of 1 percent of GNP is not exactly negligible, though. In 1981, 1 percent of GNP was $29 billion. And as we will see below, there are other problems with monopoly.

Other Welfare Costs of Monopoly

We have emphasized two consequences of monopoly that are widely viewed as undesirable: the restriction of output and the redistribution of income in favor of the owners of the monopoly. Only the restriction of output involves a net loss, and both theoretical considerations and the available evidence suggest that it is not very large compared with GNP. Other potential effects of monopoly should be mentioned.

When we compared monopoly and competition, we assumed that the costs of production under monopoly would be the same as they were under competition. If the monopoly maximizes profits, this assumption would be correct. For example, the monopoly would produce the 1000 units of good X in Figure 11–7 at a cost of $5000. If profits are to be maximized, whatever output the firm produces must be produced at the lowest possible cost. The pressure on a monopoly to keep production costs down, however, is not as strong as the pressure on a competitive firm. If costs should increase because of slack cost controls in a competitive firm, losses are unavoidable, and the firm will be unable to continue

---

[8] *Gallup Opinion Index*, Report no. 123 (Princeton, N.J., September 1975).

to operate very long with losses. For the monopolist, on the other hand, higher-than-necessary costs may just mean lower profits, not losses. In the absence of competition with other firms, the monopolist is under less pressure to minimize costs. As Adam Smith observed, "monopoly . . . is a great enemy to good management."[9]

If production costs are unnecessarily high under monopoly, this result represents another welfare cost. For example, if in Figure 11–7 the monopoly produces 1000 units at a cost of $5.50 per unit, the total cost of producing 1000 units is therefore $500 higher under monopoly than under competition. Part of the potential monopoly profit of $2000 dissipates through cost increases. Some of the profits in the $2000 profit rectangle, $P_M BAP$, are not a transfer of income from consumers to the monopolist; instead the money is absorbed by unnecessary costs and is a net loss.

A similar outcome is produced if the monopoly incurs costs in acquiring, maintaining, or extending its market position. Our analysis implicitly assumed that the only costs of the monopoly were those associated with production of the product. But a monopoly may have to expend resources to ensure continuation of its monopoly power. A lobbying effort may be necessary to secure or maintain favorable government policies to block competition by other firms. Management may spend more time in determining how to insulate their market from encroachers than in making business decisions regarding output and cost. Legal and accounting staffs may be required to fend off antitrust suits of the Justice Department. Since it takes an average of seven years to see an antitrust suit through to its conclusion, litigation can be quite costly for both the government and the firm. For instance, the Justice Department brought an antitrust suit against American Telephone and Telegraph (AT&T) in 1974. By 1981 AT&T estimated that it had spent $250 million on the case — $25 million in direct legal costs, such as lawyers' fees and briefs, and another $225 million on supporting paperwork — and that pretrial discovery proceedings had involved more than 40 million pages.[10] In January 1982, as the trial was nearing its conclusion, AT&T and the Justice Department settled the case out of court.

For both of these reasons, costs may be higher than necessary under monopoly. Insofar as this is true, measures of the welfare cost of monopoly based on the welfare triangle, which considers only the output restriction, will underestimate the true welfare cost of monopoly. We must emphasize that the analysis does not imply that costs *will* be higher under monopoly, only that they *may* be higher. At the present time there is little evidence to suggest how quantitatively important these other costs under monopoly really are, but we suspect they are not trivial. In fact, some economists believe the other welfare costs are actually larger than the cost arising from the output restriction under monopoly.

[9] Adam Smith, *The Wealth of Nations* (New York: Modern Library, 1937), p. 147.
[10] "Out of the Quagmire," *Wall Street Journal*, January 30, 1981.

Summary

A monopoly is a single seller of some product with no close substitutes. Instead of many sellers, the characteristic of competitive markets, only one seller supplies the entire market. Thus, a monopoly will confront the market demand curve for the product it sells, and that demand curve slopes downward. With a downward-sloping demand curve, the monopolist will recognize that marginal revenue is less than price, since the price must be reduced to sell a larger output.

A monopolist maximizes profits by producing the output for which marginal cost equals marginal revenue. As we saw, though, having monopoly power does not guarantee that economic profits will be made; the average cost curve may lie entirely above the demand curve. But if a product that could be produced under competitive conditions is instead produced by a monopoly, the monopolist will make economic profits. The price of the product will be higher and its output lower under monopoly than under competitive conditions.

The restriction in output characteristic of monopoly represents a misallocation of resources and therefore involves a welfare cost. Since price is above marginal cost, greater output would be worth more to consumers than it would cost to produce. The size of the welfare cost due to the restricted output is shown by the triangular area between the demand and marginal cost curves over the range of output from the monopoly level to the competitive level (where price equals marginal cost). Theoretical reasoning and empirical evidence suggest that the aggregate welfare cost due to monopolistic output restrictions in the United States economy is not large relative to GNP, but it may still be large relative to the individual markets that are involved. Moreover, monopoly may produce other types of welfare costs that are not measured by the welfare triangle, such as unnecessarily high costs of producing whatever level of output it does produce.

Review Questions and Problems

1. Using the monopoly's short-run AVC, AC, and MC curves, show how a monopoly may operate at a loss in the short run. Identify the size of the loss in the diagram. (Hint: Draw the AC curve so that it lies entirely above the demand curve but with the AVC curve lying below the demand curve at some points.)

2. You, too, can be a monopolist! For example, you could write a novel (and copyright it) or be the first to produce a long-lasting, 2-foot-long pencil. Use a diagram to explain why you prefer not to engage in these monopolistic practices.

3. In the text we stated that "if the demand curve [facing a monopoly] shifts outward parallel to the original curve, or if it rotates [outward] about the price axis, output will rise, and so will price, as long as the marginal cost curve slopes upward." Confirm this statement with a diagram using linear demand curves.

*4. Suppose we, as consumers, have the options of having commodity X produced by a monopoly or of not having commodity X produced at all. Under which arrangement would we be better off? Why?

5. "Since a monopoly is the only source of supply, consumers are entirely at its mercy. There is no limit to the price the monopoly can charge." Evaluate this statement.

6. Draw a linear demand curve and its associated marginal revenue curve. Give the formula that relates marginal revenue, price, and elasticity of demand, and explain how the curves illustrate the relationship identified by the formula.

7. Why will a monopolist never set a price at which the demand curve is inelastic? Use the total revenue and total cost curves to illustrate your answer.

*8. At the profit-maximizing output a certain monopolist's price is exactly twice as high as marginal cost. What is the elasticity of demand? (Hint: Solve $MR = P[1 - (1/\eta)]$ for η, and remember $MC = MR$.)

9. A small town has one grocery store, one service station, and one restaurant. Are these businesses properly described as monopolies? If they are, why don't new firms enter the market? If they are not, what is it that prevents them from raising prices sharply?

10. What are the major sources of monopoly power? Is it correct to say that in some cases the government is responsible for the creation of monopoly power? Is it correct to say that in some cases monopoly is unavoidable?

11. Explain why a monopolist maximizes profits by producing at the point where $MC = MR$. What price is charged? Why isn't a higher price charged?

*12. "When a monopolist is maximizing profits, price is greater than marginal cost. This means consumers will pay more for additional units of output than they cost to produce." So why doesn't the monopolist produce more?

13. "A monopoly's profits are not necessarily bad, but its reduction in output is." Evaluate this statement.

*14. "The concept of opportunity cost teaches us that producing more of any good, including a good produced by a monopoly, means that we can produce less of other goods. Thus, there is no objective basis for saying that an increase in a monopolist's output is worthwhile." Evaluate this statement.

15. Explain why a certain triangular area is a measure of the welfare cost of monopoly. What information do you need to estimate the size of the triangle?

Supplementary Readings

Dewey, D. *Monopoly in Economics and Law.* Chicago: Rand McNally, 1959.

Harberger, Arnold. "Monopoly and Resource Allocation." *American Economic Review,* 44 (May 1954): 77–87.

Mansfield, Edwin. *Monopoly Power and Economic Performance.* 4th ed. New York: Norton, 1978.

Posner, Richard. "The Social Costs of Monopoly and Regulation." *Journal of Political Economy,* 83 (August 1975): 137–169.

Scherer, F. M. *Industrial Market Structure and Economic Performance.* 2nd ed. Chicago: Rand McNally, 1980.

Tullock, Gordon. "The Welfare Costs of Tariffs, Monopolies, and Theft." *Western Economic Journal,* 5 (June 1967): 224–232.

Using Monopoly Theory
12

As we learned in the last chapter, prices tend to be higher, output lower, and profits greater under monopoly than they are under competitive conditions. The theory of monopoly, however, provides more insight than these well-known conclusions; it also provides an analytical framework that we can use to investigate issues where monopoly power is significant. In this chapter we include several examples.

DO MONOPOLIES SUPPRESS INVENTIONS?
12.1

A common bit of American folklore has it that businesses sometimes suppress inventions that would benefit consumers. Books, movies, and TV shows occasionally contain story lines involving a business's attempt to purchase or steal an invention with the purpose of destroying it to avoid having the new product ruin the market. This thesis was advanced on a grander scale in the 1980 movie *The Formula*, in which greedy oil men deliberately withhold a secret Nazi formula for making cheap synthetic fuel from coal.[1] The formula was to be kept a secret until the Mideast oil fields dried up because the oil companies did not want to reduce the demand for oil. Milder versions of this idea include the belief that manufacturers design products to wear out quickly (planned obsolescence) so that consumers will frequently have to replace the worn-out product.

In evaluating such propositions, the first thing economists do is evaluate the internal consistency of the argument. The basic premise is that a business will make greater profits by suppressing a worthwhile invention than by marketing it. Let's see under what conditions this will be true.

As a first step, we must define a "worthwhile" invention. In some sense this term must mean that a firm can produce a better-quality product by using the invention. We must be careful here since it is almost always possible to produce higher-quality products, but doing so generally involves greater costs. In that case the better quality may not be worth its extra cost to consumers. To most people, for example, the better quality of a Mercedes is not worth paying three or four times as much as for a Honda. Thus, it is easy to understand why most manufacturers choose not to produce the highest-quality product that is technically feasible: few, if any, people would purchase it, given the price producers would have to

[1] The movie is based on the novel *The Formula*, by Steven Shagan.

332

charge to cover costs. To avoid any ambiguity, a "worthwhile" invention will be one that makes it possible for a firm to produce a higher-quality product at an unchanged cost or to produce the same-quality product at a lower cost. Suppression of invention in these cases would be unambiguously harmful.

Under competitive conditions a firm would never suppress a worthwhile invention. Suppose that the invention permits the production of the same-quality product at a lower cost. The first firm to introduce the process will have lower production costs than its rivals, and this result guarantees a profit. Even if the invention cannot be patented, the firm can earn profits until other firms have had time to copy the invention (much like the Reynolds ball-point pen case).

The monopoly case is where we would expect to find worthwhile inventions being suppressed, if they are going to be suppressed at all. Let's look at an example and see whether it's likely that a monopoly will suppress a worthwhile invention. Suppose that the market for light bulbs is monopolized and that the monopoly sells light bulbs that last for 1,000 hours. Then the monopolist acquires an invention that makes it possible to produce bulbs that last for 10,000 hours at the same unit cost as the 1,000-hour bulbs. Obviously, consumers would probably purchase many fewer light bulbs per year if each one lasted ten times as long. Does this mean that the monopoly will make more money if it continues to sell the 1,000-hour light bulb and withholds the superior product?

The answer is no. The monopolist will always make more money by producing and selling the superior light bulb because consumers will pay more for a 10,000-hour light bulb than for a 1,000-hour light bulb. What if consumers want 10,000 hours of light per year? Initially, they purchase ten 1,000-hour bulbs at $1.00 each, involving a total outlay of $10.00. If it costs the monopolist $0.50 to make each bulb, the firm makes a profit of $5.00 per consumer. Each consumer would be willing to pay at least $10.00 (more if convenience counts) for one 10,000-hour bulb, since a 10,000-hour bulb yields the same light as ten 1,000-hour bulbs that together cost $10.00. The monopolist, however, can produce each 10,000-hour bulb for $0.50, so profit would be $9.50 on the sale of one 10,000-hour bulb but only $5.00 on the sale of ten 1,000-hour bulbs.

This example assumes that customers continue to purchase just enough light bulbs for 10,000 hours of light in both cases. Let's drop this unrealistic assumption and develop a more general graphical treatment. There are two equivalent ways to proceed. One is to consider the demand curve for light bulbs but to recognize that the demand curve for 10,000-hour light bulbs differs from the curve for 1,000-hour bulbs. A simpler approach is to recognize that what consumers are really purchasing is the services of light bulbs — that is, hours of lighting — and the demand curve defined in this way does not shift. What changes when we switch from 1,000- to 10,000-hour bulbs is the cost and price per hour of lighting, not the demand curve itself.

Figure 12–1 illustrates this approach. On the horizontal axis we measure kilohours of lighting; each kilohour is 1,000 hours, the service provided by each of the initial bulbs. For simplicity average and marginal cost
are assumed constant at $0.50 per 1,000-hour bulb (per kilohour).

The initial preinvention equilibrium at Q_1 involves 100 kilohours (one
hundred 1,000-hour bulbs) sold for $1.00 each. Each 1,000-hour bulb costs
$0.50 to produce, so total profit is $50. The invention of the 10,000-hour
bulb that the firm can produce at the same unit cost ($0.50) means that the
cost per kilohour falls to $0.05. Thus, the average cost curve if the new
light bulb is produced is AC′. Operating with this lower-cost curve, the
monopolist can make more profit, and the new profit-maximizing output

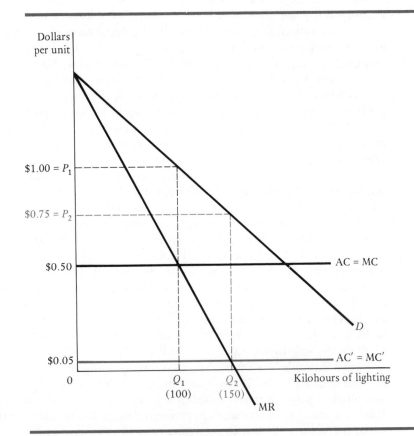

FIGURE 12–1
Monopoly and Inventions

If a monopoly can produce a 10,000-hour light bulb at the same cost as a
1,000-hour light bulb, the invention effectively reduces the cost per kilohour of
light from $0.50 to $0.05. The monopoly will make a larger profit by producing
and selling the superior light bulb.

of kilohours (not bulbs) is $0Q_2$. Price falls to $0.75 per kilohour. Profit rises from $50 to $105: the cost per kilohour is $0.05, and the price is $0.75, so the profit per kilohour is $0.70; and $0.70 times 150 kilohours yields a total profit of $105. Note that the new equilibrium corresponds to the sale of fifteen 10,000-hour bulbs at $7.50 each; fewer bulbs are sold.

This analysis suggests that a monopolist has no reason to suppress a worthwhile invention — just the reverse, in fact. We have examined the more difficult case of a higher-quality product to illustrate how we can analyze quality changes by focusing on the services of the product (hours of lighting) rather than on the product itself. The same conclusion results for an invention that lowers the cost of producing a product of unchanged quality. In that case the cost curves for an unchanged-quality product shift downward if the invention is utilized, which necessarily implies more profit for a monopolist.

Since a monopolist can increase profits by marketing a worthwhile invention, economists tend to be skeptical of allegations that businesses suppress inventions. Like many generalizations in economics, though, it is possible to conceive of a situation where a monopoly would find it profitable to suppress an invention. This could happen if the monopoly would lose its monopoly position by introducing the invention. For instance, if, once the invention of the 10,000-hour light bulb is known, other firms could produce and sell it for $0.50, the monopoly would find itself in a competitive market if it uses the invention. If the firm can patent the invention, however, the monopoly may be able to retain its monopoly position and market the invention.[2]

There have been innumerable instances where worthwhile inventions were marketed, both by competitive firms and by firms with various degrees of monopoly power. Thus, the generalization that profit incentives will lead to the introduction of worthwhile inventions seems reliable. Several problems can be laid at the door of monopoly, but widespread suppression of inventions does not appear to be one of them.

EXCISE TAXATION: COMPETITION AND MONOPOLY COMPARED
12.2

Let's see how the results of a per-unit excise tax levied on a competitive industry differ from the results of an identical tax levied on a monopoly. A per-unit excise tax requires the seller or sellers of a product to remit a certain sum to the government for each unit of the product sold. For example, a tax of $0.20 per gallon of gasoline is a per-unit excise tax on

---

[2] This analysis is a long-run analysis. In the short run, firms — whether they are monopolistic or competitive — may not introduce an invention immediately. When it is time to replace worn-out equipment, however (and that time will come more quickly when a lower-cost process is available), the firm will introduce the invention.

gasoline. (An ad valorem excise tax, in contrast, is a certain percentage of the market price, like a sales tax; both types of excise taxes have similar effects.) In the United States the most important per-unit excise taxes are levied on gasoline, cigarettes, and liquor. While these industries are not pure monopolies, it is still of interest to contrast the responses of monopolistic and competitive markets to excise taxation.

Suppose that we have an excise tax of $3 per unit of output. A basic question to ask is, Will the price to consumers rise by more if the industry is competitive or if it is monopolistic? The typical noneconomist's response to this question is that the price will rise by more under monopolistic conditions. Because a monopoly has greater market power, it seems plausible that it will respond by raising its price by $3 per unit to preserve its profits. By contrast, firms in a competitive market have no market power and are therefore less able to pass the tax on to consumers. Although this reasoning may seem sound, the following analysis indicates that price will rise by more under competitive conditions than under monopolistic conditions.

In making this comparison, we must compare a monopoly and a competitive industry operating under the same cost conditions. Consequently, we will assume that the competitive industry is a constant-cost industry (horizontal long-run supply curve) and, similarly, that the monopoly can produce at a constant average cost per unit. Figure 12–2a illustrates the competitive case. Before the tax is applied, output is $0Q_1$, and price is $6.00 per unit. A tax of $3.00 per unit adds $3.00 to unit costs at every rate of output and produces a vertical upward shift in the supply curve to S'. Price rises to $9.00 per unit, and output falls to $0Q_2$. In the end, price to consumers has risen by the amount of the tax; the net-of-tax price to producers is still $6.00, which just covers their unit production costs.

Before turning to the monopoly case, note that the implication of a price increase exactly equal to the tax is valid only for a constant-cost industry. If the supply curve slopes upward (increasing-cost case), the price will rise by less than the tax because unit production costs fall as the industry reduces output, so price need not rise by as much as the tax to enable firms to cover costs. Even in this case, however, the price increase under competition will be more than the increase under monopoly if the monopoly also has an upward-sloping marginal cost curve.

Figure 12–2b illustrates the monopoly case. Average and marginal costs are constant at $6.00 per unit, and the initial profit-maximizing position is the point where $MC = MR$, at point A. Output is $0Q_1$, and price is $10.00. When the $3.00 excise tax is imposed, the marginal cost curve shifts upward vertically by $3.00 to MC'. Marginal cost and marginal revenue are now equal at point B. Thus, the output that maximizes profits after the tax is $0Q_2$, and price is $11.50. The price has risen from $10.00 to $11.50, or by only half as much as the $3.00 tax. The monopolist's profits decrease from the larger striped rectangle to the smaller shaded rectangle, so the monopolist is, in effect, bearing part of the burden of the tax.

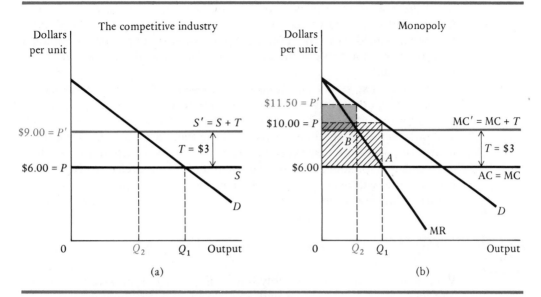

FIGURE 12-2

An Excise Tax: Monopoly Versus Competitive Industry

(a) An excise tax of $3 per unit applied to a constant-cost competitive industry will increase price by the full amount of the tax. (b) The $3 tax applied to a monopoly with the same demand and cost conditions will increase price by less than the amount of the tax.

Geometrically, price rises by less than the tax because the marginal revenue curve is steeper than the demand curve. After the tax (point *B*), marginal revenue is $3.00 higher than it was before the tax (point *A*), but because the MR curve is steeper than the *D* curve, price rises by less than $3.00. In fact, with a straight-line demand curve, the marginal revenue curve is exactly twice as steep as the demand curve, so a movement up the MR curve by $3.00 corresponds to a movement up the demand curve by exactly half that amount.

Why doesn't the monopoly raise price by the full amount of the tax? The monopolist has the ability to set any price, and charging $13 would mean that profit per unit of output would remain constant. The monopoly, however, is interested in total profit, and total profit would be lower at $13 because consumers would purchase fewer units at the higher price. If the price were set at $13, the monopoly would sell fewer than $0Q_2$ units; and at an output lower than $0Q_2$, marginal revenue would be greater than marginal cost. Consequently, it is not in the monopolist's interest to raise price by the amount of the tax; profits are higher at a lower price.

Note that the tax sharply reduces monopoly profits. The monopoly could have charged a price other than $10.00 before the tax was imposed, but it did not because profits would have been lower at any other price. Consequently, we know that before-tax profits are lower at $11.50 than they are at $10.00. After the monopoly pays the tax, net profits are reduced even further. As a result of the tax, the monopolist suffers an unavoidable loss in profits.

Thus, an excise tax on monopoly raises price by less than an excise tax on a competitive industry. Basically, this result occurs because the tax is paid partly out of the monopoly profits, so price does not rise as much as it does in the competitive industry where there are no economic profits to absorb part of the tax. The same analysis is relevant when unit production costs rise for some reason other than a tax. An increase in wage rates, for example, will also lead to a greater price increase for a competitive industry than for a monopoly.

REGULATING THE PRICE OF A MONOPOLY
12.3

Price is higher under a monopoly than it is under competitive conditions, and one approach to dealing with that problem is for the government to regulate the price the monopoly may charge. If a monopoly would normally charge a price of $15, for example, the government might impose a price ceiling of $12 in an attempt to reduce the cost of the product to consumers. We have already analyzed the effects of a price ceiling in a competitive market and have seen that the results include reduced output, a shortage at the controlled price, and nonprice rationing. A monopoly, however, may not respond to a price ceiling in the same way as a competitive industry. Indeed, under certain conditions it is possible that a mandatory price reduction for a monopoly will induce an increase in monopoly output.

How can a lower price lead to greater output? Recall that a monopoly restricts output in order to charge a higher price. A price ceiling means that a restriction in output cannot result in a higher price, so the price ceiling eliminates the monopolist's reason for restraining output.

We can achieve a fuller understanding of the problem by focusing on how a price ceiling affects the profit-maximizing output of a monopoly. In Figure 12–3 the demand curve is AD, and the marginal revenue curve is AM. In the absence of any regulation the most profitable output is $0Q_1$ since marginal revenue and marginal cost are equal at that output, and the firm will charge a $15 price. Now the government imposes a maximum price of $12. *As a result, the monopoly demand curve effectively becomes P_1CD.* Any output between zero and 150 units can be sold for a price of $12, but no higher, so the demand curve relevant for the monopolist's decision on output is the horizontal line P_1C over that range of output. Higher levels of output beyond Q_2 can still be sold for prices lower than $12, so the CD segment of the demand curve is still relevant.

When the demand curve changes, so does the marginal revenue curve. Over the range where the demand curve is horizontal, price equals

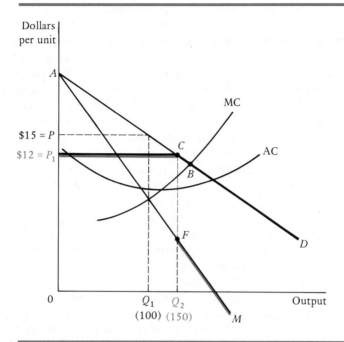

FIGURE 12-3
Regulation of the Price Charged by a Monopoly
With a maximum price of P_1 applied to the monopoly, the demand curve becomes P_1CD and the marginal revenue curve becomes P_1CFM. The profit-maximizing output is $0Q_2$: the output is higher even though the government has reduced the price the monopoly may charge.

marginal revenue since the firm can sell additional units without lowering price. Thus, P_1C is also the marginal revenue curve up to 150 units of output. At greater outputs the original demand curve is unchanged, so the *FM* segment of the original marginal revenue associated with the *CD* portion of the demand curve is still relevant. The entire marginal revenue curve is therefore P_1CFM. The curve is discontinuous at an output of 150. Think about what the discontinuous (*CF*) segment of the new marginal revenue curve means. If output increases from 149 to 150 units, the marginal revenue of the 150th unit is $12 (equal to CQ_2) since both 149 and 150 units can be sold for a price of $12. To sell 151 units, the firm must reduce price, to $11.94, for example. Thus, the marginal revenue of the 151st unit is only about $3 (equal to FQ_2).[3] Marginal revenue drops abruptly from $12 to $3 at an output of $0Q_2$.

[3] Total revenue from the sale of 150 units at $12.00 per unit is $1800. Total revenue from the sale of 151 units at $11.94 per unit is $1802.94. Thus, the marginal revenue from selling the 151st unit is $2.94.

Once we recognize the way the price regulation affects the marginal revenue curve, the remainder of the analysis is straightforward. When the price ceiling is imposed, profits are reduced at the initial output of $0Q_1$. Output $0Q_1$, however, is no longer the profit-maximizing level of output because at this output marginal revenue along P_1C is now greater than marginal cost. Consequently, the monopolist can recoup some of the lost profits by expanding production. Note that marginal revenue exceeds marginal cost as the monopolist increases output from 100 to 150 units, implying that profits rise as output expands over that range. But the marginal revenue associated with the sale of the 151st unit, FQ_2, is less than its marginal cost, so the firm will not produce that unit. Output $0Q_2$ is the new profit-maximizing output since marginal cost intersects the CF portion of the marginal revenue curve at this level of output.

In this case the mandatory lower price leads to greater output and reduced profits for the monopoly. Although the firm recoups some of the initial loss in profits by expanding output from $0Q_1$ to $0Q_2$, the net result is still a loss in profits. The monopoly could have produced $0Q_2$ at a price of $12 before the price control, but it chose not to because profits were higher at an output of $0Q_1$. The regulation essentially confronts the monopoly with a horizontal demand curve over the zero to Q_2 range of output, just like the demand curve of a competitive firm, and therefore eliminates the reason for restricting output.

Some practical difficulties arise in using this strategy to regulate monopoly. First of all, the outcome depends on where the maximum price is set. In this example the highest level of output the monopolist can be induced to produce occurs when the maximum price is set at the level where the marginal cost curve intersects the demand curve at B. If the price is set lower than that, output will decrease and a shortage will result. Since the demand and cost curves are not known to regulators, setting the correct price presents a problem. Second, the price must not be lowered to the point where the monopolist incurs losses and goes out of business. As the cost curves are positioned in the diagram, the firm can realize profits over a wide range of prices, but that is not always the case. Third, the monopoly has incentive to reduce the quality of the product since the price it may charge has been lowered. Producing a lower-quality, lower-cost product is one way the monopolist can avoid the sharp drop in profits that the price control would otherwise produce.

NATURAL MONOPOLY
12.4

Most of the disadvantages attributable to monopoly result from the absence of any firms that actively compete with it. If competitors are actually or potentially on the scene, no single firm will have much ability to influence price and the total output of the product. This line of thought sometimes leads to the conclusion that the solution to all monopoly problems is simply to break the monopoly up into several smaller independent and competing units. Unfortunately, in some situations this solution will make matters worse rather than better.

In some cases a monopoly position may result because one large firm can produce at a lower per-unit cost than can several smaller firms each producing a lower output. If the technology of production is such that economies of scale (declining average cost per unit of output) extend to very high output levels, a large firm could undersell small firms, and one or a few large firms would eventually dominate the industry. The extreme case is one where the average cost of a single enterprise declines over the entire range of market demand. As we saw earlier, this situation is called a *natural monopoly.*

Figure 12–4 illustrates the natural monopoly case. Graphically, a natural monopoly exists when the long-run average cost curve of a single firm is still declining at the point where it intersects the total market demand curve for the product — at point *A* in the diagram. One firm could

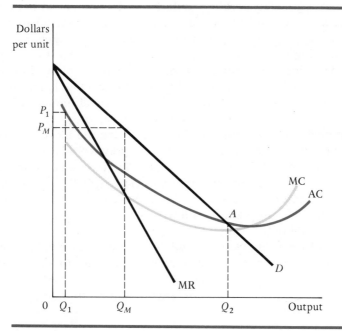

FIGURE 12–4

Natural Monopoly

When the average cost of producing a good is declining over the entire range of market demand, a natural monopoly exists. It is then cheaper for one firm to produce the entire market output than for several small firms to share the market. One firm can produce $0Q_2$ at a unit cost of AQ_2, which is lower than the cost when several firms each produce $0Q_1$ at a unit cost of P_1. However, if it is allowed to produce monopolistically, output will be $0Q_M$ and price will be P_M.

produce an output of $0Q_2$ at an average cost of AQ_2. In this situation the market, if unregulated, would tend to become dominated by a single firm. If instead there were several small firms, each producing $0Q_1$, for example, price would have to be at least P_1. Yet any one firm could expand output, sell at a lower price, and ultimately drive the smaller firms out. Monopoly is the "natural" result. Moreover, it would be undesirable to force a competitive structure on this market. The real cost of serving the market would be higher than necessary if there were several small high-cost firms.

It is easy to draw cost curves that imply a natural monopoly, but the important question is whether there are many real world instances of the phenomenon. Fortunately, natural monopoly conditions are not common, but they do exist for several products. Economists believe, for example, that natural monopoly conditions are approximated in the provision of electricity, water, natural gas, telephone services, and possibly cable television to specific geographic localities. Consider electricity. Providing electricity to a home requires that the home be physically connected to the generating facility through underground or overhead lines. If several separate firms served homes in a given community, each firm would have to run its own connecting power lines. The cost of duplicating connecting lines (implying higher average costs) could be avoided by using just one set of power lines. This situation is precisely what is shown in Figure 12–4. Unit costs are higher when several firms supply a few homes ($0Q_1$) rather than when one operation provides electricity to all homes ($0Q_2$).

When natural monopoly conditions exist, there are three feasible ways to deal with the situation. One is to leave the market alone. In this case a monopoly will result, and the monopoly would not choose to supply $0Q_2$ at a cost of AQ_2 per unit (in Figure 12–4). Instead, it would choose the profit-maximizing output of $0Q_M$ with a price of P_M. The second option is to permit a monopoly to operate but to have the government regulate its activities. The third option is to have government ownership and operation of the facility (for example, the post office).

In the United States, the regulatory option has generally been pursued. A privately owned firm is given the legal right to a monopoly in the provision of the service, but a public agency is created to regulate the firm's behavior. Now let's see how such a natural monopoly can be regulated.

Regulation of Natural Monopoly

The public agencies charged with regulating the behavior of natural monopolies, usually called public utilities, generally set the prices that may be charged. Before investigating the way they accomplish this, let's examine the economic principles behind the price-setting approach.

In Figure 12–5 the natural monopoly's average and marginal cost curves are AC and MC (ignore AC' for the moment). If we have complete

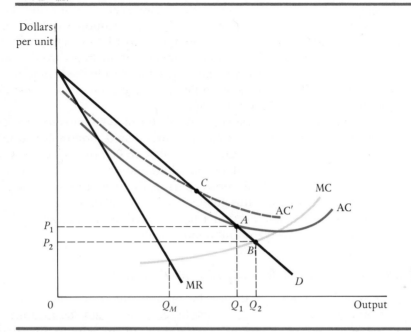

FIGURE 12-5

Regulation of Natural Monopoly

If price is set equal to MC at P_2, the monopoly could not cover its production costs. If price is set equal to AC at P_1, output will be inefficient, the monopoly may have little incentive to hold costs down, and the average cost curve could rise to AC′.

knowledge of cost and demand conditions, there are two logical prices that could be set. One is the price at the level where the average cost curve intersects the demand curve, a price of P_1. This solution is called *average cost pricing*. If the monopoly produces $0Q_1$, the price of P_1 will just cover its average cost, implying zero economic profit, or a normal rate of return. Moreover, the monopoly would have incentive to produce $0Q_1$ if a maximum price of P_1 can be charged. As explained in Section 12.3, with a price ceiling the demand curve facing the monopoly would become P_1AD, so marginal revenue (equal to P_1 up to an output of $0Q_1$) exceeds marginal cost as output expands to $0Q_1$, but MR drops below MC at higher output levels. Indeed, when a price of P_1 is set, any output other than $0Q_1$ yields a loss since average cost is above P_1 at lower rates of output.

At an output of $0Q_1$ price is greater than marginal cost (since average cost is falling at point A, marginal cost must be below it). This means that consumers value additional units of output at more than they cost to produce and suggests a second option; that is, to set price at the level where the marginal cost curve intersects the demand curve (point B). This is called *marginal cost pricing*. There is, however, a major obstacle to marginal cost pricing: if we set price at P_2, the monopoly would incur a loss at every level of output.[4] Because marginal cost is below average cost at all relevant outputs, setting a price equal to marginal cost would put the firm out of business. A subsidy could be used to enable the firm to produce $0Q_2$ at a price of P_2, but costs of implementing and financing the subsidy generally make this solution impractical.

Consequently, the most practical alternative seems to be average cost pricing. Output is greater than the unregulated monopoly output of $0Q_M$, and since expansion of output from $0Q_M$ to $0Q_1$ provides benefits to consumers that are greater than the additional production costs, there is an efficiency gain. (Put differently, part of the welfare cost arising from restricted output by an unregulated monopoly is eliminated.) Price to consumers is lower than it is under unregulated monopoly, and the owners of the monopoly receive no monopoly profit.

Regulation of Natural Monopoly in Practice

In practice, regulators do not have complete knowledge of cost and demand conditions. They generally attempt to attain the average-cost-pricing outcome by focusing on the rate of return on invested capital (accounting profits) earned by the monopoly. It works this way. If the realized rate of return is higher than what is thought to be a normal return (suggesting economic profits), then the current price must be above average cost, and the result signals regulators to reduce the price. Conversely, if the realized rate of return is lower than normal (suggesting economic losses), then regulators raise the allowed price. Proceeding in this trial and error fashion, regulators locate the price at which profits are normal — that is, where price equals average cost.

There are several problems with this approach, but perhaps the most serious is that it gives the monopolist little incentive to hold down costs. If costs rise, the regulators permit a higher price so that the monopoly still earns a normal rate of return. Thus, managers have a positive incentive to pad expense accounts, pay themselves and their friends higher-than-necessary wages, and incur numerous other costs that would normally be avoided because they cut into profits. Unnecessary costs will not reduce profits if the regulatory agency permits a price increase to cover higher costs.

Figure 12–5 also illustrates the consequences of this behavior. The AC curve continues to show the *minimum* unit costs of production, but cost padding shifts the *actual* cost curve to AC'. Since losses would occur at a

---

[4] Note that this is not true in Figure 12–3 when we follow this approach. The difference results from the fact that average cost is rising where it intersects the demand curve, so marginal cost is above average cost at the point where the MC curve intersects the demand curve.

price of P_1, regulators grant a price increase to cover the higher costs (point C). Most regulatory agencies recognize the perverse incentive of the regulation, and to overcome it, they frequently become involved in monitoring the costs of the monopoly. It is not easy, however, to determine whether a particular cost is necessary or not, so costs probably drift upward to some degree.

This form of regulation may also lead the monopoly to suppress or slow down the introduction of inventions, which would not occur under unregulated monopoly. The slowness with which AT&T has introduced automated switching equipment is a good example. Automatic panel switches to replace operators were first introduced in the 1920s, but it wasn't until the mid-1970s, fully fifty years later, that AT&T replaced all the old switches — despite the fact that further improvements in automatic switches permitted more rapid connections between telephones connected to the same switch and an increase in the number of connections a single switch could handle at a much lower cost and with much simpler maintenance. Recent advances in switching equipment, primarily using digital technology, have produced further speed and cost economies and make possible additional services, such as call waiting, call forwarding, and international direct dialing. AT&T does not expect to convert all local exchanges to digital switching until the turn of the century; thus, even though the relevant technology exists, some customers will be unable to purchase these services for more than twenty-five years.

The slowness with which regulated monopolies introduce new products and technology may be a natural response to a price ceiling. If a monopoly discovers a cost-saving technology, it is unable to keep the increased profits since the regulatory agency will in turn reduce its rates. Similarly, the monopoly will have reduced incentives to engage in research and development activities designed to reduce costs. Furthermore, a monopoly is under no competitive pressure to offer new services to consumers quickly since its customers are unlikely to have a better alternative.

For reasons such as these, economists have become increasingly critical of the regulation of natural monopoly in recent years. One famous study compared electric rates in regulated and unregulated states between 1912 and 1937 — before all states regulated rates — and found no difference in the rates charged.[5] The extent to which regulation today is successful in keeping rates down is not known. However, the alternatives to regulation when natural monopoly conditions prevail — unregulated monopoly and government ownership — are not particularly attractive either. Unfortunately, there may be no completely satisfactory solution to the natural monopoly problem.

---

[5] George Stigler and Claire Friedland, "What Can Regulators Regulate?: The Case of Electricity," *Journal of Law and Economics*, 5 (October 1962): 1–16.

CARTELS: COLLUDING TO ACHIEVE MONOPOLY POWER
12.5

Any business firm interested in making profits would like to be a monopoly, but most firms have little practical hope of becoming one. An alternative approach to attaining some monopoly profits, though, is to form a cartel. A *cartel* is an agreement among independent producers to coordinate their output and pricing decisions so each of them will earn monopoly profits.

Let's see how a group of firms in a competitive market can earn monopoly profits by coordinating their activities. We will assume that the industry is initially in long-run equilibrium, and then we will identify the short-run adjustments (with existing plants) that the firms in the industry can make to produce monopoly profits for themselves. Figure 12–6b shows the industry equilibrium with a price of P and an output of 1000 units. Figure 12–6a shows the competitive equilibrium for one of the firms in the industry. Note that initially the firm faces the horizontal demand

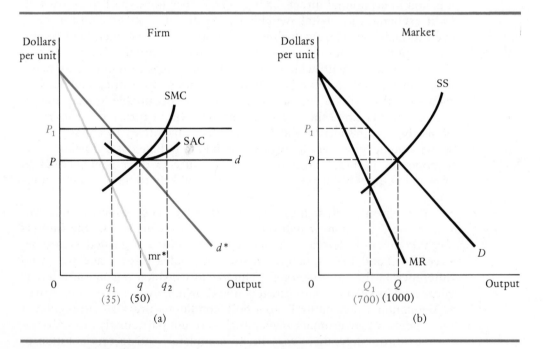

(a)   (b)

FIGURE 12–6
The Cartel

Under competitive conditions output is $0Q$ and price is P. If the firms form a cartel, output is restricted to $0Q_1$ in order to charge price P_1: the monopoly outcome. Each firm produces $0q_1$ and makes a profit at price P_1.

curve d at the market-determined price and produces an output of 50 units. To simplify matters, suppose that there are 20 identical firms in the industry, each producing 50 units of output.

Next the firms form a cartel and agree simultaneously to restrict output to attain a higher price. Each firm agrees to produce an identical level of output, equal to a twentieth of total industry output since there are 20 firms. The cartel agreement has the effect of changing the demand curve facing each firm. Before the agreement, if one firm alone reduced output, its action would not appreciably affect price, as shown by the firm's horizontal demand curve d. Now, however, other firms match a restriction in output by one firm. So when one firm cuts back output by 15 units, all firms would match the reduction, industry output would fall by 300 units, and price would rise significantly. The demand curve showing how price varies with output when firms' output decisions are coordinated in this way is the downward-sloping curve d^* in Figure 12–6a. At any price the quantity on the d^* curve is $1/20$ that on the industry demand curve.

Faced with this downward-sloping demand curve, the firm's profit-maximizing output occurs where its short-run marginal cost curve SMC intersects the new marginal revenue curve mr*. Output is 35 units; and since all 20 firms reduce production to the same output level, total output falls to 700 units and the price rises to P_1. Each firm is now making economic profits. Indeed, the idealized cartel result is just the same as if the industry were supplied by a monopoly that controlled the 20 firms. Figure 12–6b illustrates the result, with the short-run supply curve SS (the sum of the SMC curves of the firms) intersecting the industry marginal revenue curve MR at an output of 700 units and a monopoly price of P_1. By forming a cartel and restricting output to achieve the monopoly equilibrium, the firms maximize their combined profits. Figure 12–6b shows the total market effect of the coordinated output reduction by the 20 firms; Figure 12–6a shows the effects on each individual firm.

Firms can always make larger profits by colluding rather than by competing. Acting individually, they are unable to raise price by restricting output; but when they act jointly to limit the amount supplied, price will increase. Achieving a successful cartel in practice, however, is not as simple as it may seem.

Why Cartels Fail

If cartel agreements are profitable for the members, why aren't there many cartels? One reason is that in the United States they are illegal. But even before there were laws against collusive agreements, cartels were rare except when actually supported by government, and when they did exist, they were short-lived. A more important reason than illegality, many economists believe, is that several economic forces inhibit the formation, and encourage the breakdown, of cartels. Three factors contribute to cartel instability.

1. *Each firm has strong incentive to cheat on the cartel agreement.* A cartel achieves monopoly profits by having its members restrict output below the levels that each would individually choose, and this results in a higher price. Once a higher price is achieved, individual cartel members could earn even greater profits by expanding output. Each firm would like to enjoy the benefit of the cartel — a higher price — without paying the price — holding down output. If only one firm expands output, price will not fall appreciably, but the additional sales at the monopoly price will add significantly to the firm's profits. It is thus in each firm's self-interest to violate the cartel agreement to restrict output.

Figure 12–6 illustrates the incentive to cheat on the cartel agreement. If the firm in Figure 12–6a adheres to the cartel agreement, it will produce $0q_1$ and sell at price P_1. However, note what happens if the firm expands output beyond $0q_1$ while the other firms continue to abide by the cartel agreement and restrict output. In this event the firm faces a horizontal demand curve at price P_1; that is, one firm expanding output alone will not affect price. Remember that the downward-sloping demand curve is relevant only for simultaneous expansion and contraction of output by all firms. The firm acting alone can increase its profits significantly by expanding output since marginal revenue (equal to price with the horizontal demand curve) is above marginal cost at $0q_1$. Individual profits will be higher if the firm increases sales to $0q_2$ at the price of P_1.

Every firm has the same incentive to expand output and cheat on the cartel agreement. Yet if many firms do so, industry output will increase significantly, and price will fall below the monopoly level. It is in each firm's interest to have other firms restrict their output while it increases its own output. Every firm's self-interest is therefore a threat to the survival of the cartel. To be successful, the cartel must have some means of enforcing and monitoring the cartel agreement.

2. *Members of the cartel will disagree over appropriate cartel policy* regarding pricing, output, allowable market shares, and profit sharing. In Figure 12–6 we assumed that the firms had identical cost curves, making agreement on the profit-maximizing cartel output and price relatively easy. But when firms differ in size, cost conditions, and other respects, agreement will not come as easily since the firms will have different goals. If, for example, the cartel members' costs differ, they will disagree on what price the cartel should set. The problems become even more acute when the firms must make long-run investment decisions. Every cartel member will want to expand its capacity and share of total output and profits, but not all can be allowed to do so.

These problems are basically political in nature, and no matter what policy the cartel follows, it will reflect some sort of compromise among divergent views. As happens with any compromise, some firms will be unhappy with the outcome, and those firms are all the more likely to refuse to join the cartel, or join but violate the cartel policy and expand output.

3. *Profits of the cartel members will encourage entry into the industry.* If the cartel achieves economic profits by raising the price, new firms have incentive to enter the market. If the cartel cannot block entry of new firms, price will be driven back down to the competitive level as production from the "outsiders" reaches the market. Indeed, if an increase in the number of firms in the market causes the cartel to break down, price will temporarily fall below the cost of production, forcing losses on the cartel members. The prospect of entry by new competitors eager to share in the profits is probably the most serious threat to cartel stability.

To be successful, therefore, a cartel must be able to induce its members to comply with cartel policy (holding down output) and to restrict entry into the market. These tasks are not easily accomplished, and history is strewn with examples of cartels that flourished for a short time only to disintegrate because of internal and external pressures. Before concluding that cartels are always short-lived and unstable, though, let's consider the most famous cartel of recent history.

OPEC: *The Exception?*

When the Organization of Petroleum Exporting Countries (OPEC) was formed in 1960, few Americans took notice.[6] Originally containing only 5 members, the cartel grew to an ominous 13 by 1973. During these years, however, OPEC could not be judged a successful cartel. World oil prices actually declined slightly over the 1960–1970 decade — OPEC had not yet learned to use its potential market power.

All that changed in 1973 with the Arab-Israeli War. During the war, the Arab members of OPEC temporarily cut off oil exports. The results were dramatic: oil prices more than tripled in a matter of months. The estimated price of a barrel of oil on the world market was $2.91 in 1973 but jumped to $10.77 in 1974, providing a graphic demonstration of what an output restriction could accomplish. OPEC continued to hold down output after resuming exports; by accident, OPEC learned how to run a cartel! Subsequently, oil prices remained relatively stable (in real terms) until they received another jolt in 1978, when revolution swept Iran. Iranian exports, which accounted for 20 percent of all OPEC exports, fell almost to zero. Prices jumped once again and the new government in Iran continued to hold down exports, keeping prices at high levels. In addition, the Iran-Iraq War, which began in the summer of 1980, resulted in the widespread destruction of oil-producing facilities in both countries and reduced oil exports further.

In the mid-1970s some economists, familiar with the theory of cartels and the numerous historical instances of cartel collapse, predicted that OPEC would be short-lived. Since OPEC has been a successful cartel for

---

[6] For a more detailed discussion of OPEC, see James M. Griffin and Henry B. Steele, *Energy Economics and Policy* (New York: Academic Press, 1980), Chap. 4.

less than a decade, it may yet succumb to the same economic factors that destroyed other cartels. OPEC, however, has some advantages that may make it a more durable cartel than most.

1. The price elasticity of demand for oil, especially in the short run, is quite low, meaning that moderate output restrictions will produce large price increases — a favorable environment for a cartel. Fortunately, the effect of a low price elasticity is moderated by the fact that OPEC produces only half the world oil output. So when it restricts output by 10 percent, world output falls by, at most, 5 percent.

2. In 1975, OPEC countries contained 70 percent of the world's proven oil resources. Although OPEC does not control total world output, as an ideal cartel would, a 70 percent share of the stock of oil gives it substantial market power.

3. Because OPEC has only a few members, many of the internal problems that plague a cartel are minimized. Reaching agreements, as well as monitoring the output and price policies of individual members, is easier when there are only a few members involved. In fact, since just four countries (Saudi Arabia, Kuwait, Iran, and Venezuela), control three-fourths of OPEC's oil reserves, the number of effective members is quite small, a definite advantage for a cartel.

4. The biggest threat to a cartel is increased production by nonmembers. Since the impact on price depends on total (OPEC and non-OPEC) output, if restrictions in output by OPEC were matched by increases in output by others, price would not increase. In the case of oil, however, it takes a long time to locate and bring new supplies of oil into production, a situation that gives OPEC considerable short-run power.

Such natural advantages have rarely, if ever, been enjoyed by another cartel, and they help to explain OPEC's success. OPEC has also enjoyed another advantage: oil-importing nations have frequently adopted policies that strengthened OPEC's position. In the United States, for example, price controls on oil kept the price received by domestic oil producers artificially low and discouraged production and exploration. Price controls on natural gas discouraged production of this alternative energy source. Similarly, tough environmental restrictions on the mining and use of coal slowed the transition to coal as another energy alternative. In addition, the complicated system of pricing oil, involving different prices for "old" oil, "new" oil, and imported oil, kept the consumer prices of oil products below world market prices and encouraged consumption. Encouraging domestic consumption and discouraging domestic production implies an increase in demand for oil from OPEC, and the United States inevitably became more dependent on imported oil during the 1970s.

Will OPEC eventually go the way of previous cartels? As recently as 1981, few economists believed a collapse was imminent. But the situation had changed dramatically by early 1982.[7] In March 1982 the price for Saudi Arabian light crude oil was $29 a barrel, down in real terms more than 30 percent from a year earlier. OPEC oil production was down to 19 million barrels per day from 30.9 million in 1979, and yet oil markets were still characterized by surpluses. Experts were predicting that oil prices would fall further unless OPEC cut production even more.

What had happened was almost a textbook case of the operation of economic forces that undermine cartels. According to *Business Week,*

> The OPEC cartel is facing strains that it has never experienced before ... OPEC is so divided by cutthroat competition and internal political bickering that the organization is unlikely to find a way to agree anytime soon.... Under-the-table discounts already are common.[8]

(Cheating and disagreements over policy threaten cartels, as we explained earlier.)

External pressures that diminished OPEC's power were also at work.

> Demand for OPEC oil ... has collapsed under the combined impact of lower economic growth, surprisingly high conservation, expanded use of alternative energy sources such as coal and gas, and rising non-OPEC production of oil from Mexico, the North Sea, and the North Slope of Alaska.[9]

(Long-run price elasticities of demand are higher than short-run price elasticities and were being felt as consumers switched to substitutes. Entry at the high cartel price was taking place.)

To this list of external pressures we should also add that the United States removed crude oil price controls in 1981, which encouraged domestic oil production while further discouraging consumption.

The final chapter on the OPEC cartel has probably not yet been written, and it should prove to be a fascinating case to observe in the coming months and years.

PRICE DISCRIMINATION
12.6

Until now in our discussion of monopoly, we have assumed that the monopoly sets one uniform price for its product. Sometimes, a firm with some monopoly power can do even better by charging different prices to different groups of buyers. This pricing technique is called *price discrimination* when the differing prices do not correspond to different costs associated with serving the various groups of buyers.

---

[7] The discussion draws on "The Leverage of Lower Oil Prices: On World Economies, on OPEC Countries, on the Oil Industry," *Business Week,* March 22, 1982, pp. 66–73.
[8] Ibid., p. 69.
[9] Ibid., p. 69.

It is easy to find examples of price discrimination. Your college bookstore quite possibly sells books to faculty members at a discount, charging them a lower price than it charges students for the same books. Telephone companies charge higher monthly rates for business phones than for home phones. Electric companies frequently charge lower rates to businesses than to homeowners. Many drugstores offer senior citizen discounts on drug purchases. Movie theaters sometimes charge lower prices to children, senior citizens, and students. In all these cases the same product is sold to different groups for different prices.

Although there are many examples of price discrimination, products selling at the same price for all customers are far more common. Why does this difference in pricing techniques exist? There are three conditions that must be satisfied before price discrimination is to be expected.

First, the seller of the product must possess some degree of monopoly power. In the absence of monopoly power a seller is not able to charge some customers higher prices than others. If a drugstore charges women a higher price for toothpaste than it charges men, women would simply shop somewhere else. Under competitive conditions a single price tends to prevail regardless of whether some sellers wish to charge a higher price to some individuals or groups. To practice price discrimination, therefore, sellers must have some degree of monopoly power.

Second, the seller must be able to separate customers into two or more identifiable groups and prevent resale of the product among the groups. This condition is frequently violated and makes price discrimination a relatively rare occurrence. Suppose, for example, that General Motors tries to price-discriminate by selling automobiles to senior citizens at a 20 percent discount. How many automobiles would it sell at the higher, normal price? Very few, we would predict. Senior citizens would simply buy cars at a discount and then resell them at a higher price (but still below GM's normal price). A similar result would occur if people got their parents or grandparents to purchase cars for them. Resale of the product undermines the seller's ability to sell at the higher price.

If resale of the product is relatively easy, price discrimination can't be very effective. How, then, can resale be prevented? Sometimes the nature of the product itself prevents resale. Electricity provided to a local business can't be resold to a nearby homeowner. If you receive a medical checkup, there is no way you can transfer it to a friend. Children who attend movies can't reproduce the entertainment for their parents. In general, goods that are immediately consumed — a common characteristic of services — are not susceptible to resale. In contrast, manufactured items, like automobiles, appliances, and clothes, can be purchased by one person and later turned over to someone else. As a result, price discrimination is uncommon in the sale of manufactured goods.

These first two conditions are necessary to make price discrimination *possible;* a third condition is necessary to make it *profitable:* the price elasticity of demand must differ among the groups of buyers. As we will explain in more detail below, this condition makes it profitable for the seller to charge a higher price to the group with the more inelastic demand.

Price and Output Determination

Imagine a monopoly that is initially selling 1500 units of output at a single price of $10. Suppose it can separate the customers into two identifiable groups, group A and group B, and that resale of the product between the groups is not possible. Therefore, the monopolist may charge a different price to each group. However, if price discrimination is to be worth doing, the monopolist must be able to sell the 1500 units for a higher total revenue by charging each group a different price.

When the demand elasticities differ for the two groups, the monopolist can increase total revenue from selling a given quantity by charging different prices. Suppose that when both groups are charged the $10 price, the elasticity of demand for group A is 1.25 and for group B it is 5.0. Recall from Section 11.3 that the formula for marginal revenue is $MR = P[1 - (1/\eta)]$. A difference in elasticities means that the marginal revenue from selling in the two markets differs. For group A

$$MR_A = \$10[1 - (1/1.25)] = \$2.$$

For group B

$$MR_B = \$10[1 - (1/5)] = \$8.$$

This means that if one unit less is sold to group A, the monopolist loses $2 in total revenues, but if that unit is sold to group B, revenues from that group will rise by $8. Transferring a unit of output from group A to group B thus increases total revenues by $6. Reducing sales to group A raises the price to group A while group B's price falls as sales increase there. This policy means that the group with the more inelastic demand, group A, pays a higher price.

Figure 12–7 illustrates the way to divide 1500 units of output between the two groups to maximize total revenue. Group A's demand curve is to the left of the origin, and group B's is to the right. Initially, the monopolist is charging a flat $10.00 price, and at that price group A purchases 500 units and group B, 1000 units. Total revenue is $15,000. Because group A's demand curve is less elastic than group B's, however, marginal revenue is lower for group A, $2.00 compared with $8.00 per unit for group B. Shifting sales from the market where the marginal revenue is low to where it is higher increases total revenue. As long as marginal revenue is higher for group B, a further reallocation will continue to increase total revenue, so it should continue until the marginal revenues in the two markets are equal.

When the monopolist transfers 200 units from group A to group B, marginal revenue in both markets is equal at $7.50. The restriction of sales in market A, where demand is less elastic, raises price for this group

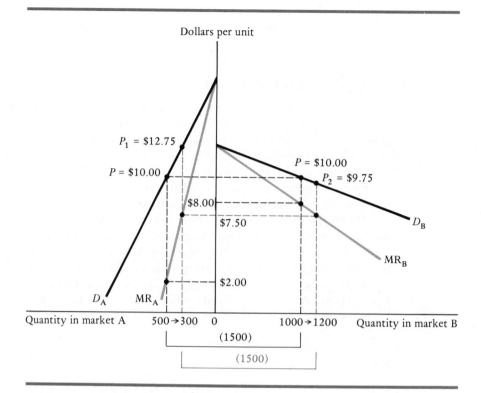

FIGURE 12-7

Gains from Price Discrimination

If demand elasticities differ and if the seller can separate markets, it pays the
seller to charge a higher price in the market with the less elastic demand. To
maximize revenues from the sale of 1500 units, the seller divides output between
the markets so that the marginal revenues are equal: 1200 units in market B and
300 units in market A. The seller charges a higher price in market A ($12.75)
than in market B ($9.75).

sharply, to $12.75. But the increase in sales in market B, where demand is
highly elastic, reduces price only slightly, to $9.75. The relative differences
in the price changes explain why total revenue increases. Price rises
sharply for the less elastic demand group but falls only slightly for the
highly elastic demand group. With sales allocated so that marginal revenue is equal, total revenue is now $15,525 [(300 × $12.75) + (1200 ×
$9.75)], up from the $15,000 in revenues the monopolist earned when both
groups were charged the same price.

When the monopolist can charge different prices to the two groups,
total revenue from the sale of any given quantity of output is highest when
the marginal revenues are equal. This result always means a higher price
for the group with the less elastic demand. Note, however, that the rule of
equating marginal revenues holds for *any* output, but it does not tell us

what level of output is most profitable. Should the monopolist produce more than 1500 units? The marginal revenue from an additional unit of output is now $7.50 whichever market it is sold in, so if marginal cost is less than $7.50, profits will be higher if output increases. When sales are divided between markets in this way, the decision on how much output to produce is made by comparing the common value of marginal revenue (since it is equal in both markets) with marginal cost.

Figure 12–8 shows how the monopolist determines the most profitable level of total output. As we just explained, the monopolist should compare the marginal cost to the common value of marginal revenue for the two separate markets. The common value of marginal revenue is derived by horizontally summing the separate marginal revenue curves, and the result is the darker curve ΣMR. This curve shows one value of marginal revenue (since it is the same in both separate markets) for each level of total output. The output level where MC equals ΣMR is consequently the most profitable output.

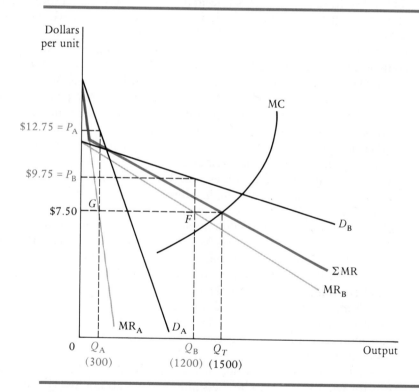

FIGURE 12–8

Price and Output Determination Under Price Discrimination

The most profitable output occurs where the sum of the separate MR curves, ΣMR, intersects MC at $0Q_T$. Thus, the monopolist sells $0Q_B$ in market B at P_B and $0Q_A$ in market A at P_A.

In the diagram the most profitable output is 1500 units where marginal cost is \$7.50 and equals the marginal revenue in both markets. To determine how this total output is divided between groups A and B, we identify the output at which marginal revenue is equal to \$7.50 in each market. To do so, we move horizontally to the left from the intersection of MC and ΣMR until we reach each group's separate marginal revenue curve. This occurs at points *F* and *G*, so sales to group A are 300 units and sales to group B are 1200 units. Price is higher for A than for B.

Evaluating Price Discrimination

Whether a monopolist who price-discriminates is in some sense worse than one who charges a uniform price is not clear. Compared to a single price monopoly, price discrimination benefits one group of consumers — those with the more elastic demand who are charged a lower price — and harms the other group. Frequently, those who benefit have lower incomes than those harmed since in some markets low-income persons are more sensitive to price (have higher demand elasticities), so perhaps this outcome is favorable. The monopoly also benefits from price discrimination with higher profits (or else it wouldn't price-discriminate), and that outcome is generally regarded as undesirable. Matters become more complicated when we recognize that total output may be greater — that is, more efficient — under price discrimination than under single-price monopoly. For these reasons no blanket condemnation of price discrimination seems appropriate, and each case should be judged on its own merits.

The identities of the monopoly and the customers may also play a role in evaluating price discrimination, as a further example will suggest. Price discrimination is sometimes found in international markets when a firm charges a higher price in its domestic market than it charges in foreign markets. This procedure is sometimes called "dumping," and it occurs when the international demand for a product is more elastic than the demand in the domestic market. The difference in elasticities occurs because there is more competition in world markets. Japan has often been charged with dumping products in the United States by charging lower prices here than it charges in Japan. In this case of price discrimination United States consumers should applaud the practice since they are the ones who benefit. If we can get TVs, stereos, radios, steel, and cars from Japan more cheaply than we can produce them here, the average real income of Americans rises.

One final point about price discrimination should be made: different prices for what appears to be the same product do not always imply price discrimination. Different prices may reflect different costs. When supermarkets in the inner city charge higher prices for food than supermarkets in the suburbs charge (as we discussed in Section 9.8), the price differential may just reflect higher costs of providing retailing services in the inner city. In that case there is no price discrimination involved.

Let's analyze a more subtle example. Sometimes a product's price differs at different times of the day or year. Telephone companies charge lower rates at night than during the day. Hotels frequently charge more during the tourist season than at other times of the year. Movie theaters may charge a lower price for matinee showings than for evening showings. These differences are probably not examples of price discrimination but are instead the result of differences in the level of demand at different times. Demand for telephone calls is high during the day, and since the telephone company operates near capacity, its marginal cost is higher during the day. Late at night demand is much lower, capacity is not strained, and marginal cost is lower. Price differences that reflect cost differences are not price discrimination and can occur in competitive markets, as the hotel and movie theater examples suggest.

MONOPOLY AND EXHAUSTIBLE RESOURCES
12.7

In Section 10.7 we examined the way a competitive market would allocate a fixed quantity of an exhaustible resource like oil over time. In the absence of technological progress and new discoveries, the price of the resource would tend to rise gradually over time at a rate equal to the interest rate. What happens, however, if the entire amount of the exhaustible resource is controlled by a monopoly rather than by several independent enterprises? Since OPEC does, in fact, control a large part of known oil reserves, this question is of more than abstract interest, and the answer may tell us something about future oil prices and availability in the event that OPEC continues to be a successful cartel.

We can extend the analysis of Section 10.7 to include the effect of monopoly on exhaustible resource prices and use over time. The major difference here is that the monopolist makes decisions on the basis of marginal revenue rather than on the basis of price in each time period.

In Figure 12–9 the total amount of oil is $0Q_T$. The firm will divide sales between year 1 (the present) and year 2 (the future). Production costs are assumed to be negligible. Demand in year 1 is shown by the curve D_1, with consumption of oil in year 1 measured from left to right. We measure consumption in year 2 from right to left, and we assume that the demand curve in year 2, D_2, is perfectly elastic. The assumption of a perfectly elastic demand curve in year 2 is somewhat unrealistic, but it simplifies the diagram since the demand and marginal revenue curves coincide when the demand curve is horizontal.

Recall from Section 10.7 that under competitive conditions equilibrium occurs at the intersection of D_1 and $D_2/(1 + i)$, where $D_2/(1 + i)$ gives next year's price in terms of its value in year 1 by using the interest rate to discount the year 2 price; this intersection occurs at point A. Under competitive conditions $0Q_C$ units of oil are sold in year 1 at a price of $40, and $Q_T - Q_C$ units are sold in year 2 at a price of $48. Since the interest

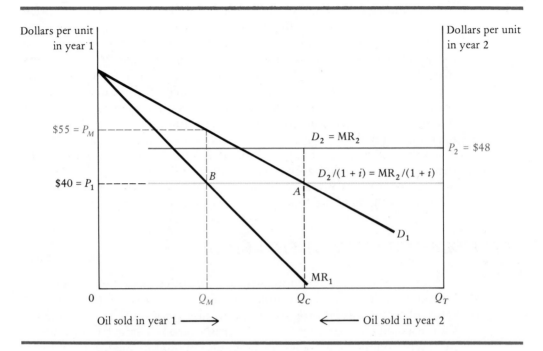

FIGURE 12-9

Monopoly and Exhaustible Resources

A monopoly supplying an exhaustible resource divides sales between periods so that MR$_1$ equals MR$_2$/(1 + i), at point B. In comparison with competitive conditions (point A), output is lower and price higher in year 1 under monopoly, but output is greater in year 2.

rate is 20 percent, price in year 2 is 20 percent greater than the price in year 1.

Under conditions of monopoly the contribution to the monopolist's revenues is the marginal revenue in each year. Each barrel of oil in year 1 adds an amount equal to MR$_1$ in revenues but involves giving up MR$_2$ in revenues in year 2. To maximize profits, the monopolist will divide sales between the two time periods so that marginal revenue in year 1 equals the present value of marginal revenue in year 2. This division of sales occurs where MR$_1$ intersects MR$_2$/(1 + i) [equal to D_2/(1 + i), since the demand curve is horizontal], at point *B*. The monopolist will sell 0Q_M in year 1 at a price of $55 and $Q_T - Q_M$ in year 2 at a price of $48.

Compared with competition, monopoly produces a lower output and a higher price in year 1 *but a higher output in year 2.* Price is the same in year 2 because of our assumption of a perfectly elastic demand curve. If we, more realistically, assume the demand curve to slope downward, the greater output of the monopolist in year 2 will be sold at a lower price than the price under competitive conditions. This peculiar result — lower future prices under monopoly than under competition — occurs because we are dealing with an exhaustible natural resource. When the monopolist sells less in year 1, there is necessarily more left to be sold in later years, and the greater quantity (compared with what would be available under competition) can only be sold at a lower price.

We may also view the monopoly outcome as a form of price discrimination. A fixed quantity of output must be allocated between the two "markets," present and future sales, and the goal is to achieve the highest total revenue possible. In contrast to the single-price (in present-value terms) competitive result, the monopolist should restrict sales in the market with the less elastic demand and increase sales in the market with the more elastic demand. If the monopolist perceives demand to be less elastic in the present, it reduces current sales and raises the present price. Future sales will be higher and price lower. And it is safe to assume that the monopolist will view present demand as more inelastic. The immediate, or short-run, present demand is likely to be quite inelastic (as the OPEC case demonstrated). The demand elasticity in the future will probably be greater because of the possibilities of future discoveries of the natural resource, the development of substitute products, and the breakup of the monopoly position. All these factors would limit the monopolist's ability to influence price by changing output in the future.

How does this discussion relate to OPEC? If OPEC is behaving monopolistically in selling oil, our analysis suggests that while present oil prices are higher than they would be under competitive conditions, future prices will be lower. OPEC conserves more oil for the future than competitive markets would, so oil prices on average in the future must be lower. In one sense monopoly in the supply of an exhaustible resource like oil is preferable to other monopolies; although consumers pay more in the present, they or their descendants will pay lower prices later on.

How long will it be before oil prices are lower under OPEC than they would have been if competitive conditions had prevailed? The answer depends heavily on the amount of oil reserves in existence relative to the present and future demands for oil. One study has tried to compare prices over time when OPEC members behave monopolistically with prices when they operate competitively. Using a computer simulation model and making specific assumptions about reserves, demand elasticities, and the like, Robert Pindyck estimated that the crossover date will be the late 1990s.[10] In other words, monopoly pricing of oil leads to higher prices until the late 1990s, but thereafter prices will be lower than they would have been if oil had been priced competitively over the entire period. Needless to say, the accuracy of such long-term projections depends on the validity of the assumptions used in the calculations, but it will be interesting to watch future price trends.

[10] Robert S. Pindyck, "Gains to Producers from Cartelization of Exhaustible Resources," *Review of Economics and Statistics,* 60 (May 1978): 238–251.

Review Questions and Problems

1. Will an excise tax applied to a monopoly cause price to rise by more or less when the monopoly's marginal cost curve slopes upward rather than when it is (as in Figure 12–1) horizontal? Show the result in a diagram.

*2. Compare the effects of an excise subsidy when applied to a monopoly and to a competitive industry with the same cost and demand conditions. In which case will price fall more? In which case will output increase more?

3. "If a business sells a product that wears out in a month, you will have to buy twelve a year, and the business will make twelve times as much money as it would selling a product that lasts a year." Evaluate this statement. Why don't businesses sell products that wear out in a day? In an hour?

4. A crucial assumption in the light bulb example is that consumers recognize the higher-quality product when they see it and therefore will pay a higher price for it. Do you think this assumption is generally true? If not, could consumer ignorance delay the introduction of worthwhile products?

5. "Price ceilings cause shortages." Is this statement always true when the price ceiling applies to a monopoly? Is it ever true in the monopoly case?

*6. Use total revenue and total cost curves to show how a price ceiling can lead a monopoly to increase output. (Hint: Draw the total cost curve as a straight line through the origin for simplicity.)

*7. In Figure 12–3, if the government sets a maximum price at the level where the average cost curve intersects the demand curve, would the monopolist make zero economic profit?

8. Explain what natural monopoly is in the relationship between cost curves and the demand curve. If the market is left to itself, what price and output would result?

9. Use a diagram to illustrate the "hoped for" result of regulation of natural monopoly that attempts to fix a price equal to average cost. What are the difficulties in achieving this outcome? Is it possible that unregulated natural monopoly could be preferable to regulated natural monopoly?

10. "Since firms in any industry can always make greater profits by colluding and acting as a monopoly, there is an inevitable tendency for competitive industries to become monopolies (or cartels) over time." Is the first part of this statement correct? Is the second part? Explain.

11. What problems usually make cartels collapse? How has OPEC been able to avoid this fate (if it still has)?

12. Mergers are another way firms may attempt to monopolize a market. Explain why the same factors that contribute to cartel instability will operate to frustrate the attempt to monopolize a market through mergers.

13. "It never pays a monopolist to sell at a low price in one market when he can get a higher price in another market." Evaluate this statement.

*14. Apply the theory of price discrimination to a monopoly that faces a downward-sloping demand curve for its domestic (home country) sales but a horizontal demand curve for sales in international markets. (Do you see how tariffs and trade restrictions could produce this situation?)

15. "People who believe that competitive markets can't be trusted to conserve enough of an exhaustible resource for future generations should be grateful to OPEC." Evaluate this statement.

16. Use Figure 12–9 to explain why the discovery of new oil fields in, say, Mexico would be expected to affect OPEC's current oil prices even though Mexico won't actually be producing oil for several years. (Hint: How will the discovery affect the future demand curve confronting OPEC?)

Supplementary Readings

Bork, Robert. *The Antitrust Paradox.* New York: Basic Books, 1978.

Demsetz, Harold. "Why Regulate Utilities?" *Journal of Law and Economics,* 11 (April 1968): 55–66.

Goodman, John, and Dolan, Edwin. *Economics of Public Policy: The Micro View.* St. Paul: West, 1979.

Griffin, James, and Steele, Henry. *Energy Economics and Policy.* New York: Academic Press, 1980.

Hirshleifer, Jack. "Suppression of Inventions." *Journal of Political Economy,* 79 (March/April 1971): 382–383.

Kahn, Alfred. *The Economics of Regulation: Principles and Institutions.* New York: Wiley, 1970.

Stigler, George. "The Theory of Economic Regulation." *Bell Journal of Economics and Management Science,* 1 (1) (Spring 1971): 3–21.

Monopolistic Competition and Oligopoly

13

Competition and monopoly lie at opposite ends of the market spectrum. Competition is characterized by many firms, unrestricted entry, and a homogeneous product while a monopoly is the sole producer of a product with no close substitutes. Yet many real world market structures seem to be incompatible with either the competitive or the monopoly model. How do we analyze a situation, for example, if a dozen similar, but slightly different, brands of aspirin are on the market, or if only three automobile companies supply most of the domestically produced cars?

Between competition and monopoly are two other types of market structures, monopolistic competition and oligopoly, which describe the major remaining market forms. In substance, monopolistic competition is closer to competition; it has many firms and unrestricted entry, like the competitive model, but its product is differentiated. Fast-food chains, for example, may be viewed as monopolistic competitors. They supply the same general product, fast food, but many people would say that a Big Mac is "different" from a Burger King Whopper. Oligopoly, on the other hand, is more like monopoly; it is characterized by a small number of large firms producing either a homogeneous product like steel or a differentiated product like automobiles. Because these market structures differ in some ways from competition and monopoly, economists have developed specific models to analyze them, models that take these differences into account. Unfortunately, economists have had less success developing and refining models to deal with these market structures than they have had with the competitive and monopoly models. In this chapter we will examine the state of the art, noting the similarities as well as the differences between monopolistic competition and oligopoly and the competitive and monopoly models. In addition, we will evaluate the importance of these models as descriptive and predictive modes of analysis.

PRICE AND OUTPUT DETERMINATION UNDER MONOPOLISTIC COMPETITION

13.1

For many years economists believed that either the competitive or the monopoly model could be used to analyze most markets. In 1933, Edward Chamberlin challenged this belief when he published *The Theory of Mo-*

nopolistic Competition.[1] Because his model of monopolistic competition seemed to describe many real world markets better than the competitive model did, it was enthusiastically received by some economists. Chamberlin's work was also widely criticized, and in recent years economists seem to be losing interest in monopolistic competition and returning to their earlier reliance on the competitive and monopoly models. In this section we will look more closely at Chamberlin's model, and in the next section we will review some of the criticisms of his work.

The Nature of Monopolistic Competition

As the term suggests, *monopolistic competition* contains elements of both competition and monopoly. Like the competitive model, it includes a large number of independent sellers, and entry into and exit from the industry is unrestricted. However, the firms produce differentiated products, meaning that consumers do not view the product of one firm as identical to the product of another firm. When firms make a product that is different from, but still similar to, that of other firms, they will have a small degree of monopoly power. For example, only McDonald's can sell a Big Mac. Unlike a monopoly product, however, a Big Mac has fairly close substitutes, which limits McDonald's' control over price. Customers may have a yen for a Big Mac when the price of a Big Mac and a Whopper are about the same, but what would happen if McDonald's tripled the price of its big burger?

Product differentiation may be real or it may be based on perceived differences by consumers. For instance, aspirin is aspirin, but many customers pay a premium for brand names such as Bayer or Anacin although government regulations require that each tablet contain the same basic mix of ingredients. Products may be differentiated on the basis of physical features such as function, design, or quality; or on the basis of advertising, brand names, logos (a smiling alligator), or packaging (L'eggs panty hose encased in a plastic egg or Flintstones vitamins shaped like Fred and the gang); or on the basis of conditions related to the sale, such as credit terms, availability or congeniality of sales help, convenience (a nearby 7–11), servicing, and so on. Clothing, drug, and liquor stores are examples of markets that are typically categorized as monopolistically competitive.

Despite some degree of product differentiation in these industries, Chamberlin reasoned that if each firm faced competition from close substitutes, all these similar products could be aggregated into "product groups" and examined. To analyze monopolistically competitive industries, Chamberlin assumed the following: (1) a large number of firms produce the product (which is differentiated); (2) the product has close substitutes; (3) the number of firms in the product group is sufficiently large so that each firm expects its actions to be ignored by its rivals; (4) the

---

[1] Edward H. Chamberlin, *The Theory of Monopolistic Competition* (Cambridge, Mass.: Harvard University Press, 1933).

cost and demand conditions are the same for all firms in the product group. The first step in analyzing monopolistic competition is to think about what these assumptions imply about the demand curve facing the individual firm.

Demand Curves under Monopolistic Competition

Because the monopolistic competitor produces a differentiated product, its demand curve slopes downward. Since it is the sole producer of that product, to sell more, it must lower price. In contrast, a competitive firm's demand curve is horizontal; consumers perceive no differences among the products sold by the various producers and are indifferent to which firm they buy from. The competitive firm has no control over price; if, for example, it tried to charge a higher price, consumers would buy elsewhere. A monopolistic competitor has some control over price, but it is limited by the availability of fairly close substitutes, which implies a high elasticity of demand.

Because a monopolistic competitor produces a product that may be unique but also has close substitutes, Chamberlin asserted that, in fact, two demand curves are relevant for the analysis. Figure 13–1 shows both demand curves. We have drawn the demand curves for one of the firms in

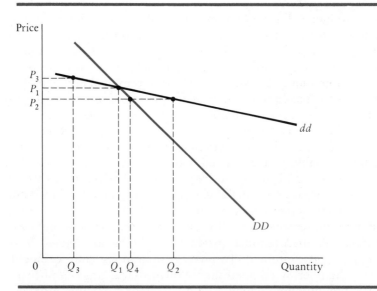

FIGURE 13–1

The Demand Curves Facing a Monopolistically Competitive Firm

The firm's demand curve when it changes its price but other firms do not is *dd*. When all firms charge the same price, the firm's sales are indicated by *DD*.

the industry, the "representative firm," but we assume that all the firms in the industry have identical demand curves. One demand curve, *dd*, shows the relevant price and output combinations if the representative firm changes price and output and its rivals ignore the changes. The second demand curve, *DD*, shows the outcomes if rival firms match any price increases or decreases.

Initially we assume that the representative firm is in equilibrium at P_1 and Q_1. The demand curve *dd* reflects the assumption that the price set by the representative firm will be ignored by its rivals. If, for example, the firm reduces its price to P_2, and other firms maintain their prices, the representative firm will be able to expand its sales noticeably to $0Q_2$ by drawing customers from rival firms. On the other hand, if the firm raises its price to P_3, sales will decrease appreciably to $0Q_3$ since customers will patronize its lower-priced rivals. Note that *dd* is quite elastic because there are close substitutes.

The second demand curve, *DD* in Figure 13–1, indicates how much the firm can sell at various prices when all firms in the industry charge the same price. For example, if all firms reduce the price from P_1 to P_2, the representative firm will sell $0Q_4$. Sales will increase by less when all firms reduce the price (as shown by *DD*) than when just one firm does it (as shown by *dd*). Curve *DD* is relevant for industrywide price changes, while curve *dd* shows the effects of price changes by one firm acting alone.

Once we understand the demand curves facing the monopolistic competitor, we can proceed to examine how the equilibrium price and output are determined. There are two equilibrium positions to consider with monopolistic competition, the short run and the long run. In the short run the equilibrium can be much like the monopoly equilibrium, with firms earning economic profit. In the long run, though, economic profit attracts entry, and profits fall until the firms just earn a normal rate of return.

Short-run Equilibrium

To determine the equilibrium price and output in the short run, look at Figure 13–2. Initially, we assume that the market price charged by all firms is P_1, and the representative firm is selling Q_1. Since the firm must take the price of the other firms as beyond its control, the relevant demand curve is *dd*, with its associated marginal revenue curve mr. At output $0Q_1$, the firm is not maximizing profits since marginal revenue is greater than marginal cost (MC), indicating that profits would be greater at a higher output. Consequently, the firm will equate marginal cost and marginal revenue by increasing production to $0Q_2$ and charging a price of P_2.

Recall, however, that all firms in the industry face identical cost and demand conditions. All will be in the same situation; all will react in the same way by expanding production; and all will charge a price of P_2. As a

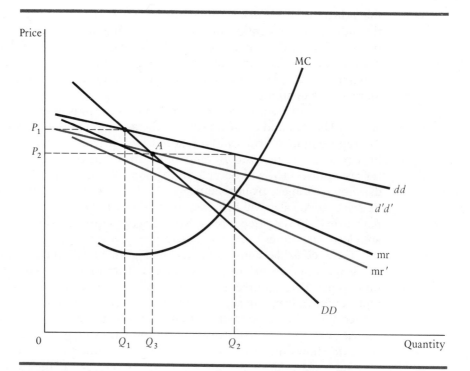

FIGURE 13-2

Short-run Adjustments for a Monopolistically Competitive Firm

With P_1 and Q_1 initially, the firm has incentive to expand output to Q_2, where MC = mr, and charge P_2. All firms, however, have this incentive to lower price. When all firms charge P_2, the firm can sell only Q_3 at point A on DD. As a result of other firms' lowering price to P_2, this firm's demand curve shifts downward to $d'd'$, passing through point A on DD.

result, when the price is P_2, the representative firm will only sell $0Q_3$ instead of $0Q_2$, as shown by the DD demand curve. What happens is that as all firms expand output and lower price, the individual firm's demand curve dd shifts downward to $d'd'$, where it intersects DD at A. The $d'd'$ curve shows how much the representative firm can sell at various prices when rival firms are selling at a price of P_2. Now P_2, not P_1, is the industry (group) price. A new marginal revenue curve mr' will be associated with $d'd'$, and given these relationships, the firm has still not achieved a profit-maximizing output. Output and price will change further.

This process of adjustment continues until price and output reach the point where the DD and dd curves' intersection coincides with the profit-maximizing position for the representative firm. This outcome occur at P^* and Q^* in Figure 13-3. With the demand curve d^*d^* the firm is maximizing profits at Q^* and P^*. In addition, since the P^* and Q^* combination

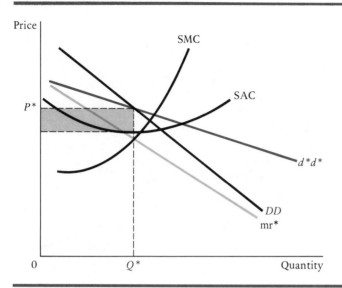

FIGURE 13-3

Short-run Equilibrium for a Monopolistically Competitive Firm

In the short run a monopolistically competitive firm may temporarily make profits, as shown by the shaded area. However, the existence of profits will induce new firms to enter the market until profits are eliminated.

lies on *DD*, this outcome is consistent with other firms' charging the same price. There is no further incentive for this firm, or any other firm, to change its price or output so this point represents a short-run equilibrium. In Figure 13–3 the average cost curve has been drawn in, and the firm is making economic profits, as indicated by the shaded area.

Long-run Equilibrium

As long as firms are earning economic profits, further adjustments will occur in the long run that will tend to eliminate those profits. Since entry is unrestricted, firms seeking higher-than-normal returns will enter — a situation just like that in the competitive industry. As entry occurs, each firm will be able to sell less at each price than it could before, and both the *DD* and *dd* curves will shift inward toward the origin, reflecting the fact that more firms are now sharing the existing market. As this occurs, profits will fall until, in long-run equilibrium, the firms all earn a normal return (zero economic profit).

Figure 13–4 illustrates the adjustment process. In the short run the demand curves are dd_{SR} and DD_{SR}, and equilibrium occurs at P_{SR} and Q_{SR} (which correspond to P^* and Q^* in Figure 13–3), with the firm earning

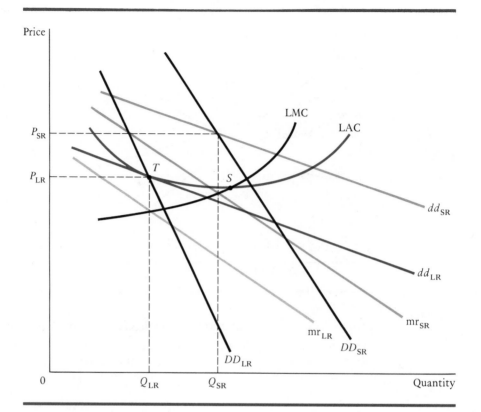

FIGURE 13–4
Long-run Equilibrium for a Monopolistically Competitive Firm

A long-run equilibrium in a monopolistically competitive market implies zero profit, as illustrated by the tangency between dd_{LR} and LAC at point T. If short-run profits initially exist, as they do when dd_{SR} confronts the firm, new firms entering the market cause dd_{SR} to shift downward until firms can just cover their average costs.

economic profits. In the long run, entry occurs, which gradually shifts the demand curves inward as market shares fall. Eventually, the demand curves shift to DD_{LR} and dd_{LR}, with a long-run equilibrium at P_{LR} and Q_{LR}. At this price and output the representative firm is earning a normal return. Demand curve dd_{LR} is tangent to the firm's long-run average cost curve LAC, indicating that average cost and average revenue are equal. Note that this equilibrium has similarities to the equilibrium in both competition and monopoly. As is true in the competitive case, each firm's demand curve is tangent to its LAC curve, and zero economic profit results. As is true in the monopoly case, the demand curve slopes downward, so price is greater than marginal cost at the equilibrium.

MONOPOLISTIC COMPETITION: AN EVALUATION
13.2

In long-run equilibrium monopolistic competition differs in three respects from the competitive long-run equilibrium: the industry is characterized by excess capacity, the industry produces an inefficient level of output, and the industry engages in nonprice competition (advertising, packaging, and other types of product differentiation).

Excess Capacity

The industry has excess capacity because each firm is not producing at the minimum point on its LAC curve. Look at Figure 13–4 again. Notice that in long-run equilibrium the firm operates to the left of the minimum point, S, on its long-run average cost curve, and this outcome will be true as long as the firm's *dd* curve has a downward slope. This means that the firm's per-unit production costs are higher than the minimum cost possible. Thus, in a monopolistically competitive industry there are many firms, each with excess capacity.

Is excess capacity bad? Some economists believe it is, pointing out that it would be possible to have the same total output with fewer firms, each producing a larger output. This would lower the unit cost of production since each firm would produce at point S (in Figure 13–4) rather than point T. Although the same total output at a lower cost sounds attractive, this argument is not conclusive. Other economists respond that this outcome can only be achieved by reducing the number of firms and thereby reducing the variety of products available to consumers. If product variety is itself valuable, then we must weigh reduced variety against lower unit production costs. For this reason it is not clear that the excess capacity related to monopolistic competition is really a defect — it may be the necessary cost associated with achieving a desirable degree of product variety.

We also note that the degree of excess capacity depends on how elastic the firms' *dd* curves are. With highly elastic demand curves (to be expected when there are many close substitutes), the difference in per-unit production costs between S and T in Figure 13–4 will be small, and the outcome seems quite close to the competitive result.

Efficiency

In long-run equilibrium the monopolistic competitor produces at the point where long-run marginal cost equals marginal revenue. Note, however, that price and marginal cost are not equal. Price is greater than marginal cost, indicating that additional units of output are worth more to consumers than it costs firms to produce them. In contrast, the competitive firm in long-run equilibrium produces the efficient output where price equals long-run marginal cost. The level of output produced by the monopolistic competitor may not differ a great deal from the efficient output, however. The more elastic *dd*, the closer price will be to marginal cost and the smaller the restriction in output will be.

Nonprice Competition

Up to now we have emphasized competition on the basis of price, implicitly assuming that nonprice characteristics of products were constant. But firms can attempt to attract customers by varying the quality of the product, the location at which it is sold, servicing, packaging, and so on. Competition of this sort is referred to as nonprice competition. It occurs in both competitive and imperfectly competitive markets but is likely to be more common in the latter.

We can analyze nonprice competition in much the same way we analyzed competition on the basis of price. Firms are still conceived to be profit maximizers, but now we consider how changes in the characteristics of the product will affect profits. For example, if the additional amount consumers will pay for a higher-quality product is greater than the additional cost of producing it, firms have incentive to produce the higher-quality product. Once again, thinking of marginal revenue and marginal cost is the method of analysis.

Economists tend to look favorably on nonprice competition, at least as long as it occurs in the context of fairly competitive markets. When competitive firms offer different qualities of products or servicing arrangements, it is reasonable to suppose that they are catering to the variety of consumer preferences that exists. It is much less clear that nonprice competition among monopolistically competitive firms — or, to an even greater degree, oligopolistic firms — works so well.

Advertising is an important form of nonprice competition. Firms incur advertising costs because they believe that by using advertising, revenues will increase more than costs, so profits will be higher. Advertising is supposed to increase revenues by shifting the demand curve facing the firm outward, so consumers will buy more at each price than before.

For economists, the basic issue in evaluating advertising is not whether it increases or decreases a firm's profit but whether it makes markets work more or less efficiently. That is, can advertising induce consumers to purchase products they don't really want or need — or does advertising actually help people become better-informed consumers?

That controversial issue will not be resolved here, but it is helpful to distinguish between two types of advertising: informative advertising and persuasive advertising. Informative advertising contains information about new products, prices, qualities, location, availability, and so on that helps consumers make better-informed choices. Persuasive advertising, on the other hand, contains little objective information; rather it attempts to convince consumers of the desirability of products by using all the subtle methods at Madison Avenue's disposal.

Economists believe that informative advertising makes markets function more effectively since it seems to be a low-cost method of providing information that consumers require to make buying choices that serve their preferences. The benefits of persuasive advertising are more dubious. Do consumers receive helpful information when they hear "Be a Pepper," "Ring around the collar," or "Oh, what a feeling . . . Toyota!"? Undoubtedly, some advertisers believe that repetitive, and even irritating and offensive, advertising helps to sell products! In a recent survey respondents cited the following commercials as offensive: Calvin Klein and Jordache jeans, Underalls panty hose, Playtex bras and girdles, and Pepto-Bismol and Rolaids antacids. Despite the negative reaction, the products sell well.[2] Do irritating ads help sell these products, as some marketing experts believe, by implanting "name recognition" in the consumer's mind, or would the products sell well anyway, despite, for example, the obnoxious Mr. Whipple's warning shoppers not to squeeze the Charmin?

A basic difficulty in evaluating advertising is that most advertising includes both informative and persuasive elements. Television is, to many people, the major source of the most mindless, tasteless, and irritating types of persuasive advertising. It is well to remember, however, that television advertising only accounts for a fifth of total advertising expenditures in the United States. In fact, total advertising outlays of all types are only about 2 percent of gross national product.[3] Other forms of advertising, such as those found in newspapers, the yellow pages, trade journals and magazines, and mail-order advertising, are more likely to be informative advertising.

Does advertising lead to higher consumer prices? Even if it did, that would not make it undesirable if the information conveyed to consumers were worth the increments in prices. Surprisingly, it is possible for advertising to lead to lower prices. This situation can occur when advertising helps consumers locate low-priced sellers and allows the sellers to move down their average cost curves and increase sales volume. Several studies have provided evidence on this point. One study compared the prices of eyeglasses in states that restricted advertising with prices in states without advertising prohibitions. On average, the prices of eyeglasses were about 25 percent higher in states that prohibited advertising.[4] Another study found that retail prescription drug prices were lower in states that did not restrict drug advertising.[5]

---

[2] Bill Abrams, "Polls Suggest TV Advertisers Can't Ignore Matters of Taste," *Wall Street Journal*, July 23, 1981, p. 25.

[3] "Estimated Annual U.S. Ad Expenditures: 1959–1977," *Advertising Age*, September 4, 1978, p. 33.

[4] Lee Benham, "The Effect of Advertising on the Price of Eyeglasses," *Journal of Law and Economics*, 15 (2) (October 1972): 337–352.

[5] John F. Cady, "An Estimate of the Price Effects of Restrictions on Drug Price Advertising," *Economic Inquiry*, 14 (4) (December 1976): 493–510.

There is no question that advertising also frequently leads to higher prices. For instance, in the case of "defensive advertising" firms may advertise only because their rivals are also advertising, and the result can be higher costs for all firms but no overall expansion in sales: each firm just holds onto its market share. Such advertising is clearly wasteful.

As these remarks suggest, advertising has both good and bad aspects, which makes an overall appraisal difficult. No doubt advertising will remain a controversial issue.

CRITICISMS OF THE THEORY
OF MONOPOLISTIC COMPETITION
13.3

For a number of years after its introduction, economists enthusiastically received the theory of monopolistic competition as an important attempt to analyze the "gray" areas between the extremes of competition and monopoly. In recent years, the theory has received less and less attention, and many economists have concluded that it does not further our understanding of economic phenomena to any significant degree. In part, this view reflects the surge in empirical research by economists over the last two decades, which has lent substantial support to the simpler competitive model. In addition, some economists have criticized the theory of monopolistic competition on other counts.

One of its most prominent critics is George Stigler. Among other things, Stigler emphasizes, as we did in Chapter 1, that the test of a theory is not whether it is descriptively accurate but whether it accurately predicts the effects of changes in the economic environment. Stigler believes that economists initially accepted the theory of monopolistic competition because it seemed more realistic: "A good deal of support for this theory stems from the mistaken demand for a correspondence between 'reality' and premises. The theory is further supported by the erroneous view ... that if the premises of competitive theory depart (in a descriptive sense) from the facts, the implications must be wrong."[6] In Stigler's view the implications of the Chamberlin model are not significantly different from those of the competitive model, and he leaves it to empirical research to resolve the issue of which is the better predictor. As noted above, many economists now believe that the evidence favors the conclusion that the competitive model predicts more accurately.

To expand somewhat on Stigler's criticism, we will turn to the analysis of some simple policies like excise taxes or subsidies, price ceilings or supports. We have seen how the competitive and monopoly models can be used to analyze these policies. Using the framework of monopolistic competition, can we predict what the effects of an excise tax will be, for

---

[6] George Stigler, "Monopolistic Competition in Retrospect," *Five Lectures on Economic Problems* (New York: Macmillan, 1950), pp. 12–24.

example, and do these effects differ from those implied by the competitive model? Actually, it is extremely difficult to use monopolistic competition theory to analyze an excise tax or any of the other policies mentioned. Our intuition suggests that a higher price will result, but we are unaware of any economist who has been able to demonstrate this result by using the theory of monopolistic competition. With an excise tax, for example, we know some firms will incur losses and leave the industry, causing both demand curves to shift. Unfortunately, we can't determine exactly how they will shift, and without knowing that, we are unable to determine the aftertax equilibrium. In addition to the difficulty of applying the theory to analyze even simple economic phenomena, we must also ask whether the theory of monopolistic competition would imply consequences that differ from those of the competitive model. If we get basically the same predictions as the competitive model, what are the advantages of using a more complicated model?

The theory of monopolistic competition is a good example of the difficulties encountered when we try to make our theories more "realistic." There is little doubt that in the real world many products are differentiated and firms face less than perfectly elastic demand curves. However, adding these features to the competitive model — which is what the monopolistic competition model essentially does — produces a very unwieldy theory, and, moreover, one whose predictions in many cases do not appear very different from those of the competitive model.

OLIGOPOLY
13.4

Oligopoly is an industry structure characterized by a few large firms producing most, or all, of the output of some product. In the United States some important industries fit this description, such as the automobile, steel, breakfast cereal, and electrical equipment industries. Unfortunately, there is no one widely accepted theory of oligopoly that can be used to analyze these markets. Economists have developed several different theories of oligopoly, but none seems to be universally applicable. The difficulty in developing a theory of oligopoly lies in the relationships among the firms in the industry.

The Nature of Oligopoly

The characteristic of oligopoly that distinguishes it from other forms of market structures, and makes it so difficult to analyze, is the *mutual interdependence* of firms in the industry. Because there are only a few firms, each realizes its actions will affect its rivals, and vice versa. If, for example, General Motors decided to cut the prices on all its new cars by 50 percent, its decision would clearly influence the sales of Chrysler and Ford products — and how Chrysler and Ford respond (matching GM's price cut or ignoring it) would in turn affect GM's sales. Therefore, any price or output decision a firm makes must be made with the thought of its rivals in mind and with some sort of guess about how rivals will respond. Since firms can never be sure how rivals will react, they will make decisions in the presence of uncertainty.

Economists have developed several theories of oligopoly, each with different behavioral assumptions about how an oligopolist believes its rivals will react and how they actually do react. The implications of these models vary since the outcome depends crucially on the assumptions made, and when the assumptions are varied, many solutions become possible. Some of the models have seemed to describe the behavior of firms in specific industries over particular periods of time, but none appears to have widespread applicability.

Oligopolistic industries usually exhibit economies of scale — which may explain the relatively small number of firms in the industry (see Section 7.6). Prices in oligopolistic industries sometimes tend to be fairly stable, and if competition occurs, it frequently takes the form of nonprice competition. Price wars seldom break out, but if they do, they tend to be fairly short-lived. To deal with the problem of mutual interdependence, firms in oligopolistic industries often attempt to coordinate their pricing and output decisions. Sometimes this coordination, or collusion, is highly organized in the form of a cartel, and sometimes it takes the less structured form of price leadership. In the next two sections we will examine both types of market coordination.

FORMALIZED MARKET COORDINATION: CARTELS
13.5

We discussed cartels in some detail in Section 12.5. We saw that if a group of firms can agree to form a cartel and coordinate their pricing and output decisions, they will earn monopoly profits. Because firms agree to restrict output to attain a higher price, industry (and individual) profits are greater than they would be if firms actively competed against each other. By its nature, an oligopolistic industry is conducive to cartel formation. If each firm in the industry belongs to the cartel, there is no uncertainty about how rival firms will react to price changes. Cartel pricing and output agreements are one way of resolving the problems inherent in mutual interdependence. In addition, because the industry contains relatively few firms, it may be easier to organize a cartel and to monitor cartel members to ensure they abide by the agreement.

In the United States cartels are viewed as a "conspiracy in restraint of trade" and are expressly forbidden by law. Nevertheless, some firms do collude and agree to fix prices and restrict output, but as noted in Section 12.5, cartels are usually short-lived. Cartels fail because each cartel member can earn higher profits if it cheats on the cartel arrangement by lowering its price while the remaining cartel members charge the cartel price;

because cartel members will disagree over pricing, output, market-sharing and profit-sharing decisions; and because profits of the cartel will attract new firms to the industry.

INFORMAL MARKET COORDINATION
13.6

Now we will examine several types of informal market collusion. As we discuss the models, keep in mind the importance of the assumptions made to the actual outcomes. In some cases we are dealing with just one firm's expectations about rival firms' reaction patterns, and in others with the interaction of reaction patterns for all the firms in the industry.

The Kinked Demand Curve Model

In the 1930s Paul Sweezy developed the kinked demand curve model in an attempt to explain why prices in oligopolistic industries apparently remained rigid despite moderate changes in cost and demand conditions.[7] The setting is a mature oligopolistic industry where price has already been determined, either by independent action or by collusion. We begin by considering one firm's expectations about the way its rivals will react to a price change it initiates. The firm's rivals have two options: they can match the price change or ignore it. In effect, the oligopolist faces the two demand curves shown in Figure 13–5. One curve, Jd_M, reflects the price and output combinations if rivals *match* the price changes; the second curve, Ad_I, shows the relevant combination if rivals *ignore* the price changes. Initially, we assume that price is at P_1 and output at $0Q_1$. If the oligopolist were to lower price below P_1, and none of its rivals matched the price cut, the firm would greatly expand its share of the market (along Ad_I), partly at its rivals' expense. If the firm increased price above P_1, and none of its rivals followed, the firm would lose a large share of the market. On the other hand, if the oligopolist increases or decreases price, and its rivals match those changes, the changes in sales will be much smaller (along Jd_M) since all firms in the industry would share any decrease or increase in sales.

Our oligopolist, it turns out, is pessimistic about the way it expects rivals to behave. No matter what decision the firm makes, it expects its rivals to react in the least favorable way. If the firm lowers its price below P_1, the firm believes its rivals will all match the price cut (so its sales would only increase slightly along Jd_M). If the firm increases its price, it believes rivals will ignore the price increase (so the firm would lose a large share of the market along Ad_I). Given these specific assumptions about the reaction patterns of its rivals, the firm will face a kinked demand curve for its

---

[7] Paul Sweezy, "Demand Under Conditions of Oligopoly," *Journal of Political Economy,* 47 (August 1939): 568–573.

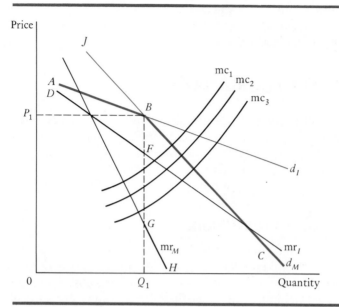

FIGURE 13-5
The Kinked Demand Curve

If the oligopolist expects other firms to match its price reductions but not its price increases, it will perceive a kinked demand curve like *ABC* with a corresponding marginal revenue curve *DFGH*. In this situation moderate changes in costs (mc_1, mc_2, mc_3) would not cause the firm to change its price or output.

product, composed of the *AB* segment of Ad_I (if the firm increases price) and the *BC* segment of Jd_M (if the firm lowers price).

To determine the profit-maximizing price and output for the firm in this setting, we must first identify the relevant marginal revenue curve. Both demand curves, Ad_I and Jd_M, have their own marginal revenue curves, mr_I and mr_M. Since the kinked demand curve is composed of segments of two demand curves, so is its marginal revenue curve. Recall that at each level of output, marginal revenue lies directly below its price. Consequently, the *DF* segment of the marginal revenue curve mr_I is the marginal revenue curve associated with the *AB* segment of the kinked demand curve, and the *GH* segment of mr_M is the marginal revenue curve associated with the *BC* segment of the kinked demand curve. The marginal revenue curve is thus the discontinuous curve *DFGH*.

To maximize profits, the firm will operate at the point where marginal cost equals marginal revenue. Given marginal cost mc_1, the firm will operate at Q_1, charging price P_1. Note that if the marginal cost shifts upward (mc_2) or downward (mc_3) between *F* and *G*, the firm will not change its price or output. Hence, changing cost conditions in an oligopolistic industry of this type can occur without accompanying changes in price or output.

Initially, many economists regarded the kinked demand curve model as a general theory of oligopoly, but empirical evidence raised doubts. Stigler, for example, examined seven oligopolistic industries and found little evidence that rival firms were reluctant to match price increases of other firms.[8] Later empirical work lent further support to Stigler's findings.[9] Moreover, economists have criticized the model on more fundamental grounds: although the kinked demand curve model explains price rigidity when cost and demand conditions change, it does not explain how the original price is determined. One purpose of microeconomic theory is to explain how prices and outputs are determined, and since the kinked demand curve model does not do this, critics claim it is nothing more than an ex post rationalization of price rigidity. And, in fact, some evidence exists that prices are not really any more "rigid" in oligopolistic markets than they are in other markets.

Price Leadership

Price leadership is another way to resolve the uncertainty of rivals' reactions to price changes. If one firm in the industry initiates a price change, and the rest of the firms traditionally follow the leader, there is no uncertainty about rival behavior. In effect, price leadership eliminates any kink in the demand curve since all firms in the industry will match any price changes, either upward or downward. Price leadership has another advantage: since no formal cartellike agreement is necessary to fix prices, a conspiracy in violation of antitrust laws is difficult to prove.

One firm may traditionally act as a price leader, such as GM in the automobile industry, or the leader may change over time. Firms may informally agree to this arrangement, or there may be no collusion at all.

PRICE LEADERSHIP BY THE LOW-COST FIRM. In an industry where the costs of production differ among firms, the low-cost firm might determine prices. The market is divided up among the firms, with the low-cost firm setting the price that will maximize its profits and the rest of the firms charging the same price. Since their production costs are higher, rival firms are willing to go along with the arrangement, fearing that if active price competition developed, they would be more vulnerable than their lower-cost rival.

Figure 13–6 illustrates this arrangement. Assume just two firms are in the industry (a duopoly), firms A and B, producing a homogeneous product. The market demand curve for the product is D. The cost curves for the firms are MC_A, AC_A, MC_B, and AC_B. Note that firm A's production costs are significantly higher than firm B's. Further, assume that the firms agree to split the market in half, so the relevant demand curve for each

[8] George Stigler, "The Kinky Oligopoly Demand Curve and Rigid Prices," *Journal of Political Economy*, 55 (October 1947): 432–449.
[9] Julian Simon, "A Further Test of the Kinky Oligopoly Demand Curve," *American Economic Review*, 59 (December 1969): 971–975.

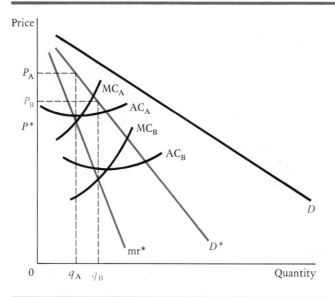

FIGURE 13-6
Price Leadership by the Low-cost Firm
If firms A and B agree to share the market equally, each firm will confront the demand curve D^*. Firm B, the low-cost firm, would then select price P_B. Firm A would be unable to charge the price it would prefer. P_A, so P_B becomes the industry price.

firm is D^*, which is equal to half the total market demand D. The marginal revenue curve associated with D^* is mr*.

If firm A had its preference, it would produce at the point where marginal cost and marginal revenue were equal and sell $0q_A$ units at a price of P_A. Note, however, that P_A is not consistent with the profit-maximizing price and output for firm B. With its lower production costs, firm B will produce $0q_B$ and charge P_B. If the two prices persisted, firm A would lose its customers to its lower-priced rival. Instead, according to the price leadership model, firm A will lower its price to P_B.

It is possible for the lower-cost firm to drive its rival out of business. If, for example, firm B set a price at P^*, firm A would shut down in the long run. Why the low-cost firm doesn't decide to eliminate its rival rather than agree to share the market equally is one puzzling aspect of this model. Perhaps the threat of antitrust action may constrain the firm's competitive urges.

PRICE LEADERSHIP BY THE DOMINANT FIRM. Another type of price leadership, also called umbrella pricing, occurs when the dominant firm in the industry sets a price that maximizes its profits and lets its smaller rivals sell as much as they want at the set price. Historically, there have allegedly been instances of price leadership by the dominant firm in industries such as virgin aluminum (Alcoa), tin cans (American Can and Continental Can), and cigarettes (American Tobacco and Reynolds).

The dominant firm price leadership model is developed in Figure 13–7. The industry demand curve is DD. Since the other smaller firms in the industry will follow any price change initiated by the dominant firm, they become price takers, just as competitive firms do, and they adjust output until price equals their marginal cost. It is possible, therefore, to derive an industry supply curve for these firms (excluding the dominant firm), as shown by S_O. The curve S_O reflects the output responses of the smaller firms in the industry to whatever prices are set by the dominant firm. Before we can determine what price will be set by the dominant firm, we must introduce a new concept, the residual demand curve. The *residual demand curve* indicates how much output the dominant firm can sell at various prices, taking into account the amounts the smaller firms

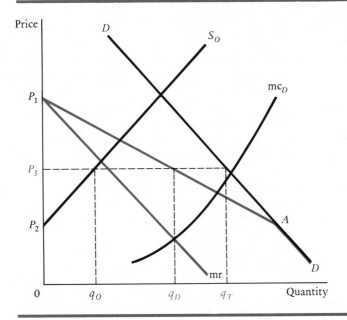

FIGURE 13–7
Price Leadership by the Dominant Firm

In an industry with one dominant firm and several smaller firms, the residual demand curve confronting the dominant firm is obtained by subtracting the quantity the other smaller firms will produce (shown by S_O) from market demand, yielding P_1AD. The dominant firm produces $0q_D$, where mc_D equals mr, and charges P_3. Smaller firms produce $0q_O$.

will produce at each price. Suppose, for example, that at a price of $10 the total quantity demanded is 20,000 units. If smaller firms supply 12,000 units when the price is $10, then 8,000 units are left for the dominant firm.

To obtain the residual demand curve, we have to subtract the amount supplied by the smaller firms from the market demand curve at each price. If, for instance, the price were set at P_1 where S_O intersects DD, smaller firms would supply the entire market, and the quantity demanded of products supplied by the dominant firm would be zero. If, instead, the price were set at P_2 or below, the dominant firm would supply the entire market since none of its smaller rivals would be willing to produce any output at a price of P_2 or lower. Intermediate points on the residual demand curve are obtained by subtracting S_O from DD, yielding P_1A as the residual demand curve. Below A, the dominant firm continues to supply the entire market, so the entire demand curve confronting the dominant firm is P_1AD.

With the dominant firm's residual demand curve and the marginal revenue curve mr associated with it, we can now find the equilibrium price and output for the dominant firm, the smaller firms, and the industry. The dominant firm will produce at a level where its marginal cost mc_D equals marginal revenue, at $0q_D$, and will charge P_3. Note that price is determined by the residual demand curve, not the market demand curve. Setting price at P_3 means that the dominant firm will supply $0q_D$ units of output and the smaller firms will supply q_Dq_T. The sum of $0q_D$ plus q_Dq_T equals the total quantity demanded at P_3. Another way to see this result is to note that at P_3 the smaller firms will supply $0q_O$ along S_O, and $0q_O + 0q_D$ also equals $0q_T$ ($0q_O$ equals q_Dq_T since both represent the amount supplied by the smaller firms when price is P_3).

Price leadership by the dominant firm need not imply active collusion among firms in the industry. Some economists suggest that smaller firms may have simply found a way to economize on information costs. By letting the "richer" dominant firm research the market to determine the profit-maximizing price and output, small firms are in effect free riding on the information generated by the dominant firm.

Entry-limit Pricing

Entry-limit pricing occurs when firms already in the industry agree to set prices high enough to earn economic profits but low enough to deter entry. Instead of maximizing short-run profits, the firms take a longer-run view. By discouraging entry, the firms may obtain higher profits over the long run. Entry-limit pricing is sometimes regarded as a variant of price leadership.

Three assumptions underlie this analysis: (1) existing firms and potential entrants to an industry want to maximize long-run profits; (2) existing firms think potential entrants expect them to maintain their present level of production so that when entry occurs, price will fall; and (3) existing firms are able to collude to set an entry-limiting price. In this setting we are considering the expectations of a potential entrant to an industry about the behavior of firms already established in the industry, and the expectations of existing firms about the potential newcomer's reactions. The potential entrant is trying to determine whether or not to enter the market, and the established firms are trying to determine what price to set to keep the newcomer out.

To begin the analysis, we need to see what the demand curve looks like for the potential entrant. In Figure 13–8 curve D represents the total market demand for the product. If firms already in the industry are producing Q_1, price will be P_1. The potential entrant does not expect to attract customers from existing firms but instead expects to add its output to the total industry output, so price will fall if it enters the market. Therefore, the new entrant perceives its potential demand curve to be the segment of the market demand curve below point A on D. By subtracting the amount sold by existing firms, $0Q_1$, from the market demand curve for each price below P_1 (corresponding to point A), we obtain d_1, the demand curve for

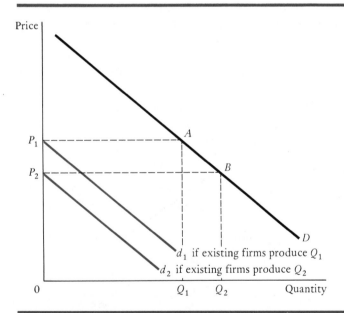

FIGURE 13–8

Entry-limit Pricing: The Demand Curve Facing the Potential Entrant

The demand curve perceived by the potential entrant is obtained by subtracting the output of existing firms from the market demand. If existing firms are producing Q_1, the potential entrant's demand curve would be d_1, which is really the AD portion of the market demand curve displaced leftward until it touches the vertical axis at P_1.

the potential entrant when existing firms produce $0Q_1$. If instead, existing firms produce $0Q_2$ at a price of P_2, we can use the same technique to obtain d_2.

To simplify the analysis, let's assume that the costs of production are constant over the range of output being discussed for both the potential entrant and the existing firms. Let's suppose, though, that the newcomer's costs are higher. With these assumptions the long-run average cost curves of the potential entrant and the existing firms are LAC_{PE} and LAC_{EF}, respectively, in Figure 13–9. If average costs are constant, then marginal costs will coincide with average costs.

Under the cost and demand conditions we have assumed, if existing firms attempt to maximize short-run profits, they will produce $0Q_{SR}$ and charge P_{SR}. At that price and output the demand curve facing the potential entrant is d_1. Price exceeds average cost over a significant level of output, so the firm would find it profitable to enter the industry. As entry occurs, price falls, cutting into the profits of already established firms. To prevent this from happening, existing firms may try to block the newcomer's entry. If they lower their price to P_D, they can deter entry. Price P_D

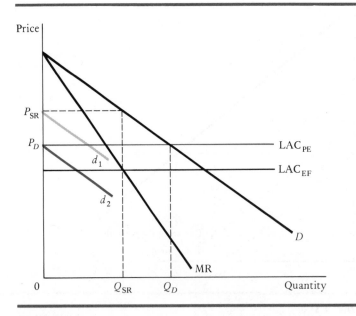

FIGURE 13–9

Entry-limit Pricing: Setting an Entry-deterring Price

If existing firms have the costs shown, and they set a price low enough so that potential entrants could not make a profit at that price, they will set the price P_D. The threat of entry can lead existing firms to charge lower prices than they would if entry could not occur.

corresponds to an output level of $0Q_D$. If existing firms produce $0Q_D$, the potential entrant's demand curve is d_2. Note that d_2 lies below the potential entrant's average cost curve, meaning that if the firm entered, it would incur losses. P_D therefore is the entry-limiting price. At a higher price, entry will occur.

The entry-limit pricing model predicts that existing firms will set a long-run price just low enough to deter entry. Does this predicted outcome describe the behavior of firms in oligopolistic industries? Not always. Instead of setting an entry-limiting price and maintaining it indefinitely, firms are often observed lowering their prices when entry appears imminent and raising them again when the threat subsides. Take, for example, Shop-Rite's attempted entry into the retail grocery market in Washington, D.C., in 1967. Prior to Shop-Rite's entry, two leading Washington chains (Safeway and Giant) built stores near Shop-Rite's new locations and cut their prices substantially below those charged in the rest of the metropolitan area. In doing so, the stores operated with abnormally low margins and sustained losses, but in the end Shop-Rite withdrew from the market.[10]

Alternatively, other evidence indicates that existing firms may actually cut back output and give up part of their market share to accommodate a newcomer rather than have the new entrant's added output depress price. In general, evidence suggests that the reactions of existing firms to the threat of entry are varied.

It is also worth stating that there is no difference between the entry-limiting price set by the existing firms and the price that would be established in the long run if the firms did nothing to impede entry. That is, if the price is initially set high enough to attract entry, entry will occur until the price falls to a level where entry is naturally deterred, and this price is the same price that established firms would use to block new entry. The only difference is that if existing firms did not attempt to deter entry, there would be a larger number of firms in the industry.

OLIGOPOLY: AN EVALUATION
13.7

We have surveyed several well-known models designed to analyze oligopolistic markets. Economists have developed many other oligopoly models, but space limitations preclude our discussing them here. The variety of these models and their implications makes it very difficult to generalize about the effects of oligopoly; no agreement has been reached that any of these models is universally applicable, and there is not even much agreement that any specific industry can be analyzed with a particular

---

[10] Federal Trade Commission, *Economic Report on Food Selling Practices in the District of Columbia and San Francisco* (Washington, D.C.: U.S. Government Printing Office, 1969), pp. 4, 23.

model. In addition, the implications of these models differ significantly. In some cases oligopoly prices are predicted to be near the monopoly level and in other cases, near the competitive level. Almost all we can say with much confidence is that oligopolistic outcomes lie somewhere between the monopoly and competitive results and that the outcomes are likely to differ from one industry to another.

In Section 11.7 we discussed empirical estimates of the welfare cost of monopoly output restrictions. As noted there, the industries studied were not single-firm industries (pure monopolies) but were instead industries dominated by a few large firms. In other words, the estimates of welfare costs really pertain to oligopolistic industries. Since the available estimates indicate that the output reductions are fairly modest, they suggest that, on average, oligopoly outcomes are probably closer to the competitive results than to the pure monopoly outcome. Don't forget, though, that these estimates do not take into account nonprice competition, like advertising, and this competition is likely to be prevalent in some oligopolistic markets.

Summary

A monopolistically competitive market is one in which there are a large number of competing firms, but each firm produces a differentiated product. Each firm thus confronts a demand curve that is highly, but not perfectly, elastic. In long-run equilibrium, firms make zero economic profit, but they are not producing at the minimum points on their long-run average cost curves since the LAC curve is tangent to a downward-sloping demand curve.

Monopolistic competition theory is somewhat controversial. On the one hand, it paints a picture that seems to describe many real world markets. On the other hand, the theory is difficult to apply to concrete problems, and its implications do not appear to differ greatly from those of the competitive model.

Oligopoly is characterized by a few firms that together produce all or most of the total output of some product. A pronounced mutual interdependence among the decisions of firms in the industry is the result. What one firm does has a decided impact on other firms, but the way the others will react is uncertain. Of the many oligopolistic models developed, no single model seems to apply to all, or even most, oligopolistic industries.

We surveyed several of the most common oligopoly models in this chapter: the kinked demand curve model, models of price leadership, and the entry-limit pricing model. Whether any of these models help us to understand how oligopolistic markets function is debatable. Some economists believe that we can analyze oligopoly adequately by using either the competitive or the monopoly models, depending on whether rivalry or cooperation characterizes the relationships among the firms.

Review Questions and Problems

1. What are the assumptions of the theory of monopolistic competition? In what way do these assumptions differ from those of the perfectly competitive model?

*2. Explain the two demand curves that are used in the analysis of monopolistic competition. Which of these curves guides the firm's price-quantity decisions? Why is the other curve necessary?

3. Draw a diagram that shows a monopolistically competitive firm in long-run equilibrium making zero economic profit. Describe the process by which the industry will attain a new long-run equilibrium following a shift upward in the firms' cost curves. Does this process differ from the competitive adjustment process?

4. What do we mean when we say that monopolistic competition leads to "excess capacity"? Is this outcome necessarily undesirable?

5. In this chapter we stated, "There is little doubt that in the real world many products are differentiated and firms face less than perfectly elastic demand curves." Does this statement imply that monopolistic competition theory should be used to analyze markets such as these?

6. What assumptions underlie the kinked demand curve model of oligopoly? What determines the price at which the kink in the demand curve occurs?

*7. Using the kinked demand curve model, explain how a reduction in costs might lead to no change in price or output. Do profits increase? If so, why are new firms not induced to enter the market?

8. Explain the determination of price and output in the model in which the dominant firm is the price leader.

*9. Suppose the supply curve of the "follower" firms in the dominant firm model is perfectly horizontal. Does the dominant firm still have effective power to set the industry price?

10. The threat of entry exists whenever firms are making economic profits. According to the entry-limit pricing model, how does this threat affect the price and output decisions of firms in the industry?

11. Under which oligopoly model does the outcome most nearly resemble that of pure monopoly? Under which oligopoly model does the outcome most nearly resemble that of perfect competition?

12. In analyzing the automobile industry, what factors would you consider in determining whether to use the competitive model, the monopoly model, or one of the oligopoly models?

Supplementary Readings

Chamberlin, Edward. *The Theory of Monopolistic Competition*. 8th ed. Cambridge, Mass.: Harvard University Press, 1962. Chaps. 4, 5.

Nutter, G. Warren. "The Plateau Demand Curve and Utility Theory." In *Readings in Microeconomics*, edited by William Breit and Harold Hochman. New York: Holt, Rinehart and Winston, 1968.

Scherer, F. M. *Industrial Market Structure and Economic Performance*. 2nd ed. Chicago: Rand McNally, 1980.

Stigler, George. "Monopolistic Competition in Retrospect." *Five Lectures on Economic Problems*. New York: Macmillan, 1950. Pp. 12–24.

Sweezy, Paul. "Demand Under Conditions of Oligopoly." *Journal of Political Economy*, 47 (August 1939): 568–573.

Employment and Pricing of Inputs

14

In this and the next two chapters, the emphasis shifts from product markets to input markets. In the last several chapters we have emphasized the factors that determine the output and price of final products; now we will begin to look more closely at the factors that determine the level of employment and prices of inputs used to produce these products. There is much similarity in the nature of the analysis of product and input markets since both involve the interaction of potential buyers and sellers. The roles of the leading actors, however, are reversed. Firms are suppliers in product markets, but they are demanders in input markets. Households and individuals are the demanders in product markets and the suppliers in input markets.

The operation of input markets has a major impact on the level and distribution of real income. An examination of these markets can help us answer many questions, such as, why are real incomes higher in the United States than they are in the less developed countries? Why do real wage rates generally tend to rise over time? Why did real wages rise so little during the 1970s and early 1980s? Why does a doctor earn three times as much as an accountant and an accountant earn three times as much as a sales clerk? These are important questions, and they suggest why there is such interest in the workings of input markets.

In this chapter we will discuss the basic principles common to all input market analysis, whether the input is labor, capital, raw materials, or land. We begin by examining the demand for inputs by competitive firms, then turn to the supply of inputs, and finally bring the two together to complete the general model. The last two sections of the chapter deal with the analysis of input markets under noncompetitive conditions.

THE INPUT DEMAND CURVE OF A COMPETITIVE FIRM
14.1

In the analysis of input markets the market demand curve is of primary importance. The market demand curve shows the total quantity of an input that will be hired or purchased at alternative prices by all demanders together. First, it is necessary to begin on a smaller scale with the factors influencing the employment decision of the individual demander, usually the business firm; then we can aggregate the demands of individual firms to obtain the demand for the input by all the firms in the industry. This treatment is similar to the derivation of the market demand curve for a consumer good; first we explained why an individual consumer would purchase more at a lower price, and then we aggregated to obtain the market demand curve.

In this section we will see how a change in the price of some input will affect its employment by a single competitive firm. At the outset, note that there are no new assumptions in the analysis. We will use the same competitive model developed in Chapters 8–10, but now our focus will be on input markets rather than the output market. For example, we still assume profit maximization is the goal of the firm, but we now want to see why profit maximization, along with the other assumptions of the competitive model, implies that a firm will employ more of an input when its price is lower.

How does a single firm determine how many workers to hire when its goal is to maximize its profits? For now, we will assume workers to be homogeneous — that is, interchangeable as far as the firm is concerned — so the only question is how many the firm should employ. Each additional worker hired adds to the firm's costs since the firm must pay the going wage rate. At the same time, each additional worker also adds to the firm's revenues since a larger work force produces greater output. Thus, there are benefits (greater revenues) and costs (wages) associated with the firm's employment decision. The firm will increase profits by hiring additional workers as long as the additional revenues generated by the expansion in output exceed the wages that must be paid. A comparison of the marginal benefit of hiring workers, in the form of added revenues, with the marginal cost of hiring workers, in the form of added wage costs, will guide the firm's decision concerning how many workers to employ.

The Firm's Demand Curve: One Variable Input

To give more content to this analysis, imagine a situation where the quantities of nonlabor inputs (such as raw materials and machines) are fixed and only the number of workers can be varied. Think of this as a short-run setting in which labor is the only variable input. In this situation the law of diminishing marginal returns will apply to labor: beyond some point, each additional worker will result in a smaller addition to output. The contribution to output made by increasing the number of workers is an important determinant of the firm's demand for labor, and the marginal physical product curve (as described in Section 6.4) contains the relevant information. In Figure 14–1 the downward-sloping portion of the marginal physical product curve for labor is MP_L. The marginal physical product curve indicates that when the firm employs 20 workers per day, the additional output produced when the firm employs one more worker (MP_L) is 3 units of output; if employment increases to 25 workers, the

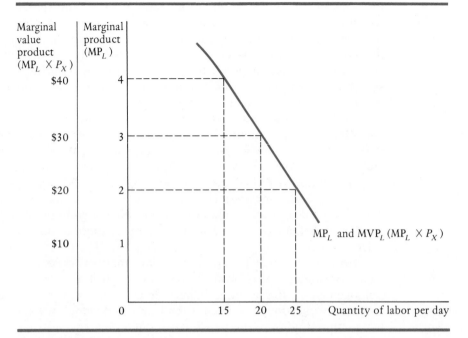

FIGURE 14-1

The Competitive Firm's Demand for Labor: One Input Variable

With labor as the only variable input, we can convert labor's marginal product curve MP$_L$ into the marginal value product curve MVP$_L$ by multiplying the marginal product of labor by the price of the commodity produced. The MVP curve is the competitive firm's demand curve for labor if other inputs cannot be varied.

marginal product of labor will be lower, at 2 units of output per worker, because of the law of diminishing marginal returns.

Starting from any given level of employment, let's consider how hiring an additional worker will affect the firm's revenues. If the firm is employing 20 workers, one more worker will increase output of the product (call it X) by 3 units, or by the marginal product of labor when 20 workers are employed. If good X sells for $10 per unit, the additional 3 units of output generated by hiring the twenty-first worker will add $30 to revenue. Multiplying the marginal physical product by the price per unit of output (MP$_L$ × P$_X$) gives us the *marginal value product of labor (MVP$_L$).* In general, the marginal value product of labor measures the extra revenue the competitive firm can receive by selling the additional output generated when it increases employment of the input by one unit.

A downward-sloping marginal value product curve is derived by multiplying the constant price of good X (recall that we are dealing with a competitive firm, so the price is unchanged when more X is sold) by the declining marginal product of labor. The marginal value product curve coincides with the marginal product curve. The only difference is that now we are measuring the marginal product of labor in terms of what it sells for on the vertical axis. For example, when 20 workers are employed, MP_L is 3 units and MVP_L is $30; when 25 workers are employed, MP_L declines to 2 units of output, so MVP_L falls to $20.

The marginal value product curve is the firm's demand curve for a given input when all other inputs are fixed. To see this, suppose that the daily wage rate is $30 per worker. The firm can hire as many workers as it wants at this wage rate, so each additional employee adds $30 to the firm's costs. Every extra worker, however, also adds an amount equal to the marginal value product to the firm's revenues. Comparing the effects on costs and revenues tells the firm how many workers to hire. For example, if the firm is currently employing 15 workers, the marginal value product of an additional worker is $40. Hiring an additional worker will therefore add more to revenues ($40) than to costs ($30), so profits will increase by employing more workers. The firm should expand employment up to the point where the marginal value product has fallen to $30, the wage rate. In Figure 14–1 the most profitable level of employment is 20 workers when the wage rate is $30. If the firm hires more than 20 workers, costs will go up by more than revenues (the wage rate, $30, is greater than MVP_L at any number in excess of 20 workers), so profits will decline.

Note that at a lower wage rate it would be profitable to hire more workers. For instance, if the wage rate were to drop to $20 per day, the firm would maximize profits by expanding employment to 25 workers. At the initial employment level of 20 workers and the lower wage rate, the marginal value product of hiring another worker ($30) would now be greater than the wage cost ($20), so the firm adds more to revenues than to costs by employing 5 more workers.

Two important conclusions emerge from this analysis. First, the marginal value product curve identifies the most profitable employment level for the input at each alternative cost. The firm will hire up to the point where the input's marginal value product is just equal to its cost. Second, the marginal value product curve — the firm's demand curve when other inputs are not varied — must slope downward. This conclusion follows directly from the law of diminishing marginal returns: if an input's marginal physical product declines as more is used, so must the marginal value product.

The preceding analysis follows from the assumption that the firm is a profit maximizer in a competitive market. It may be helpful to relate this analysis to our earlier discussion in Chapter 8 that emphasized the most profitable output level for the competitive firm. We have just seen that the firm will maximize profits by employing an input — in this case labor — up to the point where its MVP equals the cost of the input — in this case the wage rate w. When profits are at a maximum, therefore, the following condition holds:

$$w = MVP_L. \tag{1}$$

Since MVP_L equals $\mathrm{MP}_L \times P_X$, if we divide both sides of equation (1) by MP_L, we obtain

$$w/\mathrm{MP}_L = P_X. \tag{2}$$

Recall from Section 7.3 that the ratio w/MP_L is equal to the marginal cost (MC) of producing one more unit of X using additional amounts of labor. Therefore, equation (2) is equivalent to the price-equal-marginal-cost condition for profit maximization in the output market. *When the competitive firm is hiring workers so that $w = \mathrm{MVP}_L$, then $P_X = \mathrm{MC}_X$, and vice versa.* We have been looking at the same process of profit maximization that we did in earlier chapters, but now from the perspective of its implications for the employment decisions of the firm.

The Firm's Demand Curve: All Inputs Variable

In identifying the firm's MVP curve as its demand curve for an input, we assumed that the quantities of other inputs were fixed. Generally, however, a change in the price of an input will lead the firm to alter its employment not only of that input but of other inputs as well. For example, a reduction in the cost of computers may lead not only to the purchase or leasing of more computers but also to the employment of more computer programmers. Consequently, the demand curve for an input should allow the firm to adjust its use of other inputs as well as adjust the use of the one whose price has changed.

We can easily extend the analysis to allow for variation in the quantities of all inputs. Suppose the firm is initially in equilibrium, employing the appropriate quantities of all inputs. The daily wage rate is $30, and the firm employs 20 workers. In Figure 14–2 the firm is operating at point A on MVP_L. Note that the quantity of capital, assumed to be the only other input, is constant at 10 units at all points along MVP_L. Now suppose the wage rate falls to $20. If the quantity of capital is kept constant at 10 units, the firm will increase its employment of workers to 25 units, at point B on MVP_L. This increased employment will not represent a complete adjustment to the lower wage rate since it will normally be in the interest of the firm to expand its employment of capital too.

An increase in the quantity of capital, though, shifts the MVP_L curve upward. If the quantity of capital increases to 12 units, the MVP_L curve shifts to MVP'_L. With 12 units of capital, at every level of employment of labor each worker has more "tools" to work with than before, so the marginal physical productivity of workers is greater. Perhaps an example will help clarify this relationship. Suppose we employ one person with one unit of capital (a shovel) to dig a ditch. Next let the wage rate fall so that it becomes worthwhile to hire a second ditchdigger. If we have two people and one shovel, they can take turns using the shovel, and output will increase. However, if we combine the extra labor with more capital by pur-

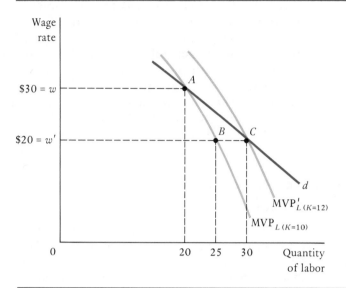

FIGURE 14-2

The Competitive Firm's Demand for Labor: All Inputs Variable

When all inputs are variable, an input's MVP curve shifts with changes in the employment of other inputs. The firm's demand curve for labor is then the *d* curve, which takes into account the way changes in the amount of capital employed affect the MVP of labor.

chasing a second shovel, the productivity of labor will increase. In other words, an increase in capital shifts the entire marginal physical product curve of labor upward, and with an unchanged product price the MVP_L shifts upward too. This adjustment leads to a further increase in the employment of workers, to point *C* on the marginal value product curve for a constant 12 units of capital. Thus, the full response of the firm to the lower wage rate is an increase in employment from 20 to 30 workers.[1]

Points *A* and *C* are two points on the firm's demand curve for labor, *d*, when the firm is able to adjust its employment of all inputs in response to a change in the wage rate. The firm still employs workers up to the point

---

[1] The analysis here deals with the situation, thought to be typical, where labor and capital are complements. (Two inputs are complements if an increase in the quantity of one leads to an increase in the marginal product of the other.) When the firm uses more labor and the same amount of capital at point *B*, the marginal product curve of capital increases, so the firm also expands its use of capital. The demand curve for labor, however, will still slope downward if the two inputs are substitutes. (They are substitutes if an increase in the quantity of one decreases the marginal product of the other.) In that case, when the firm increases labor (point *A* to point *B*), the marginal product of capital will be lower, and the firm will employ less capital. A reduction in capital, however, increases the marginal product of labor when the inputs are substitutes, so the MVP_L curve shifts upward in this case also, just as it does in Figure 14–2.

where their marginal value product equals the wage rate, but we have now allowed for the effect of induced variations in the firm's employment of other inputs on the marginal productivity of labor. We can think of the demand curve d, therefore, as a generalized marginal value product curve. Since this curve allows the firm to vary all inputs, it is the competitive firm's long-run demand curve for an input.

In deriving this demand curve for labor, we assumed that the prices of other inputs remain unchanged (only the quantities employed are allowed to vary) and that the price of the product the firm sells is also constant.

The Firm's Demand Curve: An Alternative Approach

By using an alternative approach, we can gain further insight into the adjustment of a firm to a change in the price of an input. Our original approach has the advantage of linking the demand for an input to its marginal productivity but has the disadvantage of obscuring what happens in the output market and in the market for other inputs. The approach we will now develop will also show that the demand curve for an input will slope downward, but it gives more explicit attention to the output market and the demand for other inputs.

Figure 14–3b shows the firm's position in its output market where its marginal cost curve mc crosses the horizontal demand curve at point E. Figure 14–3a shows the same initial situation from the perspective of the firm's employment of inputs. The production of output X_1 at the least possible cost occurs at the tangency between the X_1 isoquant and the isocost line MN at point E. The firm employs 20 workers and 10 units of capital in the production of X_1 units of output.

Now let's work through the effects of a reduction in the wage rate. First, how will a lower wage rate affect the firm if we *tentatively* assume it continues to produce the same output? Recall that the slope of the isocost line equals the ratio of the wage rate to the price of capital. A lower wage rate and an unchanged price of capital imply that isocost lines will be flatter because labor becomes cheaper relative to capital when the wage rate falls. Isocost line $M'N'$ in Figure 14–3a reflects the lower wage rate, and the least costly way of producing X_1 units of output occurs at the point where $M'N'$ is tangent to the isoquant, at point E_1. *To produce an unchanged output, the firm uses more labor and less capital when the relative cost of labor falls; that is, the firm substitutes labor for capital.*

In Figure 14–3b point E_1 on mc' shows the same adjustment. A reduction in the wage rate lowers the entire marginal cost curve to mc' (see Section 7.7 for a more detailed discussion), so when X_1 units are produced, the price of the product is greater than the marginal cost. The firm, therefore, has incentive to expand output as a result of the lower wage rate. Now consider the subsequent effects as the firm expands output

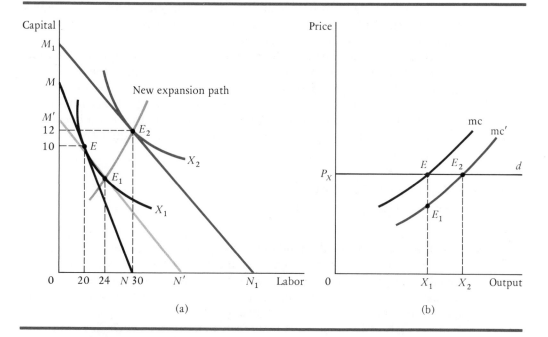

FIGURE 14-3

The Competitive Firm's Demand for Labor: All Inputs Variable

(a) A lower wage rate for labor causes the firm to employ more labor as it substitutes labor for capital — the movement from E to E_1. (b) At a lower wage rate output will expand from X_1 to X_2, as the lower wage rate causes the marginal cost curve to shift downward. This output effect further increases the employment of labor — the movement from E_1 to E_2 in part a.

from X_1 to the new profit maximizing level X_2. Figure 14–3a shows this effect as the movement along the new expansion path (based on the lower wage rate and unchanged price of capital) from point E_1 to point E_2. As the firm produces more output, it moves to a higher isocost line, M_1N_1, and it employs more of both inputs than it did at point E_1. At E_2 the firm employs 30 workers and 12 units of capital. The reduction in the wage rate has increased the employment of labor from 20 to 30 workers.

This approach to the demand curve for an input involves separating the total effect of a change in an input's price into two components, which is similar to what we did with a consumer's demand curve. The increase in the quantity employed when output is held constant and labor substituted for capital is called the *substitution effect* associated with the change in the wage rate. The movement along the X_1 isoquant from point E to point E_1 (from 20 to 24 workers) shows the substitution effect. The increase in the quantity employed when output is increased is called the *output effect,* and it is shown by the movement along the new expansion path from point E_1 to point E_2 (from 24 to 30 workers).[2] The sum of these two effects identifies the full response to the change in the price of the input on its employment by the firm.

Since both the substitution and the output effects imply greater employment at a lower input price, and lower employment at a higher input price, the firm's demand curve for an input must slope downward. The firm will employ more workers at a lower wage rate both because it will use more labor per unit of output (the substitution effect) and because it becomes profitable to produce more output when production costs fall (the output effect).

THE INPUT DEMAND CURVE
OF A COMPETITIVE INDUSTRY
14.2

We have seen that the demand curve for an input for a single competitive firm will have a negative slope, but the firm's demand curve is only a building block in the development of the more important construct, the industry demand curve for an input. We were concerned with the individual firm primarily because that is the level where employment decisions are actually made, and if we can be sure that each firm will hire more of an input at a lower price, then we have reason to believe that the total quantity demanded will increase at a lower price, that is, that the industry demand curve for an input will slope downward.

The total quantity of an input hired by an industry is the sum of the quantities employed by the firms in the industry. To derive the industry demand curve, we must therefore aggregate the demand curves of the firms. First, we must recognize one problem. When we derived the firm's demand curve, we assumed that the price of the product remained unchanged. Recall, though, that when the wage rate fell, the firm expanded output and sold the larger output at an unchanged price. The assumption of a given product price is appropriate when we are dealing with just one firm. But now we are interested in the response of all the firms in an industry to a lower wage rate, *and when all firms simultaneously increase output, they can sell more output only at a lower price.*

Figure 14–4 illustrates how this factor affects the derivation of the industry demand curve. In Figure 14–4a, d is the demand curve for labor for a single firm, and we assume that the price of the product X is \$10 at all points along d. If we suppose initially that when the wage rate is \$30, the equilibrium price of X is \$10, then the firm in Figure 14–4a will hire out to point A on its demand curve d and employ 20 workers. If there are

---

[2] In contrast to a consumer's demand curve, the demand curve for labor is not derived by pivoting the isocost line at point M in Figure 14–3a. That approach would be correct only if the firm had to continue operating at the same total cost, which is generally untrue. The total cost that is most profitable for the firm to incur depends on demand and cost conditions, which are shown in Figure 14–3b.

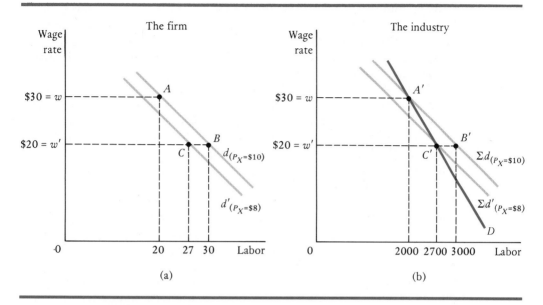

FIGURE 14–4

The Competitive Industry's Demand for Labor

(a) The competitive firm's demand curve for labor assumes a *given* product price.
(b) In deriving the industry demand curve for labor, we must take into account
the fact that as industry output changes, so will the product price. The industry
demand curve is *D*.

100 identical firms in the industry, total employment will be 2000 workers
at the $30 wage rate, point *A'* in Figure 14–4b. Point *A'* lies on the Σd
curve, which is the horizontal summation of the *d* curves of the firms in
the industry.

By assumption, point *A'* in Figure 14–4b is a point on the industry
demand curve for labor. The simple summation of the firms' demand
curves, Σd, does not, however, indicate the quantity of labor demanded by
the industry at any other wage rate. To see this, suppose that the wage rate
to all firms in the industry falls to $20. In Figure 14–4a individual firms will
begin to expand employment from point *A* toward point *B*, and in the
process output will rise. As all firms in the industry place more output on
the market, the price of *X* will fall since consumers will only purchase the
larger output at a lower price. But a lower price for *X* shifts each firm's
demand curve downward since labor's marginal *value* product curve will
be lower when the value (price) of the product is reduced. (Recall that the
marginal value product of labor is equal to the marginal product of labor
multiplied by the price of the output. Since the price of the output has
fallen, the marginal value product of labor is lower for each level of input
use.) If the price of *X* declines to $8 a unit, for example, the firm's demand

curve becomes d' in Figure 14–4a, and the firm will employ 27 workers. In Figure 14–4b all the firms together begin by expanding employment from point A' toward B', but this expansion is cut short by the declining price of X, and they end up at point C'. Point C' is a second point on the industry demand curve for labor, D.

This derivation of the industry demand curve takes into account the effect of increased employment, and hence output, on the price of the product. The industry demand curve will be less elastic than the Σd curve, which is based on an unchanged price of X, but it will still slope downward. This is easiest to see by recognizing that there will still be a substitution effect and an output effect, implying greater employment at the lower wage rate even when the declining price of X is taken into account. The price of X falls only because more X is produced, and greater production involves the use of more labor (the output effect). In addition, firms will use more labor per unit of X produced when the wage rate is lower because they will substitute labor for other inputs (the substitution effect) at each given output level.

Note that we assume the demand curve for the product produced by the industry is fixed when deriving the industry demand curve for any input. In fact, economists sometimes refer to the demand curve for an input as a *derived demand:* the demand for textile workers, for example, is derived from the demand of consumers for textiles. Firms will pay workers to produce textiles only because consumers are willing to pay for textiles. If the demand curve for textiles shifts, the demand curve for textile workers will also shift. The consumer demand curve for a product is therefore an important determinant of the position of the demand curve for an input used in the production of the product.

COMMENTS ON THE INDUSTRY DEMAND CURVE FOR AN INPUT
14.3

Fortunately, once we understand the theoretical underpinnings of the industry demand curve for an input, we can use it directly for analytical purposes without reproducing the somewhat complicated derivation. Several further points deserve attention.

1. The number of jobs is not fixed. A downward-sloping demand curve for labor (or any other input) means that the number of workers firms will hire depends on the wage rate. At a lower wage rate more jobs will exist. There can never be a shortage of jobs. (There may be fewer higher-paying jobs than we would like, but this is a different matter.)

Although this point is obvious, noneconomists frequently deny it, implicitly assuming a vertical demand curve for labor — a fixed number of jobs. For example, you may have heard someone say that automation destroys jobs. Automation can sometimes make certain jobs no longer worth filling, thus displacing some workers. These same workers, however, can find employment elsewhere because demand curves in other industries slope downward — employment will increase if the wage rate goes down. Similarly, you may have heard an observer, noting that the labor force will grow by 10 million in the next decade, ask the rhetorical question: "How can we 'create' 10 million new jobs?" Jobs don't have to be created. Innumerable unfilled jobs already exist — that's what downward-sloping labor demand curves imply. The real problem is to see that the most worthwhile jobs are filled.

2.   Economic profits of firms are zero at all points along the industry demand curve for an input. The industry demand curve derived in the previous section is a long-run demand curve, since it allows time for all inputs to be varied. A lower wage rate does not mean firms earn economic profit because with greater employment and output the price of the product will be lower too. The competitive adjustment process that eliminates economic profit is still at work, but it fades into the background when we focus on the input markets. It is true, however, that the short-run effect of a change in input prices can lead to losses or profits, but these losses or profits signal the need for a further adjustment before the industry returns to a long-run equilibrium.

3.   For some purposes it is necessary to use an input demand curve that summarizes the responses of a large number of industries. The automobile industry is not the only purchaser of steel or employer of engineers. When asking what determines the price of steel or the wage rate of engineers, it is important to recognize that the total demand of all industries using these inputs interacts with the total supply to all industries to determine input prices. We will explain this point in more detail later. For now we note that it is frequently necessary to take a perspective broader than the group of firms that produce the same product (the industry) since many firms producing different products may compete for the same inputs.

4.   Several factors interact to determine the price elasticity of demand for an input. The price elasticity of demand for an input is defined and measured the same way as for a consumer demand curve (Section 3.7). The price elasticity of demand for an input measures the responsiveness of quantity demanded to a change in price, and its magnitude is frequently quite important. For example, in evaluating the minimum wage law, it makes a difference whether a 10 percent increase in the legal minimum reduces employment of low-wage workers by 20 percent (an elasticity of 2.0) or by 5 percent (an elasticity of 0.5). Four major factors affect the elasticity of demand for an input.

First, the input demand curve will be more elastic the greater the elasticity of demand for the product produced. Recall that the input demand curve is a derived demand curve. If consumers will purchase a great deal more of the good at a slightly lower price (highly elastic product demand), firms will produce much more when an input price falls, and employment will increase sharply. An elastic product demand gives rise to a large output effect, which in turn contributes to the elasticity of demand for inputs. For instance, consider Figure 14–4b, and suppose the wage rate falls from $30 to $20. If the consumer demand curve was perfectly elastic, the greater output could be sold at an unchanged $10 price. The firms would expand employment to point B, and, in fact, Σd would be the industry demand curve in this case.

Second, the input demand curve will be more elastic when it is easier to substitute one input for another in production. This condition refers to the technology of production reflected in the curvature of the production isoquants. When it is technically easy to substitute among inputs, the substitution effect of an input price change will be large, implying a large (elastic) employment change. For example, if machines can adequately do the work performed by workers and at only a slightly higher cost, an increase in the wage rate can lead firms to switch entirely to machines and reduce employment of workers to zero — implying a highly elastic demand for workers.

Third, the demand for an input will be more elastic when the supply curve of other inputs is more elastic. If machines rise sharply in price when firms switch from workers to machines (implying an inelastic supply of machines), there is a limit on the amount of profitable switching that can occur, giving rise to a small substitution effect and a low elasticity of demand for workers. The output effect reinforces this impact. If machines rise in price as more are used when output is increased, there is a limit on how much additional output firms can profitably produce when the wage rate falls.

Fourth, the input demand curve will be more elastic the longer the time allowed for adjustment. Once again we make a distinction between long-run and short-run effects. Long-run demand curves are more elastic than short-run demand curves. Figure 14–2 shows this feature explicitly if we assume that labor but not capital can be varied in the short run. Then MVP_L is the short-run labor demand curve, and d is the long-run labor demand curve. The input demand curve will be more elastic in the long run, because substitution possibilities among inputs are greater in the long run. For example, a rise in the wage rate may make it profitable for firms to replace workers with machines. It takes time, however, for machines to be built and installed, so in the short run few workers will be discharged.

THE SUPPLY OF INPUTS
14.4

The supply side of input markets deals with the quantities of inputs available at alternative prices. This subject is somewhat complicated because the shape of the supply curve is likely to differ from one input to another. In this section we will make some general observations that are applicable to all inputs; we defer a discussion of specific inputs until the next chapter.

Like most things, inputs can be broadly or narrowly defined. A broad definition might classify all inputs as either labor, land, or capital. A narrow definition might distinguish between skilled and unskilled workers, land in New York City and Iowa, buildings and trucks, and so on. The appropriate definition depends on the problem at hand. The broad classification will serve to make the general points here, but in the next two chapters we will see examples of cases where it is fruitful to be more specific.

People own the inputs used by firms to produce goods and services. Our problem is to understand the conditions under which the owners of inputs will offer them for sale or rent. At the outset it is important to distinguish between the amount of inputs in existence at any given time — the stock of resources — and the amount offered for sale or rent. At any time there are a fixed number of people capable of working, a fixed area of land, and a fixed amount of buildings, vehicles, machinery, and other capital equipment. The amount in existence can differ significantly from the amount the owners will offer for employment. Since the amount that owners will provide is likely to depend on the price they will be paid, we must be concerned with the supply curves of inputs, not just the stock of inputs in existence.

The general shape of supply curves of inputs depends crucially on the market for which the supply curve is drawn. Take the supply curve of labor to all industries in the economy. To simplify, suppose that all workers are identical, so there will only be one wage rate. If that wage rate goes up, will the total amount of labor offered increase? We will give a fuller analysis in the next chapter, but here we note simply that the total amount of labor can increase only if workers decide to work longer hours or if more people enter the labor force. It is possible, though, that such responses to a higher wage rate will be so small that the supply curve of labor to all industries together would be approximately vertical, as in Figure 14–5a. A vertical supply curve indicates that an increase in the wage rate from w_1 to w_2 will leave the number of workers unchanged at 100 million. We are not asserting that the supply curve will necessarily be vertical like this, but it could be; so for the moment let's suppose it is.

Although the supply of labor to *all industries taken together* may be vertical, this fact does not mean that the supply curve of labor confronting *any particular industry* is vertical. Even though the total number of workers employed in the economy may not change, the number employed by one particular industry is subject to great variation. If the wage rate paid to workers in the shoe industry should increase, workers in other industries would leave their jobs to go to work making shoes. This adjustment doesn't change the total number of workers employed, but it does change employment in the shoe industry. The supply curve of workers to the shoe industry will therefore slope upward (or possibly be horizontal), as illustrated in Figure 14–5b. An increase in wage rates in the shoe industry from w_1 to w_2 will induce 10,000 workers to move from other jobs into the shoe industry.

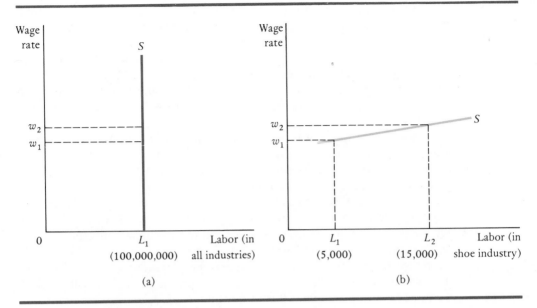

FIGURE 14-5

The Supply Curve of Labor to the Economy and to a Particular Industry

It is important to distinguish (a) the supply curve of an input to all industries together from (b) the supply curve of the input to one industry. The supply curve to one industry will always be more elastic than the supply curve to the economy as a whole.

Both labor supply curves in Figure 14–5 are correct in the sense that they can both exist simultaneously. Figure 14–5a shows the supply of labor *to the entire economy;* Figure 14–5b shows the supply curve of labor *to the shoe industry.* This situation is analogous to one we saw earlier, where the supply curve of labor facing a single firm is horizontal at the same time that the supply curve of labor to the industry slopes upward. Because the shoe industry is only a small part of the entire (economywide) labor market, its labor supply curve will be more elastic than the supply curve of labor for the economy. Indeed, if its share were as small as the numbers used in Figure 14–5 indicate, for all practical purposes the shoe industry would probably face a horizontal labor supply curve.

This discussion indicates why it is ambiguous to refer to *the* supply curve of an input. We must always specify that it is the input supply curve to a particular set of demanders. Otherwise, it is easy to fall into the trap of thinking that the supply curve of engineers to the automobile industry, for example, is vertical because in the short run there are only a limited number of trained engineers. In fact, the supply curves of *most* inputs to *most* industries are likely to be either perfectly horizontal or gently upward-sloping, as in Figure 14–5b, regardless of the shape of the supply curve of the input to the economy as a whole because most industries employ only a small portion of the total amount of any input.

These remarks apply to other inputs as well as labor. Although the total supply of land to the economy may plausibly be fixed (a vertical supply curve, as in Figure 14–5a), the supply available to any given industry is not. The corn industry can bid land away from other uses if it expands, just as homeowners can bid land away from farmers to build homes on.

Consequently, for individual industries, input supply curves will generally be quite elastic. However, supply curves of inputs to more broadly defined markets will be less elastic, and there are some situations where we should use this type of supply curve. The proper pairing of supply and demand concepts is important in the analysis of input markets, as examples given later will show in more detail.

INDUSTRY DETERMINATION OF PRICE AND EMPLOYMENT OF INPUTS
14.5

Firms in an industry compete with one another to acquire inputs, and the industry demand curve for the input summarizes the way the price of an input influences the firms' hiring decisions. Individuals and other firms provide resources to firms in the industry, and the supply curve of an input to the industry reflects the way the owners' decisions depend on the price they receive. As is true in other markets, the interaction of supply and demand determines price and quantity. Figure 14–6 illustrates this process, once again using labor as an example. As before, we assume that all workers are identical.

Figure 14–6b shows the industry demand and supply curves for labor. Market forces in the industry would tend to produce an equilibrium where firms employ 10,000 workers at a (daily) wage rate of $30. To understand fully why the behavior of firms and workers tend to produce this outcome, it is helpful to think about what would happen if some other wage rate prevailed. Suppose, for example, that the wage rate was $25 instead. At that wage only 6,000 workers would agree to work in the industry. With such low labor costs, firms would find it profitable to employ 12,000 workers, but only 6,000 are available. A shortage of labor would exist at the $25 wage rate, resulting in a tight labor market. Firms would advertise for workers but have too few applicants at the current wage. Workers presently employed by some firms in the industry would receive job offers from other firms at higher wages. Firms unable to recruit workers from within the industry would try to hire workers from firms in other industries, but to do so, they would have to offer higher wage rates. Firms, however, would be willing to pay higher wages because the marginal value productivity of workers when 6,000 are employed is above $25.

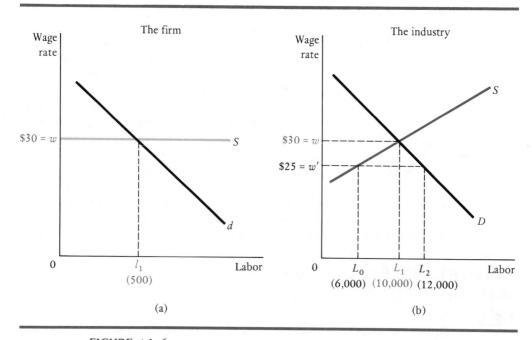

FIGURE 14-6
The Equilibrium Wage and Employment Level for a Competitive Industry

(b) Supply and demand in an industry determine the wage rate and employment: employment will be 10.000 workers at a wage rate of $30. (a) The position of the firm in equilibrium is shown. Each firm faces a horizontal supply curve at the industry-determined wage rate of $30.

As a result, the wage rate would not stay at $25; it would rise. As firms bid the wage up, workers would quit their jobs in other industries to seize the better opportunity in this market, resulting in an increase in the quantity supplied — a movement up the supply curve. As the wage increases, firms find that it is no longer profitable to try to fill 12,000 jobs, and the quantity demanded decreases — a movement up the demand curve. This process continues until the wage rate reaches the point where the number of workers willing and able to work for firms in this industry is equal to the number of workers the firms are willing to employ. Graphically, the equilibrium is shown by the intersection of the industry demand and supply curves.

When the industry market for labor is in equilibrium, the situation from the perspective of an individual firm in the industry is as shown in Figure 14–6a. The market-determined wage rate is $30, and each firm faces a horizontal supply curve at that wage. The individual firm is a small part of the total market, so it has no option but to pay the going wage rate determined in the broader market (illustrated in Figure 14–6b). And at the equilibrium wage it can hire more or fewer workers without appreciably affecting the wage rate. Faced with the $30 wage, the firm in Figure 14–6a would maximize its profits by hiring 500 workers.

One implication of this analysis is that the market-determined input price is equal to the marginal value product of the input. Each firm is in the position shown in Figure 14–6a, employing the quantity of the input at which the marginal value product equals the price. Recall that the marginal value product of an input is the value that consumers place on the contribution to output made by the input. Thus, in any competitive market the owners of inputs tend to be compensated according to how much value the inputs they provide contribute toward output. Basically, this outcome results because input demands are derived demands. Consumers, in their purchases of products, are indirectly expressing how valuable the services of the inputs are to them.

Because input suppliers in competitive markets are "paid their marginal products," some people interpret wage rates and other input prices as ethically just. This conclusion does not necessarily follow. A person fortunate enough to be intelligent and healthy may well be able to produce more than a person who is ignorant and sickly, but few people interpret justice to mean that it is necessarily desirable for the intelligent, healthy person to receive a much higher income than the ignorant, sickly person receives. For this and other reasons the ethical significance of the way competitive markets mete out rewards to those who supply inputs is open to debate. The statement that input prices tend to equal marginal value products is a positive statement about the way competitive input markets work, not an ethical judgment.

Process of Input Price Equalization Across Industries

In most cases several different industries employ some of the same inputs. Most industries, for example, use some quantities of land, electricity, unskilled labor, and buildings. To understand how the prices of these widely used inputs are determined, we must look beyond the confines of a single industry and recognize that there is competition among many industries for these inputs. We will emphasize one characteristic of this situation here: the tendency for identical inputs to receive the same prices regardless of which industry employs them.

Suppose that the aerospace industry and the telecommunications industry both employ computer programmers. Further suppose that for some reason wages are higher in the aerospace industry. The wage difference between the two industries won't persist for long because programmers can move from one industry to another. Programmers in the low-paid telecommunications industry will leave their jobs and seek work in the aerospace industry where pay is better. This movement simultaneously reduces the supply of programmers to the telecommunications industry and increases the supply of programmers to the aerospace industry. With more programmers seeking employment in the aerospace industry, the wage rate there will come down, and the wage rate will rise in the telecommunications industry where supply has fallen. This process continues until wages in the two industries are equal since only then will programmers have no further incentive to change jobs.

Figure 14–7 illustrates the process of input prize equalization. Let's assume that industry A and industry B together employ 1500 workers and that initially industry A employs 500 and industry B employs 1000. At their respective levels of employment, the wage rate is $40 in industry A (Figure 14–7a) and $30 in industry B (Figure 14–7b). To show why these markets are not in equilibrium and how they will ultimately adjust to an equilibrium, we will find it convenient to use a specially defined supply curve. Consider the momentary, or very short-run, supply curve of workers that identifies the number of workers in each industry at a specific time. These

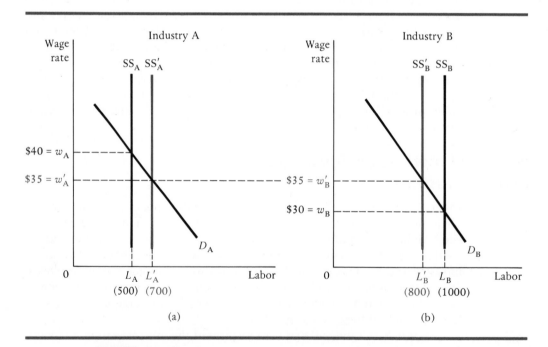

FIGURE 14–7
Input Price Equalization Across Industries
When several industries employ the same input. the input tends to be allocated among industries so that its price is the same in every industry. If this were not true — if workers were receiving $40 in industry A and $30 in industry B — input owners would have incentive to shift inputs to industries where pay is higher. and this process tends to equalize input prices.

supply curves will be vertical; that is, at a particular time each industry employs a given number of workers. These are not the supply curves we use in most applications. We use them here for the very specific purpose of illustrating explicitly how the movement of workers from one industry to another affects both markets.

Initially, the momentary supply curve of workers in industry A is SS_A, and in industry B it is SS_B. Given the initial allocation of workers between the industries, the wage rate of the 500 workers in industry A is $40, and the wage rate of the 1000 workers in industry B is $30. Clearly this result is not an equilibrium since workers in industry B have incentive to quit their jobs and seek employment in industry A. Shifts in the SS curves show the movement of workers between industries. The momentary supply curve in industry B shifts to the left as workers leave. And when these workers seek jobs in industry A, the momentary supply curve there shifts to the right. The movement of workers decreases the difference in wages between the two industries: wages fall in A and rise in B. Moreover, the movement of workers will persist as long as the wage rate is higher in industry A, which means it will continue until wages are equal in the two industries. In the diagram equilibrium occurs when 200 workers have moved from B to A, and the common wage rate of $35 is established.

Note that for this process to work it is generally not necessary for all workers to be willing to change jobs to secure higher wages. Usually only relatively few workers need relocate to bring wages in the two industries into equilibrium. In our example only 200 of the 1500 workers had to change jobs to produce a uniform wage rate. In fact, in some cases it is unnecessary for the workers to move — in the sense of changing their place of residence — at all. Suppose that industry A is in California and industry B is in North Dakota. At the outset let's suppose workers in North Dakota are paid less but are unwilling to relocate to California to work for industry A. Labor immobility of this sort, however, does not forestall the adjustment process. Because of the wage differential, firms in industry A have incentive to relocate in North Dakota to take advantage of the lower wage rate there, and the resulting impact on wages will be the same as if workers had moved from North Dakota to California — that is, a uniform wage will be established. (Wages can in some cases differ between locations because of geographic preferences of workers, but we defer that topic to the next chapter.)

The North-South Wage Differential

As the preceding remarks suggest, input prices should be equalized across industries and regions. This conclusion is seemingly at variance with the widely held view that wages in the North are higher than they are in the South. In making such comparisons, we must compare wages for comparable workers since northern and southern workers may differ, on average, in education, age, experience, and the like. Several empirical studies have controlled for these factors, and they have still found that wages of comparable workers are about 10 percent higher in the North. Since this differential has persisted for many years, it is apparently not a short-run disequilibrium.

How can this be? For many years labor economists have cited the North-South wage differential as an example of the immobility of labor, but if this reasoning were correct, why didn't firms relocate to the South to take advantage of lower-cost labor? Why didn't wages between the two regions adjust the way the preceding analysis predicted? Our theory asserts that over time *real* wages across industries and regions will be equalized. Looking more closely at the empirical work, we find the studies compared *money* wages. Since prices tend to be lower in the South, lower money wages there don't necessarily mean lower purchasing power. In fact, two recent studies that adjusted for regional differences in the cost of living found that real wages for comparable workers were the same in both regions.[3] The economic forces emphasized by economic theory were working all along; it was only the interpretation of the "facts" that was wrong.

As this discussion illustrates, markets tend to establish uniform input prices across firms, industries, and regions when identically productive inputs are compared. Competitive markets, therefore, tend to lead automatically to "equal pay for equal work." At least, this conclusion is true if we interpret *equal work* to mean equally productive work from the viewpoint of consumers; that is, equal in terms of marginal productivity. The possibility that discrimination by employers may lead to differences in wage rates among groups of workers, an apparent exception to this conclusion, is discussed in Chapter 16.

INPUT PRICE DETERMINATION IN A MULTI-INDUSTRY MARKET
14.6

When several industries compete for the available supply of a particular input, the impact of any one industry on the input's price is likely to be slight since it usually comprises only a small part of the economywide demand. The broader multi-industry conditions of demand and supply determine the input's price. Now we wish to see how a single industry fits into this broader input market and, in particular, to identify the factors that determine the shape and position of the input supply curve confronting each industry.

[3] P. R. P. Coelho and M. A. Ghali, "The End of the North-South Wage Differential," *American Economic Review*, 61 (December 1971): 932–937; and D. Bellante, "The North-South Wage Differential and the Migration of Heterogeneous Labor," *American Economic Review*, 69 (March 1979): 166–175.

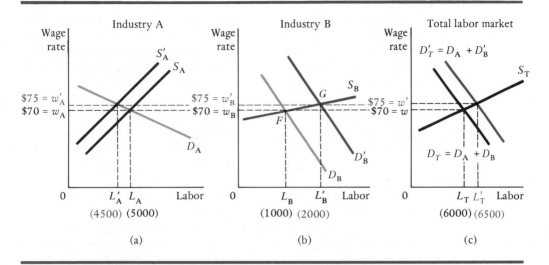

FIGURE 14-8
Input Price Determination in a Multi-industry Setting

Total labor demand D_T is the sum of the demands of industries A and B, and it intersects with total supply S_T in part c to determine the uniform wage rate. In part b the supply curve confronting industry B alone is derived by assuming that D_B increases. Supply curve S_B is highly elastic because industry B is a small part of the total labor market.

Let's consider the hypothetical market for engineers, a group of workers we assume are identical. Several industries employ engineers. Industry B's demand curve for engineers is D_B in Figure 14–8b, and D_A in Figure 14–8a reflects the demand for engineers by all other industries, *excluding* industry B. Think of industry A as a *group* of industries; each has a demand curve for engineers, and their demands are aggregated as D_A. Therefore, A and B together constitute the total market demand for engineers. The total market demand curve for engineers, the sum of D_A and D_B, is D_T in Figure 14–8c. The market supply curve of engineers to all industries together is S_T, and we have drawn it upward sloping on the assumption that higher wage rates will be needed to encourage more people to enter the engineering profession rather than some other. (Note that we are looking at a time period long enough for people to be trained as engineers. In the short run the market supply curve for engineers will be more inelastic.)

The interaction between the number of people willing and able to work as engineers and the total demand for engineers by all firms and industries determines the wage rate for engineers. This interaction is shown in Figure 14–8c, with an equilibrium involving employment of 6000 engineers at a daily wage rate of w, or \$70. Each individual industry will then employ the number of engineers they want at that wage. Industry B will hire 1000 engineers and industry A, 5000, for a total of 6000.

Our primary purpose in this section is to explain what determines the shape of the supply curve of engineers to a particular industry, in this example, industry B. We have already identified one point on this supply curve, point F. At F, 1000 engineers are willing to work in industry B at a wage of \$70. Recall that we derive the supply curve of an *output* for an industry by assuming a shift in the demand curve and tracing the consequences. We can use the same approach here to derive the supply curve of an *input* to an industry; that is, the supply curve of engineers to industry B.

Let's assume that the demand for engineers in industry B increases to D'_B, perhaps because of an increase in consumer demand for the output in industry B. As a result, the total market demand for engineers increases, but the effect on the market demand is proportionately less pronounced because demand has increased in only one segment of the market. With the market demand rising to D'_T (equal to D_A plus the new demand by B, D'_B), the wage rate of engineers is bid up to w', and total employment increases to 6500. At the new wage of \$75, industry B will hire 2000 engineers, at point G. Point G is a second point on the supply curve of engineers to industry B; that is, at \$75, 2000 engineers are willing to work in industry B. In industry A, where the demand curve has not shifted, employment falls to 4500 when the wage rate rises to \$75.

Note that the additional 1000 engineers employed in industry B come partly from industry A, where 500 fewer are employed, and partly from an expansion in the total number of engineers from 6000 to 6500. In effect, as industry B bids for more engineers by offering higher wages, it attracts some engineers from industry A and also induces some new entrants into the engineering profession.

Having derived the supply curve of engineers to industry B, we can understand more easily why the supply curve of an input to a particular industry will normally be highly elastic. In the example given here, when the wage rate in industry B rose from \$70 to \$75, the number of engineers willing to work there increased from 1000 to 2000, implying an elasticity of supply of about 10 (using the formula for arc elasticity). The elasticity of the supply curve of engineers to the total market, however, is only about 1. The reason for this difference is straightforward: industry B is only a part of the market for engineers, and it can bid engineers away from other industries — perhaps only a few from each of dozens of industries — without greatly affecting the general wage level for engineers. The smaller the share of the total market accounted for by industry B, the more elastic is its input supply curve. In our example industry B initially employed a sixth of the total number of engineers, but this proportion rose to nearly a third after the demand increase. In many real world cases a single industry will comprise a much smaller part of the total market, so its input supply curves can easily be perfectly elastic (horizontal). Recall the significance of high input supply elasticities for the elasticity of the output supply curve, as discussed in Sections 9.4 and 9.5.

We should also note that the increase in demand by industry B causes the supply curve of engineers to industry A to shift. An input supply curve to a given industry is based on given demand conditions in other industries (in drawing S_B, we assumed D_A was fixed). When other industries compete more aggressively for inputs, industry A will find its workers being bid away, causing a reduction in input supply to industry A. The result is a higher wage in industry A also. Remember that input prices will be equalized across industries, so industry A will be unable to retain engineers if it pays them less than industry B.

If we were just concerned with industry B, we would only need to consider Figure 14–8b. It is important, however, that we integrate the supply of an input to a particular industry into the broader market for the input, a market that usually contains several industries. Indeed, the concept of an industry — a group of firms producing the same product — was designed primarily to study how output markets work. For that purpose grouping together the firms producing the same product makes sense. Relying on the same classification scheme when analyzing input markets is much less helpful since many different industries compete for the same supply of inputs. The notion of an input market (Figure 14–8c) is more appropriate.

INPUT DEMAND AND EMPLOYMENT BY MONOPOLY
14.7

A monopoly is defined as a firm that is the sole seller of some product, but a firm that has monopoly power in its output market does not necessarily have market power in its input markets. A firm can be the sole seller of a product and still compete with a large number of firms in hiring inputs. In that event the firm is a monopoly in its output market and a competitor in its input markets, the case we will discuss in this section.

Like a competitive firm, a monopoly bases its decisions about input use on the way its profit is affected. A monopoly will expand employment of inputs as long as hiring one more unit adds more to revenues than to costs. The price that must be paid for inputs measures the added costs of employing another unit — just as it did for a competitive firm. The difference in the two market settings rests on the way hiring one or more unit of an input will affect the revenues of the firm.

For a competitive firm, employing one more unit of an input adds an amount equal to the marginal value product to revenues. The marginal value product is the additional output produced multiplied by the price at which it can be sold. For a monopoly one more unit of an input also adds to revenues by expanding output, but revenues do not increase by the price at which the additional output is sold. Recall that to sell more, the monopoly must reduce the price for all its output; that is, the price received for the hundredth unit of output, for example, is greater than its contribution to revenues. Marginal revenue, which is always lower than price, measures the effect on revenues of selling one more unit. Consequently, for a monopoly the contribution to revenues from employing one more unit of an input is the additional output (the marginal product of the input) multiplied by the marginal revenue associated with the additional output. The product of marginal product and marginal revenue is called the *marginal revenue product* of an input. Marginal revenue product measures the contribution to revenues from employing one more unit of the input when the price of the product falls as more is produced.

Consider a situation in which all inputs but labor are fixed in quantity for the firm. In Figure 14–9 the marginal value product curve MVP_L would be the demand curve for the input under competitive conditions, as we explained in Section 14.1. If the firm is a monopoly, the marginal revenue product curve MRP_L is the demand curve for the input. For a monopoly marginal revenue is below price at each level of output and at each level of employment of labor, so the MRP_L curve lies below the MVP_L curve. The monopoly's demand for labor curve, the MRP_L curve, slopes downward for two reasons. First, the marginal physical product of labor declines as more labor is employed (this result is true also for the competitive case). Second, the marginal revenue associated with selling more is also declining as more labor is employed since the additional output can only be sold at a lower price.

In Figure 14–9, at a wage rate of $40, the monopoly would employ $0L_1$ workers. This is the profit-maximizing level of employment. At any lower level of employment the revenues generated by hiring another worker are greater than the costs ($MRP_L > w$ at an employment of less than $0L_1$), so profits increase if employment increases to $0L_1$, where $MRP_L = w$. If the monopoly employed more workers, they would add more to costs (w) than to revenues (MRP_L), and profits would be lower.

The employment of labor, or any other input, is lower under monopolistic conditions than under competitive conditions. Under competition $0L_2$ workers would be employed at the point where $w = MVP_L$; only $0L_1$ workers would be employed under monopoly. This result should come as no surprise since it was already implicit in our conclusion in Chapter 11 that a monopoly produces less output than does a competitive industry. To produce less, it uses fewer inputs. Figure 14–9 therefore depicts the monopolistic reduction in output from the perspective of the input market.

Figure 14–9 also illustrates the welfare cost of monopoly discussed in Section 11.6. The marginal value product of labor measures how much the additional output of one more worker is worth to consumers. At the mo-

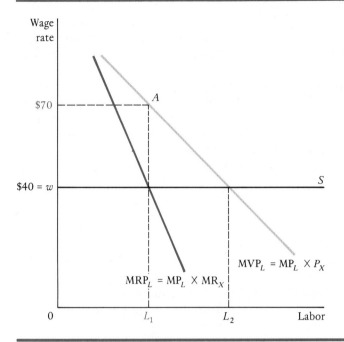

FIGURE 14-9

The Monopolist's Demand for an Input

For one input variable we derive a monopoly's input demand curve by multiplying the input's marginal product by the marginal revenue from selling the commodity produced: $MRP_L = MP_L \times MR_X$. The marginal revenue product curve MRP_L is the monopoly's demand curve, and it lies below the competitive demand curve MVP_L.

nopoly outcome, $0L_1$, MVP_L equals $70, indicating that consumers would be willing to pay more for the services of another worker than it costs the monopolist to hire the worker (the wage of $40). The benefit to consumers of more output is greater than the cost of producing more output, but the monopoly does not hire more workers to expand output. This discussion describes the same welfare cost due to monopoly that was explained in Section 11.6, but it focuses on the input side of the picture.

We can easily extend the preceding analysis of the monopoly demand for inputs to the case where all inputs are variable by proceeding in the same manner as we did for the competitive firm. No significant new conclusions emerge from this analysis. There are still just two important points. First, the input demand curves of a monopoly slope downward, both because marginal productivity of inputs decline and because marginal revenue from selling the output declines as more of any input is hired. Second, the input demand curves of a monopoly are lower than they would be if the output market were competitive.

In the case examined here the wage rate remains the same whether the market is monopolized or competitive. This outcome is implied by the assumption of a horizontal supply curve of the input. Recall that the wage rate is determined by the broader labor market composed of all the demanders of labor, not just by the hiring decisions of the single monopolistic firm. It is possible that a monopoly will be a large enough part of the overall labor market to appreciably affect the wage rate, but it need not be.

MONOPSONY
14.8

Monopsony means "single buyer." A monopsony is a single firm that is the sole purchaser of some type of input. As the sole purchaser, the monopsony faces the *market* supply curve of the input, a curve that is frequently upward sloping. An upward-sloping supply curve means that the monopsonist has market power in the input market and can reduce the price paid without losing all the input.

Monopsony in an input market is therefore analogous to monopoly in output markets. A monopoly has some discretion over the price charged for its output (as determined by the downward-sloping demand curve), while a monopsony has some discretion over the price paid for an input (as determined by the upward-sloping supply curve of the input).

Graphically, an upward-sloping supply curve for an input confronting the firm indicates the presence of monopsony. We'll use labor once more as an example. An upward-sloping supply curve means that the firm must pay a higher wage rate to increase the number of workers it employs. (Up until now we have assumed that every *firm* faces a horizontal supply curve for each input.) When the firm faces an upward-sloping supply curve for labor, the marginal cost of hiring another worker is not equal to the wage rate it must pay to all workers. For example, suppose that the firm employs 10 workers at a wage of $30, but to employ 11 workers, the firm must pay a wage rate of $31 to all 11 workers. The marginal cost of hiring the eleventh worker is therefore $41 because total labor costs rise from $300 to $341 when employment increases by one worker. Put differently, we can think of the wage rate as the average cost of labor, but when the average cost rises as more workers are employed (upward-sloping supply curve), the marginal cost of labor must be greater than average cost. In this case the $31 wage rate is equal to the average cost of labor, or the total wage bill divided by the number of workers, and the marginal cost is $41, or the additional cost of hiring an extra worker.

We can identify the profit-maximizing level of employment of a monopsony by comparing the contribution to revenues from a change in employment with the effect on costs, just as we did in previous cases. Now, however, the effect on costs is determined by the marginal cost of labor, which is not equal to the wage rate. Figure 14–10 illustrates how we determine the profit-maximizing level of employment. The demand curve of the firm indicates the amount that hiring an additional worker adds to revenues. (The demand curve will be the generalized MVP_L curve if the firm is a competitor in its output market; it will be the MRP_L curve if the firm is a monopoly in its output market. It is conceivable that a firm is competitive in its output market and has monopsony power in its labor market although this situation is admittedly unlikely.) The supply curve to the firm slopes upward — the graphical characteristic of monopsony — so the marginal cost of labor curve MC_L lies above the supply curve.

The firm maximizes profits by employing $0L_1$ workers. At that point the marginal cost of labor is equal to the addition to revenues from hiring

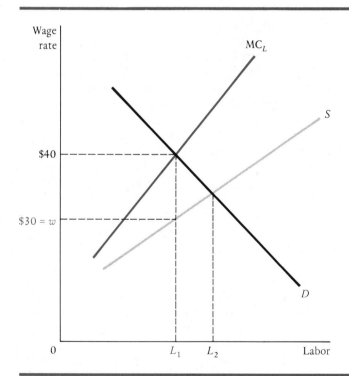

FIGURE 14–10
Monopsony

A monopsony faces an upward-sloping input supply curve, so the marginal cost of employing the input is greater than the input price: MC_L lies above S. The intersection of MC_L and D determines employment, but the wage rate is determined by the height to the supply curve.

one more worker. The firm, however, does not pay an amount equal to the worker's marginal contribution to revenues ($40). Instead, the firm pays a wage of $30. The intersection of MC_L and the demand curve determines the most profitable level of employment, while the wage rate is determined by the height to the supply curve at the corresponding level of employment.

In comparison with competitive input market conditions, employment is lower under monopsony and so is the wage rate paid. If there were competition in the input market in Figure 14–10, employment would be $0L_2$, and the wage would be higher since the supply curve slopes upward. A similarity between monopsony and monopoly is apparent from this conclusion. A monopoly restricts output in order to obtain a higher price; a monopsony restricts employment in order to pay a lower wage. A monopoly is able to charge a higher price because it faces a downward-sloping demand curve; a monopsonist is able to pay a lower wage because it faces an upward-sloping supply curve.

The analysis of monopsony is straightforward. The only difference from previous cases is that the supply curve has a positive slope instead of being horizontal. The more difficult issue is how important this type of input market structure is in the real world. Most economists believe that monopsony in input markets (particularly labor markets) is quite rare, certainly more uncommon than monopoly power in output markets. Very few workers have employment opportunities limited to a single firm. If workers' skills are sufficiently unspecialized that they can work for more than one firm, and if they are willing to change jobs, then the labor market is likely to be competitive, regardless of the size of the firm that initially employs them. Even industrial giants like General Motors, AT&T, and Exxon would lose most of their labor force if they were to cut wages below competitive levels.

Monopsony may arise in certain local labor markets because of geographic immobility of workers. Historically, the "company town" has played a role in fiction, if not in fact. Better transportation now makes it possible for people to work fifty miles or more from the place where they live. Moreover, many workers are willing to relocate to obtain better job opportunities. Remember also that it is unnecessary for all workers to relocate for competition to establish uniform wages among industries, firms, or regions (Section 14.5). Finally, firms could move into regions where wage rates are low, even if the workers can't relocate.

For these reasons the monopsony model probably has little applicability to most input markets. We do not rule out the existence of monopsony since a few cases have been cited in the economics literature, but monopsony is probably not a quantitatively important problem in the American economy. Nonetheless, it is worthwhile to understand how a monopsonist can use its buying power to affect input prices if only because this situation is the counterpart to the selling power of a monopoly.

Summary

In this chapter we saw that a competitive firm's demand curve for any input slopes downward. This result can be shown in two equivalent ways: by focusing on the marginal value product curve and by considering the substitution and output effects of a change in the input's price. We obtained the industry demand curve by aggregating the firms' demand curves, but this summation is not a simple one since the price of the product changes as total industry employment varies.

For the supply of an input, we saw that we must specify the demander or set of demanders involved. The supply curve of an input to a competitive firm is horizontal; the supply curve to an industry may be either horizontal or upward sloping. At the same time the supply curve to the economy as a whole may be quite inelastic.

In competitive markets the interaction of supply and demand determines input prices and employment. Care must be taken, though, to recognize that the relevant input market is frequently broader than a single industry. When many industries employ the same input, the input price tends to be equalized across industries. Moreover, in this case the supply curve of the input to a single industry will be very elastic: any single industry will have little effect on the input price.

Monopolies also have downward-sloping demand curves for inputs, as determined by the marginal revenue product curve. Compared with demand curves for competitive input markets, the monopoly demand curve for an input is lower. This outcome does not necessarily imply that a monopoly will pay lower prices for inputs since it may face horizontal input supply curves and thus have to pay the going market price.

A monopsony is the sole employer of some input, and so faces the market supply curve. If that supply curve slopes upward, the monopsony's employment decision will affect the price of the input: the monopsonist has market power in the input market. In comparison with competitive conditions, employment of an input will be lower, and so will its price, under monopsony.

Review Questions and Problems

1. Using the data in Table 6–2, which relate the output of wheat to the amount of labor when land is fixed, answer the following: If the price of wheat is $5 per bushel and the wage rate is $25, how many workers will be hired?

2. In question 1 suppose the price of wheat is $7 per bushel. How many workers will be hired at a $35 wage rate? At a $25 wage rate? Illustrate your answers to both questions in a diagram like Figure 14–1.

3. Why does a competitive firm's demand curve for an input slope downward? Explain, and compare the two ways of deriving the firm's demand curve.

4. Why can't we simply add up the demand curves of the firms in an industry to obtain the industry demand curve for an input?

*5. If the demand for clothing rises, the productivity of workers engaged in making clothing does not necessarily increase. Why then does the demand for workers increase?

6. Distinguish between the short-run and the long-run supply curves of geologists to the United States economy. Which curve will be more inelastic? Why?

7. Distinguish between the supply curves — either short-run or long-run — of geologists to the United States economy, to the oil industry, and to Exxon Corporation. Which is the most elastic? The least elastic? Why?

8. Discuss the determination of equilibrium input price and employment by a competitive industry. Concerning the equilibrium, firms would prefer to pay a lower price for the input; why don't they? Owners of inputs would prefer to receive a higher

price; why don't they refuse to supply the input unless the price is higher?

*9. "Employers set wage rates equal to marginal value products." True or false? Explain.

*10. "If the supply of labor increases and depresses wages in an industry, this outcome will benefit firms at the expense of workers." True or false? Explain.

*11. Writing about the closing decades of the nineteenth century, C. Vann Woodward observes: "There was nothing but the urging of conscience and the weak protest of labor to keep employers from cutting costs at the expense of their workers." Analyze this statement. Was it conscience that kept wage rates from being zero?

12. Writing in 1881, W. T. Thornton argued: "If among many liberal employers there be one single niggard, the niggardliness of that single one may suffice to neutralize the liberality of the rest. If one single employer succeeds in screwing down wages below the rate previously current, his fellow-employers may have no alternative but to follow suit, or to see themselves undersold in the product market." Why is this conclusion wrong?

13. "Automation destroys jobs and is therefore the enemy of labor." Discuss this issue, explaining how automation affects not only workers in the automated industry but also workers in the industry that produces the equipment and consumers. Does automation make it impossible for any workers to find jobs?

14. Explain why monopoly will employ more of an input when its price is lower in terms of the substitution and output effects of the lower input price. Hint: How would Figure 14–3a and b be different for a monopoly?

*15. Do monopolies cause unemployment?

16. What is a monopsony? Graphically, what distinguishes a monopsony from a competitive employer of inputs? What does this difference imply for the relative levels of employment and input prices under monopsony and under competition?

Supplementary Readings

Alchian, Armen, and Allen, William. *Exchange and Production: Competition, Coordination and Control.* 2nd ed. Belmont, Calif.: Wadsworth, 1977. Chap. 15.

Bronfenbrenner, Martin. *Income Distribution Theory.* Chicago: Aldine-Atherton, 1971.

Lester, Richard. "Shortcomings of Marginal Analysis for Wage-Employment Problems." *American Economic Review,* 36 (March 1946): 63–82.

Machlup, Fritz. "Marginal Analysis and Empirical Research." *American Economic Review,* 36 (September 1946): 519–554.

Wages, Rent, Interest, and Profit

15

The general principles discussed in the last chapter apply to the analysis of the market for any type of input. However, some special issues arise in conjunction with particular input markets, and these deserve further attention. In this chapter we will extend the general analysis to specific input markets to see how wages, rent, interest, and profits are determined. We will continue to emphasize labor markets because of the importance of labor markets in the United States economy. Labor earnings account for 75 to 80 percent of total national income; in contrast, the sum of all other types of income is only 20 to 25 percent of national income. These percentages have been fairly stable for many years. For the overwhelming majority of Americans labor earnings account for the bulk of total family income.

THE INCOME-LEISURE CHOICE OF THE WORKER
15.1

In our discussion of consumer demand in Chapters 2 and 3, we assumed the consumer's income to be fixed. Now we wish to recognize that for most people income is not fixed but depends instead on, among other things, the decision about how much time the person will work. To investigate the worker's decision concerning how many hours of work to supply, we will assume that the individual worker is paid a fixed hourly wage rate and can work any number of hours desired at the given wage.

This analysis utilizes the indifference curve–budget line technique developed earlier in the analysis of consumer choice. In Figure 15–1 the vertical axis measures the individual worker's total weekly income, and the horizontal axis, from left to right, measures the worker's leisure time. The term *leisure* refers to the portion of the worker's time when the individual receives no compensation by an employer. The worker has 168 hours a week available, 24 hours a day, 7 days a week. We will divide this time into two mutually exclusive categories, work and leisure. The working time plus leisure time per week must equal 168 hours. In Figure 15–1, $0N$ is the total time available, and a point like L_1 indicates that the individual consumes $0L_1$ hours of leisure and supplies the remaining time, NL_1

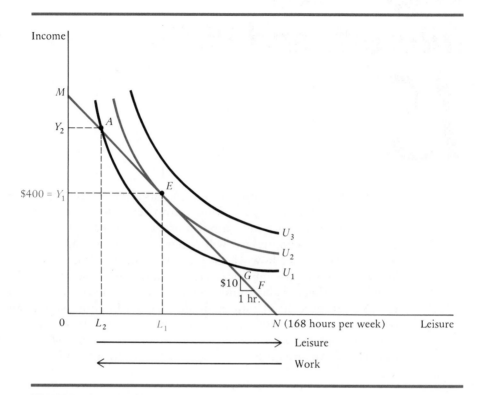

FIGURE 15-1

Income-leisure Choice of the Worker

Measuring leisure from left to right is the same as measuring hours worked from right to left from point N. The budget line MN has a slope equal to the hourly wage rate. Equilibrium is at point E, with the individual working NL₁ hours and earning $400 per week.

hours, to an employer as work effort. Measuring leisure in this way from left to right is therefore equivalent to measuring work effort (hours of labor supplied) to the left from point N.

With income and leisure measured on the axes, a worker's budget line reflects the wage rate received for each hour of work provided. In the diagram the budget line is MN, and it shows the combinations of income and leisure available to the worker. Note that the more hours the individual works (that is, the less leisure time consumed), the higher is the worker's income. For example, if NL_1 hours are worked (leisure of $0L_1$), income is $0Y_1$; but if work effort increases to NL_2 hours (leisure decreases to $0L_2$), income rises to $0Y_2$. If no work is done (point N), income will be zero since we assume that the worker has no nonlabor sources of income. Also observe that the slope of this budget line equals the worker's wage rate. For example, a movement from point F to point G indicates that the worker is providing one more hour of labor (giving up one more hour of leisure) and in return receives an additional $10 in wage income. Thus, the hourly wage rate is $10 per hour.

To the worker, both income and leisure are desirable economic goods. For a given amount of leisure (work), a higher income is preferred to a lower one; and for a given amount of income, less work (more leisure) is preferred to more. As we pointed out in Chapter 2, whenever economic goods are measured on the axes, the indifference curves will have their normal shapes (downward sloping, convex, and nonintersecting). The slope of an indifference curve relating income and leisure measures the willingness of the worker to give up leisure for more money income and therefore indicates the relative importance of these two goods to the individual. Figure 15–1 shows three of the worker's income-leisure indifference curves.

The equilibrium for the worker is at point E since this point represents the most preferred combination of income and leisure from among those on the budget line. Work effort is NL_1 (40 hours per week, for example) and income is $0Y_1$ ($400). As usual, the equilibrium is the point of tangency between the budget line and an indifference curve. In this case the tangency indicates that the subjective marginal valuation of the worker's own leisure time is equal to the market valuation of the individual's work time, the wage rate. At point E the worker must be paid at least $10 to give up one more hour of leisure since the marginal rate of substitution (MRS) between income and leisure is $10 per hour at that point.

In passing, note that we are not assuming that workers maximize their incomes. The worker could earn a higher income by working longer hours, at point A for example. But the extra Y_1Y_2 income is worth less than the L_1L_2 hours of leisure time that must be sacrificed to earn the additional income, as shown by the fact that point A is on a lower indifference curve than point E.

Is This Model Plausible?

The analysis just presented rests on the assumption that the worker is able to choose how many hours to work. A common objection to this analysis is that workers don't really have the ability to vary their work hours. Most employment contracts specify that the worker will work a certain length of time, perhaps 35 hours per week, for example. Even if an individual employee prefers a 30-hour week combined with a one-seventh reduction in pay, the employer may not give the worker the option of choosing a shorter workweek. In short, the argument holds that the workweek is fixed by the employer and beyond the control of the individual worker. There is an element of truth to this point, but it is a less damaging criticism than might be thought at first glance.

One way to justify the assumption of variable work effort is to recognize that most workers can, in fact, exercise some degree of control over how much they work although perhaps not on a daily or weekly basis. Overtime, vacation leave, leaves without pay, moonlighting, sick leave, and early retirement are options available to many workers. At a more basic level each person has a wide range of options in selecting a job in the first place. Some jobs entail long hours, some short, some permit great individual variation in work effort.

Another justification for the variable work effort assumption is that at a more fundamental level the analysis may still be valid for many purposes even if it is impossible for a worker to vary his or her workweek even slightly. Although the employer fixes the workweek, consider the economic factors that determine the level at which it is set. Employers are profit maximizers, and it is therefore in their interest to cater to the preferences of workers, just as they are led by profit motives to cater to the preferences of consumers. If a firm's employees prefer a 35-hour workweek, but the firm requires them to work 45 hours, it will lose workers to other firms that do a better job of satisfying the employees' preferences. Competition among firms for workers thus leads to the setting of workweeks that correspond to what workers want. Consequently, assuming that workers can choose how much they will work should yield a reasonably correct analysis although it does not precisely describe reality.

One qualification should be mentioned. Employers have incentive to cater to workers' preferences on the average, but not necessarily to each separate employee's preferences. For reasons related to the technology of production, most firms must have a common workweek for all employees (though it can, and does, differ among firms). A set workweek means that workers with preferences different from the group average are likely to find the workweek fixed at a level they don't like. Thus, our model may not be especially accurate for any specific worker, but it should provide a solid basis for analyzing work effort decisions by groups of workers.

THE SUPPLY OF HOURS OF WORK
15.2

One important question we can investigate by using this model is, Will workers work longer hours at a higher wage rate? Figure 15–2 examines the effect of a higher wage rate for a particular worker. When the wage rate is $5 per hour, the budget line is MN, and the worker's preferred point is E with NL_1 hours of work supplied (remember that we measure work effort from right to left in the diagram). If the wage rate rises to $8 per hour, the budget line rotates about point N and becomes steeper. The new budget line is $M'N$, with a slope of $8 per hour. Note that at the higher hourly wage, income is greater for any level of work effort. Given the specific preferences of this worker, when confronted with the higher wage rate, the new equilibrium point E' involves an increase in hours of work from NL_1 to NL_2.

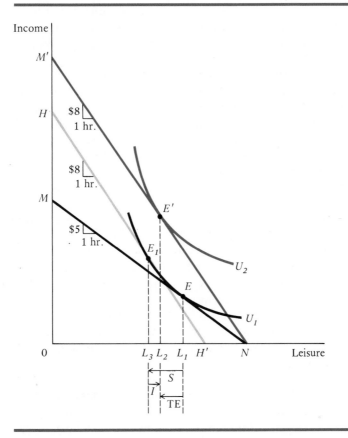

FIGURE 15-2

Worker's Response to a Change in Wage Rates

A higher wage rate shifts the budget line from *MN* to *M'N*, and work effort
increases from *NL₁* to *NL₂*. We show the income and substitution effects of the
change in wage rate by using the hypothetical budget line *HH'* that is parallel to
the *M'N* budget line but just tangent to the initial indifference curve *U₁*. The
substitution effect, *L₁L₃*, involves more work, but the income effect *L₃L₂*, involves
less. In this case the combined effect implies greater work effort at the higher
wage rate.

Does a higher wage rate always lead a worker to work more? As we
shall see, the answer is no, and we can see why by considering the income
and substitution effects associated with a change in the wage rate.

The substitution effect of a higher wage rate encourages a worker to
supply more hours of labor. When the wage rate rises from $5 to $8 per
hour, the sacrifice in consuming leisure increases since each hour of leisure consumed now means giving up $8 in income instead of $5. Since

leisure has become relatively more expensive in terms of forgone income, the worker is encouraged to substitute away from leisure toward income — that is, to work more.

An income effect is also associated with a higher wage rate. A wage increase makes the individual better off, permitting the worker to reach a higher indifference curve. A higher real income tends to increase the consumption of all normal goods, and leisure for most people is a normal good. The income effect of a wage rate increase therefore encourages the consumption of leisure and leads the worker to work less. Because of the higher wage, the worker can afford to work less; it is possible to work fewer hours and still achieve a higher money income than before the wage rate increase.

The substitution effect of a higher wage rate encourages more work, and the income effect encourages less work. Figure 15–2 also identifies the income and substitution effects of a wage rate increase. The hypothetical budget line HH' is drawn tangent to the worker's original indifference curve U_1. Its slope reflects the higher wage rate of \$8. The substitution effect is shown as the movement along U_1 from E to E_1. Because leisure time has become relatively more expensive, the worker consumes less, and work effort increases from NL_1 to NL_3. The income effect is shown as the movement from E_1 to E' when we allow the individual to move from the HH' budget line to the parallel $M'N$ budget line reflecting the increase in real income associated with the rise in the wage rate. Because leisure is a normal good, the pure income effect involves more leisure, from $0L_3$ to $0L_2$, which is the same as saying it encourages less work, NL_2 instead of NL_3. The total effect of the higher wage rate is the sum of the income and substitution effects. Although these effects operate in opposite directions, in this case the substitution effect is larger, so the total effect is an increase in hours of work from NL_1 to NL_2.

Is a Backward-bending Labor Supply Curve Possible?

For the worker whose preferences are depicted in Figure 15–2, we have seen that the supply curve of hours of work would slope upward, at least between wage rates of \$5 and \$8, since a higher wage rate led to a greater quantity of labor supplied. This outcome need not always be the case, though. It is possible for the income effect of a higher wage to be larger than the substitution effect, resulting in a reduction in hours of work at a higher wage rate.

To see intuitively how this can happen, jot down on a piece of paper alternative wage rates from \$5 to \$100 an hour and then beside each wage specify how many hours per week you would choose to work. If you start at 30 or 40 hours a week at the \$5 wage and decide to work longer hours at higher wage rates, you will soon be working 70 hours or more a week. A 70-hour workweek is near the capacity of most people for effective work.

Well before that point you may ask yourself how you will be able to enjoy your high earnings with so little free leisure time. Why not work a little less, take some time off, and enjoy your high income? After all, 30 hours a week at a wage of $30 per hour means more income *and* more leisure time to enjoy it in when compared with 40 hours at a $5 wage. Beyond some wage rate, most people will prefer to work fewer hours, earning more in total but still having more free time to spend that income.

Figure 15–3a shows an individual who would choose to work longer hours when the wage rate increases from $5 to $8 but who then decides to work somewhat less when the wage rises again. When the wage increases from $5 to $8, hours of work increase from NL_1 to NL_2; but at a wage of $11 hours worked fall to NL_3. (We have not separated the income and substitution effects in the diagram, but you may wish to do so yourself.) Figure 15–3b shows the same information but plotted as a labor supply curve of hours of work. The supply curve slopes upward between wage rates of $5 and $8 and bends backward as the wage rate rises further.

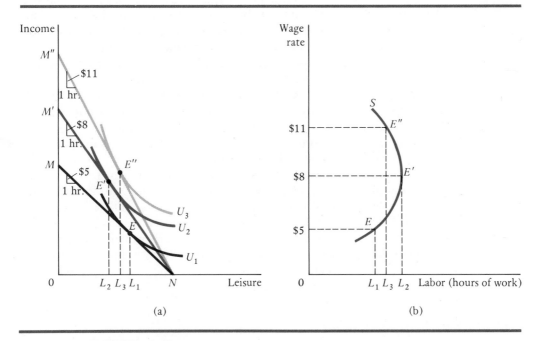

(a) (b)

FIGURE 15–3

Individual Worker's Supply of Hours of Work

(a) An individual's choices of how much to work at three alternative wage rates are represented by E, E', and E''. (b) These labor supply choices are plotted as the supply curve of hours of work. When the income effect exceeds the substitution effect, the supply curve becomes backward bending.

A supply curve of hours of work can therefore be backward bending beyond some wage rate. Note that a backward-bending supply curve of labor does not depend on an unusual combination of circumstances, as an upward-sloping demand curve did; instead it just requires that the normal income effect of a higher wage rate be larger than the substitution effect. Since leisure is a normal good, the income and substitution effects work in opposing directions in this case because the worker is a *seller* of labor services. When the price of something you sell goes up, you are better off (a positive income effect), permitting greater consumption of all goods, including leisure. (In contrast, when the price of something you purchase as a *buyer* increases, you are worse off; the income effect is negative and therefore reinforces the substitution effect.) Moreover, the income effect of a wage rate change is likely to be large relative to the substitution effect since most income derives from providing labor.

Do Pigeons Have Backward-bending Labor Supply Curves?

In Chapter 3 we discussed an experimental study that suggested that the consumption choices of rats can be analyzed using the theory of consumer choice. Animal experiments have also been undertaken to study the labor supply behavior of various animals. One recent study used male White Carneaux pigeons as subjects.[1] The pigeons were confronted with a budget line by making access to a food hopper containing mixed pigeon grains dependent on performance of a job: pecking a response key. The wage rate was changed by varying the number of pecks per payoff, with the payoff being access to the food hopper for three seconds.

The pigeons were found to have backward-bending supply curves like the one shown in Figure 15–3b. At low wage rates the pigeons would work more as the wage was increased, but beyond some level the quantity of labor supplied fell as wages were increased further. In addition, the researchers were able to isolate the income and substitution effects of a change in the wage rate. Lower wage rates produced a substitution effect involving less work effort, even "... in an environment which is designed to promote key pecking [labor supply] since there is little else for the birds to do except preen themselves and walk about."[2] Leisure was also found to be a normal good for pigeons.

The Market Supply Curve

To go from an individual's supply curve of hours of work to the market supply curve, we need only add up (horizontally sum) the responses of all workers competing in a given labor market. Thus, the market supply

[1] Raymond Battalio, Leonard Green, and John Kagel, "Income-Leisure Tradeoffs of Animal Workers," *American Economic Review*, 71 (September 1981): 621–632.
[2] Ibid., p. 630.

curve can also slope upward, bend backward, or show a combination of the two, as illustrated in Figure 15–3b. Theoretical considerations alone do not permit us to predict the exact shape of the market supply curve. A recent survey of the empirical evidence, however, suggests that the aggregate supply curve of hours of work slopes upward (at least for wage rates near present levels), with an elasticity of somewhere between 0.1 and 0.3.[3] An elasticity of 0.1 would mean that a 10 percent increase in the wage rate would increase the quantity of labor supplied by 1 percent. Such an inelastic supply curve would slope upward and be almost vertical.

A highly inelastic aggregate supply curve, as suggested by the empirical evidence, appears plausible. Casual observation suggests that the amount of time most people work does not undergo large changes over moderate periods of time when wage rates change. If individual supply curves were sharply upward sloping or backward bending, we would expect to see substantial changes in individuals' hours of work in particular jobs where market forces have produced large changes in wage rates. Hours of work per worker in most jobs and industries seem to be quite stable over time, suggesting that the effect of changes in wage rates on hours of work is not pronounced. This result does not mean that people are completely unresponsive to changes in wage rates, only that the responses that do occur are modest.

When should we use the aggregate labor supply curve? In the last chapter we emphasized that the labor supply curve *to a particular industry or occupation* is likely to slope upward and be quite elastic. We must distinguish that type of labor supply curve, however, from the one discussed here. In looking at the supply to an industry or occupation, we see that the quantity of labor services *can* increase sharply with a rise in the wage rate in that job, but the increase results mainly from an influx of workers from other jobs or industries and not from a change in hours of work of current workers. The supply curve of labor to a specific job or industry therefore depends mainly on how the number of workers varies with wage rates in those specific occupations.

The aggregate supply curve of hours of work is used in cases where the movement of workers among jobs is not likely to be important but the possible change in the amount of work done by workers in their current jobs is. For example, how would a 10 percent increase in all wage rates affect the total quantity of labor supplied? Since all jobs will pay proportionately more, people will have little or no incentive to change jobs. The only way the total labor supply will increase, therefore, is if people work longer hours (which includes the possiblity that some people will enter the labor force for the first time at the higher wage rate). For this type of aggregate analysis, which involves the total quantity of labor supplied aggregated across all industries, the market supply curve of hours of work is

---

[3] Congressional Budget Office, *An Analysis of the Roth-Kemp Tax Cut Proposal* (Washington, D.C.: U.S. Government Printing Office, October 1978).

appropriate. We will discuss an example using this supply curve in the next section and will offer several more examples in Chapter 16.

THE GENERAL LEVEL OF WAGE RATES
15.3

In analyzing further the determination of wage rates, we will find it convenient to divide the subject into two parts: the determination of the general level of wage rates and a consideration of why wage rates differ widely among jobs. In this section we will concentrate on the factors that influence the level of real wages, or the average wage rate; we defer until the next section a discussion of the factors that cause a variation in wage rates around the average.

Supply and demand are still the organizing concepts used when investigating the level of wage rates. The supply curve of labor for this problem should indicate the total quantity of labor services that will be supplied by all persons at various wage levels. The appropriate supply concept is therefore the aggregate supply curve of hours of work discussed in the previous section. For reasons given there, this supply curve is probably quite inelastic, like curve S_1 in Figure 15–4.

The aggregate demand curve for labor reflects the marginal productivity of labor to the economy as a whole. Indeed, it is convenient for this analysis to think of the wage rate as being paid in units of national output (each unit composed of the combination of goods and services consumed by the average person) to emphasize that we are dealing with the level of *real* wage rates. In constructing the demand curve relevant for a particular time period we must hold the following factors constant: the amount of real capital available (including land, buildings, equipment, roads, and so on), the level of technology, and the skills, knowledge, and health of the labor force. If these factors are fixed, an increase in the total quantity of labor is subject to the law of diminishing marginal returns. As a consequence, the aggregate marginal product curve will slope downward, and this curve is the aggregate demand curve for labor.

At a particular time, if the supply curve is S_1 and the demand curve is D_1 in Figure 15–4, then the (average) real wage rate is w_1 and employment is $0L_1$. At the high degree of aggregation used in this analysis, the model is necessarily abstract and ignores a multitude of factors that could conceivably have some effect on the positions of the demand or supply curves. Yet it serves to highlight the central importance of the productivity of labor in influencing the level of wages. National output and national income are two sides of the same coin, and with labor receiving about 80 percent of national income (output), it is clear that the factors that determine the level of output produced from a given quantity of labor play a central role in the analysis. These factors are primarily (but not exclusively) technology, the skill level of the labor force, and the amounts of other inputs, which in this example we will refer to as "capital."

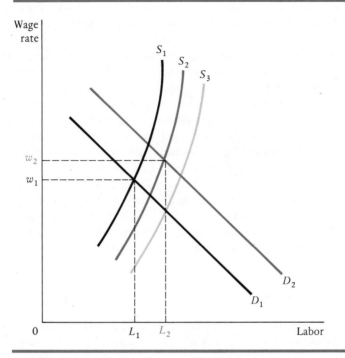

FIGURE 15-4

Determination of the General Wage Level

The aggregate demand curve for labor interacts with the aggregate supply curve to determine the general level of wage rates. Over time, normally both supply and demand increase. If demand increases faster than supply, wage rates tend to rise over time.

This analysis explains why real wage rates are so much higher in the United States than in the less developed countries — the (marginal) productivity of labor is greater. Marginal productivity is higher because of the factors that determine the position of the demand curve: capital, technology, and skills. In United States manufacturing industries the amount of capital per worker was about $60,000 in 1980, which contributes to a high average and marginal productivity of labor. Technological knowledge is superior, and the labor force is well educated and highly skilled by international standards. Consequently, output per worker is much higher in the United States. Other factors, such as climate, efficiency of the economic system in allocating the available resources, the degree of political stability, and attitudes toward work, also play a role in determining national real wage levels. And we can analyze their influence on the productivity of the labor force by examining the way they affect the positions of the demand or supply curves.

Over time, the positions of both the demand and supply curves will generally change. Because of saving and investment, the amount of capital tends to grow over time, and this shifts the demand curve outward: more capital per worker at each level of employment increases marginal productivity. Similarly, technological progress and improvements in the skill level of the labor force also increase marginal productivity. On the supply side the supply curve shifts to the right as the population grows over time. Whether or not these changes lead to rising or falling real wage rates over time depends on how much demand shifts relative to supply. In Figure 15–4, if demand increases relatively more, to D_2, while supply increases to S_2, the real wage goes up to w_2. Historically, this outcome has been the experience in most industrial countries over the past two centuries. Because of capital accumulation, technological progress, and workers with greater skills, the demand for labor has increased faster than the supply, pulling real wages and living standards up in the process. Unfortunately, this happy outcome is not inevitable.

The Malaise of the 1970s

To most Americans, who had become accustomed to uninterrupted economic progress since the 1930s, the decade of the 1970s was a shock. Foremost among the many economic woes of the last decade was a failure of the incomes of many families to keep pace with inflation. Median family income in constant dollars increased by 33 percent during the 1950s and by another 33 percent in the 1960s. In the 1970s, however, real median family income increased less than 1 percent before taxes. After taxes were paid, many families had lost ground.

What went wrong with the American economy in the 1970s? Observers point out a variety of possible culprits: inflation, government deficits, higher energy prices, rising taxes, reduced national saving and investment, Japanese imports, increased government regulation, and others. The basic problem was a failure of the real wage rates to rise as much as they had in previous decades. Thus, an explanation of the situation should concentrate on what happened to the supply of and demand for labor. Focusing on supply and demand conditions doesn't rule out the possibility that some of the factors mentioned above could have caused wages to grow less rapidly, but it suggests that a major role may have been played by a factor that most commentators failed to recognize.

During the 1970s the United States labor force grew by an unprecedented amount. Following increases of 12 percent in the 1950s and 19 percent in the 1960s, the labor force increased by more than 29 percent in the 1970s. In absolute terms the labor force grew from 82.8 million persons in 1970 to 106.9 million in 1980, an increase of more than 24 million — the largest increase on record in a single decade. Referring to Figure 15–4, we can see what the consequences of such a large increase in the labor force would be. If the normal increase in supply due to labor force growth over a decade is from S_1 to S_2 (by about 15 percent, for example), then the increase during the 1970s would be shown as the much greater shift in labor supply from S_1 to S_3. With the same increase in demand from D_1 to D_2, the greater-than-normal increase in labor supply means that over that period wage rates would not rise nearly as much as usual, or might not rise at all.

Table 15–1 provides data on the growth in the labor force and real hourly earnings for the 1950–1980 period. The labor force began to grow more rapidly in the 1960s, and real wages rose less than they had in the previous decade. The large increase in the labor force in the 1970s was associated with a 2.3 percent decrease in real wages over the entire decade. Simple supply and demand forces were at work.

The increase in the labor force in the 1970s was primarily the result of two factors. First, the number of young persons reaching working age during the decade was unusually large. The "baby boom" generation of the 1950s had grown up. Second, the percentage of females in the labor force increased from 43.3 percent in 1970 to 51.5 percent in 1980. (The labor force participation rate of females never exceeded 40 percent before 1966.) Each of these factors was significant in itself, but together they spelled an unusually large increase in labor supply. Labor markets, however, adjusted to accommodate this influx of workers, and employment increased by millions more than it had in any previous decade. But the relatively large shift in supply meant that wage rates rose less than they had in previous decades.

What roles did inflation, energy prices, decreased saving and investment, and the other factors so frequently mentioned play in affecting the growth in real wage rates? Several of these factors would have caused the demand for labor to grow less rapidly than it had in previous decades and therefore would have reinforced the tendency for wage rates to rise more

TABLE 15–1

Size of Labor Force and Wage Rates

Year	Labor Force (millions)	Increase Over Previous Period (percentage)	Index of Real Hourly Earnings (1977 = 100)	Increase Over Previous Period (percentage)
1950	62.2	—	64.0	—
1960	69.6	11.9	81.4	27.2
1970	82.8	19.0	95.7	17.6
1980	106.9	29.1	93.5	− 2.3

Source: Economic Report of the President, 1982, Tables B–29 and B–38.

slowly. For example, a reduced rate of investment and a higher price of oil — an input we purchase in large quantities from other countries — would both operate to depress the rate of increase in labor demand. On the other hand, theory suggests that some of the other factors frequently mentioned, like inflation and higher imports of consumer goods from Japan, would have little effect since they do not significantly affect productivity. The exact quantitative contribution of each of these factors to the slowdown in the growth of real wages is an unresolved issue and has been the subject of much debate in recent economic literature.[4]

The major points emphasized here still remain valid — namely, that the supply and demand model is the correct way to approach the question, and that the massive increase in the number of workers in the labor force in the 1970s had a significant impact on real wages.

WHY WAGES DIFFER
15.4

From the market forces that determine the general level of wage rates, we turn now to the question of why there is such wide variation in the wage rates received by different individuals. In Section 14.5 we explained why there is a tendency for wage rates among firms or industries to equalize. That analysis depended on the assumption that workers were identical and that they evaluated the desirability of the jobs only in terms of the money wage rates. Dropping these assumptions, as we must for a fuller understanding of labor markets, leads to the conclusion that wage rates can differ among jobs and among people employed in the same line of work. People are different, both in the type of work they are able to perform and in the type of work they are willing to perform, and these differences on the supply side of labor markets produce differences in wage rates.

Perhaps the best way to see what is involved is to take a hypothetical, but plausible, example. Figure 15–5a shows the labor market for clerks, and Figure 15–5b shows the labor market for engineers. As drawn, the intersection of supply and demand in each market yields a wage rate for engineers that is twice that for clerks. We suggest that these markets are in full equilibrium with no tendency for the wage rates to equalize. Is this result possible, and if so, why? Why don't some clerks leave their low-paying jobs and become engineers, a movement that would tend to equalize wage rates in the two occupations? Why don't employers of engineers seek out workers presently employed as clerks and offer them better-paying (but at wage rates slightly below w_E) jobs as engineers since their demand curve indicates they would be willing to hire more engineers at a lower wage?

[4] See "The Productivity Growth Slowdown," *American Economic Review*, 71 (May 1981): 314–331, and the papers cited there.

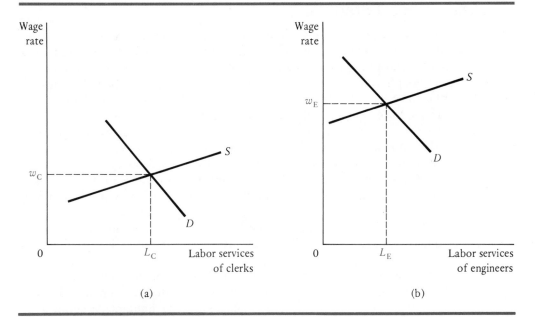

FIGURE 15-5

Equilibrium Wage Differences

(a) The labor market for clerks results in wage rate w_C. (b) The labor market for engineers results in wage rate w_E. Although the wage rate for engineers is higher, there is no tendency for these wage rates to equalize: they are equilibrium wage differences.

Thinking about these questions suggests several possible answers. First, workers currently employed as clerks may prefer their current jobs despite the financial difference; that is, they don't want to work as engineers. Second, acquiring the skills to become an engineer may have a significant cost. The wage for engineers may not be sufficiently high to compensate clerks for the training costs they would have to bear to become engineers. Third, even if there were no training costs, clerks may not have the aptitude for science and mathematics necessary to work as engineers.

These three reasons correspond to the more important causes of differences in wage rates that economists have identified. Where operative, these factors lead to wage rates that differ among persons and jobs. We refer to these differences as *equilibrium differences in wage rates* because there is no tendency for adjustments to occur that would wipe out wage differentials due to these factors. Now let's take a somewhat more detailed look at these factors.

Equalizing Wage Differentials

Monetary considerations aside, the innate attractiveness of jobs varies widely. The monetary compensation is not the only factor, and sometimes not the most important factor, that influences the job choices of individuals. People routinely make decisions to take jobs that pay them less in monetary terms than they could earn elsewhere. Many academic economists, for example, could earn 50 percent more working for government or industry, but they choose to remain in academic surroundings. Similarly, some people might agree to work at the same job for less money if they could live in the Sun Belt instead of the Northeast.

When workers view some jobs as intrinsically more attractive (or less unattractive) than other jobs, supply and demand forces produce differences in the money wage rates paid. These differences are called *equalizing wage differentials* because the less attractive jobs must pay more to equalize the real (monetary and nonmonetary) advantages of employment among the jobs.

An example will illustrate the implications of differences in job attractiveness. Suppose a certain number of potential workers are identical in their abilities to work as police officers or fire fighters. At equal wage rates, they would all prefer to be fire fighters, perhaps because they think police work is more dangerous. Only if the wage rate for police work is at least 25 percent higher than the wage paid fire fighters would they choose to enter the police force. If market conditions determine wage rates, then wage rates for police officers will be 25 percent higher than those for fire fighters. Only then would the *real* wage, in the eyes of the workers, be the same for the two jobs.

Differences in money wage rates are necessary to equate the quantity of labor supplied and demanded in different occupations when the nonmonetary attractiveness of jobs differs. Some cities have ignored this fact and have set the same wage rates for police officers and fire fighters. The outcome? There are more than enough applicants for the fire fighters' positions (a surplus) while the cities are unable to attract enough people to work in the police force (a shortage).

Differences in Human Capital Investment

Our ability to perform useful services is not fixed but can be augmented through training, education, and experience. People can become more productive workers, and more productive workers receive higher wage rates. The process by which people augment their earning capacity is sometimes called *human capital investment.* Human beings are viewed as capable of generating a flow of productive services over time, much as capital assets can. When they bear the costs of training or education themselves, they are investing in their own earning capacity by attempting to increase the productive services they can provide as workers.

Education and training are much like other investments. Initially people incur costs. For those attending college the costs include tuition, fees, and more importantly, the sacrificed income they could have earned by working. (Forgone earnings are an opportunity cost of education.) The payoff to the investment comes several years later; then you find out how profitable the investment was. If earning capacity has increased, the higher earnings in later years will cover the initial costs of the investment. No student needs to be told that this form of investment, just like many others, is risky.

Jobs that require a great deal of training or formal education — large human capital investments — will tend to pay higher wage rates. The reason is simple: if the wage rates weren't higher, few people would be willing to incur the necessary training costs. The higher wage rates associated with highly skilled work are in part the return on past investments in human capital. According to this view, it is no accident that college graduates on average earn more than high school graduates and that neurosurgeons earn more than typists.

In terms of our labor supply-demand model, the supply curve tells us that the amount of labor supplied to jobs that require large investments in human capital will be forthcoming only at higher wage rates. Thus in Figure 15–5 the supply curve of engineers is positioned higher (vertically) than the supply curve for clerks.

Differences in Ability

The productive capacity of a person depends not only on the amount of training and experience (human capital investment) but also on certain inherited traits. The relative importance of these two factors is greatly disputed. For years people have debated whether genetic or environmental factors are more important in explaining IQs. There is no doubt, however, that inherited abilities play a significant role in determining what we are capable of doing. No amount of training would allow some of us to become nuclear physicists, basketball stars, entertainers, models, politicians, or business executives. People differ in strength, stamina, height, mental ability, physical attractiveness, motivation, creativity, and numerous other respects. These characteristics, or the lack of them, have a bearing on the work we are capable of accomplishing or of learning to accomplish.

Possessing abilities that are scarce is no guarantee of a high wage. For example, the ability to wiggle your ears may be unique, but it is unlikely to generate a high income. What matters is the supply of persons with abilities required to perform certain jobs relative to the demand for their services. If consumers were not willing to pay to watch athletes throw balls through a hoop, being able to slam-dunk in twelve different ways would not command a million dollar salary. It is obvious, then, that some human characteristics are in limited supply relative to demand, and the result is that those endowed with such characteristics will be able to command higher wage rates.

The three factors discussed here produce equilibrium differences in wage rates, but the relative importance of each of these factors is generally difficult to determine precisely. What is clear is that when wage differentials persist over time — suggesting that the individual labor markets are in equilibrium, with no shortages or surpluses at the going wage rates — one or more of these factors are likely to be responsible.

ECONOMIC RENT
15.5

In ordinary usage the term *rent* refers to payments made to lease the services of land, apartments, equipment, or some other durable asset. Economists frequently use the term differently. *Economic rent* is defined as that portion of the payment to the supplier of an input that is in excess of the minimum amount necessary to retain the input in its present use.

In the history of economics the term *rent* was originally associated with the payments to landowners for the services of their land. To see why, let's suppose that the supply of land to the economy is fixed, so its supply curve is vertical. (This assumption is a slight exaggeration since the supply of usable land is not absolutely fixed; without care land can erode, become overgrown, or lose its fertility.) A vertical supply curve means that the owners of land would place the same quantity on the market regardless of its price. Even at a zero price the same amount of land would be available. Thus, the minimum payment necessary to retain land in use is zero, and any actual payment above zero exceeds the minimum amount necessary to call forth the supply. *All the payments to the owners of land would therefore satisfy the definition of economic rent.*

Figure 15–6 illustrates this point. The vertical supply curve of land interacts with the demand curve for the services of land to determine its price. The price and quantity are specified per month to indicate that we are not concerned with the sale price of the land but with the price for the services yielded by the use of land. The shaded area indicates the monthly income received by the suppliers of the input.[5] The shaded area also equals the economic rent received by landowners, because all payments for the services of land exceed the (zero) amount necessary to have a supply of $0Q$. The position of the demand curve determines the amount

---

[5] In practice, owners frequently do not receive the income from the use of their land in monetary form. Homeowners, for example, secure the services of the land on which their houses rest. Since they own the land, the income from its use is in the form of these services directly received, but these services have a monetary value determined by supply and demand.

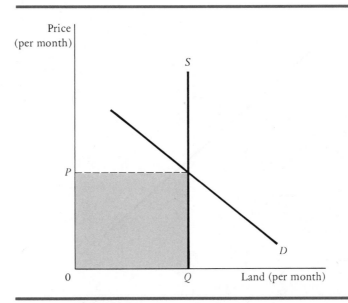

FIGURE 15–6

Economic Rent with Vertical Supply Curve

When the supply curve of an input is vertical, the entire remuneration of the input (the shaded area) represents economic rent since the same quantity would be available even at a zero price.

of economic rent. If demand increased, the price of the services of land would rise and the shaded area would be larger, but the larger shaded area would still be all rent.

Because the economists of the nineteenth century regarded the supply of land as fixed, they viewed the payments to landowners as economic rents. Today economists recognize that the suppliers of other inputs may receive rents as well. The prices received by the owners of any input in fixed supply are entirely rent, and part of the prices received by inputs with upward-sloping supply curves are also rents. Consider the supply of college professors. For clarity we will examine the discrete case involving a small number of persons. The supply curve is then the steplike relationship in Figure 15–7. In equilibrium five professors are working: individuals A, B, C, D, and E. They are assumed identical in their productivities as professors but not identical in their abilities to perform other jobs.

Individual A will be *willing* to work as a professor if paid the area A_1. Even at a very low wage he would choose to become a professor because his best employment opportunity elsewhere is as a dishwasher where he would earn very little. Individual B has a better alternative; she could sell used cars. She will work in academe if she receives at least area B_1. And so

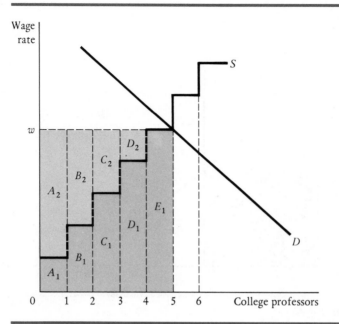

FIGURE 15-7
Economic Rent with an Upward-sloping Supply Curve
With an upward-sloping input supply curve, part of the payment to input owners represents rent. In this case individuals A, B, C, and D receive rents equal to areas A_2, B_2, C_2, and D_2, respectively.

we progress up the supply curve. The supply curve slopes upward because to attract more people, the college must bid them away from more and more attractive alternative employments.

When this labor market is in equilibrium, individuals A to E will all be paid a wage of w. A wage equal to w means that professor A will receive an amount greater than the minimum amount necessary to induce him to work as a professor. Recall that the minimum amount is area A_1, but he is being paid area A_1 plus area A_2, so area A_2 represents an economic rent. Professors B, C, D, and E receive rents equal to areas B_2, C_2, D_2, and zero, respectively. Professor E receives just enough pay to induce him to supply his services as a professor. If the wage were any lower, he would work elsewhere, so none of his earnings represents rent.

In this example part of the earnings of professors (except for E) are economic rents, and the remainder is the payment required to keep the professors from leaving their academic jobs and working elsewhere. The total rent received is the sum of the shaded areas. Whenever the supply curve of any input slopes upward, part of the payments to inputs will be rents, as in this example. The more inelastic the supply curve, the larger rents are as a fraction of total payments. In the extreme case of perfectly inelastic supply (Figure 15–6), all the payments represent rent.

Rents are the net benefits received by owners of inputs from their current employment. They measure the extent to which input owners gain from selling their services in a particular input market: the gains from voluntary exchange. Rent to the owner of an input is thus analogous to consumer surplus for a consumer (Section 4.7). Most input suppliers receive rents. Whenever musicians, journalists, or politicians say they like their present jobs so much they would continue to do them for nothing (usually an exaggeration), they are saying their earnings are entirely rents.

Rent is an ambiguous concept. As we emphasized in the last chapter, there is no such thing as *the* unique supply curve of an input. We have to specify the supply to particular uses. If we are speaking of the supply of labor to the economy as a whole, that supply curve is quite inelastic, indicating that almost all labor earnings are rent. The supply to one job or industry, however, will be quite elastic, suggesting that rents are small. The amount of rent therefore varies, depending on the alternatives. In the analysis of the supply of labor to all industries together, the alternative is no employment and a significant loss, so the rent is large. In the analysis of the supply of labor to one industry, the alternative is employment in other industries, generally at the same or only slightly lower wages, so the rent is small.

BORROWING, LENDING, AND THE INTEREST RATE
15.6

In economics the term *interest rate* is used with two apparently different meanings. The interest rate sometimes refers to the price paid by borrowers for the use of funds. When a person borrows $100 this year and must return $110 to the lender a year later, the additional $10 is interest; and the ratio of the interest to the principal amount, 10 percent, is the annual interest rate. The interest rate can also refer to the rate of return earned by capital as an input in the production process. When a person purchases a machine for $5,000, and the use of that machine generates $500 in income each year thereafter, the rate of return is 10 percent. The reasons economists frequently designate both the return on loaned funds and the return on invested capital as interest rates is that there is a tendency for those rates of return to become equal.

To begin our discussion of the determinants of the interest rate, we will use a highly simplified example. Let's suppose that no capital investment is taking place; that is, no investors are using borrowed funds to finance building construction or equipment purchases. Although there is no borrowing for investment purposes, there will still be people who wish to lend money and others who wish to borrow. Households whose current incomes are high in comparison with their expected future incomes may be willing to lend some of their current income to others and use the repayment of the loan to augment their otherwise lower ability to consume in the future. Other households may wish to borrow in order to consume more than their current income in the present, repaying the loan in the future. (Households may, of course, have other reasons for wishing to borrow or lend.) These households are the potential suppliers and demanders of consumption loans, and their interaction will determine a price, or interest rate, for borrowed funds.

The level of the interest rate affects both the supply of loanable funds and the demand for them. The suppliers of funds are saving — that is, consuming less than their current income permits. As we saw in Section 4.6, a higher interest rate has opposing income and substitution effects on the amount saved. The substitution effect of a higher interest rate encourages less present consumption (more saving) because each dollar saved will return more in the future. The income effect of a higher interest rate, however, increases the real incomes of savers, encouraging more present consumption (less saving). On balance, a higher interest rate may lead to more or less saving. The supply of loanable funds from savers is likely to slope upward at low interest rates but could become backward bending at sufficiently high interest rates. This curve is analogous to the supply curve of hours of work.

On the other side of the market, the demand curve for funds from borrowers must slope downward. To a borrower, a higher interest rate has income and substitution effects that both reduce the level of desired borrowing. The substitution effect reflects the fact that a higher interest rate makes it more expensive to finance increased consumption from borrowed funds, which inhibits borrowing. The income effect reflects the fact that a higher interest rate reduces the real income of borrowers, so they cannot afford to borrow as much.

Figure 15–8 illustrates the interaction of borrowers and lenders in the market for consumption loans. The supply of saving (funds to lend) is S_S, and the demand for these funds by borrowers for consumption purposes is D_C. Equilibrium occurs when lenders provide \$10 million to borrowers in the present time period, with borrowers agreeing to repay the loans at an interest rate of 5 percent.

Even though in this simplified example the funds saved are not used in a way that increases the output of goods and services through capital accumulation, saving is productive. Saving provides the means for borrowers to attain a consumption pattern over time that is more to their liking than having to live within their current incomes each year, and these preferences explain why borrowers are willing to pay for the use of borrowed funds. A positive interest rate emerges because lenders must receive compensation for sacrificing their use of the funds for present consumption.

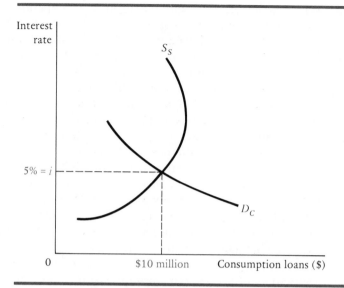

FIGURE 15–8

A Borrowing-lending Equilibrium

If there is no investment demand for funds, the demand for consumption loans and the supply of saving determine the interest rate. Here people borrow $10 million to finance present consumption with the commitment to repay it plus 5 percent interest.

INVESTMENT AND THE MARGINAL PRODUCTIVITY OF CAPITAL

15.7

In the consumption loan example the only outlet for the funds supplied by savers was the borrowing by other households to finance consumption. Now let's expand the analysis to account for the fact that saving also provides funds used to finance investments. Firms may borrow money for the purpose of enlarging their stock of capital equipment, and they must compete for the limited supply of saving with households that are borrowing to finance consumption.

Why are firms willing to incur interest costs to finance investments in capital? Basically, the reason is that capital contributes sufficiently to production to repay the interest costs. The important notion of the productivity of capital can be illustrated with a simple example. If Robinson Crusoe fishes by hand, he may be able to catch 20 fish per week. If he takes one week off to weave a net, he can then catch 25 fish a week with the net until it wears out, in 10 weeks. The 5 additional fish caught per week for 10 weeks (50 fish) is a measure of the *gross marginal productivity* of the net. Whether the net (the capital) is productive depends on balancing the gain in output against the cost of constructing the net. Since Crusoe could have caught 20 fish during the week he constructed his net, the cost of the net is a sacrifice of 20 fish. By sacrificing 20 fish during week 1, however, he gains 50 more fish during weeks 2 to 11, representing a net gain of 30 fish. In this example capital — the net — is productive in the sense that its *net* (no pun intended) *marginal productivity* is 30 fish. When capital's net marginal productivity is positive, investment — the act of adding to the amount of capital — makes it possible to produce a larger output even after "netting" out the cost of the capital.

Next we need a measure for the net productivity of investment in capital that allows us to compare the productivity of various projects. The annual percentage rate of return is convenient for this purpose. Suppose a machine costs $100 to construct this year and its use next year will add $120 to output. For simplicity we will let the machine wear out after one year's use. Then the net gain is $20 in one year, an annual rate of return on the initial $100 investment of 20 percent. The 20 percent figure is the net marginal productivity of investment, and it measures how much the capital investment will add to output one year hence per unit of present cost. It is essentially the rate of return on the investment. Denoting this rate of return measure of productivity by g, we calculate it from the formula

$$C = R/(1 + g) \qquad \text{or} \qquad \$100 = \$120/(1 + g), \tag{1}$$

where C is the initial cost and R is the resulting addition to output (capital's gross marginal value product) the next year.

When capital equipment yields services over more than one year, the normal case, the principle is the same but the formula is slightly more complicated. Suppose the equipment lasts for two years before wearing out and adds $60 to the output in the first year (R_1) and $81 in the second year ($R_2$). Then we calculate the rate of return from

$$C = [R_1/(1 + g)] + [R_2/(1 + g)^2] \tag{2}$$

or

$$\$100 = [\$60/(1 + g)] + [\$81/(1 + g)^2].$$

Given the initial cost of the equipment and the contribution to output in each year, we can solve this expression for g. In this example the rate of return is 0.25, or 25 percent per year.[6]

The Investment Demand Curve

The net productivity of an investment in capital, g, depends on the value of additional output generated (the R terms) and on the initial cost (the C term). In turn, the C and R terms depend on many factors, among them

[6] In the general case where the equipment lasts n years, the formula is
$$C = [R_1/(1 + g)] + [R_2/(1 + g)^2] + [R_3/(1 + g)^3] + \cdots + [R_n/(1 + g)^n].$$

the size and skills of the labor force, the amount and costs of other inputs such as natural resources, technology, and the degree of political stability. When we hold these other factors constant, the net productivity of investment also depends on the rate of investment undertaken per time period. The greater the rate of investment, the lower is the net *marginal* productivity of still more investment.

Consider the rate of aggregate investment for the economy as a whole. As investment increases, each additional dollar's worth of capital will add less to output than the previous dollar's worth because of the law of diminishing marginal returns; that is, more capital applied to a given labor force and quantity of land causes its marginal physical product to decline. This reduces the R terms in the formula and contributes to a lower rate of return. In addition, an increase in investment also means more demand for machinery, vehicles, buildings, and other types of capital, which will tend to raise their prices. This increases the initial cost of investment, the C term, and also contributes to a lower rate of return.

Taken together, these factors imply that a lower rate of return will be associated with a greater amount of investment, other things being equal. The downward-sloping D_I curve in Figure 15–9 illustrates this concept.

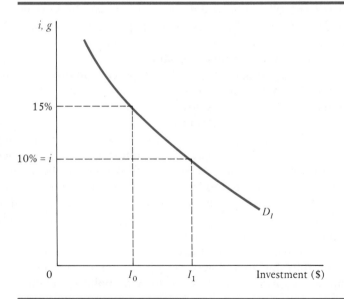

FIGURE 15–9
Investment Demand Curve
The D_I curve shows the rate of return generated by each alternative level of investment. It is the investment demand curve, and it shows the amount invested at each interest rate.

When investment is at a level of $0I_0$, g is equal to 15 percent. If investment increases to $0I_1$, the rate of return on invested capital falls to 10 percent.

The D_I curve, indicating the rate of return generated by investment at different levels, is the *investment demand curve*. This idea is easiest to understand if we suppose that firms (and individuals) finance their investment by borrowing. If the interest rate is 10 percent, investment will expand to $0I_1$, where the return on the investment just covers the cost of the borrowed funds. At any lower level of investment, $0I_0$, for example, the rate of return on investment will be 15 percent, yielding a pure economic profit to the firms and individuals who are only paying 10 percent for the funds they are investing. An expansion in investment in capital will occur as long as the rate of return is greater than the cost of borrowed funds, and such an expansion causes the rate of return to fall. Equilibrium results when investments yield a return just sufficient to cover the interest rate on borrowed funds, at $0I_1$ when the interest rate is 10 percent. *Thus, the rate of return on investment in capital tends to become equal to the interest rate for borrowed funds.*

Even if firms choose not to finance their investment activities by borrowing, $0I_1$ will still be the equilibrium level of investment when the interest rate is 10 percent. A firm with $1 million in retained earnings could use this sum to finance the acquisition of equipment, but it would not purchase more equipment unless the firm expected the investment to yield at least 10 percent. Why? Because the firm could loan the $1 million at the 10 percent interest rate; if the investment project yields less than 10 percent, the firm can do better by lending funds rather than investing them. The opportunity cost of investing is the same whether the funds are borrowed or acquired in any other way, so the 10 percent interest rate will guide investment decisions in either case.

We have been discussing investment decisions assuming firms and individuals know the rate of return that would be generated by investments in capital. In most cases they do not since the yields depend on what happens in the future. The investment demand curve reflects what investors *expect* the outcome of investment projects to be. After the fact, some investments expected to yield 10 percent will fail to, and others will do better. For given expectations on the part of actual and potential investors, the demand curve will still slope downward. A change in expectations will cause the entire curve to shift. If investors expect nationalization of industry or violent revolution to occur in a country, the demand will shift far to the left, which is one reason many firms are reluctant to invest in countries with unstable political regimes.

SAVING, INVESTMENT, AND THE INTEREST RATE
15.8

Households with a demand for consumer loans and firms and persons with investment projects compete for funds supplied by savers. So far we have discussed these elements separately; Figure 15–10 brings them to-

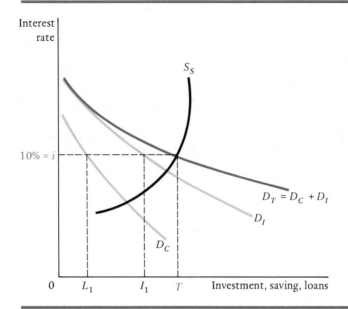

FIGURE 15-10
Determination of the Equilibrium Levels of Saving, Investment, and the Interest Rate

The total demand for funds supplied by savers, D_T, is the sum of the investment demand curve, D_I, and the demand for consumer loans, D_C. The intersection of D_T and S_S determine the interest rate. Investment is $0I_1$, saving is $0T$, and consumption loans are $0L_1$.

gether. The demand curve for consumer loans is D_C, and D_I is the investment demand curve. The horizontal summation of these curves yields D_T, the total demand for funds supplied by savers. The total demand in conjunction with the supply of savings determines the interest rate. At the market-determined interest rate of 10 percent, consumer loans are $0L_1$ and investment is $0I_1$, with the sum equal to $0T$. As drawn, the investment demand is much greater than the demand for consumer loans. This tends to be true in practice.

In this model the gross saving of households and firms, $0T$, is not equal to investment, $0I_1$ — consumer loans account for the difference. Economists sometimes define saving as net of consumer loans ($0T - 0L_1$), and with that meaning net saving is equal to investment. (We have also ignored the demand by government to borrow to finance budget deficits. Including that would create another demand for funds supplied by savers.)

The analysis in Figure 15–10 corresponds to the aggregate demand and supply of labor model since we are talking about the supply and demand for funds aggregated across all individual saving-lending and borrowing-investment markets. It is important to recognize that there is not just one big special market that determines *the* interest rate but many closely interrelated markets that we are summarizing. Bond markets, stock markets, mortgage borrowing, credit card loans, bank deposits and loans, investment of retained earnings by firms, and others are all involved in this process of allocating funds provided by a multitude of sources among different competing uses. We lose some detail by using an aggregated model (as we did in the labor market), but it has the important advantage of emphasizing the common underlying factors that affect all the interrelated markets; namely, the willingness to consume less than current income and the existence of profitable investment opportunities.

Investment in excess of the amount required to replace worn-out capital adds to the stock of productive capital, which in turn increases the productive capacity of the economy in subsequent periods. Figure 15–11 illustrates this effect. In the present year the society's production possi-

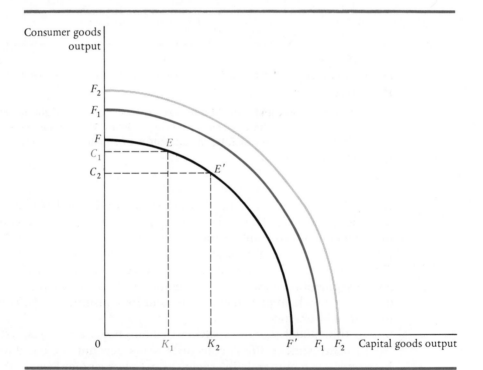

FIGURE 15–11
The Level of Investment and Productive Capacity

Greater investment in the present — E' rather than E — means less current consumption — C_2 rather than C_1 — but greater capacity to produce goods in the future. When firms invest OK_1 in year 1, the production frontier in year 2 is F_1F_1; if they invest OK_2, it is F_2F_2.

bility frontier relating the attainable output of consumer goods and capital goods is FF'. The production of capital goods requires the use of resources (inputs) that could otherwise be used to produce consumer goods, so if more capital goods are produced, fewer consumer goods are available, and vice versa. The market forces summarized in Figure 15–10 determine where we are located on this frontier. Investment of $0I_1$ in Figure 15–10 means an addition to the stock of capital of that amount and corresponds to a point such as $0K_1$ in Figure 15–11. With more capital available the following year, the productive capacity of the economy increases. When firms invest $0K_1$ in year 1, the production frontier becomes F_1F_1 in year 2. If investment were greater in year 1, for instance, at $0K_2$ (point E'), then the production frontier would move out even farther, to F_2F_2. The effect of capital investment on the position of the production frontier in subsequent periods is due to the productivity of capital discussed in Section 15.7. (There are also other reasons why the production frontier shifts outward over time, most importantly growth in the labor force, investment in human capital, and technological progress.)

Investing more in the present time period thus means that incomes and consumption will be greater in the future. Still, we should avoid drawing the conclusion that an ever-increasing expansion in investment is desirable. There is an equilibrium level of saving and investment. To invest more, we have to consume less; that is, for an increase in investment from $0K_1$ to $0K_2$, consumption must fall from $0C_1$ to $0C_2$. Thus, the cost of augmenting productive capacity and achieving higher future incomes is reduced consumption (increased saving) in the present. The saving supply curve shows how much households must be compensated in return for providing funds for investment purposes. At the equilibrium in Figure 15–10, households would supply more saving than $0T$ only if they received an interest rate higher than 10 percent. Investors, however, will be unwilling to pay savers more than 10 percent for additional investment funds since the increased investment will yield less than a 10 percent return. As a result, the market is in equilibrium with investment of $0I_1$.

Equalization of Rates of Return

Pure economic profits are the excess yield over a normal return on invested capital. The model just described determines what the normal return on invested capital will be; in our example it is equal to a yield of 10 percent. A normal return on invested capital is the payment necessary to persuade the owners of capital to provide that input. Recall that economic profits are zero when a firm or industry is earning a normal return. The normal return on invested capital is, in effect, the opportunity cost of capital since it identifies the rate of return investors can generally expect to earn on capital invested elsewhere.

There is a tendency for capital to be allocated among firms and industries so that the rate of return is equal everywhere. This tendency parallels that of labor to be allocated so that wage rates are equal. In the case of labor, however, we pointed out a number of reasons why wages differ because of differences in the productivities and preferences of people. With capital fewer qualifications are necessary. A firm purchasing a machine is indifferent to whose funds provide the financing; one person's money can purchase as much capital as another's. Moreover, a person investing funds usually doesn't care whether the funds are used to finance a computer in the aerospace industry or a truck in the construction industry; all that matters is the rate of return earned on the saving. There are, of course, some reasons why rates of return won't be exactly equal, such as differing degrees of risk, but they are generally not quantitatively as important as the factors that produce differences in wage rates.

The process by which rates of return tend to equalize is much like the process for labor. Let's say that two industries, X and Y, are initially in equilibrium earning the same rates of return on invested capital. Next let an unexpected shift in demand occur. Suppose consumers' demand for X increases and their demand for Y falls. As we explained in Chapter 9, the short-run effects are economic profits in industry X and economic losses in industry Y. In terms of the return to capital, capital now earns a rate of return above the normal level in industry X but below the normal level in industry Y. The owners of capital in industry Y have incentive to shift their investments to industry X, where the return is higher. As capital (and other resources, too) moves from Y to X, the output of industry X expands, and price falls until the industry earns a normal return (zero profit). The opposite happens in industry Y: the industry contracts, investors withdraw capital, price rises, and once again the industry earns a normal return. This process describes how industries adjust in response to a change in consumer demands from the perspective of the market for the input, capital.

Table 15–2 presents evidence of this process at work in the real world. It gives the rate of return on net worth of forty industries for three selected years. In any given year these rates of return vary significantly but tend to cluster around the average value for all industries. For instance, in 1956, thirty of the forty industries had returns within four percentage points of the average return of 13.9 percent. Does the existing variation in rates of return mean that the market forces that tend to equalize rates of return are not working properly? Not necessarily. We should consider the possibility that the rate of return in a given year may indicate a disequilibrium. In our example after demand shifted from industry Y to industry X, the rates of return between the two industries were quite different, but that difference occurred in the short run and was part of the long-run adjustment process, which eventually brought the rates of return between X and Y into equality.

To see whether there is a long-run tendency for rates of return to equalize, suppose we rank the industries in Table 15–2 by their rate of return in 1956 from first to fortieth. The top twenty industries then have

TABLE 15-2
Ranking Industries by Rates of Return on Investment, 1956, 1966, 1976

Industry	Return on Net Worth (in percentages)			Rank by Return		
	1956	1966	1976	1956	1966	1976
Drugs and medicine	21.9	21.0	20.0	1	3	3
Aircraft and parts	21.4	15.7	13.6	2	12.5	27.5
Cement	20.6	7.0	9.8	3	39	34.5
Nonferrous metal	17.8	15.7	8.5	4	12.5	39
Glass	17.7	12.7	17.3	5	28	9
Paint and varnish	17.5	13.9	10.9	6.5	21.5	33
Office equipment, computers	17.5	18.1	17.4	6.5	5.5	7.5
Instruments, photo goods	16.3	21.2	15.7	8	2	17
Soap, cosmetics	16.2	17.9	18.3	9	7	4.5
Other stone and clay	15.8	9.2	10.6	10	37	34
Chemical	15.5	15.1	16.1	11	14	15
Machinery	14.9	16.0	13.6	12	10	27.5
Automobiles and trucks	14.6	17.8	18.3	13.5	8	4.5
Petroleum products (and refining)	14.6	12.6	14.8	13.5	29	23.5
Soft drinks	14.3	22.0	22.4	15	1	1
Iron and steel	13.9	9.3	8.7	16	36	38
Paper	13.8	11.8	14.8	17.5	33	23.5
Printing and publishing	13.8	18.1	13.9	17.5	5.5	26
Tires, rubber products	13.6	13.0	7.5	19	26	40
Automotive parts	13.3	14.5	15.3	20	17	19
Lumber and wood products	12.6	11.0	15.5	21	34	18
Dairy products	12.4	12.4	14.7	22	30	25
Baking	12.2	13.9	16.1	23.5	21.5	15
Hardware and tools	12.2	19.2	16.3	23.5	4	11.5
Household appliances	12.1	15.0	17.4	26	15	7.5
Other metal products	12.1	14.0	15.0	26	20	21.5
Tobacco products	12.1	13.8	17.2	26	23	10
Furniture	11.8	14.2	9.8	28.5	18.5	34.5
Electronic equipment, radio and television	11.8	16.7	16.2	28.5	9	13
Other food products	11.7	13.3	16.1	30	24	15
Building, heating, and plumbing equipment	12.2	11.9	21.0	31	31.5	2
Shoes, leather	10.3	13.1	15.0	32	25	21.5
Railway equipment	9.9	14.2	15.1	33	18.5	20
Agricultural implements	8.3	14.7	17.9	34	16	6
Brewing	8.1	12.8	11.5	35	27	31
Clothing and apparel	7.8	15.9	12.3	36	11	30
Meat packing	7.7	5.5	12.9	37	40	29
Distilling	6.8	10.6	16.3	38	35	11.5
Textile products	6.6	11.9	9.6	39.5	31.5	37
Sugar	6.6	9.1	11.4	39.5	38	32
TOTAL	13.9	14.2	15.0			

Note: The average rank of the industries may be summarized as follows:

	Average Rank			Average Rank	
	1956	1966		1966	1976
Industries 1–20	10.5	17.4		10.5	16.7
Industries 21–40	30.5	23.6		30.5	24.1
All industries	20.5	20.5		20.5	20.5

Source: First National City Bank Monthly Economic Letter, April 1957, 1958, 1967, 1968, 1978.

an average rank in 1956 of 10.5, and the bottom twenty, an average rank of 30.5. Now compare the rankings of the same industries in 1966. The industries that were in the top twenty in 1956 — those with higher-than-median rates of return — tended to be ranked lower in 1966. In fact, their average ranking fell from 10.5 to 17.4, near the average. This comparison suggests that over time industries with unusually high rates of return see these returns decline toward the average level, exactly as our analysis would predict. Note also that those industries with lower rates of return in 1956 did better on average in 1966; their average ranking rose from 30.5 to 23.6.

The same process repeats between 1966 and 1976. Taking industries that were ranked in the top twenty in 1966, we find that the average ranking falls from 10.5 in 1966 to 16.7 in 1976.

The data in Table 15–2 seem to imply a strong tendency for rates of return to converge toward the normal level. The differences that exist in any given year probably reflect, at least in part, the fact that long-run equilibrium is not simultaneously attained by all industries in any given year.

WHY INTEREST RATES DIFFER
15.9

Although we have been discussing *the* rate of interest and its relationship to *the* rate of return on capital, you should realize that this is a simplification, just as it was when we discussed *the* wage rate in the aggregate labor supply-demand model. There is, in fact, a range of interest rates, and *the* interest rate in an aggregate model is best thought of as shorthand for "the general level of interest rates." In that sense the model developed in the preceding sections is extremely helpful in pinpointing important determinants of the level of interest rates.

Differences can exist in specific interest rates in equilibrium although the differences are less pronounced than differences in wage rates. We will discuss four of the most important reasons for these differences.

1. Differences in risk. There is always the possibility that a loan will not be repaid. The greater the risk that the borrower will default on the loan, the higher is the interest rate a lender will charge. If there is a one-in-five chance of a default, for example, the lender will have to charge an interest rate about 25 percent higher than that for completely riskless loans to receive the same expected return. This is one reason why corporate bonds pay higher interest rates than do government bonds, and why loans secured by collateral (like home mortgages) involve lower interest rates than installment credit.

2. Differences in the duration of the loan. Borrowers will generally pay more for a loan that does not have to be repaid for a long time since

that gives them greater flexibility. Usually lenders also must receive a higher interest rate to part with funds for extended periods. This is one reason why savings accounts, where the funds can be withdrawn on short notice, pay lower interest rates than six-month certificates of deposit.

3.   Cost of administering loans. A small loan usually involves greater bookkeeping and servicing costs per dollar of the loan than a large loan. Loans repaid in frequent installments, such as automobile loans, also involve higher administrative costs. When greater costs are associated with administering loans, the borrower must cover these costs and thus pay a higher interest rate.

4.   Differences in tax treatment. The way the tax system treats interest income and investment income is very complex, and it sometimes leads to divergences in interest rates that would otherwise be more nearly equal. In the next chapter we will discuss one important, but complex, example concerning the tax treatment of corporate income, but here we will mention briefly the tax treatment of state and municipal bonds. The interest paid by state and local governments on these bonds is not taxable under the federal income tax, but the interest on otherwise comparable corporate bonds is. The after-tax returns are what guide lenders' decisions, and they will tend to be brought into equality, implying a difference in the before-tax (market) rates of interest. The result is that state and local governments can borrow at lower rates of interest than corporations can.

Although these factors lead to divergences in interest rates in specific credit markets, they should not obscure the common factors that affect all interest rates. For example, if the public should decide to save less (a leftward shift in the S_S curve), all these rates would go up, as would the rate of return on invested capital.

Real versus Nominal Interest Rates

Our analysis of interest rates has focused entirely on what economists refer to as the *real* rate of interest. The *nominal*, or money, rates of interest are more commonly quoted. The difference between the two measures depends on what is happening to the price level; that is, to the purchasing power of money. If you borrow $100 this year and agree to pay back $110 next year, the nominal rate of interest is 10 percent. If prices rise by 10 percent over the year, however, the $110 you repay has the same purchasing power as the $100 you borrowed, so the real rate of interest paid is actually zero.

As this example may suggest, the real rate of interest equals the nominal rate of interest minus the rate of change in the price level. If the interest on home mortgages is 15 percent but prices rise 12 percent a year, the real interest rate is only 3 percent. And it is the real interest rate that affects incentives to save and invest, borrow and lend — which is why we concentrate on it. Let's suppose a person will save $100 this year only if he or she receives 5 percent more purchasing power next year. If the expected inflation rate is 10 percent, the individual will save only if the money interest rate is 15 percent, implying a real interest rate of 5 percent. If a borrower has an investment project that will yield 5 percent per year when prices are stable, it will yield, in money terms, 15 percent per year if prices rise by 10 percent per year. As a result, the borrower will be willing and able to pay a 15 percent nominal rate.

Inflation, that is, a rising price level — causes money rates of interest to rise but has little or no independent effect on the underlying real rates of interest and consequently has little impact on real saving and investment. (This has to be qualified somewhat when government tax policies are taken into account.) In the early 1980s when money interest rates exceeded 15 percent, many journalists and politicians anguished over how anyone could afford to borrow at such high rates. People continued to borrow because they correctly took into account the real rates of interest they had to pay. With inflation running at 12 percent or more, the real rates of interest were, in fact, no higher than they were in most previous years. In addition, with interest payments tax-deductible, what really matters to borrowers is the real aftertax interest rates, and these were actually negative for some borrowers.

Summary

In this chapter we examined the aggregate labor supply curve, which identifies the total number of hours of work that will be supplied to the economy as a whole at different levels of wage rates. We derived it from the income-leisure choices of individual workers. Since the income and substitution effects operate in opposing directions, this supply curve is likely to be quite inelastic and probably bends backward beyond some wage rate.

A major use of the aggregate labor supply curve, in conjunction with the aggregate labor demand curve, is in analyzing the determination of the general level of real wages. The aggregate demand curve is essentially the marginal product of labor curve. Its position depends on the amount of real capital (other inputs) available, the level of technology, and the productive characteristics of the labor force.

As we saw, wage rates can differ among jobs and workers for several reasons, with no tendency for the rates to become equal. These equilibrium wage differences can be due to equalizing wage differentials, differences in human capital investments, differences in ability, or a combination of these factors.

Economic rent arises whenever the supplier of an input is paid more than the minimum amount necessary to retain the input in its present use. We used supply and demand analysis to show that part of an input's price will represent rent whenever the input is in less than perfectly elastic supply.

Borrowing-lending and saving-investment markets interact to determine both the interest rate on loaned funds and the rate of return on invested capital. In equilibrium the interest rate on loaned funds and the rate of return on invested capital will tend to be equal, at least when we ignore differences in risk, tax treatment, and the like. The interest rate thus acts to equalize the willingness of people to give up present consumption for future consumption (marginal rates of substitution) and the real net marginal productivity of investment. The factors emphasized in microeconomic theory interact to determine the real interest rate and rate of return; during inflationary periods the nominal rate will exceed the real rate by the rate of inflation.

Review Questions and Problems

1. Sam works at a $7 wage rate and chooses to work 35 hours per week at that wage rate. Show and explain her equilibrium with a budget line and indifference curves. Identify the following in your diagram: the wage rate, Sam's total weekly income, hours worked, and Sam's MRS.

2. Some people say they like their work and would continue to work even if they weren't paid for it. Does this statement mean that leisure is an economic "bad" for them? Can you show the equilibrium for such a worker as a tangency between the budget line and an indifference curve?

3. Show the income and substitution effects of a higher wage rate for a worker who prefers to work shorter hours at the higher wage rate (backward-bending supply curve).

*4. John works 40 hours a week at a $7.50 wage rate. He unexpectedly inherits a trust fund that pays him $200 per week. How does this inheritance affect John's budget line? Will he continue to work 40 hours a week? Will his total income rise by $200 a week?

5. Explain why the supply curve of labor based on the income-leisure choices of workers is the relevant supply curve to use in analyzing problems involving the economywide level of wage rates.

6. Over time, generally both the aggregate demand for and supply of labor increases. Can we predict what will happen to real wage rates and employment over time?

What factors are responsible for the shift in the demand curve? The supply curve?

*7. "Since only few people have the ability to become nuclear physicists, the long-run supply curve of nuclear physicists is vertical." True or false? Explain.

8. Discuss the three reasons for equilibrium wage rate differences given in the text. Which one, or more, of these reasons accounts for differences in wage rates between engineers and school teachers; college teachers and high school teachers; basketball superstars and basketball coaches; doctors and lawyers?

9. Henry George, in *Progress and Poverty* (1879), advocated a "single tax" on land rents because he believed these to be economic rents that could be taxed without affecting the quantity of land employed. Could we apply the same argument to labor incomes? That is, could a large part of labor incomes be taxed away without significantly affecting the quantity of labor supplied?

10. What do we mean when we say that capital is productive? How do we measure this productivity? What does productivity have to do with the investment demand curve?

11. "In equilibrium the interest rate equates the willingness of people to give up present goods in return for future goods and the ability of the economy to transform present goods into future goods." Explain.

12. In what sense does the interest rate serve to bring into equality the desired rate of saving and the desired rate of investment? Would the interest rate serve this function if the government placed an upper limit on the interest rate lenders could charge? How would such a law affect the amount of investment undertaken?

*13. In Figure 15–11, will the aggregate demand for labor in year 2 be higher if investment is $0K_1$ or $0K_2$ in year 1? Why?

14. Distinguish between the real and nominal rate of interest. Which interest rate does microeconomic theory attempt to explain? Why?

Supplementary Readings

Alchian, Armen, and Allen, William. *Exchange and Production: Competition, Coordination and Controls.* 2nd ed. Belmont, Calif.: Wadsworth, 1977. Chaps. 16, 17.

Bellante, Don, and Jackson, Mark. *Labor Economics.* New York; McGraw-Hill, 1979.

Bronfenbrenner, Martin. *Income Distribution Theory.* Chicago: Aldine-Atherton, 1971.

Fisher, Irving. *The Theory of Interest.* New York: Macmillan, 1930.

Solow, R. M. *Capital Theory and the Rate of Return.* Amsterdam: North Holland, 1964.

Using Input
Market Analysis

16

Some of the most interesting and important issues in economics center around the way input markets function. This fact is not surprising. People understandably have great interest in the market or markets to which they supply inputs, since the functioning of that market largely determines their standard of living. As consumers, we have only a small stake in each of many product markets, but as producers, we have a great interest in one or a few markets. Few people (except possibly dairy farmers) are sufficiently motivated to stage demonstrations over milk price supports that raise the cost of milk by 20 percent, but the prospect of a 20 percent gain or loss in *your* wage rate will not leave you so unmoved.

In addition to our personal interest in matters that affect our own incomes, the operation of input markets is important for another reason. The way input markets work strongly influences the distribution of income among persons and families. Some people are poor because the wage rates they receive are low; others are wealthy because their wage rates are high. Increasingly in recent years public policy measures have been designed to redistribute income in favor of low-income households, and input market analysis is almost invariably necessary to understand the likely consequences of such policies. In this chapter we will use input market analysis to examine several policies and institutions that affect the incomes of workers and investors, among them the minimum wage, the Social Security tax, discrimination, unions, and the corporation income tax.

MINIMUM WAGE LAW
16.1

In 1938 Congress passed the Fair Labor Standards Act, which established a nationwide minimum wage of 25 cents per hour. By 1981 the federal minimum wage had risen to $3.35 per hour. While that increase may seem large, we should view it relative to the increase in average wage rates since 1938. In 1938, the minimum wage of 25 cents was 42 percent of the average manufacturing wage while in 1981 the minimum wage of $3.35 stood only modestly higher at approximately 50 percent of the average wage in manufacturing.

Most people think of the minimum wage as a policy designed to help low-wage workers. If some people are poor because of low wage rates, requiring employers to pay a living wage seems a straightforward remedy. Some simple economic analysis (together with a great deal of empirical evidence), however, has convinced most economists that minimum wages are not the best way to help the poor.

Only about 15 percent of all workers have wage rates low enough to be directly affected by the minimum wage at its current level. For convenience we shall refer to this group as unskilled workers. The remaining 85 percent of workers, the skilled workers, would have wages in excess of the minimum even without the law. Therefore, our analysis of the minimum wage law will focus on the unskilled labor markets where wages would normally be below the level specified by the law.

For simplicity let's assume that unskilled workers are identical in all relevant respects so that a single wage rate will prevail; we will relax this assumption later. Figure 16–1 depicts the labor market conditions for unskilled workers. Almost all jobs and industries are covered by the minimum wage law; that is, by law they must pay the minimum wage. A few industries and jobs, such as domestic workers, baby-sitters, hospital and nursing home employees, and workers in seasonal amusement parks, are exempt. Because of the broad coverage of the law, an aggregate analysis is appropriate. As a result, the supply curve of unskilled labor to all jobs will be fairly inelastic. In the absence of the minimum wage the wage rate would be \$3.00 per hour, and total employment would be $0L_1$. Next, let the government impose a minimum wage of \$4.00. In accordance with the law of demand, employers will hire fewer workers at a higher wage rate. Employment falls from $0L_1$ to $0L_2$. This quite predictable response of employers to a higher wage rate is frequently overlooked in popular discussion of the minimum wage. Economists refer to the reduction in employment of L_1L_2 as the *disemployment effect* of the minimum wage. Note also that at the \$4.00 wage the number of workers looking for work has increased to $0L_3$, which exceeds the number employed, $0L_2$, by L_2L_3. This is the unemployment created by the minimum wage.[1] The higher wage rate has induced more people to enter the job market, but because of the increase in the wage rate, employers will hire fewer people.

Do unskilled workers benefit from the minimum wage? On the basis of this analysis, it is not possible to give an unqualified answer. Workers who are able to secure employment at the \$4.00 wage do indeed benefit, but another group of unskilled workers, those who lose their jobs or who are unable to find jobs, are made worse off. Some people have argued that if the total earnings of unskilled workers as a group rise, we should say

---

[1] Official unemployment statistics may not accurately measure this unemployment. Some workers unable to find jobs at the \$4.00 wage may stop looking for work. Since the government records as unemployed only those who are actively seeking employment but unable to find it, workers who have dropped out of the labor force would not be counted.

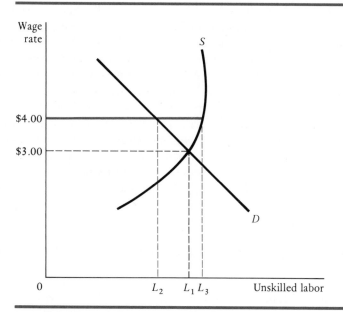

FIGURE 16-1

The Minimum Wage

A minimum wage rate of $4 reduces employment of unskilled workers from OL_1 to OL_2 and increases the quantity of labor supplied from OL_1 to OL_3. The difference between quantity demanded and quantity supplied, L_2L_3, is the unemployment created by the minimum wage law.

that they gain as a group. (Note that this outcome depends on the elasticity of demand. If demand is inelastic, total earnings will rise after a wage rate increase.) Whether or not you take that position, you should recognize that a sizable number of unskilled workers are, in fact, made worse off, and individually they suffer a major loss.

We gain more insight into who is likely to lose jobs when we drop the assumption that all unskilled workers are identical. Suppose, in the absence of the minimum wage, some unskilled workers would earn slightly below the minimum, $3.90, for example, while others would earn much less, $2.00, for example. With a minimum wage of $4.00 the wage rate for employees formerly earning $3.90 rises less than 3 percent, but for workers earning $2.00 the wage rate employers must pay doubles. Employment will therefore decline much more for workers whose wages are initially the lowest because the minimum wage increases most sharply the cost of hiring these workers. In other words, among the unskilled workers, the most disadvantaged, unproductive workers will be the ones most likely to lose their jobs and be priced entirely out of the market by the minimum wage. Since this group is presumably most in need of assistance, the fact that the harmful effects of the law hit them the hardest is relevant in reaching any overall evaluation of the minimum wage.

Apart from those who lose their jobs, who else bears a cost from the minimum wage? Most people just assume that employers or business bears the cost of paying the higher wage. This conclusion is unlikely to be true. The costs of the minimum wage are certain to be spread more widely through society in the form of higher prices for products produced using large numbers of unskilled workers and lower input prices for complementary factors of production. No one knows exactly who finally bears these costs. Perhaps the most accurate statement is that the rest of society (other than the unskilled workers) is the ultimate employer of unskilled workers, so it must bear the cost of a higher wage rate in some form.

Further Considerations

We ignored several complications in the preceding analysis. Among them are:

1. The reduction in employment could take the form of a reduction in hours each worker is employed rather than a reduction in the number of workers employed. In other words, instead of one out of ten workers losing a job, each worker might only be able to work 90 percent as many hours as desired. The response that is more profitable to employers will determine the outcome. Since some overhead costs are associated with hiring each worker, regardless of hours worked, employers will probably cut back on workers rather than on hours of work. Nonetheless, there is some evidence of reductions in hours per worker. For example, about half of all low-wage workers work only part time — although this practice is surely, at least in part, a matter of choice.

2. When the government requires firms to pay a higher *money* wage, employers will respond, if possible, by reducing fringe benefits of employment. Reducing fringe benefits means that the real wage employers must pay will rise by less than the money wage. While employment would not fall as much, the intended impact of the minimum wage is mitigated: if employers reduce fringe benefits, the real wage (minimum wage plus fringe benefits) may not change at all. It is not clear how important this reaction is, but it could partly explain why low-wage workers tend to have such poor (or nonexistent) private pension and health insurance coverage.

3. Our analysis assumed that the minimum wage law covered all jobs. Actually, not all employers must pay the minimum wage; about 15 percent of all workers have uncovered jobs. For the 85 percent of all workers in covered jobs, the analysis of Figure 16–1 still holds: employment will fall. With an uncovered sector, workers who are unable to find jobs at the minimum wage in the covered sector may seek employment in uncovered jobs. This would reduce wages in uncovered jobs, harming workers already employed in that sector. However, the uncovered sector

is now so small that we cannot say how important it is in absorbing workers who can't find jobs in the covered sector at the minimum wage. (In the past the uncovered sector was much larger: nearly 50 percent of jobs were uncovered in the 1950s.)

4.   With a surplus of workers created by the minimum wage (L_2L_3 in Figure 16–1), employers can be more selective about whom they hire. If employers have prejudices relating to the sex, race, age, weight, or religion of their workers, they are in a better position to indulge their "tastes." When there is a glut of workers to choose from, employers can more easily hire someone with characteristics they prefer. That is, if there are more applicants than jobs, the cost of discriminating falls. Insofar as employers have prejudices, the harmful effects of the minimum wage are more likely to be borne by workers with undesirable characteristics in the eyes of employers.

How Large Are the Effects of the Minimum Wage?

Most of the economic research on the minimum wage has concentrated on its effect on employment. Does the minimum wage reduce employment, and if so, by how much? Researchers have conducted scores of studies, and the evidence strongly supports the proposition that the minimum wage reduces employment, especially among the least skilled workers. But no consensus has been reached concerning the size of the disemployment effect.

Most studies have attempted to identify groups of workers who are on average less skilled and who should be most affected by the law. For example, Yale Brozen concentrated on teenage employment since teenagers frequently lack the skills, experience, and long-term job attachment necessary to earn high wages. Brozen found that teenage unemployment rates typically rose following each increase in the legal minimum. Other, more sophisticated econometric studies have supported Brozen's results.[2]

Particularly striking has been the trend in black teenage employment rates relative to white teenage employment rates. In 1948, when the minimum wage was about 40 percent of the average manufacturing wage and only 50 percent of jobs were covered, black and white teenage unemployment rates were nearly the same: 9.4 percent for blacks and 10.2 percent for whites. By the late 1970s, when the minimum wage was 50 percent of the average manufacturing wage and 85 percent of jobs were covered, white teenage unemployment stood at 15 percent, but black teenage unemployment was 35 percent. Whether black teenage unemployment rose more sharply because black teenagers are relatively less skilled (possibly because of poor schooling) or because of the way the minimum wage

---

[2] Yale Brozen, "The Effects of Statutory Minimum Wage Increases on Teen-Age Unemployment," *Journal of Law and Economics,* 12 (April 1969): 109–122; also see Finis Welch, *Minimum Wages* (Washington, D.C.: American Enterprise Institute, 1978).

lessens the cost of discrimination is not clear. Other factors, such as changed attitudes about what jobs are acceptable, may also be involved, but most economists believe the minimum wage played a significant role in increasing black teenage unemployment rates.

More recently, several studies have examined wage rate and income data to obtain a clearer picture of just who is likely to benefit from minimum wages.[3] The results were surprising. The studies found that low wage rates and low family incomes are not closely correlated. Among workers with wage rates low enough to be affected by the minimum wage, fully half were members of families in the wealthier half of the income distribution. This result occurs because some high-income families have individual members who work at low wages, such as teenage children. On the other hand, many poor families have low incomes not because of low wage rates but because they do not work or they work only part time. (A third of low-income households, for example, are elderly and retired.) And less than 20 percent of families in the bottom fifth of the income distribution have family members who work at a wage rate as low as the minimum wage, so only a minority of low-income families could potentially benefit from the minimum wage.

Most economists believe that the minimum wage is an unwise policy, not because they are against helping the poor but because the minimum wage is such an ineffective way to achieve this goal. Most low-income families are not poor because of low wage rates, and some of those who are may well end up with a zero effective wage rate (unemployed) as a result of the policy.

WHO REALLY PAYS THE SOCIAL SECURITY TAX?
16.2

The Social Security payroll tax is actually composed of two equal-rate levies, one collected from the employer and the other from the employee. In 1981 each rate was 6.65 percent. For a worker earning $10,000 a year, then, $665 is deducted from his or her paycheck to cover the employee portion of the tax, and this amount is matched by a $665 payment collected from the employer. The total tax would thus be $1330.

By splitting the tax between the employer and the employee, Congress apparently intended to divide the burden, or cost, of the tax between them. Whether or not this has actually been accomplished is far from clear. Many economists believe that the way the tax is divided into employer and employee portions has no effect on who actually bears its burden. In fact, the analysis supporting this view is just an extension of what we discussed in Section 10.1 in connection with an excise subsidy.

[3] See William R. Johnson and Edgar K. Browning. "The Distributional and Efficiency Effects of Increasing the Minimum Wage: A Simulation," *American Economic Review* (1983, forthcoming); and Edward M. Gramlich, "Impact of Minimum Wages on Other Wages, Employment and Family Incomes," *Brookings Papers on Economic Activity*, 2 (1976): 409–451.

Before discussing who actually pays the Social Security tax, we first need to see whether the way the tax is divided into employer and employee portions makes any difference to wage rates and employment levels. Therefore, we will compare the two extreme cases, one where employees pay the entire tax and the second where employers pay it. In Figure 16–2, before any tax is levied, the supply and demand curves for labor are S and D, the wage rate is \$10 per hour, and employment is $0L_1$. Now suppose government levies a payroll tax on *employers*, which requires them to pay \$2.00 to the government for each hour of labor they employ.

To understand how we incorporate the tax into the analysis, recall that the demand curve for labor shows the maximum amount per hour that employers will pay for each alternative quantity of labor. For example, the demand curve in Figure 16–2 means that employers will pay a maximum of \$10.00 per hour to hire $0L_1$ units of labor. With the tax in

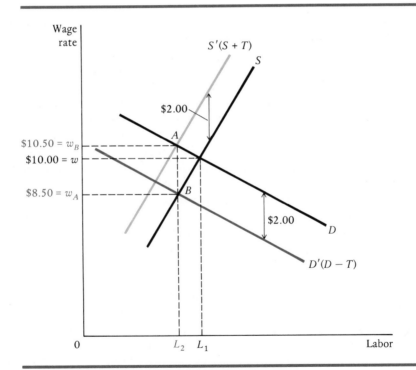

FIGURE 16-2

Tax on Employers versus Tax on Employees

A tax of \$2.00 per hour on employment has the same effects regardless of whether it is collected from employees or employers. When collected from employers, it is analyzed with a \$2.00 downward shift in demand to D'; when collected from employees, with a \$2.00 upward shift in supply to S'. In both cases workers receive \$8.50 per hour and firms pay \$10.50 per hour.

place employers will still pay no more than $10.00 per hour for the quantity $0L_1$, but since they must pay $2.00 to the government, then the amount that employers will be willing to pay workers for $0L_1$ units of labor will fall to $8.00 per hour. In the diagram the effect of the tax is therefore shown as a vertical shift downward by $2.00 in the demand curve to D'. The downward shift in the demand curve means that with a $2.00 per-hour tax, employers will pay $2.00 less to workers at each level of employment. With the supply curve S, the tax reduces employment to $0L_2$, and the wage rate paid to workers falls to w_A, or $8.50. To employers the cost of labor *including the tax* is now $10.50 per hour.

Alternatively, if employees pay the $2.00 per-hour tax entirely, the supply curve shifts vertically upward by $2.00, or to S', without affecting the demand curve. The shift in supply reflects the fact that workers must receive $2.00 more per hour to yield to necessary aftertax wage to compensate them for supplying each alternative quantity of labor. For example, if workers must pay the $2.00 per-hour tax, they will continue to supply $0L_1$ only if they receive a $12.00 wage. That is, they will provide $0L_1$ hours of labor only if they receive a net (aftertax) payment of $10.00 per hour. When workers pay the tax, the intersection of S' and D determines the new equilibrium, involving employment of $0L_2$ and a wage rate of $10.50. Since workers must remit $2.00 to the government, their take-home pay is $8.50.

Note that the real effects of the tax are exactly the same whether the tax is collected from employers or employees. When collected from employers, employment is $0L_2$, and firms pay a wage of $10.50 per hour, with $2.00 going to the government and workers receiving the remaining $8.50. When employees pay the tax, employment is again $0L_2$, and firms pay $10.50 as before; although the workers receive $10.50, they only keep $8.50 since they must remit $2.00 to the government. In both cases the $2.00 per-hour tax, the distance AB, reflects the difference between the gross-of-tax cost of labor to employers and the net-of-tax payment to workers.

The government therefore really has no control over who ultimately bears the cost of the tax by the way the tax is collected. The results are the same whether employers or employees pay the tax. Although we have shown that the effects are identical for the extreme cases (when the employer or when the employee pays the tax), this holds for the intermediate cases too. For instance, if $1.00 of the tax is collected from employers and $1.00 from employees, firms would pay $9.50 to workers (plus $1.00 to the government for a total unit cost of labor of $10.50, as before), and workers would receive a gross wage of $9.50 and get to keep $8.50 since they would turn over $1.00 to the government.

But Do Workers Bear All the Burden?

What we have just shown is that the real effects of the payroll tax are the same regardless of how it is divided, for collection purposes, between employers and employees. This is not the same as saying that workers bear all the burden of the tax. Note that in our example the $2.00 per-hour tax led to a $1.50 reduction in the net wage rate ($10.00 to $8.50), so in that case workers did not bear the full burden of the tax in the form of a lower wage rate. Most economists specializing in tax analysis, however, believe that workers bear most, if not all, of the cost of the tax in the form of reduced wages.

Exactly how much (net-of-tax) wage rates will fall when a payroll tax is collected depends on the elasticities of supply and demand. Of particular importance in the case of the payroll tax is the elasticity of supply. In Figure 16–2 we drew the supply curve of labor as moderately elastic, with lower wage rates leading to significant reductions in the quantity of labor supplied. We did so only to simplify the graph for the point being made; now let's look at the supply curve of labor that is relevant for analyzing the payroll tax.

The payroll tax applies to virtually all jobs, industries, and occupations. Since it applies economywide, the relevant supply curve for use in analyzing the payroll tax is the aggregate supply curve of hours of work. As we explained in Section 15.2, the aggregate labor supply curve is likely to be quite inelastic and, in fact, could be vertical if income and substitution effects exactly offset each other. Consequently, let's examine the impact of the payroll tax when the supply curve is vertical.

Figure 16–3 illustrates this case. In the absence of the tax employment is $0L_1$, and the wage rate is $10. Next, the government levies a tax of $2 per hour. Since it makes no difference whether the tax is collected from employers or workers, let's assume employers pay the entire tax. As a result, the demand curve shifts vertically downward by $2 to D'. With a vertical supply curve the wage rate received by workers falls by $2 — the amount of the tax — to $8. Employment, however, does not fall because workers choose to supply the same number of hours at the lower wage rate. *When the supply curve is vertical, the net wage rate received by workers falls by the full amount of the tax, so workers bear the entire burden of the tax.*[4] (If the supply curve has an elasticity of 0.1 instead of 0, workers will still bear almost all the burden of the tax unless the elasticity of demand is unusually low. You may wish to verify this result for yourself.)

Note that the cost of labor including the tax to employers has not risen; it is still $10. Now, however, $2 goes to government and $8 to workers, rather than $10 to workers. Since costs associated with hiring labor have not risen, there is no effect on the prices of products. Much popular discussion of payroll taxes, especially the employer portion, holds that higher employer payroll taxes add to labor costs and thus contribute to higher prices. The analysis here indicates that total labor costs do not rise: when taxes go up, wage rates go down. (Perhaps most plausibly in a dy-

---

[4] If the tax is collected from workers, the supply curve shifts vertically upward by $2, which means that it does not visibly shift at all. Workers still continue supplying $0L_1$, and employers still pay $10 per hour. But after sending $2 per hour to the government, workers will keep $8 per hour, just as when the tax is collected from employers.

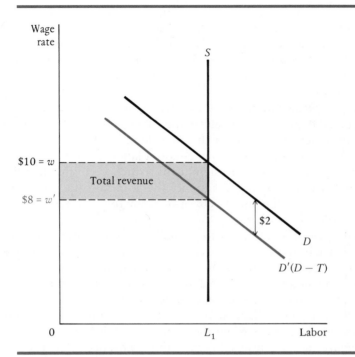

FIGURE 16–3
The Burden of the Social Security Tax
When the supply curve of labor is vertical, a tax on wage income reduces the
wage rate workers receive by the amount of the tax, from $10 to $8.

namic setting, when employer payroll taxes go up, wage rates do not rise
over time as much as they would have otherwise. The final result, however, is the same.)

This analysis suggests two conclusions, both important and both routinely misunderstood in most discussions of the payroll tax. First, it makes
no difference how the tax is divided between employers and employees.
The employer portion is no more borne by business than is the employee
portion. Second, if the aggregate supply of labor is highly inelastic, workers bear all, or virtually all, the burden of the tax in the form of lower
aftertax wage rates. In particular, workers bear the cost of the employer
portion to the same degree they bear the cost of the employee portion.
Many people are probably unaware of the existence of the employer portion of the tax, but it depresses their take-home pay just as much as the
employee portion of the tax. These are important points to keep in mind.
Recent advocates of national health insurance, for example, have proposed to finance the program through increased payroll taxes, with employers paying a disproportionately larger share. As our analysis indicates,

the cost of any national health insurance scheme financed through payroll taxes would be borne by workers in the form of lower wages, regardless of how the tax is initially assigned.

LABOR UNIONS
16.3

According to a poll conducted in 1977, nearly 50 percent of American adults believe that in the absence of labor unions living standards of workers in the United States would be no higher than for workers in underdeveloped countries.[5] Most respondents to the poll were probably unaware that real wages in underdeveloped countries are typically less than a fifth of those in the United States, but even so it seems clear that many people think unions have raised real wages significantly. To see whether this belief is warranted, let's take a look at how unions affect wage rates and employment.

In recent years only about 20 to 22 percent of American workers have been members of labor unions. The existence of a large nonunion sector in labor markets is highly relevant in analyzing the consequences of unions, as we will see. To simplify matters, let's assume that union and nonunion workers are, on average, identical in their productive characteristics. In the absence of unions, therefore, all workers would receive the same wage rate, as we explained in Section 14.5. Figure 16–4a depicts the demand curve for labor by industries in the sector that will become unionized; Figure 16–4b identifies the demand conditions for labor in the nonunion sector. A uniform wage w_1 prevails. Each sector has a downward-sloping demand curve, and workers allocate themselves among jobs so that $0L_U$ work in the sector to be unionized and $0L_N$ work in the nonunion sector. We will once again use the momentary, or very short-run, supply curves that identify the number of workers in each sector at a particular point in time, since the shifting of workers from one sector to another is important to emphasize here.

Now suppose that a labor union forms in the union sector with the objective of increasing the wage rate of its members. Basically, the union can follow one of two strategies. One is to bargain collectively with employers (armed with the threat of a strike) to secure agreement on a higher wage rate, such as w_U. At the higher wage rate, however, the downward-sloping demand curve means that fewer workers will be employed, and employment would fall to $0L_U'$. A second strategy is to limit access of workers to jobs in the union sector; that is, to reduce the supply of workers and let competition among employers bid up the wage rate. For example, if supply is limited to SS_U', the wage rate would be bid up to w_U.

In either case unions can only obtain a higher wage rate by accepting reduced employment. The downward-sloping demand curve means that

[5] "Labor Letter," *Wall Street Journal,* October 25, 1977, p. 1.

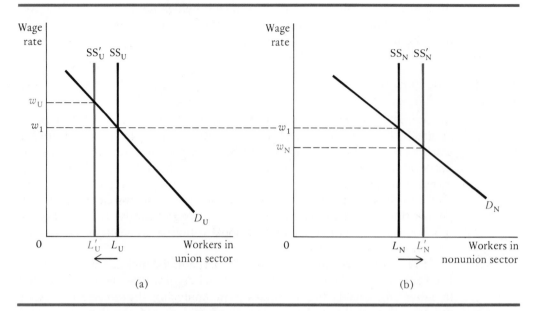

FIGURE 16-4
The Impact of Unions on Wage Rates and Employment in the Union and Nonunion Sectors
(a) Formation of a union increases the wage rate in the union sector, but only at the cost of reduced employment from $0L_u$ to $0L_u'$. (b) Workers unable to find a job in the union sector increase the supply of labor to the nonunion sector, and wages go down in that sector.

the more the unions push wage rates upward, the fewer workers the firms will employ. Any union must, therefore, contend with this trade-off. Another problem is to keep the wage rate from being pushed back down to the competitive level, w_1. At a wage of w_U there are many more workers who would like to work in the union sector than there are jobs available. Why don't firms hire some of those workers at lower wage rates? As this question suggests, the biggest threat to a union's ability to maintain a wage that is above the competitive level is competition from nonunion workers.

A labor union is to labor markets what a cartel is to a product market. A union is an association of workers who engage in coordinated activities designed to raise the price of what they sell, just as a cartel is a group of firms that collude to raise their price. Many of the problems associated with the formation of an effective cartel (Section 12.5) also plague labor unions, the most notable being the threat of entry of nonunion workers undercutting the union wage. Different unions have handled this problem in different ways, some more successfully than others. Unions have been helped by favorable legislation under which a majority of workers can vote to establish a union that becomes the sole legal negotiating agent for purposes of establishing wage rates. For our purposes here we will just take for granted the ability of unions to effectively prohibit employment of any worker at a wage lower than w_U.

If unions raise wage rates, they do so by restricting employment. What happens to the disemployed workers? Possibly they remain out of work, waiting for a job to become available at the union wage, but more likely they will try to find employment in the nonunionized sector of the economy. When employment falls by $L_U L'_U$ (Figure 16–4a) in the union sector, disemployed workers seek jobs in other industries, so the supply of workers increases from SS_N to SS'_N in Figure 16–4b. As employment increases in the nonunion sector, the wage rate falls because a larger number of workers are competing for jobs. Assuming that no workers remain unemployed (that is, no worker waits for a union job at a wage of w_U instead of accepting a nonunion job at a wage of w_N), the reduction in employment in the union sector, $L_U L'_U$, equals the increase in employment in the nonunion sector, $L_N L'_N$.

Many people think that unions gain at the expense of consumers, but our analysis suggests that this view is largely mistaken. Although labor costs rise in the union sector, causing the prices of products produced with union labor to increase, labor costs fall in the nonunion sector, so the prices of the products produced there will fall. Consequently, there is no reason to expect the average price of a market basket composed of union and nonunion sector products to necessarily be higher.

Do Unions Benefit Workers?

It will now be clear why care must be taken in assessing whether unions raise the living standards of "workers"; union workers and nonunion workers are affected quite differently. Unions can raise the real wages of some workers, but the result is a decrease in the real wages of other workers. Some workers gain and some lose.

Several economists have examined the extent to which unions have been successful in raising their workers' wages in comparison with comparable nonunion workers' wages. Not surprisingly, the impact different unions have had on wage rates has varied enormously. Some unions have had almost no effect on wage rates while others have been successful in raising wages above the competitive level by nearly 50 percent. Perhaps the best estimate is that unions on average have increased the relative wages of their members by 10 to 15 percent.[6] This estimate would suggest that real wages of union workers have increased approximately 12 percent, while nonunion workers (who are four times as numerous) bear a loss of about 3 percent in real wages.

[6] G. Lewis, *Unionism and Relative Wages in the United States* (Chicago: University of Chicago Press, 1963).

Since union workers gain and nonunion workers lose, it is not clear whether the total labor earnings of all workers taken together rise or fall. As we mentioned earlier, total labor earnings constitute about 75 to 80 percent of national income, and this percentage has been constant for many years. The share of national income going to workers as a group was just as high before unionism became prevalent as it has been since. This suggests, but does not prove, that unions have not raised the average standard of living of workers.[7] What union members have gained has come largely at the expense of nonunion workers.

This conclusion should come as no surprise. As we saw in Section 15.3, the average level of real wages in the economy depends largely on the physical productivity of labor. Unions seldom engage in activities that increase the productive abilities of workers, and sometimes (through strikes or featherbedding) unions actually diminish labor productivity.

It does not seem likely, therefore, that unions increase the average wage rate of all workers. There is, in fact, one way in which unions contribute to a lower average standard of living. As we have seen, unions cause lower employment in the unionized sector and higher employment in the nonunion sector, and this result constitutes a misallocation of labor resources. In Figure 16–4 note that the movement of labor from the union to the nonunion sectors means workers leave jobs where their marginal value products (MVP) are higher (Figure 16–4a) and fill jobs where their MVPs are lower (Figure 16–4b), indicating that the total value of goods and services produced is reduced. This is the welfare cost attributable to unions' obtaining wage rates above competitive levels, and it is analogous to the welfare cost of monopolies that obtain prices above competitive levels for the products they sell. Estimates of the welfare cost due to unions suggest it is comparable in magnitude to the welfare cost of monopolies.

DISCRIMINATION IN EMPLOYMENT
16.4

Discrimination can take many forms, but in this section we shall only be concerned with one aspect of this complex issue: how discrimination in employment by firms can affect wage rates and employment. Our main concern will be with whether, and under what circumstances, wage rates of equally productive workers will differ because some or all employers discriminate in their hiring practices against persons on grounds unrelated to their productivity, such as race, religion, or sex. If wage rate dif-

[7] To conclude from the fact that labor's share of income has not risen since the advent of unionism that unions have not had any effect would be to commit the logical fallacy *post hoc ergo propter hoc* (after this, therefore because of this). It is conceivable that labor's share would have declined over time in the absence of unions, and if so, the fact that the share has been constant would mean that unions did raise labor's share of national income. As far as we know, there is no evidence supporting this position.

ferentials unrelated to productivity can result from discrimination, we will need to qualify the analysis in Section 14.5, where we concluded that there was a tendency for wage rates to equalize.

The analysis will concentrate on employment of male and female workers by firms in a particular industry. We assume the workers to be equally productive. To begin, let's see how employment and wage rates are determined in the *absence* of discrimination based on the sex of the employees. In Figure 16–5 the supply curves of men and women to the industry are S_M and S_F. With no discrimination, however, it is the total supply of all workers that is relevant, and this curve is S_T, the sum of S_M and S_F. With the industry demand curve for labor, D_L, equilibrium occurs with total employment of $0L_T$ and a wage rate of w. Employment of female workers is $0L_F$ and of male workers, $0L_M$ ($0L_F + 0L_M = 0L_T$). Note that both groups receive the same wage rate.

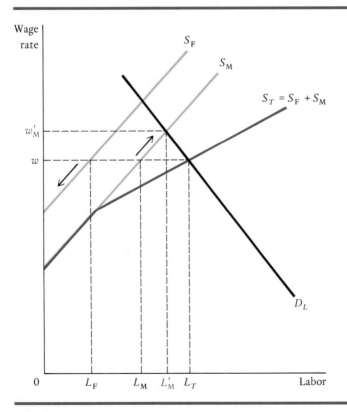

FIGURE 16–5

The Effects of Discrimination on Wages and Employment

Without employment discrimination both male and female workers will receive the same wage rate, w. If females are excluded from these jobs, the wage rate of men would rise to w'_M.

Now suppose that employers in this industry begin to discriminate against women in their hiring practices. To take an extreme case, let's suppose employers refuse to hire any women at all. Since firms will only hire men, the relevant supply curve is S_M alone. The wage rate of men will be bid up to w'_M, and employment of men will increase to $0L'_M$; no women will be employed. Because no women will be hired in this industry, they will have to find jobs in other industries, presumably at lower wage rates. Discrimination against one type of worker therefore tends to benefit other workers. In this case male workers gain and female workers lose.

We have taken the extreme case, assuming that employers refuse to hire any women regardless of whether they can be hired at a lower wage rate than men. A less extreme assumption would be that employers prefer men to women *at equal wage rates,* but they would prefer to hire women at a wage rate that was, perhaps, 10 percent lower than that of men. In that case, compared with the initial no-discrimination equilibrium, employment of men would expand, and employment of women would contract (but not to zero) until there was a 10 percent difference in wage rates. Note that as more men are hired, we move up the S_M curve, and w_M rises; as fewer women are employed, we move down S_F, and w_F falls. When there is a 10 percent differential in wage rates, the industry will be in equilibrium. Once again men gain and women lose — but the extent of the gains and losses depends on how much employers discriminate.

Market Pressures That Limit Discrimination

Some economists object to the analysis just presented on the grounds that it neglects two ways in which markets can limit the effect of discriminatory behavior on wage rates.

First, in the preceding discussion we implicitly assumed that *all* employers actively discriminate against women. It makes a great deal of difference to the analysis how many employers engage in discrimination. Suppose that in the initial no-discrimination situation in Figure 16–5, one-third of the workers are women and two-thirds are men. If half the employers (accounting for half of total employment) begin to discriminate by just hiring men, will this practice lead to higher wage rates for men and lower wage rates for women? Perhaps surprisingly, the answer is no.

The employers that discriminate will fire women and hire men away from nondiscriminating employers, but the nondiscriminating employers will replace the men they lose with the women discharged by the other firms. Since there are enough nondiscriminating employers to absorb all the women at the initial wage rate, the wage rate of women will not fall. To see this, suppose that, to the contrary, the wage of women actually fell below that of men. Because the women's wage rate was lower, nondiscriminating employers would just hire women, and as more women were hired, their wage would be bid up. Not until the wages of female workers rose to equal the wages of male workers would any men be hired by non-discriminating employers.

Discrimination in employment by only some employers will tend to produce segregated employment patterns, not wage rate differences. Discriminating employers will just hire favored groups, while nondiscriminating employers will hire disproportionate numbers of groups that are discriminated against, and wage rates of comparable workers will remain equal. Wage rates will be affected only if a sufficiently large proportion of all employers discriminate against the same group of workers. Another relevant factor is the behavior of both actual and potential employers. If all existing firms in a market discriminated against women, and their wage rate fell, the lower wage for women would give nondiscriminating firms incentive to enter the market and hire women. As a result, nondiscriminating firms would be able to operate at lower costs than discriminating firms and as more nondiscriminating firms entered the market, women's wages would rise.

A second limit on the effect of discrimination is the profit motive. Firms that engage in discrimination in employment bear a cost in the form of sacrificed profits. For example, suppose there is widespread discrimination against women and their wage rates are lower as a result. To be specific, assume that firms can hire male workers for $20,000 a year and can hire equally productive female workers for $15,000. For every male worker hired in this situation, the firm loses $5,000 in profits since it is incurring higher costs than necessary. If the firm is a profit maximizer, it would just hire female workers, which would give it a cost advantage compared with firms that hire male workers. It is this incentive that firms have — to employ the lowest-cost inputs (of comparable productivity) available — that normally tends to produce equality in input prices.

The stronger the profit motive, the less likely it is that discrimination will exist or affect wage rates. Even a moderate difference in wage rates creates the opportunity for a firm to greatly increase its profits by not discriminating. Recall that, on average, labor costs account for about 80 percent of all production costs, while before-tax corporate profits amount to 9 percent. If the average firm could reduce its labor costs by just 10 percent, it could approximately double its profits, a possibility that would produce a strong incentive to hire lower-priced labor. Discrimination in employment practices when there is a difference in wage rates among equally productive groups of workers, therefore, imposes a significant cost in sacrificed profits. It is generally inconsistent to hold that firms are greedy for profits and also that they hire high-wage workers when there are comparable low-wage workers available who could do the same work.

These arguments do not mean that discrimination in employment is nonexistent or that discrimination can have no effect on wage rates, particularly when we recognize that discrimination in employment can be due to preferences of consumers or co-workers rather than preferences of employers. (For example, employers may discriminate against certain groups if their customers are likely to refuse to purchase goods or services provided by that group of workers or if some workers are unwilling to work with another group of workers.) The analysis does suggest, however, that discriminatory attitudes must be quite widespread and that discriminators must be willing to bear substantial costs to indulge their prejudices before significant wage rate differentials for equally productive workers will result.

What Are the Facts?

As usual, the facts are not easy to interpret. In recent years black males have earned about 75 percent as much on average as white males. Women in the labor force have averaged about 60 percent as much as men. Before accepting these statistics as evidence of discrimination, though, here are some other facts. Japanese American families earn 28 percent more than the average of all white American families; Chinese American families earn 8 percent more; Jewish families earn 80 percent more than non-Jewish families. Blacks of West Indian descent actually have slightly higher incomes than whites.[8]

Discrimination may account for some of the difference in average incomes of ethnic groups, but it is clearly not the whole story. These broad averages conceal many significant differences that have important implications for earnings, quite apart from possible discrimination based on race, sex, or religion. The median age of blacks, for example, is 22, but for whites it is 30. Since earnings rise with age and experience, whites would be expected to have higher earnings because of the median age differential. Half of all blacks live in the South where money wage rates (and living costs) are lower. Blacks, especially older blacks, also bear the lingering effects of past discrimination by schools and by labor unions. Moreover, the percentage of black men who are single is double the percentage for white men, and single men on average work 20 percent fewer hours than married men.

What about women? Women are eleven times more likely than men to voluntarily quit a job; on average, they work eight months in each job, while men work three years; and they are more likely to be part-time workers. Sustained work experience has an important effect on earnings, so these differences between women and men are relevant. Marriage also seems to affect women and men differently. Married men earn more than single men, but single women earn more than married women. Perhaps this is because historically, at least, marriage has freed men of household duties and permitted more single-minded attention to jobs, while it has had the opposite effect for women. Actually, women in their thirties who

---

[8] Thomas Sowell, ed., *Essays and Data on American Ethnic Groups* (Washington, D.C.: Urban Institute, 1978), pp. 44, 258–260.

have worked without interruption since high school earn slightly more than men with the same background. Unmarried female faculty members at colleges and universities earn slightly more than unmarried male academics with similar credentials (and this was true before affirmative action).[9]

In trying to determine whether wage differences are due to discrimination, we must compare groups of workers who are equally capable, experienced, and motivated. This is not easy to do, given the numerous factors that affect the current earnings potential of any worker. Using statistical techniques, economists have tried to take into account easily measured factors like age, years of schooling, region, and hours of work. They have generally found that from one-half to three-fourths of the gross differences in earnings between blacks and whites, and between men and women, can be explained by these factors.[10] Whether the remaining differences are due to discrimination, or to as yet unquantified productivity differences, is, and probably will continue to be, a controversial issue.

THE NEGATIVE INCOME TAX
16.5

The negative income tax, or NIT for short, is the name economists give to a type of welfare program involving cash transfers to low-income families. In its pure form, any family with a sufficiently low income, for whatever reason, would be eligible to receive cash assistance. Currently, the United States does not have a pure form of NIT, but many economists have urged that it should replace the wide variety of uncoordinated welfare programs now in use.

An NIT is distinguished by the way transfers are related to the level of income: the greater the income of a family, the lower is the transfer. Table 16–1 illustrates this relationship for a hypothetical NIT. Any family with a zero annual income would receive a transfer of $4000, effectively a guaranteed minimum level of income. At higher levels of income the transfer is smaller. For example, at an income of $1000 the transfer is $3500, yielding a total disposable income of $4500. In the table the transfer is reduced by $0.50 for each additional dollar of income earned, so the transfer would become zero at an income level of $8000. Reducing the transfer as income rises guarantees that the neediest families receive the most help. The rate at which the transfer is reduced as a family's own earnings rise is called the *benefit reduction rate,* or the *marginal tax rate.* In this example the marginal tax rate is 50 percent. Calling the rate by which the benefits are reduced a marginal "tax" rate may seem inappropriate,

[9] Thomas Sowell, *Knowledge and Decisions* (New York: Basic Books, 1980), pp. 246–268. Sowell discusses some of the evidence bearing on differences in earnings due to race and sex.

[10] Ronald Ehrenberg and Robert Smith, *Modern Labor Economics* (Glenview, Ill.: Scott, Foresman, 1982), Chap. 14.

TABLE 16-1
Hypothetical Negative Income Tax

Before Transfer Income	Transfer	Total Disposable Income
$ 0	$4000	$4000
1000	3500	4500
2000	3000	5000
3000	2500	5500
4000	2000	6000
5000	1500	6500
6000	1000	7000
7000	500	7500
8000	0	8000

but the result of reducing benefits as income increases is the same as if the government gave every family $4000 and then taxed 50 percent of the family's own earnings up to a level of $8000.

One of the most important questions about the NIT is how it will affect the work incentives of transfer recipients. Before turning to that issue, we should emphasize that the question is of more than academic interest. While the United States has no pure form of NIT, several major welfare programs are, in reality, minor variants of the NIT theme. For example, under the food stamp program the transfer is reduced as earnings rise, the key feature of the NIT. Although the transfer is in food stamps, it is largely equivalent to a cash transfer under an NIT. The same is true of Aid to Families with Dependent Children (AFDC is really an NIT given to female-headed families with children), Supplemental Security Income (SSI is an NIT for the elderly poor), and several other smaller entitlement programs. Consequently, a large part of the United States welfare system already relies on NIT types of programs, so the analysis that follows is also relevant to these programs.

The NIT and Work Incentives

To examine the way an NIT affects the incentive to work, we must consider the income-leisure choice of workers. Sections 15.1 and 15.2 developed the framework for analyzing the work effort decision. As we saw, a change in the budget line relating income and leisure affects a worker's choice through income and substitution effects. Therefore, we will begin by considering the income and substitution effects of the NIT.

The income effect of a transfer program results from the fact that a cash transfer enriches the recipient. When a worker receives a transfer, he can afford to work less. Put differently, a transfer increases the real income of the recipient, and with a higher real income, consumption of normal goods, including leisure, will increase. (Recall that an increase in leisure is the same as a reduction in hours worked.) As a result, the income effect associated with the provision of an NIT transfer favors less work.

The substitution effect of the NIT relates to the way it reduces benefits as a worker's earnings rise. The marginal tax rate under the NIT reduces the net contribution to income that comes from working an additional hour. For example, if a person's wage rate is $4 under the NIT of Table 16–1, working an additional hour adds $4 to earnings but results in a $2 reduction in the transfer, so the net gain associated with an extra hour's work is only $2. In effect, the NIT reduces workers' net wage rates, which creates an incentive to substitute leisure for income. The relative cost of consuming leisure — the income sacrificed by not working — is reduced from $4 an hour to $2 an hour. Thus, the substitution effect of the NIT encourages more consumption of leisure — that is, less work — since the net compensation from work is reduced.

Both the income effect and the substitution effect of the NIT encourage less work effort, so the total effect of the program is to reduce work effort. Figure 16–6 illustrates this result. (The income and substitution effects are not shown separately in the diagram; this is left as an exercise for the reader.) Before the worker receives a transfer, the budget line is MN with a slope of $4 per hour, reflecting the hourly rate. Equilibrium is initially at point E, with work effort of NL_1 and total earnings of $4000. Under the NIT the budget line changes to MBT. If earnings are above $8000 (point B), it has no effect. (We are ignoring the taxes needed to finance the program.) When earnings are below $8000, however, the worker receives a transfer, which makes total money income greater than earnings. For example, if earnings are zero (point N), disposable income will be $4000 ($TN$); if earnings are $3000 (point S), disposable income will be $5500 ($RL_2$), equal to earnings plus a $2500 transfer ($RS$). Notice that the BT portion of the new budget line is flatter than the initial budget line, reflecting the way the NIT reduces the net wage from $4 to $2.

Faced with this change in the budget line, the worker selects point R as the new equilibrium. Work effort declines from NL_1 to NL_2 (earnings fall from $4000 to $3000), but total disposable income rises from $4000 to $5500. Note that even though the worker receives a $2500 transfer, total income only rises by $1500 since the recipient responds to the program by earning $1000 less than before. Reduced work incentives therefore make it more costly to raise the incomes of low-income households, which is one reason we are interested in this question.

Economic theory predicts that there will be a reduction in work effort under the NIT, not necessarily that people will quit working altogether.

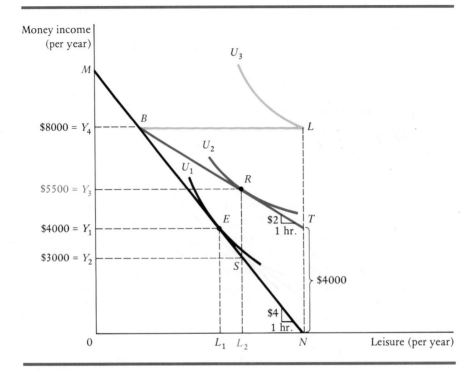

FIGURE 16–6
The Negative Income Tax

A negative income tax shifts the worker's budget line from *MN* to *MBT*. Both the income and substitution effects reduce work effort. At the equilibrium point *R* the worker is earning *SL₂* and receiving a government transfer of *RS*.

Many people think of the work incentive question as an all-or-nothing choice, arguing that if the recipient can receive as much income when not working as when working, there will be no reason to work at all. In our example in Figure 16–6, the worker would receive $4000 by quitting work, which is as much as was earned initially, but the recipient continues to work in response to the program.

Exactly how much work effort will decline depends on both the specific design of the program and on the preferences of the recipients. One type of program has seemed to some people a logical solution to the welfare problem. Suppose the government poverty line is $8000, and our goal is to raise families at least to this level. We could do so by giving each family that earns less than $8000 a transfer just large enough to raise its income to $8000 and no more. No one earning above $8000 would receive any assistance. Sound like a reasonable approach? Think about what it means. If you earn $1000, the transfer is $7000, and your total income is $8000; but if you work harder and earn $5000, the transfer falls to $3000.

Despite increased work effort, your total income does not rise at all. If your income is unaffected by how much you work, why work?

This fill-the-gap (the gap between $8000 and a family's income) approach describes a program that produces a budget line of MBL in Figure 16–6. Over the BL region the net wage rate from working falls to zero. Stated differently, the marginal tax rate is 100 percent. Faced with this budget line, most low-income families, including many who could earn above $8000, would quit work altogether. To avoid this outcome, we must keep the marginal tax rate (benefit reduction rate) well below 100 percent so that recipients' total income will go up by some amount if they earn more.

In our initial example in Figure 16–6 the NIT increased the disposable income of the recipient from $4000 to $5500. Actually, an NIT may lead to a lower total money income. Figure 16–7 illustrates this possibility. This worker earns $7500 prior to the NIT but in response to the program moves

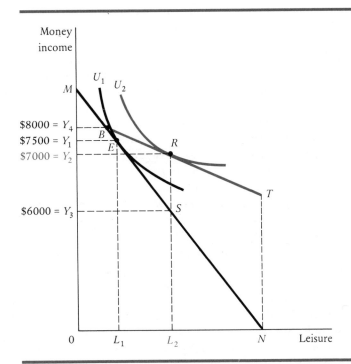

FIGURE 16–7

NIT Subsidy Can Reduce Recipient's Total Income

The NIT shifts the budget line to MBT, and this worker reduces work effort and earnings so much that total money income is lower after the subsidy than it was before. Earnings of SL_2 ($6000) plus the transfer of RS ($1000) are less than the initial earnings of $7500.

to point R, which involves earnings of $6000. Total income, $6000 in earnings plus a $1000 transfer, is actually below the level of earnings in the absence of the NIT. This outcome is possible but probably not very likely. Households initially earning close to the point where benefits are cut off ($8000) are those most likely to respond in this way since a moderate reduction in earnings at this level can lead to total money income being reduced. Note that a 20 percent reduction in earnings in Figure 16–7 produces this result, but the 25 percent reduction in earnings in Figure 16–6 for the worker initially earning less still results in an increase in total income.

Social Experimentation and the NIT

The social sciences can rarely rely on experimental methods to measure the responses of people to various stimuli, but researchers have conducted experiments to evaluate the labor supply effects of the NIT. In the late 1960s Congress authorized funds to finance a series of social experiments in which random samples of low-income families were granted NIT transfers and their responses recorded. The first of these experiments was in New Jersey and Pennsylvania and was completed in 1973; the last, and largest, of the experiments was in Seattle and Denver and ended in 1980.

Although it might be thought that such field tests would easily resolve the question of just how large the labor supply effects of an NIT would be, such has not been the case. Responses under the four experiments varied widely, and statistical problems developed in evaluating the results. For husbands, labor supply reductions (in hours of work) varied between 1 and 8 percent; for wives, responses ranged from a labor supply increase of 1 percent to a reduction of 55 percent; for female family heads, the reductions varied from 12 to 26 percent. An interim report on the Seattle-Denver experiment, the largest and probably most reliable experiment, found labor supply reductions of 5.3 percent, 14.6 percent, and 11.9 percent for husbands, wives, and female family heads, respectively.[11] The average NIT used for these experiments involved a marginal tax rate of 50 percent and an income guarantee — the amount received by a family with zero earnings — equal to the official poverty line.

One problem with the experiments was their short duration. Except for the Seattle-Denver case, the experiments lasted three years, and participants knew that benefits would terminate at the end of that period. Understandably, participants might respond differently to a short-run experiment than they would to a permanent program. Some participants in the Seattle-Denver experiment received benefits for five years, and the responses of that group in the third year were a 13 percent, 21 percent, and 23 percent reduction in hours worked by husbands, wives, and female

[11] Robert Moffitt, "The Labor-Supply Effects of an NIT: The Findings of the Income Maintenance Experiments," unpublished manuscript (New Brunswick, N.J.: Rutgers University, 1980).

family heads, respectively. These results suggest that a permanent program might produce larger effects than the earlier experiments implied.

The experimental NITs have not, therefore, completely resolved the issue of exactly how large a work disincentive effect the NIT, or similar existing programs, is likely to have. Nevertheless, they have provided some convincing evidence that the basic labor supply model of economic theory yields correct qualitative predictions.

Why do many economists favor this type of welfare program if it will reduce the incentives of the poor to work? Basically, it is because an examination of the alternative ways to help the poor reveals that they all have some undesired effects, and the NIT tends to look good in comparison. For example, most economists favor the NIT over a minimum wage law as a means of helping the poor — not because the NIT is perfect but because it appears to be better than the alternative in their judgment.

TAX RATES AND TAX REVENUES
16.6

In the late 1970s, and particularly during the 1980 presidential campaign, the public became aware of something called supply-side economics. At the risk of oversimplifying, *supply-side economics* emphasizes the way government programs, especially taxes, can reduce national output (and hence national income) by reducing the incentive of people to work, save, and invest. Supply-siders pointed out that a higher tax rate does not necessarily produce more tax revenue if the base of the tax (income or whatever) falls significantly in response to the higher rate. Moreover, a lower tax rate might actually increase revenues if enough additional productive activity was stimulated by the lower rate. To be able to lower tax rates and still get more revenue would seem to be the ideal free lunch, and some people thought that the supply-side approach might work in the United States.

To evaluate this possibility, let's examine the relationship between tax rates and tax revenues by considering an income tax on earnings applied to an individual worker. Then we will examine the implications of this analysis for the economy as a whole. Let's begin by assuming that the government levies an income tax at a flat rate of 25 percent; the tax would affect the worker just like a 25 percent reduction in the wage rate. At any level of work effort net earnings would be 25 percent lower. Thus, an income tax that reduces the taxpayer's wage rate has income and substitution effects on work effort. The substitution effect encourages less work effort because the net wage rate falls and leisure becomes relatively less costly (just like the substitution effect of the lower net wage rate under the NIT). The income effect, though, encourages more work effort since the tax reduces the taxpayer's income, and when income falls with the wage rate unchanged, there is incentive to consume less of all normal goods, including leisure. (Note that in this case the income effect is in the opposite direction from the income effect of the NIT, since the NIT increases the worker's income while the regular income tax reduces it.) Since the income and substitution effects of a tax on income are in opposite directions, the net effect of the tax on work effort can't be predicted on theoretical grounds. It is possible, though, that an income tax may lead people to work more if the income effect dominates.

We can go a bit further with the analysis. Although an income tax levied at a low rate might increase the taxpayer's work effort, as the rate becomes increasingly higher, we will ultimately reach a point where work effort will fall. We know, for example, that a 100 percent tax on earnings, which implies the worker gets to keep no income regardless of how much is earned, would lead a person to stop work altogether. Therefore, as the tax rate becomes higher, the substitution effect will probably dominate, and work effort will decline. Predictably, work effort will decline to zero by the time the rate reaches 100 percent.

Figure 16–8a shows what this implies for the relationship between tax rates and tax revenue. The before-tax budget line is *MN*. A 25 percent

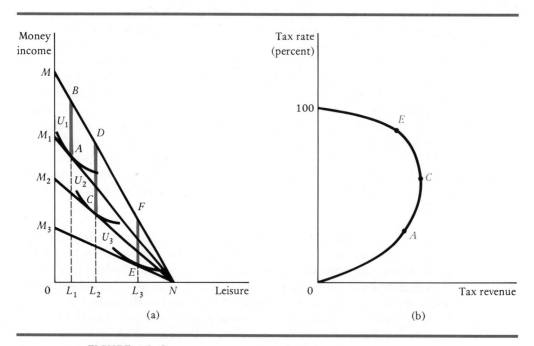

FIGURE 16–8

Derivation of the Laffer Curve

(a) Taxes on earnings of 25, 50, and 75 percent result in budget lines of M_1N, M_2N, and M_3N, respectively. The tax revenue from the 50 percent tax, *CD*, is greater than that from the 25 percent tax, *AB*; but the 75 percent tax produces less revenue than does the 50 percent tax. (b) The Laffer curve illustrates that an increase in tax rates beyond some point reduces tax revenues.

income tax rotates the budget line to M_1N, and the worker chooses to work NL_1 hours. Tax revenue, the difference between before-tax earnings when work effort is NL_1 (BL_1) and aftertax earnings (AL_1), is the distance AB. If the tax rate increases to 50 percent, the budget line becomes M_2N. With the 50 percent tax on earnings let's assume the worker reduces work effort moderately to NL_2, so tax revenue is the distance CD. Even though the worker's earnings are lower under the 50 percent tax, tax revenue is still higher (CD is greater than AB) because the doubled rate applied to a moderately smaller earnings still yields more tax revenue. When the tax rate increases to 75 percent and the budget line becomes M_3N, work effort drops more sharply, to NL_3, and tax revenue, EF, is lower than it was at the 50 percent rate. In this example if the tax rate on the worker is initially 75 percent, a reduction in the rate will increase the government's tax revenue and also benefit the worker — just as the supply-siders predicted.

This suggests a general relationship: at low tax rates an increase in the tax rate will increase tax revenues, but beyond some point, a further increase in the tax rate will reduce tax revenues. Figure 16–8b illustrates this relationship; the points A, C, and E correspond to the three tax rates depicted in Figure 16–8a. The curve in Figure 16–8b, well known among economists for many years, is now popularly known as the Laffer curve, after the contemporary economist Arthur Laffer. Rumor has it that Laffer drew the curve on a napkin for some politicians in a posh Washington restaurant sometime in the 1970s, and those politicians were never the same again.

Where Are We on the Laffer Curve?

There is no doubt that a relationship of the general shape shown in Figure 16–8b exists. The crucial question is to determine where we are on the curve. If at current tax rates we are at a point like A, then higher tax rates will produce more tax revenue (despite a reduction in work effort) and lower tax rates will mean less revenue. If we are at a point like E, however, taxes have so far depressed productive activity that a reduction will spur sufficiently greater output to increase tax revenues.

Some politicians (but very few economists) have argued that the United States is at a point like E, where lower tax rates will increase revenues. To evaluate this possibility, let's see how much work effort would have to increase at a lower tax rate to generate more revenue. Take a family earning $30,000 — slightly higher than the median income in 1982. Let's simplify matters slightly by assuming that the combined effect of federal income, state income, and Social Security taxes is equivalent to a flat rate tax of 40 percent.[12] At a 40 percent rate the family's taxes would

---

[12] In this example we will ignore the fact that state and federal income taxes are progressive, that is, use marginal tax rates that rise with income. Interpreted as a marginal tax rate, the 40 percent figure is probably not too far off for a family with earnings of $30,000.

be $12,000. If the tax rate falls to 30 percent, how much would earnings have to rise to keep tax revenue from falling? A 30 percent tax rate produces $12,000 in revenue if earnings are $40,000, so the family would have to increase its earnings from $30,000 to more than $40,000 if the lower tax rate is to produce more revenue. Put differently, the reduction in the tax rate from 40 to 30 percent would have to stimulate a 33-1/3 percent increase in earnings to keep tax revenue from falling. For the average person working a 35–40-hour week, work effort would have to increase to 47–53 hours a week. Such a large response to a ten-percentage-point reduction in the tax rate seems unlikely.

We can also look at the response to lower tax rates in terms of the supply elasticity of hours of work. A cut in the tax rate from 40 to 30 percent raises the aftertax rate of pay from 60 to 70 percent of the market wage, an increase of 16.7 percent. Since work effort must increase by 33.3 percent to keep revenues constant, the supply elasticity must be more than 2.0 [$33.3/16.7 = (\Delta L/L) \big/ (\Delta w/w)$] if tax revenues are to rise. Since the empirical evidence suggests that the overall labor supply elasticity is between 0.1 and 0.3, the possibility that tax rate reductions will generate more revenue by increasing work effort seems remote.

For reasons such as these, most economists do not believe we are on the upper part of the Laffer curve, at least when talking about the current level of taxes on earnings for most workers. It is possible, however, that for some people, especially those in very high tax brackets, a tax rate reduction could increase revenue. It is also possible that for some other taxes this statement is true. Recall, for example, our discussion of the excise tax on gasoline in Washington, D.C. (Section 3.8).

CORPORATION INCOME TAXES
16.7

Incorporated businesses are subject to a special tax in the United States, the corporation income tax. In 1982 this tax was the third largest source of tax revenue for the federal government, following the personal income tax and the Social Security payroll tax. Although the corporation income tax is commonly referred to as a tax on corporate profits, this is correct only in the accounting sense; economic profits are not really the base of the tax. Even if all corporate industries were competitive and in long-run equilibrium so that there were no economic profits, there would still be accounting profits in the form of a normal return to invested capital, and these profits would be subject to the corporation income tax. To avoid confusion, we should, perhaps, think of the tax as being levied on the net income of capital invested in corporations. The tax rate structure of the corporation income tax is slightly progressive. The first $25,000 in net income is taxed at 15 percent; the next $25,000, at 18 percent; the next, at 30 percent; the next, at 40 percent; and all net income in excess of $100,000 is subject to a rate of 46 percent. Since the bulk of the tax revenue comes from firms with net incomes above $100,000, the effective marginal tax rate for most corporate income is 46 percent.

One of the most interesting questions about tax policy concerns identifying who ultimately bears the burden of the corporation income tax. To investigate this issue, let's assume that corporations, taken as a group, are sufficiently competitive for the competitive model to apply. In addition, the analysis must recognize the existence of a large noncorporate sector in the economy. Although corporations are perhaps the most highly visible form of business organization, actually the noncorporate sector of the economy employs about half of all invested capital. The noncorporate sector includes most of the agriculture and real estate industries and a scattering of firms in other industries.

The corporation income tax is applied to the income from capital in the corporate sector but not to the income of capital employed elsewhere. To analyze this, the key factor to consider is the tendency for capital to be allocated among alternative uses so that its return is the same. We discussed this factor in Section 15.8, and at this point we should add that it is the net (aftertax) return to capital that will tend to be equalized. Investors will channel their funds into those uses that yield the highest aftertax returns, which creates a tendency for the net return on capital to be equalized in all sectors.

In the absence of the corporation income tax, suppose that the rate of return on capital is 10 percent in both the corporate and noncorporate sectors of the economy. Then the government levies a corporation income tax at a rate of 50 percent on the income of capital in the corporate sector. The immediate, or very short-run, effect is to tax away half the returns of investors in the corporate sector, leaving them with a net yield of only 5 percent. Note what this implies: capital invested in the corporate sector now earns a 5 percent return for investors, while investment in the noncorporate sector, which is untaxed, still yields 10 percent. Investors, therefore, have incentive to shift capital into the noncorporate sector, where they can realize a higher return. A reduction in capital invested in the corporate sector increases the net return there at the same time that an increase in capital invested in the noncorporate sector reduces the return there. *The shifting of capital between the corporate and noncorporate sectors will continue until the net return earned by investors is the same in both sectors.*

The movement of capital from the corporate to the noncorporate sector cannot occur instantaneously. Capital in the form of factories and equipment designed to produce automobiles probably could not be used in agricultural industries to produce food. Over time, though, capital can move from the automobile industry to other uses. Owners can allow factories and equipment in the automobile industry to wear out without replacement, reducing capital in that industry. New investment demand can channel resources that would have produced equipment for automobile production into production of tractors for farms. Thus, the passage of time allows the stock of capital to be reallocated, in effect, by channeling more new investment toward the sector with the higher net return.

A graphical analysis can be used to show more clearly how the shifting of capital induced by the corporation income tax affects both sectors. Figure 16–9a shows the employment of capital in the corporate sector, and Figure 16–9b shows the employment of capital in the noncorporate sector. The demand curves for capital showing the rates of return associated with different levels of capital use in each sector are D_C and D_N. Before the corporation income tax is in effect, capital will be allocated so that the returns are equal in both sectors, as shown by the momentary, or very short-run, supply curves SS_C and SS_N. With capital of $0K_C$ employed in the corporate sector and $0K_N$ in the noncorporate sector, the rate of return is 10 percent in both sectors.

The demand curve D'_C shows the effect of the corporation income tax on investment returns in the corporate sector. This curve indicates that the net, or aftertax, return to capital at each level of employment is now

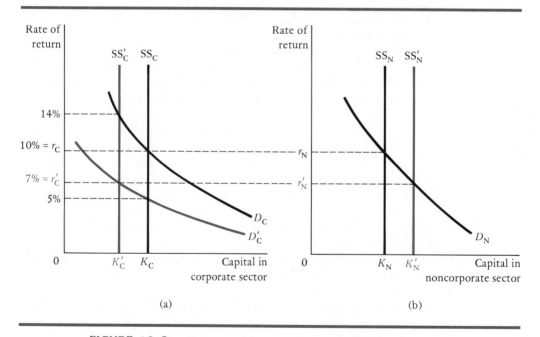

FIGURE 16–9

The Corporation Income Tax

The corporation income tax reduces the net return to capital invested in the corporate sector. Here $K_C K'_C$ units of capital will shift from the corporate to the noncorporate sectors, and the net return to capital will once again be equal across sectors at 7 percent. Investors in both sectors receive a lower rate of return because of the tax.

half as large as it was before. For example, the immediate effect of the tax, before enough time has passed for any capital to shift from one sector to another, is to reduce the return on the $0K_C$ units of capital from 10 percent to 5 percent. The government has, in effect, acquired half the gross 10 percent return to capital as tax revenues, leaving a 5 percent return for the owners of capital in the corporate sector.

Since investors are, in the short run, receiving a lower return on their investment in the corporate sector than they are receiving in the noncorporate sector, capital moves from the corporate to the noncorporate sector. This result produces a leftward shift in SS_C and a rightward shift in SS_N. A reduction in capital in the corporate sector increases the net (and gross) return there, while the return falls in the noncorporate sector as more capital is used there. The adjustment process continues until the net returns are the same in both sectors. Graphically, this equality occurs when SS_C has shifted to SS'_C and SS_N has shifted to SS'_N. With $0K'_C$ in the corporate sector and $0K'_N$ in the noncorporate sector, capital owners will receive a 7 percent return in both sectors. In the corporate sector the before-tax, or gross, return is 14 percent, but since the government receives half of this amount, the return investors receive is 7 percent, the same return that investors receive in the noncorporate sector.

Note that this analysis relies heavily on the tendency for input prices to be equalized across the relevant industries or sectors. Understanding this process is frequently essential in analyzing input market phenomena, as this and the earlier examples dealing with unions and discrimination illustrate.

Do You Bear a Burden from Corporate Taxes?

You do not have to own stock in a corporation to bear a cost from the corporation income tax. Note what the equilibrium just identified in Figure 16–9 implies. Before the tax, the investors in corporations received a return of 10 percent on their investments, but after the tax, they earn a return of 7 percent. This, however, is also true for investors in the noncorporate sector. All investors in noncorporate uses of capital also earn 7 percent rather than the previous 10 percent return. Thus, the corporate income tax places a burden on all owners of capital regardless of whether or not their capital is employed in the corporate sector.

In the broadest sense, no matter where you invest your funds, you can't escape bearing a cost. Savings accounts, government bonds, and certificates of deposit will carry lower interest rates since they must compete with corporations for funds. Home ownership, one of the major forms of investment in capital in the noncorporate sector, will be a less profitable way to hold wealth. Pension funds will yield a lower rate of return, regardless of whether they are invested in stocks, bonds, or other assets. In short, the burden of the corporation income tax is spread widely through the population so that it falls on everyone who has capital income in any form. All this is the result of the tendency for capital to receive the same net returns in all sectors.

Possibly you may also bear some burden of the corporation income tax as a consumer, but the situation here is less clear. Because the use of capital in the corporate sector must generate a higher gross return (14 percent in our example), the cost of this input has risen, and as a consequence, the prices of products produced by corporations will be somewhat higher. In the noncorporate sector, however, the opposite has happened. The cost of capital has fallen, so the prices of noncorporate products will be lower. With some products up in price and others down, whether you are harmed or benefited as a consumer depends on how much of the various products you purchase.

In the analysis so far we have ignored one other potential type of burden of the corporation income tax. We implicitly assumed that the total amount of capital was unaffected by the tax, with the reduction in capital employed in the corporate sector ($K_C K_C'$) just equal to the increase in capital employed in the noncorporate sector ($K_N K_N'$). Since the return on capital received by investors has decreased, however, it is possible that the total amount of capital will be smaller because people may save less at a lower rate of return. If that happens, the total output of the economy will fall (or grow less rapidly over time). With less capital per worker, labor productivity and wage rates would be lower than they were in the absence of the tax. Whether this outcome happens depends on the shape of the supply curve of saving (see Section 4.6).

PERSONAL INVESTMENT ADVICE: AN ECONOMIC PERSPECTIVE

16.8

Economists and economics students frequently get requests from their noneconomist friends for advice on how to invest wisely. Is it better to invest in stocks, bonds, land, houses, gold, or *objets d'art?* Most of us respond to such questions by explaining that economics is not *really* the study of these matters — which often leads the questioner to wonder why we bother studying economics at all. Still, economic theory does provide an answer of sorts to questions about which assets are the best investments. The answer is, All assets can be expected to be equally good or equally poor investments! This answer is nothing more than the observation that rates of return on various investments tend to equalize.

Let's turn to the stock market briefly to see how this tendency works there. A share of stock represents partial ownership of a company, and its price is determined in a highly competitive market with many buyers and sellers. Shareholders are the owners of the company, and they are the claimants to the (economic and accounting) profits. The price of a share of stock will generally reflect the current and expected future profitability of the company in the views of participants in the market.

Like any other investors, traders in the stock market shift their funds in an attempt to receive the highest yields possible. Assume initially that at current prices all stocks will yield the same rate of return (in the form of dividends or appreciation in the price of the shares or both). Then comes a change in the tax law, which will harm firm X and benefit firm Y. Firm Y's expected future profitability rises, so the price of its stock will be bid up to a higher level, causing its yield to fall. Firm Y's stock price will continue to rise until the expected return on the stock is comparable to that of other stocks. Similarly, firm X's expected future profitability declines, and the price of its stock will fall, causing its yield to rise until at the lower price it too will have an expected return comparable to that of other stocks. Once the stock prices adjust, shares of stock in firm Y are no better investments than shares of stock in firm X.

Adjustments in stock prices occur very rapidly in response to any information that bears on the future profitability of companies so naturally the strategy is to move on the stock before the prices change. Many professionals, such as brokers, security analysts, and pension fund managers, keep a close watch on the numerous factors that influence profitability of the various companies. They, and their clients, respond quickly to changes in market conditions, management, tax laws, foreign competition, and anything else that is likely to affect future prospects for profit. As a result, stock prices adjust quickly to levels that yield only a normal expected return.

The same principles apply to investments in other assets, whether they are oriental rugs, antiques, art, stamps, gold, or land. If someone offers to sell you a piece of land and "guarantees" that it will double in value in the next year, you should ask two questions. First, why is the land still unsold at its present asking price if it offers a return so much higher than other investments? Second, why is the owner of the land willing to sell now if he or she could wait and sell the property for twice the price in a year? For the same reason you should be properly skeptical of get-rich-quick schemes. The tendency for all investments to yield the same return means that the operation of the market rarely leaves any prospects for above-average gains.

The returns that are equalized by the market are the *expected future returns*. Since no one knows the future with any certainty, some investments will do much better than the average because of unforeseen changes in circumstances. Also, other investments will perform more poorly than the average. Thus, it is possible to receive above-normal returns if you purchase the right assets at the right time. You might achieve this result by luck (and later probably attribute your success to your superior business sense).

Apart from luck, there are probably only two ways to make a killing by investing. One is to have access to more or better information sooner than other investors. For example, if you know of an impending change in tariff policy before other people, you can purchase stock in companies that will benefit before the market price is bid up. Second, if you are able to evaluate publicly known information better than other investors, you have an advantage. Everyone may know of the forthcoming change in tariff policy, but only you know that it will benefit the Ampex Corporation in some way.

Economic theory, therefore, with its implication of a tendency for rates of return on various investments to equalize, is of some relevance in making personal investment decisions. But basically it just cautions against the prospects of making a killing.

Review Questions and Problems

1. "Proponents of minimum wage laws stressed society's obligation to act through its elected representatives to ensure an adequate standard of living for all working citizens." Evaluate the extent to which minimum wages achieve this goal.

2. Why does economic theory imply that the most harmful effects of the minimum wage will fall on the most disadvantaged and least productive workers?

*3. "The employer Social Security tax is just like any other labor cost to firms. A higher employer tax will therefore increase labor costs, reduce employment, and increase prices." Explain why this reasoning is incorrect.

4. When the Social Security Administration attempts to compare the retirement benefits a worker receives with the taxes paid, it usually bases the comparison on only the employee portion of the tax. Do you think this comparison is appropriate?

5. Do unions benefit workers? In answering this question, why is it important to distinguish between union and nonunion workers?

*6. If the entire labor force became unionized, and if the unions were successful in raising the average level of real wage rates, what would the effects be? Would the average income of people rise or fall?

7. What market forces operate to limit the effect that employers' discriminatory behav-

ior will have on the wage rates of workers who are discriminated against?

*8. Suppose that industry A and industry B together employ all workers in the economy. Wage rates for all workers, male and female, are initially equal. Then Congress passes a law that denies women the right to work in industry A. How will this law affect the allocation of workers between the two industries? Will men receive higher wage rates than women?

9. Show the income and substitution effects of a negative income tax on the quantity of labor a recipient would choose to supply.

*10. For a fill-the-gap welfare program that raises each person's income up to, say, $8,000, show how a worker (who, in the absence of the program, would earn $10,000) could be led to quit work.

11. Why is it unclear that a lower tax rate on labor income will lead to an increase in the quantity of labor supplied?

12. Mr. Moneybags earns $100,000 and pays taxes at a rate of 60 percent. If his tax rate goes down to 50 percent, and his labor supply elasticity equals 1, will the tax revenue collected from him go up or down?

13. When government levies a tax on corporate net income, capital shifts from the corporate to the noncorporate sector. Does the capital that flees the corporate sector thereby avoid bearing a burden from the tax?

14. Explain how the tendency for input prices to be equalized plays a major role in

determining the effects of the corporation income tax.

15. Gold has been falling steadily in price over the past month, while silver has been rising in price. Should you purchase gold or silver?

16. What piece of microeconomic theory is most relevant in evaluating get-rich-quick schemes?

Supplementary Readings

Bellante, Don, and Jackson, Mark. *Labor Economics.* New York: McGraw-Hill, 1979.

Browning, Edgar, and Browning, Jacquelene. *Public Finance and the Price System.* 2nd ed. New York: Macmillan, 1983. Chaps. 8, 9.

Ehrenberg, Ronald, and Smith, Robert. *Modern Labor Economics.* Glenview, Ill.: Scott, Foresman, 1982.

Goodman, John, and Dolan, Edwin. *Economics of Public Policy: The Micro View.* St. Paul: West, 1979.

Rees, A. *The Economics of Trade Unions.* Chicago: University of Chicago Press, 1962.

Sowell, Thomas. *Markets and Minorities.* New York: Basic Books, 1981.

Welch, Finis. *Minimum Wages: Issues and Evidence.* Washington, D.C: American Enterprise Institute, 1978.

General Equilibrium Analysis

17

Most of the analysis developed in previous chapters concentrated on one market at a time. Price and quantity in each market, whether it was a product or an input market, were determined by supply and demand conditions in that specific market. The analysis largely ignored what was happening in other markets. Each separate market was, in fact, conceived to be more or less independent of other markets.

We know, however, that markets are interrelated. Changes in the market for gasoline, for example, affect the automobile market, and changes in the automobile market in turn affect the gasoline market. Consequently, an analysis that focuses on one market in isolation is incomplete. To see how the various individual markets fit together to form an interconnected economic system, economists use general equilibrium analysis, the study of how equilibrium is determined in all markets simultaneously. It builds on what we have already learned about the ways individual markets function and goes one step further by incorporating into the analysis the mutual interdependence among markets.

In this chapter we provide a brief introduction to general equilibrium analysis, beginning with a comparison of general and partial equilibrium analysis. Then we develop a general equilibrium analysis of a simple competitive economy, and, finally, we discuss the question of which framework for analysis — partial or general equilibrium — is most appropriate for the examination of specific issues.

PARTIAL EQUILIBRIUM ANALYSIS AND GENERAL EQUILIBRIUM ANALYSIS COMPARED

17.1

In previous chapters we have employed partial equilibrium analysis almost exclusively. *Partial equilibrium analysis* focuses on the determination of an equilibrium price and quantity in a given product or input market, where the market is viewed as largely self-contained and independent of other markets. An analysis of the gasoline market using supply and demand curves, for example, is a partial equilibrium analysis. The supply and demand curves for gasoline are drawn on the assumption of given and unchanging prices in other product and input markets. In effect, these assumptions allow us to focus on the gasoline market and ignore other markets.

Characteristic of a partial equilibrium approach is the assumption that *some things* — like other prices — *that conceivably could change do not*. In many situations this assumption may be reasonable. For example, a tax on gasoline that raises its price is unlikely to have a measurable effect on the price of wristwatches, diapers, or bowling balls. A change in the price of gasoline could conceivably cause a change in the price of wristwatches by raising or lowering its demand, but in a partial equilibrium analysis of the gasoline market, we assume it does not. On the other hand, a higher price of gasoline would probably have a significant effect on the market for automobiles. In that case the partial equilibrium assumption that the price of automobiles does not change could be seriously inadequate.

Partial equilibrium analysis therefore tends to ignore some of the interrelationships among prices and markets. Formally, this is accomplished through the "other things equal," or *ceteris paribus*, assumptions. By contrast, in a *general equilibrium analysis* all prices are considered variable, and the analysis focuses on the simultaneous determination of equilibrium in all markets. Interrelationships among markets are taken explicitly into account. A broad view of how the interrelated markets fit together in a consistent picture is emphasized.

In a sense, general equilibrium analysis is a more comprehensive framework since it takes into account more of the interrelationships in the economy than does partial equilibrium analysis. The difference between the two modes of analysis is really one of degree. No analysis is capable of incorporating all the complex interrelationships among the thousands of real world markets. What economists call general equilibrium analysis usually involves studying the relationships among a few highly aggregated markets. In taking such a broad view, we necessarily sacrifice much detail about individual markets. On the other hand, we can adapt partial equilibrium analysis to take into account many specific factors that are important to the working of an individual market, but at the cost of neglecting some of the relationships with other markets. Both types of analysis make important contributions to economic theory, and a choice between them should depend on the type of problem investigated. Later in the chapter we will weigh the advantages and disadvantages of each type of analysis.

The Mutual Interdependence of Markets Illustrated

Before turning to the discussion of a model of general equilibrium, let's examine what is meant by the interrelationships, or *mutual interdependence*, among markets. Consider two markets where the interdependence on the demand sides of the markets is likely to be fairly pronounced, the markets for margarine and butter. Margarine and butter are close substitutes, so a higher price for margarine shifts the demand curve for butter upward; similarly, a higher price for butter would cause the demand for margarine to increase.

Figure 17–1a shows the margarine market, and Figure 17–1b shows the butter market. Initially, assume both markets are in equilibrium with the price of margarine at $2.00 per pound and the price of butter at $3.00 per pound. From our earlier analysis of demand curve relationships, recall that the prices of other goods are assumed to be fixed at all points along a given demand curve, as are consumers' incomes and tastes. Our emphasis here will be on prices in other markets. Thus, at all points along D_M the price of butter is $3.00 per pound, and at all points along D_B the price of margarine is $2.00 per pound.

To illustrate the significance of mutual interdependence, let's examine the effects of an excise tax of $0.75 per pound on margarine. Using the familiar partial equilibrium approach, we could analyze an excise tax by shifting the supply curve in Figure 17–1a upward to S'_M, which causes the price to rise to $2.50 and the quantity to fall to $0Q'_M$. Now, however, let's

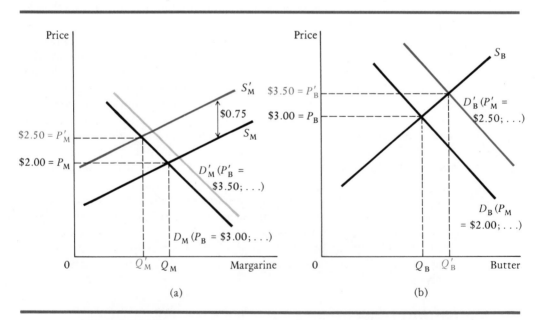

(a)   (b)

FIGURE 17–1

Mutual Interdependence Between Markets: Butter and Margarine

By raising the price of margarine, a tax on margarine increases the demand for butter. The higher price of butter causes the demand curve of margarine to shift to D'_M. This result illustrates economic interdependence between markets.

see how the partial equilibrium approach ignores the mutual interdependence between the margarine and butter markets and what implications this has for the analysis.

The foregoing partial equilibrium analysis neglects two types of consequences. *First, the change in the margarine market will have a spillover effect on other markets, which disrupts the equilibria there.* In our example the higher price of margarine will cause the demand for butter to rise because butter and margarine are substitutes. Don't forget that in drawing D_B, we held the price of margarine fixed at $2.00 per pound; when the tax raises the price of margarine to $2.50 per pound, we must redraw the demand curve for butter on the basis of the higher margarine price. Thus, D_B' is the demand for butter when the price of margarine is $2.50. In short, the tax on margarine leads to an increase in the demand for butter, which in turn increases the price of butter to $3.50 a pound.

If this type of spillover effect from the margarine market to the butter market were the only effect neglected by partial equilibrium analysis, there would be little cause for concern since the analysis of the margarine market would remain exactly correct. But there is a second type of effect neglected: *the induced change in the butter market has a feedback effect on the margarine market.* So far, the tax on margarine has led to a higher price for butter. Now consider the demand curve for margarine once again. We constructed the original demand curve, D_M, on the assumption that the price of butter was $3.00. Since the price of butter has risen, the demand curve for margarine will shift upward. When the price of butter is $3.50, for example, the demand curve for margarine is D_M'. This means that the partial equilibrium analysis of the margarine market, which identified P_M' and $0Q_M'$ as the equilibrium price and quantity, does not correctly identify the final result. Partial equilibrium analysis, by assuming that prices in other markets remain unchanged, rules out the possibility of such a feedback effect. What is the final equilibrium in the margarine and butter markets in this example? Actually, it is impossible to determine the final outcome without more information on the cross price elasticity of demand for butter and margarine and without using more complicated techniques of analysis.

This example illustrates what economists mean by mutual interdependence among markets: what happens in one market affects other markets (spillover effects) and is affected by other markets (feedback effects). Although the supply and demand conditions determine the price in each market, the positions of the supply and demand curves for any specific market may not stay put as neatly as our conventional partial equilibrium models suggest. Instead, the positions of the supply and demand curves for one product depend on supply and demand conditions in other markets, and vice versa.

The margarine-butter example is a very simple case of interdependence since just two markets are involved, and they are only related on the demand side of the market. In the real world a change in one market may affect the operation of hundreds of other markets and, in turn, be affected by conditions in those markets. In addition, the interdependence need not be restricted to the demand side of the markets. The employment and pricing of inputs in one market will affect other markets that employ the same or closely related inputs. Although the example in Figure 17–1 only deals with shifts in demand curves, the position of the supply curve also depends on what happens in other markets.

GENERAL EQUILIBRIUM AND PRODUCTION
17.2

In principle, the equilibrium in any one market depends to some degree on what happens in every other market in the economy. Given this mind-boggling complexity, how can we make sense of the real world? One way is to use a general equilibrium model that attempts to take such mutual interdependence into account. Instead of viewing each market in isolation, we treat every market as part of an interconnected system, with the mutual interdependencies explicitly spelled out.

Our approach to general equilibrium analysis will be to develop a theoretical model of a very simple economy. We will assume that only two consumer goods are produced and only two inputs are used in the production process. Concentrating on just two products and inputs allows us to capture the essential nature of interdependence among markets in the simplest possible setting, but many of the results generalize to a world of many products and inputs.

To begin with, let's describe the basic assumptions in more detail.

1. Corn and wine are the only two consumer goods produced. Consumers spend their entire incomes on these two goods.

2. Land and labor are the only two inputs, or productive resources, used to produce corn and wine. The consumers own these inputs, and they earn their incomes through the sale of the services of these resources. All inputs are homogeneous; each worker, for instance, is interchangeable with any other. Most importantly, we assume that the total quantities of land and labor are fixed in supply to the economy as a whole. In other words, the aggregate labor supply curve is vertical, and so is the supply curve for land.

3. Although the total supply of each input is fixed, the amount employed in each industry is not. The corn industry can employ more labor, for instance, but only by bidding workers away from the wine industry, since the total employment by the two industries together is fixed.

4. Only long-run effects will be considered. Both land and labor can be freely transferred from the production of one good to the other.

5. All markets are competitive.

Although these assumptions describe almost the simplest economy imaginable, understanding how the pieces fit together is still not easy. Note that there are six identifiable markets: for labor employed in producing corn; for labor employed in producing wine; for land employed in producing corn; for land employed in producing wine; and the two product markets for corn and wine. Moreover, these markets are interrelated, as we already emphasized. Consequently, we must determine a pattern of prices and quantities in which the quantities demanded and supplied in each of the six markets are brought into equality simultaneously; that is, a general equilibrium.

Production and the Edgeworth Production Box Diagram

The available quantities of land and labor will be divided between the wine and corn industries. A boxlike apparatus called the Edgeworth production box (similar to the Edgeworth exchange box diagram in Chapter 5) identifies all the ways labor and land can be allocated between the two industries. Figure 17–2 shows the box diagram for the case when the total quantity of labor is 80 units and the total quantity of land is 50 units. The horizontal and vertical dimensions of the box indicate the total quantities of the two inputs. The length of the box diagram shows the amount of labor employed by the two industries together, 80 units; the height of the box diagram shows the amount of land employed by the two industries together, 50 units.

Because of the construction of the box diagram, we can determine the quantities of labor and land employed by both industries. Let's measure the employment of labor in the production of wine horizontally from the southwestern corner, point 0_W, and the employment of land in the production of wine vertically from the same point. Point B, for example, indicates that 40 units of labor and 10 units of land are used in wine production; point C implies 60 units of labor and 20 units of land. Because the total available quantities of inputs are indicated by the dimensions of the box, a given point also identifies employment levels in the corn industry. Since total employment of labor in both industries together is 80 units, if the wine industry employs 40 units, the corn industry must be employing the remaining 40 units. In the diagram we measure the employment of labor in the corn industry to the left from the northeast corner, point 0_C. Similarly, we measure the employment of land in the corn industry downward from point 0_C. Thus, at point B the wine industry employs 10A and 40L, and the corn industry employs the remaining 40A and 40L. A movement from B to C would indicate an expansion in employment of both inputs in wine production to 20A and 60L coupled with a decline in employment of both inputs in corn production to 30A and 20L. Put differently, a movement from B to C shows that the wine industry has bid 20

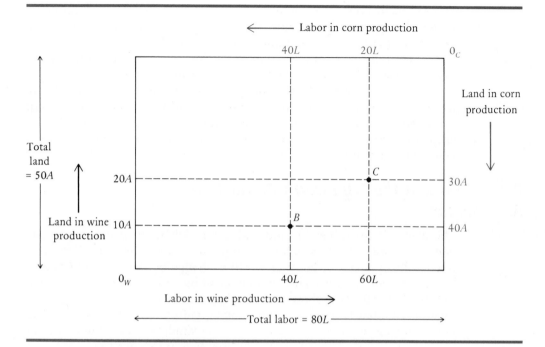

FIGURE 17-2
Edgeworth Production Box

With fixed total input supplies we can show all possible ways of allocating inputs between wine and corn production with the Edgeworth production box diagram. Point *B*, for example, indicates employment of 10*A* and 40*L* in wine production; the remaining inputs, 40*A* and 40*L*, are employed in corn production.

units of labor and 10 units of land away from the corn industry although the total employment in both industries remains unchanged.

Any point in the box diagram therefore represents a specific allocation of labor and land between the two industries. Every possible way in which the fixed quantities of labor and land can be allocated between the production of the two goods is shown by a point on or inside the box diagram. From among all these *possible* allocations of inputs, we now want to identify the one unique allocation that is determined by a general competitive equilibrium.

The Edgeworth Production Box with Isoquants

Having shown how the allocation of inputs is indicated by a point in the Edgeworth production box diagram, the next step is to identify the levels of output of corn and wine that correspond to each possible allocation of inputs. This is accomplished by incorporating the production isoquants for wine and corn into the diagram since these curves identify the level of output associated with each combination of inputs. In Chapter 6 we explained how the production function of a *firm* could be graphed as a set of isoquants. Now, though, isoquants will be used to represent the production function of an entire *industry* composed of all the separate firms producing each good. The industry isoquants have the same characteristics as those of individual firms.

Figure 17–3 incorporates the production isoquants for wine and corn into the box diagram. For wine, several isoquants are drawn with their origin at point 0_W — $100W$, $150W$, $160W$, and so on — each labeled to indicate the amount of wine produced with each combination of land and labor. Note that these isoquants have the familiar shapes discussed in Chapter 6. The isoquants for corn are drawn relative to the origin at point 0_C, with the employment of labor measured to the left and the employment of land measured down from 0_C. In effect, the isoquants for corn are turned upside down, which accounts for their unconventional appearance

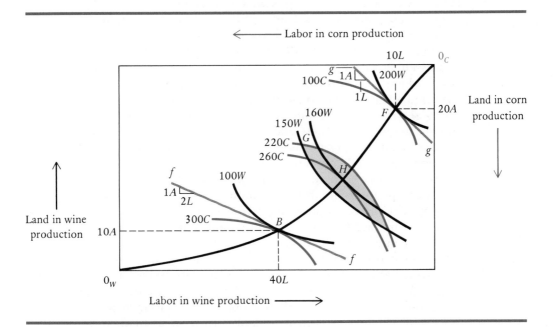

FIGURE 17–3

General Equilibrium in Input Markets

A competitive equilibrium involves an allocation of inputs that lies somewhere on the contract curve that connects points of tangency between corn and wine isoquants. Input prices depend on exactly where on the contract curve the equilibrium lies.

(unless the diagram is turned upside down). Nonetheless, the corn iso-quants embody the familiar properties, with isoquants lying closer to the origin at point 0_c representing lower outputs of corn. Several corn iso-quants are shown — $100C$, $220C$, $260C$, and so on — each labeled to show the output of corn.

With the isoquants drawn in, each point in the box diagram indicates the employment of labor and land in both industries as well as the output level of corn and wine. For example, point B implies employment of $40L$ and $10A$ by the wine industry, with an output of 100 bottles of wine; point B also indicates employment of $40A$ and $40L$ by the corn industry (see point B in Figure 17–2 to see this explicitly; to avoid cluttering the dia-gram, we have not identified these figures for corn on the axes in Figure 17–3), with an output of 300 bushels of corn. In the same way point F shows employment of $20A$ and $10L$ producing 100 bushels of corn, with the remaining $30A$ and $70L$ used to produce 200 bottles of wine.

General Equilibrium in Input Markets

The box diagram shows every conceivable way of allocating labor and land between the two industries. Still, only some of these resource alloca-tions are consistent with a competitive equilibrium in input markets. To eliminate some of the possibilities, note that every resource allocation identified by a point in the diagram occurs where the corn and wine iso-quants either intersect or are tangent. For example, points B, H, and F occur where corn and wine isoquants are tangent to one another, while the isoquants passing through point G intersect. *Only allocations of inputs where the isoquants are tangent to one another are possible competitive equilibrium positions.* These allocations include points B, H, and F, as well as other points of tangency not drawn in. The *contract curve* running from one origin to the other and passing through points B, H, and F connects all the points where corn and wine isoquants are tangent.

A competitive equilibrium in input markets must lie somewhere on the contract curve. To prove this, we need to demonstrate that competi-tive input markets could not be in equilibrium at a point like G where isoquants intersect. There are two ways to do so. First, observe that whenever two isoquants intersect, as at point G, there is a lens-shaped area lying between them. The significance of the lens-shaped area is that every allocation of inputs identified by a point inside the area involves larger outputs of both goods than at point G. For instance, point H implies greater production of both wine and corn than point G. If competitive firms were operating at point G, they could, by simply rearranging or trading the inputs they have already hired, move to point H and increase the output of both goods at no additional cost. Competitive firms could not be in equilibrium when an unexploited opportunity exists to increase output at no cost, and this is true at every point in the box diagram where isoquants intersect. Thus, any resource allocations where corn and wine isoquants intersect, which includes all points not on the contract curve, cannot represent a competitive equilibrium.

Of course, we don't often observe competitive firms directly trading inputs with each other because they generally hire the appropriate quantities of inputs in the first place. This brings us to the second, and somewhat more direct, way to show that a competitive equilibrium must lie on the contract curve. Recall that in competitive markets the price of an input tends to be equalized across firms and industries (Section 14.5). In the present case, this tendency means that the wage rate earned by workers in the wine industry will equal the wage rate of workers employed in the corn industry, and similarly for the rental price of land in both markets. Furthermore, every firm will minimize costs by employing inputs in quantities so that the ratio of marginal physical products *(MP)* equals the ratio of input prices (Section 7.4). For a wage rate of w and a rental price of land of v, the condition for cost minimization is

$$w/v = \mathrm{MP}_L/\mathrm{MP}_A = \mathrm{MRTS}_{LA}. \tag{1}$$

Geometrically, this equality is shown by the tangency between an isocost line, with a slope of w/v, and an isoquant where its slope, the marginal rate of technical substitution (MRTS_{LA}), is equal to the ratio of marginal products.

In equilibrium, each firm producing corn will operate at a point where the slope of the corn isoquant equals the ratio of input prices, w/v. In addition, each firm producing wine will operate at a point where the slope of the wine isoquant also equals the *same* ratio of input prices. *Therefore, the slopes of the wine and corn isoquants must equal one another since both are equal to the same input price ratio.* As a consequence, the equilibrium must lie on the contract curve, which identifies resource allocations where the slopes of wine and corn isoquants are equal. For example, if the wage rate is half the rental price of land, isocost lines have a slope of $1/2$, as illustrated by line *ff* in Figure 17–3. To minimize the cost of producing 100 bottles of wine, wine producers would operate at point *B* where the 100*W* isoquant is tangent to *ff*. Similarly, corn producers also minimize the costs of producing 300 bushels of corn when they use the remaining inputs since the 300*C* corn isoquant is also tangent to *ff* at point *B*. Only when the isoquants are tangent can both industries be minimizing costs when confronted with the same input prices.

For these reasons the competitive equilibrium can only exist at a point on the contract curve in Figure 17–3. Exactly where on the contract curve the equilibrium will lie depends on the consumers' demands for wine and corn, which have yet to be identified. It is intuitively clear, however, that if the demand for wine is relatively high, equilibrium will occur at a point like *F* where a large quantity of wine and very little corn is produced. On the other hand, if the demand for wine is relatively small (which is equivalent to saying the demand for corn is relatively great), not much wine and a large quantity of corn will be produced, as at point *B*.

Before leaving the box diagram, it is worth noting that input prices, and hence the incomes of the owners of land and labor services, depend on the composition of output actually produced. In Figure 17–3 if $100W$ and $300C$ are produced at point B, the ratio of input prices is indicated by the common slopes of the isoquants. At point B the wage rate would be half as large as the rental price of land since the slope of ff is $1/2$. But if $200W$ and $100C$ are produced at point F, the relative price of labor would be higher since the wage rate equals the rental price of land at point F. We will look further at the relationship between what is produced and input prices a bit later; for now it is important to recognize that input prices, and hence incomes, are likely to change when the composition of output varies.

THE PRODUCTION POSSIBILITY FRONTIER
AND OUTPUT MARKETS
17.3

To bring the output markets for corn and wine clearly into the picture, we will use the *production possibility frontier*, which shows the alternative combinations of corn and wine that can be produced with the fixed supplies of labor and land. The same information is already contained in the production box diagram, but the production possibility frontier presents it more clearly. Glance once again at the contract curve in Figure 17–3. Each point identifies a certain combination of corn and wine output that can be produced with available input supplies. A movement from one point to another on the contract curve, as from B to H, shows that as more wine is produced, corn output must fall.

The production possibility frontier is derived from the contract curve in Figure 17–3 by plotting the various possible output combinations directly. In Figure 17–4 the frontier is the bowed-out curve ZZ'. Points B, H, F, and G in Figure 17–4 correspond to these same points in Figure 17–3. For example, point B indicates an output combination of $100W$ and $300C$ in both diagrams. The frontier slopes downward, indicating more wine can be produced only by giving up corn output since land and labor must be transferred from the corn industry to the wine industry to produce more wine.

With the available quantities of labor and land, it is possible to produce any combination of output lying on or inside the production possibility frontier. Here we need only be concerned with points on the frontier since a point inside the frontier cannot be a competitive equilibrium. That is, in Figure 17–4 a point like point G inside the frontier corresponds to a point where isoquants intersect in the box diagram of Figure 17–3. As we explained in the last section, such a point cannot represent a competitive equilibrium in input markets. Only points along the contract curve are compatible with competitive equilibrium, and output combinations along the contract curve are shown as points on, not inside, the production possibility frontier.

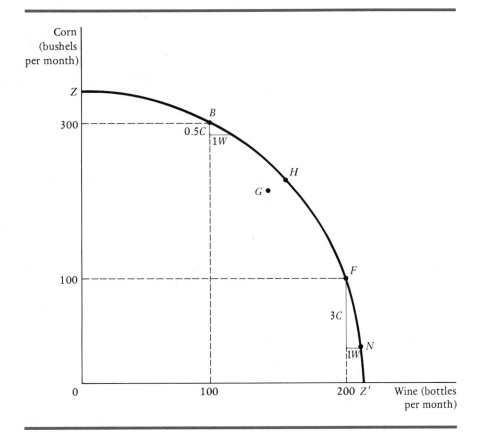

FIGURE 17–4
Production Possibility Frontier

The production possibility frontier plots the output combinations from the contract curve in Figure 17–3. It is normally bowed outward from the origin. The slope of the frontier, called the marginal rate of transformation, shows how much of one good must be given up to produce more of the other.

A common characteristic of the production possibility frontier is that it is bowed out, or concave to the origin. In our example this shape results from the differing input requirements for the two goods. Wine is a labor-intensive good in the sense that its production requires more labor applied to each unit of land, while corn is a land-intensive good requiring less labor per unit of land.[1] Think about what this means as we move

[1] The production box diagram of Figure 17–3 indicates this result by the fact that the ratio of labor to land is higher in wine production than in corn production. At point *B*, for example, 4 units of labor are employed for every unit of land in the wine industry, but only 1 unit of labor is employed per unit of land in the corn industry.

down the frontier starting from point Z (where just corn is produced). To produce the first few units of wine, only a small reduction in corn output is necessary since we can shift primarily labor from corn to wine production, and labor is more crucial to wine production than to corn production. Since a large increase in wine production results with a relatively small sacrifice in corn output, the frontier is relatively flat near point Z. As we increase wine production more and move toward point Z', it becomes more expensive in terms of sacrificed corn to increase wine production still further. At point F, for example, nearly all the available labor is already in wine production, so more of the less well-suited input, land, must be used to increase wine output further, and that necessitates a large reduction in corn output. Thus, the slope of the frontier is quite steep at point F.

The slope of the production frontier becomes steeper in absolute value as we move down the curve. Like many slopes in economics, the slope of the production frontier has a special name, the *marginal rate of transformation*, or MRT. At any point on the frontier the MRT indicates the rate at which one product can be "transformed" into the other. Of course, once corn is produced, it can't be changed into wine, but wine output can be increased by transferring land and labor from corn production to wine production, thereby gaining more wine at a cost of reduced corn output. At point B the marginal rate of transformation is $0.5C/1.0W$, indicating that production of one more unit of wine requires removing resources from corn production by an amount that will reduce corn output by 1/2 unit. Further down the frontier, at point F, the MRT is $3C/1W$, implying that one more unit of wine output necessitates a sacrifice of 3 units of corn.

In effect, the marginal rate of transformation, or the slope of the production possibility frontier, measures the marginal cost of one good in terms of the other. At point B the marginal cost of one more bottle of wine is half a bushel of corn. At point F, when wine output is higher at 200 units, the marginal cost is greater: 3 bushels of corn must be given up to produce one more bottle of wine. The curvature of the frontier reflects the assumption that the marginal cost of each good in terms of the other rises as more is produced.

The slope of the production frontier relates to marginal cost in still another way. In fact, the slope is equal to the ratio of the monetary marginal cost *(MC)* of wine production to the monetary marginal cost of corn production. *At any point on the frontier the slope, or MRT, equals* MC_W/MC_C. Let's look at an example. Suppose that at current output levels the marginal cost of wine is $10 and the marginal cost of corn is $20. How much corn would we have to give up to produce one more bottle of wine? (That is, what is the MRT between wine and corn?) Producing one more bottle of wine utilizes $10 worth of resources (labor and land), so $MC_W = \$10$. If we remove $10 worth of resources from corn production, corn output will fall by half a unit since the marginal cost of 1 unit of corn is \$20. Thus, we must give up half a unit of corn to produce one more unit of wine — that is, $MRT = 0.5C/1.0W = 1C/2W$. This ratio is also equal to the ratio of marginal costs: $MC_W/MC_C = \$10/\$20 = 1C/2W$.

When the marginal cost of corn is twice that of wine, we know that one more unit of wine requires a sacrifice of half a unit of corn. Point *B* illustrates this situation. As we move down the frontier, the marginal cost of wine increases as more is produced, and the marginal cost of corn declines as less is produced. (This means that the ratio MC_W/MC_C rises since the numerator increases and the denominator decreases.) At point *F*, for example, $MC_W/MC_C = 3C/1W$, showing that the marginal cost of wine is three times the marginal cost of corn, so 3 units of corn must be given up to produce 1 more unit of wine.[2]

General Competitive Equilibrium Illustrated

We are now in a position (finally!) to illustrate a competitive economy in which all markets simultaneously achieve equilibrium. To begin, let's assume that the equilibrium levels of output of wine and corn are indicated by point *B* on the production possibility frontier in Figure 17–5. Our goal is to show that this combination of output is consistent with a simultaneous equilibrium in all the interdependent product and input markets.

Recall from our analysis of a competitive industry that when the industry is in equilibrium, the price of the product will equal the marginal cost of producing it. Since there are two markets in our example, each market must satisfy this equality. Thus,

$$MC_W = P_W, \tag{2}$$

$$MC_C = P_C. \tag{3}$$

Dividing equation (2) by equation (3), we obtain

$$MC_W/MC_C = P_W/P_C. \tag{4}$$

That is, when each product's marginal cost equals its price, the ratio of marginal costs also equals the ratio of prices. From the previous section we know that the ratio of marginal costs equals the slope of the production frontier; thus, the slope of the production frontier at point *B*, indicated by the slope of the tangent line *ff*, is also equal to the ratio of prices.

From our discussion of consumer behavior in earlier chapters, we know that each consumer's budget line has a slope equal to the ratio of product prices. In our example here each consumer's budget line will have a slope of $1C/2W$, implying that the price of corn is twice the price of wine. *The budget line for a typical consumer is MN in the diagram with a*

---

[2] It is possible for the production possibility frontier to be a straight line with a constant slope at all points. This result occurs when both industries are constant-cost industries so that the marginal cost of each good is constant over all levels of output. The ratio MC_W/MC_C is constant at all combinations of output, implying a linear production frontier.

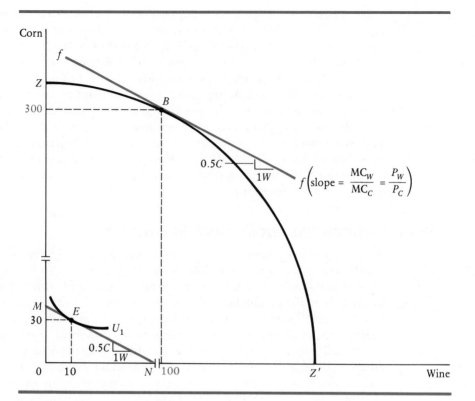

FIGURE 17-5

General Competitive Equilibrium

The competitive equilibrium output combination is at point *B*. The slope of the production frontier at point *B* equals the slope of each consumer's budget line: the slope of *MN* and *ff* are both 0.5C/1W.

slope equal to the slope of the production function at point B since both slopes equal P_W/P_C. The consumer's equilibrium is shown by the tangency between *MN* and the indifference curve U_1 at point *E*.

For the wine and corn markets to be in equilibrium, the total quantities of wine and corn demanded by all consumers together must exactly equal the quantities supplied — 100*W* and 300*C* — at the prevailing prices. If we assume that there are ten consumers, each identical to the representative consumer, this condition will be fulfilled. With each consumer desiring to consume 10*W* and 30*C* when $P_W/P_C = 1C/2W$, the total quantities demanded would be 100*W* and 300*C*, equal to the total quantities supplied. The product markets would then be in equilibrium.

The input markets must also be simultaneously in equilibrium. When we are at point *B* in Figure 17–5, we are also at point *B* in the production box diagram in Figure 17–3. Production at this point on the contract curve in Figure 17–3 determines the relative input prices of labor and land; the ratio of the wage rate to the rental price of land is 1/2. Given this input price ratio and the individual levels of employment in the two industries, the input markets are in equilibrium.

There is another sense in which the various markets must be in balance. Each consumer's income derives from providing labor or land or both to input markets. The input prices determine, in part, the position of the consumer's budget line. Each consumer's budget line must therefore be consistent with the amount of labor or land owned and the prices of these inputs.

Only when all these component parts of the economy mesh perfectly is a state of general equilibrium achieved. Admittedly, even though we are dealing with a simple economy, these interrelationships among markets make it difficult to understand fully how the various pieces fit together. Our primary purpose here, however, is to convey an intuitive appreciation for the interdependence among markets and for the nature of a position of general equilibrium in all markets.

EFFECTS OF A CHANGE IN DEMAND
17.4

We can also use the general equilibrium approach to economic analysis to investigate how the economy responds to a change that disrupts the initial equilibrium. Because of the mutual interdependence among markets, a change in one market will have repercussions to some degree on the operation of all markets. Even a seemingly simple change, such as the change in product demands that will be discussed in this section, entail fairly complex interactions that must be taken into account.

Let's start from the initial equilibrium described in the last section. For the output combination produced, this equilibrium in Figure 17–6 is again at point B on the production possibility frontier, with the price ratio, P_W/P_C, equal to $0.5C/1.0W$. Now suppose that consumer preferences change so that at the current product prices consumers wish to consume more than 100 bottles of wine and less than 300 bushels of corn. The demand for wine has increased and the demand for corn has fallen. Let's trace out the effects, keeping in mind the interdependencies between the product and input markets.

In the short run the shift in demand would raise the price of wine above long-run production costs, creating short-run profits in the wine industry. The decline in demand for corn creates short-run losses. In the long run the wine industry would expand by increasing employment of both labor and land, while the corn industry would contract, reducing its employment of inputs. In terms of Figure 17–6, the actual output combination produced moves down the production frontier from B toward point F, involving more wine and less corn production. Let's assume that the final equilibrium occurs at point F.

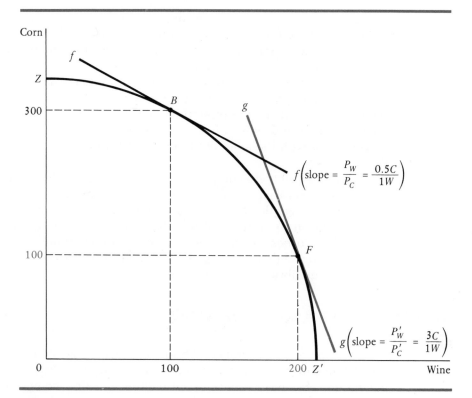

FIGURE 17–6

Effects of a Change in Demand

A shift in demand from corn to wine changes the equilibrium from point B to point F. The relative price of wine rises, as does the wage rate.

Wine production therefore increases from 100 to 200 bottles, and corn output falls from 300 to 100 bushels. As a result, the relative price of wine increases. At point F the price of wine has risen to three times the price of corn ($P'_W/P'_C = 3/1$), whereas the initial price ratio was 1/2.

The change in the output mix also has implications for the prices of inputs. Refer to Figure 17–3 and note that a move from point B to point F in that diagram (corresponding to the movement from B to F in Figure 17–6) causes the wage rate to rise in comparison with the rental price of land. The reason is that wine is naturally more labor-intensive than corn, so when more wine is produced, greater pressure is put on the limited amount of labor. Labor becomes scarcer relative to consumers' demands when consumers want more wine, so the wage rate naturally tends to rise. Land becomes less scarce relative to consumers' demands when consumers want less corn, and corn is land-intensive.

The change in input prices means that the incomes of some consumers change. Consumers who just supply labor services, for example, earn higher incomes when the economy operates at point F because wage rates are bid up. At the same time, those who only supply land suffer a loss in income because of the lower relative rental price of land. Moreover, this change in the distribution of income also influences the appropriate output mix on the production frontier since some consumers will have higher incomes and hence greater demands than before while others will have lower incomes and lower demands.

Consequently, a simple shift in demand changes not only product prices and output but also input prices and the distribution of income. In the end, when a new general equilibrium is achieved, these changes all must fit together in the manner described in the previous section.

Only Relative Prices Are Determined

At various places in this text we have stated that microeconomics is concerned with the factors that determine relative prices, not absolute prices. In the context of our general equilibrium analysis, the meaning and significance of this point becomes clear. In our analysis here only the price ratios are determined, not the absolute prices — even though we used a few dollar figures for illustrative purposes. When the equilibrium is at point B in Figure 17–6, all we know is that $P_W/P_C = 1/2$, and from the related point B in Figure 17–3 that $w/v = 1/2$. (It is also possible to determine the input prices relative to output prices, but we did not go into that.[3]) The various price ratios are relative prices: the price of one good or input in comparison with the price of another good or input.

We cannot determine the absolute level of prices by using the techniques of microeconomics. If one set of absolute prices yields relative prices that are consistent with a general equilibrium, then a doubling or halving of all prices would also be compatible with general equilibrium. For example, suppose our equilibrium at point B is associated with the following prices: $P_W = \$10$, $P_C = \$20$, $w = \$40$, and $v = \$80$. If all absolute prices are doubled ($P'_W = \$20$, $P'_C = \$40$, $w' = \$80$, and $v' = \$160$), all the relative prices — the price ratios — would be unaffected. *In real terms, nothing would have changed.* Each consumer would have twice the earnings and would purchase exactly the same quantities of corn and wine at the doubled product prices. Each firm would receive twice the revenue in dollars and would hire the same quantities of inputs at the doubled input prices. Thus, it is relative prices that are crucial in determining the real outcome — outputs, employment, well-being of people, and so on — which is why microeconomics emphasizes relative prices.

It is difficult to think always in terms of relative prices or price ratios. One convenient simplification is to assume that the price level, the

---

[3] In a competitive equilibrium we know that the input price equals the marginal value product. So the wage rate of workers producing wine will be given by $w = \text{MVP}_L^W = \text{MP}_L^W \cdot P_W$. From this equation it follows that $w/P_W = \text{MP}_L^W$, or the ratio of the wage rate and the price of wine equals the marginal product of labor in producing wine.

weighted average of product prices, remains constant. While these days that assumption may appear farfetched, it is a harmless simplification that permits us to think in dollar prices. Referring to Figure 17–6, we could then say that the movement from point *B* to point *F* involves an increase in the dollar price of wine and a reduction in the dollar price of corn. For example, the price of wine might rise from $10 to $30, while the price of corn falls from $20 to $10. These figures yield the appropriate price ratios necessary to attain a general equilibrium. This is just a way of ensuring that a change in dollar prices corresponds to a change in relative price.

WHEN SHOULD GENERAL EQUILIBRIUM ANALYSIS BE USED?
17.5

The first sixteen chapters of this book have concentrated on partial equilibrium analysis, and it would not have received such emphasis if economists believed that it was an unreliable framework for analysis. Yet we have seen that partial equilibrium analysis neglects some types of interdependence among markets that can have an impact on the way a given market functions. General equilibrium analysis, in contrast, takes into account the interrelationships among markets. On these grounds the general equilibrium approach would appear superior, so it may be worthwhile to explain why economists familiar with both approaches continue to rely on partial equilibrium analysis to study many issues.

Partial equilibrium analysis explicitly ignores some factors that could have a bearing on the analysis, but in many cases these neglected factors may be *quantitatively* unimportant in the sense that if they were taken into account, the conclusions would only be affected to a trivial degree. In our butter-margarine example at the beginning of the chapter, the excise tax on margarine may affect the price of butter only slightly, and this in turn will have an even smaller effect on the demand curve for margarine. In that case ignoring the market interdependencies and assuming that the margarine demand curve "stays put" may yield a result that is a sufficiently close approximation to the true outcome. Recognizing the much greater difficulty of using general equilibrium analysis (we didn't want to tell you that at the beginning of the chapter!), we can justify the partial equilibrium approach on pragmatic grounds: it works well enough for the problem at hand.

In many cases the conclusions of a partial equilibrium analysis differ only in minor respects from the conclusions of a general equilibrium analysis. For example, by using a general equilibrium approach in the last section, we examined what happens when demand shifts from corn to wine. The results included an increase in the (relative) price of wine and the output of wine, and a decrease in the (relative) price of corn and the output of corn. The same results would be obtained from using two supply-demand diagrams when one demand curve shifts up and the other shifts down. The two analyses are not identical in all respects since the general equilibrium treatment also identifies effects on input prices and the income distribution that are not obvious from the partial equilibrium approach. But if we are mainly concerned with what happens in the product markets, the partial equilibrium analysis would be adequate.

We do not mean to say that partial equilibrium analysis can always be used. There are some cases where the implications of a partial analysis differ from those of a general equilibrium treatment in important respects. It is not possible, however, to lay down firm rules that tell us when to use one approach and when the other since we are dealing with matters of degree. A reasonable guideline is that partial analysis is usually accurate in cases that involve a change in conditions that primarily affect one market among many, with repercussions on other markets dissipated throughout the economy. When a change in conditions will affect many, or all, markets at the same time and to the same degree, a general equilibrium analysis is more appropriate.

An example will clarify this distinction. Suppose that a price control is applied to one product, perhaps rental housing. (See the rent control example in Section 10.3.) Rent controls are sure to have a major impact on the rental housing market, but the impact on other markets is likely to be slight and uncertain. Most economists would agree that a partial equilibrium analysis focusing on the rental housing market would be adequate to investigate this issue.

By contrast, say that the government applies price controls to all goods and services simultaneously. With all markets affected at the same time, and to a large degree, a general equilibrium analysis is required. In fact, a partial equilibrium analysis can give results that are misleading in this case. Suppose, for example, that the government mandates a 50 percent reduction in the (dollar) prices of all goods except good X and a 5 percent reduction for good X. If we looked at the market for X using partial equilibrium analysis, we would be tempted to say the output of X would fall and a shortage would result. The opposite is more likely to be the actual result since this set of price controls actually *increases* the *relative* price of X compared with all other goods. Resources would shift from industries where prices are depressed the most to industries where they are depressed the least, increasing output in the latter industries. Only a general equilibrium analysis would be capable of accurately evaluating this situation.

So both general and partial equilibrium approaches are quite valuable, with their relative usefulness depending on the issue being investigated. Previous chapters have given numerous examples of topics that can be fruitfully studied by using the partial equilibrium approach. This chapter has shown how the separate markets form an interconnected system and attain a general equilibrium. In the next chapter we will see how we can use the general equilibrium model to evaluate the efficiency with which an economy allocates resources.

Summary

We have seen that partial equilibrium analysis concentrates on one market at a time, viewing that market, to an extent, as independent from other markets. In contrast, general equilibrium analysis views the economy as a network of interconnected markets, with what happens in one market affecting other markets and in turn being affected by other markets. Mutual interdependence among markets is emphasized.

To introduce general equilibrium analysis, we developed a simple two-input, two-output model. We used the Edgeworth production box diagram to analyze the input markets. A competitive equilibrium lies somewhere on the contract curve in the box diagram; exactly where depends on conditions of demand for the products.

The production possibility frontier is derived from the contract curve in the production box diagram; it shows the alternative combinations of the two goods that can be produced. The slope of the production frontier, the marginal rate of transformation, measures the marginal cost of one good in terms of the other and equals the ratio of the marginal costs of the two goods. In a general competitive equilibrium the slope of each consumer's budget line will be equal to the slope of the production possibility frontier at the output mix produced. Input prices are simultaneously determined, as shown by the slope of the isoquants in the production box diagram. Input markets and output markets must all be in equilibrium for a general equilibrium to exist.

General equilibrium analysis is necessary to analyze some types of issues, especially those that involve sizable changes that affect most or all markets. Partial equilibrium analysis is adequate to analyze phenomena that primarily involve a single market.

Review Questions and Problems

1. What do economists mean when they say markets are "mutually interdependent"? Give an example to support your explanation.

2. Distinguish between partial equilibrium and general equilibrium analysis. What assumptions in partial equilibrium analysis make it possible to ignore the mutual interdependence among markets?

*3. In the butter-margarine example of Figure 17–1, would there be any feedback effect on the butter market from the margarine market if the supply curve of margarine were horizontal?

4. What is the Edgeworth production box diagram? What six variables does a point in the box diagram identify?

5. Why must a general competitive equilibrium lie on the contract curve in the production box diagram?

6. How do we identify the relative prices of inputs for an allocation of inputs lying on the contract curve?

7. Define the *production possibility frontier*. What is the relationship between the frontier and the contract curve in the production box diagram?

8. Define *marginal rate of transformation*. How is it related to the production possibility frontier? How is it related to the marginal costs of producing the two goods?

*9. If all industries are in equilibrium, and the price of refrigerators is ten times the price of toasters, what is the marginal rate of transformation between the two goods? How do you know?

10. "In a competitive equilibrium every consumer's budget line has a slope equal to the slope of the production possibility frontier at the point indicating the output mix being produced." Explain.

11. Using the production possibility frontier and the exchange box diagram, illustrate a position of general competitive equilibrium. How are output prices shown? How are input prices implicitly determined at this point of equilibrium?

12. "A shift in consumer demand will cause a movement along the production possibility

frontier." Explain why. What other economic variables (other than the outputs of the goods) will be affected by this change in demand?

*13.   How would an increase in the supply of labor affect the production box diagram? The production possibility frontier?

14.   What factors are important in deciding whether a particular economic issue can be adequately analyzed by using a partial equilibrium approach or a general equilibrium approach?

Supplementary Readings

Kraus, Melvyn, and Johnson, Harry. *General Equilibrium Analysis.* Chicago: Aldine, 1975.

Quirk, J., and Saposnik, R. *Introduction to General Equilibrium Theory and Welfare Economics.* New York: McGraw-Hill, 1968.

Scherer, F. M. "General Equilibrium and Economic Efficiency." *American Economist* (Spring 1966): 54–70.

Welfare Economics

18

Most people think that economics is important because it deals with matters that strongly affect the well-being of members of society. Ideally, we would like economics to provide assistance in answering questions such as, Should the minimum wage law be repealed? Is it better to tax corporate profits or personal incomes? Will rent controls improve the way rental housing markets work? Should government strictly limit environmental pollutants emitted by factories? As we emphasized in Chapter 1, though, questions like these concerning the desirability of various policies cannot be answered by economics alone — or by any other social science. Economics can help to identify some of the consequences of various policies, but evaluating these consequences requires individual, subjective value judgments.

The branch of economics that bears most directly on the evaluation of economic phenomena is called *welfare economics*. To avoid confusion at the outset, we should point out that welfare economics is not concerned exclusively, or even primarily, with government welfare programs for low-income households. Instead, it deals with the way various economic arrangements affect the welfare, or well-being, of all members of society.

A central concept in welfare economics is the notion of economic efficiency. Indeed, it would be little exaggeration to define welfare economics as the study of how alternative economic arrangements promote or hinder the attainment of efficiency in the way resources are allocated. Since the concept of efficiency plays such a major role in welfare economics, we begin by discussing it in some detail. After that, we determine when economic resources are allocated efficiently, and then we examine whether a competitive economy operates efficiently. Finally, we show how monopolies and labor unions affect the efficiency with which resources are allocated.

THE NATURE OF ECONOMIC EFFICIENCY
18.1

We first introduced the concept of economic efficiency in Chapter 5 in the context of an analysis of the distribution of fixed quantities of goods among consumers. Now we are concerned with efficiency in a more general sense. In our discussion, the terms *efficient* and *optimal* are used interchangeably; some economists prefer instead to use the term *Pareto*

510

optimality, after the Italian economist Vilfredo Pareto who first gave careful attention to the concept.[1]

Let's begin with a formal definition of economic efficiency and its corollary, economic inefficiency. *An allocation of resources is efficient when it is not possible, through any feasible change in resource allocation, to benefit one person without making some other person, or persons, worse off.* This definition is based on how well the economy caters to the well-being of people. Put most simply, when the economy is operating efficiently, there is no scope for further improvements in anyone's welfare or well-being unless they are benefited at the expense of other people.

An allocation of resources is inefficient when it is possible, through some feasible change in the allocation of resources, to benefit at least one person without making any other person worse off. Inefficiency implies waste in the sense that the economy is not satisfying the wants of people as well as it could.

These abstract definitions become clearer with the aid of a diagram. To simplify matters, let's assume that society consists of only two people, Hank and Monica, although we can easily extend the analysis to larger numbers. In Figure 18–1 the well-being, or welfare, of Hank is measured horizontally and the welfare of Monica, vertically. Since no objective way exists to attach units of measurement to a person's utility or well-being, the measure of well-being is entirely ordinal. In other words, a rightward movement in the diagram implies that the resource allocation has changed in a way that benefits Hank, but it does not tell us how much better off Hank is. All we know from the diagram is that the farther to the right we are, the higher is the indifference curve Hank attains. Upward movements similarly imply a change that benefits Monica.

The levels of well-being attained by Hank and Monica depend on their consumption of goods and services. There are limits, though, to how much they can consume because limited quantities of resources are available to produce goods and services. Scarcity ultimately places upper limits on the well-being of Hank and Monica, and these limits are shown in Figure 18–1 by the welfare frontier *WW'*, which is also sometimes called the utility frontier. The *welfare frontier* separates welfare levels that are attainable from those that are impossible to reach, given the quantities of resources available. Any point lying on or inside the frontier is attainable. For example, different allocations of resources would place Hank and Monica at points *A*, *B*, *C*, or *D*. Any point lying outside the frontier, like point *L*, is unattainable. The economy cannot produce enough goods and services to make Hank and Monica as well off as the point indicated by *L*.

A welfare frontier can be used to illustrate how the allocation of resources affects the well-being of members of society. To use it correctly, we must understand how it is derived from the underlying characteristics of an allocation of resources, and we will do this in the remainder of the

[1] Vilfredo Pareto, *Manuel d'Economie* (Paris: V. Giard and E. Briere, 1909).

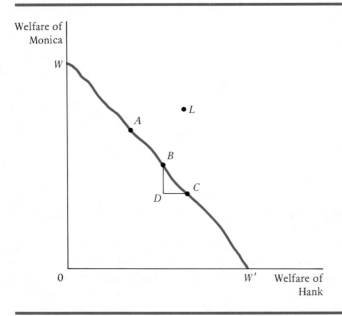

FIGURE 18–1
The Welfare Frontier
The welfare frontier shows how any allocation of resources affects the well-being of both consumers. Any point lying on the frontier is an efficient, or optimal, point. Points lying inside the frontier, like point *D*, are inefficient since it is possible to make both parties better off.

chapter. For now, let's take the existence of the frontier for granted and use it to illustrate several points about the nature of economic efficiency.

Any allocation of resources that implies a point lying on the *WW'* frontier is efficient, or optimal; that is, it satisfies the definition of efficiency given earlier. Consider point *A*, for example. Since it is impossible to move beyond the frontier, there is no possible movement from point *A* that would benefit one person without making the other person worse off. The resource allocation identified by point *A* is efficient by definition. The same is also true of point *B*: any possible move from point *B* harms at least one of the two persons. Thus, point *B* also represents an efficient allocation of resources. Indeed, *every point lying on the welfare frontier satisfies the definition of economic efficiency.* In fact, all points on the frontier are equally efficient, and no point on the frontier is more efficient than any other.

Any point lying inside the welfare frontier represents an inefficient allocation of resources. Point *D*, for instance, is inefficient because it is possible to change the allocation of resources to benefit one person without harming the other. A vertical move from point *D* to point *B* makes

Monica better off and leaves Hank's welfare unchanged, so Monica has benefited with no harm to Hank. Alternatively, a horizontal move from *D* to *C* benefits Hank without harming Monica. *Every point lying inside the welfare frontier represents an inefficient allocation of resources.* Note also that an inefficient point means it is possible to change the resource allocation in a way that makes *both* Hank and Monica better off, such as a move from point *D* to a point between *B* and *C* on the welfare frontier.

Efficiency as a Goal for Economic Performance[2]

The notions of efficient and inefficient resource allocations, as summarized by the points on and inside the welfare frontier, naturally lead to an emphasis on the factors that affect the level and distribution of well-being. But this focus does not allow us to identify one resource allocation as better than any other. To see this point clearly, consider a choice among the points on the welfare frontier, all of which are efficient. Is one better than another? Note that the points differ in terms of the distribution of well-being: a movement from one point to another — for example, from *A* to *C* — benefits one person and harms another. On the principle that there is no objective way to compare one person's gain with another person's loss — interpersonal utility comparisons can't be made objectively — economics must remain silent on this issue. There is no economic basis for preferring one efficient point to another. As individuals we might believe, for example, that point *C* is better than point *A*, but we can't rest our judgment on efficiency considerations.

To see that economic efficiency is a reasonable goal, notice what an inefficient allocation of resources, like point *D*, implies. Inefficiency, by definition, indicates that it is possible to change the allocation of resources in a way that benefits some, perhaps all, people without harming anyone — a seemingly desirable goal. Since a move from inside the frontier at *D* to a point on the frontier between *B* and *C* benefits both parties, would anyone oppose such a change? In this context we must realize that when we talk about people being better off, we mean better off according to their own preferences: Monica views herself as better off at *B* than at *D*. Accepting efficiency as a goal means accepting the premise that each person is the best judge of his or her own welfare. One could quarrel with this view, but it appears a reasonable assumption in most situations. If granted, we could conclude that changes benefiting some and harming no one — a move from inefficient to efficient points — are desirable, which is why we use efficiency as a goal.

We must not conclude, however, that *any* efficient position is better than *any* inefficient position. For example, although a move from inefficient point *D* to efficient point *A* is from an inefficient allocation to an efficient allocation, the change in this case benefits Monica but makes

---

[2] This section repeats much the same material we covered on pages 144–146.

Hank worse off. In comparing these points it is not enough to note that one is efficient and the other inefficient; we must also take into account the change in the distribution of well-being. If Hank is very poor and Monica very wealthy, we might judge point *D* to be preferred overall. By making such a judgment, however, we recognize that efficiency is not the only goal: the distribution of well-being counts too. Even so, efficiency goals are not irrelevant since there are still efficient points between *B* and *C* that make both Hank and Monica better off than point *D*.

Almost all real world changes in resource allocation involve both a movement to a more (or less) efficient position and a change in the distribution of well-being, like the movement from *D* to *A* in the diagram. In these cases demonstrating that there is a gain (loss) in efficiency does not prove that the change is desirable (undesirable) since distributional effects are important too. As a consequence, economists are generally reluctant to claim that economics can prove that one set of economic arrangements is superior to any other. Economics can sometimes prove that one situation is more efficient than another, but there are other goals besides efficiency.

CONDITIONS FOR ECONOMIC EFFICIENCY

18.2

As every student of introductory economics learns, every economy must solve three fundamental economic problems:

1. How much of each product to produce.
2. How much of each input to use in the production of each product.
3. How to distribute the products among consumers.

Each of these problems can be solved in different ways, but not all solutions are equally efficient. In this section we will assume that there are only two consumer products, wine and corn, and two inputs, land and labor — the basic assumptions of the model developed in the last chapter. In addition, we will now assume only two consumers, Hank and Monica. In this simple economy, we can restate the three basic economic problems as follows: how to divide whatever amounts of corn and wine are produced between Hank and Monica; how to allocate the fixed quantities of land and labor between corn and wine production; and what mix of corn and wine to produce. Now let's consider the efficient resolution of each problem.

1.   Efficiency in the distribution of products among consumers. We discussed this issue in Chapter 5 (especially Section 5.2) and will deal with it briefly here. Recall that an Edgeworth exchange box diagram shows all possible distributions of the products between consumers. Only some of these distributions, however, are efficient. The contract curve identifies

which distributions of output are efficient. At all points along the contract curve, the marginal rates of substitution between wine and corn (MRS_{WC}) are the same for both consumers. Thus, we can concisely express the condition for efficiency in the distribution of products as

$$MRS_{WC}^{H} = MRS_{WC}^{M}. \tag{1}$$

If this condition does not hold, both Hank and Monica can be made better off with a change in the distribution of products.

  2. Efficiency in the allocation of inputs. With fixed quantities of land and labor that can be used in the production of corn and wine, an Edgeworth production box diagram shows all possible ways of allocating inputs. We discussed this device in the previous chapter (Section 17.2) although our emphasis there was not explicitly on efficient input allocation. Remember from that discussion that when the input allocation does not lie on the contract curve, more of both products can be produced by moving to the contract curve. The contract curve in the production box diagram identifies the efficient input allocations. At all points along the contract curve, the marginal rates of technical substitution between labor and land ($MRTS_{LA}$) are equal in the production of both corn and wine. Thus, the condition for efficiency in the allocation of inputs is

$$MRTS_{LA}^{C} = MRTS_{LA}^{W}. \tag{2}$$

If this condition does not hold, more of both corn and wine can be produced by an appropriate change in the allocation of inputs. In effect, efficiency in the allocation of inputs means we are operating on, rather than inside, the production possibility frontier.

  3. Efficiency in output mix. Now we come to the question of where on the production possibility frontier we should operate — that is, what combination of corn and wine should be produced. Producing an efficient output mix involves balancing the subjective wants, or preferences, of consumers with the objective conditions of production. It will be convenient here to begin with a numerical example.

  In Table 18–1 the three entries in column 1 describe a specific allocation of resources. Total outputs of wine and corn are $100W$ and $300C$, which are divided between our two consumers so that Monica has $40W$ and $100C$ and Hank has $60W$ and $200C$. We assume this distribution of products is efficient, so the marginal rates of substitution are equal for the two consumers at $3C/1W$. We also assume that we are operating on the production possibility frontier at a point where its slope, the marginal rate of transformation, is $1C/1W$. Our problem is to determine if this is an efficient output mix. In other words, is it possible to change the output mix by moving to another point on the production frontier and distribute the new levels of output between Hank and Monica so both are better off? If it is possible, then the initial allocation cannot be efficient.

  Let's examine this question by changing the output mix in a specific way and seeing how it affects Hank and Monica. Since the MRT_{WC} is $1C/$

TABLE 18-1

An Inefficient Output Mix

	(1) Output Mix	(2) MRS_{WC}	(3) MRT_{WC}	(4) New Output Mix $(-2C + 2W)$	Equally Preferred Output Mix
Monica	$40W + 100C$	$3C = 1W$		$41W + 99C$	$41W + 97C$
Hank	$60W + 200C$	$3C = 1W$		$61W + 199C$	$61W + 197C$
Total	$100W + 300C$		$1C = 1W$	$102W + 298C$	$102W + 294C$

$1W$, it is possible to increase the output of wine by 2 bottles by reducing the output of corn by 2 bushels. The new output mix of $102W$ and $298C$ can be divided between Hank and Monica as shown in column 4. Both Hank and Monica are better off with their new consumption bundles. Recall that we assumed that Hank's and Monica's marginal rates of substitution were $3C/1W$, so we can compare the consumption combinations of columns 1 and 4. With her initial bundle of $40W$ and $100C$, Monica was willing to give up 3 bushels of corn for one more bottle of wine, but the combination of $41W$ and $99C$ gives her one more bottle of wine at a cost of only one bushel of corn. She is thus on a higher indifference curve. The same is also true for Hank.[3]

It is always possible to change the output mix and leave both consumers better off whenever their common marginal rates of substitution are not equal to the marginal rate of transformation. We can see this result intuitively from the meanings of the terms. When MRS_{WC} is $3C/1W$, then the marginal benefit of one more bottle of wine is equal to 3 bushels of corn since this is the maximum amount of corn that would be given up for one more bottle of wine. When MRT_{WC} is $1C/1W$, the marginal cost of one more bottle of wine is only one bushel of corn. Thus, when MRS_{WC} is greater than MRT_{WC}, the marginal benefit to consumers of more wine output is greater than the marginal cost of producing it — both expressed in units of corn. More wine is worth more to consumers than it costs to produce, and they can be better off by moving along the production frontier to a point where more wine and less corn is produced.

As more wine and less corn is produced, MRT_{WC} rises; and as Hank and Monica consume more wine and less corn, their marginal rates of substitution tend to decline. The process of producing more wine and less corn tends to bring MRT_{WC} and MRS_{WC} closer together. This movement

[3] We can show the same point somewhat differently by identifying the consumption bundle for each consumer that is equally preferred to the initial one. This result is shown in column 5, where each consumer has 3 bushels of corn less and 1 bottle of wine more than in column 1. Since the market baskets they can achieve, shown in column 4, contain the same amount of wine but *more* corn, they must be preferred to the baskets in column 5 and thus preferred to the initial ones in column 1.

along the production frontier can continue to benefit both consumers until the two terms are exactly equal.

Efficiency in the output mix requires that the marginal benefit to consumers of one good in terms of the other (MRS_{WC}) be exactly equal to the marginal cost of producing that good in terms of the other (MRT_{WC}). The condition for efficiency in the output mix is, then,

$$[MRS_{WC}^i] = MRT_{WC}. \tag{3}$$

The term $[MRS_{WC}^i]$ refers to the marginal rate of substitution that is equal for all i consumers. When this equality holds, it is impossible to change the output mix in a way that benefits all consumers. Any possible change will harm at least one consumer, so the output mix is by definition efficient.

We have discussed three conditions for efficiency. Only when all three hold simultaneously is the allocation of resources fully efficient, and there is then no possible change that will benefit one consumer without harming the other.

Graphical Analysis of Efficiency Conditions

We can illustrate much of this analysis in a single diagram. In Figure 18–2 the production possibility frontier ZZ' has an Edgeworth exchange box diagram inside it. Remember that the dimensions of the box diagram show the total quantities of the two goods available. The point on the production frontier where the economy operates determines the total quantities of the two goods. At point B, for instance, 100 bottles of wine and 300 bushels of corn are produced, so a box diagram with these dimensions is OC_1BW_1. In interpreting this box as an Edgeworth exchange box, we treat point 0 as the origin for Hank's indifference curves and point B as the origin for Monica's indifference curves.

Now let's examine the same allocation of resources described in Table 18–1. The output mix is at point B with $100W$ and $300C$, and the marginal rate of transformation at B is $1C/1W$, shown by the slope of the line ff. Wine and corn are divided between Hank and Monica so that Hank has $60W$ and $200C$ and Monica has the remaining $40W$ and $100C$, shown by point E in the box diagram. In addition, we assumed earlier that the consumers' marginal rates of substitution were equal at those consumption levels, and this is shown by a tangency between Hank's and Monica's indifference curves at point E. The equal MRSs are $3C/1W$, shown by the slopes of the indifference curves at E; they are also equal to the slope of the tangent line gg.

This diagram contains a great deal of information about our hypothetical economy. It shows the total outputs of the two goods as well as the market baskets of each of the two consumers. Since the indifference curves are tangent at point E, the distribution of the $100W$ and $300C$ be-

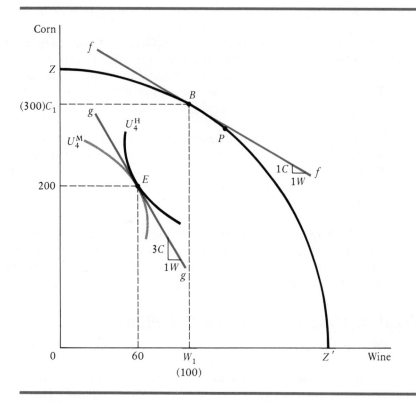

FIGURE 18-2
An Inefficient Output Mix
The output combination at point *B*, with the products distributed as shown by point *E* in the box diagram, represents an inefficient output mix. The consumers' common MRS, 3*C*/1*W*, is greater than the economy's MRT, 1*C*/1*W*, which implies that more wine and less corn can make both consumers better off.

tween the consumers is efficient: there is no way to alter the distribution of the *given* outputs that would benefit both. Since we are operating on, rather than inside, the production frontier, the allocation of inputs is efficient. Two of the three efficiency conditions are satisfied. What about the third? Determining if the output mix is efficient involves comparing the common MRS of the consumers with the MRT. In the diagram this comparison is equivalent to comparing the slope of *gg* with the slope of *ff*. Since *gg* is steeper than *ff*, [MRS^i_{wc}] > MRT_{wc}. Consumers place a higher value on more wine than it costs to produce. This result is not surprising because we have simply graphed the same information presented in Table 18–1. Figure 18–2, therefore, shows an inefficient output mix, so an increase in wine output combined with the required reduction in corn output — moving toward point *P* — could benefit both consumers. Note that a movement toward point *P* will involve an increase in marginal cost (MRT), and at the same time marginal benefit (MRS) will tend to diminish until the two become equal at an efficient output mix.

Can we use Figure 18–2 to show both consumers better off when the output mix is at point *P?* By some careful geometry, it is possible to do so, but the difficulty is that when the output mix moves from *B* to point *P,* the dimensions of the Edgeworth box diagram are altered. This in turn means we would have to carefully redraw Monica's indifference curves since the origin of her indifference map has moved from point *B* to point *P.* For example, Monica's indifference curve U_4^M would then be located farther to the southeast. When the origin shifts, the entire set of indifference curves must shift with it. (Hank's indifference curves stay put since his origin remains at point 0.) As mentioned, this manipulation requires some careful geometry and results in a very cluttered diagram, so instead we will use a separate diagram.

Figure 18–3 shows the Edgeworth box diagram associated with point *P* on the production possibility frontier. One way of distributing the 150*W*

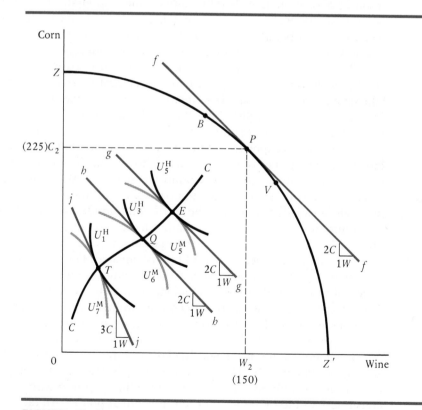

FIGURE 18–3

Efficient Output Mix Depends on Distribution

The output mix at point *P,* with the distribution shown at point *E,* is an efficient allocation since MRS = MRT. Distribution of the same outputs at point *Q* is also efficient, but the distribution at point *T* is not since at this point MRS > MRT.

and $225C$ is shown at point E on the contract curve for the relevant Edge-worth box diagram $0C_2PW_2$. The output mix (point P) combined with the specific distribution of that output (point E) is an efficient, or Pareto op-timal, allocation of resources. (In fact, it illustrates a resource allocation in which both consumers are better off than they are at point E in Figure 18–2 when the output mix at point B was produced.) All three efficiency conditions are satisfied. The $150W$ and $225C$ are distributed so that the consumers' MRSs are equal, the economy is producing on the production frontier at point P, and the consumers' MRSs are equal at $2C/1W$ to the economy's MRT, also $2C/1W$.

From the resource allocation just identified, and with the available quantities of land and labor and known production technology, there is no conceivable way the economy could be restructured so that one person is better off unless it comes at the expense of some other person. Con-sequently, this resource allocation places us on the welfare frontier dis-cussed in the previous section, and illustrated in Figure 18–4. The resource allocation described by points P and E in Figure 18–3 is shown as point E on the welfare frontier in Figure 18–4. We have identified how resources must be allocated to achieve one point on the welfare frontier; that is, one efficient, or optimal, allocation of resources.

There is more than one allocation of resources for which all three conditions for efficiency are satisfied. To see that there are other efficient allocations, look at Figure 18–3 again. Suppose we hold the output mix fixed at point P and redistribute the fixed quantities of wine and corn so that we move to point Q on the contract curve. This distribution benefits Monica at Hank's expense, but that by itself does not tell us whether it is a movement along the welfare frontier or to a point inside it. Are all three efficiency conditions satisfied at point Q? Since the MRSs are equal, and since we are still on the production frontier, the first two conditions are necessarily satisfied. Whether the third condition is satisfied depends on the common slopes of the indifference curves at point Q — the slope of the line hh. If this slope is equal to the marginal rate of transformation, $2C/1W$, then the third efficiency condition is satisfied. For the specific sets of preferences graphed, this is true. Thus, we have identified a second allo-cation of resources that is fully efficient, with all three conditions satisfied. This allocation is shown as point Q on the welfare frontier in Figure 18–4.

Let's go through this exercise once more by moving along the con-tract curve in Figure 18–3 to point T, benefiting Monica at Hank's expense. At point T the common MRS is $3C/1W$, and that is not equal to the MRT at point P, which is $2C/1W$. Since $[MRS_{wc}^i] > MRT_{wc}$ with this resource allocation, it would be possible to increase the output of wine so that both consumers would be better off than they are at point T. In fact, this situa-tion is qualitatively identical to that shown in Figure 18–2 and described earlier in Table 18–1. Thus, this resource allocation satisfies two of the efficiency conditions but not the third: it is not fully efficient. In Figure 18–4 it is shown as point T *inside* the welfare frontier since we know both

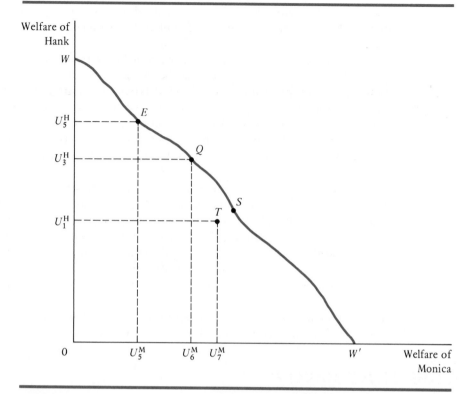

FIGURE 18–4

Various Resource Allocations Illustrated with Welfare Frontier

Points E, Q, and T in the diagram correspond to those same points in the previous diagram. Points E and Q are efficient allocations and so lie on the welfare frontier. Point T is an inefficient allocation and so lies inside the welfare frontier.

consumers can be made better off by altering the output mix whenever $[MRS^i_{WC}] > MRT_{WC}$. We would have to choose a point farther down the production frontier, like point V in Figure 18–3, and *its* associated Edgeworth box diagram to show explicitly the resource allocation at which both consumers are better off than at point T.[4] As this example shows, *no unique output mix — one point on the production frontier — is more efficient than all others.* The appropriate output mix may depend on the distribution of well-being among consumers. If Monica has a stronger

[4] An alternative way to derive the welfare frontier would be to proceed as follows. For each point on the production frontier, construct the associated Edgeworth box diagram. Plot the related welfare levels from along each one of the contract curves for each box diagram. Some of the points, such as E and Q on CC in Figure 18–3, will be on the welfare frontier. Some, like point T, will lie inside it. The welfare frontier is the locus of the extreme — or farthest out — points plotted in this way.

preference for wine than Hank, moving down the welfare frontier to a point where Monica is better off will involve increasing the output of wine, as is true of the movement from Q to T.

To sum up, we have shown what conditions must be satisfied for a particular allocation of resources to be efficient. We have, in fact, looked behind the welfare frontier to see what types of resource allocations are implied by points along the frontier. As we have seen, three conditions must hold simultaneously for a resource allocation to be efficient, or Pareto optimal. If one or more of these conditions is not satisfied, resources will be inefficiently allocated, and we will be inside the welfare frontier.

We should emphasize one final point. The concept of efficiency and the three conditions that must be satisfied for a resource allocation to be efficient are applicable to any economy, whether it is free enterprise, socialist, or centrally planned. Every economy, no matter how structured, must produce goods, distribute goods among consumers, and allocate inputs to different uses; and there are efficient and inefficient ways to accomplish these activities. A careful reading of this section will show, in fact, that no reference was made to "prices" or "markets" at any point. Thus, efficiency — how well an economy serves the wants of its consumers — is a concept that can be used to evaluate any economic system.

COMPETITIVE MARKETS AND ECONOMIC EFFICIENCY
18.3

Having just emphasized that the concept of efficiency can be used to evaluate the allocation of resources in any type of economy, we can now turn to an economy in which all markets are perfectly competitive. Let's consider each of the three efficiency conditions in turn.

1. A perfectly competitive economy results in an efficient distribution of products among consumers. This point has been discussed previously in Section 5.4, so here the argument will only be repeated briefly. When Hank is in equilibrium as a consumer, his consumption basket will be one where his MRS equals the ratio of product prices, or

$$P_W/P_C = \text{MRS}_{WC}^H. \tag{4}$$

Likewise, Monica will be in equilibrium when

$$P_W/P_C = \text{MRS}_{WC}^M. \tag{5}$$

Since competitive markets establish a uniform price for each product, the ratio P_W/P_C will be the same for both consumers, so Hank's MRS is equal to the same price ratio as Monica's, and both are equal to each other:

$$\text{MRS}_{WC}^H = \text{MRS}_{WC}^M. \tag{6}$$

This is the condition for an efficient distribution. A competitive equilibrium therefore implies an efficient distribution of products.

2. A perfectly competitive economy results in an efficient allocation of inputs. This point has also been derived previously, in Section 17.2. To prove the point, recall that each firm producing corn minimizes costs by employing inputs in quantities such that the marginal rate of technical substitution between the inputs equals the input price ratio, or

$$w/v = MRTS_{LA}^{C}. \tag{7}$$

Likewise, a firm producing wine operates where

$$w/v = MRTS_{LA}^{W}. \tag{8}$$

Since competitive markets equalize input prices across firms and industries, the ratio w/v is the same for all firms. Therefore, the right-hand sides of equations (7) and (8) are also equal to one another, so

$$MRTS_{LA}^{C} = MRTS_{LA}^{W}. \tag{9}$$

This is the condition for efficiency in the allocation of inputs.

3. A perfectly competitive economy results in an efficient output mix. This is demonstrated by considering the equilibrium conditions of firms in output markets and the equilibrium conditions of consumers. When wine producers produce the profit-maximizing outputs, they operate where marginal cost equals price, or

$$P_W = MC_W. \tag{10}$$

For corn producers the profit-maximizing condition is

$$P_C = MC_C. \tag{11}$$

Dividing equation (10) by (11) yields

$$P_W/P_C = MC_W/MC_C. \tag{12}$$

Since we know that

$$MC_W/MC_C = MRT_{WC} \qquad \text{(Section 17.3)}$$

and

$$P_W/P_C = [MRS_{WC}^i],$$

then by substitution

$$[MRS_{WC}^i] = MRT_{WC}, \tag{13}$$

and this is the condition for an efficient output mix.

These formal manipulations show that *when perfectly competitive markets are in equilibrium, all three conditions for economic efficiency are automatically satisfied.* Figure 18–5 illustrates this outcome for our two-good, two-consumer economy. Figure 18–5 looks much like Figure 18–3, as it should since the former also illustrates an efficient resource alloca-

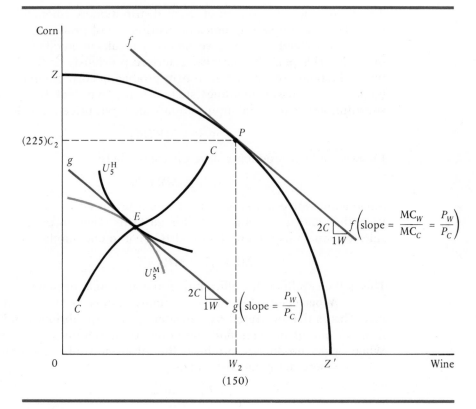

FIGURE 18–5

Economic Efficiency in a Competitive Economy

Competitive markets produce an efficient allocation of resources. The output mix at point *P*, together with the distribution shown by point *E*, illustrates a competitive equilibrium. All efficiency conditions are satisfied.

tion. The difference is that the various slopes are now identified as the ratios of prices established by competitive markets. The slope of the production frontier equals the ratio of marginal costs and the ratio of product prices. Each consumer faces a budget line with a slope equal to the slope of line *gg*, which equals the price ratio. Thus, the consumers' MRSs must equal the MRT in a competitive equilibrium. (See also Figure 17–5 and the discussion there.)

No reader need be told that this presentation is not an intuitive explanation. Instead, it builds on what was learned in earlier chapters by condensing much of the previous analysis to quickly prove the major point. How a competitive economy efficiently solves the three basic economic problems probably cannot be explained convincingly in an intuitively pleasing way. Perhaps the closest we can come is to note that a competitive economy relies on voluntary exchanges. Whenever any possible change in resource allocation promises mutual benefits to market participants, people have incentive to work out exchanges to realize these gains. If all mutually beneficial exchanges are consummated, as they would be in competitive markets, then no further change will benefit some without harming others. The outcome is efficient.

This discussion is a formal proof, at a highly abstract level, of Adam Smith's famous "invisible hand" theorem; namely, that people pursuing their own ends in competitive markets promote an important social goal — economic efficiency — that is no part of their intention, and which they may not even understand. In terms of our welfare frontier construction, it means that competitive markets automatically attain a point on the frontier. Now we see why it is misleading to describe this accomplishment of competitive markets with the phrase "maximizing society's welfare" or with similar phrases. Society does not have preferences, and the one point on the welfare frontier that represents a competitive equilibrium is not the only efficient resource allocation. Nonetheless, we should recognize that competitive markets tend to get us to a point on the welfare frontier, which is no easy task.

Partial Equilibrium Approach

So far we have used a general equilibrium approach in our discussion of efficiency since the general nature of the results is best shown this way. But it is also possible to use a partial equilibrium, or single-market, analysis to explain why the competitively determined level of output is efficient.

Previously we treated the wine and corn markets simultaneously. Now let's focus on the wine market alone. Figure 18–6 shows the supply and demand curves for wine, with an equilibrium output of 150 bottles. As we saw before, 150 bottles of wine is the efficient output of wine (see Figure 18–5), but now let's analyze this output mix in terms of the supply and demand curves. The simplest way to proceed is to show why every other level of output is inefficient. Suppose instead that only 100 bottles of wine are produced. Producers are then operating at point *A* on the supply curve, while consumers are at point *B* on the demand curve.

Let's compare the marginal benefit of more wine to consumers in relation to its marginal production costs. At point *B* on the demand curve each consumer purchases wine up to the point where its marginal benefit is $15. Monica, for example, purchases 10 bottles. As we saw in Chapter 3, the height to her demand curve d_M measures the marginal importance of the good to her. The price really represents the marginal benefit of wine relative to other goods. Monica would be willing to give up $15 worth of other goods, like corn, to have one more bottle of wine, so the height to the demand curve can be interpreted as a measure of marginal benefit in dollars.

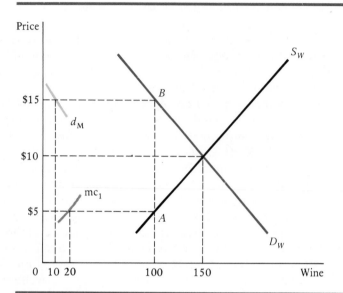

FIGURE 18-6

Efficient Output from a Partial Equilibrium Viewpoint

In partial equilibrium terms, the demand curve shows the marginal benefits of the good to consumers and the supply curve shows the marginal cost of producing it. At the intersection, marginal benefit and marginal cost are equal: an efficient level of output.

The height to the supply curve indicates the marginal cost of production. When 100 bottles of wine are being produced, each producer is in a position like firm 1, producing up to the point where marginal cost (mc) equals $5. To produce more wine, the firm must bid away $5 worth of labor and land from the production of other goods — for instance, corn. If the corn market is competitive, when $5 worth of labor and land is diverted to wine production, an amount of corn that is worth $5 to consumers must be sacrificed.

When output of wine is 100 units, consumers will give up $15 worth of other goods (corn) to get one more bottle of wine, while one more bottle of wine can be produced at a cost of only $5 worth of other goods (corn). At 100 units the marginal benefit of more wine output is greater than its marginal cost. Consumers will be better off with an expansion of wine output although this involves less of other goods. An efficient output results when the marginal benefit of more wine just equals its marginal cost, and this outcome occurs at an output of 150 units — the equilibrium level of output of the competitive wine industry.

Now let's relate this to the general equilibrium approach. In general equilibrium terms, an efficient output mix requires MRS to equal MRT.

MRS, however, is a measure of marginal benefit of one good in terms of another, and the partial equilibrium counterpart is the dollar price that consumers will pay. Similarly, MRT is a measure of marginal cost of one good in terms of another, while the partial equilibrium counterpart is the height to the supply curve showing marginal cost in dollars. *Thus, the intersection of competitive supply and demand curves is, in partial equilibrium terms, equivalent to the MRS = MRT solution in general equilibrium terms: both express an equality between marginal benefit and marginal cost.* The difference is that the general equilibrium approach explicitly considers what happens in other markets while it remains implicit in the single-market approach.

Are Competitive Markets Really So Efficient?

The demonstration that a competitive equilibrium is Pareto optimal is the basis for much of the faith economists have in competitive markets. Nevertheless, the "invisible hand" theorem should be regarded with some skepticism. It is unlikely that any real world economy could literally attain a fully efficient allocation of resources. To achieve that outcome every one of thousands of markets must be *perfectly* competitive and simultaneously attain an equilibrium. Actually, the underlying conditions — technology of production, input quantities, consumer preferences — are constantly changing, so demand and supply curves are always shifting. Equilibrium is never fully attained.

In addition, probably no real world markets are, or could be, perfectly competitive. Some minor deviations from perfect competition might only make a small difference, but some markets are noncompetitive to marked degrees. For example, monopolies and labor unions interfere with the attainment of economic efficiency, as we will see in the next section. Other impediments to efficiency include externalities and public goods, which we will discuss in the next chapter. In addition, some government policies such as the minimum wage and agricultural price supports lead markets to produce inefficient results.

For these reasons actual markets will fall short of attaining a perfectly efficient allocation of resources. The important questions, though, are how closely actual markets approximate the theoretical ideal and what the practical alternatives are. To study these questions requires the use of both theoretical analysis and empirical evidence, and the answers probably vary from case to case. An understanding of the theoretical determination of the efficiency characteristics of perfectly competitive markets, however, shows that the internal logic of the economic forces at work in markets is not perverse. Profit maximization by firms and utility maximization by consumers actually promote economic efficiency when they occur in the context of competitive markets.

Before closing our discussion of economic efficiency, we should emphasize the important role of knowledge in the process. When showing what an efficient allocation of resources looks like, we assumed that all the relevant information was known: consumer preferences, production functions, and the quantities and productive capabilities of inputs. Clearly, in the real world, with millions of consumers and hundreds of thousands of firms and products, no one person knows, or could possibly ever know, all the relevant information needed to attain economic efficiency. To emphasize this point, economists frequently point out that probably no one person knows how to make even a simple lead pencil. Producers of pencils purchase wood, graphite, steel, paint, and rubber from other people. Pencil producers do not know how to produce these inputs themselves. Despite the fact that no one knows how to make a pencil, much less an automobile, these items are produced. How?

The answer is that in a market system the partial bits of knowledge possessed by many different people are coordinated through market transactions to produce a result that no one totally comprehends.[5] Individuals only need information about their own consumption or production activities; all they need to know about the rest of the economy to adjust their behavior appropriately is conveyed through prices. For example, if new deposits of iron ore are discovered at the same time that the supply of trees declines, the price of steel desks would fall relative to the price of wooden desks. Consumers and businesses would substitute steel desks for wooden ones, thereby using more of the more plentiful iron ore and economizing on the now scarcer wood. This efficient response can, and probably would, occur without anyone knowing why prices changed in the way they did.

A market system can function efficiently, at least roughly so, without any single individual understanding how. In this sense markets economize on the knowledge that people individually require to coordinate their economic activities. An immense amount of knowledge must be utilized to achieve an efficient allocation of resources. Perhaps the most significant implication of our analysis is that in principle an efficient outcome can be accomplished by decentralized, voluntary transactions among people, each of whom has only a tiny portion of the requisite knowledge.

APPLYING WELFARE ECONOMICS: TWO EXAMPLES
18.4

We have used the production frontier and Edgeworth box apparatus to illustrate a competitive equilibrium. Now we will use it to examine the impact of monopoly and labor unions on the allocation of resources.

---

[5] This important point was emphasized by F. A. Hayek in "The Use of Knowledge in Society," *American Economic Review*, 35 (September 1945): 519–530. More recently Thomas Sowell has elaborated on the significance of this insight in *Knowledge and Decisions* (New York: Basic Books, 1980).

Monopoly

Previously, we assumed that both corn and wine were produced under competitive conditions. Suppose instead that wine is produced by a monopoly while corn continues to be produced competitively.

Our earlier analysis of profit maximization by a monopoly (Section 11.4) will help us to show what a monopoly equilibrium looks like. A monopoly in wine production maximizes profits by producing an output where marginal cost equals marginal revenue, but the price charged is higher than marginal revenue, so it is greater than marginal cost:

$$P_W > MC_W \qquad \text{(for example, \$15 > \$5).} \qquad (14)$$

Relative prices are what matter, though, so we must also include the corn market where price equals marginal cost since that market is competitive:

$$P_C = MC_C \qquad \text{(for example, \$5 = \$5).} \qquad (15)$$

Dividing equation (14) by (15), we can relate the relative price of wine to its relative marginal cost:

$$P_W/P_C > MC_W/MC_C \qquad \text{(\$15/5 > \$5/5; or } 3C/1W > 1C/1W). \qquad (16)$$

The inequality of equation (16) tells us what the situation looks like graphically: under monopoly the relative price of wine (P_W/P_C) is greater than its relative marginal cost (MC_W/MC_C). Suppose the output mix is at point M on the production frontier in Figure 18–7. The slope of the frontier at point M, shown by the slope of the line ff, equals the ratio of marginal costs — the right side of inequality (16). At M, however, the price ratio facing consumers is not equal to the ratio of marginal costs, as it is under competition. Instead, the relative price of the monopolized good is pegged artificially high, as shown by the slope of line jj, which represents P_W/P_C. Consumer equilibrium, as shown in the Edgeworth box diagram, therefore occurs at a point where budget lines have a slope of P_W/P_C. Thus, consumer equilibrium occurs at point E, where the slopes of the indifference curves equal $3C/1W$, the price ratio.

This is what a monopoly equilibrium looks like in a general equilibrium framework. Now let's see whether the three conditions for efficiency are satisfied. Since the consumers' MRSs are equal at point E, and since we are on the production frontier at point M, the first two conditions are satisfied. The third condition, however, is violated by monopoly. At point E the consumers' common MRS ($3C/1W$) exceeds the MRT [$(1C/1W) = (MC_W/MC_C)$], indicating that the output mix is inefficient. More wine and less corn should be produced since the marginal benefit of more wine in terms of corn exceeds its marginal cost at the monopoly equilibrium.

We need not explain again in detail why this resource allocation is inefficient since Figure 18–7 conforms to Figure 18–2 and Table 18–1, which first dealt with the condition for efficiency in the output mix. We

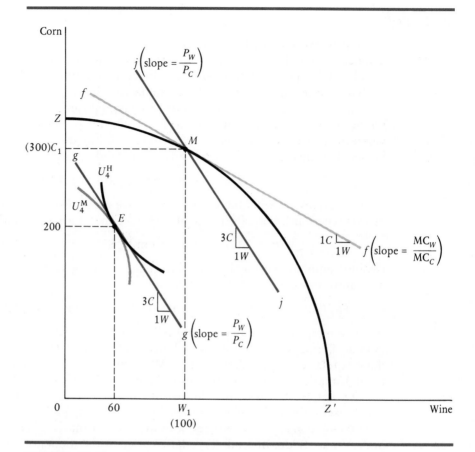

FIGURE 18–7

Monopoly and Inefficiency in the Output Mix

With wine produced by a monopoly, the equilibrium is at point *M*, with the distribution at point *E*. Since MRS > MRT, this outcome represents an inefficient allocation in which output of the monopolized good is too low.

should stress, rather, that the present analysis is simply the general equilibrium approach to the welfare cost of monopoly that was explained in Section 11.6. They are two different ways of saying the same thing — output is too low under monopoly.[6]

Labor Unions

We can also evaluate the effect of labor unions on resource allocation by using the basic principles of welfare economics. Let's suppose that in an

[6] Figure 11–7 shows the welfare cost, or inefficiency, due to monopoly from a partial equilibrium perspective. The fact that price is above marginal cost in this diagram corresponds to the difference between the slopes of *ff* and *jj* in Figure 18–7.

otherwise competitive economy workers in the wine industry form a union and establish higher wage rates. As explained in Section 16.3, at the higher wage rate employment of workers in the unionized industry will fall. We assume that disemployed workers from the wine industry secure jobs in the corn industry, although at lower wages. Thus, the same total quantity of labor is employed after the union is formed, but the distribution of workers between the unionized wine industry and the nonunionized corn industry has changed.

Now consider the efficiency implications of such a resource allocation. *The central fact to take into account is that the wage rate paid by wine producers exceeds the wage rate paid by corn producers.* Wine producers will minimize their production costs by employing labor and land in quantities such that the ratio of marginal products equals the ratio of input prices — the tangency between an isoquant and an isocost line. Wine producers will be in this situation:

$$w_U/v = \text{MRTS}_{LA}^{W}, \tag{17}$$

where w_U is the union wage, v is the rental price of land, and MRTS_{LA}^{W} is the marginal rate of technical substitution between labor and land in producing wine.

Corn producers will likewise minimize production costs, but they confront a wage rate for (nonunion) workers, w_N, that is lower than w_U. Their equilibrium in input markets appears as

$$w_N/v = \text{MRTS}_{LA}^{C}. \tag{18}$$

Both industries pay the same price for land inputs, but since w_U is greater than w_N, the relative price of labor is higher in the wine industry: $w_U/v > w_N/v$. From equations (17) and (18) above, then,

$$\text{MRTS}_{LA}^{W} = w_U/v > w_N/v = \text{MRTS}_{LA}^{C}, \tag{19}$$

or

$$\text{MRTS}_{LA}^{W} > \text{MRTS}_{LA}^{C}. \tag{20}$$

Equation (20) violates the second efficiency condition that requires inputs to be allocated between wine and corn production so that the marginal rates of technical substitution are equal. Examine this result graphically in an Edgeworth production box diagram. In Figure 18–8 point *G* illustrates the situation where a union in the wine industry establishes a higher wage rate than is paid to workers in the corn industry. In the unionized wine industry producers minimize the cost of producing 120 bottles of wine by equating the ratio of input prices, as shown by the slope of line *ff*, to the slope of the 120*W* isoquant at point *G*. The ratio of input prices in the corn industry, however, is lower, as shown by the slope of the line *gg*. When corn producers minimize costs at this lower relative cost of labor, they operate at point *G*, where the 270*C* corn isoquant is tangent to line *gg*.

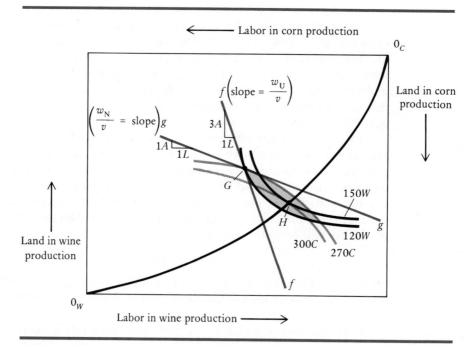

FIGURE 18-8

Labor Unions and the Allocation of Inputs

A labor union in the wine industry leads to a higher wage rate for workers in that industry than for workers in the corn industry. This results in the input allocation, point G, lying off the contract curve because the MRTSs differ.

Because the industries equate their respective MRTSs to different relative labor costs, the MRTSs themselves must differ. This result is shown by the fact that the 120*W* isoquant and the 270*C* isoquant intersect at point *G*, indicating that this is an inefficient allocation of inputs. More of both corn and wine could be produced by allocating the same total quantities of labor and land differently between the industries. For example, at point *H*, 150 bottles of wine and 300 bushels of corn could be produced. But to achieve this outcome requires increased employment of labor in the wine industry, which the union will not permit because it is holding down employment to maintain a higher wage rate.

Figure 18–9 illustrates what the union wage policy implies in terms of the production possibility frontier, the *ZZ'* curve. Point *G* in Figure 18–8 corresponds to point *G* in Figure 18–9: *the economy is operating inside the production possibility frontier.* Note that this is not because resources are unemployed (since we are assuming all inputs are employed), but because of an inefficient allocation of inputs between wine and corn production. Since total output is lower than it could be, so is total consumption, and

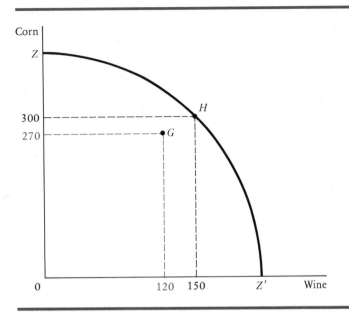

FIGURE 18-9
Labor Unions and the Production Possibility Frontier
Point *G* here corresponds to point *G* in Figure 18-8. A labor union causes the economy to operate inside the frontier because of the misallocation of inputs.

people are not as well off as they could be if the economy were operating on the production frontier.

Does this conclusion mean that unions are undesirable? Not necessarily. Unions lead to an inefficient allocation of resources, but for reasons discussed in the first section of this chapter, efficiency is not the only criterion. In particular, union members do benefit, but they do so at the expense of other people, and that change in the distribution of well-being must also be acknowledged. In terms of Figure 18–1, if Hank is the union member and Monica the nonunion worker, the formation of the union results in a movement from an efficient point like *A* to an inefficient point like *D*.

Summary

In this chapter we examined welfare economics, the study of how effectively economic arrangements promote the welfare, or well-being, of all members of society. The concept of economic efficiency, or Pareto optimality, plays a central role in the analysis since it defines a situation in which no

person's well-being can be further improved unless someone else is harmed.

Three conditions determine whether an economy is operating efficiently. First, the goods produced must be efficiently distributed among consumers. Efficient distributions occur at points on the contract curve in an exchange box diagram. Second, inputs must be allocated efficiently to the production of the goods. Efficient input allocations are shown by points on the contract curve in a production box diagram or, equivalently, by the economy's operation on, rather than inside, its production possibility frontier. Third, the output mix produced must be efficient. An efficient output mix is identified by a point on the production frontier where, when the outputs are distributed among consumers, each consumer's marginal rate of substitution equals the marginal rate of transformation.

When all markets are perfectly competitive, all three efficiency conditions are automatically satisfied: a competitive economy tends to allocate resources in an efficient way. In contrast, we saw that when a monopoly produces one product, the third efficiency condition is violated: the consumers' marginal rates of substitution will not equal the marginal rate of transformation. A monopoly produces an inefficient level of output. As another example of how certain economic arrangements can lead to inefficiency, we examined the way resource allocation is affected by labor unions. With a labor union in one of the industries, the output mix produced lies inside, rather than on, the production frontier: a violation of the second efficiency condition.

Review Questions and Problems

1. What is an efficient allocation of resources? An inefficient allocation of resources? Illustrate your answer by using a welfare frontier.

2. "If the government takes $1000 from multimillionaire Clint Eastwood and gives it to a destitute family, it is obvious that this action would increase the poor family's well-being by more than it would diminish Eastwood's, so social welfare would increase." Discuss the issue. How would you show this change in resource allocation by using a welfare frontier?

3. "Demonstrating that a policy is efficient is not the same as showing that it is desirable." Why not?

4. State and explain the three conditions that must be satisfied for the allocation of resources to be efficient.

5. The condition for an efficient rate of output of any good is, in short, MRS = MRT. From the definitions of these terms you should be able to give an intuitive explanation of why this condition must hold. Do so.

*6. Using the production possibility frontier with the exchange box diagram under it, show a situation where the output of wine is too large — that is, larger than is efficient. Does this result mean that a lower output of wine (and higher output of corn) will necessarily benefit both consumers?

*7. When the three conditions for optimal resource allocation are satisfied, where are we located in terms of the welfare frontier? Explain. If any one condition is not satisfied, where are we located in terms of the welfare frontier? Explain.

8. "The concept of efficiency has no meaning in a socialist economy; it is relevant only for a private enterprise system." Comment on this statement.

9. Explain why, when all markets are competitive and in equilibrium, all three conditions for efficiency are satisfied. Does this mean that society's welfare is maximized? What does it mean?

10. Use the partial equilibrium constructs of supply and demand curves to explain why the equilibrium rate of output of a competitive industry is also an efficient rate of output.

*11. According to Albert Einstein: "The economic anarchy of capitalist society as it exists today is in my view the main cause of our evils. Production is carried on for profit, not for use." Is there a conflict between "production for profit" and "production for use"?

12. What efficiency condition does a monopoly violate? Show the result, using both

general equilibrium and partial equilibrium approaches.

13. What efficiency condition do labor unions violate? How is the effect shown by using the production possibility frontier?

14. In terms of the welfare frontier, what is the effect of monopoly? What is the effect of labor unions? Does this analysis support the contention that both monopolies and labor unions are bad?

*15. We analyzed the policy of "target price subsidies" in agricultural markets in Section 10.5. Use the production frontier–exchange box diagram to evaluate the efficiency of resource allocation under this policy.

*16. Ignoring rationing problems and black markets, under rent controls (or any price ceiling that produces a shortage) the price paid by consumers equals the marginal cost of producing the good. Does this result mean that the output level is efficient? Explain.

Supplementary Readings

Bator, F. M. "The Simple Analytics of Welfare Maximization." *American Economic Review*, 47 (March 1957): 22–59.

Browning, Jacquelene, and Browning, Edgar. "Welfare Analytics in General Equilibrium Theory: An Improved Geometry." *Canadian Journal of Economics*, 9 (May 1976): 341–350

Harberger, Arnold. "Three Basic Postulates for Applied Welfare Economics: An Interpretive Essay." *Journal of Economic Literature*, 9 (September 1971): 785–797.

Rees, A. "The Effects of Unions on Resource Allocation." *Journal of Law and Economics*, 6 (October 1963): 69–78.

Scherer, F. M. "General Equilibrium and Economic Efficiency." *American Economist* (Spring 1966): 54–70.

Public Goods and Externalities

19

If markets, left to themselves, would always function efficiently, there would be little scope for government policy, except perhaps to alter the distribution of income. But in some situations even competitive markets are not capable of producing efficient outcomes. In this chapter we will look at two of the more important reasons why private markets fail, the presence of public goods and externalities. When public good and externality elements lead markets to generate an inefficient allocation of resources, it is possible for government to intervene with an appropriate policy that will improve matters. Much of the modern economic rationale for government intervention in the economy is based squarely on the analysis of how public goods and externalities may adversely affect the way resources are allocated by markets.[1]

WHAT ARE PUBLIC GOODS?
19.1

As economists use the term *public good*, it does not necessarily refer to a good provided by the government. Instead, they define a public good by the characteristics of the good itself. Two characteristics are important: nonrival consumption and nonexclusion.

A good is *nonrival in consumption* if, with a given level of production, consumption by one person need not diminish the quantity consumed by anyone else. Although this definition may sound peculiar, such goods do exist. Consider the way a nuclear submarine reduces the likelihood of foreign attack. Your property and person are protected, and so are others', and the protection you receive in no way diminishes the extent to which others are protected. Another example is a flood control project that reduces the probability of flood damage. Less flood damage to one home does not mean more flood damage to another: all persons in a given area simultaneously receive the benefits in the form of a reduced likelihood of flooding.

---

[1] This chapter draws heavily on material presented in Chapter 2 of Edgar K. Browning and Jacquelene M. Browning, *Public Finance and the Price System*, 2nd ed. (New York: Macmillan, 1983).

In effect, nonrival consumption means potential simultaneous consumption of a good or service by many persons. By contrast, most goods and services are rival in consumption. For a given level of production of shoes (or wine, calculators, T-shirts, cars, or hamburgers), the more you consume, the less is available for others. In these cases consumption is rival because the economic system must ration output among competing (rival) consumers. When a good is nonrival in consumption, the good need not be rationed. Once it is produced, the good can be made available to all consumers without affecting any individual's level of consumption.

The second characteristic of a public good is nonexclusion. *Nonexclusion* means that it is impossible, or prohibitively costly, to confine the benefits of a good (once produced) to selected persons. Thus, a person can benefit from production of the good regardless of whether he or she pays for it. The characteristics of nonrivalry and nonexclusion often go together, but there is a distinction between the concepts. Nonrivalry means that consumption by one person *need not* (not *does not*) interfere with consumption of others; although a good may be nonrival in consumption, it still may be possible to restrict consumption to selected persons. When a television program is broadcast, for example, any number of people in the area can watch and not interfere with the reception of others. Thus, a television broadcast is nonrival in consumption. It is possible, though, to exclude some people from viewing the program. The broadcaster could install metering devices on all TV sets so that only those paying a fee could watch the program — nonpayers would be excluded. Although the broadcast is nonrival, exclusion is possible, so it does not have both characteristics of a public good.

In contrast, national defense is an example of a good with both characteristics. A given defense effort protects (or endangers) everyone simultaneously, and it is impossible to limit the protection to certain people; that is, there is no feasible way to protect you and exclude your neighbor. The benefits of defense are nonrival to the population, and exclusion of selected persons is virtually impossible.

A good that is nonrival in consumption with high exclusion costs creates severe problems for a market system. Once such a good is produced, many people will automatically benefit, regardless of whether they pay for it because they cannot be excluded. As we will see, this feature makes it unlikely that private producers will provide the good efficiently.

The Free Rider Problem

Even when a public good is worth more to people than it costs to produce, private markets may fail to provide it. To see how, consider the construction of a dam that will lessen the probability of flooding for members of a specific community; the dam is a public good for residents of the community. The dam has a total cost of $10,000, and business firms will be willing to build it if someone will pay for it. If 10 persons live in the community and the benefit of the dam to each person is $2,000, then the total benefit of the dam to all 10 residents is $20,000 — twice as much as it costs. All 10 people would be better off if each contributes $1,000 to finance construction costs, since each would then receive a benefit valued at $2,000 from the dam.

Despite the fact that it is in each resident's interest to have the dam constructed, there is a good chance that it won't be built if private markets are relied upon to organize the construction. To finance the dam, several residents must jointly agree to contribute, and individuals will realize that they will receive the benefits of the dam once it is built regardless of whether they make any contribution toward the dam's construction. *Each resident, therefore, has incentive to understate what the dam is worth in an effort to secure the benefit at a lower, or zero, cost.* If enough people behave in this way — as *free riders* — voluntary contributions will be insufficient to finance the dam and it won't be built.

When public goods are involved, free rider behavior is rational, but it hinders the ability of private markets to cater efficiently to the demand for a public good. In the example just discussed, it is conceivable that enough people would contribute so that the dam would be financed by voluntary agreements. Because just ten people are involved, only a small number need agree to contribute. The severity of the free rider problem, however, varies with the number of people involved; and when a large number of people receive benefits from a public good, it is virtually certain that voluntary cooperation through private markets will fail to provide the good.

As the group size increases, it is more likely that everyone will behave like a free rider, and the public good will not be provided. To illustrate, let's change the dam example slightly and assume that the dam now benefits 1,000 people, each by $20. (Note that the total benefit is still $20,000, just as before.) In this case, faced with deciding whether to, or how much to, contribute voluntarily, each person will realize that one single contribution will have virtually no effect on whether the dam is built. Put differently, the outcome depends mainly on what the other 999 people do, and whether any one person contributes will not affect what others do. In this case each person will get the same benefit whether or not any contribution is made, and choosing not to contribute is the most rational behavior. Because this is true for everyone, few people would contribute, and the good would not be provided.

Many real world examples provide evidence of free rider behavior with public goods. A particularly clear-cut example occurred in 1970 when General Motors tried to market pollution control devices for automobiles at a price of $20. The emission controls would have reduced the pollution emitted by 30 to 50 percent. Pollution abatement is, of course, a public good, at least over a certain geographic area. It is reasonable to suppose that the benefits of a 30 to 50 percent reduction in automobile pollution far outweighed the cost of $20 per car. Yet GM withdrew the device from the market because of poor sales. This is an illustration of the large-group free rider problem at work. Everyone might have been better off if all drivers used the device, but it was not in the interest of any single person to purchase it because the overall level of air quality would not be noticeably improved as a result of one individual's solitary action.

When the benefits of a public good are nonrival over a large group, it is unlikely that private markets will provide the good. Even if some amount of the public good is provided through the contributions of a few people, it will be provided in a suboptimal quantity. This is true even when it is in the interest of people to have the good provided; that is, even when the benefits exceed the costs. Competitive markets cannot in general supply public goods efficiently. This fact constitutes a major justification for considering governmental alternatives. In the dam example with 1,000 persons, for instance, the government could levy a tax of $10 on each person and use the $10,000 in tax revenue to finance the dam. Each person would benefit from this policy, receiving services from the dam worth $20 at a cost of $10 in taxes. The government expenditure of $10,000 on the dam would lead to a more efficient allocation of resources than reliance on private markets.

EFFICIENCY IN THE PROVISION OF A PUBLIC GOOD
19.2

What is the efficient output of a public good? As usual, we must compare the marginal benefits and marginal costs associated with different levels of output. The marginal cost of a public good is the opportunity cost of using resources to produce that good rather than other goods, just as it was in the case of the nonpublic, or private, goods discussed in previous chapters. Because of the nonrival nature of the benefits of a public good, though, its marginal benefit differs from that of a private good. With a good like wine, the marginal benefit of producing an additional unit is the value of the wine to the single person who consumes it. With a public good like defense, the marginal benefit is not the marginal value to any one person alone since many people benefit simultaneously from the same unit. Instead, we must add up the marginal benefit of every person who values the additional unit of defense, and the resulting sum indicates the combined willingness of the public to pay for more defense — that is, its marginal benefit.

Figure 19–1 shows how we derive the demand, or social marginal benefit, curve for a public good like submarines. For simplicity, assume that only two people, Monica and Hank, benefit from the defense services of submarines. Each person has a demand curve for submarines, shown as D_M and D_H. These demand curves are derived from each person's indifference curves, just as their demand curves for a private good would be. Recall that the height to a consumer's demand curve indicates the marginal benefit of another unit of the good. *To derive the social, or com-*

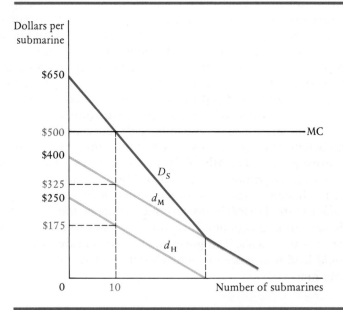

FIGURE 19-1

The Efficient Output of a Public Good

Because the benefits of a public good are nonrival, the social marginal benefit is the sum of the marginal benefits of the separate consumers. Graphically, the social demand curve is constructed by vertically summing the consumers' demand curves. The efficient output is identified by the intersection of D_S and MC.

bined, demand curve, we must add together the marginal benefits of the two consumers. Geometrically, the combined demand curve involves a *vertical summation* of the consumers' demand curves. For example, the marginal benefit to Monica of the first submarine ($400) is added to the marginal benefit Hank receives from the first submarine ($250) to determine the social marginal benefit ($650) for the first unit. This vertical addition of marginal benefits identifies one point on the social marginal benefit curve, indicating that the combined marginal benefit of Hank and Monica for the first submarine is $650. At alternative quantities of submarines we continue to add the heights to each consumer's demand curve to trace out the entire social demand curve, D_S.

We can now determine the efficient output of submarines. At any level of output where D_S lies above the marginal cost curve MC — drawn here for simplicity as horizontal at $500 — Hank and Monica are willing to pay more for an additional unit of output than its marginal cost, so efficiency requires a higher output. This means that an additional unit could be financed in a way that makes both of them better off — with each contributing somewhat less than the maximum amount he or she is willing to pay. When MC lies above D_S, however, too much of the public good is being produced — the combined marginal benefits as shown by D_S are less than marginal cost over this range of output. Therefore, the efficient rate of output is 10 submarines, where Monica's marginal benefit of \$325 plus Hank's marginal benefit of \$175 just equals the marginal cost of \$500.

In general, the efficient output of a public good occurs at the point where D_S, obtained by vertically summing the demand curves of all consumers, intersects the marginal cost curve. There is no presumption, however, that this output will be the actual, or equilibrium, output. In fact, we have already seen that the free rider problem will generally mean that private markets will not produce the efficient output. The government has the power to finance the efficient output from tax revenues, but whether it actually does so depends on how political forces determine public policy.

Government financing of a public good with taxes overcomes one aspect of the free rider problem, the tendency of people to withhold payment. There is another aspect of free rider behavior that government financing does not overcome: people would still have no incentive to reveal accurately their demands for the public good. To determine the efficient output, we must know every person's demand curve so that we can vertically add them to obtain D_S. How can we find out how much a public good like defense is worth to millions of people? This is probably the most difficult practical problem in applying the analysis to concrete cases.

In our analysis of efficiency in resource allocation in the last chapter, we pointed out that there are three conditions for efficiency. These conditions also apply to public goods. So far, we have emphasized only the condition for an efficient level of output. A second condition is that the output be produced using the least costly combination of inputs. In Figure 19–1 that condition is implicit in the assumption that a marginal cost of \$500 is the minimum cost necessary to produce a submarine. The third condition relates to the efficient rationing of the good among consumers. For a private good this condition requires an equality of marginal rates of substitution. But how is a public good rationed efficiently?

With a public good there is no rationing problem. If 10 submarines are produced, both Hank and Monica simultaneously benefit, and the benefit to one in no way diminishes the benefit to the other. To put this point differently, suppose it were possible in some hard-to-imagine way to have Monica protected by 10 submarines but Hank protected by only 5. In other words, if exclusion were possible, would there be any advantage in excluding Hank from the services of all 10 submarines? Apparently not — when 10 submarines are available, and if Hank only receives the services of 5, this does not make any more available for Monica. Consequently, Hank is harmed, and no one benefits. By definition, this outcome is clearly inefficient.

Recall our definition of a public good as one characterized by nonrival consumption and nonexclusion. When a good has both characteristics, it would be impossible to exclude anyone from the benefits even if we wanted to. What about a good with nonrival benefits where exclusion is possible? The analysis above suggests that *it is inefficient to exclude anyone even if we could.* Before accepting that as a general rule, let's examine an important public policy issue dealing with a good where benefits are nonrival but exclusion is possible.

Patents

As we explained in Chapter 11, a patent grants temporary legal monopoly power to an inventor. A patent gives the inventor the right to make and sell some new product or to use some new production process for a period of seventeen years. But what do patents have to do with the exotic world of nonrival benefits and nonexclusion? Surely, you say, a vibrating toilet seat (patent no. 3,244,168, granted in 1966) is not a public good.

Admittedly, most of the products and production processes granted patents are not themselves public goods. But what about the knowledge required to make, for example, a better mousetrap? This knowledge of "how to do it" has nonrival benefits. Once the knowledge exists, any number of people can use it without interfering with each other's use. One person's use of this special knowledge does not leave less for someone else. Simultaneous consumption of knowledge is therefore possible, but could people be excluded from the use of knowledge? Whether exclusion is possible depends to an extent on the type of knowledge involved, but in some cases the use of knowledge can be prohibited by making it illegal to produce or sell the tangible embodiment of the knowledge. For example, if it is illegal for you to manufacture and sell the better mousetrap, you would be effectively excluded from using the knowledge of how to make it. This is exactly what patents do. They exclude all but the inventor from making use of the knowledge he or she produced.

Thus, at least some types of knowledge have nonrival benefits, but exclusion is possible. Now let's consider efficiency in resource allocation in connection with knowledge. Although new knowledge is sometimes produced accidentally, much of it results from the use of resources devoted to research and development. The efficient output of new knowledge requires that the appropriate quantity of resources be devoted to producing it, and in principle this outcome is accomplished by equating the vertically summed marginal benefits with marginal cost, just as in Figure 19–1. Yet once the knowledge exists, using it efficiently requires that no one be excluded. Both aspects of efficiency are important.

To see how this discussion relates to patents, suppose that the inventor of a better mousetrap could not exclude others from copying and selling the product. Would the inventor devote a million dollars to develop an improved product? If this investment was successful, others would immediately copy and sell it, driving the price down to a level that just covered production costs and leaving no way for the inventor to recoup research costs. For this reason inventors would have little financial incentive to produce the knowledge in the first place, even though that knowledge might be highly beneficial. Too few resources would be devoted to research and development, because those who bear the costs could not charge others who use the knowledge for the benefit they receive. In other words, private markets would not produce the efficient quantity of the public good, new knowledge.

Patents can encourage a greater, more efficient output of new knowledge. Because inventors receive a temporary monopoly right, inventors of worthwhile products can get a return above the cost of producing the product to compensate for the research costs. The prospect of this gain would stimulate inventors to devote more resources to the production of new knowledge. This example illustrates how private markets can produce a good with nonrival benefits when exclusion is possible.

Encouraging a greater, more efficient output is the beneficial result of using patents, but there is a cost. Once the new knowledge is produced, it will be inefficiently used for seventeen years since some people are excluded from using it. For example, the better mousetrap would be monopolistically produced for seventeen years, which inefficiently restricts the use, or consumption, of the product. This cost must be weighed against the gain; namely, that the better mousetrap might never have been developed without the incentive created by patent protection.

Private markets can produce goods with nonrival benefits when exclusion is possible, as the patent example shows. Private markets, however, would probably not function with perfect efficiency because of the exclusion of some people who could potentially benefit but are excluded from doing so. Whether it is possible to devise some arrangement that works better is uncertain and would require a more detailed case-by-case evaluation. In any event, it is clear that the degree of inefficiency in market provision for a nonrival good will be far less when exclusion is possible than when it is not. The combination of the nonrival and nonexclusion characteristics creates the more severe problems for market provision, and in this case a more active role for government may be called for. No one has determined, for example, how national defense could be provided by private markets.

EXTERNALITIES
19.3

Sometimes in the process of producing or consuming certain goods, there are harmful or beneficial side effects called *externalities* that are borne by people who are not directly involved in the market exchanges. These side effects of ordinary economic activities are called *external benefits* when the effects are beneficial and *external costs* when they are harmful. The term *externality* stems from the fact that these effects are felt beyond, or are external to, the parties directly involved in generating the effects. A few examples will make the nature of externalities clear.

Immunization against a contagious disease is a good example of a consumption activity that involves external benefits. For instance, if Barney decides to get an inoculation, he benefits directly because his chance of contracting the disease is reduced. This benefit is not the external benefit since Barney himself receives it. The external benefit is the one other people receive in the form of a reduced likelihood they will catch the disease because the inoculated person is less likely to transmit it. The central point is that Barney's decision about whether or not to be inoculated is unlikely to be affected by how his inoculation affects other people: he is concerned mainly with the effect on his own health. Thus, the benefit his inoculation creates for others is external to, and doesn't influence, his decision.

Probably the best examples of external costs come from the area of pollution. Driving an automobile or operating a factory with a smoking chimney pollutes the atmosphere that others breathe; thus the operation of a car or factory imposes costs on people not directly involved in the activity. Similarly, operating a motorcycle produces a level of noise that is often irritating (harmful) to those nearby, just as the noise level of a supersonic or subsonic airplane may be annoying to people living near airports. Congestion is also an external cost: when a person drives during rush hour, the road becomes more congested not only for this person but for other drivers as well.

At a formal level externalities and public goods are very similar. If Barney is inoculated for a contagious disease, there are nonrival benefits: both he and others simultaneously benefit from his inoculation. In addition, it would be very difficult to exclude other people from the benefits. When a person produces new knowledge, this action also confers an external benefit on others who can utilize the knowledge profitably. Pollution is also like a public good, except here it should perhaps be called a public bad since there are nonrival costs. A large number of people are simultaneously harmed if the atmosphere is polluted, and it would obviously be difficult to have the atmosphere in a particular area polluted for some and not for others. If there is any difference between externalities and public goods, it may be the fact that external effects are *unintended* side effects of activities undertaken for other purposes. People don't pollute because they enjoy breathing polluted air — they simply want to transport themselves conveniently in a car from one place to another.

Recognizing the similarity between externalities and public goods makes it easier to understand the significance of externalities. *Externalities are likely to lead to an inefficient allocation of resources just as public goods do.* Market demands and supplies will only reflect the benefits and costs of market participants; the benefits and costs that fall on others will not be taken into account in determining resource allocation. For example,

Barney may decide against being inoculated because the improvement in his health is not worth the extra cost. If the benefits of improved health for others are added to his benefit, the combined benefit might exceed the cost. In this case Barney's decision not to be inoculated would represent an inefficient use of resources.

External Costs

A closer look at a case involving external costs will help clarify the issues involved. Suppose that firms in a constant-cost competitive industry produce some type of waste materials as a by-product of their activities. They dispose of these wastes by dumping them in a nearby river. From the firms' points of view, this method of disposal is the least costly one. People living downstream, however, suffer because the river no longer serves recreational purposes. The firms in the industry impose external costs on those living downstream. Because these external costs are not taken into account by the firms, the allocation of resources will be inefficient.

Let's see how this situation appears diagrammatically. In Figure 19–2 the competitive demand and supply curves are D and S, and the equilibrium output is Q_1 with a price of $20 per unit. Each unit of output generates a specific quantity of wastes, so the greater the industry output, the greater is the amount of water pollution. The harm done by the pollution is shown by the marginal external cost, or MEC, curve. It slopes upward, reflecting the assumption that additional amounts of pollution inflict increasing costs on people living downstream as the water becomes more polluted. The marginal external cost curve results from vertically summing the marginal cost of each person harmed since the harmful effects are nonrival over many persons. At the market output of Q_1 the marginal external cost is $7, implying that people downstream would be $7 better off with one unit less of the product and the waste associated with it.

With external costs the competitive output is too large. Firms expand output to the point where the price consumers will pay just covers *their* costs of production, but the resulting price does not cover *all* costs of production since the damage done by pollution is also a cost of producing the product. At Q_1 firms incur costs of $20 per unit, which is just covered by the price paid by consumers, but there is also a cost of $7 per unit borne by people downstream. At the competitive level of output Q_1, the product is not worth what it costs to produce. The social, or combined, marginal cost of production is $27, whereas the marginal benefit to consumers is only $20. The social marginal costs of production are shown by the curve S_S, obtained by vertically summing the MEC curve and the supply curve. It identifies all the costs associated with producing the product, not just the costs borne by producers. Efficiency requires that output be expanded to the point where the marginal benefit to consumers equals the social marginal cost of production. This is shown by the intersection of D and S_S at an output of Q_E.

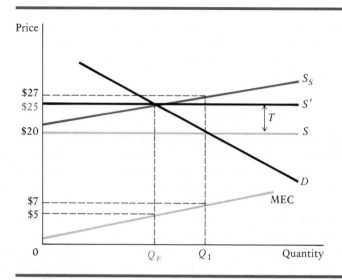

FIGURE 19-2
External Costs and Taxes

The marginal external cost curve, MEC, shows the external costs associated with production of the good. Vertically adding this curve to the private supply curve S yields the social marginal cost curve S_s. Its intersection with the demand curve identifies the efficient output Q_E, which is less than the market equilibrium output Q_1.

Competitive market pressures, however, lead to an output of Q_1, larger than the efficient output. The government could do several things to improve the situation. One policy would be to levy an excise tax on the product to induce firms to produce at the efficient level. A tax of $5 per unit would shift the supply curve up by $5 to S', and firms would curtail production to Q_E with consumers paying a price of $25. The result is the efficient level of output, where the marginal benefit to consumers equals the social marginal cost of production. Note that pollution is not completely eliminated; it is simply reduced to the point where a further reduction in production and pollution would cost more than it is worth. In general, external costs should not be totally eliminated even though those who are harmed might like to see them reduced to zero. Instead, the gain from reduced pollution to people downstream must be weighed against the cost to consumers of a reduced output.

In this example we assumed that each unit of output was invariably associated with a certain amount of pollution. In the more general case the amount of pollution per unit of output is variable. Automobiles, for example, can produce various amounts of emissions. When this situation is the relevant case, as it usually is, the tax should be levied on pollution itself, not on the product. Then firms would have incentive to curtail pollution — the external cost — in the least costly way available. We have discussed the way a tax on pollution would affect firms in Section 8.7.

External Benefits

External benefits can be analyzed in a similar fashion. Let's suppose that consumption of some product generates external benefits; that is, people other than the direct consumers of the product benefit from its consumption. The competitive supply and demand curves in Figure 19–3 are S and D. The demand curve D only reflects the marginal benefits of the good to the consumers of the product, and its intersection with the supply curve determines the market equilibrium with an output of Q_1 and a price of

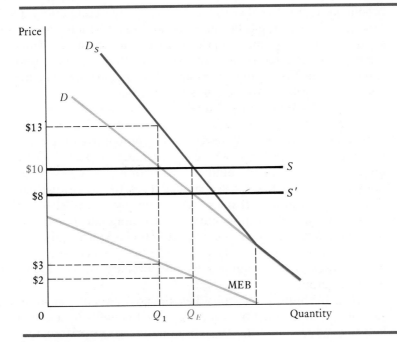

FIGURE 19–3

External Benefits and Subsidies

The marginal external benefit curve, MEB, shows the external benefits generated by consumption of the good. Vertically adding this curve to the private demand curve D yields the social marginal benefit curve D_S. Its intersection with the supply curve identifies the efficient output Q_E, which is greater than the market equilibrium output Q_1.

$10. The marginal external benefit curve, MEB, shows the external benefits per unit of consumption. This curve is derived by vertically summing the demands of people other than the immediate consumers of the product. Vertical summation is used because many people other than direct consumers simultaneously receive benefits — that is, the benefits are nonrival.

When external benefits exist, the competitive output is inefficient. At Q_1 the marginal benefit to consumers of another unit of the product is $10, as given by the height of the demand curve. If another unit is consumed, people other than the direct consumers also receive a marginal benefit valued at $3, as shown by the height of MEB at Q_1. Thus, the combined marginal benefit for all those affected by consumption of another unit is $13, and this amount exceeds the $10 marginal cost of producing an additional unit. The combined, or social, marginal benefits are shown by D_S, which is derived by vertically adding D and MEB (again because the benefits are nonrival).[2] The competitive output is too low because the marginal benefits of additional units of output exceed the marginal costs of producing them. Yet there is no tendency for competitive pressures to produce a larger output because the additional benefits to the direct consumers are less than the $10 price per unit they must pay. Thus, it is not in the consumers' interest to purchase more than Q_1 units; only when the *combined* benefits to consumers and other people are considered is it apparent why greater production is worthwhile.

Figure 19–3 illustrates the general tendency of an activity to be underproduced when external benefits are involved and when production is determined in competitive markets. The competitive output is Q_1, whereas the efficient output is Q_E, where D_S intersects S. To achieve the efficient output, the government could step in with a policy designed to increase output beyond the market-determined level. In this case an excise subsidy would be appropriate. If the government pays firms $2 for every unit of output they sell, the supply curve confronting consumers would shift to S'. Although the marginal cost of production is still $10, the government in effect bears $2 of the cost through the subsidy, so consumers only pay $8. At the lower price consumers would purchase Q_E units, and this is the efficient output.

By using appropriate subsidies, the government can stimulate expansion of output in situations where external benefits lead competitive markets to produce too little. To determine the appropriate subsidy, though, requires knowledge of the magnitude of the marginal external benefit at various output levels. Whether that information can be obtained is unclear.

---

[2] At an output in excess of the level at which the marginal external benefit becomes zero, the D_S and D curves coincide. When consumption is so great that additional consumption yields zero marginal benefits to other people, the only ones who receive any benefits from further increasing consumption are the direct consumers themselves, and their marginal benefits are shown by the D curve.

EXTERNALITIES AND PROPERTY RIGHTS
19.4

External effects may appear intrinsically different from normal costs and benefits, but that appearance is partly misleading. When a firm uses your labor services, it imposes a cost on you since you sacrifice the option to use your time in other ways. When a firm pollutes the river passing by your home, it imposes a cost on you since you sacrifice the option to use the river to fish in. These costs are not fundamentally different: they both imply that you are unable to use economic resources in ways you value. Why, then, do we call pollution, but not the firm's employment of your labor services, an external cost?

One glaring difference in these two cases is that the firm must pay you for your labor services, but you are not compensated when the river is despoiled. Since the firm must pay you at least enough to persuade you to give up alternative uses of your time, it will have incentive to take this cost into account in deciding whether to employ you; that is, when the firm bears a direct cost associated with the use of a resource, that cost enters into its production decisions. But if the firm can use the river in a way that harms you without compensating you for the damage, it has no reason to consider this cost in making its output decisions — the firm treats the river as a zero-priced input.

Next, we should ask why the firm must pay for the use of your labor services but not for the use of the river. The answer involves property rights to the use of economic resources. You have well-defined and legally enforceable rights to your own labor services, meaning that no one can use them without securing your permission, which is normally acquired by paying you. There are, however, no such clearly defined property rights to the water that flows past your home. In fact, it is not certain who "owns" the river and has the right to decide how it will be used. Consequently, the firm can use it as a convenient garbage dump. If you had property rights to pure water flowing past your home, the firm would have to buy your permission to dump waste in the river. The firm might still pollute, but it would do so only if the gain from polluting was greater than the compensation it had to pay you. Then this situation would be just like the case of your labor services: pollution would no longer be a cost external to the firm's calculations — the cost would be taken into account, and the allocation of resources would be efficient.

Reasoning along these lines suggests that externalities are intimately connected with the way property rights are defined. Indeed, in most cases dealing with externalities, we can usually trace the fundamental source of the problem to an absence or inappropriate assignment of property rights. This suggests that it may not be necessary for government to use taxes, subsidies, or regulation at all; it need only define and enforce property rights, and the resulting market exchanges would produce an efficient resource allocation. Without suggesting that this proposition is always true (it isn't), here are two examples where it is.

Sun, Surf, and Externalities

Imagine a beautiful beach on the California coast and suppose that no one owns it, just as no one owns the river. How will this scarce economic resource be used? It is not too fanciful to conceive of masses of people crowding the beach trying to enjoy the sand, sun, and surf. Radios blare, dune buggies roar up and down the beach, dirt bikes spray sand, litter lies all over the beach, surfboards crash into swimmers. Externalities are rampant.

Most would agree that this is not an efficient use of scarce beachfront property, and the reason is that no one owns it, so no one has incentive to see that the property is used in the most valuable way. The situation is different when someone has property rights to the beach. In that case the use of the property will be guided by who will pay the most for its use; that is, by who benefits most from its use. The owner may still use the property as a beach, but now it will be operated differently. The owner might charge admission which will diminish the overcrowding that reduces the attractiveness of the nonowned beach. The owner might enforce rules regarding radios, litter, surfboards, and so on, further enhancing the benefits to consumers. In short, the external costs are no longer external when someone owns the beach. The owner has incentive to see that the beach yields as much benefit to consumers as possible since they will then pay more for its use.

The beach example is hypothetical, but it helps explain why some highways, parks, and beaches are overcrowded and inefficiently utilized. "Publicly owned" property is, in effect, sometimes owned by no one in the sense that no one has the incentive and the right to see that it is used in the most valuable way.

Radio Waves and Externalities

Our second example comes from the history of United States radio broadcasting.[3] Radio began to be used commercially around the beginning of the twentieth century. In the early years there was no government involvement at all. Anyone who wanted to broadcast a message could build or buy a transmitter and broadcast on any frequency. The situation that developed before government regulation has been vividly described by Charles Siepmann:[4]

> The chaos that developed as more and more enthusiastic pioneers entered the field of radio was indescribable. Amateurs crossed signals with professional broadcasters. Many of the professionals broadcast on the same

---

[3] Ronald H. Coase, "The Federal Communications Commission," *Journal of Law and Economics*, 2 (October 1959): 1–40.
[4] Quoted in Coase, op. cit., p. 13.

wavelength and either came to a gentlemen's agreement to divide the hours of broadcasting or blithely set about cutting one another's throats by broadcasting simultaneously. Listeners thus experienced the annoyance of trying to hear one program against the raucous background of another.

Today economists would describe these events as the external costs associated with numerous people trying to use the same wavelengths simultaneously. The problem was that at the time no property rights had been established for wavelengths. No one owned any specific wavelength, just as no one owned our hypothetical beach. The market for radio wavelengths could not function properly because no property rights had been established for the resources (the radio wavelengths). In this case the "chaos" could have been avoided by creating legally enforceable property rights in wavelengths and letting the market determine who would use the various frequencies.

As it happens, the Federal Communications Commission (FCC) grew out of these events, and it has come to do more than just assign and enforce property rights in frequencies. Today one must obtain a license from the FCC to operate a broadcasting station on a specific frequency. In addition, transfers of ownership of broadcasting stations — along with the right to broadcast on a particular frequency — must be approved by the FCC. Thus, the FCC not only assigns frequencies but also decides who has the right to broadcast.

The Coase Theorem

These examples suggest that the assignment of property rights can make an important contribution to resolving issues involving externalities, but who is to have exactly what right to use the resource in question? Should the factory have the right to discharge smoke into the atmosphere, or should a nearby resident have the right to pure air? A case can certainly be made that both of these parties have a reasonable claim to use the atmosphere for their own purposes, yet giving the resident the right to clean air denies the factory the right to use a smokestack, and vice versa.

Ronald Coase resolved this issue in one of the most widely read papers in the history of economics.[5] Coase developed his analysis by considering a rancher and a farmer with adjoining properties. The rancher's cattle would occasionally stray onto the farmer's property and destroy some of his crops: an external cost associated with cattle raising if this cost is not properly taken into account. Now suppose the farmer has the right to grow his crops in a trample-free environment. The rancher would then be legally liable for the damage caused by his cattle. Since the rancher will have to compensate the farmer for the crop damage, the cost

[5] Ronald H. Coase, "The Problem of Social Cost," *Journal of Law and Economics,* 3 (October 1960): 1–45.

of straying cattle will become a direct cost to the rancher and will be taken into account in his production decision. An efficient outcome would result, probably one involving fewer straying cattle.

This conclusion is familiar, but Coase went further and argued that even if the rancher were not liable for damages, an efficient outcome would still result! This situation corresponds to giving the rancher the right to allow his cattle to stray. Coase explained that the farmer then has incentive to offer to pay the rancher to reduce the number of cattle that stray because a reduction in crop damage increases the farmer's profits. The harm done by straying cattle necessarily implies that the farmer will be willing to pay something to avoid that harm. An agreement would therefore be struck that would reduce cattle straying to the efficient level.

Insofar as efficient resource allocation is concerned, it doesn't matter who is initially assigned the property rights. As long as the property rights are clearly defined and enforced, bargaining between the parties can achieve the efficient pattern of resource use. It is true, though, that the *distributional* effects depend on the exact definition of property rights. When the rancher is liable, he will compensate the farmer; alternatively, when the rancher is not liable, the farmer will pay the rancher to reduce the cattle straying. In both cases cattle straying and crop damage are reduced to the efficient level, but different people bear the cost and secure the benefit.

Simply assigning property rights will not resolve all externality problems. In the case discussed earlier, firms pollute a river and *many* people living downstream are harmed. If downstream residents are given the right to clean water in the river, would bargaining between parties lead to an efficient level of water pollution? Definitely not. The problem here is that thousands of people are affected by the water pollution, and a firm would have to negotiate agreement with all of them simultaneously to be allowed to pollute. *Whenever the effects are nonrival over a large group and exclusion is not feasible, the free rider problem hinders the process of achieving agreement among all concerned.* The process of negotiation would be so costly and time-consuming as to become a practical impossibility. Firms wouldn't even try to bargain with thousands of people when all have to agree. If property rights were assigned in this way, there would be no pollution in the river — but that is sure to be at least as inefficient as allowing the firm to pollute freely.

Our earlier conclusion that markets would be inefficient is correct, therefore, in the case where the external effects simultaneously fall on many people. Assigning property rights can solve externality problems when there are small numbers of parties involved but not when there are large numbers, because of the free rider problem. Many issues of great importance, such as defense, pollution, and police protection, are large-group externalities or public goods, and private markets will not function effectively in these areas without some form of government intervention.

Summary

Public goods are goods with two characteristics: nonrival consumption and nonexclusion. When a good has these two characteristics, the free rider problem will arise and make it difficult for voluntary arrangements to ensure that the appropriate quantity will be produced.

An efficient output of a public good is that output at which the vertically summed demand curves of individuals intersect the marginal cost, or supply, curve. Private markets will generally not provide the efficient quantity of a public good. It is possible for government to improve the efficiency of resource allocation in this situation with suitable intervention in the private economy.

Externalities are the harmful or beneficial side effects of market activities that are borne by people who are not directly involved in the market exchanges. They represent costs or benefits that are not incorporated in the private supply and demand curves that guide economic activity. Once again, the result is an inefficient allocation of resources. In some cases it is only necessary to appropriately define property rights for these effects to be taken into account. In other cases, principally those involving large numbers of people, this solution will not work and other types of government policies should be proposed.

As we saw, when public goods and externalities exist, competitive markets cannot be counted on to generate efficient outcomes. This conclusion does not imply that government intervention will necessarily improve matters, only that it may. Whether or not it actually does depends on whether political processes have an inherent tendency to produce efficient outcomes, a subject we have not considered.

Review Questions and Problems

1. What two characteristics define a public good? Which of the following are public goods: parks, police services, welfare payments to the poor, production of energy, space exploration?

2. Why will private markets produce an inefficient output of a public good?

3. What is the condition for efficiency in the output of a public good? How is an efficient output identified graphically?

4. What is the condition for efficiency in the rationing of a public good, once it is produced?

*5. Suppose there are three consumers, two "hawks" and one "dove." The dove receives negative benefit from (is harmed by) national defense, but the hawks value defense. Show graphically how an efficient output of defense is determined in this case.

6. Since patents are legal grants of monopoly power, how is it possible to defend patents on efficiency grounds?

7. When external costs are associated with the production of some good, should the output of the good, on efficiency grounds, be limited to a level at which the external costs are zero? Use a diagram to explain your answer.

8. "External costs are bad, and government intervention to reduce them is justified. External benefits, however, are good, and there is no reason for government intervention in this case." Evaluate these statements.

9. Education is frequently cited as a source of external benefits. In what way, if at all, does your receiving a college education benefit other people?

*10. Suppose that property rights change so that students no longer have exclusive rights to the use of lecture notes they take in classes. (All notes are collected after class, and anyone can borrow notes for twenty-four hours on a first-come, first-served basis.) How would this change affect note taking, class attendance, and studying? Would students learn more or less? What does this example illustrate about the relationship between externalities and property rights?

11. In 1978 Californians were debating Proposition 5, the Clean Indoor Air Act. This bill would have banned smoking in nearly all public facilities and private businesses. The major argument for the bill was that it "is needed to protect nonsmokers from the health hazards of cigarettes." Prepare an evaluation of the economic case for Proposition 5. (Assume that it is in fact true that smoking adversely affects the health of nearby nonsmokers.)

*12. "When public goods or externalities lead to inefficient resource allocation, government intervention is justified." Is it? Why?

Supplementary Readings

Browning, Edgar, and Browning, Jacquelene. *Public Finance and the Price System.* 2nd ed. New York: Macmillan, 1983. Chap. 2.

Buchanan, James. *The Demand and Supply of Public Goods.* Chicago: Rand McNally, 1968.

Coase, Ronald. "The Problem of Social Cost." *Journal of Law and Economics,* 3 (October 1960): 1–45.

Ruff, Larry. "The Economic Common Sense of Pollution." *The Public Interest,* no. 19 (Spring 1970): 69–85.

Scherer, F. M. *Industrial Market Structure and Economic Performance.* 2nd ed. Chicago: Rand McNally, 1980.

Appendix: Answers to Selected Problems

Chapter 1

4. First, since the increase in the overall price level over the year is not given, it is not clear how the relative price of textbooks has changed. Second, it is possible that the demand curve has shifted over the year, perhaps due to such things as changes in college enrollments or greater interest in economics and business courses.

6. These statements implicitly deny the law of demand. They suggest that there is some fixed quantity of education, energy, and retirement benefits, less than which we can't do without and more than which would be worthless. In short, they seem to imply vertical demand curves.

10. Once again, such articles conceive of demand and supply as fixed quantities and neglect the fact that the quantity demanded and supplied depend on price. If the market for coal is unregulated, the market price will adjust so there is no shortage in 1990.

12. (a) $0.70 and 120,000. (b) The demand curve confronting producers becomes DAD_1.

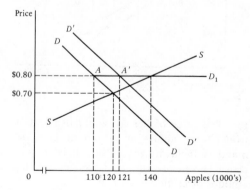

Output will be 140,000 with consumers chasing 110,000 and government 30 (equal to the output consumers don't chase — 140,000 less 110,000). (c) Consu demand becomes $D'D'$, and the dem curve confronting producers becom $D'A'D_1$. Total output and price don't char but consumer purchases rise to 121,000 a government purchases fall to 19,000 (140, less 121,000).

Chapter 2

3. The budget line line is MAN, kinked point A. Along the MA portion the slope $10/1X$ while the slope is $5/1X$ along the A portion.

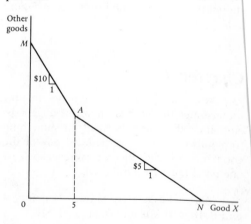

4. Income is $600, the price of A times the A intercept. The price of B is $30, income of $600 divided by the B intercept, 20. The slope is $2.5A/1B = P_B/P_A = $30/$12$.

9. Monica would be at point A on the budget line. At this point, her MRS $< P_G/P_W$: the slope of the indifference curve at A is $1W/1G$ while the budget line's slope is $3W/1G$. Thus, Monica is not in equilibrium at point A. The equilibrium is at point E.

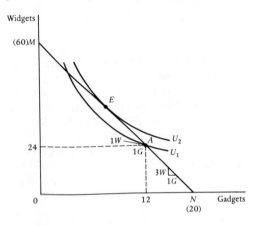

12. Not necessarily. Seat belts have costs as well as the benefit of reduced risk of injuries, and if motorists considered the marginal cost of purchasing and using them greater than the marginal benefit, they would be rational not to purchase them. This would be shown as a corner equilibrium, as in Figure 2–11.

Chapter 3

3. Yes; at a higher income it is possible for a consumer to purchase more of all goods. No; since all income is spent on something (remember, saving is considered one of the goods), at a higher income more of at least one good must be purchased.

4. Market baskets are shown as points A and B. If good X is a normal good, MRS_{XO} — the slope of the indifference curve — must be greater at B, as shown in the diagram. Otherwise the consumer wouldn't purchase more X at a higher income. If X is an inferior good, MRS_{XO} at point B would be less than at point A.

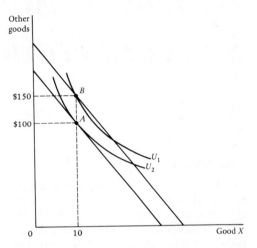

11. If the consumer could purchase as much gas as desired at a price of $1.50, the budget line would be MN. However, since only 25 gallons can be acquired at that price, the budget line is MAN', and the consumer's equilibrium is at point A. Since the MRS at A is greater than $1.50 per gallon, the consumer will pay more than $1.50 to get additional gasoline beyond 25 gallons.

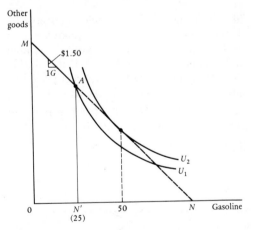

16. The price of heroin would rise and so would total outlays on heroin since its demand is inelastic. Since the funds to purchase heroin are obtained by stealing, the amount of crime would rise.

Chapter 4

2. Larry will be better off with food stamps but will consume more food with the excise subsidy. The food stamp equilibrium is point E on budget line MAN', with the $100 cost shown by the distance ET. The excise subsidy equilibrium is point E' on budget line MN_1 with the $100 cost equal to $E'T'$. The trick is to locate the size of the excise subsidy per unit that costs exactly $100, and this implies the excise subsidy equilibrium occurs where Larry's price consumption curve intersects AN'. Note that at a larger excise subsidy per unit (lower price), total cost would exceed $100, and vice versa.

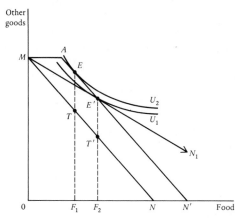

6. Harry will be better off and consume less gasoline. The price increase changes the budget line from MN to MN' and distance ET = $500 (= 1000 gallons times $0.50). Thus, a

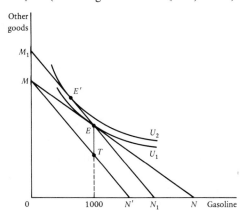

cash transfer of $500 shifts the budget line to M_1N_1, which passes through point E since $M_1M = ET = $500.

14. This may represent an intuitive feeling that consumer surplus is large, but what is relevant in deciding whether more or less is worthwhile is the marginal value of the good, not its consumer surplus.

16. With inelastic demand, a reduced supply leads to increased total outlays. Total outlays, however, do not measure the total value of the good to consumers. Total value is the area under the demand curve, and with a lower quantity that magnitude is reduced.

Chapter 5

2. Vertical and horizontal movements indicate that one party has given some of one commodity to the other party without getting anything in return. A voluntary trade would not be shown by such movements.

5. The question describes the situation shown at point A on one of the sides of the box diagram. Although the MRSs differ, the distribution is efficient since there is no way to move without harming one of the two persons. The equality-of-MRSs' condition is necessary for efficiency only when both parties consume some positive amount of both commodities.

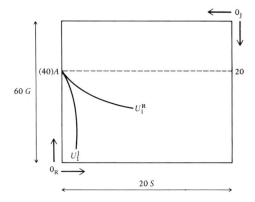

8. An equal distribution is shown at the midpoint of the diagonal line connecting the origins. This distribution would be efficient only if the consumers' MRSs happen to be equal at that point. Insofar as the consumers have different preferences, this will not be so.

10. Voluntarism in trade includes the right to stop trading with someone if you can do better disposing of the good in another way. Presumably, both the apartment owner and the future purchasers of condominiums will both benefit from the conversion if the owner's judgment is correct. Note that this situation is no different in principle than when you stop eating at McDonald's and patronize Burger King instead.

Chapter 6

3. The average and marginal product curves would coincide and be a horizontal line: AP and MP are constant regardless of the amount of input used. If the law of diminishing marginal returns holds, the total product curve could not have this shape.

4. The total product curve has the shape shown in Figure 6–6. The marginal and average product curves are shown in the diagram here. Note that AP = MP for the first unit.

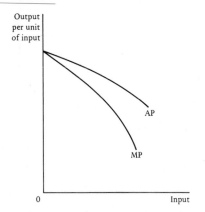

6. Since the marginal product indicates how much output will rise if the worker is hired, the employer should be concerned with the marginal product.

10. The isoquant might have a slope of (minus) one at this point, but it does not have to. If it does, it implies that the marginal products of both inputs are equal when equal quantities are employed. Remember that the slope of the isoquant equals the ratio of the marginal products.

Chapter 7

1. No interest has to be paid, but the firm does sacrifice an interest return it could receive by investing the profits in bonds, for example. If the firm could invest its profits elsewhere and receive a return of 10 percent, the opportunity cost of financing out of profits would be as high as financing by borrowing.

4. With MP falling from the start, MC and AC are rising from the start, as shown in the diagram. If MP first rises and then falls, the cost curves have their conventional U shapes.

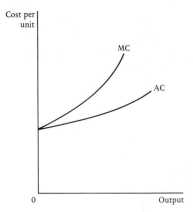

6. Basically, the reason is that we assume firms attempt to maximize profits. If it is possible to produce the same output at a lower total cost, a firm would make larger

profits by doing so. This reasoning does not provide a basis for assuming that the Post Office or the Ford Foundation minimizes costs since they are not profit-making operations.

10. The firm is at point A on isocost line MN. At point A, the isoquant has a slope of $3C/2L$, which is steeper than the isocost line with a slope of $1C/3L$. By operating at point B on the lower isocost line $M'N'$, the firm could produce the same output at a lower cost.

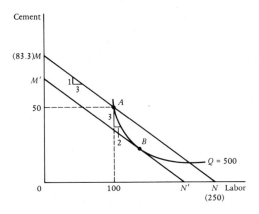

Chapter 8

2. The industry demand curve is not the horizontal sum of the demand curves facing each firm.

4. (a) Output is zero and losses equal fixed costs of $60 (profits are minus $60) since the firm can't cover AVC. (b) Output is 6 units and the firm loses $34 (profits are minus $34), but this is less than it would lose if it shut down. (c) Output is 9 units and profits are $40.

7. The price is $5 and *average* cost is $3 according to the question, but just because P is greater than AC doesn't mean it is greater than MC. (See Figure 8–5.) Profit maximization requires $P = $ MC, not $P = $ AC. In fact, if the firm did expand output until $P = $ AC, it would make no profit.

13. The LAC and LMC curves shift vertically upward by $1 to LAC' and LMC'. The profit maximizing output falls to Q_4.

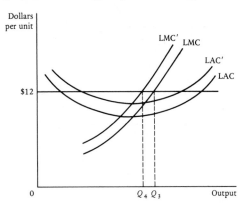

Chapter 9

4. In the long run, the industry supply curve is not the sum of the firms' marginal cost curves. The industry has a horizontal supply curve in the constant cost case because new firms can enter the market and produce at the same average cost as existing firms, and entry does not increase input prices.

6. This would be true for a constant cost industry but not for an increasing cost industry. In an increasing cost industry, when price falls, industry output will go down, leading to lower input prices and a downward shift in cost curves until remaining firms can cover costs at the lower price.

7. In this case where new firms can't enter and the cost curves don't shift as the industry expands, the curve showing the long-run response to an increase in demand is the sum of the existing firms' LR marginal cost curves. (See page 560.) The industry in part b expands along LS', and the final equilibrium involves a higher price. In part a, a typical firm produces where $P' = $ LMC and makes economic profits that are not competed away since new firms can't enter.

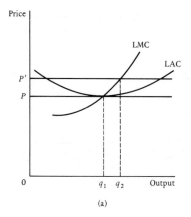

(a)

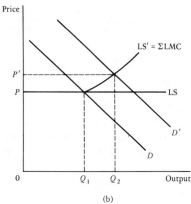

(b)

Chapter 10

3.   With a constant cost industry, with LS_1 and D, P and Q are the equilibrium price and quantity. The tax shifts LS_1 to $LS_1 + T$, and price rises to P_1, or by the amount of the tax T. With an increasing cost industry, supply curve is LS_2, and shifts to $LS_2 + T$ when the tax is applied. Price rises by less in this case to P_2.

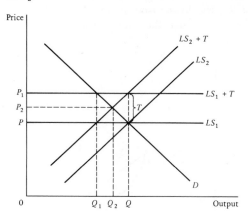

13.   (a) If the union establishes a wage rate above the competitive level, supply will fall (the supply curve shifts upward). (b) No effect on supply; demand is affected. (c) Supply will fall; costs of production increase. (d) Supply will fall; costs of production increase. (e) No effect on supply curve; will affect quantity supplied through effect on price. (f) Supply will increase as supply of labor increases and wage rates go down. (g) Supply will fall. Try this with the fixed proportions model.

17.   Output will fall and the firm will suffer losses in the short run, but price will not change. In the long run the firm will go out of business since it cannot raise the price without losing all its business to the other (untaxed) firms.

7.   Among the things that will be harmful to at least some of the tenants: the shortage of housing, making it more difficult and time consuming to find an apartment; deterioration in quality and reduction in quantity; nonprice rationing by renters; and inefficiency in the distribution. It is uncertain whether poor or nonpoor renters are more likely to be benefited, but the fact that the poor move more frequently and have characteristics that may be to their disadvantage under nonprice rationing (larger families, less steady employment) does suggest the possibility that poor tenants are less likely to benefit.

11.   On the effects of an increase in demand, see answer to question 12(b) for Chapter 1 on page 555. An increase in the target price will reduce the price paid by consumers, increase the price received by farmers, increase output, and increase total outlays by government.

15.   An increase in year 2 demand shifts D_2 to D_2' so consumption in year 1 falls from $0Q$ to $0Q'$ as price rises to P_1' in year 1. Price rises and so does consumption in year 2.

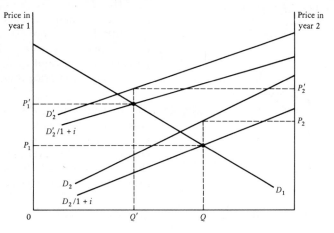

Chapter 11

4.   We would be better off having the good produced by a monopoly since a monopolistically priced good is better than having none at all.

8.   Solving $MR = P[1-(1/\eta)]$ for η yields $\eta = P/(P-MR)$. With $MC = 0.5P$ and $MC = MR$, $MR = 0.5P$. Thus, $\eta = P/(P-0.5P) = P/0.5P = 2$.

12.   To sell more, the price on all units sold must be reduced. This means that marginal revenue will be less than the price paid for an additional unit, so the monopolist will be interested in the marginal revenue generated by additional output, not the price at which it can be sold.

14.·   The welfare cost due to monopoly means that consumers would be willing to give up the necessary quantities of other goods to have more of the monopolized product. This is shown by the fact that at the monopolist's output, price (the marginal value to consumers) is greater than marginal cost (the value of other goods that are produced by the resources required to produce another unit of the monopolist's product).

Chapter 12

2.   Assume constant costs. In the competitive case, price will fall by the amount of the subsidy per unit. (See Figure 10–2.) In the monopoly case shown here, the subsidy S shifts the LMC and LAC curves down by the amount of the subsidy. Output increases from Q to Q_1, and price declines from P to P_1 or by only half as much (with a linear demand curve) as the subsidy per unit.

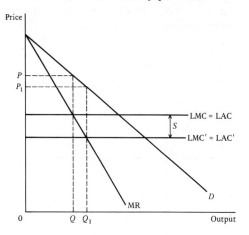

6.   Under unregulated monopoly, output is $0Q$, profit is AB, and price is P. With a price

ceiling of P', the total revenue curve becomes $0C$–TR, and profit is now greater at $0Q'$ (CD) than at $0Q$ (LB).

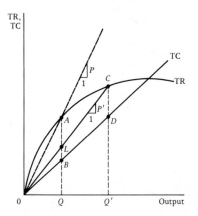

7.   No. By producing less than the output at which $P = LAC$, the monopoly can realize positive profits. (In this case, there will be a shortage at the regulated price.) To identify the profit maximizing output, draw in the LMC curve and see where it intersects the horizontal price (equal marginal revenue) line.

14.   The ΣMR curve is ABD_2. Total output is $0Q_2$. $0Q_1$ is sold in the home market at P_2 while $0Q_2 - 0Q_1$, or Q_1Q_2, is sold in the international market at the lower price, P_1.

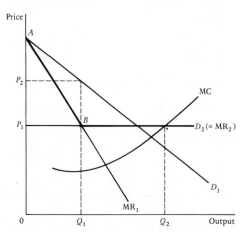

Chapter 13

2.   The *dd* curve is the one the firm perceives as its demand curve, and its price-quantity decisions are based on it. The *DD* curve is necessary because it indicates what happens to price and quantity when all the firms change the price they charge.

7.   In Figure 13–5, a shift in the marginal cost curve from mc_1 to mc_2 would lead to no change in price or quantity. Profits do increase since the average cost curve also shifts downward. Why the greater profitability in this market doesn't attract entry of new firms is another of the unanswered questions posed by this model.

9.   With the supply curve of the follower firms shown as S_0, the dominant firm faces a demand curve *PAD* and marginal revenue curve *PALM*. The dominant firm can only affect the price if it sets a price below P. If the dominant firm's marginal cost curve is mc_1, price will be P with both the dominant firm and other firms supplying a total output of Q. If mc_2 is the cost curve, the dominant firm supplies the entire market at P and produces Q. Only if the mc curve is lower than mc_3 will price and total output differ from P and Q. In most cases, then, a horizontal supply curve of other firms means that the dominant firm will have no effect on price and output.

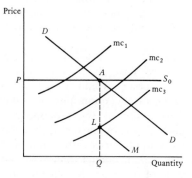

Chapter 14

5. The marginal *value* productivity of any given number of workers will be higher when product demand increases since consumers will pay a higher price for the product.

9. False. Each employer must take the market wage rate as given. Employers expand employment at the market determined wage rate up to the point where MVP equals that wage rate.

10. In the short run, an unanticipated increase in labor supply will lead to economic profits for firms and somewhat lower prices for consumers. In the long run, economic profits of the firms will be zero. Consumers, who will be able to get the product at a lower price, are the primary beneficiaries of an increase in labor supply in the long run.

11. No single firm except a monopsony has the ability to cut wage rates without losing employees. This quotation illustrates the common error of treating thousands of separate firms as if they could collude to form one gigantic monopsony. One could just as well argue that consumers force down the prices of products they buy at the expense of enormous losses to firms.

15. No. Monopolies employ fewer workers than do competitive industries, but workers could still find employment elsewhere. Even with monopolies, labor markets are only in equilibrium when the wage rate is such that quantity supplied and quantity demanded are equal.

Chapter 15

4. Initially, John is at point E on MN. The inheritance produces a parallel shift in the budget line to $M'N'N$, where $N'N = \$200$. There is only an income effect here since the wage rate has not changed. If leisure is a normal good, John will consume more of

it — that is, work less. For example, the equilibrium might be at E', and his total weekly income would be $400, up only $100 because he is earning $100 less than before.

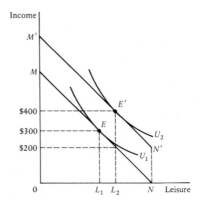

7. False. Not everyone who has the ability to be a nuclear physicist is already one. At a higher wage for physicists, others with the requisite ability would be attracted to the profession. At a lower wage rate, fewer would be.

13. Aggregate labor demand will be higher if investment is $0K_2$ in year 1. The more investment today, the greater the amount of capital per worker in the future. More capital per worker means the marginal productivity of workers will be greater, and hence demand for workers will be greater too.

Chapter 16

3. Labor costs will not increase if the money wages that must be paid go down by the amount of the increase in employer tax. As explained in the text, if the supply of labor is perfectly vertical, this will happen.

6. In this case, there would be no nonunion sector to absorb displaced workers. Thus, higher wage rates would reduce employment, and the result would be unemployment. Average *earnings* of workers would fall if demand is elastic and would rise if it is

inelastic. Average *incomes* (including capital income) of the population would necessarily fall since total output would be lower with reduced employment.

8. No women would be employed in A; all the women would be employed in B. Wage rates for men and women will remain equal, however, unless there are fewer men initially in B than there are women in A. To see this, imagine that wage rates did go down in B and up in A. Then the men initially in B have incentive to shift to A, and this process would continue until the wage rates in A and B were again equal.

10. Initially, the budget line is *MN*, and the worker is at point *E* earning $10,000. With the welfare program, the budget line becomes *MAN'*. With the worker's preferences as shown, the new equilibrium is at *N'* since the worker is on the higher indifference curve U_2 at that point.

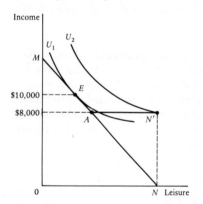

Chapter 17

3. No, at least not from the demand side of the market since the price of margarine would not change in this case, and thus the demand curve for butter would not shift.

9. Ten toasters per refrigerator. The MRT is equal to the ratio of marginal costs, and since marginal cost equals price in equilibrium, the MRT equals the ratio of the price of refrigerators to the price of toasters.

13. It would expand the size of the box diagram by increasing its length (assuming labor is measured on the horizontal axis). This would cause the PPF to shift outward since it will now be possible to produce more of both goods than before.

Chapter 18

6. With the output mix at point *E* distributed between the consumers as shown by point *A*, the output of wine is larger than efficient. This is shown by the fact that the common MRS is less than MRT: *gg* is flatter than *ff*. This does not mean that a lower output of wine will *necessarily* benefit both consumers, only that it is possible to distribute a lower output of wine (and the accompanying higher output of corn) in such a way that both consumers are better off.

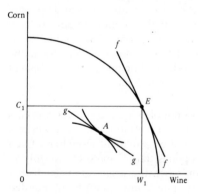

7. We are located at *some* point *on* the welfare frontier. When any condition is not satisfied, we are located at some point inside the welfare frontier.

11. No, at least not if markets are competitive.

15.   The equilibrium is one where the price to consumers is less than the price to producers and so is less than marginal cost. This means that the output of the subsidized good is too large. The outcome would look like that shown for question 6, if we assume it is wine being subsidized with a target price subsidy.

16.   No. Consumers can't purchase as much as they want at the controlled rent, and so the controlled rent does not measure the marginal value (or MRS) of rental housing to consumers. The marginal value of rental housing would be greater than the controlled rent, and therefore greater than marginal cost, so output is too low.

Chapter 19

5.   The dove, individual C, has a negative demand for defense. This must be added vertically to the demands of the hawks A and B. The result, Σd, is lower than it would be if we summed the demands of A and B only. Where Σd intersects MC identifies the efficient output. (See graph in next column.)

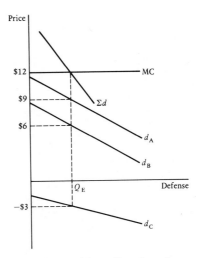

10.   We would predict that class attendance would rise, poorer notes would be taken (but maybe carbon paper would be used?), and students would study the text more. Students would probably learn less.

12.   No. Government intervention could make a bad situation worse. Only an explicit analysis of the effects of government intervention could show whether it would improve matters, in the sense of leading to a more efficient resource allocation.

Index